Dorothea Ruggles-Brise

The Vocal Magazine

Or, compleat British songster. Consisting of such English, Scotch, and Irish songs,

catches, glees, cantatas, airs, ballads

Dorothea Ruggles-Brise

The Vocal Magazine
Or, compleat British songster. Consisting of such English, Scotch, and Irish songs, catches, glees, cantatas, airs, ballads

ISBN/EAN: 9783744794145

Printed in Europe, USA, Canada, Australia, Japan

Cover: Foto ©Thomas Meinert / pixelio.de

More available books at **www.hansebooks.com**

THE

VOCAL MAGAZINE;

OR,

Compleat Britiſh Songſter.

CONSISTING OF SUCH

ENGLISH, SCOTCH, AND IRISH

SONGS,	CANTATAS,
CATCHES,	AIRS,
GLEES,	BALLADS, &c.

AS ARE DEEMED MOST WORTHY OF BEING TRANSMITTED
TO POSTERITY.

LONDON:
Printed for HARRISON and Co. Nº. 18, Paternoſter-Row.
M-DCC LXXXIV.

The beautiful Mrs. Fitzherbert resided at Richmond Hill when the Prince of Wales first paid his address to her. She was "The Lass of Richmond Hill" celebrated in the very popular song of that name.

See "Memoirs of Mrs. Fitzherbert; with an account of her marriage with H.R.H. the Prince of Wales, afterwards King George IV. By the Hon. Charles Langdale. London; Bentley; 1856."

Extracts of this in "Times" for 29th March 1856. page 5. See Cassell's Illustrated Family Paper, for Feby 27, 1864, p. 222, for different accounts of "The Lass of Richmond Hill."

THE

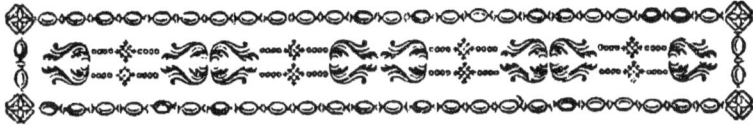

VOCAL MAGAZINE.

NUMBER I.

SONG 1.

THE APPROACH OF MAY.

Written by Mr. CUNNINGHAM.

THE virgin, when foften'd by May,
 Attends to the villager's vows;
The birds fweetly bill on the fpray,
 And poplars embrace with their boughs.
On Ida bright Venus may reign,
 Ador'd for her beauty above;
We fhepherds who dwell on the plain,
 Hail May as the mother of love.

From the Weft as it wantonly blows,
 Fond zephyr careffes the vine,
The bee fteals a kifs from the rofe,
 And willows and woodbines entwine.
The pinks, by the rivulet's fide,
 That border the vernal alcove,
Bend downward to kifs the foft tide,
 For May is the mother of love.

May tinges the butterfly's wing,
 He flutters in bridal array;
If the lark and the linnet now fing,
 Their mufic is taught them by May:
The ftock-dove, reclufe with her mate,
 Conceals her fond blifs in the grove;
And, murmuring, feems to repeat,
 That May is the mother of love.

The goddefs will vifit ye foon,
 Ye virgins be fportive and gay;
Get your pipes, O ye fhepherds! in tune,
 For mufic muft welcome the day.
Would Damon have Phillis prove kind,
 And all his keen anguifh remove,
Let him tell a foft tale, and he'll find,
 That May is the mother of love.

SONG 2.

THE ORIGIN OF ENGLISH LIBERTY.

Written by G. A. STEVENS.

ONCE the gods of the Greeks, at ambrofial
 feaft,
Large bowls of rich nectar were quaffing:
Merry Momus among them was fat as a gueft,
 (Homer fays the celeftials lov'd laughing:)
On each in the fynod the humourift droll'd,
 So none could his jokes difapprove;
He fung, repartee'd, and fome fmart ftories told,
 And at laft thus began upon Jove.

" Sire! A·las, who long has the univerfe bore,
 " Grows grievoufly tir'd of late;
" He fays that mankind are much worfe than
  " before,
 " So he begs to be eas'd of their weight."
Jove, knowing the earth on poor Atlas was
 hurl'd,
 From his fhoulders commanded the ball;
Gave his daughter, Attraction, the charge of the
 world,
 And fhe hung it up high in his hall.

Mifs, pleas'd with the prefent, review'd the
 globe round,
 To fee what each climate was worth;
Like a diamond, the whole with an atmofphere
 bound,
 And fhe varioufly planted the earth:
With filver, gold, jewels, fhe India endow'd;
 France and Spain fhe taught vineyards to rear;
What fuited each clime, on each clime fhe be-
 ftow'd,
 And freedom, fhe found, flourifh'd here.

Four cardinal virtues fhe left in this ifle,
 As guardians to cherifh the root;

The bloffoms of liberty 'gan then to fmile,
And Englifhmen fed on the fruit.
Thus fed, and thus bred, from a bounty fo rare,
O preferve it as free as 'twas giv'n !
" We will, while we've breath ; nay, we'll grafp
" it in death,
" Then return it untainted to Heav'n !"

SONG 3.

AN ELEGIAC PASTORAL BALLAD.

Written by the EDITOR.

YE fwains who inhabit the green,
You have heard that my Phillida's dead ;
In your looks the fad tidings are feen,
And her worth in your grief may be read.

Oh! was fhe not lovely and fair ;
Has fhe fcarce left fuch beauty behind?
And yet what was that to compare
With the graces which dwelt in her mind?

But let me not think of her charms!
How I lov'd her my verfe cannot tell ;
Death has fnatch'd her away from my arms ;
With angels, alone, muft fhe dwell.

In vain do I utter my grief;
Her lofs the whole world can't fupply ;
Death only will give me relief;
To him, then, with pleafure I fly.

Oh! fhew me the way to my fair;
Lead me on to the regions of blifs!
And, fure as my love was fincere,
I'll praife thee, great victor, for this.

SONG 4.

THE ROAST BEEF OF OLD ENGLAND; A CANTATA.

RECITATIVE.

'TWAS at the gates of Calais, Hogarth tells,
Where fad defpair and famine always dwells,
A meagre Frenchman, Madam Grandfire's cook,
As home he fteer'd, his carcafe that way took ;
Bending beneath the we'ght of fam'd Sir Loin,
On whom he often wifh'd, in vain, to dine :
Good Father Dominick by chance came by,
With rofy gills, round paunch, and greedy eye ;
Who, when he firft beheld the greafy load,
His benediction on it he beftow'd:
And as the folid fat his fingers prefs'd,
He lick'd his chaps; and thus the knight ad-
drefs'd.

AIR.

O rare roaft beef! lov'd by all mankind,
If I were doom'd to have thee,
When drefs'd and garnifh'd to my mind,
And fwimming in thy gravy,
Not all thy country s force combin'd
Should from my fury fave thee.

Renown'd Sir Loin, oft-times decreed
The theme of Englifh ballad ;

On thee e'en kings have deign'd to feed,
Unknown to Frenchmen's palate :
Then how much doth thy tafte exceed
Soup-meagre, frogs, and fallad !

RECITATIVE.

A half-ftarv'd foldier, fhirtlefs, pale and lean,
Who fuch a fight before had never feen,
Like Garrick's frighted Hamlet, gaping ftood,
And gaz'd with wonder on the Britifh food.
His morning's mefs forfook the friendly bowl,
And in fmall ftreams along the pavement ftole.
He heav'd a figh, which gave his heart relief;
And then, in plaintive tone, declar'd his grief.

AIR.

Ah, facre dieu! vat do I fee yonder,
Dat look fo tempting red and vite?
Begar, it is de roaft beef from Londre ;
Oh! grant to me von little bite.

But to my guts if you give no heeding,
And cruel fate dis boon denies ;
In kind compaffion unto my pleading,
Return, and let me feaft my eyes.

RECITATIVE.

His fellow-guard, of right Hibernian clay,
Whofe brazen front his country did betray,
From Tyburn's fatal tree had hither fled,
By honeft means to gain his daily bread :
Soon as the well-known profpect he defcry'd,
In blubb'ring accents dolefully he cry'd.

AIR.

Sweet beef, that now caufes my ftomach to
rife,
Sweet beef, &c.
So taking thy fight is,
My joy, that fo light is,
To view thee, by pailfulls runs out of my eyes.

While here I remain, my life's not worth a
farthing,
While here, &c.
Ah, hard-hearted Loui,
Why did I come to you!
The gallows, more kind, would have fav'd me
from ftarving.

RECITATIVE.

Upon the ground hard by poor Sawney fate,
Who fed his nofe, and fcratch'd his ruddy pate ;
But when Old England's bulwark he efpy'd,
His dear lov'd mull, alas! was thrown afide :
With lifted hand he blefs'd his native place,
Then fcrubb'd himfelf, and thus bewail'd his
cafe.

AIR.

How hard, Oh, Sawney! is thy lot,
Who was fo blythe of late ;
To fee fuch meat as can't be got,
When hunger is fo great !
O the beef! the bonny, bonny beef,
When roafted nice and brown ;
I wifh I had a flice of thee,
How fweet it would gang down !

Ah, Charley! hadft thou not been feen,
This ne'er had happ'd to me;
I would the de el had pick'd mine ey'n,
Ere I had gang'd wi' thee.
O the beef, &c.

RECITATIVE.

But fee! my mufe to England takes her flight,
Where health and plenty focially unite:
Where fmiling freedom guards great George's throne,
And whips, and chains, and tortures, are not known.
Tho' Britain's fame in loftieft ftrains fhould ring,
In ruftic fable give me leave to fing.

AIR.

As once on a time a young frog, pert and vain,
Beheld a large ox grazing o'er the wide plain,
He boafted his fize he could quickly attain.
O the roaft beef of Old England,
And O the Old Englifh roaft beef.

Then eagerly ftretching his weak little frame,
Mamma, who ftood by, like a knowing old dame,
Cry'd, " Son, to attempt it you're furely to " blame."
O the roaft beef, &c.

But deaf to advice, he for glory did thirft,
An effort he ventur'd more ftrong than the firft;
Till fwelling and ftraining too hard made him burft.
O the roaft beef, &c.

Then, Britons, be valiant; the moral is clear:
The ox is Old England, the frog is Monfieur,
Whofe puffs and bravadoes we need never fear.
O the roaft beef, &c.

For while, by our commerce and arts, we are able
To fee the Sir Loin fmoaking hot on our table,
The French may e'en burft like the frog in the fable.
O the roaft beef, &c.

SONG 5.

Written by Mr. GAY.

GO, rofe, my Chloe's bofom grace;
How happy fhould I prove,
Might I fupply that envy'd place
With never-fading love!
There, phœnix like, beneath her eye,
Involv'd in fragrance, burn and die;
Involv'd in, &c.

Know, haplefs flow'r, that thou fhalt find
More fragrant rofes there,
I fee thy with'ring head reclin'd
With envy and defpair;
One common fate we both muft prove;
You die with envy, I with love.
You die, &c.

SONG 6.

A TWO-PART SONG.

Written by Mr. PRIOR.

WHEN Bibo thought fit from the world to retreat,
As full of champaign as an egg's full of meat,
He wak'd in the boat, and to Charon he faid,
He would be row'd back, for he was not yet dead.
" Trim the boat, and fit quiet!" ftern Charon reply'd,
" You may have forgot—you was drunk when " you dy'd."

SONG 7.

Sung in Love in a Village.

CUPID, god of foft perfuafion,
'Take the helplefs lover's part;
Seize, oh! feize, fome kind occafion
To reward a faithful heart.

Juftly thofe we tyrants call,
Who the body would enthrall;
Tyrants of more cruel kind,
Thofe who would enflave the mind,
Cupid, god of, &c.

What is grandeur? Foe to reft;
Childifh mummery, at beft.
Happy I in humble ftate!
Catch, ye fools, the glitt'ring bait.
Cupid, god of, &c.

SONG 8.

THE CRYING AND LAUGHING SONG,

Sung at VAUXHALL.

WHEN I awake, with painful brow,
Ere the cock begins to crow;
Toffing, tumbling in my bed,
Aching heart, and aching head;
Pond'ring over human ills,
Cruel bailiffs, taylors bills;
Flufh and Pam thrown up at Loo:
When thefe forrows ftrike my view,
I cry——
And, to ftop the gufhing tear,
Wipe it with the pillow-bier.

But when fportive ev'ning comes,
Routs, ridottos, balls, and drums;
Cafinos here, Feftinos there,
Mirth and paftime ev'ry where;
Seated by a fprightly lafs,
Smiling with the fmiling glafs:
When thefe pleafures are my lot,
Taylors, bailiffs, all forgot,
I laugh——
Carelefs, then, what may befal,
Thus I fhake my fides at all.

Then, again, when I perufe,
O'er my tea, the morning news;
Difmal tales of plunder'd houfes,
Wanton wives, and cuckold fpoufes;
When I read of money lent,
At fixteen and a half per cent,
I cry——

But if, ere the muffin's gone,
Simp'ring enters honeft John;
" Sir, Mifs Lucy's at the door,
" Waiting in a chaife and four,"
Unftant vanifh all my caies,
Swift I fcamper down the ftairs,
And laugh——

So may this indulgent throng,
Who now, fmiling, grace my fong,
Never more cry, Oh! oh! oh!
But join with me in, Ha! ha! ha!

SONG 9.

Sung in the *Beggar's Opera*.

IF you at an office folicit your due,
And would not have matters neglected,
You muft quicken the clerk with the perquifite
too,
To do what his duty directed.

Or would you the frowns of a lady prevent,
She, too, has this palpable failing,
The perquifite foftens her into confent;
That reafon with all is prevailing.

SONG 10.

A PASTORAL BALLAD.

Written by Mr. WOTY.

YE fwains that infult o'er my woe,
And make me the jeft of the green,
What I fuffer ye fienderly know,
My Phillis ye never have feen.
O! fhe's lovely as thought can exprefs,
As gentle and mild as the dove:
I faw her—and who could do lefs—
I faw, and I could not but love!

I ne'er told her the anguifh I bear,
She might think me prefumptuous and bold;
Ah! what need of words to declare
What my eyes muft fo often have told!
How fhall I my love recommend!
I may rob all her heart of it's cafe;
And, fure, I muft dread to offend,
Whofe ftudy is only to pleafe.

They tell me I'm penfive and grave,
Not, as formerly, chearful and free;
All pleafures contented I wave,
That fpring not, my Phillis, from thee.
Nor riches nor grandeur I mind,
Nor titles to flattter my pride;
To me, if the nymph is unkind,
All the world's a defart befide.

At each fcene of the well-fabled woe,
Which forrow fo forcibly fpeaks,

I mark'd the foft current o'erflow,
And the tear gently fteal down her cheeks.
I mark'd it! and, truft me, ye fair,
It pleas'd me fuch foftnefs to fee!
Can fhe melt at a fancy'd defpair,
And not have compaffion for me?

Her voice founds fo filverly fweet,
When fhe tells me there's hope for her fwain,
My life I'd lay down at her feet
But to hear the dear accents again.
In expreffion let others excel,
My love is a ftranger to art:
Tho', may be, I fpeak not fo well,
Yet, truft me, I fpeak from the heart.

May thy days to thy wifhes be bleft!
May'ft thou never have caufe to repine!
Or, if forrows thy bofom moleft,
O tell them, and they fhall be mine.
Will my fair-one my fervice deny?
My prefumption will Phillis forgive?
Contented for her I could die,
With whom 'twould be heaven to live.

SONG 11.

A favourite Song in *Tamerlane*.

TO thee, O gentle fleep, alone,
Is owing all our peace;
By thee our joys are heighten'd fhewn,
By thee our forrows ceafe.

The nymph, whofe hand by fraud or force
Some tyrant has poffefs'd,
By thee obtaining a divorce,
In her own choice is blefs'd.

Oh! ftay, Arpafia bids thee ftay;
The fadly weeping fair
Conjures thee not to lofe, in day,
The object of her care.

To grafp whofe pleafing form fhe fought;
That motion chas'd her fleep:
Thus by ourfelves are ofteneft wrought
The griefs for which we weep.

SONG 12.

THE STATE OF A LOVER.

HOW happy a lover's life paffes,
When beauty returns figh for figh!
He looks upon all men as affes,
Who have not fome girl in their eye.

With heart full as light as a feather,
He trips to the terras or parks,
Where fwains croud impatient together,
And maidens look out for their fparks.

What fweet palpitation arifes,
When Chloe appears full in view!
Her fmiles at more value he prizes,
Than mifers the mines of Peru.

Tho' fwift-winged time, as they're walking,
Soon parts them, alas! by his flight;

By reflection he still hears her talking,
And absent he keeps her in sight.
Whenever abroad he regales him,
And Bacchus calls out for his lass;
His love for his Chloe ne'er fails him,
Her name gives a zest to his glass.

No other amusements he prizes,
Than those that from Chloe arise;
She's first in his thoughts when he rises;
And last when he closes his eyes.
Then let not ambition distress us,
Or fortune's fantastical chance;
Love only with Chloe can bless us,
And give all we want to embrace.

SONG 13.

Written by G. A. STEVENS.

Sung at VAUXHALL.

CONTENTED I am, and contented I'll be;
For what can this world more afford,
Than a girl that will sociably sit on my knee,
And a cellar that's plenteously stor'd ?

See! my vault door is open, descend ev'ry guest,
Tap the cask, for the wine we will try ;
'Tis as sweet as the lips of your love to your taste;
And as bright as her cheeks to your eye.

In a piece of flit-hoop I my candle have stuck,
'Twill light us each bottle to hand ;
The foot of my glass for the purpose I've broke,
For I hate that a bumper should stand.

Sound that pipe—'tis in tune, and the binns
are well fill'd,
View that heap of Champaigne in the rear ;
Those bottles are Burgundy see how they're pil'd,
Like artillery, tier over tier.

My cellar's my camp, and my soldiers my flasks,
All gloriously rang'd in review ;
When I cast my eyes round, I consider my casks
As kingdoms I've got to subdue.

'Tis my will, when I die; not a tear shall be shed,
No hic jacet be grav'd on my stone ;
But pour on my coffin a bottle of red,
And say that my drinking is done.

SONG 14.

Sung in the Capricious Lovers.

FOR various purpose serves the fan ;
As thus—a decent blind,
Between the sticks to peep at man,
Nor yet betray your mind.

Each action has a meaning plain,
Resentment's in the snap ;
A flirt expresses strong disdain,
Consent a gentle tap.

All passions will the fan disclose,
All modes of female art ;

And to advantage sweetly shews,
The hand, if not the heart.

'Tis folly's sceptre, first design'd
By love's capricious boy,
Who knows how lightly all mankind
Are govern'd by a toy.

SONG 15.

Sung at VAUXHALL.

O Give me that social delight
Which none but true lovers receive,
When Luna bedecks the still night,
And glances her smiles on the eve :
When to the fair meadows we go,
Where peace and contentment retire ;
Or down the smooth current we row,
In time with the flutes and the lyre.

By nature these pictures are drawn :
How sweet is each landscape dispos'd !
The prospect extends to the lawn,
Or by the tall beeches is clos'd.
Come, Strephon, attend to the scene :
The clouds are all vanish'd above ;
The objects around are serene,
As modell'd to music and love.

SONG 16.

Sung in Love in a Village.

IN love should there meet a fond pair,
Untutor'd by fashion or art,
Whose wishes are warm and sincere,
Whose words are th' excess of the heart.
If aught of substantial delight;
On this side the stars can be found ;
'Tis, sure, when that couple unite,
And Cupid by Hymen is crown'd.

SONG 17.

CORYDON AND PHILLIS; A PASTORAL.

Written by Mr. CUNNINGHAM.

HER sheep had in clusters crept close to a
grove,
To hide from the heat of the day ;
And Phillis herself, in a woodbine alcove,
Among the sweet violets lay !
A young lambkin, it seems, had been stole from
it's dam,
('Twixt Cupid and Hymen a plot)
That Corydon might, as he search'd for his
lamb,
Arrive at the critical spot.

As thro' the green hedge for his lambkin he
peeps,
He saw the fair nymph with surprise ;
Ye gods, if so killing, he cry'd, while she sleeps,
I'm lost if she opens her eyes ;
To tarry much longer would hazard my heart,
I'll homeward my lambkin to trace.

B

But in vain honeft Corydon ftrove to depart,
For love held him faſt to the place.
Ceaſe, ceaſe, pretty birds, what-a chirping you keep,
I think you too loud on the fpray;
Don't you fee, foolifh lark, that the charmer's aſleep,
You'll wake her as fure as 'tis day.
How dare that fond butterfly touch the fweeſ maid !
Her cheeks he miſtakes for the rofe :
I'd put him to death, if I was not afraid
My boldnefs would b eak her repofe.
Then Phillis lɔok'd up with a languifhing fmile,
Kind fhepherd, ſaid fhe, you miſtake ;
I laid myf lf down for to reſt me awhile,
But truſt me I was not aſleep.
The fhepherd tuok courage, advanc'd with a bow,
He plac'd himfelf down by her fide;
And manag'd-the matter, I cannot tell how,
But yeſterday made her his bride.

SONG 18.

Sung at VAUXHALL.

WHERE fhall Celia fly for fhelter ?
In what fecret grove or cave ?
Sighs and fonnets fent to melt her,
From the young, the gay, the brave.
Tho' with prudifh airs fhe ſtarch her,
Still fhe longs, and ſtill fhe burns :
Cupid fhoots like Hymen's archer,
Wherefoe'er the damfel turns.

Virtue, youth, good-fenfe, and beauty,
(If difcre ion guide us not)
Sometimes are the ruffian's booty,
Sometimes are the booby's lot;
Now they're purchas'd by the trader,
Now commanded by the peer;
Now fome fubtle, mean invader,
Wins the h art, or gains the ear.

O difcretion! thou'rt a jawel,
Or our grand-mamas miſtake,
Stinting flame by bating fewel,
Always careful and awake.
Would you keep your pearls from tramplers,
Weigh the licence, weigh the banns;
Mark my fong upon your famplers,
Wear it on your knots and fans.

SONG 19.

Song in the Padlock.

SAY, little foolifh fluit'ring thing,
Whither, ah ! whither would you wing
Your airy flight ?
Stay here and fing,
Your miſtrefs to delight.
N , no, no,
Sweet Robin, you fhall not go !
Where you wanton, could you be
Half fo happy as with me ?

SONG 20.

Sung in High Life below Stairs.

COME here, fellow-fervants, and liſten to me,
I'll fhew you how thofe of fuperior degree,
Are only dependents, no better than we,
Are only dependents, &c.
Both high and low in this do agree,
'Tis here, fellow-fervant, and there, fellow-fervant, and all in a livery.
'Tis here, fellow-fervant, &c.

See yonder fine fpark in embroidery dreſt,
Who bows to the great, and if they fmile, is bleſt ;
What is he, i'faith, but a fervant at beſt ?
Both high, &c.

Nature made all alike, no diſtinction fhe craves;
So we laugh at the great world, it's fools and iɔs knaves ;
For we are all fervants, but they are all flaves.
Both high, &c.

The fat fhining glutton looks up to his fhelf,
The wrinkled lean mifer bows down to hispeff,
And the curl-pated beau is a flave to himfelf.
Both high, &c.

The gay fparkling belle, who the whole town alarms,
And with eyes, lips and neck, fets the fmarts all in arms,
Is a vaffal herfelf, a mere drudge to her charms.
Both high, &c.

Then we'll drink like our betters, and laugh, fing, and love ;
And when fick of one place, to another we'll move,
For with little and great the beſt joy is to rove.
Both high, &c.

SONG 21.

Sung in Thomas and Sally.

FROM ploughing the ocean, and thrafhing Monfieur,
In old England we're landed once more;
Your hands, my brave comrades; halloo, boys, what cheer
For a failor, that's juſt come on fhore ?
Thofe hectoring blades thought to fcare us, no doubt,
And to cut us, and flafh us—morbleau !
But hold there—avaſt—they were plaguily out;
We have flic'd them and pepper'd them too.

Then courage, my hearts, yourr own confequence know,
You invaders fhall foon do you right ;
The lion may roufe, when he bears the cock crow,
But fhall never be put in a fright.

You've only to fhun your nonfenfical jars,
Your damn'd party and idle conteſt ;
And let all your ſtrife be, like us honeſt tars,
Who fhall fight for their country beſt.

A sea-faring spark if the maids can affect,
Bid the simpering gypsies look to't ;
Sound bottoms they'll find us in ev'ry respect,
And our pockets well laden to boot.

The landsmen mayhap, in the way of discourse,
Have more art to persuade, and the like ;
But 'ware those false colours——for better for
worse,
Is the bargain we're willing to strike.

Now long live the king! may he prosperous
reign,
Of no power, no faction, afraid ;
May Britain's proud flag still exult o'er the main,
At all points of the compass display'd !

No quickfands endanger, no storms overwhelm,
Steady, steady, and safe may she fail ;
No ignorant pilots e'er fit at her helm,
Or her anchor of liberty fail !

SONG 22.

THE NOD, WINK, AND SMILE.

Sung at VAUXHALL.

LET fusty old grey-beards of apathy boast,
And Venus and Bacchus revile ;
In spite of their books, they are slaves to some
toaft,
The dupes of a nod, wink, or smile.

Some snug sober citizens here may repair,
Without an idea of guile ;
But what with the music, and what with the
fair,
They follow the nod, wink, and smile.

Let men boast of titles, of honours, renown ;
The females of this happy isle.
Can vanquish the victors, nay kill with a frown,
Or save, by a nod, wink, or smile.

These gardens of pleasure the beauties approve,
Who the dulleft of moments beguile ;
Here Cupid unfurls the white standard of love,
And commands with a nod, wink, and smile.

SONG 23.

BLYTHE JOCKEY ; A SCOTCH BALLAD.

Sung at VAUXHALL.

BLYTHE Jockey, young and gay,
Is all my heart's delight ;
He's all my talk by day,
And all my dreams by night.

If from the lad I be,
'Tis winter then with me ;
But when he tarries here,
'Tis summer all the year.

When I and Jockey met
First on the flow'ry dale,
Right sweetly he me tret,
And love was all his tale.

You are the lass, said he,
That flaw my heart frae me ;

O ease me of my pain,
And never shew difdain.

I'm glad when Jockey comes,
Sad when he gangs away ;
'Tis night when Jockey glooms,
But when he smiles 'tis day.

Well can my Jockey kyth
His love and courtesie ;
He made my heart full blythe,
When he first spake to me.

His suit I ill deny'd,
He kifs'd and I comply'd ;
Sae Jockey promis'd me,
That he would faithful be.

When our eyes meet I pant,
I colour, sigh, and faint ;
What lafs that would be kind,
Can better speak her mind ?

SONG 24.

THE ABSENT LOVER.

WHILE Celia's remote from my sight,
In vain to be chearful I try ;
Nor the verdure of spring can delight,
Or the want of her presence supply.

No flow'r that the lawn dscape arrays,
With the bloom of her cheeks can compare ;
Nor the blufhes Aurora di'plays
Can equal the looks of my fair.

The bird that so sweetly complains,
Each night to the liftening grove,
Sings not in such soft melting strains
As are those of the virgin I love !

The charms that embellish her mind,
What numbers wou'd serve to exprefs ?
Whofe converse, so sweet. fo refin'd,
Can soften the deepeft diftrefs!

Each other bright fair I'd refign,
With whatever the gay world can give,
Would fortune but make Celia mine,
With enough independent to live.

No monarch would, then, be more bleft ;
Nor wuu'd I, a throne to enjoy,
Exchange the dear nymph I pofsefs'd,
Whofe love ev'ry wish cou'd supply.

Then say, cruel fate ! why so long
I am doom'd ftill to languifh in vain ?
You either must soften my fong,
Or foon I muft die with my pain.

SONG 25.

Sung at RANELAGH.

NOT on beauty's tranficnt pleafure,
Which no real joys impart ;
Nor on heaps of fordid treasure,
Did I fix my youthful heart.

'Twas not Chloe's perfect feature
Did the fickle wand'rer bind ;

Not her form, the beaſt of nature,
  'Twas alone her ſpotleſs mind.
    Not on beauty's, &c.

Take, ye ſwains, the real bleſſing,
  That will joys for lifeinſure ;
The virtuous mind alone poſſeſſing,
  Will your laſting bliſs ſecure.
    Not on beauty's, &c.

S O N G 26.

Sung in the *Padlock.*

DEAR heart! what a terrible life am I led ?
  A dog has a better, that's ſhelter'd and fed ;
Night and day 'tis the ſame.
My pain is dere game ;
Me wiſh to de Lord me was dead.

Whate'er's to be done,
Poor black muſt run ;
Mungo here, Mungo dere,
Mungo every where.
Above, or below,
Sirrah, come, ſirrah, go ;
Do ſo, and do ſo.
Oh ! Oh !
Me wiſh to de Lord me was dead.

S O N G 27.

Written by Mr. GAY.

RECITATIVE.

'TWAS when the ſeas were roaring,
  With hollow blaſts of wind,
A damſel lay deploring,
  All' on a rock reclin'd !
Wide o'er the foaming billows
  She caſt a wiſtful look ;
Her head was crown'd with willows,
  That trembled o'er the brook.

AIR.

Twelve months are gone and over,
  And nine long tedious days ;
Why didſt thou, vent'rous lover,
  Why d'oſt thou truſt the ſea ?
Ceaſe, ceaſe, thou troubled ocean,
  And let my lover reſt ;
Ah ! what's thy troubled motion,
  To that within my breaſt ?

The merchant robb'd of pleaſure,
  Views tempeſts with deſpair :
But what's the loſs of treaſure
  To loſing of my dear ?
Should you ſome coaſt be laid on,
  Where gold and diamonds grow,
You'd find a richer maiden,
  But none that loves you ſo.

How can they ſay that nature,
  Has nothing made in vain ;
Why, then, beneath the water,
  Do hideous rocks remain ?'

No eyes thoſe rocks diſcover,
  That lurk beneath the deep,
To wreck the wand'ring lover,
  And leave the maid to weep.

Thus melancholy lying,
  Thus wail'd ſhe for her dear,
Repaid each blaſt with ſighing,
  Each billow with a tear :
When o'er the wide waves ſtooping,
  His floating corſe ſhe ſpy'd ;
Then like a lily drooping,
  She bow'd her head—and dy'd.

S O N G 28.

SPRING.

Sung at RANELAGH.

HAIL, young Spring, the earth adorning,
  Drive old Winter far away ;
Call the roſy-finger'd morning,
  Deck the ſun in radiance gay,

Flora, bring thy ſweeteſt treaſure ;
  Zephyrs, waft thy ſofteſt gale ;
Chant, ye birds, the ſong of pleaſure ;
  Echo, tell it thro' the vale.

Leafleſs, tuneleſs, unendearing,
  Mourn'd the long-deſerted grove ;
But, ſweet Spring, at thy appearing,
  All is harmony and love.

S O N G 29.

Sung in the *Waterman.*

AND did you not hear of a jolly young wa-
  terman,
Who at Black-Friars Bridge us'd for to ply ?
He feather'd his oars with ſuch ſkill and dex-
  terity,
Winning each heart, and delighting each eye :
He look'd ſo neat, and row'd ſo ſteadily,
The maidens all flock'd in his boat ſo readily ;
And he ey'd the young rogues with ſo charm-
  ing an air,
That this waterman ne'er was in want of a
  fare.

What ſights of fine folks he oft row'd in his
  wherry ;
'Twas clean'd out ſo nice and ſo painted
  withal !
He was always firſt oars, when the fine city
  ladies,
In a party to Ranelagh went, or Vauxhall.
And oftentimes wou'd they be giggling and
  leering,
But 'twas all one to Tom, their gibing and
  jeering ;
For loving, or liking, he little did care,
For this waterman ne'er was in want of a fare.

And yet, but to ſee how ſtrangely things
  happen ;
  As he row'd along, thinking of nothing
    at all,

Had I a Heart for Falshood framd

Song 30.

Publishd by Harrison & C? N°18 Paternoster Row.

He was ply'd by a damsel so lovely and charm-
ing,
That she smil'd, and so straightway in love
he did fall.
And would this young damsel but banish his
sorrow,
He'd wed her to-night, before it was morrow:
And how should this waterman ever know care,
When he's marry'd, and never in want of a
fare?

SONG 30.

Sung in the *Duenna*.

HAD I a heart for falshood fram'd,
I ne'er could injure you:
For tho' your tongue no promise claim'd,
Your charms would make me true.

To you no soul shall bear deceit,
No stranger offer wrong:
But friends in all the ag'd you'll meet,
And lovers in the young.

But when they learn that you have blest
Another with your heart,
They'll bid aspiring passion rest,
And act a brother's part.

Then, lady, dread not here deceit,
Nor fear to suffer wrong:
For friends in all the ag'd you'll meet,
And brothers in the young.

SONG 31.

Written by Dr. SMOLLET.

Sung at VAUXHALL.

THY fatal shafts unerring move;
I bow before thine altar, love!
I feel thy soft, resistless flame,
Glide swift thro' all my vital frame.

For while I gaze my bosom glows,
My blood, in tides impetuous flows;
Hope, fear, and joy. alternate roll,
And floods of transports whelm my soul.

My falt'ring tongue attempts, in vain,
In soothing murmurs to complain;
My tongue some secret magic ties,
My murmurs sink in broken sighs.

Condemn'd to nurse eternal care,
And ever drop the silent tear;
Unheard I mourn, unknown I sigh,
Unfriended live, unpity'd die!

SONG 32.

THE INCURIOUS.

GIVE me but a wife, I expect not to find
Each virtue and grace in one female com-
bin'd.
No goddess for me; 'tis a woman I prize,
And he that seeks more is more curious than
wise.

Be she young, she's not stubborn, but easy to
mould;
Or she claims my respect, like a mother, if old:
Thus either can please me, since woman I
prize,
And he, &c.

Like Venus she ogles, if squinting her eye;
If blind, she the roving of mine cannot spy:
Thus either is lovely; for woman I prize,
And he, &c.

If rich be my bride, she brings tokens of love;
If poor, then the farther from pride my re-
move;
Thus either contents me; for woman I prize,
And he, &c.

I ne'er shall want converse, if tongue she pos-
sess;
And if mute, still the rarity pleases no less;
I'm suited to either; for woman I prize,
And he, &c.

Then cease, ye profane, on the sex to descant;
If you've wit to discern, of charms they've no
want;
Each fair can make happy, if woman we prize;
And he, &c.

SONG 33.

Sung in *Eliza*.

MY fond shepherds of late were so blest,
Their fair nymphs were so happy and gay,
That each night they went safely to rest,
And they merrily sung thro' the day;
But, ah! what a scene must appear?
Must the sweet rural pastimes be o'er?
Shall the tabor no more strike the ear?
Shall the dance on the green be no more?

Must the flocks from their pastures be led?
Must the herds go wild straying abroad?
Shall the looms be all stopp'd in each shed,
And the ships be all moor'd in each road?
Must the arts be all scatter'd around,
And shall commerce grow sick of the tide?
Must religion expire on the ground,
And shall virtue sink down by her side?

SONG 34.

A HUNTING SONG.

YE sportsmen draw near, and ye sportswomen
too,
Who delight in the joys of the field;
Mankind, tho' they blame, are all eager as you,
And no one the contest will yield.
His lordship, his worship, his honour, his grace,
A hunting continually go;
All ranks and degrees are engag'd in the chase;
Hark forward, huzza, tally ho.

The lawyer will rise with the first of the morn,
To hunt for a mortgage or deed;
The husband gets up, at the sound of the horn,
And rises to the Commons full speed;

The patriot is thrown in purfuit of his game;
The poet, too, often lays low,
Who, mounted on Pegafus, flies after fame,
With hark forward, huzza, tally ho.

While, fearlefs, o'er hills and o'er woodlands
we fweep,
Tho' prudes on our paftime may frown,
How oft do they decency's bounds over-leap,
And the fences of virtue break down.
Thus, public or private, for penfion, for place,
For amufement, for paffion, for fhew,
All ranks and degrees are engag'd in the chace,
With hark forward, huzza, tally ho.

SONG 35.

FEMALE LIBERTY REGAINED.

Sung at VAUXHALL.

THO' man has long boafted an abfolute fway,
While woman's hard fate was love, ho-
nour, obey;
At length over wedlock fair liberty dawns,
And the lords of creation muft pull in their
horns;
For Hymen among ye proclaims his decree,
When hufbands are tyrants, their wives will
be free.

Away with your doubts, your furmifes, and
fears,
'Tis Venus beats up for her gay volunteers;
Enlift at her banner, you'll vanquifh with eafe,
And make of your hufbands what creatures you
pleafe;
To arms then, ye fair ones, and let the world
fee,
When hufbands are tyrants, their wives will
be free.

The rights of your fex, wou'd you e'er fee re-
ftor'd,
Your tongues fhou'd be us'd as a two-edged
fword,
That ear piercing weapon each hufband muft
dread,
Who thinks of the marks you may place on
his head;
Then wifely unite, till the men all agree,
That woman, that woman, fhall ever be free.
No more fhall the wife, all meek as a lamb,
Be fubject to, Zounds! do you know who I am?
Domeftic politenefs fhall flourifh again,
When women take courage to govern the men;
Then ftand to your charter, and let the world
fee,
Tho' hufbands are tyrants, their wives will be
free.

SONG 36.

Sung in Artaxerxes.

IN infancy our hopes and fears
Were to each other known;
And friendfhip, in our riper years,
Has twin'd our hearts in one;

O! clear him, then, from this offence;
Thy love, thy duty prove;
Reftore him with that innocence
Which firft infpir'd my love.

SONG 37.

Sung in the Way to Keep Him.

Written by DAVID GARRICK, Efq.

YE fair marry'd dames, who fo often deplore,
That a lover once bleft, is a lover no more;
Attend to my counfel, nor blufh to be taught,
That prudence muft cherifh what beauty has
caught.

The bloom of your cheek, and the glance of
your eye,
Your rofes and lilies may make the men figh;
But rofes and lilies, and fighs pafs away,
And paffion will die as your beauties decay.

Ufe the man that you wed like your fav'rite
guittar;
Tho' there's mufic in both, they are both apt to
jar!
How tuneful and foft from a delicate touch,
Not handled too roughly, nor play'd on too
much!

The fparrow and linnet will feed from your
hand,
Grow tame by your kindnefs, and come at
command:
Exert with your hufband the fame happy fkill;
For hearts, like your birds, may be tam'd to
your will.

Be gay and good-humour'd, complying and kind;
Turn the chief of your care from your face to
your mind;
'Tis there that a wife may her conqueft improve,
And Hymen fhall rivet the fetters of love.

SONG 38.

Sung at VAUXHALL.

ON pleafure's fmooth wing how old time
fteals away,
Ere love's fatal flame leads the fhepherd aftray!
My days, O ye fwains! were a round of delight,
From the cool of the morn to the ftillnefs of
night:
No care found a place in my cottage or breaft;
But health and content all the year was my gueft.
'Twas then no fair Phillis my heart could en-
fnare,
With voice, or with feature, with drefs, or
with air:
So kindly young Cupid had pointed the dart,
That I gather'd the fweets, but I mifs'd of the
fmart:
I toy'd for a while, then I rov'd like a bee;
But ftill all my fong was, I'll ever be free.

'Twas then ev'ry object frefh raptures did yield;
If I ftray'd thro' the garden, or travers'd the
field,

Ten thoufand gay fcenes were difplay'd to my
    fight;
If the nightingale fung, I could liften all night;
With my reed I could pipe to the tune of the
    ftream,
And wake to new life from a rapturous dream.

But now, fince for Hebe in fecret I figh,
Alas, what a change! and how wretched am I!
Adieu to the charms of the valley and glade;
Their fweets now all ficken, their colours all
    fade;
No mufic I find in foft Philomel's ftrain,
And the brook o'er the pebbles now murmurs
    in vain.

They fay that fhe's kind, but no kindnefs I
    fee;
On others fhe fmiles, but fhe frowns upon me;
Then teach me, bright Venus, perfuafion's
    foft art,
Or aid me, by reafon, to ranfom my heart!
To crown my defire, or to banifh my pain,
Give love to the nymph, or give eafe to the
    fwain.

SONG 39.

Sung in *Cymon.*

IF fhe whifpers the judge, be he ever fo wife,
    Tho' great and important his truft is;
His hand is unfteady, a pair of black eyes
Will kick up the balance of juftice.

If his paffions are ftrong, his judgment grows
    weak,
    For love through his veins will be creeping;
And his worfhip, when near to a round dimpl'd
    cheek,
Though he ought to be blind, will be peeping.

SONG 40.

A MARTIAL SONG.

HOW ftands the glafs around?
    For fhame, ye take no care, my boys;
How ftands the glafs around?
Let mirth and wine abound.
The trumpets found,
The colours they are flying, boys,
    To fight, kill, or wound;
May we ftill be found,
Content with our hard fate, my boys,
On the cold ground.

Why, foldiers, why,
Shou'd we be melancholy, boys?
    Why, foldiers, why,
Whofe bus'nefs 'tis to die?
What, fighing, fie!
Drown fear, drink on, be jolly, boys,
    'Tis he, you, or I!
Cold, hot, wet, or dry,
We're always bound to follow, boys,
And fcorn to fly.

'Tis but in vain,
I mean not to upbraid ye, boys;

'Tis but in vain
For foldiers to complain;
Should next campaign
Send us to Him who made us, boys,
We're free from pain!
But if we remain,
A bottle and kind landlady
Cure all again.

SONG 41.

Sung in *Mother Shipton.*

TO heal the fmart a bee had made
    Upon my Chloe's face,
Honey upon her cheek fhe laid,
    And bade me kifs the place.

Pleas'd, I obey'd, and from the wound
    Imbib'd both fweet and fmart;
The honey on my lips I found,
    The fting within my heart.

SONG 42.

VILLAGE COURTSHIP; A PASTORAL GLEE.

Sung at VAUXHALL.

HOW harmlefs and fweet are the joys of the
    plain,
When, quitting the village, each nymph and
    her fwain
    The piper's loud fummons obey;
While fhines the bright moon, radiant queen
    of the night,
And filv'ring the meadows, looks down with
    delight,
    To fee jolly mortals fo gay!

AURELIA.

Come, Julia, add one to the throng
That trip it the valley along:
    The found of our feet,
    Pleas'd echo fhall beat,
And mimic each clofe of our fong.

DAMON.

Aurelia, my charmer, away!
For once turn the night into day;
    The joys of the wake,
    Ale, cyder, and cake,
Forbid any longer delay.

MORSUS.

Bold youth, your addreffes decline;
The choice of thefe damfels refign:
    Tho' grey are my locks,
    The herds and the flocks
That graze round the village are mine.

DAMON.

Permit me to afk, as a friend,
To which of thefe girls you pretend?
    Your plea fhould be try'd,
    The fair-one decide,
And conteft in union fhall end.

DELIA.

Tho', Mopſus, your riches I know,
That plea I ſhall never allow;
For while a full bowl
My thirſt can controul,
Unheeded a river may flow.

PHILLIS.

Good farmer! ſince female decree
All parties muſt bring to agree;
Let Colin be mine,
Thy pelf I decline;
Content and a cottage for me.

JULIA.

To end fruitleſs cavils and noiſe,
Take, Strephon, my hand and my voice:
Away age and croſſes,
A coach and ſix horſes
Shan't draw me away from my choice.

SONG 43.

THE COMPARISON.

PARTING to death we will compare;
For, ſure, to thoſe who love ſincere,
So dreadful is the pain,
Such doubts, ſuch horrors, rend the mind!
But, oh! when adverſe fate grows kind,
How ſweet to meet again!

To thoſe try'd hearts, and thoſe alone,
Who have the pangs of abſence known,
The bliſsful change is given;
And who—oh! who wou'd not endure
The pangs of death, if they were ſure
To reap the joys of heaven?

SONG 44.

Written by Mr. SHENSTONE.

WHEN forc'd from dear Hebe to go,
What anguiſh I felt at my heart!
And I thought—but it might not be ſo—
She was ſorry to ſee me depart.
She caſt ſuch a languiſhing view,
My path I could ſcarcely diſcern;
And ſo ſweetly ſhe bade me adieu,
I thought ſhe had bade me return.

Methinks ſhe might like to retire
To the grove I had labour'd to rear;
For whatever I heard her admire,
I haſted, and planted it there.
Her voice ſuch a pleaſure conveys,
So much I her accents adore,
Let her ſpeak, and whatever ſhe ſays,
I'm ſure ſtill to love her the more.

And now, ere I haſte to the plain,
Come, ſhepherds, and tell of her ways;
I could lay down my life for the twain
Who would ſing me a ſong in her praiſe.
While he ſings may the ruins of the town
Come flocking, and liſten the while;

Nor on him let Hebe once frown,
Tho' I cannot allow her to ſmile.
To ſee when my charmer goes by,
Some hermit peeps out of his cell;
How he thinks of his youth with a ſigh!
How fondly he wiſhes her well!
On him ſhe may ſmile if ſhe pleaſe,
It will warm the cool boſom of age—
Yet ceaſe, gentle Hebe, O ceaſe,
Such ſoftneſs will ruin the ſage.

I've ſtole from no flow'rets that grow,
To deck the dear charms I approve;
For what can a bloſſom beſtow,
So ſweet, ſo delightful as love!
I ſing in a ruſtical way,
A ſhepherd, and one of the throng;
Yet Hebe approves of my lay:
Go, poets, and envy my ſong.

SONG 45.

THE LINNETS.

AS bringing home, the other day,
Two linnets I had ta'en,
The little warblers ſeem'd to pray
For liberty again:
Unheedful of their plaintive notes,
I ſung acroſs the mead;
In vain they tun'd their pleaſing throats,
And flutter'd to be freed.

As paſſing thro' the tufted grove,
Near which my cottage ſtood,
I thought I ſaw the queen of love,
When Clora's charms I view'd;
I look'd, I gaz'd, I preſs'd her ſtay,
To hear my tender tale;
But all in vain—ſhe fled away,
Nor could my ſighs prevail.

Soon, thro' the wound which love had made,
Came pity to my breaſt;
And thus I (as compaſſion bade)
The feather'd pair addreſs'd;
Ye little warblers, chearful be,
Remember not ye flew;
For I, who thought myſelf ſo free,
Am far more caught than you.

SONG 46.

Sung at VAUXHALL.

TO make the moſt of fleeting time,
Shou'd be our great endeavour;
For love we both are in our prime,
The time is now or never.

A thouſand charms around you play;
No girl more bright or clever;
Then let us both agree to-day,
To-morrow will be never.

I ne'er ſhall be a better man,
I burn with love's high fever;
Pray now be kind, I know you can,
You muſt not anſwer never.

Whilſt you, thus, Chloe, turn aſiJe,
　You fruſt.ate my endeavour;
That face will fade, come down that pride,
　Your time is now or never.

Ere for yourſelf or me too la`e,
　Say now, you're mine for ever;
I may be ſnatch'd by care or fate,
　My time is now or never.

SONG 47.

Sung at RANELAGH, after the Regatta.

YE lords, and ye ladies, who form this gay
　throng,
Be ſilent a moment, attend to my ſong;
And while you ſuſpend your fantaſtical round,
Come bleſs your ſweet ſtars, that you're none of
　you drown'd.
Derry down, down; down, derry down.

As you've long been detain'd with daughters and
　ſpouſes,
From your parks, and your lawns, and your fine
　country houſes;
Ere for ſummer's dull ſeaſon you bid us adieu,
We preſent you a feaſt, and a novelty too.

Enough of feſtinos, champetres enough,
Bal parés, and freſcos, and ſuch worn-out ſtuff;
But how to amuſe ye! aye, there was the
　queſtion;
A Regatta was thought of, oh! lucky ſug-
　g ſtion.

From the lagunes of Venice we've ſtolen the
　hint,
And hope you'll acknowledge there's ſome merit
　ir.'t;
Nay, we truſt you'll pronounce it cool, uſeful,
　and hearty,
As old father Thames is made one of the party.

For ſay, ſhould Britannia ungratefully treat
The friend of her commerce, the nurſe of her
　fleet?
Shall he who with toil wafts your treaſures to
　ſhore,
In her hours of amuſement be thought of no
　more?

Array'd in his beſt, in hiꞏ holiday cloaths,
To-night the gay Thames his aſſiſtance beſtows;
And, as uſual to render the ſhew more compleat,
We have ranſack'd the wardrobe of Taviſtock
　Street.

We've friends in the court, and we've friends
　in the city;
No doubt, then, our plan is both uſeful and
　pretty;
Since the ſix clubs have join'd to defray all the
　charges,
And the lord-mayor and aldermen lent us their
　barges.

Did ye mind how each candidate tugg'd at the
　oar?
How the managers ſtorm'd, how the conſtables
　ſwore?

Shall ye ever forget how the mob was delighted,
When the boats all run foul, and the ladies were
　frighted?

But the races are o'er, the procⱥſſion is cloſ'd,
The landing effected, the clamour compoſ'd;
The fare that's before ye, we hope you'll agree,
Is better than coffee, rolls, butter, and tea.

But ere ye return, and your faces vermilion,
With twiſting allemand, and friſking cotillion,
Thus with crotchet and ballad we greet every
　gueſt,
And welcome you all to our otter-like feaſt.

We've ſtrove to amuſe you by water and land,
Once Torre, to pleaſe ye, had fire at command;
To charm ye ſhould be all the elements care,
So next time we ll fix on a plan in the air.

SONG 48.

Written by Mr. CONGREVE.

Sung at VAUXHALL.

O What joy does conqueſt yield,
　When returning from the field?
Shining in his glitt ring arms,
　How the god-like warrior charms!
Laurel-wreaths his head ſurrounding,
　Banners waving in the wind;
Fame her golden trumpet ſounding,
　Ev'ry voice in concert join d.

SONG 49.

Sung in the Oratorio of SUSANNA.

ASK if yon damaſk roſe is ſweet,
　That ſcents the ambient air,
Then aſk each ſhepherd that you meet,
If dear Suſanna's fair.

Say, will the vulture quit his prey,
　And warble thro' the grove?
Bid wanton linnets quit the ſpray,
　Then doubt thy ſhepherd's love.

The ſpoils of war let heroes ſhare,
　Let pride in ſplendor ſhine;
Ye bards, unenvy'd, laurels wear,
　Be fair Suſanna mine.

SONG 50.

HOPE; A PASTORAL.

Written by Mr. SHENSTONE.

MY banks are all furniſh'd with bees,
　Whoſe murmur invites one to ſleep;
My grottos are ſhaded with trees,
　And my hill's are white over with ſheep.
I ſeldom have met with a loſs,
　Such health do my mountains beſtow;
My fountains are border'd with moſs,
　Where the hare-bells and violets blow.

I've found out a gift for my fair;
　I've found where the wood-pigeons breed,

C

But, let me that plunder forbear,
  She'll fay 'twas a barbarous deed:
He ne'er could be true, fhe averr'd,
  Who could rob a poor bird of it's young;
And I lov'd her the more when I heard
  Such tendernefs fall from her tongue.

But where does my Phillida ftray,
  And where are her grots and her bow'rs;
Are the groves and the vallies as gay,
  And the fhepherds as gentle as ours?
The groves may perhaps be as fair,
  The face of the vallies as fine;
The fwains may in manners compare,
  But their love is not equal to mine.

SONG 51.

A TOUCH ON THE TIMES.

Written by JAMES WORSDALE, Efq.

COME liften, and laugh at the times,
  Since folly was never fo ripe;
For ev'ry man laughs at thofe rhimes
  That give his own follies a wipe :
We live in a kind of difguife;
  We flatter, we lye, and proteft,
While each of us artfully tries
  On others to faften the jeft.

The virgin, when firft fhe is woo'd,
  Returns ev'ry figh with difdain;
And while by her lover purfu'd,
  Can laugh at his folly and pain:
But when from her innocence won,
  And doom'd for her virtue to mourn,
When fhe finds herfelf loft and undone,
  He laughs (though unjuft) in his turn.

The fools, who at law do contend,
  Can laugh at each other's diftrefs,
And while the dire fuit does depend,
  Ne'er think how their fubftance grows lefs;
Till hamper'd by tedious expence,
  Altho' to compound they are loth,
They'll find, when reftor'd to their fenfe,
  The lawyers fit laughing at both.

But while we perceive it the fafhion
  For each fool to laugh at the other,
Let us ftrive, with a gen'rous compaffion,
  To correct, not contemn, one another.
We all have fome follies to hide,
  Which, known, would difhonour the beft;
And life, when 'tis thoroughly try'd,
  Like friendfhip, will feem but a jeft.

SONG 52.

Sung at VAUXHALL.

I Do as I will with my fwain,
  He never once thinks I am wrong;
He likes none fo well on the plain,
  I pleafe him fo well with my fong.
A fong is the fhepherd's delight;
  He hears me with joy all the day;
He's forry when comes the dull night,
  That haftens the end of my lay.

With fpleen and with care once opprefs'd,
  He afk'd me to footh him the while;
My voice fet his mind all to reft,
  And the fhepherd would inftantly fmile.
Since when, or in mead, or in grove,
  By his flocks on the clear river-fide,
I fing my beft fongs to my love,
  And to charm him is grown all my pride.

No beauty had I to endear,
  No treafure of nature, or art;
But my voice, which had gain'd on his ear,
  Soon found out the way to his heart:
To try if that voice would not pleafe,
  He took me to join the gay throng;
I won the rich prize with much eafe,
  And my fame's gone abroad with my fong.

But let me not jealoufy raife;
  I wifh to enchant but my fwain?
Enough then for me is his praife,
  I fing but for him the lov'd ftrain.
When youth, wealth, and beauty, may fail,
  And your fhepherds elude all your fkill,
Your fweetnefs of fong may prevail,
  And gain all your fwains to your will.

SONG 53.

THE SONS OF NEPTUNE.

WHAT cheer, brother tars! our toils are
    all o'er,
The high foaming billows difturb us no more;
Rude Boreas now ruffles the ocean in vain,
We are clear of the danger attending the main.
Now each honeft heart take his bottle and lafs,
For life is a moment that quickly will pafs.

Since life's but a moment, how fenfelefs are they
Who loiter and trifle that fhort fpace away?
We will, my brave boys, our time nobly employ,
For in women and wine are the charms that
    ne'er cloy:
Our hours, then, in freedom and pleafure we'll
    pafs,
And our care will be loft betwixt love and our
    glafs.

Can the politick ftatefman, tho' ever fo great,
Be free from the cares and the turmoils of ftate?
Or can they, like feamen, enjoy while they live,
The pleafures that honour and honefty give?
'Tis out of their fphere, confcience will inter-
    lope,
But liquor and love are our anchor and hope.

SONG 54.

THE RATIONAL LOVER.

AWAY, let nought to love difpleafing,
  My Winifrida, move thy fear;
Let nought delay the heav'nly bleffing,
  Nor fqueamifh pride, nor gloomy care.

What tho' no grants of royal donors
  With pompous titles grace our blood,

We'll shine in more substantial honours,
And to be noble, we'll be good.

What tho' from fortune's lavish bounty
No mighty treasures we possess;
We'll find within our pittance plenty,
And be content without excess.

Still shall each kind returning season
Sufficient for our wishes give;
For we will live a life of reason,
And that's the only life to live.

Our name, whilst virtue thus we tender,
Shall sweetly sound where er 'tis spoke;
And all the great ones much shall wonder,
How they admire such little folk.

Through youth and age, in love excelling,
We'll hand in hand together tread;
Sweet smiling peace shall crown our dwelling,
And babes, sweet smiling babes, our bed.

How should I love the pretty creatures,
Whilst round my knees they fondly clung;
To see 'em look their mother's features,
To hear 'em lisp their mother's tongue.

And when with envy time transported
Shall think to rob us of our joys,
You'll in your girls again be courted,
And I go wooing in my boys.

SONG 55.

SERENADE.

Sung at MARYBONE.

AWAKE, my charmer, my Rosalind wake,
Thy shepherd, thy Paridel's here;
Come shake off thy slumber, thou queen of my
heart,
And let me thy beauties revere:
Thy dearest companions of mirth are all up,
Lo! yonder they trip o'er the plain;
Oh! come, or they'll chide the neglect of thy
vow,
And never believe thee again.

Oh! come, while the birds are all whistling
around,
And teaching soft echo to sing:
While morning, profuse of unparallel'd sweets,
Drops spice on the zephyr's cool wing:
Oh! now, while the sun at thy window peeps in,
And shoots his bold rays at thine eyes;
Oh! now, while thy shepherd, thy Paridel's
here,
Arise, my dear Rosalind, rise.

SONG 56.

Sung in the *Padlock*.

WAS I a shepherd's maid, to keep
On yonder plains a flock of sheep;
Well pleas'd I'd watch, the live long day,
My ewes at feed, my lambs at play:
Or, would some bird, that pity brings,
But for a moment lend it's wings;

My parents they might rave and scold,
My guardian strive my will to hold;
Their words are harsh, his walls are high,
But, spite of all, away I'd fly.

SONG 57.

A HUNTING SONG.

COME, rouze, brother sportsmen, the hunters all cry,
We've got a good scent, and a fav'ring sky;
The horn's sprightly notes, and the lark's early
song,
Will chide the dull sportsman for sleeping so
long.

Bright Phœbus has shewn us the glimpse of his
face,
Peep'd in at our windows, and call'd to the
chace;
He soon will be up, for his dawn wears away,
And makes the fields blush with the beams of
his ray.

Sweet Molly may teaze you, perhaps, to lie
down;
And if you refuse her, perhaps she may frown:
But tell her, that love must to hunting give
place;
For as well as her charms, there are charms in
the chace.

Look yonder, look yonder, old Reynard I spy,
At his brush nimbly follow brisk Chanter and
Fly;
They seize on their prey, see his eye balls they
roll;
We're at in the death—now let's home to the
bowl.

There we'll fill up our glasses, and toast to the
king;
From a bumper fresh loyalty ever will spring;
To George, peace and glory may heaven dispense,
And fox-hunters flourish a thousand years hence.

SONG 58.

A PASTORAL SONG.

Sung at RANELAGH.

WHAT shepherd or nymph of the grove
Can blame me for dropping a tear,
Or lamenting aloud, as I rove,
Since Phœbe no longer is here?
My flocks, if at random they stray,
What wonder, if she's from the plains!
Her hand they were wont to obey:
She rul'd both the sheep and the swains.

Can I ever forget how we stray'd
To the foot of yon neighbouring hill,
To the bow'r we had built in the shade,
Or the river that runs by the mill!
There, sweet, by my side as she lay,
And heard the fond stories I told,
How sweet was the thrush from the spray,
Or the bleating of lambs from the fold?

How oft wou'd I fpy out a charm,
　Which before had been hid from my view!
And, while arm was infolded in arm,
　My lips to her lips how they grew!
How long the fweet conteft would laft!
　Till the hours of retirement and reft;
What pleafures and pain each had paft,
　Who longeft had lov'd, and who beft.

No changes of place, or of time,
　I felt when my fair-one was near;
Alike was each weather and clime,
　Each feafon that chequer'd the year:
In winter's rude lap did we freeze,
　Did we melt on the bofom of May?
Each morn brought contentment and eafe,
　If we rofe up to work or to play.

She was all my fond wifhes could afk;
　She had all the kind gods could impart;
She was nature's moft beautiful tafk;
　The defpair and the envy of art;
There all that is worthy to prize,
　In all that was lovely was dreft;
For the graces were thron'd in her eyes,
　And the virtues all lodg'd in her breaft.

SONG 59.

ARTFUL CHLOE.

AS once on Chloe's knee, in chat,
　The little playful Cupid fat;
His arrows tipt with fmiles he found,
And fhot the random fhafts around.

Young Strephon fmil'd the god to fee;
And cry'd, Blind archer, fhoot at me.
Full oft the wanton, touch'd with pride,
Took aim, but Strephon ftepp'd afide.

Defigning Chloe cry'd, Forbear;
And vow'd their conteft now unfair.
As Cupid's blind, young fwain, faid fhe,
Unjuft it is that you fhould fee.

The darling fhepherd ftraight comply'd,
And blindfold now the god defy'd;
While Chloe level'd right his dart,
And ftruck out-witted Strephon's heart.

SONG 60.

Sung in the Chaplet.

PUSH about the brifk bowl, 'twill enliven
　the heart,
　While thus we fit round on the grafs:
The lo'er, who talks of his fuff'rings and
　fmart,
　Def'rves to be reckon'd an afs, an afs;
　Deferves to, &c.

The wretch, who fits watching his ill-gotten
　pelf,
　And wifhes to add to the mafs,
Whate'er the curmudgeon may think of him-
　felf,
　Deferves to be reckon'd an afs;
　Deferv es to, &c.

The beau, who fo fmart, with his well-pow-
　der'd hair,
　An angel beholds in his glafs,
And thinks with grimace to fubdue all the fair,
　Deferves to be reckon'd an afs;
　Deferves to, &c.

The merchant from climate to climate will
　roam,
　Of Crœfus the wealth to furpafs;
And oft, while he's wand'ring, my lady at home,
　Claps the horns of an ox on the afs;
　Claps the, &c.

The lawyer fo grave, when he puts in his plea,
　With forehead well cover'd with brafs,
Tho' he talks to no purpofe, he pockets your fee;
　There you, my good friend, are the afs;
　There you, &c.

The formal phyfician, who knows ev'ry ill,
　Shall laft be produc'd in this clafs;
The fick man awhile may confide in his fkill,
　But death proves the doctor an afs;
　But death, &c.

Then let us, companions, be jovial and gay,
　By turns take our bottle and lafs;
For he who his pleafure puts off for a day,
　Deferves to be reckon'd an afs, an afs;
　Deferves to, &c.

SONG 61.

CONTENT; A PASTORAL BALLAD.

Written by Mr. CUNNINGHAM.

O'ER moorlands and mountains, rude, bar-
　ren, and bare,
　As wilder'd and weary'd I roam,
A gentle young fhepherdefs fees my defpair,
　And leads me o'er lawns to her home;
Yellow fheaves, from rich Ceres, her cottage
　had crown'd,
　Green rufhes were ftrew'd on the floor;
Her cafement fweet woodbines crept wantonly
　round,
　And deck'd the fod feats at her door.

We fat ourfelves down to a cooling repaft,
　Frefh fruits, and fhe cull'd me the beft;
While thrown from my guard, by fome glan-
　ces fhe caft,
　Love flily ftole into my breaft.
I told my foft wifhes, fhe fweetly reply'd,
　(Ye virgins her voice was divine)
I've rich ones rejected, and great ones deny'd,
　Yet take me, fond fhepherd, I'm thine.

Her air was fo modeft, her afpect fo meek,
　So fimple, yet fweet were her charms;
I kifs'd the ripe rofes that glow'd on her cheek,
　And leck'd the lov'd maid in my arms.
Now jocund together we tend a few fheep;
　And if, on the banks by the ftream,
Reclin'd on her bofom I fink into fleep,
　Her image ftill foftens my dream.

Together we range o'er the flow-rifing hills,
　Delighted with paftoral views;

Or reft on the rock where the ftreamlet diftils
And maik out new themes for my mufe.
To pomp or proud titles fhe ne'er did afpire,
The damfel's of humble defcent;
The cottager Peace is well known for her fire,
And fhepherds have nam'd her Content.

SONG 62.

THE LITTLE COQUETTE.

Sung at VAUXHALL.

THO' ftill fo young, and fcarce fifteen,
   Yet fweethearts I have plenty;
And if more forward I had been,
   Ere this they had been twenty.
Like buzzing flies, or wafps with ftings,
   In fwarms they hover round me:
I brufh away thofe humming things,
   They have no power to wound me.

I furely am not much to blame,
   To fport with one and t'other;
My lovers raife no reddifh fhame,
   'Tis playing with one's brother.
I like to hear what each can fay,
   To fee what they'd be doing;
And when they think me moft their prey,
   I'm fartheft off from ruin.

What, tho' in crowds I pafs the day,
   And all my joy is teizing,
To one alone I'd not be gay,
   Left one fhould be too pleafing.
They fondly flutter here and there,
   And take their idle ftation;
They only catch my eye and ear,
   But raife no palpitation.

Then welcome, Harry, Tom, and Phil,
   Your numbers won't alarm me;
For, truft me, I'm in fafety ftill,
   'Tis only one can harm me.
Then to this folly, nymphs, be kind,
   Coquetting's but a feafon;
When older grown, to one refign'd,
   I'll yield to love and reafon.

SONG 63.

A PASTORAL BALLAD.

Sung at VAUXHALL.

TO pleafe me the more, and to change the
   dull fcene,
My fwain took me oft to the fports on the green;
And to ev'ry fine fight would he tempt me to
   roam,
For he fear'd left my heart fhould grow weary
   of home.

To yield to my fhepherd, fo fond and fo kind,
I left my dear cot and true pleafures behind;
And oft, as I went, faw 'twas folly to roam,
For falfe all the joy was that grew not at home.

To flirt, to be prais'd, was to me no delight,
I figh'd for no fwain with my own in my fight;

Then how could I wifh all abroad thus to roam,
When love and contentment were always at
   home?

Like the bird in the cage, who's been kept
   there too long,
I'm bleft as I can be, and fing my glad fong;
I afk not again in the woodlands to roam,
Nor chufe to be free, nor to fly from my home.

Ye nymphs, and ye fhepherds, fo frolick and
   gay,
Who in roving now flutter your moments away;
Believe it, my aim fhall be never to roam,
But to live my life through, and be happy at
   home.

SONG 64.

FRIENDSHIP.

THE world, my dear Mira, is full of deceit,
   And friendfhip's a jewel we feldom can meet;
How ftrange does it feem, that in fearching
   around,
This fource of content is fo rare to be found!
Oh! friendfhip, thou balm, and rich fweet'ner
   of life,
Kind parent of eafe, and compofer of ftrife;
Without thee, alas! what are riches and pow'r,
But empty delufions, the joys of an hour.

How much to be priz'd and efteem'd is a friend,
On whom we may always with fafety depend?
Our joys when extended will always increafe,
And griefs, when divided, are hufh'd into peace.
When fortune is fmiling, what crowds will
   appear,
Their kindnefs to offer, and friendfhip fincere;
Yet change but the profpect, and point out
   diftrefs,
No longer to court you they eagerly prefs.

SONG 65.

Sung in the Elopement.

COME hafte to the wedding, ye friends and
   ye neighbours,
The lovers their blifs can no longer delay;
Forget all your forrows, your care and your
   labours,
And let ev'ry heart beat with rapture to day:
Ye vot'ries all, attend to my call,
   Come revel in pleafures that never can cloy.
Come, fee rural felicity,
   Which love and innocence ever enjoy.

Let envy, let pride, let hate and ambition,
   Still crowd to, and beat at the breaft of the
   great;
To fuch wretched paffions we give no admiffion,
   But leave them alone to the wife-ones of
   ftate;
We boaft of no wealth, but contentment and
   health,
   In mirth and in friendfhip our moments em-
   ploy.
Come, fee rural felicity, &c.

With reason we taste of each heart-stirring plea-
sure,
With reason we drink of the full-flowing
bowl;
Are jocund and gay, but all within measure,
For fatal excess will enslave the free soul.
Then come at our bidding to this happy wed-
ding,
No care shall intrude, here, our bliss to annoy.
Come, see rural felicity, &c.

SONG 66.

THE HAPPY SURPRIZE.

WHILE autumn weighs down the late year,
    And harvest is thick on the ground,
The grapes in thick clusters appear,
    The village with plenty is crown'd;

I tell to the lone woods my grief,
    For Laura so fair fled away;
Nor music can yield me relief,
    I sigh for her all the long day.

I rov'd o'er the once happy plain,
    The woodlands and vales in despair;
The nightingale echo'd my strain,
    But Laura, alas! was not there.

I turn'd from the dew-weeping grove,
    I saw her resplendent in charms:
'Twas she, or the goddess of love;
    'Twas Laura return'd to my arms!

No longer my fair-one will stray,
    Tho' winter's approaches I see,
I bask on the bosom of May,
    'Twill always be summer with me.

SONG 67.

A BACCHANALIAN BALLAD.

O Greedy Midas, I've been told,
    That what you touch you turn to gold;
Oh! had I but a power like thine,
    I'd turn whate'er I touch to wine.

Each purling stream should feel my force,
Each fish my fatal power mourn;
And, wond'ring at the mighty change,
    Should in their native regions burn.

Nor should there any dare approach
Unto my mantling, sparkling vine,
But first should pay their rites to me,
    And stile me only god of wine.

SONG 68.

Sung at MARYBONE.

WHEN courted by Strephon, what pains
    then he took,
Each day on my charms to refine;
So much of an angel he saw in my look,
    That he swore I was something divine.
Like Venus in beauty, like Juno in gait,
    Like Pallas most wonderful wise;

And thus of three deities fairly, in prate,
    He purloin'd, to please me, the skies.
But when I was marry'd, more trouble he found,
    To make me a woman again;
My notions celestial so much did abound,
    That a goddess I still would remain.
But finding that his adoration would cease,
    My senses at last were restor d;
From sublimity gently descending to peace,
    I begg'd to be lov'd, not ador'd.

Be cautious, ye youths, with the nymph that
    you prize,
Nor too much her beauty commend;
When once you have rais'd the fair maid to
    the skies,
To the earth she'll not easy descend.

SONG 69.

WILLY; A SCOTCH BALLAD.

Sung at VAUXHALL.

WITH tuneful pipe and merry glee,
    Young Willy won my heart,
A blyther swain you could na see,
    All beauty without art.
Willy's rare, and Willy's fair,
And Willy's wond'rous bonny;
    And Willy says he'll marry me
Gin e'er he'll marry ony.

O came you by yon water-side,
    Pull'd you the rose or lily,
Or came you by yon meadow green,
    Or saw you my sweet Willy.
Willy's rare, and Willy's fair, &c.

Syne now the trees are in their bloom,
    And flow'rs spread o'er ilka field,
I'll meet my lad among the broom,
    And lead him to my summer's shield.
Willy's rare, and Willy's fair, &c.

SONG 70.

CORYDON; A PASTORAL.

To the Memory of W. SHENSTONE, Esq.

Written by Mr. CUNNINGHAM.

COME, shepherds, we'll follow the hearse,
    We'll see our lov'd Corydon laid;
Tho' sorrow may blemish the verse,
    Yet let the sad tribute be paid.
They call'd him the pride of the plain;
    In sooth he was gentle and kind;
He mark'd, in his elegant strain,
    The graces that glow'd in his mind.

On purpose he planted yon trees,
    That birds in the covert might dwell;
He cultur'd his thyme for the bees,
    But never once rifled their cell.
Ye lambkins, who play'd at his feet,
    Go bleat, and your master bemoan;
His music was artless and sweet,
    His manners as mild as your own.

No verdure fhall cover the vale,
No bloom on the bloffoms appear;
The fweets of the foreft fhall fail,
And winter difcolour the year.
No birds in our hedges fha'll fing,
(Our hedges fo vocal before)
nce he that fhould welcome the fpring,
Can greet the gay feafon no more.

His Phillis was fond of his praife,
And poets came round in a throng;
They liften'd—they envy'd his lays,
But which of them equal'd his fong?
Ye fhepherds, henceforward be mute,
For loft is the paftoral ftrain;
So give me my Corydon's flute,
And thus—let me break it in twain.

SONG 71.

A HUNTING SONG.

WHEN Phœbus begins juft to peep o'er the
hills,
With horns we awaken the day,
And rouze brother fportfmen, who fluggifhly
fleep,
With hark! to the woods, hark away!
See the hounds are uncoupled in mufical cry,
How fweetly it echoes around;
And high-mettled fteeds with their neighing all
feem
With pleafure to echo the found.

Behold where fly Reynard, with panick and
dread,
At diftance o'er hillocks doth bound;
The pack on the fcent fly with rapid career,
Hark! the horns! O how fweetly they found!
Now on to the chace, o'er hills and o'er dales,
All dangers we nobly defy;
Our nags are all ftout, and our fports we'll
purfue,
With fhouts that refound to the fky.

But fee how he lags, all his arts are in vain,
No longer with fwiftnefs he flies;
Each hound in his fury determines his fate,
The traitor is feiz'd on and dies.
With fhouting and joy we return from the field,
With drink crown the fports of the day;
Then to reft we recline, till the horn calls again,
Then away to the woodlands, away.

SONG 72.

THE COMPLAINING MAID.

Sung at VAUXHALL.

YE fhepherds, who ftray with my fwain,
Companions in fport, and in youth,
O! tell him how great is my pain!
How I grieve for the lofs of his truth!
O! tell him, how oft has he fwore
He never would ceafe to be mine!
Or leave me his faith to deplore,
Or with heart-breaking anguifh repine!

Remind him how oft in the grove,
At my feet he in raptures would kneel,
And implore me to pity his love,
Till he taught me, fond foul, how to feel!

O! tell him, 'tis now he muft come,
For more my fond heart cannot bear;
Or the maidens will carry me home,
The victim of love and defpair.

SONG 73.

A SCOTCH BALLAD.

Sung at VAUXHALL.

LOVE never more fhall give me pain,
My fancy's fix'd on thee;
Nor ever maid my heart fhall gain,
My Peggy, if thou die.

Thy beauties did fuch pleafure give,
Thy love fo true to me:
Without thee I fhall never live,
My deary, if thou die.

If fate fhall tear thee from my breaft,
How fhall I lonely ftray;
In dreary dreams the nights I'll wafte,
In fighs the filent day.

I ne'er can fo much virtue find,
Nor fuch perfection fee;
Then I'll renounce all woman-kind,
My Peggy, after thee.

No new-blown beauty fires my breaft
With Cupid's raving rage;
But thine, which can fuch fweets impart,
Muft all the world engage.

'Twas this that, like the morning fun,
Gave joy to life and me;
And when it's deftin'd day is done,
With Peggy let me die.

Ye pow'rs that fmile on virtuous love,
And in fuch pleafures fhare;
You, who it's faithful flames approve,
With pity view the fair.

Reftore my Peggy's wonted charms,
Thofe charms fo dear to me;
Oh! never rob them from thefe arms,
I'm loft if Peggy die.

SONG 74.

THE EFFORTS OF LOVE AND MUSIC.

THE morning op'd fmiling, all nature was
gay,
And Flora had chequer'd the grove;
The thrufh and the linnet were heard on the
fpray,
Attuning their voices to love.

Young Damon, well pleas'd, in a woodbine
retreat,
To Phillis unbofom'd his mind;
But his paffion in vain did the fhepherd repeat,
With coolnefs his fuit fhe declin'd.

In murmurs foft mufic now glides thro' the air,
To harmony wakens the vale;
The nymph caught the found, when her rap-
    tures declare
Full hopes of fuccefs to his tale.

Exulting, thus Damon his wifhes exprefs'd—
    Thofe notes breathing love's gentle fire,
Speak joy to Alexis, with Sylvia blefs'd,
    And love all their virtues infpire:

O ceafe then, my deareft, to treat with dif-
    dain,
An heart fway'd by virtue and love;
But hafte to yon fane at the top of the plain,
    And Hymen's mild influence prove.

Thus mufic and love were too much for the fair;
    In vain fhe her wifhes would hide;
Her blufhes the ftate of her bofom declare,
    And Damon could not be deny'd.

SONG 75.

A MASQUERADE SONG.

Written by the EDITOR.

JOIN with me, ye motley band,
    And the pleafures of the night,
Let the mufe, by your command,
    Give their tributary right.

Youth and beauty here are feen,
    Where full threefcore years have paft;
And the maid that's fcarce fifteen,
    By her grandame is furpafs'd.

Bucks, that fifty years ago
    Boafted joys they ne'er obtain'd,
Now are found as youthful beaux,
    And their folly have regain'd.

All conditions may appear
    In what charaéter they pleafe;
And the wretched here may wear
    Features bleft with health and eafe.

In the world at large, we fee,
    Many do their hearts difguife;
But, in our epitome,
    No fuch foul deception lies.

Here we only feek to hide
    Faults of age with charms of youth,
While within our breafts refide
    Hearts that facred are to truth.

SONG 76.

A FREE-MASON'S SONG.

COME, let us prepare,
    We brothers that are
Met together on merry occafion;
    Let's drink, laugh, and fing,
    Our wine has a fpring;
Here's a health to an accepted mafon.

    The world is in pain
    Our fecret to gain,
But ftill let them wonder and gaze on;

    Till they're fhewn the light,
    They'll ne'er know the right
Word or fign of an accepted mafon.

    'Tis this, and 'tis that,
    They cannot tell what,
Why fo many great men in the nation
    Should aprons put on,
    To make themfelves one
With a free and an accepted mafon.

    Great kings, dukes, and lords,
    Have laid by their fwords,
This our myft'ry to put a good grace on;
    And ne'er been afham'd
    To hear themfelves nam'd
With a free and an accepted mafon.

    Antiquity's pride
    We have on our fide,
It makes each man juft in his ftation;
    There's nought but what's good
    To be underftood
By a free and an accepted mafon.

    We're true and fincere,
    We're juft to the fair,
They'll truft us on ev'ry occafion;
    No mortal can more
    The ladies adore,
Than a free and an accepted mafon.

    Then join hand in hand,
    To each other firm ftand,
Let's be merry, and put a bright face on;
    No mortal can boaft
    So noble a toaft,
As a free and an accepted mafon.

SONG 77.

ABSENCE.

HOW heavy the time rolls along,
    Now Julia is out of my fight!
How dull is the nightingale's fong,
    That once us'd to give fuch delight!

The meadows that feemed fo green,
    Now lofe all the verdure of May;
The cowflip and violet are feen
    To droop, fade, and wither away.

Bright Phœbus no longer can pleafe!
    Gay profpeéts no longer can charm!
E'en mufic affords me no eafe,
    Tho' wont ev'ry paffion to calm.

My flocks, too, diforderly ftray,
    And bleat their complaints in my ear;
No more they leap, frolic, and play,
    But fad, like their mafter, appear.

But ah! if my Julia were feen,
    My flocks, how they'd fkip o'er the plain!
Each flow'ret would fpring on the green,
    And nightingales charm me again.

For her a green arbour I've made,
    Enrich'd with each fragrant flow'r,
The fun's fcorching heart it will fhade,
    And her beauty preferve from his pow'r.

Return then, my fair-one, return,
Your coming no longer delay;
O leave not your fhepherd to mourn,
But haften, my charmer, away.

S'O N G 78.

Sung in the *Metamorphofes.*

WHAT ftate of life can be fo bleft
As love that warms the lover's breaft;
Two fouls in one the fame defire,
To grant the blifs, and to require!
But if in heav'n a hell we find,
'Tis all from thee, oh! jealoufy,
Thou tyrant of the mind.

Falfe in thy glafs all objects are,
Some fet too near, and fome too far;
Thou art the fire of endlefs night,
The fire that burns, and gives no light.
All torments, ev'ry ill, we find
In only thee, oh! jealouty,
Thou tyrant of the mind.

S O N G 79.

GRAMACHREE MOLLY; AN IRISH AIR.

AS down on Banna's banks I ftray'd, one
evening in May.
The little birds, in blytheft notes, made vocal ev'ry fpray:
They fung their little tales of love, they fung
them o'er and o'er.
Ah! gramachree, ma cholleenouge, ma Molly
afhtore!

The daify dy'd, and all the fweets, the dawn
of nature yields,
The primrofe pale, and vi'let blue, lay fcatter'd
o'er the fields:
Such fragrance in the bofom lies of her whom
I adore.
Ah! gramachree, &c.

I laid me down upon a bank, bewailing my fad
fate,
That doom'd me thus the flave of love, and
cruel Molly's hate;
How can fhe break the honeft heart that wears
her in it's core?
Ah! gramachree, &c.

You faid you lov'd me, Molly dear: Ah! why
did I believe?
Yet who could think fuch tender words were
meant but to deceive?
That love was all I afk'd on earth; nay, Heav'n
could give no more.
Ah! gramachree, &c.

O! had I all the flocks that graze on yonder
yellow hill,
Or low'd for me the num'rous herds that yon
green pafture fill;
With her I love, I'd gladly fhare my kine and
fleecy ftore.
Ah! gramachree, &c.

Two turtle-doves, above my head, fat courting
on a bough,
I envy'd them their happinefs, to fee them bill
and coo;
Such fondnefs once for me fhe fhew'd, but now,
alas! 'tis o'er.
Ah! gramachree, &c.

Then fare thee well, my Molly dear, thy lofs
I e'er fhall mourn;
While life remains in Strephon's heart, 'twill
beat for thee alone;
Tho' thou art falfe, may Heav'n on thee it's
choiceft bleffings pour.
Ah! gramachree, &c.

S O N G 80.

DELIA'S PROMISE.

Sung at VAUXHALL.

THE happy moments now are near
When Delia promis'd to be here;
Calm ftilnefs rules, no zephyrs move,
The hour is foft, and calls to love.

But hark! there's mufic, 'tis her voice,
'Tis Delia fings—ye birds, rejoice:
Hufh every breeze, let nothing move,
For deareft Delia fings of love.

Come, let the foft enchanting fcene,
Thefe many walks for ever green;
Let this light-excluding grove
Incline my fair to hear of love.

Cupid is jealous of his pow'r;
O come then, this is Hymen's hour:
If Delia does my claim approve,
This is the hour for joy and love.

S O N G 81.

Written by Mr. CUNNINGHAM.

I Said—On the banks by the ftream,
I've pip'd for the fhepherds too long:
Oh, grant me, ye mufes, a theme,
Where glory may brighten myfong!

But Pan bade me ftick to my ftrain,
Nor leffons too lofty rehearfe;
Ambition befits not a fwain,
And Phillis loves paftoral verfe.

The rofe, tho' a beautiful red,
Looks faded to Philis s bloom;
And the breeze from the bean-flow'r bed,
To her breath's but a feeble perfume:

The dewdrop fo limpid and gay,
That loofe on the violet lies,
Tho' brighten'd by Phœbus's ray,
Wants luftre, compar'd to her eyes.

A lily I pluck'd in full pride,
It's frefhnefs with her's to compare;
And foolifhly thought, (till I try'd)
The flow'ret was equally fair.

How, Corydon, could you miſtake?
Your fault be with ſorrow confeſt,
You ſaid, the white ſwans on the lake
For ſoftneſs, might rival her breaſt.

While thus I went on in her praiſe,
My Phillis paſs'd ſportive along:
Ye poets, I covet no bays,
She ſmil'd—a reward for my ſong!
I find the god Pan's in the right,
No fame's like the fair-one's applauſe!
And Cupid muſt crown with delight
The ſhepherd that ſings in his cauſe.

SONG 82.

THE ROSY DAWN.

Sung at VAUXHALL.

WHEN primroſe ſweet bedecks the year,
    And ſportive lambkins play,
When lilies in each vale appear,
    And muſic wakes the day;
With joy I meet my ſhepherd ſwain
    Come tripping o'er the lawn;
Then hand in hand we range the plain,
    To hail the roſy dawn.

Well pleas'd I hear his artleſs tale,
    While rural ſcenes delight;
Beneath the beech in yonder dale,
    His muſic charms the night.
When morn returns, I meet my ſwain
    Come tripping o'er the lawn;
Then hand in hand we range the plain,
    To hail the roſy dawn.

Without a bluſh to church I'll haſte
    With him who has my heart;
While love invites, no time I'll waſte,
    No more we'll ever part;
And when returning with my ſwain,
    We trip it o'er the lawn;
While hand in hand we range the plain,
    We'll hail the roſy dawn.

SONG 83.

A SCOTCH BALLAD.

Sung at VAUXHALL.

ON Tay's green banks I'll boldy tell
    The love I have for Jockey;
Attend my ſong each blythſome belle,
    And ſhepherds, hither flock ye.
I gave my heart to that fond ſwain,
    Who won it of me fairly;
I'd do t if 'twere t do again,
    I love him ſtill ſo dearly.

His manners ſofe, tho' ſtrong his mind,
    Not fickle like the weather;
Not croſs to-day, to-morrow kind,
    And lighter than a feather;
His words and actions both agree,
    His temper's warm, not heady;
He's always good and juſt to me,
    To love and honour ſteady.

For his own ſelf, I like my ſwain,
    I know his worth and nature:
I'll give him not a moment's pain,
    Nor wrong ſo ſweet a creature.
No girl on Tweed, or Clyde, or Spey,
    Is born to ſo much pleaſure,
As is the merry laſs of Tay,
    Or cloſer hugs her treaſure.

SONG 84.

Sung in the Metamorphoſes.

I Am a tinker by my trade,
    Each day I live I mend?
I'm ſuch an univerſal friend,
I hide the faults by others made.
    Work for the tinker, ho! good wives;
'Twere well, while I your kettles mend,
    if you d amend your lives.

The beſt that's going is my trade,
    'Tis even better than the law;
By them are breaches wider made,
    I daily ſtop up many a flaw.

That we ſhould mend, is each man's cry,
    A doctrine 'tis that all will teach;
Then how much better, pray, am I,
    Who practiſe what they only preach?

SONG 85.

Sung in the Devil to Pay.

YE gods! ye gave to me a wife,
    Out of your grace and favour,
To be the comfort of my life,
    And I was glad to have her:

But if your providence divine
    For greater bliſs deſign her;
To obey your will, at any time,
    I'm ready to reſign her.

SONG 86.

THE CROSS-PURPOSES.

Sung at RANELAGH.

TOM loves Mary paſſing well,
    And Mary ſhe loves Harry;
But Harry ſighs for bonny Bell,
    And finds his love miſcarry;
For bonny Bell for Thomas burns,
    Whilſt Mary ſlights his paſſion:
So ſtrangely freakiſh are the turns
    Of human inclination.

Moll gave Hal a wreath of flowers,
    Which he, in am'rous folly,
Conſign'd to Bell, and in few hours
    It came again to Molly:
Thus all by turns are woo'd and woo,
    No turles can be truer;
Each loves the object they purſue,
    But hates the kind purſuer.

As much as Mary, Thomas grieves,
Proud Hal defpifes Mary;
And all the flouts which Bell receives
From Tom, fhe vents on Harry.
If one of all he four has frown'd,
You ne'er faw people grummer;
If one has fmil'd, it catches round,
And all are in good-humour.

Then, lovers, hence this leſſon learn,
Throughout the Britiſh nation;
How much 'tis ev'ry one's concern
To fmile at reformation
And ſtill, thro' life, this rule purfue,
Whaſever objects ſtrike you,
Be kind to them that fancy you,
That thoſe you love may like you.

SONG 87.

Sung at VAUXHALL.

I Winna marry ony mon but Sandy o'er the
Lee,
But I will ha my Sandy Lad, my Sandy o'er
the Lee;
For he's aye a kiffing, kiffing, aye a kiffing me.

I will not have the minifter, for all his godly
looks;
Nor yet will I the lawyer have, for all his wily
crooks;
I will not have the plowman lad, nor yet will
I the miller,
But I will have my Sandy Lad, without one
penny fiɗler:
For he's aye a kiffing, &c.

I will not have the foldier lad, for he gangs to
the war;
I will not have the failor lad, becaufe he fmells
of tar;
I will not have the lord nor laird, for all their
mickle gear;
But I will have my Sandy Lad, my Sandy o'er
the meir:
For he's aye a kiffing, &c.

SONG 88.

THE CAPTIVE.

Sung at VAUXHALL.

WHILST a captive to your charms,
I enfold you in my arms;
When I figh and fwear I'm true,
Think I love no girl but you;
But when I fay your face is fair,
And all of you beyond compare,
Praife your mind and temper too,
Love but him who loves but you.

Whilft I doat upon you more
Than fhepherd did on nymph before,
Can you bid the world adieu,
Can you love, as I love you?

O'er lands and waves with you I'll fly,
With you I'll live, with you I'll die;
What'er you'll have of me I'll do;
Then think I none can love but you.

Whilft I breathe my ardent flame,
Has your bofom caught the ſame?
Let me have, dear girl, my due;
Love him, then, who loves but you.
Sweet your look, and fond your figh,
To my wiſhes now comply;
Hymen claims, to-day, his due;
Love me, then, as I love you.

SONG 89.

THE INCONSTANT.

Sung at MARYBONE.

YOUNG Damon, with feducing art,
His deathlefs paſſion pleads;
Bids Sylvia take his conſtant heart;
She loves, and he fucceeds.
Yet he her kifs-imprinted lips
Forſakes within the hour;
And apes the roving bee, that fips
The fweets of ev'ry flow r.

New objects now attract his eyes,
Subdu'd by other charms;
While hapleſs Sylvia vainly tries
To lure him to her arms.
Of this, ye blooming fair, be fure,
If virtue once give way,
The heart you think you hold fecure,
No longer owns your fway.

SONG 90.

Written by G. A. STEVENS.

WHEN Jove was refolv'd to create the
round earth,
He fub-œna'd the virtues divine;
Young Bacchus he fat præcedentum of mirth,
And the toaſt was, wit, women, and wine.

The fentiment tickled the ear of each g d;
Apollo he wink d to the nine;
And Venus gave Mars, too, a fly wanton nod,
When fhe drank to wit, women, and wine.

Old Jove fhook his fides, and the cup put around,
While Juno, for once, look'd divine:
Thefe bellings, fays he, fhall on earth now
abound,
And the toaſt is, wit, women, and wine.

Thefe are joys worthy gods, which to mortals
are giv'n,
Says Momus: who will not repine?
For what's worth our notice, pray tell me, in
heav'n,
If men have wit, women, and wine.

This joke you'll repent, I'll lay fifty to feven;
Such attractions no pow'r can decline;
Old Jove, by yourfelf you'll foon keep houfe in
heav'n,
For we follow wit, women, and wine.

D 2

Thou'rt right, fays old Jove, let us hence to
   the earth,
Men and gods think variety fine;
Who'd ſtay in the clouds, when good-nature
   and mirth
Are below, with wit, women, and wine?

SONG 91.

THE FORSAKEN NYMPH.

GUARDIAN Angels now protect me,
   Send, ah! ſend the youth I love;
Deign, O Cupid, to direct me,
   Lead me thro' the myrtle grove.
Bear my fighs, ſoft-floating air,
Say I love him to deſpair;
Tell him 'tis for him I grieve,
For him alone I wiſh to live.

'Mid ſecluded dells I'll wander,
   Silent as the ſhades of night,
Near ſome bubbling rills meander,
   Where he erſt has bleſt my fight;
There to weep the night away,
There to waſte in fighs the day.
Think, fond youth, what vows you ſwore;
And muſt I never ſee thee more?

Then recluſe ſhall be my dwelling,
   Deep in ſome ſequeſter'd vale;
There, with mournful cadence ſwelling,
   Oft repeat my love-fick tale:
And the lark and Philomel
Oft ſhall hear a virgin tell
What the pain to bid adieu
To joy, to happineſs, and you.

SONG 92.

THE TRANSFORMATION.

WHOE'ER with curious eye has rang'd
   Thro' Ovid's tales, has ſeen
How Jove, incens'd, to monkies chang'd
A tribe of worthleſs men.
Repentant ſoon, th' offending race
   Intreat the injur'd pow'r,
To give them back the human face,
And reaſon's aid reſtore.

Jove, ſooth'd at length, his ear inclin'd,
   And granted half their pray'r;
But t'other half he bid the wind
   Diſperſe in empty air.
Scarce had the thund'rer giv'n the nod,
   That ſhook the vaulted ſkies,
With haughtier air the creatures ſtrode,
And ſtretch'd their dwindled fize.

The hair in curls luxurious now
   Around their temples ſpread;
The tail, that whilom hung below,
   Now dangled from the head.
The head remains unchang'd within,
   Nor alter'd much the face;
It ſtill retains it' native grin,
And all it's old grimace.

Thus half tranſform'd, and half the ſame,
   Jove bade them take their place,
Reſtoring them their a..cient claim
   Among the human race.
Man with contempt the brute ſurvey'd,
   Nor would a name beſtow;
But woman lik'd the motley breed,
   And call'd the thing a beau.

SONG 93.

Sung in the *Metamorphoſes*.

AH, dear Marcella! maid divine,
   No more will I at fate repine,
If I this day behold thee mine,
   For dearly do I love thee.

Thy eaſe ſhall be my ſweet employ,
My conſtant care, my ev'ry joy;
May then no chance my hopes deſtroy!
   For dearly do I love thee.

Sweet is the woodbine to the bee,
The riſing ſun to ev'ry tree,
But ſweeter far art thou to me,
   For dearly do I love thee.

And let me but behold thee mine,
No more will I at fate repine;
But while I live, thou maid divine,
   With rapture will I love thee.

SONG 94.

Written by Dr. GOLDSMITH.

WHEN lovely woman ſtoops to folly,
   And finds too l.te, that men betray;
What charms can ſoothe her melancholy?
   What art can waſh her guilt away?

The only art, her guilt to cover,
   To hide her flame from ev'ry eye,
To give repentance to her lover,
   And wring his boſom—is to die!

SONG 95.

A BACCHANALIAN SONG.

MY temples with cluſters of grapes I'll en-
   twine,
And barter all joy for a goblet of wine;
In ſearch of a Venus no longer I'll run,
But ſtop and forget her at Bacchus's tun.

Yet why this reſolve to relinquiſh the fair?
'Tis a folly with ſpirits like mine to deſpair;
For what mighty charms can be found in a glaſs,
If not fill'd with the health of ſome favourite
   laſs?

'Tis woman whoſe charms ev'ry rapture impart,
And ſend a new ſpring to the pulſe of the heart:
The miſer himſelf (ſo ſupreme is her ſway)
Grows convert to love, and reſigns her his key.

At the ſound of her voice, ſorrow lifts up her
   head,
And poverty liſtens, well pleas'd, from her ſhed;

While age, in an extafy, hobbling along,
Beats time with his crutch to the tune of her
　　fong.

Then bring me a goblet from Bacchus's hoard,
The largeft and deepeft that ftands on the board;
I'll fill up a brimmer, and drink to the fair;
'Tis the thirft of a lover; and pledge me who
　　dare!

SONG 96.

Sung in *Love in a Village.*

LET gay ones, and great,
　　Make the moft of their fate,
From pleafure to pleafure they run;
Well, who cares a jot?
I envy them not,
While i have my dog and my gun.

For exercife, air,
　To the fields I repair,
With fpirits unclouded and light;
The bliffes I find,
No ftings leave behind,
But health and diverfion unite.

SONG 97.

Sung in the *Election.*

WHILE happy in my native land,
　　I boaft my country's charter;
I'll never bafely lend my hand,
　　Her liberties to barter.

The noble mind is not at all
　　By poverty degraded;
'Tis guilt alone can make us fall;
　　And well I am perfuaded,
Each free-born Briton's fong fhould be,
　　Or give me death or liberty.

Tho' fmall the pow'r which fortune grants,
　　And few the gifts fhe fends us;
The lordly hireling often wants
　　That freedom which defends us.

By law fecur'd from lawlefs ftrife,
　　Our houfe is our caftellum:
Thus blefs'd with all that s dear in life,
　　For lucre, fhall we fell 'em?
No—ev'ry Briton's fong fhould be,
　　Or give me death or liberty.

SONG 98.

ADVICE TO THE LADIES.

YE fair, be advis'd by a friend,
　　Whofe counfel proceeds from the heart,
On beauty no longer depend,
　　Or fly to the efforts of art:
If a fhepherd you'd gain to your arms,
　　Let virtue each action approve;
Her charms the fond bofom alarms,
　　And foftens the foul into love.

To-day be not nice as a bride,
　　To-morrow untimely fevere;
Let prudence and truth be your guide;
　　Nor caprice nor folly appear:
Unlefs you thus govern your mind,
　　And banifh deceit from your breaft,
Too foon by experience you'll find,
　　Inconftancy ne'er can be bleft.

Neglected you'll wither and fade,
　　Till beauty, by age, fhall decay;
Then lonely retreat to the fhade,
　　And mourn the fad hours away:
How defp'rate will then be your fate,
　　How great your fad lofs to deplore!
Repentance, alas! is too late,
　　When the power to charm is no more.

SONG 99.

Sung in the *Chriftmas Tale.*

MY eyes may fpeak pleafure,
　　Tongue flow without meafure,
Yet my heart in my bofom lies ftill;
　　Thus the river is flowing,
　　The mill-clapper going,
But—the miller's afleep in the mill.

Tho' lovers furround me,
　　With fpeeches confound me,
Yet my heart in my bofom lies ftill;
　　Thus the river is flowing,
　　The mill-clapper going,
But—the miller's afleep in the mill.

The little god eyes me,
　　And means to furprize me,
But my heart is awake in my breaft;
　　Thus boys flily creeping,
　　To catch a bird fleeping,
But—the linnet's awake in his neft.

SONG 100.

WHAT IS THAT TO YOU; A SCOTCH SONG.

Sung at VAUXHALL.

MY Jeany and I have toil'd
　　The live-long fummer's day,
Till we were almoft fpoil'd,
　　At making of the hay.
Her kerchy was of holland clear,
　　Ty'd to her bonny brow;
I whifper'd fomething in her ear;
　　But what is that to you?

Her ftockings were of kerfey green,
　　And tight as ony filk;
O, fic a leg was never feen!
　　Her fkin was white as milk.
Her hair was black as ane could wifh,
　　And fweet, fweet was her mou!
Ah! Jeany daintily can kifs;
　　But what is that to you?

The rofe and lily baith combine
　　To make my Jeany fair:

There is nae benifon like mine,
   I have amaiſt nae care.
But when another ſwain, my fair,
   Shall ſay you're fair to view;
Let Jeany whiſper in his ear,
   Pray what is that to you?

SONG 101.

Sung at VAUXHALL.

AH! where can one find a true ſwain,
   In whom a young nymph may confide?
Men are now ſo conceited and vain,
   They no longer have hearts to divide:
Or in court, or in city, or town,
   All acknowledge how fruitleſs the ſearch;
So polite, too, each village is grown,
   Even their girls are left in the lurch.

Then adieu to the thraldom of love,
   Adieu to it's hopes and it's fear;
Henceforth I in freedom will rove,
   Who like it the willow may wear:
Yet ſhould fortune, my truth to reward,
   Send ſome youth with each talent to bleſs,
How far I my purpoſe could guard,
   Is a ſecret I need not confeſs.

SONG 102.

HOPE AND FEAR.

Sung in Lionel and Clariſſa.

HOPE and fear alternate riſing,
   Strive for empire o'er my heart;
Ev'ry peril now deſpiſing,
   Now at ev'ry breath I ſtart.

Teach, ye learned ſages, teach me,
   How to ſtem this beating tide;   /
If you've any rules to teach me,
   Haſte, and be the weak one s guide.

Thus our trials, at a diſtance,
   Wiſdom's ſcience promiſe aid;
Yet, in need of their aſſiſtance,
   We attempt to graſp a ſhade.

SONG 103.

Sung at RANELAGH.

THE gaudy tulip ſwells with pride,
   And rears it's beauties to the ſun,
With heav'n-born tints of Iris' bow;
   While low the vi'let ſprings beſide,
As in the ſhade it ſtrives to ſhun
   The hand of ſome rapacious foe.

Of worth intrinſic, ſmall the ſtore
   That from the tulip can ariſe,
When parted from it's glowing bed:
   While hid, the vi'let charms the more,
Like incenſe in it's native ſkies,
   When cropt to grace the virgin head.

Then think, ye fair-ones, how theſe flow'rs
   Are wrought in nature's various robe:

Where pride declines, and merit thrives;
   Your virgin dignity o'er-pow'rs
The heroes or the conquer'd globe:
   But ſweet compliance makes ye wives.

SONG 104.

Sung at VAUXHALL.

THE faireſt flow'rs the vale prefer,
   And ſhed ambroſial ſweetneſs there;
While the tall pine and mountain oak,
   Oft feel the tempeſt's ruder ſtroke.

So in the lowly moſs grown ſeat,
   Dear peace and quiet dwell;
The ſtorms that wreck the rich and great
   Fly o'er the ſhepherd's cell.

SONG 105.

Sung in the Oracle.

WOULD you with her you love be bleſt,
   Ye lovers theſe inſtructions mind,
Conceal the paſſion in your breaſt,
   Be dumb, inſenſible, and blind:
But when with gentle looks you meet,
   And ſee the artleſs bluſhes riſe,
Be ſilent, loving, and diſcreet;
   The oracle no more implies.

When once you prove the maid ſincere,
   Where virtue is with beauty join'd;
Then boldly like yourſelves appear,
   No more inſenſible, or blind:
Pour forth the tranſports of your heart,
   And ſpeak your ſoul without diſguiſe;
'Tis fondneſs, fondneſs muſt impart;
   The oracle no more implies.

Tho' pleaſing, fatal is the ſnare,
   That ſtill entraps all womankind;
Ladies, beware, be wiſe, take care,
   Be deaf, inſenſible, and blind:
But ſhould ſome fond deſerving youth
   Agree to join in Hymen's ties,
Be tender, conſtant, crown his truth;
   The oracle no more implies.

SONG 106.

Written by SOAME JENNYNS, Eſq.

TOO plain, dear youth, theſe tell-tale eyes
   My heart your own declare,
But for Heav'n's ſake let it ſuffice,
   You reign triumphant there.

Forbear your utmoſt pow'r to try,
   Nor farther urge your ſway;
Preſs not for what I muſt deny,
   For fear I ſhould obey.

Could all your arts ſucceſsful prove,
   Would you a maid undo,
Whoſe greateſt failing is her love,
   And that her love of you?

Say, would you ufe that very pow'r
   You from her fondnefs claim,
To ruin, in one fatal hour,
   A life of fpotlefs fame?

Ah' ceafe, my dear, to do an ill,
   Becaufe perhaps you may;
But rather try your utmoft fkill
   To fave me, than betray.

Be you yourfelf my virtue's guard,
   Defend, and not purfue;
Since 'tis a tafk for me too hard,
   To fight with love and you.

SONG 107.

Written by Mr. GARRICK.

IF truth can fix thy wav'ring heart,
   Let Damon urge his claim;
He feels the paffion void of art,
   The pure, the conftant flame.

Tho' fighing fwains their torments tell,
   Their fenfual love contemn;
They only prize the beauteous fhell,
   But flight the inward gem.

Poffeffion cures the wounded heart,
   Deftroys the tranfient fire;
But when the mind receives the dart,
   Enjoyment whets defire.

By age your beauty will decay,
   Your mind improves with years;
As when the bloffoms fade away,
   The rip'ning fruit appears.

May Heav'n and Sylvia grant my fuit,
   And blefs each future hour;
That Damon, who can tafte the fruit,
   May gather ev'ry flow'r.

SONG 108.

Sung in the Mafque of Alfred.

YE warblers, while Strephon I mourn,
   To chear me your harmony bring;
Unlefs, fince my fhepherd is gone,
   You ceafe, like poor Phillis, to fing;
Each flower declines it's fweet head,
   Nor odours around me will throw,
While ev'ry foft lamb on the mead
   Seems kindly to pity my woe.

Each rural amufement I try,
   In vain, to reftore my paft eafe;
What charm'd, when my Strephon was by,
   Has now loft the power to pleafe.
Ye feafons that brighten the grove,
   Not long for your abfence we mourn;
But Strephon neglects me and love,
   He roves, and will never return.

As gay as the Spring is my dear,
   And fweet as all flowers combin'd;
His fmiles, like the Summer, can chear;
   Ah! why then, like Winter, unkind!

Unkind is he not, I can prove,
   But tender to others can be;
To Celia and Chloe makes love,
   And only is cruel to me.

SONG 109.

ON TOBACCO.

TOBACCO's but an Indian weed,
   Grows green at morn, cut down at eve;
   It fhews our decay, we are but clay.
Think on this when you fmoke tobacco.

The pipe that is fo lily white,
   Wherein fo many take delight,
   Is broke with a touch; man's life is fuch.
Think on this when you fmoke tobacco.

The pipe that is foul within,
   Shews how man's foul is ftain'd with fin;
   It does require to be purg'd with fire.
Think on this when you fmoke tobacco.

The afhes that are left behind,
   Do ferve to put us all in mind,
   That into duft return we muft.
Think on this when you fmoke tobacco.

The fmoke that does fo high afcend,
   Shews that man's life muft have an end;
   The vapour's gone, man's life is done.
Think on this when you take tobacco.

SONG 110.

LOTHARIA.

VAINLY now you ftrive to charm me,
   All ye fweets of blooming May;
How fhould ever funfhine warm me,
   While Lotharia keeps away?

Go, ye warbling birds, go leave me;
   Shade, ye clouds, the fmiling fky;
Sweeter notes her voice can give me,
   Softer funfhine fills her eye.

SONG 111.

WOMAN.

Sung at MARYBONE.

Written by Mr. BOYCE.

SOME love to range, fo fond of change,
   Variety's their fhrine;
Each has his fcheme and fav'rite whim,
   But woman, woman's mine.

The feftive bowl, the martial foul,
   The mifer, I decline;
Like chil'ifh toys, to fome they're joys,
   But lovely woman's mine.

With various arts fhe charms our hearts,
   And makes this life divine;
For all the tricks of all the fex,
   I'd ftill have woman mine.

Let ideots rave, who what they'd have
  The fex they can't define;
Juft as fhe is, fhe's form'd to pleafe,
  And long be woman mine!

The fparkling eye, the melting figh,
  When heart and heart conjoin;
The blifs of love, all blifs above,
  Make charming woman mine.

In pomp and ftate, fucceed, ye great,
  I'll envy nor repine;
If bleft with pow'r, to life's laft hour,
  To keep dear woman mine.

S O N G   112.

THE SKY-LARK.

GO, tuneful bird, that glads the fkies,
  To Daphne's window fpeed thy way;
And there on quiv'ring pinions rife,
  And there thy vocal art difplay.

And if fhe deign thy notes to hear,
  And if fhe praife thy matin fong;
Tell her the founds that foothe her ear,
  To Damon's native plaints belong.

Tell her, in livelier plumes array'd
  The bird from Indian groves may fhine;
But afk the lovely, partial maid,
  What are his notes compar'd to thine?

Then bid her treat yon witlefs beau,
  And all his flaunting race, with fcorn;
And lend an ear to Damon's woe,
  Who fings her praife, and fings forlorn.

S O N G   113.

Sung in *Artaxerxes*.

THE foldier, tir'd of war's alarms,
  Forfwears the clang of hoftile arms,
And fcorns the fpear and fhield;
But if the brazen trumpet found,
He burns with conqueft to be crown'd,
  And dates again the field.

S O N G   114.

Sung in the *Duenna*.

O The days when I was young!
  When I laugh'd in fortune's fpight,
Talk'd of love the whole day long,
  And with nectar crown'd the night.

Then it was, old father care,
  Little reck'd I of thy frown;
Half thy malice youth could bear,
  And the reft a bumper drown.
O the days, &c.

Truth, they fay, lies in a well,
  Why, I vow, I ne'er could fee;
Let the water-drinkers tell,
  There it always lay for me:

For when fparkling wine went round,
  Never faw I falfhood's mafk;
But ftill honeft truth I found,
  In the bottom of each flafk!
O the days, &c.

True, at length my vigour's flown,
  I have years to bring decay;
Few the locks that now I own,
  And the few I have are grey!

Yet, old Jerome, thou may'ft boaft,
  While thy fpirits do not tire,
Still, beneath thy age's froft,
  Glows a fpark of youthful fire.
O the days, &c.

S O N G   115.

Written by the Duke of BUCKINGHAM.

GRAVE fops my envy now beget,
  Who did my pity move;
They, by the right of wanting wit,
  Are free from cares of love.

Turks honour fools; becaufe they are
  By that defect fecure
From flavery and toils of war,
  Which all the reft endure.

So I, who fuffer cold neglect
  And wounds from Celia's eyes,
Begin extremely to refpect
  Thefe fools that feem fo wife.

'Tis true, they fondly fet their hearts
  On things of no delight;
To pafs all day for men of parts,
  They pafs alone the night.

But Celia never breaks their reft;
  Such fervants fhe difdains:
And fo the fops are dully bleft,
  While I endure her chains.

S O N G   116.

THE FEMALE DUELLIST.

Sung at VAUXHALL.

SINCE all fo nicely take offence,
  And pinking is the fafhion,
I foon fhall find a good pretence
  For being in a paffion.

If any on my drefs or air,
  To jeft dare take occafion;
By female honour I declare,
  I'll have an explanation!

If you're too free, or full of play,
  By Jove! my lads, I'll cure ye;
And if too cold you turn away,
  You'll rouze a very fury.

A law is ev'ry thing I fay;
  No fwain fhall call me cruel;
Whoe'er my will fhall difobey,
  Gives fignal for a duel.

A very Amazon am I,
   And various weapons carry;
I've glancing lightning in my eye,
   And tongue—a sword to parry.

E'en let him arm with what he will,
   With Cupid's bow and arrow
You soon shall see my man I'll kill,
   As easy as a sparrow.

SONG 117.

A NAVAL SONG.

HOW little do the landsmen know
   Of what we sailors feel,
When waves do mount, and winds do blow!
   But we have hearts of steel:
No danger can affright us,
No enemy shall flout;
We'll make the monsieurs right us,
   So toss the cann about.

Stick close to orders, messmates,
   We'll plunder, burn, and sink;
Then France have at your first-rates,
   For Britons never shrink:
We'll rummage all we fancy,
   We'll bring them in by scores;
And Moll, and Kate, and Nancy,
   Shall roll in louis-d'ors.

While here at Deal we're lying,
   With our noble commodore,
We'll spend our wages freely, boys,
   And then to sea for more:
In peace we'll drink and sing, boys,
   In war we'll never fly;
Here's a health to George our king, boys,
   And the royal family.

SONG 118.

Sung in *Love in a Village.*

HOPE! thou nurse of young desire,
   Fairy promiser of joy;
Painted vapour, glow-worm fire,
   Temp'rate sweet, that ne'er can cloy!

Hope! thou earnest of delight,
   Softest soother of the mind;
Balmy cordial, prospect bright,
   Surest friend the wretched find!

Kind deceiver, flatter still;
   Deal out pleasures unpossess'd:
With thy dreams my fancy fill,
   And in wishes make me blest.

SONG 119.

Written by Sir JOHN SUCKLING.

I Pr'ythee send me back my heart,
   Since I cannot have thine:
For if from yours you will not part,
   Why then shou'dst thou have mine?

Yet now I think on't, let it lie;
   To find it were in vain;
For thou'st a thief in ev'ry eye
   Wou'd steal it back again.

Why should two hearts in one breast lie,
   And yet not lodge together?
Oh, love! where is thy sympathy,
   If thus our breasts thou sever?

But love is such a mystery,
   I cannot find it out:
For when I think I'm best resolv'd,
   I then am in most doubt.

Then farewel care, and farewel woe,
   I will no longer pine:
For I'll believe I have her heart,
   As much as she has mine.

SONG 120.

THE WAY TO KEEP HIM.

YE fair, possess'd of ev'ry charm
   To captivate the will;
Whose smiles can rage itself disarm,
   Whose frowns at once can kill:
Say, will you deign the verse to hear,
   Where flatt'ry bears no part;
An honest verse, that flows sincere
   And candid from the heart?

Great is your pow'r; but, greater yet,
   Mankind it might engage,
If, as ye all can make a net,
   Ye all could make a cage:
Each nymph a thousand hearts may take,
   For. who's to beauty blind;
But to what end a prisoner make,
   Unless we've strength to bind?

Attend the counsel often told,
   (Too often told in vain)
Learn that best art, the art to hold,
   And lock the lover's chain.
Gamesters to little purpose win,
   Who lose again as fast;
Though beauty may the charm begin,
   'Tis sweetness makes it last.

SONG 121.

A HUNTING SONG.

HARK! hark! the joy-inspiring horn
   Salutes the rosy, rising morn,
   And echoes thro' the dale;
With clam'rous peals the hills resound,
The hounds quick-scented scour the ground,
   And snuff the fragrant gale.

No gates nor hedges can impede
The brisk, high-mettled, starting steed,
   The jovial pack pursue;
Like lightning darting o'er the plains,
The distant hills with speed he gains,
   And sees the game in view.

E

Her path the timid hare forsakes,
And to the copse for shelter makes,
  There pants awhile for breath;
When now the noise alarms her ear,
Her haunt's descry'd, her fate is near,
  She sees approaching death.

Directed by the well-known breeze,
The hounds their trembling victim seize,
  She faints, she falls, she dies;
The distant coursers now come in,
And join the loud triumphant din,
  Till echo rends the skies.

SONG 122.

WHAT means that tender sigh, my dear?
  Why silent drops that chrystal tear?
What jealous fears disturb thy breast,
Where love and peace delight to rest;
What tho' thy Jockey has been seen
With Molly sporting on the green;
'Twas but an artful trick to prove
The matchless force of Jenny's love.

'Tis true a nosegay I had drest
To grace the witty Daphne's breast;
But 'twas at her desire, to try
If Damon cast a jealous eye.
These flow'rs will fade by morning dawn,
Neglected, scatter'd o'er the lawn;
But in thy fragrant bosom lies
A sweet perfume that never dies.

SONG 123.

Sung in the *Funeral.*

LET not love on me bestow
  Soft distress and tender woe;
I know none but substantial blisses,
Eager glances, solid kisses;
I know not what the lovers feign,
Of finer pleasure mix'd with pain;
Then pr'ythee give me, gentle boy,
None of thy grief, but all thy joy.

SONG 124.

THE topsails shiver in the wind,
  The ship she casts to sea;
But yet, my soul, my heart, my mind
  Are, Mary, moor'd with thee:
For tho' thy sailor's bound afar,
Still love shall be his leading star.

Should landmen flatter when we're sail'd,
  O! doubt their artful tales;
No gallant sailor ever fail'd,
  If love breath'd constant gales:
Thou art the compass of my soul,
Which steers my heart from pole to pole.

Sirens in ev'ry port we meet,
  More fell than rocks and waves;
But such as grace the British fleet,
  Are lovers, and not slaves:

No foes our courage shall subdue,
Altho' we've left our hearts with you.

These are our cares; but if you're kind,
  We'll scorn the dashing main,
The rocks, the billows, and the wind,
  The pow'r of France and Spain:
Now England's glory rests with you,
Our sails are full—sweet girls, adieu!

SONG 125.

Sung in the *Man of Mode.*

AS Amoret and Phillis sat
  One ev'ning on the plain,
And saw the charming Strephon wait
  To tell the nymph his pain;
The threat'ning danger to remove,
  He whisper'd in her ear,
Ah! Phillis, if you would not love
  The shepherd, do not hear.

None ever had so strange an art,
  His passion to convey
Into a list'ning virgin's heart,
  And steal her soul away:
Fly, fly, betimes, for fear you give
  Occasion for your fate.
In vain, said she, in vain I strive,
  Alas! 'tis now too late.

SONG 126.

Written by Mr. BOOTH.

CAN, then, a look create a thought
  Which time can ne'er remove?
Yes, foolish heart, again thou'rt caught,
  Again thou bleed'st for love.

She sees the conquest of her eyes,
  Nor heals the wound she gave;
She smiles, whene'er his blushes rise,
  And, sighing, shuns her slave.

Then, swain, be bold, and still adore her,
  Still her flying charms pursue;
Love and int'rest both implore her,
  Pleading night and day for you!

SONG 127.

Sung in *Orpheus and Eurydice.*

WHEN Orpheus went down to the regions
    below,
  Which men are forbidden to see,
He tun'd up his lyre, as old histories shew,
  To set his Eurydice free.

All hell stood amaz'd, that a person so wise
  Should so rashly endanger his life,
And venture so far—but how vast their surprize!
  When they heard that he came for his wife.

To find out a punishment due to the fault,
  Old Pluto long puzzled his brain;
But hell had not torments sufficient, he thought,
  So he gave him his wife back again.

But pity fucceding foon vanquifh'd his heart,
And pleas'd with his playing fo well,
He took her again, in reward for his art:
Such power had mufic in hell.

SONG 128.

WHY fhould we of humble ftate,
    Vainly blame the pow'rs above;
Or accufe the will of fate,
    Which allows us all to love?
Love (impartial, gentle boy)
    Deals his gifts as free as air;
Love is all the fhepherd's joy,
    Love is all the damfel's care.

Hope, that charmer of the foul,
    Hope in love fhould ever live;
Could our years for ever roll,
    Love would bleffings ever give:
Youth, alas! too fwiftly flies,
    Nor can Cupid bid him ftay;
Beauty like a fhadow dies,
    Love has wings and will away.

SONG 129.

Sung in the Mafque of *Alfred.*

IF thofe who live in fhepherd's bow'r,
    Prefs not the gay and ftately bed;
The new-mown hay and breathing flow'r
    A fofter couch beneath them fpread.

If thofe who fit at fhepherd's board,
    Soothe not their tafte with wanton art;
They take what nature's gifts afford,
    And take it with a chearful heart.

If thofe who drain the fhepherd's bowl,
    No high and fparkling wine can boaft;
With wholefome cups they chear the foul,
    And crown them with the village toaft.

If thofe who join in fhepherd's fport,
    Dancing on the daify'd ground,
Have not the fplendour of a court,
    Yet love adorns the merry round.

SONG 130.

A HUNTING SONG.

HARK! the huntfman's began to found
    the fhrill horn,
Come quickly unkennel the hounds:
'Tis a beautiful, glittering, golden-ey'd morn,
    We'll chace the fox over the grounds.

See! yonder fits Reynard, fo crafty and fly;
    Come faddle your courfers apace:
The hounds have a fcent, and are all in full cry;
    They long to be giving him chace.

The horfemen are mounted, the fteeds feel
    the fpur,
And fwiftly they fcour it along;
Rapid after the fox runs each mufical cur;
    Follow, follow, my boys, is the fong.

O'er mountains and vallies they fkim it away,
    Now Reynard's almoft out of fight;
But fooner than lofe him, they'd fpend the
    whole day
In hunting—for that's their delight.

By eager purfuing they'll have him at laft:
    He's fo tir'd, poor rogue, down he lies;
Now ftarts up afrefh—young Snap has him faft:
    He trembles, kicks, ftruggles, and dies.

SONG 131.

Written by the Earl of CHESTERFIELD.

MISTAKEN fair, lay Sherlock by,
    His doctrine is deceiving;
For whilft he teaches us to die,
    He cheats us of our living.

To die's a leffon we fhall know
    Too foon, without a mafter;
Then let us only ftudy, now,
    How we may live the fafter.

To live's to love; to blefs, be bleft
    With mutual inclination;
Share, then, my ardour in your breaft,
    And kindly meet my paffion.

But if thus blefs'd I may not live,
    And pity you deny;
To me, at leaft, your Sherlock give,
    'Tis I muft learn to die.

SONG 132.

BELIEVE my fighs, my tears, my dear,
    Believe the heart you've won;
Believe my vows to you fincere,
    Or, Peggy, I'm undone:
You fay I'm fickle, apt to change
    At every face that's new;
Of all the girls I ever faw,
    I ne'er lov'd one like you.

My heart was once a flake of ice,
    Till thaw'd by your bright eyes;
Then warm'd and kindled in a trice
    A flame that never dies:
Then take and try me, and you'll find
    A heart that's kind and true;
Of all the girls I ever faw,
    I ne'er lov'd one like you.

SONG 133.

WHAT ftill does dear Lucy's difdain
    Occafion this feftering fmart?
Cannot time give relief to your pain,
    And heal the flight wound in your heart?

The arrows of Cupid, I know,
    At firft are all pointed with fteel:
But how frail is the ftrength of his bow!
    How fleeting the pangs which we feel!

His wings they are fhatter'd by time,
    His quiver is foil'd in the duft;

Such, fuch is life's flowery prime,
  And beauty's moft infolent truft.

Tafte the joys a new paffion can give,
  With the nymph that's complying and kind;
Or learning more fageiy to live,
  Be bleft, and give love to the wind.

SONG 134.

Written by Mr. CONGREVE.

PIOUS Selinda goes to pray'rs,
  If I but afk the favour:
And yet the tender fool's in tears,
  When fhe believes I'll leave her.

Wou'd I were free from this reftraint,
  Or elfe had hopes to win her;
Wou'd fhe could make of me a faint,
  Or I of her a finner.

SONG 135.

A BACCHANALIAN SONG.

WE'LL drink, and we'll never have done,
    boys,
Put the glafs then around with the fun, boys;
Let Apollo's example invite us,
  For he's drunk ev'ry night,
  That makes him fo bright,
That he's able next morning to light us.
Drinking's a Chriftian diverfion,
Unknown to the Turk and the Perfian;
  Let Mahumetan fools
  Live by heathenifh rules,
And dream o'er their tea-pots and coffee;
  While the brave Britons fing,
  And drink health to the king,
And a fig for their fultan and fophy.

SONG 136.

Sung at VAUXHALL.

MORE bright the fun began to dawn,
  The merry birds to fing,
And flow'rets dappled o'er the lawn,
  In all the pride of fpring;
When for a wreath young Damon ftray'd,
  And fmiling to me brought it;
Take this, he cry'd, my deareft maid;
  And who, aye who'd have thought it!

I blufh'd the prefent to receive,
  And thank'd him o'er and o'er;
When foft he figh'd, Bright fair, forgive,
  I muft have fomething more:
One kind fweet kifs will pay me beft,
  So earneftly he fought it,
I let him take it, I proteft,
  And who, aye who'd have thought it!

A fwain that woo'd with fo much art,
  No nymph could long difdain;
A fecret flame foon touch'd my heart,
  And flufh'd thro' ev'ry vein:

'Twas love infpir'd the pleafing change,
  From his my bofom caught it;
'Twas ftrange indeed, 'twas paffing ftrange,
  And who, aye who'd have thought it!

Hark! Hymen calls, the fhepherd cry'd:
  Let us, my dear comply;
We inftant went, with love our guide,
  And bound the nuptial tie:
And ever fince that happy day,
  As mutual warmth has taught it,
We fondly kifs, and fport and play,
  And who, aye who'd have thought it!

SONG 137.

A HUNTING SONG.

O'ER the lawns, up the hills, as with ar-
    dour we bound,
Led on by the loud-founding horn;
Kind breezes ftill greet us, with chearfulnefs
    crown'd,
  And joyful we meet the fweet morn.
Rofy health blooms about us with natural grace,
  Whilft echo, re-echo'd, enlivens the chace.

Should all the gay larks, as they foar to the fky,
  Their notes in a concert unite;
The mufic of hounds, when fet off in full cry,
  Would give a more tuneful delight.
  Rofy health, &c.

'Tis over—'tis over—a pleafure divine
  Frefh air and full exercife yield:
At night, my good friends, o'er the juice of
    the vine
  We'll fing to the fports of the field.
  Rofy health, &c.

SONG 138.

COULD you guefs, for I ill can repeat,
  The fenfation I'm deftin'd to prove;
'Tis fomething than friendfhip more fweet,
  More paffionate even than love.

For ever, when abfent from you,
  Pale echo returns my fond fighs;
But when haply your beauties I view,
  On my lips the faint utterance dies.

This the fecret I had to betray;
  And the fate of my paffion is fuch,
That in what I was prompted to fay,
  Methinks I have utter'd too much.

SONG 139.

THE PERPLEX'D VIRGIN.

Sung at MARYBONE.

YOUNG Colin to our cottage came,
  And vow'd how much he lov'd;
I own I felt a fecret flame,
  Yet not his fuit approv'd:
A thoufand tender tales he told,
  I feem'd to think untrue;

And made believe my heart was cold;
 What cou'd a virgin do?

The artless mind is soon imprefs'd
 With thoughts before unknown;
When Cupid wounds the female breaft,
 He's fure to keep his throne.
In vain our fortitude we try,
 When love's refolv'd to fue;
'Tis hard thro' pity to comply:
 What can a virgin do?

SONG 140.

Sung in the *Chaplet*.

VAIN is ev'ry fond endeavour
 To refift the tender dart;
For examples move us never,
 We muft feel, to know the fmart.
When the fhepherd fwears he's dying,
 And our beauties fets to view;
Vanity, her aid fupplying,
 Bids us think 'tis all our due,
 Bids us think, &c.

Softer than the vernal breezes
 Is the mild, deceitful ftrain;
Frowning truth our fex difpleafes;
 Flatt'ry never fues in vain:
But, too foon, the happy lover
 Does our tend'reft hopes deceive:
Man was form'd to be a rover,
 Foolifh woman to believe,
 Foolifh woman, &c.

SONG 141.

THO', Flavia, to my warm defire
 You mean no kind return;
Yet ftill with undiminifh'd fire,
 You wifh to fee me burn.

Averfe my anguifh to remove,
 You think it wond'rous right,
That I love on, for ever love,
 And you for ever flight.

But you and I fhall ne'er agree,
 So, gentle nymph, adieu;
Since you no pleafure have for me,
 I'll have no pain for you.

SONG 142.

Written by Mr. BUDGELL.

WHY will Florella, when I gaze,
 My ravifh'd eyes reprove?
And hide 'em from the only face
 They can behold with love?

To fhun her fcorn, and eafe my care,
 I feek a nymph more kind;
And while I rove from fair to fair,
 Still gentle ufage find.

But oh! how faint is ev'ry joy,
 Where nature has no part;

New beauties may my eyes employ,
 But you engage my heart.

So reftlefs exiles, doom'd to roam,
 Meet pity ev'ry where;
Yet languifh for their native home,
 Tho' death attends them there.

SONG 143.

SINCE Emma caught my roving eye,
 Since Emma fix'd my wav'ring heart,
I long to fmile, I fcorn to figh,
 But nature triumphs over art.
If fuch the haplefs moments prove,
 Ah! who would give his heart to love?

If frowns and fighs, and cold difdain,
 Be meet return for love like mine;
If cruel Emma fcoffs my pain,
 And archly wonders why I pine:
 If fuch, &c.

But fhould the lovely girl relent;
 Oh!—when I wifh, and figh, and vow,
Should fhe with blufhes fmile confent,
 And heart for heart, well pleas'd, beftow;
Should fuch the blifsful moments prove,
 Who would not give his heart to love?

SONG 144.

Sung in *Comus*.

THE wanton god, who pierces hearts,
 Dips in gall his pointed darts;
But the nymph difdains to pine,
 Who bathes the wound with rofy wine.

Farewel lovers when they're cloy'd;
 If I'm fcorn'd becaufe enjoy'd,
Sure the fqueamifh fops are free
 To rid me of dull company.

They have charms, whilft mine can pleafe;
 I love them much, but more my eafe:
No jealous fears my love moleft,
 Nor faithlefs vows fhall break my reft.

Why fhould they e'er give me pain,
 Who to give me joy difdain?
All I hope of mortal man
 Is to love me while he can.

SONG 145.

A Dawn of hope my foul revives,
 And banifhes defpair;
If yet my deareft Damon lives,
 Make him, ye gods, your care.

Difpel thefe gloomy fhades of night,
 My tender grief remove;
Oh! fend fome chearing ray of light,
 And guide me to my love.

Thus, in the fecret, friendly fhade,
 The penfive Celia mourn'd,
While courtly echo lent her aid,
 And figh for figh return'd.

When, fudden, Damon's well-known face
Each riſing fear difarms ;
He eager fprings to her embrace,'
She ſinks into his arms.

SONG 146.

Sung in the *Beggar's Wedding.*

Y O U N G virgins love pleaſure,
  As miſers do treaſure,
And both alike ſtudy to heighten the meaſure ;
  Their hearts they will rifle,
  For ev'ry new trifle,
And when in their teens fall in love for a ſong:

  But foon as they marry,
  And find things mifcarry,
Oh! how they figh, that they were not more
     wary:
  Inftead of foft wooing,
  They run to their ruin,
And all their lives after drag forrow along.

SONG 147.

A CANTATA.

Sung at VAUXHALL.

AIR.

W H Y, Damon, wilt thou ſtrive in vain
  My firm refolves to move ?
My heart, alas! may feel the pain,
  But fcorns the guilt of love!

RECITATIVE, accompanied.

Perfidious, too, like all the reſt,
  Is faithlefs Damon grown!
Ah! canſt thou feek to wound the breaſt
  That pants for thee alone?

AIR.

No' for a thought fo meanly bafe,
  Ungrateful! thou ſhalt find,
The heart that could admire thy face
  Can hate thee for thy mind.

SONG 148.

AN ANACREONTIC ODE.

Written by Capt. THOMPSON.

Sung at VAUXHALL.

L AUGHING Cupids, bring me rofes,
  And my wreath, ye graces, twine;
I'm this night difpos'd for rapture,
  Having beauty, wit, and wine.

Let the fober ſtoicks wonder,
  And their apathy cefine ;
I'll not follow fuch dull doctrine,
  While I've beauty, wit, and wine.

Such old dotards well may cenfure,
  Call me thoughtlefs libertine ;

Sour's the grape when we can't reach it,
  So is beauty, wit, and wine.

Come, ye briſk Arabian laſſes,
  For that heaven you feek is mine.
Upon beds of rofes lolling,
  Blefs'd with beauty, wit, and wine.

And when this gay life is over,
  Pour libations on my ſhrine;
I've a paradife hereafter, -
  Full of beauty, wit, and wine.

SONG 149.

N O more, ye fwains, no more upbraid
  A youth by love unhappy made;
Your rural fports are all in vain,
To foothe my care, or eafe my pain.
Nor ſhade of trees, nor fweets of flow'rs,
Can e'er redeem my happy hours;
When eafe forfakes the tortur'd mind,
What pleafure can a lover find ?

Yet, if again you wiſh to fee
Your Damon ſtill reſtor'd and free,
Go try to move the cruel fair,
And gain the fcornful Celia's ear.
But, oh ! forbear with too much art
To touch that dear relentlefs heart,
Left rivals to my tears you prove,
And jealoufy fucceed to love.

SONG 150.

Sung in the *Maid of the Oaks.*

C O M E fing round my favourite tree,
  Ye fongſters that vifit the grove;
'Twas the haunt of my ſhepherd and me,
  And the bark is a record of love.

Reclin'd on the turf, by my fide,
  He tenderly pleaded his caufe;
I only with bluſhes reply'd,
  And the nightingale fill'd up the paufe.

SONG 151.

A PASTORAL BALLAD.

S I N C E Emma, the peerlefs, is flown '
  To the regions of permanent reſt,
Perverfely will Colinet moan,
  And wiſh the dear feraph unbleft !

What tho' ſhe were pride of the plain,
  What tho' ſhe were queen of the dance ;
What tho' ſhe gave joy to the fwain,
  And rival'd the flow'rs of romance !

The fair-one forfook with a fmile
  The pleafures that once ſhe held dear ;
For, Colinet, thefe are but vile,
  Compar'd with a blifs more fincere.

What tho' ſhe were joy to your heart,
  What tho' ſhe were light to your eye;
What tho' the kind fair would impart
  Each rapture, each tear, and each figh!

The end of her pilgrimage here,
Was to fit her for manfions of blifs;
Then indulge not the murmuring tear,
Nor lament fuch an exit as this.

Since Emma the peerlefs is flown
To the regions of permanent reft,
Perverfely fhould Colinet moan—
He has not a wifh to be blefs'd.

SONG 152.

THE PRUDENT BACCHANALIAN.

By the Editor.

WHERE focial mirth with pleafure reigns,
We jocundly repair;
And Bacchus fills our fprightly veins
With antidotes to care.

But, left the jolly god fhould claim
More worfhip than his due,
The glafs is held by Reafon's dame,
Who feeks her tribute too.

To pleafe them both fhould be our care,
For much to both we owe;
She arms us ftrong againft defpair,
And he difpels our woe.

Then who to either doth refufe,
Shall find this fatal truth;
A dullnefs one will fure produce.
The other rob his youth.

SONG. 153.

A SCOTCH RONDEAU.

Sung at VAUXHALL.

YE nymphs, 'tis true to Colin's ftrain
I've often liften'd in the grove;
And can you blame me, that a fwain
Like Colin fhould engage my love;

Alas! could I my heart fecure,
Unlefs to worth and merit blind;
Ah! fay could you yourfelves endure,
To flight a fwain fo true and kind?

When truth conveys the tender tale,
And honour breathes the fhepherd's figh;
Love o'er difcretion will prevail,
To fhun it's pow'r in vain we try.

SONG 154.

Sung at VAUXHALL.

ATTEND, ye nymphs, while I impart
The fecret wifhes of my heart,
And tell what fwain, if one there be,
Whom fate defigns for love and me.

Let reafon o'er his thoughts prefide,
Let honour all his actions guide;
Stedfaft in virtue let him be,
The fwain defign'd for love and me.

Let folid fenfe inform his mind,
With pure good-nature fweetly join'd;
Sure friend to modeft merit be
The fwain defign'd for love and me.

Where forrow prompts the penfive figh,
Where grief bedews the drooping eye,
Melting in fympa hy I fee
The fwain defign'd for love and me.

Let fordid av'rice claim no part
Within his tender, gen'rous heart;
Oh! be that heart from falfhood free,
Devoted all to love and me.

SONG 155.

THE SHEPHERD.

NO more the feftive train I'll join:
Adieu! ye rural fports, adieu!
For what, alas! have griefs like mine
With paftimes or delights to do!
Let hearts at eafe fuch pleafures prove,
But I am all defpair and love.

Ah, well a-day! how chang'd am I!
When late I feiz'd the rural reed,
So foft my ftrains, the herds hard by
Stood gazing, and forgot to feed;
But now my ftrains no longer move,
They're difcord ail, defpair, and love.

Behold around my ftraggling fheep,
The faireft once upon the lea;
No fwain to guide, no dog to keep,
Unfhorn they ftray, nor mark'd by me:
The fhepherds mourn to fee them rove;
They afk the caufe, I anfwer love.

Neglected love firft taught my eyes
With tears of anguifh to o'erflow;
'Tis that which fill'd my breaft with fighs,
And tun'd my pipe to notes of woe;
Love has occafion'd all my fmart,
Difpers'd my flock, and broke my heart.

SONG 156.

A HUNTING SONG.

Sung in the *Maid of the Oaks*.

COME roufe from your trances,
The fly morn advances,
To catch fluggifh mortals in bed;
Let the horn's jocund note
In the wind fweetly float,
While the fox from the brake lifts his head;
Now creeping,
Now peeping,
The fox from the brake lifts his head.
Each way to his fteed,
Your godd fs fhall lead,
Come follow, my worfhippers, follow;
For the chafe all prepare,
See the hounds fnuff the air,
Hark, hark, to the huntfmen's fweet hollow!

Hark Jowler, hark Rover,
  See Reynard breaks cover,
The hunters fly o'er the ground;
  Now they dart down the lane,
  Now they skim o'er the plain,
And the hills, woods, and vallies refound;
    With dashing
    And splashing,
The hills, woods, and vallies refound.
  Then away with full speed,
  Your goddess shall lead,
Come follow, my worshippers, follow;
O'er hedge, ditch, and gate,
If you stop you're too late;
Hark, hark, to the huntsman's sweet hollow.
  Then away with full speed, &c.

SONG 157.

Written by Mr. FALCONER.

THE smiling plains, profusely gay,
  Are drest in all the pride of May;
The birds around, in ev'ry vale,
Breathe rapture on the vocal gale.

But ah, Miranda! without thee,
Nor spring nor summer smiles on me!
All lonely, in the secret shade,
I mourn thy absence, charming maid.

O soft as love, as honour fair!
More gently sweet than vernal air!
Come to my arms, for you alone,
Can all my unguish past atone.

O come! and to my bleeding heart
Th' ambrosial balm of love impart;
Thy presence lasting joy shall bring,
And give the year eternal spring.

SONG 158.

AN ELEGIAC BALLAD.

WHERE now is that sun of repose
  That once us'd to smile on this breast,
On the morn that so genially rose,
  And at eve set so kindly in rest?

Alas! all withdrawn from my sight,
  On the morning no longer it beams;
And, instead of contentment at night,
  Spreads horror alone in my dreams.

O, Belmour! why e'er did I hear
  What I knew must be death to believe?
Or drink up a strain with my ear,
  When I saw it was meant to deceive?

To whom, tell me now, can I speak,
  That will not reproach and exclaim;
And read thro' the blush on this cheek,
  That guilt is the parent of shame?

In vain the dark grove do I try,
  Some respite from censure to find;
But, oh! from a world I may fly,
  Yet cannot escape from my mind!

In the thickest recess of the shade,
  My conscience cries, Flavia, see there,
What a wretch a fond father is made,
  What a mother is plung'd in despair!

The zephyr's most innocent gale
  Now seems at my conduct to roar;
And the stream, as it winds through the dale,
  Says, Flavia is spotless no more.

At church, in the moment of pray'r,
  Remorse lifts her terrible rod,
And harrows my soul with despair,
  Tho' I kneel at the throne of my God.

'Tis just—and I cannot upbraid,
  For Belmour yet swell in the eye;
And this bosom, tho' lately betray'd,
  Still heaves with the tender a sigh!

In spite of religion's pure breath,
  The softest ideas will rise;
And I doat to distraction and death,
  While I labour to hate and despise.

Come grave, then, thou best of reliefs,
  Regardless of season or time,
At once give an end to my griefs,
  And a Lethe to wash o'er my crime.

Yet cease not, ye tears, still to flow,
  From the fount of contrition or love;
So th' excess of my sorrows below
  May purchase my pardon above.

THE

VOCAL MAGAZINE.

NUMBER II.

SONG 159.

Written by the EDITOR.

WHEN Freedom was banifh'd from
Greece and from Rome,
And wander'd, neglected, in fearch of a home;
Jove, willing to fix her where long fhe might
ftand,
Turn'd the globe round about to examine each
land.
Derry down, down; down, derry down.

With nice circumfpection he view'd the whole
ball,
And weigh'd in his balance the merits of all;
Then quickly determin'd that England, alone,
Was the fpot well adapted for Liberty's throne.
Derry down, &c.

So inftant convening the deities round,
He told them a dwelling for Freedom he'd
found;
And begg'd that each god would fome bounty
impart
To a land from whence Liberty ne'er fhould
depart.
Derry down, &c.

Then Mars boldly ftepp'd from his miftrefs's
fide,
And fwore that the Britons in war fhould prefide;
While Bacchus declar'd that each heart chear-
ing juice,
For the ufe of true Englifhmen, he would produce.
Derry down, &c.

Merry Momus then rofe, and begg'd they would
admit
He might give them a fp'ce of the true Attic wit;
And Venus declar'd, if 'twas pleafing to Jove,
She could wifh to make England the empire of
love.
Derry down, &c.

To render compleat all the bleffings now paft,
And provide that they might to eternity laft;
It was inftant refolv'd that a toaft fhould be
giv'n,
And drank in a bumper by each one in Heav'n.
Derry down, &c.

The words of the toaft, as it ftands on record,
Were, ' Britons with Britons together accord;
' By your enemies, then, you fhall always be
' fear'd,
' And with wine, wit, and women, inceffantly
' chear'd.'
Derry down, &c.

Then let each fon of Freedom, who thefe gifts
approves,
Fill his glafs to the brim in the liquor he loves;
And join me in drinking ' Confufion to thofe
' Who, Englifhmen born, are ftill Englifhmen's
' foes!'
Derry down, down; down, derry down.

SONG 160.

COLIN; A PASTORAL.

To the Memory of Mr. CUNNINGHAM.

Written by Mr. HAWKINS.

GIVE ear, O ye fwains, to my lay;
Since Colin, alas! is no more,
I languifh and pine all the day,
In forrow my lofs to deplore:
For he was fo gentle a fwain,
His manners were ever rever'd;
So fweet was his paftoral ftrain,
So artlefs, it ever endear'd.

Ye warblers, that bill on each fpray,
Be penfive, be huff'd, and forlorn;
Ye lambkins, that wantonly ftray,
O bleat for your fhepherd that's gone!

F

So tender and loving was he,
   So faithful and firm to his truſt;
With mildneſs he liv'd, and with glee;
   A picture of all that wasjuſt.

His aſpect was meek and ſerene,
   Tranquillity dwelt in his air;
No mortal like him e'er was ſeen,
   No mortal with him could compare:
For he was ſo gentle and kind,
   That birds cluſter'd round in a throng,
And all in full harmony join'd
   To echo his elegant ſong.

But Colin from us is far borne,
   No longer he ſings thro' the grove;
No longer, beneath the gay thorn,
   He pours forth his ſonnets of love:
Then farewel, O favourite bard!
   Adieu, my dear Colin, adieu!
Thy worth I ſhall ever regard,
   To thy fame I will ever be true.

SONG 161.

THE RAPE OF THE TRAP.

Written by Mr. SHENSTONE.

'TWAS in a land of learning,
   The muſe's fav'rite ſtation,
Such pranks, of late,
Were play'd by a rat,
   As gave them conſternation.

All in a college-ſtudy,
   Where books were in great plenty,
This rat would devour,
More ſenſe in an hour,
   Than I could write—in twenty.

His breakfaſt, half the morning,
   He conſtantly attended;
And when the bell rung
For evening-ſong,
   His dinner ſcarce was ended.

Huge tomes of geo—graphy,
   And maps, lay all in flutter;
A river or a ſea
Was to him a diſh of tea,
   And a kingdom—bread and butter.

Such havock, ſpoil, and rapine,
   With grief my muſe rehearſes;
How freely he would dine
On ſome bulky ſchool-divine,
   And for deſſert—eat verſes.

He ſpar'd not even heroics,
   On which we poets pride us;
And would make no more
Of King Arthurs, by the ſcore,
   Than—all the world beſide does.

But if the deſp'rate potion
   Might chance to over-doſe him;
To check it's rage,
He took a page
   Of logic, to compoſe him.

A trap, in haſte and anger,
   Was bought, you need not doubt on't;
And ſuch was the gin,
Were a lion once in,
   He could not, I think, get out on't.

With cheeſe, not books, 'twas baited;
   The fact, I'll not belye it;
Since none, I tell ye that,
Whether ſcholar or rat,
   Minds books, when he has other diet.

But more of trap and bait, Sir,
   Why ſhould I ſing, or either?
Since the rat, with mickle pride,
All their ſophiſtry defy'd,
   And dragg'd them away together.

Both trap and bait were vaniſh'd
   Thro' a fracture in the flooring;
Which, tho' ſo trim
It now may ſeem,
   Had then a doz'n or more in.

Then anſwer this, ye ſages,
   Nor think I mean to wrong ye;
Had the rat, who thus did ſeize on
The trap, leſs claim to reaſon,
   Than many a ſage among ye?

Dan Prior's mice, I own it,
   Were vermin of condition;
But this rat, who merely learn'd
What rats alone concern'd,
   Was the greater politician.

That England's topſy-turvy,
   Is clear from theſe miſhaps, Sir;
Since traps, we may determine,
Will no longer take our vermin,
   But vermin take our traps, Sir.

Let ſophs, by rats infeſted,
   Then truſt in cats to catch 'em;
Leſt they prove the utter bane
Of our ſtudies, where, 'tis plain,
   No mortal ſits—to watch 'em.

SONG 162.

KATE OF ABERDEEN.

Written by Mr. CUNNINGHAM.

THE ſilver moon's enamour'd beam
   Steals ſoftly through the night,
To wanton with the winding ſtream,
   And kiſs reflected light.
To courts be gone, heart-ſoothing ſleep,
   Where you've ſo ſeldom been,
Whilſt I May's wakeful vigil keep
   With Kate of Aberdeen.

The nymphs and ſwains expectant wait,
   In primroſe chaplets gay,
Till morn unbars her golden gate,
   And gives the promis'd May:
The nymphs and ſwains ſhall all declare
   The promis'd May, when ſeen,
Not half ſo fragrant, half ſo fair,
   As Kate of Aberdeen.

I'll tune my pipe to playful notes,
  And rouze yon nodding grove,
Till new-wak'd birds diftend their throats,
  And hail the maid I love;
At her approach the lark miftakes,
  And quits the new-drefs'd green:
Fond birds! 'tis not the morning breaks,
  'Tis Kate of Aberdeen.

Now blithefome o'er the dewy mead,
  Where elves difportive play,
The feftal dance young fhepherds lead,
  Or fing their love-tun'd lay.
Till May in morning robe draws nigh,
  And claims a virgin queen;
The nymphs and fwains exulting cry—
  Here's Kate of Aberdeen!

SONG 163.

Sung at FREE-MASONS HALL.

A SSIST me, ye fair tuneful nine,
  Euphrofyne, grant me thy aid;
Whilft the honours I fing of the trine,
  Prefide o'er my numbers, blythe maid.
Ceafe clamour and faction, oh, ceafe!
  Fly hence, all ye cynical train;
Difturb not, difturb not the Lodge's fweet peace,
  Where filence and fecrefy reign.

Religion untainted here dwells,
  Here the morals of Athens are taught;
Great Hiram's tradition here tells
  How the world out of chaos was brought.
With fervency, freedom, and zeal,
  Our mafter's commands we obey;
No cowan, no cowan our fecrets can fteal,
  No babbler our myft'ries betray.

Here Wifdom her ftandard difplays;
  Here nob y the fciences fhine;
Here the temple's vaft column we raife,
  And finifh a work that's divine.
Illum'd from the Eaft with pure light,
  Here the arts do their bleffings beftow,
And all perfect, all perfect unfold to the fight
  What none but a mafon can know.

If on earth any praife can be found,
  Any virtue unnam'd in my fong,
Any grace in the univerfe round,
  May thefe to a mafon belong:
May each brother his paffions fubdue,
  Practife charity, concord, and love,
And be hail'd, and be hail'd by the thrice hap-
  py few
Who prefide in the Grand Lodge above!

SONG 164.

T HE bird that hears her neftling cry,
  And flies abroad for food,
Returns impatient through the fky
  To nurfe her callow brood:
The tender mother knows no joy,
  But bodes a thoufand harms,

And fickens for her darling boy,
  When abfent from her arms.

Such fondnefs with impatience join'd
  My faithful bofom fires,
Now forc'd to leave the fair behind,
  The queen of my defires:
The pow'rs of verfe too languid prove,
  All fimilies are vain
To fhew how ardently I love,
  Or to relieve my pain.

The faint with fervent zeal infpir'd,
  For Heaven, and joy divine;
The faint is not with rapture fir'd,
  More pure, more warm than mine:
I take what liberty I dare,
  'T were impious to fay more;
Convey my longings to the fair,
  The goddefs I adore.

SONG 165.

Sung in Oroonoko.

B RIGHT Cynthia's pow'r, divinely great,
  What heart is not obeying?
A thoufand Cupids on her wait,
  And in her eyes are playing.

She feems the queen of love to reign;
  For fhe alone difpenfes
Such fweets as beft can entertain
  The guft of all the fenfes.

Her face a charming profpect brings;
  Her breath gives balmy bliffes;
I hear an angel when fhe fings,
  And tafte of heav'n in kiffes.

Four fenfes thus fhe feafts with joy,
  From Nature's richeft treafure?
Let me the other fenfe employ,
  And I fhall die with pleafure.

SONG 166.

AMORET.

S WEET Phyllis, well met,
  The fun is juft fet,
To yon myrtle grove let's repair;
  All nature's at reft,
  And none to moleft;
I've fomething to fay to my fair.

PHYLLIS.

No, no, fubtle fwain,
  Entreaties are vain,
Perfuade me to go you ne'er fhall;
  Night draws on apace,
  I muft quit the place,
The dew is beginning to fall.

AMORET.

Believe me, coy maid,
  By honour I'm fway'd,
No fears need your bofom alarm;

The oak and the pine
Their leaves kindly join,
To shelter love's vot'ries from harm.

PHYLLIS.

Your arts I despise,
My virtue I prize;
Though poor, I am richer than those
Who, lost to all shame,
Will barter their fame
For purchase of gold and fine cloaths.

AMORET.

You do me much wrong;
Such thoughts ne'er belong
To the noble and gen'rous breast;
I meant but to know
If Phyllis would go
And let Hymen make Amoret blest.

PHYLLIS.

If what you now say
Your heart don't betray,
It gives me much pleasure to find
My Amoret still
A stranger to ill,
And to Wedlock's soft bondage inclin'd.

SONG 167.

THE ROAST BEEF OF OLD ENGLAND.

WHEN mighty ro.st beef was the English-
man's food,
It ennobled our veins, and enriched our blood;
Our soldiers were brave, and our courtiers were
good:
O the roast beef of Old England!
And O the Old English roast beef!

But since we have learn'd from all-conqu'ring
France,
To eat their ragoûts, as well as to dance,
We're fed upon nothing——but vain com-
plaisance.
O the roast beef, &c.

Our fathers of old were robust, stout and strong,
And kept open house with good cheer all day
long,
Which m.de the plump tenants rejoice in this
song.
O the roast beef, &c.

But now we are dwindled to——what shall I
name?
A sneaking poor race, half begotten——and
tame.
Who fully those honours that once shone in
fame.
O the roast beef, &c.

When good Queen Elizabeth sat on the throne,
Ere coffee, or tea, or such slip-slops were known,
The world was in terror if e'er she did frown.
O the roast beef, &c.

In those days, if fleets did presume on the main,
They seldom or never return'd back again;
As witness the vaunting Armada of Spain.
O the roast beef, &c.

O then they had courage to eat and to fight,
And when wrongs were a cooking to do them-
selves right;
But now we're a pack of—I could—but good
night.
O the roast beef, &c.

SONG 168.

Sung in She Wou'd if She Cou'd.

Written by Sir GEORGE ETHEREGE.

TO little or no purpose I spent many days,
In ranging the Park, th' Exchange, and the
plays;
For ne'er in my rambles, till now, did I prove
So lucky to meet with the man I cou'd love.
Oh! how am I pleas'd, when I think on this
man,
That I find I must love, let me do what I can!

How long I shall love him, I can no more tell,
Than, had I a fever, when I should be well;
My passion shall kill me before I will shew it,
And yet I would give all the world he did
know it:
But oh, how I sigh, when I think, should he
woo me,
I cannot deny what I know wou'd undo me!

SONG 169.

Written by Mr. PRIOR.

ALEXIS shunn'd his fellow swains,
Their rural sports and jocund strains,
(Heaven guard us all from Cupid's bow;)
He lost his crook, he left his flocks,
And, wand'ring through the lonely rocks,
He nourish'd endless woe.

The nymphs and shepherds round him came,
His grief some pity, others blame;
The fatal cause all kindly seek:
He mingled his concern with theirs,
He gave them back their friendly tears;
He sigh'd, but could not speak.

Clorinda came, among the rest;
And she, too, kind concern exprest,
And ask'd the reason of his woe:
She ask'd; but with an air and mien,
As made it easily foreseen,
She fear'd too much to know.

The shepherd rais'd his mournful head—
And will you pardon me, (he said)
While I the truth reveal;
Which nothing from my breast should tear,
Which never should offend your ear,
But that you bid me tell?

'Tis thus I rove, 'tis thus complain,
Since you appear'd upon the plain;
　You are the caufe of all my care:
Your eyes ten thoufand dangers dart;
Ten thoufand torments vex my heart;
　I love, and I defpair.—

Too much, Alexis, I have heard;
'Tis what I thought, 'tis what I fear'd;
　And yet I pardon you, fhe cry'd:
But you fhall promife, ne'er again
To breathe your vows, or fpeak your pain.—
He bow'd, obey'd, and dy d.

SONG 170.

ANACREONTIC.

AS wanton Cupid faw, one day,
　A linnet warbling on a fpray,
He long'd to make the bird his prey.—

See here the ftring that ties my bow;
Says he, I warrant that will do,
For fuch an artlefs bird as you.

Then round the flutterer's neck he caft
The fiiken cord, and ty'd it faft—
I've got you fafe (he cries) at laft.

In vain with out-ftretch'd wings and beak
He tries the urchin's ftring to break;
No more allow'd his flight to take.

No more he rifes from the ground,
But hops and hovers round and round,
Within his fetters, narrow bound.

So Cupid, with enfnaring arts,
Lets fly abroad his poifon'd darts,
And feizes wretched lovers hearts;

Torments them with his wanton play,
Makes them his tyrant pow'r obey,
Yet feems to rule with gentle fway.

But foon miftaken mortals find
How faft a filken cord can bind;
The lover, not the boy, is blind.

SONG 171.

WHEN firft I faw Chloe, I pray'd for a kifs;
　She frown'd, and cry'd—Pr'ythee, fwain,
　　don't;
I always think freedoms fo clofe are amifs,
　And, take my word for it, I won't.—

Too clofe! (I reply'd) Can a lover too clofe
Approach the dear charmer he loves?
He can t, ev'ry fhepherd that's happy well
　knows,
And never a damfel difproves.

Sly Cupid now whifper'd—Why beg for a kifs,
Confider, your manhood's at ftake,
Each beauty defpifes a queftion like this,
　'Tis yours, not to afk, but to take?

A lover with boldnefs the fair fhould attack;
　'Tis conduct in them to be fhy;

And once their fweet lips if you heartily fmack,
　They'll never once after deny.—

Encourag'd by this, I determin'd to prefs
　The prettieft of nymphs ever known,
Till my heart beat with tranfport, to fuch an
　excefs,
That her bofom grew warm as my own.

A manly affurance, where love is fincere,
　In lovers fhews prudence and fkill;
And now, when I cry—Shall I kifs you, my
　dear?
Her anfwer's—You may if you will.

SONG 172.

THROUGH THE WOOD LADDIE.

Sung at VAUXHALL.

O Sandy, why leav'ft thou thy Nelly to
　mourn,
　Thy prefence could eafe me,
　When naithing can pleafe me!
Now dowie I figh on the banks of the bourn,
Or through the wood, laddie, until thou return.

Tho' woods now are bonny, and mornings are
　clear,
　While lav'rocks are finging,
　And primrofes fpringing,
Yet nane of them pleafes mine eye or mine ear,
When through the wood, laddie, ye dinna ap-
　pear.

That I am forfaken fome fpare not to tell,
　I'm fafh'd wi' their fcorning,
　Baith ev'ning and morning,
Their jeering goes aft to my heart wi' a knell,
When through the wood, laddie, I wander
　myfel.

Then ftay, my dear Sandy, no longer away;
　But, quick as an arrow,
　Hafte hence to thy marrow,
Who's living in languor till that happy day,
When through the wood, laddie, we ll dance,
　fing, and play.

SONG 173.

Written by MATTHEW GREEN.

I Lately faw what now I fing,
　Fair Lucia's hand difplay'd;
　This finger grac'd a diamond ring,
　And that a fparrow play'd.

The feather'd plaything fhe carefs'd,
　And ftrok'd it's head and wings;
And while it neftled on her breaft,
　She lifp'd the deareft things.

With chizzel-bill, a fpark ill-fet
　He loofen'd from the reft,
And fwallow d down to grind his meat,
　The eafier to digeft.

She feiz'd his bill with wild affright,
　Her diamond to defcry:

'Twas gone! fhe ficken'd at the fight,
Moaning her bird would die.

The tongue-ty'd knocker none might ufe,
The curtains none might draw,
The footmen went without their fhoes,
The ftreets were laid with ftraw.

The doctor us'd his oily art,
Of ftrong emetic kind;
Th' apothecary play'd his part,
And engineer'd behind.

When phyfic ceas'd to fpend it's ftore,
To bring away the ftone,
Dicky, like people given o'er,
Picks up, when let alone.

His eyes difpell'd their fickly dews,
He peck'd behind his wing:
Lucia recov'ring at the news,
Relapfes for the ring.

Meanwhile, within her beauteous breaft,
Two diff'rent paffions ftrove;
When av'rice ended the conteft,
And triumph'd over love.

Poor little, pretty, flutt'ring thing,
Thy pains the fex difplay!
Who, only to repair a ring,
Could take thy life away.

Drive av'rice from your breafts, ye fair,
Monfter of fouleft mien;
Ye would not let it harbour there,
Could but it's form be feen.

It made a virgin put on guile,
Truth's image break her word;
A Lucia's face forbear to fmile,
A Venus kill her bird.

SONG 174.

Written by G. LYTTELTON, Efq.

THE heavy hours are almoft paft
That part my love and me,
My longing eyes may hope at laft
Their longing wifh to fee.

But how, my Delia, will you meet
The man you've loft fo long?
Will love on all your pulfes beat,
And tremble on your tongue?

Will you in every look declare
Your heart is ftill the fame;
And heal each idly anxious care
Our fears in abfence frame?

Thus, Delia, thus I paint the fcene
When fhortly we fhall meet,
And try what yet remains between
Of loit'ring time to cheat.

But if the dream that foothes my mind
Shall falfe and groundlefs prove;
If I am doom'd at length to find
You have forgot to love;

All I of Venus afk, is this,
No more to let us join;
But grant me here the flatt'ring blifs,
To die, and think you mine.

SONG 175.

Written by Mr. WHITEHEAD.

YES, I'm in love, I feel it now,
And Celia has undone me;
And yet, I'll fwear, I can't tell how
The pleafing plague ftole on me.

'Tis not her face that love creates,
For there no graces revel;
'Tis not her fhape, for there the fates
Have rather been uncivil.

'Tis not her air, for fure in that
There's nothing more than common;
And all her fenfe is only chat,
Like any other woman.

Her voice, her touch, might give th' alarm,
'Twas both, perhaps, or neither;
In fhort, 'twas that provoking charm
Of Celia all together.

SONG 176.

THE TON.

Sung at VAUXHALL.

TOO long the rhymfters of the age,
Thofe fcribbling fons of ftrife,
Have dar'd a crow-quill war to wage
With dames of higher life.
I am the fex's championefs,
And now ftand forth alone,
Prepar'd to refcue and redrefs
The ladies of the Ton.

Ye fair, who tafte and fafhion love,
I fummon to my fong;
To all the world I'll plainly prove,
We never can do wrong.
Tho' trifling duties we neglect,
To modifh life unknown,
'Tis fenfe and reafon ftill direct
The ladies of the Ton.

If glad we feek the midnight hour,
Which others fnore away,
'Tis but to reconfider more
The labours of the day.
If all the night we pafs at whift,
'Tis for reflection done,
In hopes our mem'ries to affift,
And fit us for the Ton.

If, dreading pointed ridicule,
To hufbands we feem loth,
And with our lovers play the fool,
'Tis tendernefs for both.
For kind to thefe the world derides,
And harfh to thofe they moan,
So pure compaffion only guides
The ladies of the Ton.

If in our coaches bent in two,
We're tortur'd every day,
It proves how much we can go through,
When fashion leads the way.
Then mark it's pow'r, ye belles and smarts,
For fashion, have I shewn,
May break the necks, if not the hearts,
Of ladies of the Ton.

SONG 177.

A BIRD IN THE HAND IS WORTH TWO IN
THE BUSH.

Sung at VAUXHALL.

LONG time I've enjoy'd the soft transports
of love,
I've bill'd like a sparrow, or coo'd like a dove;
In woodbine alcove, or in jessamine bow'r,
To many fond shepherds I've listen'd an hour;
But now for such pleasures I care not a rush,
One bird in the hand is worth two in the bush.

Young Colin's caresses inspir'd me with joy,
And Damon's soft vows I thought never
could cloy,
With each have I sat in a fav'rite retreat,
And beheld with delight each fond swain at
my feet;
But now for such pleasures I care not a rush,
One bird in the hand is worth two in the bush.

Gay Strephon declares I'm the girl to his mind,
If he proves sincere, I'll be constant and kind;
He vows that to-morrow he'll make me his
wife,
I'll fondly endeavour to bless him for life:
For all other swains now I care not a rush;
One bird in the hand is worth two in the bush.

SONG 178.

RURAL LIFE.

FREE from noise, free from strife,
In a sweet country life.
I could wish for to pass all my days,
Where innocence reigns,
Flocks cover the plains,
And birds sweetly echo their lays.

How contented they live,
What joys they receive,
Tho' nothing but ground for their floor;
Just before the sweet cot,
So delightful the spot,
Where jessamine grows by the door!

How early they rise,
Transported with joys,
So contented their days pass along!
And if justly combin'd,
With a true heart and mind,
To a wife whom all virtues belong.

Tho' homely their food,
Their appetite's good,
Blooming health on their cheeks doth appear;

Neither envy nor pride
With them can reside,
But happiness shines through the year.

At sun going down,
Their work being done,
They're the happiest people on earth;
By the oak on the green
Each couple is seen,
With innocent pastime and mirth.

When harvest is done,
With a formal old song,
The jolly farmer amongst all the rest,
He will laugh, drink, and say,
This is our holiday,
With beef and good ale of the best.

SONG 179.

THE LIBERTINE REPULSED.

HENCE, Belmour, perfidious! this instant
retire,
No farther entreaties employ;
Nor meanly pretend any more to admire
What basely you wish to destroy.

Say, youth, must I madly rush on upon shame,
If a traitor but artfully sighs!
And eternally part with my honour and fame
For a compliment paid to my eyes?

If a flame all dishonest be vilely profest,
Thro' tenderness must I incline,
And seek to indulge the repose of a breast
That would plant endless tortures in mine!

No, Belmour—a passion I can't but despise,
Shall never find way to my ears;
Nor the man meet a glance of regard from my
these eyes,
That would drench them for ever in tears.

Can the lover who thinks, nay, who wishes
me base,
Expect that I e'er should be kind?
Or atone with a paltry address to my face,
For the injury done to my mind?

Hence, Belmour, this instant, and cease every
dream,
Which your hope saw so foolishly born;
Nor vainly imagine to gain my esteem,
By deserving my hate and my scorn.

SONG 180.

ODE TO MAY.

Written by Miss WHATELEY.

FAIREST daughter of the year,
Ever blooming, lovely May;
While the vivid skies appear,
Nature smiles, and all is gay.

Thine the flowery painted mead,
Pasture fair, and mountain green;
Thine, with infant harvest spread,
Laughing lies the lowland-scene.

Friend of thine, the shepherd plays
Blithesome near the yellow broom;
While his flock, that carelefs ftrays,
Seeks the wild-thyme's fweet perfume.

May, with thee I mean to rove
O'er thefe lawns and vallies fair,
Tune my gentle lyre to love,
Cherish hope, and foften care.

Round me shall the village fwains,
Shall the rofy nymphs appear;
While I fing, in rural ftrains,
May, to shepherds ever dear.

I had never fkill to raife
Pæans from the vocal ftrings,
To the godlike hero's praife,
To the pageant pomp of kings.

Stranger to the hoftile plains,
Where the brazen trumpets found;
Life's red ftream the verdure ftains,
Heaps promifcuous prefs the ground:

Where the murd'rous cannon's breath
Fate denounces from afar,
And the loud report of death
Stuns the cruel ear of war.

Stranger to the park and play,
Birth-night balls and courtly trains:
Thee I woo, my gentle May,
Tune for thee my native ftrains.

Blooming groves, and wand'ring rills,
Soothe thy vacant poet's dreams,
Vocal woods, and wilds, and hills,
All her unexalted themes.

S O N G 181.

JAMIE AND SUE.

Sung at VAUXHALL.

JAMIE.
PR'YTHEE, Sufan, what doft mufe on,
By this doleful, doleful, fpring?
You are, I fear, in love, my dear,
Alas, poor thing! alas, poor thing! alas, poor
thing!

SUE.
Truly, Jamie, I muft blame ye,
'Caufe you look fo pale and wan,
I fear 'twill prove you are in love,
Alas, poor man!

JAMIE.
Nay, my Suey, now I view ye,
Well I know, I know your fmart;
When you're alone, you figh and moan,
Alas, poor heart!

SUE.
Jamie hold, I dare be bold
To fay thy heart, thy heart is ftole,
And know the fhe, as well as thee,
Alas, poor foul!

JAMIE.
Then, my Sue, tell me who,
I'll give thee beads of pearl;
And eafe thy heart of all the fmart,
Alas, poor girl!

SUE.
Jamie, no, if you fhou'd know,
I fear 'twould make you fad;
And pine away, both night and day,
Alas, poor lad!

JAMIE.
Why then, Sue, it is for you
That I am burning in thefe flames;
And when I die, I know you'll cry—
Alas, poor James!

SUE.
Say you fo; then Jamie know,
If you fhou'd prove untrue,
Then you will make me likewife cry—
Alas, poor Sue!

BOTH.
Come, then, join thy hand with mine,
And we will dance, will dance and fing;
I do agree to marry thee,
Alas, poor thing!

S O N G 182.

'TIS not my Patty's fparkling eyes,
Her air, her eafy grace,
Her thrilling accents, that I prize,
Or yet her blooming face?

Such charms as thefe in others fhine,
Whofe beauty's all they boaft;
But when that beauty does decline,
Their greateft power is loft.

But lovely Patty's wit refin'd,
Her fenfe, good-nature, eafe,
Divine perfections of the mind,
And firm defire to pleafe:

'Tis thefe that raife the maiden's fame,
That prompt defire and love,
And kindle in my breaft a flame,
That time can ne'er remove.

S O N G 183.

HE'LL STEAL YOUR TENDER HEARTS
AWAY.

Sung at VAUXHALL.

BY moffy brook and flow'ry plain,
I fondly feek my fhepherd fwain;
Tell me, fweet maidens, have ye feen
The gentle Damon on the green?
Avoid the danger while you may,
He'll fteal your tender hearts away.

Perfuafion fmiles whene'er he fpeaks,
And rofy dimples deck his cheeks,

Blooming as health, as Hebe fair,
The Graces twine his auburn hair,
Loves in his funny eye-beams play,
That ſtole my tender heart away.

Sweet wreaths of flow'rs he wove for me,
Laſt night, beneath the hawthorn tree;
Bewitching are his tales of love,
Propitious may they ever prove:
For Damon, gentle, kind, and gay,
Has ſtole my tender heart away.

SONG 184.

Sung in the *Beggar's Opera.*

HOW happy ſhould I be with either,
Were t'other dear charmer away;
But while you thus teaze me together,
To neither a word will I ſay:
But tol de rol, &c.

SONG 185.

INLAND NAVIGATION.

'TWAS juſt at the time when in ſorrowful
ſtrain,
Old England was grievouſly groaning;
Her natives in ſadneſs, to add to the ſcene,
The loſs of their trade were bemoaning:
To give ſome redreſs, in this age of diſtreſs,
Some worthies, (tho' few in the nation)
As a ſcheme that might tend to ſome favourable
end,
Were reſolv'd to promote navigation.

The loveis of commerce will freely combine,
Without any kind of evaſion,
To ſtrengthen ſo noble and brave a deſign,
And gladly embrace the occaſion:
What Briton, that knows what opulence flows
From this art, but with free approbation,
And ſpirit alert, will his int'reſt exert
To ſupport and extend navigation.

'Tis this makes our iſle, in the eyes of the world,
A bulwark of terror and wonder;
What ſtate, when our ſhipping their ſails have
unfurl'd,
But what is oblig'd to knock under!
In war or in peace, all commerce would ceaſe,
Was it not for a free navigation;
'Tis of riches the ſource, when ſuch plans we
enforce,
And of freedom our dear preſervation.

In Lancaſhire view what a laudable plan,
And brought into fine execution
By Bridgewater's duke; let us copy the man,
And ſtand to a good reſolution:
If the waters of Trent with the Merſey have
vent,
What mortal can have an objection!
So they do not proceed, to cut into the Tweed,
With the Scots to have greater connection!

A free intercourſe with our principal ports,
For trade muſt be certainly better;
When traffic's extended, and goods eaſy vended,
In conſequence things will be cheaper:
Our commerce muſt thrive, and the arts will
revive,
Which are now in a ſad ſituation;
If we follow this notion, from ocean to ocean,
To have a compleat navigation.

To the land what advantages ſoon muſt proceed,
When once we have open'd our ſluices?
Our cattle, and even the land where they feed,
Will be turn'd into far better uſes:
'Tis this will enable our merchants abroad
To vie with each neighbouring nation;
Who now, as they tell us, in faCt underſell us,
For want of this free navigation.

SONG 186.

THE ÆRIAL EMBASSY.

YE winged tenants of the wood,
Ye warbling choir, ariſe!
And ſeek the bower of my fair,
Ere ſleep forſake her eyes.

Go, ſweetly mourning Philomel,
Whoſe ſorrows never reſt;
Awake yon ſhamleſs, drowſy lark,
And force him from his neſt.

Thou, my ſoft linnet, add thy note;
And thou, melodious thruſh!
And thou, ſweet goldfinch, haſte! for ſee
The morn begins to bluſh.

Together wing your airy way
To yonder woodbine ſhade,
There ſoftly ſwell your gentle ſtrains,
And wake the lovely maid.

Through all the fragrant ſpicy grove,
Fond labour of her ſwain,
Let echo waft your vary'd notes,
And call her to the plain.

So ſhall each neſt within my meads
Be ſafe from youthful theft;
Nor ſhall your young, by cruel ſnares,
Of parents be bereft.

No miſſive tube ſhall here be ſeen,
My tender birds to ſtay:
Then haſte, O haſte, ye tuneful tribe,
And call my love away.

SONG 187.

PHILANDER AND DAPHNE.

O, Ye gods! Philander cries,
See a nymph in yonder bow'r,
Whoſe devoted, piercing eyes,
Wrapt in ſleep's enchanting pow'r,

Ceaſe at preſent to allure
Ev'ry youthful heart to love;
G

And, within the glade obfcure,
Let me all her charms approve.

Gentle zephyrs, breathe ye foft,
Careful fan her lovely form,
And around her playing, oft
Teach her dreams my inward ftorm.

O with what compofure there,
If to man fuch blifs was giv'n,
I'd replace her flowing hair,
Steal a kifs, and tafte of heav'n!

Waft me, happy fpirits! waft me,
Far from fcenes of deep defpair,
To your lovely, charming Daphne,
Thro' the fleeting, liquid air.

Like yon pretty, tender dove,
To it's faithful partner true,
I would live the life of love—
O! fhe gently wakes. Adieu.

SONG 188.

Written by Mr. SHENSTONE.

I Told my nymph, I told her true,
My fields were fmall, my flocks were few;
While faltering accents fpoke my fear,
That Flavia might not prove fincere.

Of crops deftroy'd by vernal cold,
And vagrant fheep that left my fold:
Of thefe fhe heard, yet bore to hear;
And is not Flavia then fincere?

How, chang'd by fortune's fickle wind,
The friends I lov'd became unkind:
She heard, and fhed a gen'rous tear;
And is not Flavia then fincere?

How, if fhe deign'd my love to blefs,
My Flavia muft not hope for drefs:
This too fhe heard, and fmil'd to hear;
And Flavia fure muft be fincere.

Go fhear your flocks, ye jovial fwains,
Go reap the plenty of your plains;
Defpoil'd of all which you revere,
I know my Flavia's love fincere.

SONG 189.

RALPH OF THE MILL; A PASTORAL
BALLAD.

Written by Mr. HAWKINS.

AS Hebe was tending her fheep, t'other day,
Where the warblers whiftle and fing,
A rural young fwain came tripping that way,
As brifk and as blithe as a king.
The youth was a ftranger to trouble and care,
Contentment e'er guided his will,
Yet ever regarded the fmiles of the fair,
Though always bred up in a mill.

Love ftole in his breaft at the fight of the maid,
For he could not her charms but adore—
' And if thou art cruel, dear Hebe,' he faid,
' I furely fhall love you the more.'

Such tendernefs melted her into furprize,
(For Hebe was never unkind)
And all of a fudden love glow'd in her eyes,
Which fpoke the dictates of her mind.

They fat themfelves down at the foot of a hill,
And chatted together fo free,
Till Ralph, the young fwain, made figns to the
mill,
Whilft clafping the nymph on his knee;
And thus, in a tranfport, the miller reply'd—
' Thy charms, deareft girl, are divine!'
Then prefs'd her fweet lips, and with rapture
he cry'd—
' O Hebe! confent to be mine.'

She liften'd attentive to all his requeft,
And freely comply'd to his will;
And now, to her folace, fhe's marry'd, and bleft
With honeft young Ralph of the mill.
Peace follows their footfteps wherever they go,
In blifs all their hours are fpent;
But, leaders of fafhion, I'd have you to know,
Their ' happinefs flows from content.'

SONG 190.

THE CHOICE.

A Man that's neither high nor low,
In party nor in ftature;
No noify rake, nor fickle beau,
That's us'd to cringe and flatter.

And let him be no learned fool
That nods o'er mufty books;
That eats and drinks, and lives by rule,
And weighs my words and looks.

Let him be eafy, frank, and gay,
Of dancing never tir'd;
Always have fomething fmart to fay,
But filent, if requir'd.

SONG 191.

A PASTORAL.

Written by Mr. CUNNINGHAM.

PALEMON, feated by his favourite maid,
The fylvan fcenes with extafy furvey'd;
Nothing could make the fond Alexis gay,
For Daphne had been abfent half the day;
Dar'd by Palemon for a paftoral prize,
Reluctant (in his turn) Alexis tries.

PALEMON.

This breeze by the river how charming and
foft!
How fmooth the grafs carpet! how green!
Sweet, fweet fings the lark, as he carrols aloft;
His mufic enlivens the fcene.
A thoufand frefh flow'rets unufually gay,
The fields and the forefts adorn;
I pluck'd me fome rofes—the children of May,
And could not find one with a thorn.

Alexis.

The ſkies are quite clouded——too bold is the
    breeze!
Dull vapours deſcend on the plain;
The verdure's all blaſted that cover'd yon trees,
    The birds cannot compaſs a ſtrain!
In ſearch for a chaplet my temples to bind,
    All day, as I ſilently rove,
I can't find a flow'ret, not one to my mind,
    In meadow, in garden, or grove.

Palemon.

I ne'er ſaw the hedge in ſuch excellent bloom,
    The lambkins more wantonly gay!
My cows ſeem to breathe a more pleaſing per-
    fume,
    And brighter than common the day!
If any dull ſhepherd ſhould fooliſhly aſk,
    So rich why the landſcapes appear?
To give a right anſwer, how eaſy my taſk!
    Becauſe my ſweet Phillida's here.

Alexis.

The ſtream that ſo muddy moves ſlowly along,
    Once roll'd in a beautiful tide;
It ſeem'd o'er the pebbles to murmur a ſong,
    But Dahpne ſat then by my ſide:
See—ſee—the ſweet maid o'er the meadow ſhe
    hies!
Quite alter'd already the ſcene!
How limpid the ſtream is! how gay the blue
    ſkies!
The hills and the hedges how green!

SONG 192.

THE LADY ISABELLA'S TRAGEDY.

THERE was a lord of worthy fame,
    And a hunting he would ride,
Attended by a noble train
    Of gentry by his ſide.

And while he did in chace remain,
    To ſee both ſport and play;
His lady went, as ſhe did ſeign,
    Unto the church to pray.

This lord he had a daughter dear,
    Whoſe beauty ſhone ſo bright,
She was belov'd both far and near,
    Of many a lord and knight.

Fair Iſabella was ſhe call'd,
    A creature fair was ſhe;
She was her father's only joy,
    As you ſhall after ſee:

Therefore her cruel ſtep-mother
    Did envy her ſo much,
That day by day ſhe fought her life,
    Her malice it was ſuch.

She bargain'd with the maſter-cook,
    To take her life away:
And, taking of her daughter's book,
    She thus to her did ſay—

Go home, ſweet daughter, I thee pray,
    Go haſten preſently;
And tell unto the maſter-cook
    Theſe words that I tell thee.

And bid him dreſs to dinner ſtraight
    That fair and milk-white doe,
That in the park doth ſhine ſo bright,
    There's none ſo fair to ſhow.

This lady, fearing of no harm,
    Obey'd her mother's will;
And preſently ſhe haſted home,
    Her pleaſure to fulfil.

She ſtraight into the kitchen went,
    Her meſſage for to tell;
And there ſhe ſpy'd the maſter-cook,
    Who did with malice ſwell—

Now, maſter-cook, it muſt be ſo,
    Do that which I thee tell:
You needs muſt dreſs the milk-white doe
    Which you do know full well.

Then ſtraight his cruel bloody hands
    He on the lady laid;
Who, quivering and ſhaking ſtands,
    While thus to her he ſaid—

Thou art the doe, that I muſt dreſs;
    See here, behold my knife;
For it is pointed preſently
    To rid thee of thy life—

O then—cry'd out the ſcullion-boy,
    As loud as loud might be—
O ſave her life, good maſter-cook,
    And make your pyes of me!

For pity's ſake do not deſtroy
    My lady with your knife:
You know ſhe is her father's joy;
    For Chriſt's ſake ſave her life!—

I will not ſave her life, he ſaid,
    Nor make my pyes of thee;
Yet if thou doſt this deed betray,
    Thy butcher I will be.

Now when this lord he did come home
    For to ſit down and eat;
He called for his daughter dear,
    To come and carve his meat—

Now ſit you down, his lady ſaid,
    O ſit you down to meat;
Into ſome nunnery ſhe is gone;
    Your daughter dear forget.

Then ſolemnly he made a vow,
    Before the company,
That he would neither eat nor drink,
    Until he did her ſee.

O then, beſpake the ſcullion boy,
    With a loud voice ſo high—
If now you will your daughter ſee,
    My lord, cut up that pye;

Wherein her fleſh is minced ſmall,
    And parched with the fire:
All cauſed by her ſtep-mother,
    Who did her death deſire.

And curfed be the mafter-cook,
  O curfed may he be!
I proffer'd him my own heart's blood,
  From death to fet her free.

Then all in black this lord did mourn;
  And for his daughter's fake,
He judg'd her cruel ftep-mother
  To be burnt at a ftake.

Likewife he judg'd the mafter-cook
  In boiling-lead to ftand,
And made the fimple fcullion-boy
  The heir of all his land.

SONG 193.

THE WESTERN BEAUTY.

LISTEN, Bath, and the voice of an oracle
  hear,
Nor fancy the poet in jeft:
Alarm'd for all nature, I bid thee beware
Of a fair-one that flames in the Weft.

From her cheek, tho' pale ficknefs has rifl'd
  the rofe,
And robb'd of it's l'ghtning her eye;
Lo, with graces fufficient the virgin ftill glows,
A legion of nymphs to fupply.

To recal thofe loft charms to thy fountain fhe
  wings,
But forbid her to tafte it, or lave;
For, woe to the world fhould'ft thou grant her
  thy fprings,
And health be the fruit of thy wave.

Fulfill'd would the prophefy rife, (by my foul!)
  By which poor mankind muft expire;
Which declares that the globe fhall be burn'd
  like a fcroll,
That an angel fhall fet it on fire.

SONG 194.

THE PANACEA; OR, UNIVERSAL REMEDY.

Written by Mr. EGGLESHAM.

A Doctor behold of moft extenfive credit!
  Whate'er your diforder no longer pray
  dread it;
With one fingle drug all complaints I can cure:
Tho' my med'cine is fharp, yet it's virtues are
  fure.   La, la, la, la, &c.
The body's grofs humours, and ftomach's va-
  garies,
I leave to the college, and apothecaries;
My aims are much higher, and leave them be-
  hind;
They cure but the body, I body and mind.
             La, la, la, la, &c.
This anodyne necklace (a cord to your thinking)
Apply'd to the throat, cures all ills in a twink-
  ling;
Whatever their ftation, it inftantly frees 'em,
Politician, rake, bully, fine lady, or beefom
          La, la, la, la, &c.

The judge, who 'gainft law all his life has run
  riot,
Whofe confcience and practice can ne'er be at
  quiet,
May be cur'd, by one dofe, of chagrin and repentance,
Nor ever be forc'd to reverfe his own fentence.
          La, la, la, la, &c.

The bellowing lawyer, who roars by the hour
'Gainft all things—but gold and the people in
  pow'r,
Oh, let him but once in this necklace be ftrung,
Tho' his principles hold, he will yet hold his
  tongue.   La, la, la, la, &c.

With ftar brightly fhining, the knight of long
  ftanding
Will give o'er the thoughts of your free votes
  commanding;
Only one litt'e dofe will quite fettle his brain,
Nor bruifers, nor butchers he'll think of again.
          La, la, la, la, &c.

The feeble old noble, long fince dead to pleafure,
Who ftill feels an itch for virginity's treafure,
No more difappointment or actions fhall pain,
Nor, poffefs d of the prize, fhall poffefs it in vain.
          La, la, la, la, &c.

No profit I aim at, the good of the nation
Is all my defign in this free publication;
Then hither who wifh or deferve it, repair;
You fhall all be fupply'd——I've enough and to
  fpare.   La, la, la, la, &c.

SONG 195.

WHEN I behold that angel face,
  I feel love's fierceft fire,
That form, replete with every grace,
  Was made to give defire.

Oft I effay to tell my pain,
  As oft I fear her frown;
As fatal that, as on the main
  Mad tempefts thund'ring down.

Yet could I hope the fweet relief
  Of one reviving fmile;
How would it foften all my grief,
  And ev'ry pange beguile!

Not yonder fun, that lights the fky
  Is to it's courfe more true,
Than to the laws of love am I,
  Than I fhould be to you.

SONG 196.

WHEN Celia dwells on Florio's charms,
  Commends his rofy neck and arms,
    With gloomy fpleen I fwell;
My pallid cheeks, and filent tears,
Confus'd replies, and anxious fears,
    Too plain my anguifh tell.

But when o'erpower'd by gen'rous wine,
His odious arms thy waift entwine,
    With fhame and rage I burn;

Yet ftill I cannot ceafe to love,
Vouchfafe, dear nymph, my flame t'approve,
My conftancy return.

Thrice happy they whom love unites
In mutual bonds, in pure delights,
Unbroken by complaints;
Whofe blifs nor anxious care nor ftrife
Difturbs their lateft hours of life,
Or happinefs e'er taints.

S O N G 197.

SIR DILBERRY DIDDLE, CAPTAIN OF
MILITIA.

OF all the brave captains that ever were feen,
Appointed to fight by a king or a queen;
By a queen or a king appointed to fight,
Sure never a captain was like this brave kinght.

He pull'd off his flippers, and wrapper of filk,
And foaming as furious—as whifk-pared milk;
Says he to his lady—My lady, I'll go—
My company calls me; you muft not fay no.

With eyes all in tears, fays my lady—fays fhe—
O cruel Sir Dilberry, do not kill me!
For I never will leave thee, but cling round thy middle,
And die in the arms of Sir Dilberry Diddle.

Says Diddle again to his lady—My dear!
(And with a white handkerchief wip'd off a tear)
The hotteft of actions will only be farce,
For fure thou art Venus!—Says fhe, Thou art Mars!

Awhile they ftood fimp'ring like mafter and mifs,
And Cupid thought he would have given one kifs;
'Twas what fhe expected, admits no difpute,
But he touch'd his own finger, and blew a falute.

By a place I can't mention, not knowing it's name,
At the head of his company, Dilberry came;
And the drums to the window call ev'ry eye,
To fee the defence of the nation pafs by.

Old bible-faced women, through fpectacles dim,
With hemming and coughing, cry'd, Lord! it is him!
While boys, and the girls, who more clearly could fee,
Cry'd, Yonder's Sir Dilberry Diddle—that's he.

Of all the fair ladies that came to the fhew,
Sir Diddle's fair lady ftood firft in the row—
O charming, fays fhe, how he looks all in red!
How he turns out his toes! how he holds up his head!

Do but fee his cockade, and behold his dear gun,
Which fhines like a looking-glafs held in the fun;

O! fee thyfelf now, thou'rt fo martially fmart,
And look as you look'd when you conquer'd my heart!
The fweet-founding notes of Sir Dilberry Diddle,
More ravifh'd his ears than the found of a fiddle;
And as it grew faint, that he heard it no more,
He foften'd the word of command to—encore.

The battle now over without any blows,
The heroes unarm, and ftrip off their cloaths;
The captain refrefh'd with a fip of rofe-water,
Hands his dear to the coach, bows, and then fteps in after.

John's orders were fpecial, to drive very flow,
For fevers oft follow fatigue, we all know;
But prudently cautious, in Venus's lap,
His head under apron, brave Mars took a nap.

He dream'd, fame reports, that he cut all the throats
Of the French, as they landed in flat-bottom'd boats:
In his fleep if fuch dreadful deftruction he makes,
What havock, ye gods! fhall we have when he wakes!

S O N G 198.

Sung in Thomas and Sally.

THE echoing horn calls the fportfmen abroad;
To horfe, my brave boys, and away:
The morning is up. and the cry of the hounds
Upbraids our too tedious delay.
What pleafure we find in purfuing the fox!
O'er hill and o'er valley he flies:
Then follow; we'll foon overtake him—huzza!
The traitor is feiz'd on, and dies.

Triumphant returning at night with the fpoil,
Like Bacchanals fhouting and gay,
How fweet with a bottle and lafs to refrefh,
And lofe the fatigues of the day!
With fport, love and wine, fickle fortune defy;
Dull wifdom all happinefs fours:
Since life is no more than a paffage, at beft,
Let's ftrew the way over with flow'rs.

S O N G 199.

BACCHUS TRIUMPHANT.

Sung at MARYBONE.

THE fwain with his flock by a brook loves to reft,
With foft rural lays to drive grief from his breaft;
The fop, light as air, loves himfelf to behold,
The Briton his foe, and the mifer his gold;
The pleafures I chufe yield more joy to my foul,
The delight of my heart is a full-flowing bowl.

The huntfman, fatigu'd with the toils of the chace,
By the fide of a fountain delights to folace;

At his miftrefs's feet the fond lover to whine,
The beau at the play or affembly to fhine.
The pleafures, &c.

My Chloe's in rapture to hear herfelf prais'd,
The courtier to find that his income is rais'd,
Some nymphs love the town, and in jewels to
    fhine,
And fome fpiritlefs lovers in filence to pine.
The pleafures, &c.

Some cards love, fome coffee, fome dice, and
    fome tea,
Some talking, fome fiddling, fome dancing,
    fome play.
Their choices are dull, there's a fpirit in wine,
Which always en'ivens with rapture divine.
The pleafures I chufe yield more joy to my foul,
The delight of my heart is a full-flowing bowl.

SONG 200.

THE FARMER'S SONG.

Sung at SADLER'S WELLS.

IN a fweet healthy air, on a farm of my own,
    Half a mile from the church, and juft two
    from a town,
Diverfions and bufinefs I vary for eafe,
But your fine folks of London may do as they
    pleafe.

By my freehold, 'tis true, I'm entitled to vote;
But, becaufe I will never be wrong, if I know't,
I'll adhere to no one till each party agrees;
But your fine folks at London, &c.

Tho' fixty and upwards, I never knew pain,
My Goody's as ancient, yet does not complain;
From the flocks of my own I wear coats of
    warm frize;
But your fine folks at London, &c.

I ne'er was at law in the courfe of my life,
Nor injur'd a neighbour in daughter or wife;
To the poor have lent money, but never took
    fees,
But your fine folks at London, &c.

I ne'er had ambition to vifit the great,
Yet honour my king, and will ftand by the fate,
By the church, and dear freedom, in all it's
    degrees;
But your fine folks at London may do as they
    pleafe.

SONG 201.

THE THRUSH.

Sung at VAUXHALL

SWEET thrufh, that makes the vernal year
    Sweeter than Flora can appear,
As Philomel attends thy lay,
She envies the return of day.
The tuneful lyre, and fwelling flute,
At thy rich warbling fhall be mute.
    Vocal minftrel, thy foft lay
    Treafures up and ends the May.

Hark! how the black-bird woos his love,
The fkill'd mufic an of the grove;
On thorn, as perch'd, he nobly fings,
A cadence for the ear of kings;
Sublime and foft, gay and ferene,
A virginal to hail a queen.
    Nature's mufic thus improves
    All the graces and the loves.

SONG 202.

THE INNKEEPER'S SONG.

Sung at SADLER'S WELLS.

WHAT think you, my mafters? 'tis won-
    drous to me,
That puffs are encourag'd to fuch a degree :
But puffs I deteft, fo live quiet and hufh;
I fell you good wine, and good wine needs no
    bufh.

Pofts, penfions, and votes, are oft got by a
    puff,
Bar, pulpit, and theatre, thrive by the ftuff,
But puffs I deteft, &c.

I laugh at the newfpapers till I'm half blind,
To fee how by puffing men tickle mankind;
But puffs I deteft, &c.

When great ones negociate matters by puff,
To ape them mechanics are ready enough;
But puffs I deteft, fo live quiet and hufh;
I fell you good wine, and good wine needs no
    bufh.

SONG 203.

DAMON AND SYLVIA.

DAMON.

DEAR Sylvia, no longer my paffion defpife,
    Nor arm thus with terror thofe beautiful
        eyes;
They become not difdain, but moft charming
    would prove,
If once they were foften'd with fmiles and
    with love.

SYLVIA.

While I with a fmile can each fhepherd fubdue,
O Damon, I muft not be foften'd by you;
Nor fondly give up, in an unguarded hour,
The pride of us women, unlimited pow'r.

DAMON.

Tho' power, my dear, be to deities giv'n,
Yet generous pity's the darling of Heav'n;
O then, be that pity extended to me,
I'll kneel and acknowledge no goddefs but thee.

SYLVIA.

Suppofe to your fuit I fhould liften a while,
And only for pity's fake grant you a fmile!

DAMON.

Nay ftop not at that, but your kindnefs improve,
And let gentle pity be ripen'd to love.

SYLVIA.

Well, then, faithful swain, I'll examine my heart,
And if it be poffible, grant you a part.

DAMON.

Now that's like yourfelf, like an angel exprefs'd;
For grant me but part, and I'll foon fteal the reft.

BOTH.

Take heed, ye fair maids, and with caution believe;
For love's an intruder, and apt to deceive;
When once the leaft part the fly urchin has gain'd,
You'll ne'er be at eafe till the whole is obtain'd.

S O N G 204.

PATTY OF THE MILL.

Sung at RANELAGH.

FAR fweeter than the hawthorn bloom,
  Whofe fragrance fheds a rich perfume,
  And all the meadows fill;
Much fairer than the lily blows,
More lovely than the blufhing rofe,
  Is Patty of the mill.

The neighb'ring fwains her beauty fir'd,
With wonder ftruck, they all admir'd,
  And prais'd her from the hill;
Each ftrove with all his ruftic art,
To foothe and charm the honeft heart
  Of Patty of the mill.

But vain were all attempts to move
A fixed heart, more true to love
  Than turtles when they bill;
A chearful foul, a pleafing grace,
And fweet content, fmiles in the face
  Of Patty of the mill.

The good a friend in fortune find,
Exalts the honeft, virtuous mind,
  And guards it from all ill:
Ye fair, for ever conftant prove;
Be ever kind, be true to love,
  Like Patty of the mill.

S O N G 205.

ABSENCE.

HOW fweet to recal the dear moments of joy!
'Tis this and this only can abfence employ;
Can raife my fond heart, and beguile my foft pain,
Till I fee with delight my dear charmer again.
Ah! who ever knew fuch full tranfports as I,
While with her the fwift minutes unheeded pafs'd by.
Alas, with the fweet recollection I burn:
Bring back your delights, ye dear moments return.

Ah me! what delight in my bofom would rife,
While with eager attention I've hung on her eyes;
And watch'd the kind beams of compaffion and love,
While fhe pity'd my paffion, and feem'd to approve.
Ah me! with what raptur'd attention I've hung,
To catch the fweet accents that flow'd from her tongue,
When tendernefs bade the dear maiden impart
The pleafing fenfations that glow'd in her heart.

Oh, how does my fair-one pafs off the long day!
Is the charmer quite eafy while I am away?
Indeed, if our thoughts like our hearts fhould agree,
The dear lovely creature is thinking on me.
Ah, did fhe but think with fuch fondnefs as I,
How much would fhe grieve, and how oft would fhe figh!
Yet with fo much fond love may her bofom ne'er burn,
If fhe fighs as I figh, if fhe mourns as I mourn.

Why do I thus wander? why figh thus alone?
Alas, 'tis the lofs of my fair that I moan!
Why thus ev'ry hour do my forrows increafe?
Alas, it is abfence that ruins my peace!
Why fwells my fad bofom with fear and with grief?
Ah! nought but her prefence can bring me relief.
Why thus down my cheek trickles faft the big tear?
Ah, how can I help it!—my fair is not here.

Till I nourifh'd this paffion, I all unconcern'd
Saw peace my companion wherever I turn'd;
Till now, with my heart all at eafe, I could reft,
And a figh was a ftranger unknown to my breaft.
What then is this love? and why do I endure
Thefe griefs in my bofom, nor feek for a cure?
Why thus my fond heart is o'erwhelm'd with defpair,
And I know no delight when away from my fair!

Yet, Colin, thefe pains, fpite of all thou haft faid,
By one hour of her prefence are far overpaid.
Thefe forrows, from abfence which now you deplore,
Then vanifh, are loft, and are thought of no more,
Recal thofe rafh words, and forbear to complain,
Since the next tender meeting rewards all thy pain.
Let fweet expectation, then, leffen thy care;
Let hope foften abfence, and keep off defpair.

Sure, fure, thofe dear pleafures will once more return;
How long in his abfence diftrefs'd muft I mourn?
How long muft I wifh, while my lot I deplore,
That dear angel-face!——Could I fee it once more!

That dear angel-voice!—Time, how sweet didst
　　thou seem
While I liften'd, enchanted, as love was her
　　theme!
Oh, come thofe dear hours! and to foothe my
　　fond pain,
Love again be her theme, and I liften again.

How dull and how flow do the moments retreat!
Time was when they flew—now there's lead on
　　their feet.
Ye loit'rers, be gone: why fo long do ye ftay?
Ye fly when I'm with her, ye creep when away.
Ah, Colin, how foolifh time's progrefs to blame:
His paces are equal, his motions the fame!
'Twas the joy of her prefence made time appear
　　fleet;
'Tis the pain of her abfence adds lead to his
　　feet.

SONG 206.

THE INVITATION.

Sung at MARYBONE.

COME, ye party jangling fwains,
　　Leave your flocks and quit the plains,
Friends to country, friends to court,
Nothing here fhall fpoil your fport.
　　Ever welcome to our feaft,
　　Welcome every friendly gueft!

Sprightly widows, come away,
Laughing dames and virgins gay,
Little gaudy, fluttering miffes,
Smiling hopes of future bliffes.
　　Ever welcome, &c.

All that ripening fun can bring,
Beauteous fummer, beauteous fpring,
In one varying fcene we fhow
The green, the ripe, the bud, the blow.
　　Ever welcome, &c.

Comus jefting, mufic charming,
Wine infpiring, beauty warming,
Rage and party-malice dies,
Peace returns, and difcord flies.
　　Ever welcome to our feaft,
　　Welcome every friendly gueft!

SONG 207.

O FYE FOR SHAME.

Sung at VAUXHALL.

AS thro' the grove I chanc'd to ftray,
　　I met young Phillis on her way;
I flew like lightning to her arms,
And gaz'd in rapture on her charms,
Her looks reveal'd a modeft flame,
But ftill fhe cry'd—O fye for fhame.

With eager hafte I ftole a kifs,
Which blufhing Phillis took amifs;
She pufh'd me from her with a frown,
And call'd me bold prefuming clown;
While I confefs'd myfelf to blame,
But ftill fhe cry'd—O fye for fhame.

In tender fighs I told my love,
And pledg'd my faith on things above;
But fhe, like all her fex, was coy,
And, tho' I fwore, would not comply;
Yet I perceiv'd fhe met my flame,
But ftill fhe cry'd—O fye for fhame.

When this I faw, I quickly cry'd—
Will lovely Phillis be my bride?
For hark, I hear the tinkling bell;
To church let's go?—It pleas'd her well;
And foon a kind compliance came.
But ftill fhe cry'd—O fye for fhame.

Now Hymen's bands have made us one,
The joys we tafte to few are known,
No jealous fears our bofoms move;
For conftant each, we truly love;
She now declares I'm not to blame,
Nor longer cries—O fye for fhame.

SONG 208.

THE HAPPY BACCHANALIAN.

FILL your glaffes, banifh grief,
　　Laugh, and worldly cares defpife;
Sorrow ne'er can bring relief,
Joy from drinking will arife.
Why fhould we with wrinkled care,
Change what nature made fo fair?
　　Drink, and fet your hearts at reft,
　　Of a bad bargain make the beft.

Some purfue the winged wealth,
　　Some to honour do afpire;
Give me freedom, give me health,
There's the fum of my defire.
What the world can more prefent,
Will not add to my content;
　　Drink, and fet your minds at reft,
　　Quiet of mind is always beft.

Bufy brains, we know, alas!
　　With imaginations run,
Like fand within the hour-glafs,
Turn'd and turn'd, and ftill runs on,
Never knowing when to ftay,
But uneafy every way;
　　Drink, and fet your hearts at reft,
　　Peace of mind is always beft.

Mirth, when mingled with our wine,
　　Makes the heart alert and free;
Let it rain, or fnow, or fhine,
Still the fame thing 'tis with me.
There's no fence againft our fate,
Changes daily on us wait;
　　Drink, and fet your hearts at reft,
　　Of a bad bargain make the beft.

SONG 209.

Sung in *Thomas and Sally.*

WHEN I was a young one, what girl was
　　like me;
So wanton, fo airy, and brifk as a bee!
I tattled, I rambled, I laugh'd, and where'er
A fiddle was heard—to be fure I was there.

Miss WELLER, as Polly, *in the* Beggar's Opera.

When my Hero in Court appears. Song 20.

Published by J. Bew, 1 June 1778.

To all who came near I had something to say;
'Twas this, Sir—and that, Sir—but scarce
ever Nay;
And, Sundays, drefs'd out in my filks, and my
lace,
I warrant I ftood by the beft in the place.

At twenty I got me a hufband, poor man!
Well, reft him—we all are as good as we can;
Yet he was fo peevifh, he'd quarrel for ftraws,
And jealous— tho' truly I gave him fome caufe.
He fnubb'd me, and huff'd me; but let me
alone;
Egad, I've a tongue, and I paid him his own!
Ye wives, take the hint, and when fpoufe is
untow'rd,
Stand firm to your charter, and have the laft
word.

But now I'm quite alter'd, the more to my woe;
I'm not what I was forty fummers ago:
This Time's a fore foe; there's no fhunning his
dart;
However, I keep up a pretty good heart.

Grown old, yet I hate to be fitting mum chance;
I ftill love a tune, though unable to dance;
And, books of devotion laid by on my fhelf,
I teach that to others I once did myfelf.

SONG 210.

Sung in the *Beggar's Opera.*

WHEN my hero in court appears,
And ftands arraign'd for his life;
Then think of poor Poily's tears;
For ah, poor Polly's his wife.
Like the failor he holds up his hand,
Diftreft, on the dafhing wave.
To die a dry death at land,
Is as bad as a wat'ry grave.
And alas, poor Polly!
A lack, and a well-a-day!
Before I was in love,
Oh! every month was May.

SONG 211.

THE LASS WITH THE DELICATE AIR.

Sung at MARYBONE.

YOUNG Molly, who lives at the foot of the
hill,
Whofe fame every virgin with envy does fill,
Of beauty 's blefs'd with fo ample a fhare,
That men call her the lafs with the delicate air.

One evening laft May, as I travers'd the grove,
In thoughtlefs retirement, not dreaming of love,
I chanc'd to efpy the gay nymph, I declare,
And really fhe'd got a moft delicate air.

By a murmuring brook, on a green moffy bed,
A chaplet compofing, the fair-one was laid;
Surpriz'd and tranfported, I could not forbear,
With rapture to gaze on her delicate air.

For that moment young Cupid felected a dart,
And pierc'd without pity my innocent heart:
And from thence how to gain the dear maid
was my care,
For a captive I fell to her delicate air.

When fhe faw me, fhe blufh'd, and complain'd
I was rude,
And begg'd of all things that I would not in-
trude.
I anfwer'd, I could not tell how I came there,
But laid all the blame on her delicate air;
Said, her heart was the prize which I fought to
obtain,
And hop'd that fhe'd grant it to eafe my fond
pain.
She neither rejected, nor granted my pray'r,
But fir'd all my foul with her delicate air.

A thoufand times fince I've repeated my fuit,
But ftill the tormentor affects to be mute;
Then tell me, ye fwains, who have conquer'd
the fair,
How to win the dear lafs with the delicate air.

SONG 212.

Sung at VAUXHALL.

THE woodlark whiftles thro' the grove,
Tuning the fweeteft notes of love,
To pleafe his female on the fpray;
Perch'd by his fide, her little breaft
Swells with a lover's joy confeft,
To hear and to reward the lay.

Come then, my fair-one, let us prove,
From their example, how to love;
For thee the early pipe I'll breathe,
And when my flocks return to fold,
Their fhepherd to thy bofom hold,
And crown him with the nuptial wreath.

SONG 213.

ROSY JUNE.

Written by Mr. NICHOLLS.

LET letter'd bards fing lofty ftrains,
Of Pindus' mount, of Latian plains;
I melt delight, at rifing day,
Along the Kentifh lawns to ftray;
There, whilft the birds are wrapt in tune,
To breathe the fweets of rofy June.

Or far about the hills to trace,
And fing my country's fertile face;
Her pippen-trees in filver bloom;
Her curling-hops, her golden broom;
Of fhelter, where, at fultry noon,
The ruftick fhuns the heat of June.

Of ample orchards, halefome ftreams,
Where fifhes fport in funny beams;
Of diftant meads, where flocks are feen,
Like argent fpots on pureft green;
Where (while he crops the vernal boon)
The mower fings of rofy June.

H

To fing of clover's purple dye,
Grateful to the wand'ring eye;
Of pea-blown vallies, wheat-clad fields,
Brighter fcenes than Tempe yields.
Ah! how gay, by midnight moon,
Are fcenes like thefe in rofy June!

And ftill to fing, in Dorick ftrains,
Of low-roof'd cots, where quiet reigns;
Of ruftick lads, by honour fram'd,
Of fylvan maids, for beauty fam'd,
Whofe loves will never cloy fo foon,
But ever laft as frefh as June.

And (more than many a realm can boaft)
To fing our fea-girt happy coaft,
Where, big with commerce, ev'ry tide
The fleets of diftant nations glide.
To themes like thefe my flute I tune,
Whilft rofes deck the month of June.

SONG 214.

PLATO'S ADVICE.

SAYS Plato, Why fhould man be vain,
  Since bounteous Heaven hath made him
    great?
Why looketh he with infolent difdain
  On thofe undeck'd with wealth or ftate?
Can coftly robs or beds of down,
  Or all the gems that deck the fair;
Can all the glories of a crown
  Give health, or eafe the brow of care?

The fceptred king, the burden'd flave,
  The humble and the haughty, die;
The rich, the poor, the bafe, the brave,
  In duft, without diftinction, lie.
Go fearch the tombs where monarchs reft,
  Who once the greateft titles bore;
Their wealth and glory are bereft,
  And all their honour is no more.

So flies the meteor through the fkies,
  And fpreads along a gilded train;
When fhot, 'tis gone, it's beauty dies,
  Diffolves to common air again.
So 'tis with us, my jovial fouls,
  Let friendfhip reign while here we ftay;
Let's crown our joy with flowing bowls,
  For when Jove calls we muft obey.

SONG 215.

Sung in the *Miller of Manffield*.

HOW happy a ftate does the miller poffefs,
  Who would be no greater, nor fears to be
    lefs!
On his mill and himfelf he depends for fupport,
Which is better than fervil-ly cringing at court.
What tho' he all dufty and whiten'd does go,
The more he's bepowder'd, the more like a
    beau:
A clown in this drefs may be honefter far,
Than the courtier that ftruts in his garter and
    ftar.

Tho' his hands are fo daub'd, they're not fit to
    be feen,
The hands of his betters are not very clean:
A palm more polite may as dirtily deal;
Gold, in handling, will ftick to the fingers like
  . meal.

What if, when a pudding for dinner he lacks,
He cribs without fcruple from other men's
  · facks;
In this of right noble example he brags,
Who borrow as freely from other men's bags.

Or fhould he endeavour to heap an eftate,
In this, too, he'd mimick the tools of the ftate,
Whofe aim is, alone, their own coffers to fill,
As all his concern's to bring grift to his mill.

He eats when he's hungry, he drinks when
    he's dry,
And down, when he's weary, contented does lie;
Then rifes up chearful to work and to fing:
If fo happy's a miller, then who'd be a king!

SONG 216.

Sung at RANELAGH.

ONE Midfummer morning, when nature
    look'd gay;
The birds full of fong, and the flocks full of play;
When earth feem'd to anfwer the fmiles from
    above,
And all things proclaim'd it the feafon of love;
My mother cry'd, Nancy, come hafte to the
    mill,
If the corn be not ground, you may fcold if you
    will.

The freedom to ufe my tongue, pleas'd me, no
    doubt;
A woman, alas! would be nothing without.
I went to'ard the mill without any delay,
And conn'd o'er the words I intended to fay;
But when I came near it, I found it ftock ftill;
Blefs my ftars, now I cry'd, huff 'em rarely I
    will.

The miller to market that inftant was gone,
The work was all left to the care of his fon;
Now tho' I can fcold well as any one can,
Yet I thought 'twould be wrong to fcold the
    young man.
I faid, I'm furpriz'd you can ufe me fo ill;
Sir, I muft have my corn ground, I muft and I
    will.

Sweet maid, cry'd the youth, the neglect is not
    mine,
No corn in the town I'd grind fooner than thine,
There's no one more ready in pleafing the fair,
The mill fhall go merrily round, I declare;
But hark how the birds fing, and fee how they
    bill!
Now I muft have a kifs firft, I muft and I will.

My corn being done, I to'ard home bent my
    way;
He whifper'd he'd fomething of moment to fay;
Infifted to hand me along the green mead,
And there fwore he lov'd me, indeed and indeed;

And that he'd be conſtant and true to me ſtill,
So that ſince that I've lik'd him, and like him I
will.

I often ſay, Mother, the miller I'll huff;
She laughs, and cries, Go, girl; aye, plague him
enough:
And ſcarce a day paſſes, but, by her deſire,
I ſteal a ſly kiſs from the youth I admire.
If wedlock he wiſhes, his with I'll fulfil;
And I'll anſwer, O yes, with a hearty good
will.

SONG 217.

YOUNG ROGER.

Sung at VAUXHALL.

YOUNG Roger he courted me for a whole
year,
He ſighed and made ſuch a moan,
That I lov'd him, yet dare not to tell him,
(thro' fear;)
So I vow'd that I would lie alone.
He ſaid, and he ſwore, if I'd be his bride,
He would bring me to fine London town,
I ſhould ſee Fox's Hall and the playhouſe beſide,
But I ſtill ſaid I would lie alone.

Away then he went to the dance at the fair,
Where I ſaw him give Sue a green gown;
I wiſh'd from my heart that I had not gone there,
And hop'd that ſhe might lie alone;
I redden'd and ſigh'd, I danc'd and I cry'd,
And my heart ſent forth many a groan;
To get him again all my arts they were try'd,
For I now thought I'd not lie alone.

T'other evening he came to my cot with a ſmile,
And aſk'd if I kinder was grown;
I told him no longer his hopes I'd beguile,
Nor would I lie longer alone:
To London we came, to the playhouſe I've been,
And then dear Fox Hall was I ſhewn;
Such dreſſing, ſuch dancing, ſuch ſights have
I ſeen,
That I'm glad I no more lie alone.

SONG 218.

Sung in the Oratorio of Judith.

VAIN is beauty's gaudy flow'r,
Pageant of an idle hour;
Born juſt to bloom and fade:
Nor leſs weak, leſs vain than it,
Is the pride of human wit;
The ſhadow of a ſhade.

SONG 219.

THE FRIAR OF ORDERS GREY; AN OLD
BALLAD.

IT was a friar of orders grey,
Walk'd forth to tell his beads;
And he met with a lady fair,
Clad in a pilgrim's weeds.

Now Chriſt thee ſave, thou rev'rend friar;
I pray thee tell to me,
If ever at yon holy ſhrine
My true love thou didſt ſee?

And how ſhall I know your true love
From many another one?
O by his cockle hat and ſtaff,
And by his ſandal ſhone.

But chiefly by his face and mien,
That were ſo fair to view;
His flaxen locks that ſweetly curl'd,
And eyne of lovely blue.

O lady, he is dead and gone!
Lady, he's dead and gone!
And at his head a green-graſs turf,
And at his heels a ſtone.

Within theſe holy cloiſters long
He languiſh'd, and he dy'd,
Lamenting of a lady's love,
And 'plaining of her pride.

Here bore him barefac'd on his bier,
Six proper youths and tall;
And many a tear bedew'd his grave
Within yon kirk-yard wall.

And art thou dead, thou gentle youth!
And art thou dead and gone!
And didſt thou die for love of me!
Break, cruel heart of ſtone!

O weep not, lady, weep not ſo;
Some ghoſtly comfort ſeek;
Let not vain ſorrow rive thy heart,
Nor tears bedew thy cheek.

O do not, do not, holy friar,
My ſorrow now reprove;
For I have loſt the ſweeteſt youth
That e'er won lady's love.

And now, alas! for thy ſad loſs
I'll evermore weep and ſigh;
For thee I only wiſh'd to live,
For thee I wiſh to die.

Weep no more, lady, weep no more,
Thy ſorrow is in vain;
For, violets pluckt, the ſweeteſt ſhow'rs
Will never make grow again.

Our joys as winged dreams do fly;
Why then ſhould ſorrow laſt?
Since grief but aggravates thy loſs,
Grieve not for what is paſt.

O ſay not ſo, thou holy friar;
I pray thee, ſay not ſo:
For ſince my true-love dy'd for me,
'Tis meet my tears ſhould flow.

And will he never come again?
Will he ne'er come again?
Ah! no, he's dead, and laid in his grave,
For ever to remain.

His cheek was redder than the roſe;
The comelieſt youth was he!
But he is dead, and laid in his grave,
Alas! and woe is me!

Sigh no more, lady; sigh no more;
Men were deceivers ever;
One foot on sea, and one on land,
To one thing conftant never.

Hadft thou been fond, he had been falfe,
And left thee fad and heavy;
For young men e'er were fickle found,
Since fummer trees were leafy.

Now fay not fo, thou holy friar,
I pray thee fay not fo;
My love he had the trueft heart;
O he was ever true!

And art thou dead, thou much-lov'd youth;
And didft thou die for me!
Then farewel home; for evermore
A pilgrim I will be.

But firft upon my true-love's grave
My weary limbs I'll lay;
And thrice I'll kifs the green grafs turf
That wraps his breathlefs clay.

Yet ftay, fair lady; reft a while
Beneath this cloifter wall:
See, thro' the hawthorn blows the cold wind,
'And drizzle rain doth fall.

O ftay me not, thou holy friar;
O ftay me not, I pray!
No drizzly rain that falls on me
Can wafh my fault away.

Yet ftay, fair lady; turn again,
And dry thofe pearly tears;
For fee, beneath this gown of grey,
Thy own true love appears.

Here, forc'd by grief and hopelefs love,
Thefe holy weeds I fought;
And here, amid thefe lonely walls,
To end my days I thought:

But haply, for my year of grace
Is not yet pafs'd away;
Might I ftill hope to win thy love,
No longer would I ftay.

Now farewel grief, and welcome joy
Once more unto my heart:
For fince I've found thee, lovely youth!
We nevermore will part.

SONG 220.

Sung in *Thomas and Sally.*

WHEN late I wander'd o'er the plain,
From nymph to nymph, I ftrove in vain
My wild defires to rally:
But now they're of themfelves come home,
And, ftrange! no longer feek to roam;
They center all in Sally.

Yet fhe, unkind one! damps my joy,
And cries, I court but to deftroy:
Can love with ruin tally?
By thefe dear lips, thefe eyes, I fwear,
I would all deaths, all torments bear,
Rather than injure Sally!

Come then, oh! come, thou fweeter far
Than jeffamine and rofes are,
Or lilies of the valley;
O! follow love, and quit your fear,
He'll guide you to thefe arms, my dear,
And make me bleft in Sally.

SONG 221.

THE ENGLISH PADLOCK.

MISS Danæ, when fair and young,
(As Horace has divinely fung)
Could not be kept from Jove's embrace
By doors of fteel, and walls of brafs.

Tell us, myfterious hufband, tell us,
Why fo myfterious, why fo jealous?
Can harfh reftraint, the bolt, the bar,
Make thee fecure, thy wife lefs fair?

Send her abroad, and let her fee
That all this world of pageantry,
Which fhe, forbidden longs to know,
Is powder, pocket-glafs, and beau.

Be to her virtues ever kind,
Be to her faults a little blind;
Let all her ways be unconfin'd;
And clap your Padlock—on her mind.

SONG 222.

RONDEAU.

Sung at VAUXHALL.

SINCE fweet love has had poffeffion
Of my fond and tender breaft,
Take my true and true confeffion,
Friendfhip is too cold a gueft.

Love has got the whole direction,
Friendfhip has no longer charms;
Only mutual, ftrong affection,
Now my raptur'd bofom warms.

Friendfhip now is cool as reafon;
Taftelefs all it s pleafures prove;
Love s the paffion now in feafon;
Welcome, dear bewitching love.

SONG 223.

Sung at VAUXHALL.

LOVE'S A RIDDLE.

LOVE's a bubble, courting trouble,
Whilft we love and love in vain;
When 'tis over, is the lover,
Now we've got him, worth the gain?

Is love treafure, is it pleafure,
That can pay whole years of care?
Is the bleffing worth careffing?
Speak, ye fwains; and own, ye fair.

Kind, ye're pleafing; coy, we're teazing;
Love's a fond fatiguing chace;

Smiles deceives us, hopes relieve us,
  Hearts our sport from place to place!

Cupid smiling, life beguiling,
  Tempts us with the playful toy;
Oft denying, oft complying,
  Love's our torment and our joy.

SONG 224.

PITTY PATTY.

Sung at VAUXHALL.

THE morning young Jockey would make me
    his bride,
He stole to my chamber, and sat by my side;
When he open'd the curtains, such joy 'twas
    to me,
That my heart play'd a tune that went pitty
  patty.

But feigning to sleep, (Oh, how great was my
  bliss!)
So gently, so kindly, he gave me a kiss!
Then my head to his bosom he press'd with
  such glee,
That my heart play'd a tune, that went pitty
  patty.

Grown bold with success, he ventur'd to take
A second salute—Then 'twas time to awake.
Arise, love, he said, to the kirk let us flee,
As our hearts play a tune that goes pitty patty.

SONG 225.

THE KNIFE-GRINDER.

Written by Mr. RHODES.

Sung at SADLER'S-WELLS.

THERE are grinders enough, Sirs, of ev'ry
    degree,
From jewel-deck'd great, to low poverty;
Whatever the station, it sharpens the sense,
And the wheel it goes round to wind in the
  pence.
Master grinders enough at the helm you may
  find,
Tho' I'm but a journeyman—Knives to grind.

Whatever the statesman may think of himself,
He turns fortune's wheel in pursuit of the pelf;
He grinds back and edge, Sirs, his ends to ob-
  tain,
And his country may starve, so he pockets the
  gain.
Master-grinders, &c.

The rich grind the poor, is a saying of old;
The merchant the tradesman, we need not be
  told:
Whether Pagan, Mahometan, Christian you be,
There are grinders of all sorts, of ev'ry degree.
  Master-grinders, &c.

The patriot, with zeal animated, declares
The curtain he'll draw, and display the state-
  player's;

He is a staunch grinder, to some 'tis well known,
And they are mightily gall'd by the grit of his
    stone.
  Master-grinders, &c.

I too am a grinder, what, what, Sirs, of that?
I am but in taste, since I copy the great:
To be, Sirs, ingenu us, I'll tell you my mind;
'Tis for what I can get, makes me willing to
  grind.
Master-grinders enough at the helm you may
  find,
Tho' I'm but a journeyman—Knives to grind.

SONG 226.

THE SEASONS.

WHEN the young Chloe's rising charms
    Invited lovers to her arms,
      She look'd a dainty thing;
We saw her beauty, own'd her wit;
And, as the simile most fit,
      We call'd the period Spring.

Full bloom'd, as is the ripen'd flow'r,
We saw her still maturer pow'r,
      And woman's state become her:
The prudent mother and the wife,
Dispensing round her all the life
      And all the bliss of Summer.

Advancing on in life's career,
The maids to Chloe lent an ear,
      And what she knew, she taught 'em:
Her sage advice bestowing round,
Till ev'ry prudent virgin found
      The richest fruits of Autumn.

Now Chloe's charms are faded quite,
Yet honour cannot hold it tight
      Of her due praise to stint her:
For she who Summer well employs,
Shall reap the Autumn's solid joys,
      Nor dread the frost of Winter.

SONG 227.

A PASTORAL DIALOGUE.

DAMON.

HASTE, haste, Phyllis, haste! 'tis the
    first of the May:
Hark, the goldfinches sing, to the woods let's
    away:
We'll pluck the pale primrose; nay, start not,
    my dear,
I've something to whisper alone in your ear.

PHYLLIS.

Excuse me, fond swain; it has often been said,
The wood is unsafe for a maiden to tread:
And a wither'd old gipsey, one day I espy'd,
Bade me shun the thick wood, and said some-
    thing beside.

DAMON.

'Tis all a mere fable, there's nothing to fright,
There's musick all day, and no spectres at night;

No creature but Cupid, believe me, is there;
And Cupid's an urchin you furely can't fear.

PHYLLIS.

For all I could fay, when arriv'd at the wood,
Who knows your defigns; you might dare to
be rude!
So I bid you farewel, and confefs I'm afraid,
Left Cupid and you are too hard for a maid.

DAMON.

His dictates you wifely at once fhou'd approve;
For, pray what is lif.? 'tis a pain without love:
Think how youth, like the rofe, tho' unga-
ther'd, will fade;
Then quickly comply, left you die an old maid.

PHYLLIS.

By language as artful poor Daphne was won;
Thus courted, fhe yielded, was trick'd and un-
done :
And rather than truft the fine things you have
faid,
Let my beauty decay, and I die an old maid.

DAMON.

Believe not I'm faithlefs and falfe as the wind,
I'll be true as the turtle, as fond and as kind;
Will lead you to pleafures untafted before,
And make you my bride: can a mortal do more?

PHYLLIS.

Then at once I comply, for I cannot fay, no;
To-morrow to church with my fhepherd I ll go;
To the wood next, tho' Cupid fo talk'd of be
there,
With joy I ll away, and adieu to all fear.

PHYLLIS.

Ye nymphs to the wood never venture to go;
Till the prieft joins your hand, you muft anfwer, no, no!

DAMON.

Ye fwains, fhould your fair-ones be deaf to
you ftill,
You muft wear the foft chain, then they'll go
where you will.

SONG 228.

Sung at VAUXHALL.

MY Jockey is the blitheft lad
That ever maiden woo'd;
When he appears my heart is glad,
For he is kind and good.
He talks of love, whene'er we meet,
His words with rapture flow;
Then tunes his pipe, and fings fo fweet,
I have no power to go.

All other laffes he forfakes,
And flies to me alone;
At ev'ry fair, and all the wakes,
I hear him making moan.
He buys me toys, and fweetmeats too,
And ribbands for my hair;

No fwain was ever half fo true,
Or half fo kind and fair.
Where'er I go, I nothing fear,
If Jockey is but by,
For I alone am all his care,
When any danger's nigh.
He vows to wed next Whitfunday,
And make me bleft for life;
Can I refufe, ye maidens, fay,
To be young Jockey's wife?

SONG 229.

Sung in the Padlock.

IN vain you bid your captive live,
While you the means of life deny:
Give me your fmiles, your wifhes give,
To him who muft without you die.

Shrunk from the fun's enliv'ning beam,
Bid flow rs retain their fcent and hue:
It's fource dry'd up, bid flow the ftream,
Or me exift depriv'd of you.

SONG 230.

Sung in the Deferter.

THO' prudence may prefs me,
And duty diftrefs me,
Againft inclination, ah! what can they do?
No longer a rover,
His follies are over,
My heart, my fond heart, fays, my Henry is
true.

The bee thus as changing,
From fweet to fweet rang ng,
A rofe fhould he light on, ne'er wifhes to ftray;
With raptures poffeffing
In one ev'ry bleffing,
Till, torn from her bofom, he flies far away.

SONG 231.

KITTY FELL.

Sung at RANELAGH.

WHILE beaux, to pleafe the ladies, write,
Or bards to get a dinner by't,
Their well-feign'd paffions tell;
Let me, in humble verfe, proclaim
My love for her who bears the name
Of charming Kitty Fell.
Charming Kitty, lovely Kitty,
Oh——charming Kitty, Kitty Fell.

That Kitty's beautiful and young,
That fhe has danc'd, that fhe has fung,
Alas! I know full well:
I feel, and I fhall ever feel,
The dart more fharp than pointed fteel,
That came from Kitty Fell.
Charming Kitty, &c.

Of late I hop'd, by reafon's aid,
To cure the wounds which love had made,
And bade a long farewel:
But t'other day fhe crofs'd the green;
I faw, I wifh I had not feen,
My charming Kitty Fell.
Charming Kitty, &c.

I afk'd her why fhe pafs'd that way?
To church, fhe cry'd—I cannot ftay:
Why, don't you hear the bell?
To church—oh! take me with thee there,
I pray'd: fhe would not hear my prayer;
Ah! cruel Kitty Fell.
Cruel Kitty, &c.

And now I find 'tis all in vain,
I live to love, and to complain,
Condemn'd in chains to dwell;
For tho' fhe cafts a fcornful eye,
In death my falt'ring tongue will cry,
Adieu! dear Kitty well.
Charming Kitty, cruel Kitty,
Adieu! fweet Kitty, Kitty Fell.

SONG 232.

Sung at VAUXHALL.

YES, Delia, 'tis at length too plain,
My boafted liberty how vain,
Thy eyes triumphant prove!
My freedom now I ceafe to boaft,
But think that freedom nobly loft,
By ferving thee and love.

I talk'd, I laugh'd, with ev'ry fair;
No jealous pang, no anxious care,
Did e'er my heart perplex;
Till I beheld, too lovely maid!
In thee, with ev'ry grace difplay'd,
The charms of all thy fex.

SONG. 233.

A HUNTING SONG.

Sung in Apollo and Daphne.

THE fun from the eaft tips the mountains
with gold,
And the meadows all fpangled with dew-drops
behold,
How the lark's early matin proclaims the new
day;
And the horn's chearful fummons rebukes our
delay!
With the fports of the field there's no pleafure
can vie,
While jocund we follow, follow, follow, follow,
follow, follow, follow follow, follow, fol-
low, follow, follow, follow, the hounds in
full cry.

Let the drudge of the town make riches his
fport,
And the flave of the ftate hunt the fmiles of
the court:

No care nor ambition our paftime annoy,
But innocence ftill gives it's zeft to our joy.
With the fports of the field, &c.

Mankind are all hunters in various degree;
The prieft hunts a living, the lawyer a fee;
The doctor a patient, the courtier a place;
Tho' often, like us, they're flung out with
difgrace.
With the fports of the field, &c.

The cit hunts a plum, the foldier hunts fame;
The poet a dinner, the patriot a name;
And the artful coquette, tho' fhe feems to re-
fufe,
Yet, in fpite of her airs, fhe her lover purfues.
With the fports of the field, &c.

Let the bold, and the bufy, hunt glory and
wealth,
All the bleffings we afk is the bleffing of health,
With hounds and with horns, thro' the woodlands to roam,
And, when tir'd abroad, find contentment at
home.
With the fports of the field there's no pleafure
can vie,
While jocund we follow, follow, follow, follow,
follow, follow, follow, follow, follow, fol-
low, follow, follow, follow the hounds in
full cry.

SONG 234.

Sung in the Chriftmas Tale.

O! Take this wreath my hand has wove,
The pledge and emblem of my love;
Thefe flow'rs will keep their brighteft hue,
While you are conftant, kind, and true:
But fhould you, falfe to love and me,
With from my fondnefs to be free;
Foreboding that my fate is nigh,
Each grateful flow'r will droop and die.

SONG 235.

Sung at VAUXHALL.

YE virgins attend,
Believe me your friend,
And with prudence adhere to my plan;
Ne'er let it be faid
There goes an old maid,
But get marry'd as faft as you can.

As foon as you find
Your hearts are inclin'd
To beat quick at the fight of a man;
Then chufe out a youth
Of honour and truth,
And get marry'd as faft as you can.

For age, like a cloud,
Your charms foon will fhroud,
And this whimfical life's but a fpan;
Then, maids, make your hay
While Sol darts his ray,
And get marry'd as faft as you can.

The treacherous rake
Will artfully take
Ev'ry meth·d poor g·rls to trepan;
But baffle their fnare,
Make virtue your care,
And get marry'd as faft as you ean.

And when Hymen's bands
Have join'd both your hands,
The bright flame ftil' continue to fan;
Ne er harbour the ftings
That jealoufy brings,
But be conftant, and bleft while you can.

SONG 236.

Written by Mr. HARRINGTON.

GENTLE airs fweet joys impart,
   Balm to heal the wounded mind;
Soothing founds relicve the heart,
   Sorrows here their comfort find.

Mufick, ftill thy charms difpenfe!
   O! ftill this vale of tears attend;
Lead to chearful innocence,
   Reafon's aid, and virtue's friend.

SONG 237.

Sung at VAUXHALL.

SIMPLE Strephon, ceafe complaining,
   Talk no more of foolifh love;
Think not e'er my heart to reign in,
   Think not all you fay can move.

Did I take delight to fetter
   Thrice ten thoufand flaves a day;
Thrice ten thoufand times your betters
   Gladly would my rule obey.
   Simple Strephon, &c.

Seek not her who ftill forbids you,
   To fome other tell your moan;
Chufe where'er your fancy leads you,
   Let Clorinda but alone.
   Simple Strephon, &c.

SONG 238.

Sung at VAUXHALL.

THE flame of love fincere I felt,
   And fcreen'd the paffion long;
A tyrant in my foul it dwelt,
   But awe fupprest my tongue.
At length I told the deareft maid,
   My heart was fixt upon her.
But think not I can love, fhe faid;
   I can't, upon my honour.

The heart that once is roving caught,
   All prudent nymphs diftruft;
And muft it, f r a youthful fault,
   Be ever deem'd unjuft?
So Celia judg'd, fo fenfe decreed,
   And bade me ftill to fhun her;
Yuor fuit, fh: faid, won't here fucceed,
   It won't, upon my honour.

Too long, I cry'd, I've been to blame,
   I with a figh confefs;
But thou who can ft the rake reclaim,,
   My new-born paffion blcfs.
Had ev'ry nymph like Celia prov'd,
   I cou'd not have undone her;
On thee, bright maid, thou heft-belov'd,
   I doat, upon my honour.

Awhile the nymph my fuit reprefs'd,
   My conftancy to prove;
Then with a blufh confent exprefs'd,
   And bleft me with her love.
To church I led the blooming fair,
   Enraptur'd that I'd won her;
And now life's fweeteft joys we fhare,
   We do, upon my honour.

SONG 239.

COME, fill me a bumper, my jolly brave boys,
   Let's have no more female impert'nence and
   noife ;
For I've try'd the endearments and pleafures of
   love,
And I find them but nonfenfe and whimfies,
   by Jove!

When firft I faw Betfey, I made my complaint,
I whin'd like a fool, and fhe figh d like a faint;
But I found her religion, her face, and her love,
Were hypocrify paint, and felf-intereft, by Jove!

Sweet Cecil came next, with her languifhing air,
Her outfide was orderly, modeft and fa·r;
But her mind was fophiftical, fo was her love,
For I found fhe was only a ftrumpet, by Jove!

Come fill me a bumper, then, jolly brave boys,
Here's a farewel to female impert'nence and
   noife;
I know few of the fex who are worthy my love,
And for ftrumpets and jilts, I abhor them, by
   Jove!

SONG 240.

Sung at VAUXHALL.

SURE Sally is the lovelieft lafs
   That e'er gave fhepherd glee;
Not May-day, in it's morning-drefs,
   Is half fo fair as fhe.
Let poets paint the Paphian queen,
   And fancy'd forms adore;
Ye bards, had ye my Sally feen,
   You'd think on thofe no more.

No more ye'd prate of Hybla's hill,
   Where bees their honey fip,
Did ye but know the fweets that dwell,
   On Sally's love-taught lip:
But, ah! take heed, ye tuneful fwains,
   The ripe temptations fhun;
Or elfe, like me, you'll wear her chains;
   Like me, you'll be undone.

Once in my cot, fecure I flept,
   And lark-like hail'd the dawn;

More sportive than the kid I kept,
  I wanton'd o'er the lawn:
To ev'ry maid love-tales I told,
  And did my truth aver;
Yet, ere the parting kiss was cold,
  I laugh'd at love and her.

But now the gloomy grove I seek,
  Where love-lorn shepherds stray;
There to the winds my grief I speak,
  And sigh my soul away:
Nought but despair my fancy paints,
  No dawn of hope I see;
For Sally's pleas'd with my complaints,
  And laughs at love and me.

Since these my poor neglected lambs,
  So late my only care,
Have lost their tender fleecy dams,
  And stray'd I know not where:
Alas, my ewes, in vain ye bleat;
  My lambkins lost, adieu!
No more we on the plains shall meet,
  For lost's your shepherd too.

SONG 241.

THE TEMPEST OF WAR.

Sung at VAUXHALL.

LET the tempest of war
  Be heard from afar,
With trumpets and cannons alarms:
  Let the brave, if they will,
  By their valour or skill,
Seek honour and conquest in arms.

  To live safe, and retire,
  Is what I desire,
Of my flocks and my Chloe possest;
  For in them I obtain
  True peace without pain,
And the lasting enjoyment of rest.

  In some cottage or cell,
  Like a shepherd to dwell,
From all interruption at ease;
  In a peaceable life,
  To be blest with a wife,
Who will study her husband to please.

SONG 242.

JEANY'S COMPLAINT; A SCOTCH SONG.

TO thee, sweet, chanting, warbling throng,
  I do address my plaintive lay;
Since Jockey's left me, I'm undone,
  And courts another far away;
Tho' oft he said, he'd constant be,
  And ne'er would wed a maid but me.

No more will Jockey tune his pipe,
  And on the green the dance declare:
Nor tell his tales, which gave delight;
  To Jeany and the virgins fair:
Alas! I see my pleasure's lost,
Since Jockey's gone, who pleas'd me most.

The lasses all with envy look,
  When Jockey led me to the green;
Then from my lips a kiss he took,
  And made me happy as a queen:
But, now he's left me here to mourn,
Never again for to return.

My flocks neglected leave the plain;
  While here I wander in the shade,
Making complaint to birds, in vain,
  The sorrows of a hopless maid:
Yet they alone I leave to tell
What makes me bid the world farewel.

SONG 243.

IN pity, Celia, to my pain,
  No more my heart reprove,
Nor let the blasts of cold disdain
  Destroy my rising love.
My love, as yet but newly blown,
  Must die for want of care;
'Tis your's (as you the seeds have sown)
  To save the flow'rs they bear.

When first the springing flow'r appears,
  And shews it's rising head,
Each gentlest wind it shiv'ring fears,
  And courts the gard'ner's aid.
In pity, then, no longer strive
  To grieve my faithful mind;
Since love and faith, and justice too,
  Expect you to be kind.

SONG 244.

AH, Strephon! what can mean the joy
  The eager joy I prove,
While you each tender art employ
  To win my soul to love?

So well your passion you reveal,
  So top the lover's part;
That I with blushes own, I feel
  A rebel in my heart.

Then take the heart that pines to go,
  But see it kindly us'd;
For who such presents will bestow,
  If this should be abus'd!

SONG 245.

THE HONEST CONFESSION.

Sung at RANELAGH.

MY mother cries—Betsy, be shy,
  Whenever the men would intrude—
I know not her meaning, not I,
  But I'd take her advice—if I could.

Alexis stept up t'other day
  To kiss me, and ask'd if he shou'd:
Pray what cou'd a' shepherdess say?
  But I'd fain have said no—if I could.

My mother remembers the time
  When she like a vestal was mew'd:
I

Now this I conceive was a crime,
And I'd not be ferv'd fo—if I could.

If I'm with Alexis, fhe'll chide;
She fays he perhaps may be rude:
I will not pretend to decide,
But I fancy he would—if he cou'd.

Laft May-morn I tript o'er the plain;
He faw me, and quickly purfu'd;
I heartily laugh'd at the fwain;
I'd catch you, he cry'd—if I cou'd.

Well foon he o'ertook my beft hafte,
And fwore he'd be conftant and good;
I vow I'll live decent and chafte;
But I'd marry the fwain—if I cou'd.

SONG 246.

Sung at RANELAGH.

SWEET Contentment! heav'nly bright!
Worfhipp'd through the realms of light!
Void of thee, what's pomp or pow'r?
Pageants of the faithlefs hour.
Can the fun of pomp and ftate,
Brighten through the gloom of fate?
Can the ftudious, or the gay,
Chace intruding care away?

Pomp and grandeur are thy foes,
Pride ne'er taftes thy foft repofe;
Yet within the mofs-grown cell,
Thou with poverty canft dwell;
Softly foothe the peafant's breaft;
Lull th' untutor'd mind to reft;
And, howe'er we change the name,
Virtue and Content's the fame.

SONG 247.

THE CAUTION.

SHE came from the hills of the weft,
A fmile of contentment fhe wore,
Her heart was a garden of reft;
But, ah! the fweet feafon is o'er.

How oft by the ftreams in the wood,
Delighted, fhe'd ramble and rove!
And while fhe ftood marking the flood,
Would tune up a ftanza of love.

Her drefs was a garment of green,
Set off with a border of white;
And all the day might be feen
Like a bird that is always in plight.

In rural diverfion and play
The fummers glid fmoothly along;
And her winters pafs'd brifkly away,
Chear'd up with a tale or a fong.

At length a deftroyer came by,
A youth of more perfon than parts,
Well fkill'd in the arts of the eye,
The conqueft and havock of hearts.

He led her by fountains and ftreams,
He woo'd her with novels and books;

He told her his tales and his dreams,
And mark'd their effect in her looks.
He taught her by midnight to roam
Where fpirits and fpectres affright;
For paffions increafe with the gloom,
And caution expires with the light.

At length, like a rofe from the fpray,
Like a lily juft pluck'd from the ftem,
She droop'd, and fhe faded away,
Thrown by and neglected like them.

SONG 248.

Sung at SADLER's-WELLS.

LET foldiers fight for prey or praife,
And money be the mifer's wifh,
Poor fcholars ftudy all their days,
And gluttons glory in their difh.
'Tis wine, pure wine, revives the foul;
Therefore give us the charming bowl.

Let minions marfhal every hair,
Who in a lover's look delight,
And artificial colours wear,
Pure wine is native red and white.
'Tis wine, pure wine, &c.

The backward fpirit it makes brave;
That lively, which before was dull;
Opens the heart that loves to fave,
And kindnefs flows from cup brimful.
'Tis wine, pure wine, &c.

Some men want youth, and others health,
Some want a wife, and fome a punk;
Some men want wit, and others wealth,
But they want nothing who are drunk.
'Tis wine, pure wine, revives the foul;
Therefore give us the charming bowl.

SONG 249.

NUMBERLESS KISSES.

Sung at VAUXHALL.

DEAR Chloe, come give me fweet kiffes,
For fweeter no girl ever gave;
But why, in the midft of my bliffes,
Do you afk me how many I'd have?
I'm not to be ftinted in pleafure;
Then pr'ythee, dear Chloe, be kind;
For fince I love thee beyond meafure,
To numbers I'll ne'er be confin'd.

Count the bees that on Hybla are playing,
Count the flow'rs that enamel the fields,
Count the flocks that on Tempe are ftraying,
Or the grain that rich Sicily yields;
Count how many ftars are in heaven,
Go number the fands on the fhore,
And when fo many kiffes you've given,
I ftill fhall be afking for more.

To a heart full of love let me hold thee,
A heart which, dear Chloe, is thine;
In my arms I'd for ever enfold thee,
And twift round thy neck like a vine.

What joy can be greater than this is!
My life on thy lips shall be spent;
But the wretch who can number his kisses,
Will always with few be content.

SONG 250.

WRITTEN BY MR. HARRINGTON.

HOW sweet in the woodland, with fleet
hound and horn,
To waken shrill echo, and taste the fresh morn!
But hard is the chace my fond heart must
pursue,
For Daphne, fair Daphne, is lost to my view.

Assist me, chaste Dian, the nymph to regain,
More wild than the roebuck, and wing'd with
disdain;
In pity o'ertake her, who wounds as she flies;
Tho' Daphne's pursu'd, 'tis Myrtillo that dies.

SONG 251.

NO glory I covet, no riches I want,
Ambition is nothing to me;
The one thing I beg of kind Heav'n to grant,
Is a mind independent and free.

With passions unruffled, untainted with pride,
By reason my life let me square:
The wants of my nature are cheaply supply'd,
And the rest are but folly and care.

The blessings which Providence freely has lent,
I'll justly and gratefully prize;
While sweet meditation, and chearful content,
Shall make me both healthy and wise.

In the pleasures the great man's possessions display,
Unenvy'd, I'll challenge my part;
For ev'ry fair object my eyes can survey,
Contributes to gladden my heart.

How vainly, thro' infinite trouble and strife,
The many their labours employ;
Since all that is truly delightful in life,
Is what all, if they will, may enjoy.

SONG 252.

NANCY DAWSON.

OF all the girls in our town,
The black, the fair, the red, the brown,
Who dance and prance it up and down,
There's none like Nancy Dawson:
Her easy mien, her shape so neat,
She foots, she trips, she looks so sweet,
Her ev'ry motion is compleat:
I die for Nancy Dawson.

See how she comes to give surprize,
With joy and pleasure in her eyes!
To give delight she always tires;
So means my Nancy Dawson.

Was there no task t'obstruct the way,
No Shuter droll, nor house so gay,
A bet of fifty pounds I'll lay,
That I gain'd Nancy Dawson.

See how the op'ra takes a run,
Exceeding Hamlet, Lear, or Lun,
Though in it there would be no fun,
Was't not for Nancy Dawson.

Tho' Beard and Brent charm ev'ry night,
And female Peachum's justly right,
And Filch and Lockit please the sight,
'Tis crown'd by Nancy Dawson.

See little Davy strut and puff,
Pox on the op'ra, and such stuff,
My house is never full enough;
A curse on Nancy Dawson.

Tho' Garrick he has had his day,
And forc'd the town his laws t'obey,
Now Johnny Rich is come in play,
With help of Nancy Dawson.

SONG 253.

Sung at VAUXHALL.

NOW the snow-drops lift their heads,
Cowslips rise from golden beds,
Silver lilies paint the grove,
Welcome May, and welcome love.

Now the bee, on silver wings,
Flow'ry spoils unweary'd brings,
Spoils that nymphs and swains approve,
Soft as May, and sweet as love.

Whilst a-down the slopy hill
Trickles soft the purling rill,
Balmy scents perfume the grove,
May unbends the soul to love.

Long the clay-cold maid denies,
Nor regards her shepherd's sighs;
Now your fond petitions move,
May's the season form'd for love.

On the fair that deck our isle,
Let each grace and virtue smile,
And our happy shepherds prove
Days of ease, and nights of love.

SONG 254.

Sung at VAUXHALL.

WHY, my swain, so blythe and clever,
Do you leave me all in sorrow?
Three whole days are gone for ever,
Since you said you'd come to-morrow.
If you lov'd but half as I do,
You'd been here with looks so bonny,
Love has flying wings I well know,
Not for ling'ring lazy Johnny.

What can he be now a doing?
Is he with the lasses maying?
He had better here be wooing,
Than with other damsels playing.

Tell me truly where he's roving,
    That I may no longer forrow;
If he's weary grown of loving,
    Let him tell me fo to-morrow.

Does fome favourite rival hide thee?
    Let her be the happy creature;
I'll not plague myfelf to chide thee,
    Nor difpute with her a feature.
But I can no longer tarry,
    Nor will kill myfelf with forrow;
I may lofe the time to marry,
    If I reach beyond to-morrow.

Think not, fhepherd, thus to brave me,
    If I'm your's, away no longer;
If you won't, another'll have me;
    I may cool, but not grow fonder—
If your lovers, girls, forfake ye,
    Whine not in defpair and forrow;
Bleft another lad may make ye,
    Stay for none beyond to-morrow.

SONG 255.

DEAR Nancy fir'd my artlefs breaft,
    I ne'er faw girl fo clever;
I fometimes thought fhe'd make me bleft,
    And fometimes fancy'd never:
Whene'er I told my am'rous tale,
    With fighs oft intervening—
Your fuit, fhe'd cry, won't here prevail;
    I cannot tell your meaning.

The wife remark—A man in love
    Looks wond'rous foft and filly:
The truth coy Nancy made me prove,
    For oh! her heart was chilly:
To balls and plays fhe us'd to range,
    Her company ftill feen in;
But ftill 'twas ftrange, 'twas mighty ftrange,
    She could not tell my meaning—

I love you, Nancy, oft I'd cry,
    Without you, can't be eafy;
Oh! fhall I live, or fhall I die,
    Pray tell me which will pleafe you?—
By all means live! the fair replies,
    This paffion wants a weaning;
Declare yourfelf without difguife,
    I cannot tell your meaning.

Oh! now, I thought's the lucky time;
    Although fo long I've tarried—
I hope, I anfwer'd, 'tis no crime,
    To fay, I'd fain be marry'd.
She gave her hand; nor feem'd to flight
    The love there was no fcreening;
And now we live in fweet delight,
    Vers'd in each other's meaning.

SONG 256.

I Met young Damon t'other day,
    And near me as he drew,
No fwain, methought, e'er look'd fo gay;
    Upon my word 'tis true.

With ardent blifs, my lips he preft;
    Pray, what could Phillis do?
I frown'd, but 'faith I frown'd in jeft;
    Upon my word 'tis true.

The fhepherd figh'd, and talk'd of love;
    (A theme to me quite new)
Of angels—Heaven—and pow'rs above;
    And vow'd that all was true.
My bofom throbb'd I knew not why,
    As ftill more fond he grew—
I liften'd to his tale with joy;
    Upon my word 'tis true.—

Let Damon now be bleft, he cry'd,
    And fondly to me flew;
His freedom vain I ftrove to chide;
    Upon my word 'tis true.
With blufhes fpread I look'd confent,
    Felt joys but known to few;
For then I found what Damon meant,
    And all he faid was true.

SONG 257.

THE ROVER RECLAIMED.

Sung at VAUXHALL.

I Rambled about for a twelvemonth, I vow
    In fearch of a damfel for life;
For roving perplex'd me, I could not tell how,
    So I ventur'd at laft on a wife.

The girls of the town, each rake muft well know,
    Imbitter the pleafures of life;
For evils on evils will conftantly flow,
    And make us all wifh for a wife.

A miftrefs, 'tis true, who's youthful and gay,
    May fweeten the troubles of life,
And, while fhe is conftant, drive forrow away;
    But what is all this to a wife!

In wedlock alone, true pleafures we find,
    To gild the rough paffage through life;
Then chufe out a lafs with a delicate mind,
    And make the dear charmer a wife.

And you, O ye fair, be kind to the man
    Who offers to blefs you for life;
Ee conftant and true, and as fond as you can;
    For thefe are the charms of a wife.

SONG 258.

THE CONTENTED MILLER.

IN a plain, pleafant cottage, conveniently neat,
    With a mill and fome meadows, a freehold eftate;
A well-meaning miller by labour fupplies
Thofe bleffings which grandeur to great ones denies;
No paffions to plague him, nor cares to torment,
His conftant companions are health and content;
Their lordfhips in lace may take note if they will,
He's honeft, tho' daub'd with the duft of his mill.

Ere the lark's early carols salute the new day,
He springs from his cottage as jocund as May;
He chearfully whistles, regardless of care,
Or sings the last ballad he bought at the fair.
While courtiers are toil'd in the cobwebs of
state,
Or bribing el ctions in hopes to be great,
No fraud nor ambition his bosom does fill,
Contented he works, if there's grist for his
mill.

On Sunday, bedeck'd in his home-spun array,
At church he's the loudest to chant or to pray;
Then sits to a dinner of plain English food,
Tho' simple his pudding, his appetite's good:
At night, when the priest and excisemen are
gone,
He quaffs at the alehouse with Roger and
John;
Then reels to his pillow, and dreams of no ill.
What monarch so bless'd as the man of the
mill!

SONG 259.

THE NONPAREILLE.

THE nymph whom I lov'd was as chearful as
day,
And as sweet as the blossoming hawthorn in
May;
Her temper was smooth as the down on the
doves,
And her face was as fair as the mother of love's:
Tho mild as the pleasantest zephyr that sheds,
And receives gentle odures from flowery beds,
Yet warm in affection as Phœbus at noon,
And chaste as the silver-white beams of the
moon:.

Her mind was unsully'd as new-fallen snow,
And as lively as tints from young Iris's bow;
As clear as the stream, and as deep as the flood;
She, tho' witty, was wise, and tho' beautiful,
good:
The sweets that each virtue or grace had in
store,
She cull'd as the bee does the bloom of each
flow'r;
Which, treasur'd for me, O how happy was I!
For tho' her s to collect, it was mine to enjoy.

SONG 260.

THE HONEST FELLOW.

PHO! pox o' this nonsense, I prythee, give
o'er,
And talk of your Phillis and Chloe no more;
Their face, and their air, and their mien; what
a rout!
Here's to thee, my lad, push the bottle about
Let finical fops play the fool and the ape,
They dare not confide in the juice of the grape;
But we honest fellows——'sdeath! who'd ever
think
Of puling 'or love, while he's able to drink?

'Tis wine, only wine, that true pleasure be-
stows;
Our joys it increases, and lightens our woes;
Remember what topers of old us'd to sing,
The man that is drunk is as great as a king.

If Cupid assaults you, there's law for his tricks;
Anacreon's cases see, page twenty-six:
The precedent's glorious, and just, by my soul!
Lay hold on, and drown the young dog in a
bowl.

What's life but a frolick, a song, and a laugh?
My toast shall be this, whilst I've liquor to
quaff;
' May mirth, and good fellowship always
abound!'
Boys, fill up a bumper, and let it go round.

SONG 261.

THE CHEARFUL SPRING.

SHARP Winter melts, and spreads her wing;
A pleasing change, a smiling spring;
The trees their vary'd blossoms wear,
And op'ning flow'rs perfume the air;
Sweet Philomela tunes her strain,
And warbling charms the list'ning plain.

The sun increases ev'ry round,
The snow is vanish'd from the ground,
With songs the vocal forests ring,
All to adorn the chearful spring;
The meadows all around are seen,
Covered o'er with lovely green.

The dusky clouds so swiftly fly,
And leave behind the azure sky;
The mountains smile, the hills are gay,
And vallies boast the pride of May;
The streams that overflow'd their mounds,
Now gently glide within their bounds.

SONG 262.

THE LOVER'S RECANTATION; A CANTATA

Sung at VAUXHALL.

RECITATIVE.

THE kind appointment Celia made,
And nam'd the myrtle bow r,
There, fretting, long poor Damon stay'd
Beyond the promis'd hour;
No longer able to contain
This anxious expectation,
With rage he thought t' allay his pain,
And vented thus his passion—

AIR.

To all the sex deceitful,
A long and last adieu,
Since women prove ungrateful
As long as men prove true.
The pains they give are many,
And, oh! too hard to bear;
The joys they give, if any,
Few, short, and insincere.

RECITATIVE.

Now Celia, from mamma, got loofe,
  Had reach'd the calm retreat;
With modeſt bluſh ſhe begg'd excuſe,
  And blam'd her tardy feet;
The ſhepherd, from each doubt releas'd,
  His joy could not reſtrain,
But as each tender thought increas'd,
  Thus chang'd his railing ſtrain.

AIR.

How engaging, how endearing,
  Is a lover's pain and care!
And what joy the nymph's appearing,
  After abſence or deſpair.
Women wiſe, increaſe deſiring,
  By contriving kind delays,
And, advancing or retiring,
  All they mean is—more to pleaſe.

SONG 263.

Sung at VAUXHALL.

WHEN Hobbinol intreated Doll
  Within the grove to enter,
She hung her head, and, bluſhing, ſaid,
  She was afraid to venture.—
For there poor Nan put faith in man,
  And ſorely does repent her;
Which makes me fear no good is near,
  And therefore will not venture.

His fond requeſt he eager preſs'd,
  And ſwore no harm he meant her—
By honour ſwav'd, be not diſmay'd,
  But kindly with me venture.
On wedlock bent was all he meant,
  Would that, he ſaid, content her—
To prove me true, yon ſteeple view,
  Say, will my Dolly venture?

Doubt ſtill poſſeſs'd the damſel's breaſt,
  Till virtue counſel lent her.—
Haſte, haſte, he cry'd, be made a bride,
  And after you may venture.
Doll gave conſent, to church they went,
  A wife back Hymen ſent her;
No more a maid, ſhe's not afraid
  With him alone to venture.

SONG 264.

A PRISON SONG.

WELCOME, welcome, brother debtor,
  To this poor, but merry place;
Where no bailiff, dun nor ſetter,
  Dares to ſhew his frightful face:
But, kind Sir, as you're a ſtranger,
  Down your garniſh you muſt lay,
Or your coat will be in danger;
  You muſt either ſtrip or pay.

Ne'er repine at your confinement
  From your children or your wife;

Wiſdom lives in true reſignment,
  Thro' the various ſcenes of life.
Scorn to ſhew the leaſt reſentment,
  Tho' beneath the frowns of fate;
Knaves and beggars find contentment,
  Fears and cares attend the great.

Tho' our creditors are ſpiteful,
  And reſtrain our bodies here,
Uſe will make a gaol delightful,
  Since there's nothing elſe to fear,
Ev'ry iſland's but a priſon,
  Strongly guarded by the ſea;
Kings and princes, for that reaſon,
  Priſ'ners are, as well as we.

What made the great Alexander
  Weep at his unfriendly fate?
'Twas becauſe he could not wander
  Beyond this world's ſtrong priſon-gate.
For the world is alſo bounded
  By the heavens and ſtars above;
Why ſhould we, then, be confounded,
  Since there's nothing free but Jove?

SONG 265.

Sung at VAUXHALL.

YOUNG Colin proteſts I'm his joy and
  delight;
He's ever unhappy when I'm from his ſight.
He wants to go with me wherever I go;
The deuce ſure is in him for plaguing me ſo.

His pleaſure all day is to ſit by my ſide;
He pipes and he ſings, tho' I frown and I chide.
I bid him depart; but he ſmiling, ſays No.
The deuce ſure is in him for plaguing me ſo.

He often requeſts me his flame to relieve;
I aſk him what favour he means to receive?
His anſwer's a ſigh, while in bluſhes I glow.
What mortal beſide him would plague a maid ſo?

This breaſt-knot he yeſterday brought from the
  wake,
And ſoftly intreated I'd wear for his ſake.
Such trifles 'tis eaſy enough to beſtow;
I ſure deſerve more for his plaguing me ſo.

He hands me each eve from the cot to the plain,
And meets me each morn to conduct me again;
But what's his intention I wiſh I could know,
For I'd rather be married than plagu'd with
  him ſo.   .

SONG 266.

Sung at MARYBONE.

THAT Jenny's my friend, my delight, and
  my pride,
I always have boaſted, and ſeek not to hide;
I dwell on her praiſes wherever I go,
They ſay I'm in love, but I anſwer, No, no.

At evening oft-times with what pleaſure I ſee
A note from her hand, ' I'll be with you at tea!'

My heart how it bounds when I hear her below!
But fay not 'tis love, for I anfwer, No, no.

She fings me a fong, and I echo it's ftrain;
Again, I cry—Jenny; fweet Jenny, again.
I kifs her fweet lips, as if there I could grow;
But fay not 'tis love, for I anfwer, No, no.

She tells me her faults, as fhe fits on my knee:
I chide her, and fwear fhe's an angel to me;
My fhoulder fhe taps, and fhe bids me think fo :
Who knows but fhe loves, tho' fhe anfwers,
No, no.

From beauty and wit, and good-humour, how I,
Should prudence advife, and compel me to fly.
Thy bounty, O Fortune! make hafte to beftow,
And let me deferve her, or ftill I'll fay, No.

SONG 267.

THE BRAES OF BELLADINE.

BENEATH a green fhade, a lovely young
fwain
One evening reclin'd to difcover his pain;
So fad, yet fo fweetly, he warbled his woe,
The winds ceas'd to breathe, and the fountains
to flow;
Rude winds with compaffion could hear him
complain,
Yet Chloe, lefs gentle, was deaf to his ftrain.—

How happy, he cry'd, my moments once flew,
Ere Chloe's bright charms firft flafh'd in my
view!
Thofe eyes then with pleafure the dawn could
furvey,
Nor fmil'd the fair morning more chearful than
they;
Now fcenes of diftrefs pleafe only my fight—
I'm tortur'd in pleafure, and languifh in light.

Through changes, in vain, relief I purfue,
All, all but confpire my griefs to renew;
From funfhine to zephyrs and fhades we repair,
To funfhine we fly from too piercing an air;
But love's ardent fever burns always the fame;
No winter can cool it, no fummer inflame.

But, fee the pale moon all clouded retire;
The breezes grow cool, not Strephon's defire;
I fly from the dangers of tempeft and wind,
Yet nourifh the madnefs that preys on my mind:
Ah, wretch! how can life be worthy thy care?
To lengthen it's moments but lengthens defpair.

SONG 268.

Sung at VAUXHALL.

WAS Nanny but a rural maid,
And I her only fwain,
To tend her flocks in verdant mead,
And on the verdant plain;
Oh! how I'd pipe upon my reed,
To pleafe my lovely maid;

While of all fenfe of care we're freed,
Beneath the oaken fhade.

When lambkins under hedges bleat,
And rain feems in the fky;
Then to our oaken fafe retreat,
We'd both together hie!
There I'd repeat my vows of love
Unto my charming fair,
Whilft her dear flutt'ring heart would prove
A mind, like mine, fincere.

Let others fancy courtly joys,
I'd live in rural eafe;
Then grandeur, buftle, pride, and noife,
Could ne'er my fancy pleafe.
In Nanny ev'ry joy combines,
With grace and blooming youth,
Sincerity and virtue fhines,
With modefty and truth.

SONG 269.

THE REVENGE.

WHEN I beheld you all divine,
And fondly thought your paffion true,
I, Chloe, call'd you only mine,
And lov'd no other nymph but you.
How could I think a face fo fair,
Could now fo falfe and fickle prove;
That you, who did fo often fwear,
Would ever break the bonds of love?

But I no longer feel your chain,
Nor you poffefs your wonted pow'r;
No longer I a flave remain,
A Chloe's captive, as before:
But go, and other hearts beguile,
Go, and fome other conqueft find;
'Tis you that fhew a flatt'ring fmile,
'Tis you can kill while yet you're kind.

SONG 270.

Sung at VAUXHALL.

COME, Laura, and meet your fond fwain,
Ere Phœbus declines to the weft,
Nor let me ftill languifh in pain;
Your prefence alone makes me blefs'd.
When abfent no pleafure I feel,
My paffions but ficken and die;
No power my tortures, my tortures can heal,
Unlefs my dear Laura is by.

Then hafte to yon jeffamine grove,
Enjoy what no language can tell;
'Tis the feat of contentment and love,
Where peace and tranquillity dwell:
There Cupid our hearts fhall unite,
There Hymen his altar fhall raife,
The mufes fweet fongs fhall indite,
And charm the whole grove with their lays.

O think, with fuch pleafures as thefe,
How time will glide fwiftly away,
Each ftriving the other to pleafe,
Dull winter fhall fmile as the May;

No happineſs either will taſte,
But what we both jointly approve;
Then hither, dear charmer, O haſte,
And bleſs a fond ſwain with your love.

SONG 271.

MARS TRIUMPHANT.

Sung at VAUXHALL.

NOW peace has ſpread her downy wing,
  And tuneful linnets ſweetly ſing,
No longer, Phœbe, waſte the time,
Enjoy the ſeaſon in it's prime;
No more I court the ſound of arms,
'Tis love and beauty now have charms.
No longer war my boſom fires,
'Tis love alone my ſoul inſpires:
But hark, I hear the trumpet ſound,
Loud ſhouts of war re-echo round;
I quit my love for war's alarms,
Ambition only now has charms;
'Tis war invites me to the field.
And love and beauty now muſt yield.

SONG 272.

Sung at RANELAGH.

RAIL no more, ye learned aſſes,
  'Gainſt the joys the bowl ſupplies;
Sound it's depth, and fill your glaſſes,
Wiſdom at the bottom lies;
Fill them higher ſtill, and higher,
  Shallow draughts perplex the brain;
Sipping quenches all our fire;
Bumpers light it up again.

Draw the ſcene for wit and pleaſure;
  Enter jollity and joy;
We for thinking have no leiſure,
  Manly mirth is our employ:
Since in life there's nothing certain,
  We'll the preſent hour engage;
And when death ſhall drop the curtain,
With applauſe we'll quit the ſtage.

SONG 273.

CORYDON'S REQUEST; A PASTORAL ELEGY.

Written by Mr. NICHOLS.

COME, ſhepherds, attend whilſt I ſing,
  Come, Philidel, hear me impart;
Should your Corydon die in the ſpring,
  O grant the firſt wiſh of his heart.

From the elms which embroider the mead,
  Select one whoſe trunk's undecay'd;
And (when of it's branches 'tis freed)
  Of that let my coffin be made.

Collect ev'ry flow'ret of May,
  From the hawthorn the bloſſoms divorce,

Take the lilacs ſo fragrant, ſo gay,
  And ſtrew them all over with coiſe.

E'en ſuch let the villagers have,
  The matrons who wiſh me ſo well,
To ſcatter before to my grave,
  As they move to the knoll of my knell.

Let thoſe who are conſtant in love,
  My pall to the church-way ſuſtain;
Take roſemary, freſh from the grove,
  To furniſh the funeral train.

Of flow'rs let a garland be made,
  Like that you was pleas'd to approve,
When under the ſycamore ſhade
  You taught me the language of love.

When borne by the ruſtics along,
  Let this on my coffin be plac'd,
To ſhew I was fond of the throng
  Whom truth and ſimplicity grac'd.

Then high on the church-beam, in view,
  Be't hung, that my love, when ſhe's by,
May think on a ſhepherd ſo true,
  And his mem'ry greet with a ſigh.

With the reſt, let old Colin attend;
  Bid the brighteſt young maids o'the dale;
And thus let them ſing of a friend,
  As ſlowly they move o'er the vale.

For titles he was not renown'd,
  Nor riches, nor greatneſs of blood;
But our ſhepherd was conſtantly found
  A friend to the honeſt and good.

His face wore the ſmile of content;
  To all he was gentle and kind;
To treaſure he never was bent,
  Except 'twas the goods of the mind.

His temperance oft has been try'd;
  We know he was ever ſincere;
And if he'd a tincture of pride,
  'Twas ſhewn but when folly was near.

If he knew the diſtreſs of a friend,
  He felt more than words have expreſs'd;
To relieve was his ultimate end,
  And gratitude govern'd his breaſt.

His Philidel reign'd in his heart;
  Tho' wedded, he lov'd her ſincere:
Let great ones go ſtudy the part,
  However exalted their ſphere.

His flute and his paſtoral ſong
  Have charm'd us the long ſummer's day;
The maids of the ruſtical throng
  Have made him the theme of their lay.

E'en thus you may ſing of a ſwain,
  To reſtleſs ambition unknown;
Whoſe manners were eaſy and plain,
  Whoſe faith was as pure as your own.

And then, you who wait him around,
  If your kindneſs you wiſh to increaſe,
Lay Corydon deep in the ground,
  That his body may moulder in peace.

Now bind with green ofiers the fod,
    I afk not the creft-blazon'd ftone;
Convinc'd to be known to my God,
    Is honour that's equall'd by none.

SONG 274.

DRINK to me only with thine eyes,
    And I will pledge with mine;
Or leave a kifs but in the cup,
    And I'll look not for wine:
The thirft that from my foul doth rife,
    Doth afk a drink divine;
But might I of Jove's nectar fip,
    I would not change for thine.

I fent thee late a rofy wreathe,
    Not fo much hon'ring thee,
As giving it a hope that there
    It would not wither'd be:
But thou thereon didft only breathe,
    And fent it back to me;
Since when it grows and fmells, I fwear,
    Not of itfelf, but thee.

SONG 275.

THE BIRTH OF CONTENT.

Written by Mr. NICHOLLS.

ERE Time waxed old, to divert the young
    hours,
Jove fled from his fpoufe, and empyreal bowr's,
To an ifle by all heav'n admir'd:
O'er the daify-deck'd plains as the deity trod,
The rays of his brow fo announced the god,
    Every creature with wonder retir'd.

Undiftinguifh'd from mortals he wifh'd to abide,
To that end laid his rays and his fulmen afide,
    Affuming the guife of a fwain:
To the cot of Paxella like lightning he flew,
There begg'd of the maid a retreat from the dew,
    And pleaded the length of the plain.

She welcom'd him in, and foon cover'd the board
With the beft of ripe viands Induftry had ftor'd,
    Then, with modefty, bade him partake:
From the fpring of Hygeïa frefh water was
    brought,
As foft as her lips, and as pure as her thought,
    Which, delighted, he drank for her fake.

The treat (tho' 'twas homely) was feafon'd
    with mirth;
Such as rarely obtrudes at the cupboards of
    worth;
Blue-ey'd Meeknefs was there, clad in fleece:
'Mongft the guefts rofy Temperance fat with
    delight,
Whilft true Friendfhip, a flame which for ever
    burns bright,
    Sweetly warbled the carrol of peace.

So much kindnefs with rapture the deity fills—
Say, what pow'r fhall refift when a deity wills—
He clafp'd the dear maid to his breaft:

(The while he bid Envy her adders decline;)
He gave, for her comfort, an offspring divine,
    And the fairy Simplicity drefs'd—

Hence, (he cry'd) quickly hence let the fweet-
    one be fent
'Mongft the children of earth, and be called
    Content;
Who carefs her fhall forrow no more:
Without her in vain fhall be phyfical aid;
The bloom on the face of the beauty fhall fade,
    And the wealthy be wretched and poor.

The princes of earth, where fhe deigns to abide,
Shall prefer beyond or ambition or pride;
    The wifeft fhall court her to ftay:
At her fmiles fwoln-ey'd Sorrow fhall certainly
    ceafe,
Whilft dimpled-cheek Pleafure with pleafures
    increafe,
    And the needy be jolly and gay.

SONG 276.

THE STRAWBERRY-VALE.

Written by Mr. NICHOLLS.

T'OTHER day, in the ftrawberry-vale,
    When only my Phillis was there,
I begg'd fhe'd attend to my tale,
    I long'd to unbofom my care.

With fmiles, fweet as Flora's in May,
    She bid me my pleafure impart.
I faid, (in a faltering way)
    Your eyes have ta'en captive my heart.

The dance and the tabor I fhun,
    No reft on my pillow I find;
Believe me, wherever I run,
    Your image ftill dwells in my mind.

O! foothe the keen anguifh I bear;
    Soft pity I read in thine eye;
Ah! quickly, dear charmer, declare,
    If the fhepherd who loves you muft die?

O! this was a moment of blifs;
    I vow'd to be ever fincere:
Her hand fhe prefented to kifs,
    And brighten'd her blufh with a tear.

And now, if my fheep are fecure,
    I meet her at eve in the dale,
Where fhe wifhes that flame may endure,
    She approv'd in the ftrawberry-vale.

SONG 277.

Sung at SADLER'S WELLS.

I'M a hearty good fellow, a ruby-nos'd fot,
    Who yet never thought of or treafon or plot;
A good bottle that's mellow's the chief of my
    cares,
And I guzzle each night till I'm carry'd up
    ftairs.

For the tombs of the brave ones, the wealthy
    and wife,
All the news that they tell us, is, Under he lies;

K

'Tis a hint that I like not, a trumpery tale,
So I drown all the thoughts on't in flaggons of
· ale.

They may call me fot, blockhead, or e'en what
they will;
But if wealth, nor if titles, nor wifdom or fkill,
Can their owners preferve from a church-yard
or prieft,
Why, I'll live as I like it, all method's a jeft.

On the leffon of Nature it is that I think,
For fhe taught me to love, and fhe taught me
to drink;
To my pleafures full power fhe taught me to
give,
And I'll ftick to her maxims as long as I live.

I've money good ftore on't, and fpend it I muft'
Be roaring and jolly, but honeft and juft;
That, cold in my coffin, my landlord may fay—
He's gone, and he's welcome, there's nothing to
pay.

SONG 278.

VENUS, beauteous queen of love,
In whom the charms and graces blend;
Liften from th' Idalian grove;
O liften, and my fuit befriend!

For, lo! the maid upon whofe cheek
Thou deign'ft thy matchlefs charms to fhow'r,
The vermeil boom, and dimple fleek,
Now defies thy am'rous pow'r.

Then bid the god of foft defires
Aim at her cruel breaft a dart;
Bid him light there his tender fires,
Such fires as play round Strephon's heart.

Yet, let the nymph devoted burn,
Let her confefs thy boundlefs reign,
That dares thy dove-like pow'r to fpurn,
Thy pleafing yoke and flowery chain.

SONG 279.

A MODERN COUSIN'S SONG.

Written by the EDITOR.

LET others boaft an ancient name,
From which they would derive their fame;
Regardlefs of intrinfic worth,
So they can claim a noble birth;
But Modern Coufins feek renown
From nought but merit of their own.

In lowly pofture each receives
The precepts which our order gives;
That fuch humility may fhew,
We mean to practife—when we know.
For Modern Coufins, &c.

With facred Truth our heads are crown'd,
While we the myftic Ring furround;
And, by our feeming magic art,
We banifh falfhood from the heart.
For Modern Coufins, &c.

By Friendfhip's emblem at the heart,
We do in lively terms impart,
How ftrict the union ought to be
Of our renown'd fociety;
Since Modern Coufins, &c.

Within the unpolluted breaft
Our focial myfteries we reft;
That Modern Coufins may be known
From other Coufins they difown.
For Modern Coufins, &c.

Not that the Modern Coufins need,
Or Word, or Sign; for ev'ry deed
Shews—Honour, Virtue, are their guide;
And that they do o'er all prefide.
For Modern Coufins feek renown
From nought but merit of their own.

SONG 280.

A RONDEAU.

Written by Mr. HAWKINS.

Sung at VAUXHALL.

WAFT, O Cupid! to Leander,
Sighs that rend my tender breaft;
Whilft I ftray in groves meander,
Bid him fly to make me blefs'd.

Purling rills be gently flowing,
Op'ning glades your fweets diftil;
Soothe a heart's inceffant glowing,
With content my fancy fill.

Hafte, ah, hafte! my lover to me;
Fear not, now, my cold difdain:
While, fweet fhepherd, you purfue me,
To keep my heart I ftrive in vain.

SONG 281.

THE SHEPHERD'S INVITATION.

Written by CHRISTOPHER MARLOW.

COME live with me, and be my love,
And we fhall all the pleafures prove
That vallies, groves, or hill, or field,
Or wood, or fteepy mountain, yield.

There will we fit upon the rocks,
And fee the fhepherds feed their flocks,
By fhallow rivers, to whofe falls
Melodious birds fing madrigals.

There will I make thee beds of rofes,
With a thoufand fragrant pofies,
A cap of flowers, and a kirtle
Embroider'd all with leaves of myrtle.

A gown made of the fineft wool,
Which from our pretty lambs we pull;
Slippers lin'd choicely for the cold;
With buckles of the pureft gold.

A belt of ftraw, and ivy buds,
With coral clafps, and amber ftuds;
And if thefe pleafures may thee move,
Come live with me; and be my love.

Thy silver dishes for thy meat,
As precious as the gods do eat,
Shall, on an ivory table, be
Prepar'd each day for thee and me.

The shepherd-swains shall dance and sing
For thy delight each May-morning:
If these delights thy mind may move,
Then live with me, and be my love.

SONG 282.

THE NYMPH'S ANSWER.

Written by Sir WALTER RALEIGH.

IF all the world and love were young,
  And truth in every shepherd's tongue,
These pretty pleasures might me move
To live with thee, and be thy love.

But time drives flocks from field to fold;
When rivers rage, and rocks grow cold,
And Philomel becometh dumb,
The rest complain of cares to come.

The flowers that bloom in wanton field,
To wayward Winter reckoning yield;
A honey-tongue, a heart of gall,
Is fancy's spring, but sorrow's fall.

Thy gowns, thy shoes, thy beds of roses,
Thy cap, thy kirtle, and thy posies,
Soon break, soon wither, soon forgotten,
In folly ripe, in reason rotten.

Thy belt of straw, and ivy buds,
Thy coral clasps, and amber studs;
All these in me no mind can move,
To come to thee, and be thy love.

What should we talk of dainties then,
Of better meat than's fit for men?
These are but vain; that's only good
Which God hath blest, and sent for food.

But could youth last, and love still breed;
Had joy no date, and age no need;
Then these delights my mind might move
To live with thee, and be thy love.

SONG 283.

IN IMITATION OF MARLOW.

COME live with me, and be my dear,
  And we will revel all the year,
In plains and groves, on hills and dales,
Where fragrant air breathes sweetest gales,

There shall you have the beauteous pine,
The cedar, and the spreading vine;
And all the woods to be a screen,
Left Phœbus kiss my summer's green.

The feat of your disport shall be
Over some river in a tree,
Where silver sands and pebbles sing
Eternal ditties to the spring.

There shall you see the nymphs at play,
And how the satyrs spend the day;

The fishes gliding on the sands;
Off 'ring their bellies to your hands.

The birds, with heav'nly-tuned throats,
Possess wood's echo with sweet notes,
Which to your senses will impart
A music to enflame the heart.

Upon the bare and leafless oak,
The ring-dove's wooings will provoke
A colder blood than you possess
To play with me, and do no less.

In bowers of laurel, trimly dight,
We will outwear the silent night,
While Flora busy is to spread
Her richest treasure on our bed.

Ten thousand glow-worms shall attend,
And all their sparkling lights shall spend;
All to adorn and beautify
Your lodging with more majesty.

Then in my arms will I enclose
Lilies fair mixture with the rose;
Whose nice perfections in love's play
Shall tune me to the highest key.

Thus as we pass the welcome night,
In sportful pleasure and delight,
The nimble fairies on the ground
Shall dance and sing melodious sound.

If these may serve for to entice
Your presence to Love's Paradise,
Then come with me, and be my dear,
And we will straight begin the year.

SONG 284.

Written by Sir WALTER RALEIGH.

SHALL I, like an hermit, dwell
  On a rock, or in a cell,
Calling home the smallest part
That is missing of my heart,
To bestow it where I may
Meet a rival every day?
If she undervalues me,
What care I how fair she be?

Were her tresses angel gold;
If a stranger may be bold,
Unrebuked, unafraid,
To convert them to a braid,
And, with a little more ado,
Work them into bracelets too;
If the mine be grown so free,
What care I how rich it be?

Were her hands as rich a prize
As her hairs, or precious eyes;
If she lay them out to take
Kisses for good-manners sake;
And let every lover skip
From her hand unto her lip;
If she seem not chaste to me,
What care I how chaste she be?

No; she must be perfect snow,
In effect as well as show,

K 2

Warming but as fnow-balls do,
Not like fire, by burning too:
But when fhe by change hath got
To her heart a fecond lot;
Then, if others fhare with me,
Farewel her, whate'er fhe be.

SONG 285.

THE charms which blooming beauty fhews
From faces heavenly fair,
We to the lily and the rofe
With femblance apt compare:

With femblance apt; for ah! how foon,
How foon they all decay!
The lily droops, the rofe is gone,
And beauty fades away.

But when bright virtue fhines confefs'd,
With fweet difcretion join'd;
When mildnefs calms the peaceful breaft,
And wifdom guides the mind;

When charms like thefe, dear maid, confpire
Thy perfon to approve,
They kindle generous, chafte defire,
And everlafting love.

Beyond the reach of time or fate,
Thefe graces fhall endure;
Still, like the paffion they create,
Eternal, conftant, pure.

SONG 286.

INVITATION TO THE FEATHER'D RACE.

Written by the Rev. Mr. GRAVES.

AGAIN the balmy zephyr blows,
Frefh verdure decks the grove,
Each bird with vernal rapture glows,
And tunes his notes to love.

Ye gentle warblers, hither fly,
And fhun the noon-tide heat;
My fhrubs a cooling fhade fupply,
My groves a fafe retreat.

Here freely hop from fpray to fpray,
Or weave the moffy neft;
Here rove and fing the live-long day,
At night here fweetly reft.

Amidft this cool tranflucent rill,
That trickles down the glade,
Here bathe your plumes, here drink your fill,
And revel in the fhade.

No fchool-boy rude, to mifchief prone,
E'er fhews his ruddy face,
Or twangs his bow, or hurls a ftone,
In this fequefter'd place.

Hither the vocal thrufh repairs,
Secure the linnet fings,
The goldfinch dreads no flimy fnares
To clog her painted wings.

Sad Philomel! ah, quit thy haunt,
Yon diftant woods among,
And round my friendly grotto chaunt
Thy fweetly-plaintive fong.

Let not the harmlefs red-breaft fear,
Domeftic bird, to come
And feek a fure afylum here,
With one that loves his home.

My trees for you, ye artlefs tribe,
Shall ftore of fruit preferve:
Oh, let me thus your friendfhip bribe!
Come, feed without referve.

For you thefe cherries I protect,
To you thefe plums belong;
Sweet is the fruit that you have pick'd,
But fweeter far your fong.

Let, then, this league betwixt us made,
Our mutual interefts guard;
Mine be the gift of fruit and fhade,
Your fongs be my reward.

SONG 287.

Written by Dr. O——.

NOW ev'ning had ting'd the gay landfcape
with gold,
The fwains were retir'd, and their flocks in the
fold,
When Delia complain'd in the woodland alone;
Loud echoes retain'd, and reply'd to her moan,
The warblers fat lift'ning around on the fpray,
And the gale ftole in murmurs as foft as her lay.

Ah, my Strephon! ('twas thus the fair mourner
begun)
How cruel to leave me, thus loft and undone!
Your vows like the wind you forget or defpife,
You flight my complaints, and are deaf to my
cries;
The frown once fo dreadful, ah! where is it's
pow'r?
The voice heard with tranfport, gives tranfport
no more.

Though the fylvans to pleafe me exert all their
powers,
Though the fwains crown my head with a gar-
land of flowers,
Though they fwear that my eyes like the morn-
ing are gay,
That my fong is more fweet than the nightin-
gale's lay,
Yet while Strephon is abfent, dejected, difmay'd,
I droop like a flow'r that repines in the fhade.

O return, gentle fhepherd, return to my pray'r!
Ah, think how I figh in unpity'd defpair!—
But in vain all my hopes! all my wifhes are
vain!
While the ftreams and the breezes thus hear me
complain;
While the birds to my anguifh reply from the
bough,
He flies from my arms, and regards not my woe

Ah! too eafy to truft all the oaths that he fwore,
When he vow'd that no nymph had e'er charm'd him before.
Be warn'd, then, ye fair, nor too rafhly believe;
Think the men, when they flatter but want to dec ive;
That the fond eafy promife was ne'er meant to bind;
And believe, when they fwear, that their oaths are all wind.

SONG 288.

THE INVITATION.

Written by Mr. B——Y.

AWAKE, my fair, the morning fprings,
  The dew-drops glance around;
The heifer lows, the blackbird fings,
  The echoing vales refound.

The fimple fweets would Stella tafte,
  That breathing morning yields,
The fragrance of the flow'ry wafte,
  And frefhnefs of the fields!

By uplands, and the greenwood-fide,
  We'll take our early way,
And view the valley fpreading wide,
  And op'ning with the day.

Nor uninftructive fhall the fcene
  Unfold it's charms in vain,
The fallow brown, the meadow green,
  The mountain and the plain.

Each dew-drop glift'ning on the thorn,
  And trembling to it's fall,
Each blufh that paints tha cheek of morn,
  In fancy's ear fhall call:

O ye in youth and beauty's pride,
  Who lightly dance along;
While laughter frolicks at your fide,
  And rapture tunes your fong;

What though each grace around you play,
  Each beauty bloom for you,
Warm as the blufh of rifing day,
  And fparkling as the dew;

The blufh that glows fo gaily now,
  But glows to difappear,
And quiv'ring from the bending bough,
  Soon breaks the pearly tear!

So pafs the beauties of your prime,
  That e'en in blooming die;
So, fhrinking at the blaft of time,
  The treach'rous graces fly.

Let thofe, my Stella, flight the ftrain,
  Who fear to find it true!
Each fair of tranfient beauty vain,
  And youth as tranfient too!

With charms that win beyond the fight,
  And hold the willing heart;
My Stella fhall await their flight,
  Nor figh when they depart.

Still graces fhall remain behind,
  And beauties ftill controul;
The graces of the polifh'd mind,
  And beauties of the foul.

SONG 289.

BELINDA, with affected mien,
  Tries ev'ry power and art;
Yet finds her efforts all in vain,
  To gain a fingle heart:
Whilft Chloe, in a different way,
  .ums but herfelf to pleafe,
And makes new conquefts every day,
  Without one borrow'd grace.

Belinda's haughty air deftroys
  What native charms infpire;
While Chloe's artlefs, fhining eyes,
  Set all the world on fire.
Belindá may our pity move,
  But Chloe gives us pain;
And while fhe fmiles us into love,
  Her fifter frowns in vain.

SONG 290.

BLACK-EY'D SUSAN.

Written by Mr. GAY.

ALL in the Downs the fleet was moor'd,
  The ftreamers waving in the wind,
When black-ey'd Sufan came on board,
  Oh! where fhall I my true love find?
Tell me, ye jovial failors, tell me true,
Does my fweet William fail among the crew?

William, who high upon the yard,
  Rock'd with the billows to and fro;
Soon as her well-known voice he heard,
  He figh'd, and caft his eyes below.
The cord flides fwiftly thro' his glowing hands,
And, quick as lightning, on the deck he ftands.

So the fweet lark, high pois'd in air,
  Shuts clofe his pinions to his breaft,
(If, chance, his mate's fhrill note he hear)
  And drops at once into her neft.
The nobleft captain in the Britifh fleet
Might envy William's lips thofe kiffes fweet.

O, Sufan! Sufan! lovely dear!
  My vows fha'l ever true remain;
Let me kifs off that falling tear:
  We only part to meet again.
Change, as ye lift, ye winds; my heart fhall be
The faithful compafs, that ftill points to thee.

Believe not what the landmen fay,
  Who tempt with doubts thy conftant mind;
They'll tell thee, failors, when away,
  In ev'ry port a miftrefs find—
Yes, yes, believe them, when they tell thee fo,
For thou art prefent, wherefoc'er I go.

If to far India's coaft we fail,
  Thy eyes are feen in diamond's bright:
Thy breath is Afric's fpicy gale;
  Thy fkin is ivory fo white:

Thus ev'ry beauteous object, that I view,
Wakes in my foul fome charms of lovely Sue.

Tho' battle call me from thy arms,
  Let not my pretty Sufan mourn;
Tho' cannons roar, yet fafe from harms
  William fhall to his dear return:
Love turns afide the balls that round me fly,
Left precious tears fhould drop from Sufan's eye.

The boatfwain gave the dreadful word,
  The fails their fwelling bofom fpread;
No longer muft fhe ftay-aboard:
  They kifs'd; fhe figh'd; he hung his head.
Her lefs'ning boat unwilling rows to land:
Adieu! fhe cries; and wav'd her lily-hand.

SONG 291.

WHILE filently I lov'd, nor dar'd
    To tell my crime aloud,
The influence of your fmiles I fhar'd,
  In common with the crowd:

But when I once my flame expreft,
  In hopes to eafe my pain,
You fingled me from all the reft,
  The mark of your difdain.

If thus, Corinna, you fhould frown
  On all that you adore,
Then all mankind muft be undone,
  Or you muft fmile no more.

SONG 292.

THE GARLAND.

Written by Mr. PRIOR.

THE pride of ev'ry grove I chofe,
    The violet fweet, and lily fair,
The dappled pink, and blufhing rofe,
  To deck my charming Chloe's hair.

At morn the nymph veuchfaf'd to place
  Upon her brow the various wreath;
The flow'rs lefs blooming than her face,
  The fcent lefs fragrant than her breath.

The flow'rs fhe wore along the day;
  And ev'ry nymph and fhepherd faid,
That in her hair they look'd more gay,
  Than glowing in their native bed.

Un'reft at ev'ning, when fhe found
  Their colours loft, their odours paft,
She chang'd her look, and on the ground
  Her garland and her eye fhe caft.

That eye dropt fenfe diftinct and clear,
  As any mufe's tongue could fpeak;
When from it's lid a pearly tear
  Ran trickling down her beauteous cheek.

Diffembling what I knew too well—
  My love, my life, faid I, explain
This change of humour; prythee, tell,
  That falling tear, what does it mean?

She figh'd, fhe fmil'd; and to the flow'rs
  Pointing, the lovely moralift faid—

See, friend, in fome few fleeting hours
  See yonder what a change is made!

Ah, me! the blooming pride of May
  And that of beauty are but one;
At noon both flourifh bright and gay,
  Both fade at ev'ning, pale and gone.

At dawn poor Stella danc'd and fung,
  The am'rous youth around her bow'd;
At night her fatal knell was rung,
  I faw, and kifs'd her in her fhroud.

Such as fhe is, who dy'd to-day,
  Such I, alas! may be to-morrow;
Go, Damon, bid thy mufe difplay
  The juftice of thy Chloe's forrow.

SONG 293.

THE MORNING SALUTATION.

Written by Mr. CONGREVE.

SEE! fhe wakes! Sabina wakes!
    And now the fun begins to rife;
Lefs glorious is the morn, that breaks
  From his bright beams, than her fair eyes.

With light united day they give,
  But different fates ere night fulfil:
How many by his warmth will live!
  How many will her coldnefs kill!

SONG 294.

OH! HOW HOT IT IS!

Written in June 1761.

OH, the fultry month of June!
    Sweating late and early;
Able fcarce to hum a tune,
  Oh! we fwelter rarely!

All night long we're in a fweat,
  Sweating till the morning;
Piping hot then up we get,
  Breakfaft bell gives warning.

After tea we take a walk,
  In the grove or meadow:
Oh! how hot! is all our talk;
  None e'er fweat as we do.

Then upon the grafs we're laid;
  For a while, how clever!
Soon the fun darts thro' the fhade,
  We're as hot as ever.

Panting with the noon-tide heat,
  Homeward next we ftroll, Sir,
All befmear'd with duft and fweat,
  Dolly brings the bowl, Sir.

Cooling cream, our thirft t'allay,
  Eager now we fwallow;
Cyder too, and curds and whey;
  Still we melt our tallow.

Chairs, ftools, benches, reftlefs grown,
  Now we try to eafe us;

Chairs, ftools, benches, beds of down,
Nothing now can pleafe us.

Dinner waits, and down we fit,
Fifh and flefh invite us;
Not a morfel can we eat,
Nothing can delight us.

From our liquors, ftrong or weak,
We derive no pleafure;
Cooling draughts in vain we feek,
Sweating beyond meafure.

Ev'ning now comes on apace,
Now the fun is fetting;
Shadows fkim the meadow's face,
But we ftill are fweating.

Sweating thus from day to day,
Pitying pow'rs, befriend us!
And, inftead of June fo gay,
Winter once more fend us!

SONG 295.

A BUCK'S SONG.

WOULD you tafte the perfume of the morn,
While the dew-drops befpangle the thorn;
Hark, away, when the founds
Of the merry-mouth'd hounds
Keep time with the mellow-ton'd horn;
Ere Phœbus with round ruddy face
The tops of the mountains fhall grace,
To the fports of the day
Brother Bucks hafte away,
Purfue with new vigour the chace.

It was Nimrod the jovial and gay,
Who firft taught us to hunt for the prey;
And with full-flowing bowls
To enliven our fouls,
And joyoufly finifh the day:
Due homage then pay at his fhrine,
Pour mighty libations of wine;
Fill up to the brink,
To his mem'ry let's drink,
Proclaim our great founder divine,

SONG 296.

A FREE MASON'S SONG.

WHEN quite a young fpark,
I was in the dark,
And wanted to alter my ftation;
I went to a friend,
Who prov'd, in the end,
A free and an accepted Mafon.

At a door he then knock'd,
Which quickly unlock'd,
When he bid me to put a good face on,
And not be afraid,
For I fhould be made
A free and an accepted mafon.

My wifhes were crown'd,
And a mafter I found,
Who made a moft folemn oration;

Then fhew'd me the light,
And gave me the right
Sign, token, and word, of a mafon.

How great my amaze,
When I firft faw the blaze!
And how ftruck with the myftic occafion!
Aftonifh'd! I found,
Tho' free, I was bound
To a free and an accepted mafon.

When cloathed in white,
I took great delight
In the work of this noble vocation;
And knowledge I gain'd,
When the lodge he explain'd
Of a free and an accepted mafon.

I was bound, it appears,
For feven long years,
Which to me is of trifling duration:
With freedom I ferve,
And ftrain ev'ry nerve
To acquit myfelf like a good mafon.

A bumper then fill
With an hearty good will,
To our mafter pay due veneration;
Who taught us the art
We ne'er will impart,
Unlefs to an accepted mafon.

SONG 297.

TO you, gay folks, in London town,
In fummer who refide,
Who flaunt each night in Marybone,
And each fine place befide,
While, faunt'ring here and there, you fpend
Your hours—to you thefe lines I fend.

With eafe and foft contentment blefs'd,
We laugh at folly's train,
Nor figh for joys by you poffefs'd,
French-horns or burnt Champaign;
The fragrant lily, and the rofe,
Far, far outfhine your belles and beaux.

Let Brent with fing-fong trilling note
Regale your nicer ears;
We think the blackbird's tuneful throat
The mufic of the fpheres;
The fweeter linnet and the thrufh
Our concerts make in ev'ry bufh.

While Philomel, in fhades remote,
Sweet bird of night! complains,
We liften to each warbling note,
Inchanted with her ftrains;
And when the tuneful dirge is o'er,
We cara! cry——Encore, Encore!

When fultry funs dart fiercer beams,
Thro' woods and glades we rove,
Or haunt the fide of purling ftreams,
Our pleafures to improve;
Thus, thus, we pafs the live-long day,
Nor heed we what your great ones fay.

When, pinch'd with northern blaft fo keen,
We fhun the cool retreat,

The chearful glafs diverts our fpleen,
  At dinner when we meet;
In fober chat our time we kill,
Or play at whift——or dear quadrille.

While fome with patriotic zeal
  Vouchfafe the helm to fteer,
And, ardent for the public weal,
  The pofts of honour fhare;
It matters not, to fuch as we,
Who holds the ftaff—or wears the key.

Let ftatefmen, vers'd in court grimace,
  Contend for pow'r and pay;
To get a penfion or a place,
  Cringe, flatter, and betray;
A nobler prize we have in view,
While love and friendfhip we purfue.

'Tis this that gilds our morning bright,
  And ev'ry cloud difpels;
Nor chearlefs is the gloom of night,
  Where love with friendfhip dwells.
Blefs'd fpot, where joys like thefe combine!
Such, fuch are Thomfon's joys, and mine.

SONG 298.

A SELECT ALBION'S SONG.

YE tuneful Nine, my fong infpire,
  And fill each breaft with rapt'rous fire;
Affift with ev'ry trembling ftring,
To make the vaulted cieling ring;
While we record, in choral ftrains,
The band where union truly reigns.

Here friendfhip's feen in ev'ry face,
And gives to mirth a focial grace;
Here peace and plenty ever fmile,
To blefs the fons of Albion's ifle;
And fceptred wifdom ne'er difdains
To join the band where union reigns.

With feftal fong, and rofy wine,
We offer up at Bacchus' fhrine,
Who bleeds the grape for Albion's cheer,
Tho' France, and Spain, the vineyards rear;
With Nectar he recruits our veins,
And joins the band where union reigns.

To make our happinefs compleat,
Here liberty has fix'd her feat;
And does each Albion fon infpire
With free-born courage, matchlefs fire:
No breach of honour ever ftains
The band where union truly reigns.

Should Spain with haughty ftride advance,
And proudly fhake her feeble lance ;
Or Gallia's fons (afpiring race)
Attempt to wound fair Albion's peace;

We'll dauntlefs brave the hoftile plains,
And prove, with Albions, union reigns,
Then fill the goblets to the brink,
And let each worthy brother drink
Succefs to Albion, and her caufe,
Her rights, her liberties, and laws;
And joyous fing, in choral ftrains,
The band where union truly reigns.

SONG 299.

Written by Mr. BAKER.

WOMAN! thoughtlefs, giddy creature!
  Laughing, idle, flutt'ring thing,
Moft fantaftic work of nature!
  Still, like fancy, on the wing.
Slave to ev'ry changing paffion,
  Loving, hating, in extreme;
Fond of ev'ry foolifh fafhion,
  And, at beft, a pleafing dream.

Lovely trifle! dear illufion!
  Conqu'ring weaknefs! wifh'd-for pain!
Man's chief glory, and confufion;
  Of all vanities moft vain.
Thus, deriding beauty's power,
  Bevil call'd it all a cheat;
But, in lefs than half an hour,
  Kneel'd and whin'd at Celia's feet.

SONG 300.

WHEN her beams, that late warm'd me,
  Clariffa withdrew,
How charg'd all at once, and how lifelefs I
  grew!
Quite uneafy and reftlefs, I rov'd up and down,
So ftrange a diforder fure never was known.

I fat down to write, and endeavour'd to think,
But no ufe could I make of my dear pen and ink:
I flew to my claret, that balm of the mind!
But, ah! in my claret no eafe could I find!

In diverfions I next hop'd to get fome relief;
But diverfions, how vain! to a heart full of
  grief!
Then I por'd o'er my books; fure, thought I,
  'mongft the wife,
I fhall meet with fome marvellous cure in a
  trice:

But they honeftly told me, that what I endur'd
Could, alone, by the nymph who firft caus'd it,
  be cur'd;
Then hafte, my Clariffa! to fhine on me, hafte,
Left, benighted much longer, this verfe be
  my laft.

THE

VOCAL MAGAZINE.

NUMBER III.

SONG 301.

A SONG UPON SONGS.

COME ev'ry brisk soul
　Who delights in a bowl,
In mirth, or what to it belongs;
Attend to my verse,
While here I rehearse,
　To please you, a song upon songs.

But first I declare,
To him who to hear
This little original longs;
Let him think what he will,
Nought offensive or ill
　Is contain'd in this song upon songs,

Great statesmen conceal
Their schemes, wheel in wheel,
　And under disguise commit wrongs;
I nobody hurt,
But contribute to mirth,
　By writing a song upon songs.

The boisterous knave,
Who pretends to be brave,
　And boasts of his fights and ding dongs;
When put to the test,
How fallen his crest!
　And his courage—a song upon songs.

The clergy resort
To superiors at court,
　And crave for fat livings in throngs;
While I, with low aim,
Aspire to fame,
　In scribbling a song upon songs.

Taste differs in all,
In great and in small,
　A hobby-horse to all belongs;

A girl, ball, or play,
A review, or birth-day,
　Or even a song upon songs.

Guitars with some suit,
Some a fiddle, or flute,
　And some love a poker and tongs;
Some admire duettos,
And others cantatas,
　And others, my song upon songs.

Let all who've the spleen
Buy this Magazine;
　Such property to it belongs,
It will give them a cure,
As certain and sure
　As this is a song upon songs.

But if you proceed,
And continue to read
　Each song which to this book belongs:
You'll own, I believe,
Many pleasure can give,
　Besides this our song upon songs.

SONG 302.

Sung at MARYBONE.

THE sun, like any bridegroom gay,
　Rose to salute the spring,
The flow'rets hail'd the birth of May,
And birds began to sing;
When Damon tript it o'er the plain,
　Dear Chloe's heart to win;
But at the window tapp'd in vain,
　She would not let him in.

Beside the mansions where the great
　From glorious feats retir'd,
The Druids us'd to celebrate
　The virtues they admir'd:

L

Love whifper'd then in Damon's ear,
    And bade his fong begin :
And thus he fung to pleafe the fair,
    In hopes fhe'd let him in.

So fweet his fong, the maiden rofe,
    In rural plain attire ;
And like the genial feafon glows
    With thrilling foft defire:
But, angry like, by love controul'd,
    Cry'd, Shepherd, why this din?
Why wake me thus ? I've often told
    I ne'er would let you in,

The fair-one in his arms he prefs'd,
    And kifs'd her o'er and o'er :
And who, with honour in his breaft,
    Could then have thought on more?
To church he led her in her prime,
    For pleafure void of fin ;
And now fhe hails the happy time,
    When firft fhe let him in.

SONG 303.

COLIN'S COMPLAINT.

Written by Mr. ROWE.

DESPAIRING befide a clear ftream,
    A fhepherd forfaken was laid;
And while a falfe nymph was his theme,
    A willow fupported his head.
The winds that blew over the plain,
    To his fighs with a figh did reply;
And the brook, in return to his pain,
    Ran mournfully murmuring by.

Alas ! filly fwain that I was!
    Thus fadly complaining he cry'd;
When firft I beheld that fair face,
    'Twere better by far I had dy'd:
She talk'd, and I blefs'd the dear tongue;
    When fhe fmil'd 'twas a pleafure too great:
I liften'd, and cry'd, when fhe fung,
    Was nightingale ever fo fweet!

How foolifh was I to believe
    She could doat on fo lowly a clown!
Or that her fond heart would not grieve
·   To forfake the fine folk of the town!
To think that a beauty fo gay,
    So kind and fo conftant would prove;
Or go clad like our maidens in grey,
    Or live in a cottage on love?

What tho' I have fkill to complain!
    Tho' the Mufes my temples have crown'd!
What tho', when they hear my foft ftrain,
    The virgins fit weeping around!
Ah, Colin! thy hopes are in vain,
    Thy pipe and thy laurel refign;
Thy falfe-one inclines to a fwain
    Whofe mufic is fweeter than thine.

And you, my companions fo dear,
    Who forrow to fee me betray'd,
Whatever I fuffer, forbear,
    Forbear to accufe the falfe maid;
Tho' through the wide world I fhould range,
    'Tis in vain from my fortune to fly;

'Twas her's to be falfe and to change;
    'Tis mine to be conftant and die.

If, while my hard fate I fuftain,
    In her breaft any pity is found,
Let her come with the nymphs of the plain,
    And fee me laid low in the ground,
The laft humble boon that I crave,
    Is to fhade me with cyprefs and yew;
And when fhe looks down on my grave,
    Let her own that her fhepherd was true.

Then to her new love let her go,
    And deck her in golden array;
Be fineft at ev'ry fine fhow,
    And frolic it all the long day:
While Colin, forgotten and gone,
    No more fhall be talk'd of or feen,
Unlefs when beneath the pale moon,
    His ghoft fhall glide over the green!

SONG 304.

Sung at RANELAGH.

RECITATIVE.

WHEN Bacchus, jolly god, invites,
    To revel in his ev'ning rites;
In vain his altar I furround,
Tho' with Burgundian incenfe crown'd:
No charms has wine without the lafs;
'Tis love gives relifh to the glafs.

AIR.

While all around, with jocund glee,
    In brimmers toaft the favourite fhe;
Tho' ev'ry nymph my lips proclaim,
    My heart ftill whifpers Chloe's name;
And thus, with me, by am'rous ftealth,
    Still ev'ry glafs is Chloe's health.

SONG 305.

WILLIAM AND MARGARET.

WHEN all was wrapt in dark midnight,
    And all were faft afleep,
In glided Marg'ret's grimly ghoft,
    And ftood at William's feet.

Her face was like the April morn,
    Clad in a wint'ry cloud;
And clay-cold was her lily hand,
    That held the fable fhroud.

So fhall the faireft face appear,
    When youth and years are flown;
Such is the robe that kings muft wear,
    When death has reft their crown.

Her bloom was like the fpringing flow'r,
    That fips the filver dew;
The rofe was budded in her cheek,
    And op'ning to the view.

But love had, like the canker-worm,
    Confum'd her early prime :
The rofe grew pale, and left her cheek ;
    She dy'd before her time.

Awake, she cry'd, thy true love calls,
　Come from her midnight grave;
Now let thy pity hear the maid
　Thy love refus'd to save.

This is the dark and fearful hour
　When injur'd ghosts complain ;
Now dreary graves give up their dead,
　To haunt the faithless swain.

Bethink thee, William, of thy fault,
　Thy pledge and broken oath;
And give me back my maiden vow,
　And give me back my troth.

How could you say my face was fair,
　And yet that face forsake?
How could you win my virgin heart,
　Yet leave that heart to break?

How could you promise love to me,
　And not that promise keep?
Why did you swear mine eyes were bright,
　Yet leave those eyes to weep?

How could you say my lip was sweet,
　And make the scarlet pale?
And why did I, young witless maid,
　Believe the flatt'ring tale?

That face, alas! no more is fair;
　That lip no longer red;
Dark are mine eyes, now clos'd in death,
　And ev'ry charm is fled.

The hungry worm my sister is ;
　This winding-sheet I wear;
And cold and weary lasts our night,
　Till that last morn appear.

But, hark! the cock has warn'd me hence:
　A long and last adieu !
Come see, false man! how low she lies,
　That dy'd for love of you.

Now birds did sing, and morning smile,
　And shew her glitt'ring head ;
Pale William shook in ev'ry limb,
　Then raving left his bed.

He hy'd him to the fatal place
　Where Marg'ret's body lay,
And stretch'd him on the green-grass turf
　That wrapt her breathless clay:

And thrice he call'd on Marg'ret's name,
　And thrice he wept full sore;
Then laid his cheek to the cold earth,
　And word spake never more.

SONG 306.

A HUNTING SONG.

HARK away! hark away!
　We'll chace the fleet hare by the dawn;
We're up, my brave lads, before day,
　Our sport will be over ere morn.

Pale echo, who silent has been,
　No longer in slumbers shall lie;
But, awak'd by our dogs on the green,
　From hills to the vallies reply.

The hare is put up, my brave souls,
　Lo! yonder she brushes the glade;
See Pompey how fleetly he bowls,
　Poor puss is most sadly afraid.

She turns and she doubles in vain,
　And, hoic! she now loses breath;
Huzza, she is flat on the plain,
　We'll revel, my boys, o'er her death !

SONG 307.

WHAT's all the pomps of gaudy courts,
　But vain delights, and jingling toys;
While pleasure crowns your rural sports,
　With calm content and tranquil joys!

SONG 308.

THE HAPPY LOVER.

WHILST on thy dear bosom lying,
　Celia, who can paint my bliss?
Who the transports I'm enjoying,
　When thy balmy lips I kiss?
Ev'ry look with love inspires me,
Ev'ry touch my bosom warms,
Ev'ry melting transport fires me,
　Ev'ry joy is in thy arms.

Those dear eyes, how soft they languish!
　Feel my heart with raptures beat;
Pleasure turns almost to anguish,
　When the transport is so great:
Look not so divinely on me,
　Celia, I shall die with bliss;
Yet ' yet! turn those eyes upon me,
　Who'd not die a death like this!

SONG 309.

Sung in *Artaxerxes*.

FAIR Semira, lovely maid,
　Cease in pity to upbraid
My opprss'd but constant heart;
Full sufficient are the woes,
Which my cruel stars oppose ;
Heav'n, alas! hath done it's part.

SONG 310.

Sung in *Artaxerxes*.

LET not rage, thy bosom firing,
　Pity's softer claim remove:
Spare a heart that's just expiring,
　Forc'd by duty, rack'd by love.

Each ungentle thought suspending,
　Judge of mine by thy soft breast;
Nor with rancour never ending,
　Heap fresh sorrows on th' opprest.

Heav'n, that ev'ry joy has cross'd,
　Ne'er my wretched state can mend;
I, alas! at once have lost
　Father, brother, lover, friend!

SONG 311.

Sung in *Love in a Village.*

MY heart's my own, my will is free,
   And fo fhall be my voice;
No mortal man fhall wed with me,
   Till firft he's made my choice.

Let parents rule, cry Nature's laws,
   And children ftill obey;
And is there, then, no faving claufe,
   Againft tyrannic fway?

SONG 312.

PHILLIS, I pray, what did I fay?
   That I did not adore you?
I durft not fue, as others do,
   Or talk of love before you.

Should I make known my flame, you'd frown,
   No tears could e'er appeafe you;
'Tis better I fhould filent die,
   Than talk for to difpleafe you.

SONG 313.

Sung in the *Maid of the Mill.*

IF that's all you want, who the plague will
   be forry?
'Twere better by half to dig ftones in a quarry;
   For my fhare, I'm weary of what is got by't:
'Sflefh, here's fuch a racket, fuch fcolding and
   coiling,
You're never content, but when folks are a
   toiling,
And drudging like horfes, from morning till
   night.

You think I'm afraid, but the difference to fhew
   you,
Firft, yonder's your fhovel, your facks too I
   throw you;
Henceforward take care of your matters who
   will,
They are welcome to flave for your wages who
   need em;
Tol,lol,de rol, lol, I have purchas'd my freedom,
And never hereafter fhall work at the mill.

SONG 314.

THE WISH.

IF I live to be old, for I find I go down,
   Let this be my fate: In a country town,
May I have a warm houfe, with a ftone at the
   gate,
And a cleanly young girl to rub my bald pate.
May I govern my paffion with an abfolute fway,
And grow wifer and better, as my ftrength
   wears away;
Without gout or ftone, by a gentle decay!

May my little houfe ftand on the fide of a hill,
With an eafy defcent to a mead and a mill;

That when I've a mind I may hear my boy read,
In the mill, if it rains; if it's dry, in the mead!
   May I govern, &c.

Near a fhady grove, and a murmuring brook,
With the ocean at diftance whereon I may
   look,
With a fpacious plain without hedge or ftile,
And an eafy pad-nag to rid out a mile.
   May I govern, &c.

With Horace and Petrarch, and two or three
   more
Of the beft wits that reign'd in the ages before;
With roaft mutton, rather than ven'fon or teal,
And clean, tho' coarfe linen at every meal.
   May I govern, &c.

With a pudding on Sundays, with ftout hum-
   ming liquor,
And remnants of Latin to welcome the vicar,
With Monte-Fiafcone, or Burgundy wine,
To drink the king's health as oft as I dine.
   May I govern, &c.

May my wine be vermilion, may my malt-
   drink be pale,
In neither extreme, or too mild, or too ftale:
In lieu of defferts, unwholefome and dear,
Let Lodi or Parmefan bring up the rear.
   May I govern, &c.

Nor tory, nor whig, obfervator, or trimmer,
May I be, nor 'gainft the law's torrent a fwim-
   mer.
May I mind what I fpeak, what I write, and
   hear read,
And with matters of ftate ne'er trouble my
   head!
   May I govern, &c.

Let the gods, who difpofe of ev'ry king's crown,
Whomfoever they pleafe, fet up and pull down;
I'll pay the whole fhilling impofed on my head,
Tho' I go without claret that night to my bed.
   May I govern, &c.

I'll bleed without grumbling, though that tax
   fhould appear
As oft as new moons, or weeks in a year.
For why fhould I let a feditious word fall,
Since my lands in Utopia pay nothing at all?
   May I govern, &c.

Tho' I care not for riches, may I not be fo poor
That the rich without fhame cannot enter my
   door;
May they court my converfe, may they take
   much delight
My old ftories to hear in a long winter's night!
   May I govern, &c.

My fmall ftock of wit may I not mifapply,
To flatter ill men, be they never fo high;
Nor mifpend the few moments I fteal from the
   grave,
In fawning or cringing, like a dog or a flave!
   May I govern, &c.

Mr DIBDIN as Ralph in the MAID OF THE MILL.

If that's all You want, who the
Plague will be sorry?

Song 313.

Published by J, Bew Jan 1, 1779

May none whom I love, to so great riches rise,
As to slight their acquaintance, and their old
  friends despise,
So low or so high may none of them be,
As to move neither pity nor envy in me!
    May I govern, &c.

A friendship I wish for, but alas! 'tis in vain,
  Jove's store-house is empty, and can't it sup-
  ply,
So firm, that no change of times, envy or gain,
  Or flatt'ry, or women, should have power
  to untie.
    May I govern, &c.

But if friends prove unfaithful, and fortune a
  whore,
Still may I be virtuous, tho' I am poor;
My life, then, as useless, may I freely resign,
When no longer I relish true wit and good wine!
    May I govern, &c.

To out-live my senses may it not be my fate,
  To be blind, to be deaf, to know nothing
  at all!
But rather let death come before 'tis so late,
  And while there's some sap in it, may my
  tree fall!
    May I govern, &c.

I hope I shall have no occasion to send
For priests, or physicians, till I'm so near my
  end,
That I have eat all my bread, and drank my
  last glass;
Let them come then, and set their seals to my
  pass.
    May I govern, &c.

With a courage undaunted, may I face my last
  day;
And when I am dead may the better sort say,
In the morning when sober, in the evening
  when mellow,
He's gone, and not left behind him his fellow!
    May I govern, &c.

Without any noise, when I've pass'd o'er the
  stage,
And decently acted what part fortune gave,
And put off my vest in a chearful old age,
  May a few honest fellows see me laid in my
  grave!
    May I govern, &c.

I care not whether under a turf or a stone,
With any inscription upon it, or none:
If a thousand years hence, Here lies W. P.
Shall be read on my tomb, what is it to me?
    May I govern, &c.

Yet one wish I add, for the sake of those few
  Who in reading these lines any pleasure shall
  take :

May I leave a good fame, and a sweet-smelling
  name.
Amen—Here an end of my wishes I make.
May I govern my passion with an absolute sway,
And grow wiser and better, as my strength
  wears away;
Without gout or stone, by a gentle decay!

SONG 315.

THE FORCE OF MUSIC.

WHEN Sappho tun'd the raptur'd strain,
  The listening wretch forgot his pain,
With art divine the lyre she strung,
  Like thee she play'd, like thee she sung.

For when she struck the quiv'ring wire,
  The eager breast was all on fire;
But when she tun'd the vocal lay,
  The captive soul was charm'd away!

SONG 316.

THE LOVER'S REQUEST.

TAKE, oh! take those lips away,
  That so sweetly were forsworn;
And those eyes, the break of day,
  Lights that do mislead the morn.
But my kisses give again,
Seals of love, tho' seal'd in vain.

Hide, oh! hide those hills of snow,
  Which thy frozen bosom bears;
On whose tops the pinks that grow,
  Are like those that April wears.
But from my tender bleeding heart,
Withdraw the arrow, ease the smart;
Offend no more great angry Jove,
But pity, since you cannot love!

SONG 317.

Sung at RANELAGH.

RECITATIVE.

A Wretch, long tortur'd with disdain,
  That ever pin'd, or pin'd in vain ;
At length the god of wine addrest,
Sure refuge of a wounded breast.

AIR.

Vouchsafe, O pow'r, thy healing aid,
Teach me to gain the cruel maid;
Thy juices take the lover's part,
Flush his wan looks, and chear his heart.

RECITATIVE.

To Bacchus thus the lover cry'd;
And thus the jolly god reply'd.

AIR.

Give whining o'er, be brisk and gay,
And quaff his sneaking form away ;
With dauntless mien approach the fair,
The way to conquer is—to dare.

RECITATIVE.

The fwain purfu'd the god's advice,
The nymph was now no longer nice.

AIR.

She fmil'd, and fpoke the fex's mind:
When we grow daring, you grow kind;
Men to themfelves are moft fevere,
And make us tyrants by their fear.

SONG 318.

Sung at RANELAGH.

AT Windfor, where Thames glides fo fweetly
    along,
Lives the wifh of my heart, the dear girl of my
    fong;
Her name all the day I with raptures repeat,
And am bleft when the fhepherds but talk of
    my Kate.

When my fair-one is by, the whole village is
    gay,
For 'tis fhe, not the fun, that enlivens the day:
The lads are all happy when round her they
    wait.
And the laffes learn beauty by watching my
    Kate.

Should I gain the pale lily, or blufh-painted rofe,
And with pinks and fweet woodbines a garland
    compofe,
More lovely to fight are her looks; and more
    fweet
Is the fragrance that dwells on the lips of my
    Kate.

Hufh! hufh! ye vain warblers, no more croud
    the fpray,
Nor think to divert with your love-liven'd lay;
With fuccefs each may tune the fhrill note to
    his mate,
But your notes are all harfh to the voice of my
    Kate.

As fhe fits on the bank by the fide of the ftream,
The birds, without fear, feed and play by the
    brim;
And why fhould they not? they can think no
    deceit,
Such truth is confef,'d in the looks of my Kate.

The fhepherds bring pofies of flow'rs, but the
    maid
Cries, Thefe are but emblems that I too muft
    fade:
But myrtles I'll bring, and in their happy date
Shew the unfading charms of the mind of my
    Kate.

SONG 319.

THE MAID OF THE MILL.

ATTEND all ye fhepherds and nymphs to
    my lay,
You may learn from my tale, and go wifer away;

A damfel once dwelt at the foot of a hill,
Well known by the name of the Maid of the
    Mill.

In her all the graces had jointly combin'd,
Her face to improve, and embellifh her mind;
Nor pride nor deceit e'er her bofom did fill,
'Twas nature alone in the maid of the mill:

The lord of the village beheld the fweet maid,
Each art to fubdue her was prefently laid:
With gold he endeavour'd to tempt her to ill;
But nought could prevail with the maid of the
    mill.

Her virtue fhe priz'd beyond fplendor or ftate;
Tho' poor, yet fhe never repin'd at her fate;
His proffers fhe flighted, in vain all his fkill
To ruin the fame of the maid of the mill.

Young Colin addrefs'd her with hope and with
    fear,
His heart was right honeft, his love was fincere;
With rapture his bofom each moment would
    thrill,
Whene'er he beheld his dear maid of the mill.

His paffion was founded on honour and truth,
The nymph read his heart, and of courfe lov'd
    the youth;
At church little Patty foon anfwer'd, I will;
His lordfhip was baulk'd of the maid of the mill.

What happinefs waits on the chafte nuptial pair?
Content, they are ftrangers to forrow and care;
The flame at firft rais'd in each other burns
    ftill,
And Colin is blefs'd with the maid of the mill.

SONG 320.

Sung in *Acis and Galatea*.

LOVE founds the alarm,
    And fear is a flying;
When beauty's the prize,
    What mortal fears dying?

In defence of my treafure
    I'll bleed at each vein;
Without her no pleafure,
    For life is a pain.

SONG 321.

Sung at VAUXHALL.

YE nymphs and ye fhepherds that join in the
    throng,
Pray tarry a while, and attend to my fong;
The ftory is fimple, tho' true, that I tell,
And I hope it will pleafe you all wonderful well.

I went t'other day to a wake on the green;
And met with a lafs fair as beauty's gay queen;
I afk'd for a kifs, but the damfel cry'd No!
And ftruggled and frown'd, and faid, Pray let
    me go.

I tenderly cry'd, Phillis, don't be a prude;
But ftill fhe return'd, I'll cry out if you're rude;

The more that I prefs'd her the more she cry'd
    No.
And ftruggled and frown'd, and faid, Pray let
    me go.
I found no entreaties would make her comply,
Whenever I touch'd her, 'twas, Fye, Colin,
    fye ;
So I fent for a parfon, and made her my wife,
And now I am welcome to kifs her for life.

Ye virgins that hear, learn example from this,
Take care how too freely you part with a kifs;
Conceal for a time all the favours you can,
For that's the beft way to make fure of a man.

SONG 322.

WHY fhould I now, my love, complain,
    That toil awaits thy chearful fwain;
Since labour oft a fweet beftows,
Which lazy fplendor never knows?

Hence fprings the purple tide of health,
The rich man's wifh, the poor man's wealth;
And fpreads thofe blufhes o'er the face,
Which come and go with native grace.

The pride of drefs, the pomp of fhew,
Are trappings, oft, that cover woe;
But we, whofe wifhes never roam,
Shall tafte of real joys at home !

SONG 323.
Sung at MARYBONE.

SINCE loft to peace of mind ferene,
    I drag my chain in fruitlefs hope,
I'll court each melancholy fcene,
    And give my forrows their full fcope.
My lovely, fprightly, gallant tar,
Who fports with fierce, deftructive war,
Think what I feel, where'er thou art,
Think of thy Mary's breaking heart.

Secure thy dancing caftle rides
    Upon the bofom of the deep,
The ftormy wind and wave abides,
    And navigation bids thee fleep;
But balmy fleep and downy reft
Shall fly the tempeft in thy breaft,
When jealous fears like mine fhall prove
The truth of my dear failor's love.

Hope, doubt, and fear, and winds and waves,
    More dreadful to the love-tofs'd mind,
Than thofe the fkilful feaman braves,
    Who leaves pale care and grief behind.
Th' adventurous maid embark'd like me,
That fails on fuch a troubled fea,
The ocean's rage would gladly meet,
And in his depths feek a retreat.

Yet, O be ftill, my frantic brain,
    Let reafon whifper to thy fears;
My failor may return again,
    Crown'd with fuccefs, to dry my tears;
When fame, with all her gaudy charms,
Shall yield him to my longing arms,

And one blefs'd hour together blend
The lover, hero, hufband, friend.

Britannia, hail! thou mighty queen;
    The ftrength, the power, the feas are thine;
Long may thy pow'r on juftice lean,
    To be preferv'd, they muft combine:
To courage fingly ne'er refort,
For virtue is thy true fupport;
'Tis that alone can ftrength maintain
Be virtuous, and for ever reign.

SONG 324.
Sung at VAUXHALL.

BY the fide of a ftream, at the foot of a hill,
    I met with young Phebe who lives at the
    mill;
My heart leapt with joy at fo pleafing a fight,
For Phebe, I vow, is my only delight.

I told her my love, and fat down by her fide,
And fwore the next morning I'd make her my
    bride;
In anger fhe faid, Get you out of my fight,
And go to your Phillis; you met her laft night.

Surpriz'd, I reply'd, Pray, explain what you
    mean?
I never, I vow, with young Phillis was feen;
Nor can I conceive what my Phebe is at.
Oh ! can't you? fhe cry'd; well, I love you for
    that.

Say, did you not meet her laft night on this
    fpot?
O Colin, O Colin, you can't have forgot;
I heard the whole ftory this morning from Mat,
You ftill may deny it, I love you for that.

'Tis falfe, I replied; deareft Phebe believe,
For Mat is a rover, and means to deceive ;
You very well know he has ruin'd young Pat,
And furely my charmer muft hate him for that.

Come, come then, fhe cry'd, if you mean to
    be kind,
I'll own 'twas to know the true ftate of your
    mind :
Tranfported I kifs'd her, fhe gave me a pat,
I made her my wife, and fhe loves me for that.

SONG 325.
THE CHARMS OF THE BOTTLE.

YE mortals, whom trouble and forrow attend,
    Whofe life is a feries of pain without end,
For ever depriv'd of Hope's all-chearing ray,
Ne'er know what it is to be happy a day;
Obey the glad fummons, the bar-bell invites,
Drink deep, and I warrant it fets you to rights.

When poverty enters, an unwelcome gueft,
By hard-hearted duns too con.inually preft,
When brats begin crying and fqualling for bread,
And wife's never filent till faft in her bed;
    Obey the glad fummons, &c.

Did Neptune's falt element run with frefh wine,
Tho' all Europe's powers together combine,
Our brave Britifh failors need ne'er care a jot,
Surroundéd by plenty of fuch rare grape-fhot.
' Obey the glad fummons, &c.

Was each dull, pedantical, text-fpinning vicar,
To leave off dry preaching, and flick to his li-
   quor,
O how would he wifh for that power divine,
To change, when he would, fimple water to wine!
   Obey the glad fummons, &c.

If wine, then, can miracles work fuch as thefe,
And give to the troubl'd mind comfort and eafe,
Defpair not, that bleffing in Bacchus you'll find,
Who fhowers his gifts for the good of mankind.
Obey the glad fummons, the bar-bell invites;
Drink deep, and I warrant it fets you to rights.

S O N G   326.

A GLASS OF GOOD WINE.

MY merry companions, fo jovial and free,
   You know I'm a poet, then liften to me,
Infpire my mufe, jolly Bacchus divine,
I'll chant in the praife of a glafs of good wine.

The female whofe flattering looking-glafs tells
How much all the reft of her fex fhe excels,
In vain from it's aid may attempt to outfhine;
More charms fhe'd receive from a glafs of good
   wine.

The fhort-fighted fpark with perfpective ap-
   ply'd,
In putting the fair to the blufh takes a pride;
Give o'er, bold intruder, your cruel defign,
Greater beauties you'll find in glafs of good
   wine.

Old bald-pated time, who good company fpoils,
When pleafure is reigning and good-humour
   fmiles,
With us round the bowl would moft chearfully
   join,
Was his hour-glafs chang'd to a glafs of good
   wine.

If, then, fuch perfections the grape does produce,
Ye powers above fend enough for our ufe;
Your bounty to prove drain the fea of it's wine,
And let it again ebb and flow with good wine.

S O N G   327.

ACHILLES AND PATROCLUS.

A CANTATA.

R E C I T A T I V E.

WHEN ftern Achilles left the Grecian band,
   And orders gave to feek his native land;
Juft as the naval fleet prepar'd to go,
Patroclus ftrove Achilles' grief to know.
Whence comes that figh——why heaves thy
   manly breaft,
What fiend invidious robs my friend of reft?

Divine Achilles, let Patroclus know,
For friends fhould always fhare in private woe!
Enough, Achilles faid—moft noble youth,
From thee, alas! who can conceal the truth!

AIR.

Know then, my friend, ungrateful Greece
   This day demands my Brifeis fair;
And I alas! no more fhall ceafe
   To be immers'd in endlefs care.
But mark, ye gods, fhould Hector carnage fpread,
Unmov'd Achilles will fmile o'er the dead.

RECITATIVE.

Patroclus heard, while tears half drown his
   eyes?
And could you fee your country bleed? he
   cries;
Could you relentlefs to the prayer of all,
See Hector triumph in the Grecian's fall?
Behold! they fly—to parly is difgrace;
Lend me your armour, I'll the danger face:
Hector himfelf will be alarm'd with fears,
When in the front thy blazing creft appears;
Achilles like, I'll fee my country freed,
Or bravely in the glorious combat bleed,

AIR.

Omnipotent Jove,
   And ye powers above,
From danger great Achilles fhield:
   While I, undifmay'd,
   In his armour array'd,
Seek peril and death in the field.
   Adieu then, my friend,
   I'll ftrive to defend
Thofe princes Achilles did fhield:
   Oh! may I, like you,
   Great Hector fubdue,
Or breathlefs be ftretch'd in the field.

RECITATIVE.

Alternate griefs Achilles bofom rend,
He fcarce can fay, Farewel, adieu, my friend.
Patroclus clad in godlike armour bright,
Each Trojan trembles at the boding fight.
The fight began; but oh! the fates decreed,
Patroclus for ungrateful Greece fhould bleed.
He fell—yet ere an herald could difclofe
What caufe Achilles had for inward woes,
The godlike warrior the fad tidings guefs'd,
And thus the anguifh of his foul exprefs'd.

AIR.

My friend, I conceive, by the afpect you wear,
   Your meffage my peace may deftroy!
But Achilles is proof againft forrow and care,
   And never again will know joy.
If Patroclus is dead, oh! ye powers divine,
   The hand that depriv'd him of breath,
Let it feel, in return, the vengeance of mine,
   And death be aton'd for in death.

Once more, in the field, cruel Hector fhall find
   Achilles his valour will try;
Achilles will prove him, no fkulking behind
   Shall enable the traitor to fly.

Then grant, potent Jove, fince Patroclus is flain,
This arm may the wretch's blood fpill;
When re-enge is comoleat, on yon hoftile plain,
Do with me, great Jove, what you will.

SONG 328.

Sung in *Love in a Village.*

GENTLE youth, ah! tell me why,
  Still you force me thus to fly.
Ceafe, oh! ceafe to perfevere;
Speak not what I muft not hear:
To my heart it's eafe reftore;
Go, and never fee me more.

SONG 329.

THE HAPPY SHEPHERD; A PASTORAL.

Written by Mr. HAWKINS.

HOW happy a fhepherd am I,
  With Laura, the pride of my heart!
I'll never more languifh nor figh,
  For know, fhe has cur'd all my fmart:
She vows that fhe will be my wife,
  By all that is honeft and fair;
Then I'll be her hufband for life,
  And never know forrow nor care.

Brother fhepherds, who toil on the plain,
  By me take example, I pray;
Throw off all your trouble and pain,
  And ever be chearful and gay.
Then, nymphs, who are modeft and fhy,
  For once hear young Damon's advice,
The reafon I tell you for why,
  As happy you'll be in a trice.

Give each of your hands to your fwain,
  Then drive away faction and ftrife;
Bid adieu to all anguifh and pain,
  And be happy the reft of your life.
Such is Damon's advice, my kind fair,
  Then take it moft freely, I pray;
So fly from all forrow and care,
  Henceforward be merry and gay.

SONG 330.

WINE AND MUSIC: A CANTATA.

RECITATIVE.

AS I fat joyous in a pleafant room,
  Where none but choiceft fpirits ever come,
A fong was call'd; filence aloud proclaim,
For mirth and joy was ev'ry hum'rift's aim:
Up ftarts a genius, and he thus began,
Hoping to pleafe each focial fon;
To wine and mufic he addrefs'd his fong,
In words like thefe, or thefe, he fung:

AIR.

O bring me mufic, bring me wine,
  Go fill the fprightly bowl:
'Tis only wine and mufic can
  Relieve the wounded foul.

Apollo, tune thy trembling lyre;
  Great Bacchus, found thy tun;
And while thou doft the chorus fill,
  Our joys can ne'er be done.

Then take the cup and fill it high,
  Such joys to us belong;
Then let us all with chearful hearts
  Invoke the god of fong.
Come, god of mirth and revelry,
  Come bring thy merry round,
And fh-w the cynic fool, that he
  Such joys has never found.

Sacred to mirth, this fpot, my friends,
  Ye focial fons decree;
Let us, then, confecrate this night
  To wit and jollity:
Come let the cup with wine o'erflow;
  The bottle pufh about;
Come fill, my brother bloods around,
  The ftarry liquor out.

SONG 331.

SHEPHERD, would'ft thou here obtain
  Pleafure unally'd with pain,
Joy that fuits the rural fphere,
Gentle fhepherd, lend an ear:
  Artlefs deed, and fimple drefs,
  Mark the chofen fhepherdefs.

Learn to relifh calm delight,
Verdant vales, and fountains bright;
Trees that nod on floping hills,
Caves that echo, tink'ling rills.
  Artlefs deed, &c.

If thou canft no charm difclofe
In the fimpleft bud that blows,
Go, forfake thy plain and fold,
Join the crowd, and toil for gold.
  Artlefs deed, &c.

Tranquil pleafures never cloy;
Banifh each tumultuous joy;
All but love—for love infpires
Fonder wifhes, warmer fires.
  Artlefs deed, &c.

Love, and all it's joys, be thine;
Yet, ere thou the reins refign,
Hear what reafon feems to fay,
Hear attentive, and obey.
  Artlefs deed, &c.

Crimfon leaves the rofe adorn,
But beneath them lurks the thorn;
Fair and flow'ry is the brake,
Yet it hides the vengeful fnake.
  Artlefs deed, &c.

Think not fhe, whofe empty pride
Dares the fleecy garb decide;
Thinks not fhe, who, light and vain,
Scorns the fheep, can love the fwain.
  Artlefs deed, &c.

Let not lucre, let not pride,
Draw thee from fuch charms afide;

M

Have not thofe their proper fphere?
Gentler paffions triumph here.
    Artlefs deed, &c.

See, to fweeten thy repofe,
The bloffom buds, the fountain flows,
Lo, to crown thy healthful board,
All that milk and fruits afford.
    Artlefs deed, &c.

Seek no more—the reft's in vain;
Pleafure, ending foon in pain;
Anguifh, lightly gilded o'er;
Clofe thy wifh, and feek no more.
    Artlefs deed, &c.

SONG 332.

AS griev'd Britannia ey'd the main,
    Deploting there her loft command,
(Her trade deftroy'd, her children flain)
    And wet with briny tears the fand;
The world's recorder, Time, appears,
And thus the drooping matron chears.

Why, Albion's genius, this difmay,
    Thefe trickling tears, this vifage fodden?
Where are your fmiles to hail the day,
    That William fav'd thee at Cuiloden?
Difpel thy fears, and with thy fmiles
Enliven this bleft queen of ifles.

When William fought, and Charles gave way,
    Is this the day? fhe rofe and faid,
Is this the happy, glorious day,
    When freedom triumph'd, flav'ry fled?
Oh! be this day for ever bleft,
Which gave to frighted Albion reft.

As when fome ravifher alone
    Has caught a fair incautious maid,
Intent his beaftly will to crown;
    She cries for, but defpairs of aid:
When ftraight the much-lov'd youth appears,
The favage kills, and ends her fears.

Like her, by Charles and flavery caught,
    I cry'd for aid and liberty:
William, like him, arofe and fought,
    And fet his beft lov'd miftrefs free.
For this may ftill the hero's name
Be foremoft in the lifts of fame.

Would all, like him, my caufe maintain,
    Making my weal their chiefeft care,
Soon fhould they humble France and Spain,
    And Europe learn again to fear:
Br tain her Empire then fhould fee
Enduring, mighty Time, with thee.

SONG 333.

A PASTORAL.

Sung at RANELAGH.

OH, Damon, believe not your Jenny's untrue,
    Nor think that fhe's falfe and inconftant
        to you;
Think yon tow'ring mount of itfelf fhall remove,
Ere, Damon, you doubt of the truth of my love.

Yon clear cryftal ftream fhall the mountains
        o'erflow,
And on the hard rock the pale primrofe fhall
        blow;
In queft of the lion the lamb'.in fhall range,
Ere Jenny's fix'd paffion fhall leffen or change.

Upon the fmooth green, when the fhepherds
        advance,
To hail May's return, with the tabor and
        dance.
If Damon is abfent, I quit the glad throng,
And join my complaints to the nightingale's
        fong.

The pain which I fuffer my flock feems to know,
And frolick and play as to leffen my woe;
I cry, Ceafe, dear lambkins, your fporting and
        play,
You cannot delight while my Damon's away.

No toil fhall difcomfort while Damon's in fight,
The fun s piercing rays can in fummer delight;
And winter's rude tempefts fhall ftill find me
        gay,
For, bleft with my fhepherd, each month will
        be May.

SONG 334.

A CANTATA.

Sung at RANELAGH.

RECITATIVE.

ALL in her fair fequefter'd cell,
    Where happinefs was wont to dwell,
Contentment fat, with down-caft look;
And thefe, or words like thefe, fhe fpoke:
Genius of Albion! wake thy queen,
Lo, Gallia clouds the peaceful fcene!
Bid her arife, her wrongs to fee,
Protect herfelf, and cherifh me.

Britannia, alarm'd at Contentment's requeft,
In a voice that confefs'd her, her people addreft.

AIR.

Caft the olive wreath off! arm, ye Britons,
        advance!
Sound the trump! beat the drum!—point your
        thunder at France!
By defiance convince 'em their efforts are vain,
For that George, King of England, is king of
        the main;
And that great, like your fathers, thofe heroes
        of old,
As you're born to be free, you've the fenfe to
        be bold.

SONG 335.

WHEN hope was quite funk in defpair,
    My heart it was going to break,
My life appear'd worthlefs my care,
    But now I will fav't for thy fake.

Where'er my love travels by day,
    Wherever he lodges by night,

With me his dear image fhall ftay,
And my foul keep him ever in fight.

With patience I'll wait the long year,
And ftudy the gentleft charms,
Hope time away till thou appear,
To lock thee for ay in my arms.

Whilft thou waft a fhepherd I priz'd
No higher degree in this life,
But now I'll endeavour to rife
To a height that's becoming a wife.

For beauty, that's only fkin deep,
Muft fade like the gowans in May,
But inwardly rooted will keep
For ever without a decay.

Nor age nor the changes of life
Can quench the fair fire of love,
If virtue's ingrain'd in the wife,
And the hufband have fenfe to approve.

SONG 336.

Sung at VAUXHALL.

I Have rambled, I own it, whole years up and
down,
And figh'd o'er each beautiful nymph of the
town;
Such fancies have plagu'd me, that oft in my
life
I've been ready to ftart at the name of a wife.

But afham'd of my fears that have oft broke
my reft,
And wearied with roving, both cloy'd and un-
bleft;
I'll try to be happy the reft of my life,
And venture, tho' late, yet at laft, on a wife.

Then farewel the jilt, and the fool, and the
bold,
I quit you with pleafure before I grow old;
One girl of my heart i will take to for life,
And enough, of all confcience, I hold, is one
wife.

I'll fearch the town over this fair one to find,
Nor fickle, nor jealous, nor vain, nor unkind;
Whofe wit and good-humour may hold out
for life;
And then, if fhe'll have me, I'll make her my
wife.

'Tis time that the follies of life had an end,
And foon, nay, this inftant, I'm ready to mend:
What wonder there ll be at fo alter'd a life!
If your're wife, you, like me, will refoire on a
wife.

SONG 337.

Sung at VAUXHALL.

NIGHT, to lovers joys a friend,
Swiftly thy affiftance lend;
Lock up envious, feeing day,
Bring the willing youth away;

Hafte, and fpeed the tedious hour,
To the fecret happy bow'r;
Then, my heart, for blifs prepare,
Thyrfis furely will be there.

See the hateful day is gone,
Welcome evening now comes on;
Soon to meet my dear I fly,
None but love fhall then be by;
None fhall dare to venture near,
To tell the plighted vows they hear;
Parting thence will be the pain,
But we'll part to meet again.

Don't you feel a pleafing fmart,
Gently ftealing to your heart?
Fondly hope, and fondly figh?
For, my fhepherd, oft do I;
With in Hymen's bands to join,
I'll be yours, and you be mine?
Tell me, Thyrfis, tell me this,
Tell me, then, and tell me yes.

Farewel, loit'ring idle day!
To my dear I hie away;
On the wings of love I go,
He the ready way will fhow:
Peace, my breaft, nor danger fear;
Love and Thyrfis both are near;
'Tis the youth! I'm fure 'tis he!
Night, how much I owe to thee!

SONG 338.

BEAUTEOUS nymph, approve the flame
Thy merit rais'd within my breaft,
Let ev'ry tender thought proclaim
How much I love, and how diftrefs'd:
Since words themfelves want energy to prove
What Damon fuffers by capricious love.

Supprefs not, then, the pleafing thought,
Which thy foft nature muft advance,
Nor blufh if in the conteft caught,
The pureft minds have fell by chance;
Then deign, Belinda, generous and kind,
To fmile compliance on the humble mind.

SONG 339.

FRIENDSHIP AND WINE.

Sung at VAUXHALL.

LET the grave, and the gay,
Enjoy life how they may,
My pleafures their pleafures furpafs;
Go the world well or ill,
'Tis the fame with me ftill,
If I have but my friend and my glafs.

The lover may figh,
The courtier may lie,
And Crœfus his treafure amafs;
All the joys are but vain,
That are blended with pain;
So I'll ftand by my friend and my glafs.

New life wine infpires,
And creates new defires,
And oft wins the lover his lafs,

Or his courage prepares
To difdain the nymph's airs;
So I'll ftand by my friend and my glafs.

The earth fucks the rain,
The fun draws the main,
With the earth we are all in a clafs;
Then enliven the clay,
Let us live while we may,
And I'll ftand by my friend and my glafs.

'Tis friendfhip and wine,
Only, life can refine:
We care not whate'er comes to pafs
With courtiers, or great men,
There's none of us ftatefmen:
Come, here's to our friend and our glafs.

SONG 340.

Sung at VAUXHALL.

A S I went to the wake that is held on the
    green,
I met with young Phebe, as blithe as a queen;
A form fo divine might an anchoret move,
And I found (tho' a clown) I was fmitten with
    love;
So I afk'd for a kifs, but fhe, blufhing, reply'd,
Indeed, gentle fhepherd, you muft be deny'd.

Lovely Phebe, I cry'd, don't affect to be fhy,
I vow I will kifs you—here's nobody by;
No matter for that, fhe reply d, 'tis the fame;
For know, filly fhepherd, I value my fame:
So pray let me go, I fh ll furely be mifs'd;
Befides, I'm refolv'd that I will not be kifs'd.

Lord blefs me! I cry'd, I m furpriz'd you re-
    fufe;
A few harmlefs kiffes but ferve to amufe:
The month it is May, and the feafon for love,
So come, my dear girl, to the wake let us rove.
No, Damon, fhe cry'd, I muft firft be your wife,
You then fhall be welcome to kifs me for life.

Well, come then, I cry'd, to the church let
    us go,
But after dear Phebe muft never fay no.
Do you prove but true, (fhe reply c) you fhall
    find
I'll ever be conftant, good-humour'd and kind.
So I kifs when I pleafe, for the ne'er fays fhe
    wo 't,
And I kifs her fo much that I wonder fhe don't.

SONG 341.

THE MODEST QUESTION.

C AN love be controul'd by advice,
    Can madnefs and reafon agree?
O Molly; who'd ever be wife,
    If madnefs is loving of thee?
Let fages pretend to defpife
    The joys they want fpirits to tafte;
Let me feize old Time as he flies,
    And the bleffings of life while they laft.

Dull wifdom but adds to our cares;
    Brifk love will improve ev'ry joy;
Too foon we may meet with grey hairs,
    Too late may repent being coy:
Then, Molly, for what fhould we ftay
    Till our beft blood begins to run cold;
Our youth we can have but to-day;
    We may always find time to grow old.

SONG 342.

Sung in Midas.

L OVELY nymph, affuage my anguifh,
    At your feet a tender fwain
Prays you will not let him languifh;
    One kind look wou'd eafe his pain.

Did you know the lad that courts
    You, he not long need fue in vain;
Prince of fong, of dance, of fports,
    You fcarce will meet his like again.

SONG 343.

Sung in the Maid of the Mill.

W HEN you meet a tender creature,
    Neat in I mb, and fair in feature,
Full of kindnefs and good-nature;
    Prove as kind again to fhe.
Happy mortal! to poffefs her,
In your bofom warm and prefs her,
Morning, noon, and night, carefs her,
    And be fond as fond can be.

But if one you meet that's froward,
Saucy, jilting, and untoward,
Shou'd you act the whining coward,
    'Tis to mend her ne'er the whit.
Nothing's tough enough to bind her;
Then agog when once you find her,
Let her go, and never mind her;
    Heart alive, you're fairly quit.

SONG 344.

Sung at SADLER'S WELLS.

M Y dog and my miftrefs are both of a kind,
    As fickle as fancy, inconftant as wind;
My dog follows ev'ry ftrange heel in the ftreets,
And my miftrefs as fond of each fellow fhe
    meets;
Yet, in fpite of her arts, I'll not make the leaft
    ftrife,
But be cherry, and merry, and happy thro' life.

Go Mifs where fhe will, and whenever fhe
    pleafe,
Her conduct fhall ne'er my philofophy teaze;
Her fried m fhall never embitter my glee,
One woman's the fame as another to me.
So, in fpite of her airs, I'll not make the leaft
    ftrife,
But be cherry, and merry, and happy thro' life.

I laugh at the wretches who ftupidly pine
For falfe-hearted gipfeys they title divine;

At worſt of my love-fits no phyſic I aſk,
But that which is found in the bowl or the
 flaſk.
For go things how they will, I'll not make the
 leaſt ſtrife,
But be cherry, and merry, and happy thro' life.

The girl that behaves with good-humour and
 ſenſe,
Shall ſtill to my heart have the warmeſt pre-
 tence;
And for thoſe who would ji't me, deceive, and
 betray,
In honeſter bumpers I'll waſh them away.
'Tis my final reſolve, not to make the leaſt ſtrife,
But be cherry, and merry, and happy thro' life.

SONG 345.

Sung in *Thomas and Sally*.

THE May-day of life is for p'eaſure,
 For ſinging, for dancing, and ſhow;
Then why will you waſte ſuch a treaſure,
 In ſighing and crying—Heigho!

Let's copy the bird in the meadows,
 By h r's tune your pipe when 'tis low;
Fly round and coquette it as ſhe does,
 And never ſit crying—Heigho!

Though, when in the arms of a lover,
 It ſometimes may happen, I know,
That, ere all our toying is over,
 We cannot help crying—Heigho!

In age ev'ry one a new part takes;
 I find to my ſorrow 'tis ſo:
When old, you may cry till your heart aches,
 And no one will mind you—Heigho!

SONG 346.

ADVICE TO THE FAIR-SEX.

Sung at VAUXHALL.

FORGIVE, ye fair, nor take it wrong,
 If aught too much I do;
Permit me, while I give my ſong,
 To give a leſſon too:
Let modeſty, that heav'n-born maid,
 Your works and actions grace;
'Tis this, and only this, can add
 New luſtre to your face.

'Tis this which paints the virgin cheeks
 Beyond the power of art;
And every real bluſh beſpeaks
 The goodneſs of the heart.
This index of the virtuous mind
 Your lovers will adore;
'Tis this will leave a charm behind,
 When bloom can charm no more.

Inſpir'd by this, to idle men
 With nice reſerv behave;
And learn, by diſtance, to maintain
 The pow'r your beauty gave:
For this, when beauty muſt decay,
 Your empire will protect;

The wanton pleaſes for a day,
 But ne'er creates reſpect.
With this their ſilly jeſts reprove,
 When coxcombs dare intrude;
Nor think the man is worth your love,
 Who ventures to be rude:
Your charms, when cheap, will ever pall;
 They ſully with a touch;
And tho we mean to grant not all,
 We often grant too much. .

But patient let each virtuous fair
 Expect the gen'rous youth,
Whom heav'n has doom'd her heart to ſhare,
 And bleſs'd with love and truth;
For him alone preſerve her hand,
 And wait the happy day,
When he with juſtice can command,
 And ſhe with joy obey.

SONG 347.

IANTHE the lovely, the joy of the plain,
 By Iphis was lov'd, and lov'd Iphis again;
She liv'd in the youth, and the youth in the
 fair;
Their pleaſure was equal, and equal their care;
No time nor enjoyment their dotage withdrew,
But the longer they liv'd ſtill the fonder they
 grew.

A paſſion ſo happy alarm'd all the plain:
Some envy'd the nymph; but more envy'd the
 ſwain.
Some ſwore 'twould be pity their loves to in-
 vade;
That the lovers alone for each other were made:
Bu all, all conſented that none ever knew
A nymph yet ſo kind, or a ſhepherd ſo true.

Love ſaw them with pleaſure, and vow'd to
 take care
Of the faithful, the tender, the innocent pair:
What either did want he bid either to move;
But they wanted nothing but ever to love:
Said 'twas all that to pleaſe them his god-head
 cou'd do,
That they ſtill might be kind, and ſtill might
 be true.

SONG 348.

DAMON AND PHILLIS.

DAMON.

WHEN Phillis was faithful, and fond as
 ſhe's fair,
With a chaplet of roſes I braided my hair;
But the willow, ſad ſhepherd, muſt ſhadow thy
 brow,
For Phillis no 'onger remembers her vow.
To the groves, with fond Colin, my ſhepherdeſs
 flies,
While Damon diſturbs the ſtill plains with his
 ſighs.

PHILLIS.

Bethink thee, falfe Damon, before you upbraid,
When Phebe's fair lambkins had yefterday
   ftray'd,
Thro' the woodlands you wander'd, poor Phillis
   forgot,
And drove the gay ramblers quite home to her
   cot;
But a fwain fo deceitful no damfel can prize,
'Tis Phebe, not Phillis, lays claim to your
   fighs.

DAMON.

Like fummer's gay feafon young Phebe was
   kind,
And her manners were graceful, untainted her
   mind;
Though the fweets of contentment her cottage
   adorn,
Tho' fhe's frefh as the rofe-bud, and fair as
   the morn,
Tho' fhe fmiles like Pomona—thofe fmiles I'd
   refign,
Would Phillis be faithful, and deign to be mine.

PHILLIS.

On his pipe though blithe Colin fo prettily
   plays,
Though he fings fuch fweet fonnets, and writes
   in my praife,
Tho' he chofe me his true-love laft Valentine's
   day,
When birds fat like bridegrooms all pair'd on
   the fpray,
I could drive the gay fhepherd far far from my
   mind,
If Damon, the rover, were conftant and kind.

DAMON.

Fine folks, my dear Phillis, may revel and range,
But how fleeting the pleafure that's founded
   on change!
The villager's cottage fuch happinefs brings,
That peafants with pity may look upon kings.

PHILLIS.

To the church then let's haften, our tranfports
   to bind,
And Phillis will always prove conftant and kind.

DAMON.

To the church then let's haften, our tranfports
   to bind,
And Damon will always prove conftant and kind.

SONG 349.

O Lovely maid! how dear thy pow'r!
   At once I love, at once adore;
With wonder are my thoughts poffeft,
While fofteft love infpires my breaft:
This tender look, thefe eyes of mine,
Confefs their am'rous mafter thine;
Thefe eyes with Strephon's paffion play,
Firft make me love, and then betray.

Yes, charming victor, I am thine;
Poor as it is, this heart of mine
Was never in another's pow'r,
Was never pierc'd by love before:
In thee I've treafur'd up my joy;
Thou can'ft give blifs, or blifs deftroy:
And thus I've bound myfelf to love,
While blifs or mifery can move.

Oh! fhou'd I ne'er poffefs thy charms,
Ne'er meet my comfort in thy arms;
Were hopes of dear enjoyment gone,
Still wou'd I love, love thee alone;
But, like fome difcontented fhade,
That wanders where it's body's laid,
Mournful I'd roam with hollow glare,
For ever exil'd from my fair.

SONG 350.

THE hounds are all out, and the morning
   does deep;
Why, how now, you fluggardly fot!
How can you, how can you lie fnoring afleep,
   While we all on horfeback are got,
      My brave boys?

I cannot get up, for the over-night's cup
   So terribly lies in my head;
Befides, my wife cries, My dear, do not rife,
   But cuddle me longer in bed,
      My dear boy.

Come, on with your boots, and faddle your
   mare,
   Nor tire us with longer delay;
The cry of the hounds, and the fight of the
   hare,
   Will chace all dull vapours away,
      My brave boys.

SONG 351.

Sung in *Lethe.*

YE mortals, whom fancies and troubles per-
   plex,
Whom folly mifguides, and infirmities vex ;
Whofe lives hardly know what it is to be bleft;
Who rife without joy, and lie down without
   reft;
Obey the glad fummons, to Lethe repair,
Drink deep of the ftream, and forget all your
   care.

Old maids fhall forget what they wifh for in
   vain,
And young ones the rover they cannot regain;
The rake fhall forget how laft night he was
   cloy'd,
And Chloe again be with paffion enjoy'd:
Obey then the fummons, to Lethe repair,
And drink an oblivion to trouble and care.

The wife at one draught may forget all her
   wants,
Or drench a fond fool to forget her gallants;

The troubled in mind fhall go chearful away,
And yefterday's wretch be quite happy to-day:
Obey then the fummons, to Lethe repair,
Drink deep of the ftream, and forget all
    your care.

SONG 352.

MUSIC has pow'r to melt the foul;
    By beauty nature's fway'd;
Each can the univerfe controul,
    Without the other's aid.

But here together both appear,
    And force united try;
Mufic enchants the lift'ning ear,
    And beauty charms the eye.

What cruelty thefe pow'rs to join!
    Thefe tranfports who can bear?
Oh! let the found be lefs divine,
    Or look the nymph lefs fair!

SONG 353.

FROM morning till night, and wherever I
    go,
Young Colin purfues me, though ftill I fay no;
Ye matrons experienc'd, inform me, I pray,
In a point, that's fo critical, what fhall I fay?

Soft fonnets he makes on my beauty and wit,
Such praifes a bofom that's tender muft hit;
He vows that he'll love me for ever and aye:
In a point, that's fo critical, what can I fay?

He brought me a garland, the fweeteft e'er feen,
And, faluting me, call'd me his heart's little
    queen;
In my breaft, like a bird, I found fomething
    play;
Inftruct a young virgin, then, what fhe muft fay.

But vain my petition, you heed not my call,
But leave me unguarded, to ftand or to fall;
No more I'll folicit, no longer I'll pray;
Let prudence inform me in what I fhall fay.

When next he approaches with care in his
    eye,
If he afks me to wed, I vow I'll comply;
At church he may take me for ever and aye,
And, I warrant you, then I fhall know what to
    fay.

SONG 354.

THE VINDICATION.

Sung at VAUXHALL.

THE wicked wits, as fancy hits,
    All fatirize the fair;
In profe and rhyme, and ftrains fublime,
    Their foibles they declare:

The kind are bold, the chafte are cold;
    Thefe prudifh, thofe too free:
Ye curious men, come tell us, then,
    What fhould a woman be?

But hard's the tafk, and vain to afk,
    Where optics are untrue;
The mufe fhall here th'indicted clear,
    And prove the crimes on you:
The rake is cloy'd, when fhe's enjoy'd
    On whom his wifh was plac'd;
The fool, deny'd, affects the pride,
    And rails, to be in tafte.

But, not like thefe, the men of blifs
    Their fure criterion fix:
No; wifdom cries, My fons, arife,
    And vindicate the fex:
'Tis theirs to prove thofe fweets of love
    Which others never fhare;
And evidence, that none have fenfe
    But who adore the fair.

Ye blooming race, with ev'ry grace
    Celeftially impreft,
'Tis yours to quell the cares that dwell
    Within the human breaft!
At beauty's voice our fouls rejoice,
    And rapture wakes to birth;
And Jove defign'd th'enchanting kind
    To form an Heav'n on earth.

Oh! ev'ry art, to win the heart,
    Ye dear infpirers try;
Each native charm with fafhion arm,
    And let love's lightning fly:
And hence, ye grave, your counfels fave,
    Which youth but fets at nought;
For woman ftill will have her will,
    And fo I think fhe ought.

SONG 355.

NOW the hill-tops are burnifh'd with azure
    and gold,
And the profpect around us moft bright to be-
    hold;
The hounds are all trying the mazes to trace,
The fteeds are all neighing, and pant for the
    chace.
Then roufe each true fportfman, and join, at
    the dawn,
The fong of the hunters and found of the horn.

Health braces the nerves, and gives joy to the
    face,
Whilft over the heath we purfue the fleet chace;
See the downs now we leave, and the coverts
    appear,
As eager we follow the fox or the hare.
    Then roufe, &c.

Wherever we go pleafure waits on us ftill,
If we fink in the valley, or rife on the hill;
O'er hedges and rivers we valiantly fly,
For, fearlefs of death, we ne'er think we fhall die.
    Then roufe, &c.

From ages long paſt, by the poets we're told,
That hunting was lov'd by the ſages of old;
That the ſoldier and huntſman were both on
    a par,
And the health-giving chace made them bold
    in the war.
    Then rouſe, &c.

When the chace is once over, away to the
    bowl,
The full-flowing bumpers ſhall chear up the
    ſoul;
Whilſt, jocund, our ſongs ſhall with choruſſes
    ring,
And toaſts to our laſſes, our country, and king.
    Then rouſe, &c.

SONG 356.

THE COUNTRY WEDDING.

Sung at RANELAGH.

WELL met, pretty nymph, ſays a jolly
    young ſwain,
To a beautiful ſhepherdeſs, croſſing the plain;
Why ſo much in haſte? (now the month it was
    May)
Shall I venture to aſk you, fair maiden, which
    way?
Then ſtraight to this queſtion the nymph did
    reply,
With a ſmile on her look, and a leer in her eye,
I came from the village, and homeward I go;
And now, gentle ſhepherd, pray why wou'd you
    know?

I hope, pretty maid, you won't take it amiſs,
If I tell you the reaſon of aſking you this;
I wou'd ſee you ſafe home, (now the ſwain was
    in love)
Of ſuch a companion if you wou'd approve.
Your offer, kind ſhepherd, is civil, I own;
But I ſee no great danger in going alone:
Nor yet can I hinder; the road being free
For one as another, for you or for me.

No danger in going alone, it is true;
But yet a companion is pleaſanter too;
And if you could like (now the ſwain he took
    heart)
Such a ſweetheart as me, why we never wou'd
    part:
Oh! that's a long word, ſaid the ſhepherdeſs
    then;
I've often heard ſay, there's no minding you
    men;
You'll ſay and unſay, and you'll flatter 'tis true,
Then leave a young maiden the firſt thing
    you do.

Oh! judge not ſo harſhly, the ſhepherd repiy'd,
To prove what I ſay, I will make you my bride;
To-morrow the parſon (well ſaid, little ſwain)
Shall join both our hands, and make one of us
    twain;

Then what the nymph anſwer'd to this is not
    ſaid;
But the very next morn to be ſure they were wed:
Sing hey diddle, ho diddle, hey diddle down,
O when ſhall we ſee ſuch a wedding in town?

SONG 357.

Sung in the *Jubilee.*

BEHOLD this fair goblet, 'twas carv'd from
    the tree,
Which, oh! my ſweet Shakeſpeare, was planted
    by thee;
As a relick I kiſs it, and bow at thy ſhrine;
What comes from thy hand muſt be ever
    divine.
    All ſhall yield to the mulberry-tree;
       Bend to thee
       Bleſs'd mulberry;
       Matchleſs was he
       Who planted thee,
    And thou, like him, immortal ſhalt be.

Ye trees of the foreſt ſo rampant and high,
Who ſpread round your branches, whoſe heads
    ſweep the ſky;
Ye curious exotics, whom taſte has brought
    here,
To root out the natives at prices ſo dear:
    All ſhall yield, &c.

The oak is held royal, is Britain's great boaſt,
Preſerv'd once our King, and will always our
    coaſt:
Of the fir we make ſhips: there are thouſands
    that fight,
But one, only one, like our Shakeſpeare can
    write.
    All ſhall yield, &c.

Let Venus delight in her gay myrtle bow'rs,
Pomona in fruit-trees, and Flora in flow'rs;
The garden of Shakeſpeare all fancies will ſuit,
With the ſweeteſt of flow'rs, and the faireſt of
    fruit.
    All ſhall yield, &c.

With learning and knowledge the well-letter'd
    birch
Supplies law and phyſic, and grace for the
    church;
But law and the goſpel in Shakeſpeare we find,
He gives the beſt phyſic for body and mind.
    All ſhall yield, &c.

The fame of the patron gives fame to the tree;
From him and his merits this takes it's degree:
Give Phœbus and Bacchus their laurel and
    vine,
The tree of our Shakeſpeare is ſtill more
    divine.
    All ſhall yield, &c.

As the genius of Shakeſpeare outſhines the
    bright day,
More rapture than wine to the heart can
    convey;

So the tree which he planted, by making his
 own,
Has the laurel and bays, and the vine, all in one.
 All shall yield, &c.

Then each take a relic of this hollow tree,
From folly and fashion a charm let it he;
Let's fill to the planter the cup to the brim,
To honour your country, do honour to him.
 All shall yield, &c.

SONG 358.

Sung in *Cymon*.

IF pure are the springs of the fountain,
 As purely the river will flow;
If noxious the stream from the mountain,
 It poisons the valley below:
  So of vice, or of virtue, possest,
  The throne makes the nation,
  Thro' ev'ry gradation,
  Or wretched, or blest.

SONG 359.

THE HAPPY SHEPHERDESS; A PASTORAL.

Written by Mr. HAWKINS.

SINCE Jockey of late is so kind,
 My poor panting heart is at rest;
Such peace and contentment I find,
 No maiden so happy and blest:
For sweetly my days pass away,
 With joy I attend on my sheep;
And though they should happen to stray,
 I'll never once offer to weep.

Such bliss do I find from my swain,
 For he is so bonny and gay,
He meets me each night on the plain,
 And calls me the flower of May.
He took me last week to the fair,
 And gave me a top-knot beside;
Then kiss'd me, and call'd me his care,
 And vow'd I should soon be his bride.

Then tell me, ye maidens, I pray,
 How can I my Jockey deny,
Who chearfully sings through the day,
 And charms me whenever he's nigh?
On the banks of the soft-flowing Tweed,
 Whenever we happen to meet,
So pleasingly plays on his reed,
 No shepherd like Jockey so sweet.

SONG 360.

COME, Clio. come, and with thee bring
 The little loves on downy wing!
Haste thee from the realms above;
Haste, and let us sing of love.

And lo! to join the am'rous theme,
 Light tripping o'er the verdant clod,
Comes the laughter-loving dame,
 And the mischief-making god.

And with them come the graces three,
And the muse of comic glee;
While, behind, to close the rear,
See Hymen, saffron-rob'd, appear.

Hail! fair Venus, beauty's queen;
 All subduing Cupid, hail!
Haste, and take thy arrows keen,
 And Chloe's flinty breast assail.

For lo! of every charm possest
To captivate the feeling breast,
Her youthful heart elate with pride,
She dares thy matchless power deride.

And while thy golden-pointed dart
Unnoted, more arded flies,
She vend the most obdurate heart,
And scatters love from both her eyes.

Then haste and light thy tender fire,
And all her soul with love inspire;
Far off each stubborn passion drive:
Yes, let her burn—but burn alive.

SONG 361.

Sung in *Elfrida*.

HAIL to thy living light,
 Ambrosial morn! all hail thy roseat ray,
That bids gay nature all her charms display,
 In varied beauty bright!
  Away, ye gobblins all!
Wont the traveller to daunt,
Whose vagrant feet have trac'd your haunt,
 Beside some lonely wall!
  Away, ye elves, away,
Shrink at ambrosial morning's living ray.

SONG 362.

THE BUSH ABOON TRAQUAIR.

HEAR me, ye nymphs, and ev'ry swain,
 I'll tell how Peggy grieves me,
Tho' thus I languish, thus complain,
 Alas! she ne'er believes me.
My vows and sighs, like silent air,
 Unheeded, never move her;
At the bonny bush aboon Traquair,
 'Twas there I first did love her.

That day she smil'd, and made me glad,
 No maid seem'd ever kinder;
I thought myself the luckiest lad,
 So sweetly there to find her.
I try'd to soothe my am'rous flame,
 In words that I thought tender;
If more there pass'd, I'm not to blame,
 I meant not to offend her.

Yet now she scornful flees the plain,
 The fields we then frequented;
If e'er we meet she shews disdain;
 she looks as ne'er acquainted.
The bonny bush bloom'd fair in May,
 It's sweets I'll ay remember;
But now her frowns make it decay,
 It fades as in December.

N

Ye rural powers, who hear my ftrains,
　Why thus fhould Peggy grieve me?
Oh! make her partner in my pains,
　Then let her fmiles relieve me.
If not, my love will turn defpair,
　My paffion no more tender,
I'll leave the bufh aboon Traquair,
　To lonely wilds I ll wander.

SONG 363.

THE CORDELIER.

Written by Mr. PRIOR.

WHO has e'er been at Paris muft needs know
　the Greve,
The fatal retreac of th' unfortune brave,
Where honour and juftice moft oddly contribute
To eafe heroes pains by a halter and gibbet.
　Derry down, down, hey derry down.

There death breaks the fhackles which force
　had put on,
And the hangman compleats what the judge
　but begun:
There the fquire of the pad, and the knight of
　the poft,
Find their pains no more baulk'd, and their
　hopes no more croft.
　Derry down, &c.

Great claims are there made, and great fecrets
　are known;
And the king, and the law, and the thief has
　his own:
But my hearers cry out, What a deuce doft
　thou ail?
Cut off thefe reflections, and give us thy tale.
　Derry down, &c.

'Twas there, then, in civil refpect to harfh laws,
And for want of falfe witnefs to back a bad
　caufe,
A Norman of late was oblig'd to appear,
And who to affift, but a grave cordelier.
　Derry down, &c.

The fquire, whofe good grace was to open the
　fcene,
Seem'd not in great hafte that the fhew fhould
　begin:
Now fitted the halter, now travers'd the cart,
And often took leave, but was loth to depart.
　Derry down, &c.

What frightens you thus, my good fon, fays
　the prieft;
You murder'd, are forry, and have been con-
　feft?
O, father! my forrow will fcarce fave my bacon,
For 'twas not that I murder'd, but that I was
　taken.
　Derry down, &c.

Poh! pr'ythee, ne'er trouble thy head with fuch
　fancies;
Rely on the aid you fhall have from St. Francis:

If the money you promis'd be brought to the
　cheft,
You have only to die, let the church do the reft.
　Derry down, &c.

And what will folks fay, if they fee you afraid?
It reflects upon me, as I knew not my trade:
Courage, friend; to-day is your period of for-
　row,
And things will go better, believe me, to-
　morrow.
　Derry down, &c.

To-morrow! our hero reply'd in a fright;
He that's hang'd before noon, ought to think of
　to-night.
Tell your beads, quoth the prieft, and be fairly
　tuck'd up,
For you furely to-night fhall in paradife fup.
　Derry down, &c.

Alas! quoth the fquire, howe'er fumptuous the
　treat,
Parbleu! I fhall have little ftomach to eat:
I fhould therefore efteem it a favour and grace,
Would you be fo kind as to go in my place.
　Derry down, &c.

That I wou'd, quoth the father, and thank
　you to boot,
But our actions, you know, with our duty
　muft fuit:
The feaft I propofe to you I cannot tafte,
For this night by our order is mark'd for a faft.
　Derry down, &c.

Then turning about, to the hangman he faid,
Difpatch me, I pr'ythee, this troublefome blade;
For thy cord, and my cord both equally tie,
And we live by the gold for which other men
　die.
　Derry down, &c.

SONG 364.

Sung in the *Rofe*.

THE nobleft heart, like pureft gold,
　Refifts impreffions whilft 'tis cold;
But melted down in love's bright flame,
　Soft and complying to the teft,
　It takes the image firft impreft,
　And bears it in the faithful breaft,
Through circling years the fame.

SONG 365.

SYLVIA TO ALEXIS.

ALEXIS, how artlefs a lover!
　How bafhful and filly you grow!
In my eyes can you never difcover,
　I mean Yes when I often fay No?

When you pine and you whine out your paffion,
　And only entreat for a kifs,
To be coy and deny is the fafhion;
　Alexis fhould ravifh the blifs.

In love, as in war, 'tis but reafon
To make fome defence for the town:
To furrender without it were treafon,
Before that the outworks were won.

If I frown, 'tis my blufhes to cover,
"Tis for honour and modefty's fake;
He is but a pitiful lover,
Who's foil'd by a fingle attack.

But when we by force are o'erpower'd,
The beft and the braveft muft yield;
I am not to be won by a coward
Who hardly dares enter the field.

SONG 366.

WHAT various expreffions our language allows
To a lover, a bridegroom, and veteran fpoufe!
How diff'rent their thought, and how diff'rent
their carriage,
In courtfhip, at wedding, and after their marriage!

The lover whines out in a languifhing air,
My beauty, my angel, my charmer, my fair;
Her cheeks are like rofes, her lips are like ruby;
He makes her a goddefs, fhe makes him a booby.

The bridegroom now thinks he more freedom
can take,
And calls her his deary, his duck—and his
drake;
He fwears time itfelf his love cannot cool;
He thinks her an angel, fhe thinks him a fool.

The hufband in fhort time can clearer perceive,
For what people fee, they are apt to believe;
He thinks her a compound of mifchief and evil,
He calls her a ftrumpet, and fhe him a devil.

SONG 367.

BONNY CHRISTY.

HOW fweetly fmells the fummer green!
Sweet tafte the peach and cherry;
Painting and order pleafe our een,
And claret makes us merry:
But fineft colours, fruits and flowers,
And wine, tho' I be thirfty,
Lofs a' their charms and weaker powers,
Compar'd with thofe of Chrifty.

When wand'ring o'er the flow'ry park,
No nat'ral beauty wanting,
How lightfome is't to hear the lark,
And birds in confort chanting;
But if my Chrifty tunes her voice,
I'm rapt in admiration,
My thoughts with extafies rejoice,
And drap the hale creation.

Whene'er fhe fmiles a kindly glance,
I take the happy omen,
And aften mint to make advance,
Hoping fhe'll prove a woman:

But, dubious of my ain defert,
My fentiments I fmother;
With fecret fighs I vex my heart,
For fear fhe love another.

Thus farg blate Edie by a burn,
His Chrifty did o er-hear him;
She doughtna let her lover mourn,
But e'er he wift drew near him.
She fpake her favour with a look
Which left nae room to doubt her;
He wifely this white minute took,
And flung his arms about her.

My Chrifty!—witnefs, bonny ftream,
Sic joys frae tears arifing,
I wifh this may na be a dream;
O love the maift furprifing!
Time was too precious now for tauk;
This point of a' his wifhes
He wadna with fet fpeeches bauk,
But war'd it a' on kiffes.

SONG 368.

Sung in *Alfred.*

A Youth adorn'd with ev'ry art,
To warm and win the coldeft heart,
In fecret mine poffeft,
The morning bud that faireft blows,
The vernal oak that ftraighteft grows,
His face and fhape exprest.

In moving founds he told his tale,
Soft as the fighings of the gale
That wakes the flow'ry year;
What wonder he could charm with eafe,
Whom happy nature form'd to pleafe,
Whom love had made fincere?

At morn he left me—fought and fell.
The fatal ev'ning heard his knell,
And faw the tears I fhed;
Tears that muft ever, ever fall;
For, ah! no fighs the paft recal,
No cries awake the dead.

SONG 369.

THE MAN TO HER MIND.

LEAVE party difputes, your attention I pray,
All you who to mirth are inclin'd,
And of thofe I diflike when you hear what I fay,
You may guefs at the man to my mind.

Ye felf-loving coxcombs, whofe fondnefs is feen
From the form your falfe mirrors difplay,
When you talk of a paffion, as nothing you mean,
So all goes for nothing you fay.

No pretenfion I boaft to the aukward young heir,
Tho' born to a wealthy eftate,
Who paying no court to the charms of the fair,
Buys a wife, like a calf, by her weight.

The old batter'd rake fure no woman can love,
Who has long reckon'd marriage a curfe;
Tho' his great condefcenfion he's ready to prove,
By his taking a wife for a nurfe.

A fool for a husband some females have chose,
And repentance oft rues what is past,
Tho' he turns for a season which way the wind
   blows,
The weathercock's rusty at last.

But the man that has sense, with a heart that's
   sincere,
Where passion and reason agree,
Whose fortune's sufficient to combat with care,
—Can't you guess at the lover for me?

SONG 370.

Sung at RANELAGH.

AWAKE, thou blithesome god of day,
   I vite each fo gster round,
Let ev'ry heart be blithe and gay,
   The world with mirth abound;
Betsy s sweet seraphic charms
   In raptures now ' sing,
Soon let her prison be my arms,
   And I'll thy tribute bring.

Ye regents, who the realms above
   With godlike sweetness guard,
Far Besy s heart invade with love,
   Her faithful twain reward;
If not, avaunt! ye gods divine,
   Contented et me die,
My Betsy's eyes much brighter shine
   Than all your spangled sky.

No longer boast your lilies fair,
   Nor russet seems your snow,
With Betsy's skin their white compare,
   Where new-born roses grow;
Your sun that gilds the realms above,
   A distant heat may give,
But Betsy's eyes will always prove
   How sweet it is to live.

SONG 371.

THE NIGHT MAGISTRATE; A CANTATA.

RECITATIVE.

'TWAS at the dreary hour when sprites
   abound,
And nimble fairies trip enchanted ground;
When none but rogues and vagrants walk the
   streets,
And watchmen snore, regardless of their beats;
When wearied hackney-horses slowly move,
And on their boxes coachmen sleep above:
In elbow-chair, and awful state compos'd,
The midnight mogistrate his will disclos'd;
The hobbling, drowsy, walking dials, head
His words with wonder, and his anger fear'd;
In admiration of his wisdom stood,
Then cry'd his honour was as wise as good;
Well pleas'd he nod, and hums his joy to
   show,
Then thus his own importance lets them know.

AIR.

Attend, my friends, while I display,
   And make you understand,
The reason why you must obey,
   And why I will command.
Know, then, I represent the king,
   Tho' you may think it odd;
And I can affidavits bring,
   That kings descend from God.

RECITATIVE.

Thus having spoke with countenance quite big,
He blow'd his nose, took snuff, and plac'd his
   wig;
Then sunk supinely in the elbow-chair,
To snore away the tedious hours, and care;
But envious of his ease, and drowsy joys,
Two buckish sparks molested him with noise;
The rattles turn—girls scream—and oaths re-
   found,
And lamps demolish'd jingle on the ground;
The veterans sally out, and leave their beer,
And to the assistance of their brothers steer;
O'er-power'd by numbers, though they bravely
   fought,
The bucks were to the round house safely
   brought;
Th' awaken'd chief, with anger in his face,
Thus with the sparks expostulates the case:

AIR.

Disturbances of the public peace,
   And of the peace of me;
Shall such disorders never cease,
   And I in office be!

Can't you go quiet to your beds,
   As other people do?
No, you must break my watchmen's heads,
   And beat them black and blue.

Hand-cuff, and put them in the hole—
   Unless they'll tip some chink;
Which if they do, upon my soul,
   I think we'll have some drink.

RECITATIVE.

The cash produc'd, they are allowed to stay,
And drink, and sing, until returning day.

SONG 372.

THE SORROWFUL SHEPHERD; A PASTORAL.

Written by Mr. HAWKINS.

AH! whither, alas! shall I fly?
   What clime shall I seek for relief?
Since Phillis no longer is nigh,
   O! how shall I smother my grief?
The sweetest, the fairest was she,
   So sweetly she tript o'er the plain;
But now she ne'er smiles upon me,
   She's faithless—and false to her swain.

With Strephon she's gone far away,
   With him is contented and blest;
While I am distracted all day,
   And ruin'd for want of my rest.

No heed can I take of my sheep,
　They ramble and roam as they pleafe,
For I can do nothing but weep,
　Till Phillis my forrows appeafe.

Dear nymph, hear thy shepherd complain,
　Return and fubdue all my care;
No longer torment me with pain,
　Nor drive me thus into defpair:
Thy charms ever shall be my pride,
　Thy fmiles I will ever admire;
Then deign for to be but my bride,
　And fatisfy all my defire.

SONG 373.

Sung in the *Summer's Tale.*

WHEN love at firft approach is feen,
　His dang'rous form he veils;
A playful infant's harmlefs mien,
　The playful god conceals.

When foon, by us fond dupes careft,
　He acts his trait'rous part;
And as we prefs him to the breaft,
　He fteals into the heart.

SONG 374.

AN AMERICAN SONG.

SURE never was picture drawn more to the
　life,
Or affectionate hufband more fond of his wife,
Than America copies, and loves Britain's fons,
Who, confcious of freedom, are bold as great
　guns.
　Hearts of oak are we ftill, for we're fons of
　　thofe men
　Who always are ready, fteady, boys, fteady,
　To fight for their freedom again and again.

Tho' we feaft and grow fat on American foil,
Yet we own ourfelves fubjects of Britain's fair
　ifle;
And who's fo abfurd to deny us the fame,
Since true Britifh blood flows in every vein.
　Hearts of oak, &c.

Then cheer up my lads, to your country be firm,
Like kings of the ocean we'll weather each ftorm;
Integrity calls out, Fair Liberty, fee,
Waves her flag o'er our heads, and her words
　are, Be free.
　Hearts of oak, &c.

To King George, as true fubjects, we loyal bow
　down,
But hope we may call magna charta our own;
Let the reft of the world flavifh worfhip decree,
Great Britain has order'd her fons to be free.
　Hearts of oak, &c.

Poor Efau his birth-right gave up for a bribe,
Americans fcorn the foul felling tribe;
Beyond life our freedom we chufe to poffefs,
Which thro' life we'll defend, and abjure the
　broad S.
　Hearts of oak, &c.

On our brow while we laurel-crown'd liberty
　wear,
What Englifhmen ought, we Americans dare?
Though tempefts and terrors around us we fee,
Bribes nor fears can prevail o'er the hearts that
　are free.
　Hearts of oak, &c.

With loyalty liberty let us entwine,
Our blood fhall for both flow as free as our wine;
Let us fet an example what all men fhould be,
And a toaft give the world, 'Here's to thofe
　dare be free!'
　Hearts of oak are we ftill, for we're fons of
　　thofe men
　Who always are ready, fteady, boys, fteady,
　To fight for their freedom again and again.

SONG 375.

A DRINKING SONG.

COME, my never-frowning glafs,
　Always welcome to my lip;
Here's to Delia, lovely lafs,
　Oh, how grateful is the fip!
This is pleafure to the foul,
　This will banifh care away;
He who hates the fmiling bowl,
　What's he fit for, topers, fay?

SONG 376.

A PASTORAL BALLAD.

BY the banks of a murmuring brook,
　Where fpring fhed it's fragrance around,
Neglecting his flock and his crook,
　Alexis lay ftretch'd on the ground;
Quite dumb with his forrows oppreft,
　Till woe from his tears had relief,
Then wildly he beats on his breaft,
　And thus difemburden'd his grief.

Ah, fate too unkind and fevere!
　Untimely to fnatch to the grave,
In Daphne, my all that was dear,
　And all my fond wifhes could crave:
Ye bow'rs that have witnefs'd each fcene,
　Where woodbine and jefs'mine entwine,
To a flame more ye confcious e'er been
　So fpotlefs as Daphne's and mine?

What tho' o'er this daify-deck'd mead
　A thoufand fair lambkins do rove,
Tho' well thou canft breathe on the reed,
　What mufic's a medicine for love?
Alexis, doom'd ever to wail,
　Oh, think of thy treafures no more!
For what would ten thoufand avail,
　They cannot thy Daphne reftore.

Ye hills, and ye vallies, adieu,
　Adieu to each youth on the plain;
Since nought will my pleafure renew,
　Ah, why fhould I linger in pain?
My lambkins, forfaken by me,
　Let fome happier fhepherd enjoy;

For all with frefh anguifh I fee
That Daphne's joint cares did employ.

This faid, from the margin he fprung,
Grown frantic with love and defpair;
Yet Daphne, tho' dying, he fung,
Till falter'd the name of his fair:
The ftreams as they murmur along,
The forrowful ditty relate,
And zephyr, the willows among,
Still fighs the fad tale of his fate.

SONG 377.

THE JOVIAL PHILOSOPHER.

BE content in your ftation, my friend,
  The maxim it *probatum eft*;
Life's fhort from beginning to end,
  Then let us pafs thro' it with zeft.

The monarch, furrounded by fame,
  Can afte no more pleafure than you;
His paffions and feelings the fame,
  Defires and wifhes as few.

The cobler who hugs his brown lafs,
  Feels emotions of love full as ftrong
As thofe of a much higher clafs,
  And glories he won her by fong.

For the lofs of a nail tinker's rage,
  As much as for realms a great king;
With clamours our ears both engage,
  And much the fame peal they both ring.

On my word, my good friend, we're a crowd,
  Variegated among great and fmall;
We take it by turns to be proud,
  And likewife by turns rife and fall.

Like actors, who ftrut for an hour
  In all the grand flav'ry of ftate;
Next day, abdicated from power,
  With pages o'er porter they'll prate.

Then from an enlivening bowl,
  While your reafon holds good, never flinch;
For life's but a fpan, my brave foul,
  Then faith we'll enjoy ev'ry inch.

SONG 378.

BACCHUS, when merry, beftriding his tun,
  Proclaim'd a new neighbourly feaft:
The firft that appear'd was a man of the gown,
  A jolly parochial prieft;
He fill'd up his bowl, drank healths to the
    church,
  Preferring it to the king,
Altho' he long fince left both in the lurch,
  Yet he canted like any thing.

The next was a talkative blade, whom we call
  A doctor of the civil law,
Who guzzled and drank up the devil and all,
  As faft as the drawers could draw :
But healths to all nobles he ftiffly deny'd,
  Tho' luftily he could fwill,
Becaufe ftill the fafter the quality dy'd,
  It brought the more grift to his mill.

The next was a phyfician to ladies and lords,
  Who eafes all ficknefs and pain,
And conjures diftempers away with hard words,
  Which he knows is the head of his gain:
He ftepp'd from his coach, fill'd his cup to the
    brim,
  And quaffing did freely agree,
That Bacchus, who gave us fuch cordials to
    drink,
  Was a better phyfician than he.

The next was a juftice who never read law,
  With twenty informers behind,
On free-coft he tippl'd, and ftill bid 'em draw,
  Till his worfhip had drunk himfelf blind;
Then reeling away, they all rambled in queft
  Of drunkards and jilts of the town,
That they might be punifh'd to frighten the reft,
  Except they wou'd drop him a crown.

The fifth was a tricking attorney at law,
  By tally-men chiefly employ'd,
Who lengthen'd his bill with co-hy and maw-
    draw,
  And a hundred fuch items befide ;
The healths that he drank were to Weftminfter-
    Hall,
  And to all the grave dons of the gown;
Rependum & Petro, dorendum & Paul,
  Such Latin as never was known.

The laft that appear'd was a foldier in red,
  With his hair doubled under his hat;
Who was by his trade a fine gentleman made,
  Tho' as hungry and poor as a rat:
He fwore by his God, tho' he liv'd by his king,
  Or the help of fome impudent punk,
That he wou'd not depart till he made the butt
    fing,
  And himfelf moft confoundedly drunk.

SONG 379.

THE HAPPY LOVER.

THROUGHOUT the nation, Sir, find
  me a lafs,
  That's loving, engaging, and pretty;
She freely into my affection fhall pafs,
  As fure as there's fools in the city.

And if fhe proves kind, Sir, why I fhall prove
  true,
  And juftly efteem her my treafure;
But fhould fhe be fcornful, what then fhall I
  do?
  Why, faith, I'll difmifs her with pleafure.

SONG 380.

THE DAY MAGISTRATE; A CANTATA.

RECITATIVE.

ABOUT the time when bufy faces meet,
  And carts and coaches rumble in each ftreet;
When madam rifes, and the tea things rattle;
And all the fex prepare for general tattle,
The maudlin libertines are let to know,
They muft, attended, to the juftice go;

A coach is call'd—they to his worship steer,
To be or sent to Bridewell or set clear.
His worship o'er his chocolate attends,
To punish foes and to oblige his friends;
With air important, then demands the cause
Why they are brought, and for what breach of
    laws;
In sober sadness the grave chief explains
The bucks transgression, and his——want of
    brains.

AIR.

Your worship must know,
Ten hours ago.
    Which was in the dead of the night;
    These sparks play'd the devil,
    In manner uncivil,
        And throw'd us all into a fright.

My men's heads they broke,
And call'd it a joke,
    And made twenty lamps for to rattle;
But being surrounded,
They soon were confounded,
    And vanquish'd and taken in battle.

RECITATIVE.

His worship heard, and strok'd his under-jaw,
Then look'd authority, and gave an haw;
Turn'd o'er the statutes, and the riot act,
And talk'd of quint, and quart, and doubt,
    and fact:
But the young blades, to mollify the cause,
And smooth the aspect of hard-featur'd laws,
Begg'd that they might a private word express,
Which was acceded to with readiness;
Then, humbly pray'd, their rashness he'd forget,
And they'd remain for ever in his debt;
And with respect, and great submission shewn,
They hop'd he'd make a trifling gift his own:
This generous spirit in each culprit spark,
Produc'd these orders to his worship's clerk.

AIR.

Clerk, write a discharge,
And set these at large,
    For, faith, they are men of condition:
'Tis true, they transgress'd,
But now they've express'd
    For their folly much grief and contrition.

For justice, sometimes,
Should wink at small crimes,
    Of rigour relax, and be kind:
The poor I commit;
But pay, and submit,
    You'll find me, as painted, quite blind.

SONG 381.

WEDLOCK.

OF all the various states of life,
    Sure wedlock is the best,
For in a faithful loving wife,
    A man is surely blest.

Of all the joys this world can give,
    All kinds of earthly bliss,

There's none can equal, as I live,
    The matrimonial kiss.

How sweetly glides the time away,
    When sitting by his wife,
The happy spouse with joy can say,
    Come kiss me, my dear life.

Tho' worldly cares perplex and gall,
    And threaten rude alarms,
The married man forgets them all,
    When in his wife's dear arms.

Not Hybla's fam'd poetic grove,
    With all it's fabled sweets,
Can equal those of wedded love,
    Betwixt the lawful sheets.

How joyous is the happy dad,
    How swells his heart with glee,
When little Poll, or Sall, or Ned,
    He dandles on his knee!

And now to pay me for my song,
    Pray, all your wishes join,
That ere the time be very long,
    Some sweet girl may be mine.

SONG 382.

Sung in *Artaxerxes.*

WATER, parted from the sea,
    May increase the river's tide,
To the bubbling fount may flee,
    Or thro' fertile vallies glide:

Though, in search of lost repose,
    Thro' the land 'tis free to roam,
Still it murmurs as it flows,
    Till it reach it's native home.

SONG 383.

THE BROOM OF COWDENKNOWS.

HOW blithe was I each morn to see
    My swain come o'er the hill!
He leap'd the brook, and flew to me:
    I met him with good will.
I neither wanted ewe, nor lamb,
    While his flocks near me lay;
He gather'd in my sheep at night,
    And chear'd me all the day.
Oh! the broom, the bonny bonny broom,
    Where lost was my repose;
I wish I was with my dear swain,
    With his pipe and my ewes.

He tun'd his pipe and reed so sweet,
    The birds stood list'ning by:
The fleecy flock stood still and gaz'd,
    Charm'd with his melody:
While thus we spent our time, by turns,
    Betwixt our flocks and play,
I envy'd not the fairest dame,
    Tho' e'er so rich and gay.
O the broom, &c.

He did oblige me ev'ry hour,
    Cou'd I but faithful be?

He ftole my heart; cou'd I refufe,
Whate'er he afk'd of me?
Hard fate! that I muft banifh'd be,
Gang heavily and mourn,
Becaufe I lov'd the kindeft fwain
That ever yet was born.
O the broom, &c.

SONG 384.

SERENADE.

Written by the EDITOR.

SLEEP! thou halm of human woe,
Quit, O quit my charming maid;
To fome wretched mortal go,
Who may want thy lenient aid.

See where anguifh and defpair
For thy kind affiftance cries;
Thither, fleep, with fpeed repair,
And relieve their weary'd eyes.

Thus, kind god of foft repofe,
Praifed fhalt thou ever be;
When they wake, by fongs of thofe,
While they fleep, with voice of me.

SONG 385.

Written by Mr. POPE.

SAYS, Phebe, Why is gentle love
A ftranger to that mind
Which pity and efteem can move,
Which can be juft and kind?

Is it becaufe you fear to prove
The ills that love moleft;
The jealous cares, the fighs that move
The captivated breaft?

Alas! by fome degree of woe,
We every blifs muft gain;
That heart can ne'er a tranfport know,
That never felt a pain.

SONG 386.

A WELCH SONG.

COT fplutter o'nails,
Hur was come from North Wales,
To try hur good fortune in London;
But oh! hur poor heart,
Hur fears, for hur part,
Alas! hur for ever is undone.

For as hur was coing,
With Shenkin and Owen,
To pray to goot Tavit hur faint, Sir;
A young tamfel hur met,
Put hur all in a fweat,
Good lack hur was ready to faint, Sir.

So pright was hur eyes,
As the ftars in the fkies,
Hur lips were like rupies fo fine, Sir;
Hur cheeks were o'erfpread
With a fweet white and red,
She look't like an angel divine, Sir.

When fhe fpoke, how hur voice
Made her pofome rejoice!
So charming and prafe were hur words,
Sir;
The wood-lark or thrufh,
That fing on a pufh,
No accents fo fweet can afford, Sir.

Since that lucklefs hour,
So creat is love's power,
Hur croans and fays nothing put Heigh
day!
Put hur paffion, hur fear,
Hur can never declare,
For the lafs was as crand as a lady.

Yet true lovers all,
When you hear of hur fall,
O'er her crave fhed a tear out of pity;
For fo earneft hur crieves,
Hur fhall tie, hur believes,
And fo there's an end to hur ditty.

SONG 387.

WHAT tho' the fun withdraws his ray,
And clould bedark the fky,
Yet foon fhall winter pafs away,
And fpring falute the eye.

The clouds, diffolv'd by chearful fun,
Soft pleafures will encroach,
The fun obfcur'd, the clouds return,
As winter does approach.

But ah! when wint'ry age draws on,
A dreary fcene's in ftore,
Life's fun, that warpn'd the heart, is gone,
And fpring returns no more.

SONG 388.

Sung at MARYBONE.

STINT me not in love or wine,
I'll have full draughts of either;
Round me fprings the mantling vine;
Bacchus, hafte you hither.

See the grape bleeds to replenifh my cup,
I'll drink it, Silenus, I'll drink it all up:
And tho' my feet ftagger, and tho' my eyes roll,
Ye Bacchanals bring me another full bowl.

Truce with your bumpers, Venus now,
The ruddy victor chaces;
Send fome nymph with graceful brow
To my warm embraces.

See blooming young Hebe is now on the wing,
As ripe as full fummer, as wanton as fpring;
Ye fawns and ye dryads, far hence from the
grove,
'Tis filence and gloom that is facred to love.

Steering thus from joy to joy,
Careful thoughts I banifh;
Time this flame fhall ne'er deftroy,
Others blaze and vanifh.

Ye graces and fatyrs, my chaplet prepare,
With myrtle and ivy come bind up my hair;
While I in due juftice your pains will requite,
By drinking all day, and by loving all night.

SONG 389.

A SAILOR'S SONG.

ON Old England's bleft fhore
We are landed once more,
Secure from the ftorms of the main;
For great George, and his caufe,
For our country and laws,
We have conquer'd, and will do again.

Where the fun's orient ray
Firft opens the day,
On India's extended domain,
The fwarthy fac'd foes
Who dar'd to oppofe,
We have conquer'd, and will do again.

Come, my brave hearts of oak,
Let us drink, fing, and joke,
While here on the fhore we remain;
When our country demands,
With hearts, and with hands,
We are ready to conquer again.

SONG 390.

WHAT is beauty, when virtue's away!
A fhort blooming flower of youth!
A flower that blooms to decay,
E'en when it's fupported by truth!

But virtue, when beauty is gone,
Shines lovely for ever confeft,
Gives majefty grace on a throne,
And banifhes care from the breaft.

Ye nymphs, then, regard the fond mufe;
Tho' now you are blooming and gay,
Be your mind your chief care to purfue,
For beauty can laft but a day.

SONG 391.

EV'RY mortal fome favourite pleafure pur-
fues,
Some to White's run for play, fome to Batfon's
for news;
To Shuter's droll phiz others thunder applaufe,
And fome triflers delight to hear Nichols's
noife:
But fuch idle amufements I'll carefully fhun,
And my pleafures confine to my dogs and my
gun.

Soon as Phœbus has finifh'd his fummer's career,
And his maturing aid bleft the hufbandman's
care;
When Roger and Nell have enjoy'd harveft-
home,
And, their labours being o'er, are at leifure to
roam;

From the noife of the town and it's follies I run,
And I range o'er the fields with my dogs and
my gun.

When my pointers around me all carefully
ftand,
And none dares to ftir, but the dog I command;
When the covey he fprings, and I bring down
my bird,
I've a pleafure no paft'me befide can afford:
No paftime nor pleafure that's under the fun,
Can be equal to mine with my dogs and my
gun.

When the covey I've thinn'd, to the woods I
repair,
And I brufh thro' the thickets devoid of all
fear;
There I exercife freely my levelling fkill,
And with pheafants and woodcocks my bag
often fill;
For death (where I find them) they feldom can
fhun,
My dogs are fo fure, and fo fatal my gun.

My fpaniels ne'er babble, they're under com-
mand;
Some range at a diftance, and fome hunt at
hand;
When a woodcock they flufh, or a pheafant they
fpring,
With heart-chearing notes, how they make the
woods ring!
Then for mufic let fribbles to Ranelagh run,
My concert's a chorus of dogs and a gun.

When at night we chat over the fport of the
day,
And, fpread o'er the table, my conquer'd fpoils
lay,
Then I think of my friends, and to each fend a
part;
For my friends to oblige is the pride of my
heart:
Thus the vices of town, and it's follies, I fhun,
And my pleafures confine to my dogs and my
gun.

SONG 392.

YE lads, and ye laffes, who bloom in your
prime,
I love and regard ye, the jewels of time;
Then lift, and attend to the words that I fay,
For life's a mere vapour, a thing of decay.

As now let me find ye with fmiles on your brows,
Each nymph prove indulgent, each youth keep
his vows;
Save love and good-humour, with hearts tnat
true chime,
All joys that men boaft of are infults of time.

What a wretch muft he be, who fo doats upon
pelf,
To think that no mortal feels want but himfelf;

Who ftarves 'midft the guineas he counts o'er
  with glee,
Such, fuch are the vileft abufers of me.

The girl that is fqueamifh, the icy-fac'd prude,
The man that is flinty, remorfelefs, and rude;
With him that's a milkfop, and baulks the full
  toaft;
As time they abandon, by time fhall be loft.

But ftill to the chearful, the good, and the gay,
December fhall meet them ftill mild as the
  May:
Hand in hand I'll conduct them who live
  without crime,
From the fons of the earth, to the father of
  time.

SONG 393.

Sung at RANELAGH.

BY the dew-befprinkled rofe;
  By the blackbird piping clear;
By the weftern gale, that blows
  Fragrance on the vernal year:
Hear, Amanda, hear thy fwain,
Nor let me longer figh in vain.

By the cowflip, clad in gold;
  By the filver lily's light;
By thofe meads, where you behold
  Nature rob'd in green and white:
Hear, Amanda, hear thy fwain,
And to his fighs, oh! figh again.

By the riv'let's rambling race;
  By the mufic that it makes;
By bright Sol's inverted face,
  Who for the ftream his fky forfakes;
Hear, Amanda, hear thy fwain,
And into joy convert his pain.

SONG 394.

Sung at VAUXHALL.

FLATT'RING hopes, the mind deceiving,
  Early faith too often cheat;
Woman, fond and all-believing,
Loves and hugs the dear deceit.

Empty fhew of pomp and riches,
  Cupid's trick to catch the fair,
Lovely maids too oft bewitches;
Flatt'ry is the beauty's fnare.

SONG 395.

THE FAITHFUL SHEPHERD.

WHEN flow'ry meadows deck the year,
  And fportive lambkins play,
When fpangled fields renew'd appear,
  And mufick walk'd the day;
Then did my Chloe leave her bower,
  To hear my am'rous lay,
Warm'd by my love, fhe vow'd no power
  Should lead her heart aftray.

The warbling choirs from ev'ry bough
  Surround our couch in throngs,
And all their tuneful arts beftow,
  To give us change of fongs:
Scenes of delight my foul poffefs'd,
  I bleis'e, then hugg' i my maid;
I rou d the kiffes from her breaft,
  Sweet as a noon-day's fhade.

Joy fo tranfporting never fails
  To fly away as air;
Another fwain with her prevails,
  To be as falfe as fair.
What can my fatal paffion cure?
  I'll never woo again;
All her difdain I muft endure,
  Adoring her in vain.

What pity 'tis to hear the boy
  Thus fighing with his pain;
But time and fcorn may give him joy,
  To hear her figh again.
Ah! fickle Chloe, be advis'd,
  Do not thyfelf beguile;
A faithful lover fhould be priz'd,
  Then cure him with a fmile.

SONG 396.

Sung in the *Wedding Ring*.

THE trav'llers, that through defarts ride
  By conduct of fome friendly ftar;
When clouds obfcure their trufty guide,
  Out of their courfe muft wander far:

So I, with penfive care and pain,
  In abfence ftill muft ftray,
Till you, my ftar, fhine out again,
  And light me on my way.

SONG 397.

THE MARRIED MAN.

I AM marry'd and happy; with wonder hear
  this,
  Ye rovers and rakes of the age,
Who laugh at the mention of conjugal blifs,
  And who only loofe pleafures engage:
You may laugh, but believe me you're all in
    the wrong
  When you merrily marriage deride;
For to marriage the permanent pleafures be-
    long,
  And in them we can only confide.

The joys which from lawlefs connections arife,
  Are fugitive, never fincere;
Oft ftolen with hafte, or fnatch'd by furprize,
  Interrupted by doubts, and by fear:
But thofe which in legal attachments we find,
  When the heart is with innocence pure,
Are from ev'ry imbitt'ring reflection refin'd,
  And to life's lateft hour will endure.

The love which ye boaft of, deferves not that
  name,
  True love is with fentiment join'd;

But yours is a paffion, a feverifh flame,
Rais'd without the confent of the mind.
When, dreading confinement, ye miftreffes hire,
With this and with that ye are cloy'd;
Ye are led, and mifled, by a flatt'ring falfe fire,
And are oft by that fire deftroy'd.

If you afk me from whence my felicity flows,
My anfwer is fhort—from a wife;
Who for chearfulnefs, fenfe, and good-nature,
I chofe,
Which are beauties that charm us for life.
To make home the feat of perpetual delight,
Ev'ry hour each ftudies to feize;
And we find ourfelves happy, from morning to
night,
By our mutual endeavours to pleafe.

SONG 398.

Sung in the *Royal Shepherd*.

VOWS of love fhould ever bind
Men who are to honour true;
They muft have a favage mind,
Who refufe the fair their due.

Scorn'd and hated may they be,
Who from conftancy do fwerve;
So may ev'ry nymph agree
All fuch faithlefs fwains to ferve.

SONG 399.

LONG at thy altar, God of love,
I paid a double duty;
A flave to Celia's voice and wit,
To Chloe's tafte and beauty:

Fain would I fix my reftlefs heart,
While they, with aukward feature,
Dif.uis'd, in affectation's mafk,
The genuine gifts of nature.

SONG 400.

THE SYCAMORE SHADE.

T'OTHER day as I fat in the fycamore fhade,
Young Damon came whiftling along,
I trembled, I blufh'd—a poor innocent maid!—
And my heart caper'd up to my tongue.
Silly heart, I cry'd, fie what a flutter is here!
Young Damon defigns you no ill;
The fhepherd's fo civil, you've nothing to fear,
Then pr'ythee, fond urchin, lie ftill.

Sly Damon drew near, and knelt down at my
feet,
One kifs he demanded—no more!
But urg'd the foft preffure with ardour fo fweet,
I could not begrudge him a fcore.
My lambkins I've kifs'd, and no change ever
found,
Many times as we play'd on the hill;
But Damon's dear lips made my heart gallop
round,
Nor would the fond urchin lie ftill.

When the fun blazes fierce, to the fycamore
fhade,
For fhelter, I'm fure to repair;
And, virgins, in faith I'm no longer afraid,
Altho' the dear fhepherd be there.
At ev'ry fond kifs that with freedom he takes,
My heart may rebound if it will;
There's fomething fo fweet in the buftle it
makes,
I'll die ere I bid it lie ftill.

SONG 401.

A PASTORAL.

Sung at VAUXHALL.

FAREWEL, ye green fields and fweet
groves,
Where Phillis engag'd my fond heart;
Where nightingales warble their loves,
And nature is drefs'd without art:
No pleafure ye now can afford,
Nor mufic can lull me to reft;
For Phillis proves falfe to her word,
And Strephon can never be bleft.

Oft-times, by the fide of a fpring,
Where rofes and lilies appear,
Gav Phillis of Strephon would fing,
For Strephon was all fhe held dear:
But as foon as fhe found, by my eyes,
The paffion that glow'd in my breaft,
She then, to my grief and furprize,
Prov'd all fhe had faid was a jeft.

Too late, to my forrow, I find,
The beauties alone that will laft,
Are thofe that are fix d in the mind,
Which envy or time cannot blaft:
Beware, then, beware how ye truft
Coquettes, who to love make pretence;
For Phillis to me had been juft,
If nature had blefs'd her with fenfe.

SONG 402.

A FREE-MASON'S SONG.

HAIL, mafonry, thou craft divine!
Glory of earth, from heav'n reveal'd;
Which doft with jewels precious fhine,
From all but mafon's eyes conceal'd;
Thy praifes due who can rehearfe,
In nervous profe, or flowing verfe!

As men from brutes diftinguifh'd are,
A mafon other men excels;
For what's in knowledge choice and rare,
But in his breaft fecurely dwells?
His filent breaft, and faithful heart,
Preferve the fecrets of the art.

From fcorching heat, and piercing cold,
From beafts whofe roar the foreft rends,
From the affaults of warriors bold,
The mafon's art mankind defends:
Be to this art due honour paid,
From which mankind receives fuch aid,

O 2

Enfigns of ftate that feed our pride,
Diftinctions troublefome and vain!
By mafons true are laid afide;
Art's free-born fons fuch toys difdain,
Ennobl'd by the name they bear,
Diftinguifh'd by the badge they wear.

Sweet fel'owfhip, from envy free,
Friendly converfe of brotherhood,
The lodge's lafting cement be!
Which has for ages firmly ftood.
A lodge thus buil', for ages paft
Has lafted, and will ever laft.

Then in our fongs b juftice done,
To thofe who have enrich'd the art,
From Adam to great Leven down,
And let each brother b ar a part;
Let our grand-mafter's health go round,
His praife in every lodge refound.

SONG 403.

Sung at VAUXHALL.

IN vain I feek to calm to reft
The heart that flutters in my breaft!
I fee. my foul with fears opprefs'd,
Yet know not wh nce they flow:
How anxious is the lover's fate!
Ten thoufand doubts perplex his ftate:
Fond hopes of future blifs create
But certain prefent woe.

SONG 404.

Sung at VAUXHALL.

TO reafon, ye fair-ones, affert your pretence.
Nor hearken to language beneath common-
  fenfe:
When angels men call ye, and homage would
  pay,
If you credit the tale, you're as faulty as they.

Ten thoufand gay fcenes are prefented to view,
Ten thoufand oaths fworn, but not one of them
  true;
Such paffions, O heed not, unlefs to deride,
Left a victim you fall to an ill-grounded pride.

Prefer ye the dictates of virtue to found,
True bleffings can ne'er without goodnefs be
  found;
Leave folly and fafhions, mifguiders of youth,
And ftick to their oppofites, freedom and truth.

SONG 405.

Sung at RANELAGH.

THE fmiling morn, the blooming fpring,
  Invite the chearful birds to fing;
And, while they warble on each fpray,
Love melts the univerfal lay:
Let us, Amanda, timely wife,
Like them improve the hour that flies,

And in foft raptures wafte the day,
  Among the birks of Endermay.

For foon the winter of the year,
And age, life's winter, will appear:
At this thy living bloom will fade,
As that will ftrip the verdant fhade:
Our tafte of pleafure then is o'er,
The feather'd fongfters are no more;
And when they droop, and we decay,
Adieu the birks of Endermay.

Behold the hills and vales around,
With lowing herds and flocks abound;
The wanton kids, and frifki g lambs,
Gambol and dance about their dams;
The bufy bee, with humming noife,
And all the reptile kind rejoice:
Let us, like them, then, fing and play,
About the birks of Endermay.

SONG 406.

Sung in Almena.

AS flows the cool and purling rill,
In filver mazes down the hill,
It chears the myrtle, and the vine,
That in each other's foliage twine:

So ftreams from the maternal heart,
What tender nature can impart;
Thus happy, in my arms to fold,
And to my heart Almena hold.

SONG 407.

THE FRIAR AND NUN; A CANTATA.

RECITATIVE.

IN Paris city, they report for truth,
  There dwelt an active prieft, in prime of
  youth.
And in the convent, as fome others fay,
There liv'd a nun as blooming as the May:
The rev'rend father figh d for her in vain,
He dar a not openly his love explain;
Her beauty fann d the embers of defire,
But looks auftere quite damp'd the rifing fire.
At length kind fortune did his wifhes blefs,
For the fair nun came to him to confefs;
With great devotion fhe her forehead fign'd,
And thus reveal'd the troubles of her mind:

AIR.

Holy father, believe, for my forrows I grieve,
  And fincerely repent each tranfgreffion;
One fault, above all, my mind does enthral,
  And torments me furpaffing expreffion.
Tho' to Heav'n I'm bound, yet Cupid has found
  The method to lead me aftray;
Alas! I am frail; for love would prevail,
  Tho' confcience cry'd, fternly, Stay, ftay!

RECITATIVE.

The jolly prieft, as near the fair he ftood,
Feels genial warmth ftir up his youthful blood;

Then fmiling on the lovely fuppliant fair,
He chuck'd her chin, and bade her not defpair.
I know no harm there is in love, he faid,
Each fex, my dear, was for the other made;
The church ordains it, and you do no fault,
If to the church you yield up what you ought:
But 'tis a fin if any one fhould fraft
Upon thofe charms, unlefs he is a prieft.

AIR.

Confider how happy will be your condition,
  If once you will form refolution
To bed with a prelate—You need no contrition,
  For prelates can give abfolution :
Then yield to my arms thy ravifhing charms,
  Permit me thy beauties to rifle;
You know I can blefs you, as well as confefs you ;
  Befides, it is only a trifle.

SONG 408.

Sung in the *Maid of the Mill.*

WITH the man that I love, was I deftin'd
    to dwell,
On a mountain, a moor, in a cot, in a cell;
Retreats the moft barren, moft defert, would be
More pleafing than courts or a palace to me.
Let the vain and the venal in wedlock afpire,
To what folly efteems, and the vulgar admire;
I yield them the blifs where their wifhes are
    plac'd;
Infenfible creatures! 'tis all they can tafte.

SONG 409.

THE SISTERS.

YOUNG Arabella, mama's care,
    And ripe to be a bride,
Had charms a monarch might enfnare,
    But beauty mix'd with pride:
And ftill to blaft that happinefs,
    Her pride each lover cool'd;
The number of her flaves was lefs,
    And lefs the tyrant rul'd.

Her fifter Charlotte, tho' not blefs'd
    With beauty's potent fpell,
The virtues of the mind poffefs'd,
    And bore away the belle:
Knights, Earls, and Dukes, like fummer-flies,
    Around the maiden flew;
They prefs'd to tell ten thoufand lies,
    As men are apt to do.

Fond Celadon addrefs'd the fair,
    Refolv'd no time to lofe;
A youth with fuch a fhape and air,
    What female could refufe!
Like all the reft, he own'd his flame,
    His artlefs flame alone;
The blufhing maid confefs'd the fame,
    The prieft foon made them one.

Poor Arabella, vex'd to find
    Her fifter made a wife,
Pretends to rail at all mankind,
    And praife a fingle life.

Ye virgins, Charlotte's plan purfue,
  Shun Arabella's fate;
Accept the man that's worthy you,
  Before it is too late.

SONG 410.

THE SORROWFUL SHEPHERDESS.

Written by Mr. HAWKINS.

MY Jockey is fled from the plain,
    And left me in forrow to mourn;
Was ever fo cruel a fwain,
    To leave me, and will not return!
No longer he pipes on his reed,
    No longer his praifes I'll tell;
Yet dull are the banks of the Tweed,
    Since Jockey has bade them farewel.

His crook he has broken in twain,
    His fheep and his lambkins now ftray;
They bleat for their mafter in vain,
    And carelefsly wander away.
Then hafte thee, fome fhepherd fo free,
    And call the poor flocks to their home,
O! be to them kinder than he
    Who caus'd the dear wand'rers to roam.

Each virgin, fo happy and gay,
    Attend to the words I impart,
Be careful and cautious, I pray,
    How you give a young fhepherd your heart.
Tho' Jockey was rural and neat,
    To me was moft loving and kind ;
His manners were gentle and fweet,
    Till cruelty grew in his mind.

SONG 411.

Sung in *Thomas and Sally.*

WERE I as poor as wretch can be,
    As great as any monarch, he,
Ere on fuch terms I'd mount his throne,
I'd work my fingers to the bone.

Grant me, ye pow'rs, (I afk not wealth)
Grant me but innocence and health;
Ah! what is grandeur, link'd to vice?
'Tis only virtue gives it price.

SONG 412.

A PINERIAN SOCIETY SONG.

IF the annals we read in the days of King
    John,
'Bout the year of our æta twelve hundred and
    one,
We fhall find that weak prince was about to in-
    vade
The rights of his people, their commerce and
    trade.
Derry down, &c.

His fubjects perceiving what muft be their fate,
If not timely prevented, before 'twas too late;

Refolv'd, like true Britons, not tamely to yield;
So the commons unite, and the lords take the
field.
Derry down, &c.

All ranks and all ftations concern'd in the caufe,
Refolving to ftand by their rights and their laws;
Tradefmen now a fraternity firft did begin,
And ev'ry good member was named a Pin.
Derry down, &c.

Now chapters they had, and good orders they
made,
In which were confulted the good of the trade ;
With a firm refolution to ftand by each other,
Which ftill is the bus'nefs of ev ry true brother.
Derry down, &c.

Tho' the time is long fince, yet all of us know
What benefit from this firm union did flow;
For the king was obliged to grant them, foon
after,
That blefling of England, our great Magna
Charta.
Derry down, &c.

Since now you have heard from what laudable
caufe,
The term of Pinerian, fo ancient, arofe;
Then let us, who zealoufly keep up that name,
Be emulous of their good purpofe and fame.
Derry down, &c.

Since our inftitution enjoins the fame ends,
To confirm us as brothers, and make us all
friends,
With a true honeft zeal let us act our part,
And ftand by each other with hand and with
heart.
Derrry down, &c.

Let us no contention nor envying know,
But mirth and good-humour continually flow ;
Then all focial happinefs here will be fix'd,
And harmony always with intereft be mix'd.
Derry down, &c.

Then rife, my good brethren, and join hand in
hand,
And as firm to each other, as now, let us ftand ;
Then what fhall fuch mutual friendfhip disjoin ?
The world muft admire us, and praife our de-
fign.
Derry down, &c.

Now fill up your glafs, and about let it flow,
To our noble grand, and ancients alfo;
And to all abfent brothers, wherever they be;
And thus may Pinerians for ever agree.
Derry down, &c.

SONG 413.

Sung in the *Capricious Lovers.*

WHEN late, a fimple ruftic lafs,
I rov'd without conftraint,
A ftream was all my looking-glafs,
And health my only paint.

The charms I boaft, alas! how few,
I gave to nature's care;
As vice ne'er fpoil'd their native hue,
They could not want repair.

SONG 414.

Sung at VAUXHALL.

YE belles and beaux, attend my fong,
I'll tell you fomething new:
Perhaps you'll fmile, and think me wrong,
Though ftrange, you'll find it true.

In days of yore, hiftorians fay,
'Twas wifdom bore the prize;
But modern times have chang'd the lay,
'Tis folly to be wife.

Let no grave Cynic take offence,
And think me too unkind;
All boaft of wifdom's but pretence,
Our paflions make us blind.

Obferve at church the learned prieft,
He bids you temp'rance prize;
Yet o'er his bottle, at a feaft,
'Tis folly to be wife.

No more thofe mufty rules purfue,
Once taught in heathen fchools;
Believe me, (for I tell you true)
The ancients were but fools.

As thro' life's ftream we glide along,
We diff'rent paffions prize;
But be the burden of my fong,
'Tis folly to be wife.

SONG 415.

MY cautious mother, t'other day,
Cry'd, Polly, mind me, do;
I faw young Damon come this way,
And fear he came to you:
You know he's gay, and thought a rake,
So never welcome make him.
Thus I got fcolded for his fake,
I wifh the deuce may take him.

It's true I met him in a grove,
He gently clafp'd my hand,
Then figh'd, and talk'd more things of love
Than I could underftand;
And who'd have thought that we were feen?
But of fuch tricks I'll break him;
If he won't tell me what they mean,
The deuce, fure, ought to take him.

I often feel my bofom glow
With warmth I never knew;
If this be love that haunts me fo,
What can a virgin do?
Indeed, for pipe, for dance and fong,
'Gainft ev'ry fwain I'd take him,
But if he tantalizes long,
I hope the deuce will take him.

They fay, from wedlock fprings delight,
Then let him fpeak his mind,

I've no objection to unite
  With one fo fond and kind:
My mother, tho' too apt to pry,
  To difoblige I'm lothe;
Howe'er, I'll wed, then all her cry
  Will be, Deuce take you both.

SONG 416.

Sung in *Poor Vulcan*.

THESE mortals fay right, in their jovial
    abodes,
That a glafs of good punch is the drink of the
    gods;
        Take only a fmack of
        The nectar we crack of,
You'll find it is punch, and no more:
    The ingredients they mingle,
    Are contraries, fingle;
So are ours, they're the elements four.
Then, Bacchus, for thou art the drunkard's
    protector,
        Iffue inftant a fiat.
        And let who dare deny it,
That nectar's good punch, and that good punch
    is nectar.

SONG 417.

Sung at VAUXHALL.

PHOEBUS, meaner themes difdaining,
  To the lyrift's call repair,
And the ftrings to rapture ftraining,
  Come and praife the Britifh fair.

Chiefs throughout the land victorious,
  Born to conquer and to fpare,
Were not gallant, were not glorious,
  'Till commanded by the fair.

All the works of worth and merit,
  Which the fons of art prepare,
Have no pleafure, life, or fpirit,
  But as borrow'd from the fair.

Reafon is as weak as paffion,
  But if you for truth declare,
Worth and manhood are the fafhion,
  Favour'd by the Britifh fair.

SONG 418.

Sung at MARYBONE.

THE fprightly horn awakes the morn,
  And bids the hunter rife;
The op'ning hound returns the found,
  And echo fills the fkies.
See ruddy health, more dear than wealth,
  On yon blue mountain's brow;
The neighing fteed invokes our fpeed,
  And reynard trembles now.

In ancient days, as ftory fays,
  The woods our fathers fought;
The ruftic race adorn'd the chace,
  And hunted as they fought.

Come let's away, make no delay,
  Enjoy the foreft's charms;
Then o'er the bowl expand the foul,
  And reft in Chloe's arms.

SONG 419.

THE eaftern fky was purpled o'er,
  The lark, high pois'd in air,
Pour'd forth her foft, enchanting fong,
  The morn was frefh and fair;
When Colin to the mead convey'd
  His gentle fleecy charge,
Then to the lovely Delia's praife,
  Tun'd forth the fong at large.

My Delia is as Venus fair,
  As Hebe young and gay;
Would fhe but deign my flocks to fhare,
  I'd praife her all the day:
From morn to eve, from eve to morn,
  The woods, the groves fhould ring;
Would fhe to Colin give her hand,
  E'en winter would feem fpring.

She looks on a fhepherd as mean,
  Yet knows not the cares of the great;
A fhepherdefs is like a queen,
  But never knows envy nor hate:
Her flocks are her fubjects around,
  Her crook is her fceptre conteft,
Content is her glittering crown,
  And fimplicity makes up the reft.

Come, then, my fweet maid, to the plain,
  O come, let ambition fubfide,
Thro' pleafure's fmooth courfe you fhall go,
  And Colin fhall ftill be your guide:
The meads are enamel'd with flow'rs,
  And feem thy fair hand to invite;
O fly then, my fair to the grove,
  And feaft ev'ry fenfe with delight.

SONG 420.

TO love and be lov'd, how tranfporting the
    blifs,
To give, and receive, the foft conjugal kifs;
To fee a young race of fweet prattlers around,
Is a pleafure fuperior to all can be found!

Let libertines rail at the joys they ne'er know,
Such joys as from rambling can fure never flow;
A bottle and Thais may pleafe for a night,
But wedlock affords never-fading delight.

Tho' cenfure may feem to have room for it's
    rage,
In this money-jeb, fcandalous, match-making
    age;
When parents and guardians their children dif-
    pofe,
As chapmen at Smithfield buy horfes and cows.

But calmly confider true love as the fource,
And wedlock will furely be happy of courfe;
Yet a competent fortune will certainly pirate,
For life is fcarce life unlefs pafs'd thro' with eafe.

'Tis prudent, I own, ere you marry, to fee
If your means will fupport a wife eafy and free;
For cavils in wedlock will rife, to be fure,
When induftry can t keep the wolf from the
   door.

But when fortune and love both together com-
   bine,
And beauty and fenfe, too, as mutually join;
Let them rail on who will, I am certain of this,
That wedlock, fo plann'd, is the height of all
   blifs.

SONG 421.

Written by Mr. CHURCHILL.

A Jolly brifk tar, but a little time fince,
   As bold as a beggar, as drunk as a prince,
Fell foul of au ale-houfe, and thinking it fin
To pafs without calling, reel'd jovially in.
   Derry down, &c.

Scarce feated was he, when the landlord pafs'd
   by,
With pudding and beef, which attracted Jack's
   eye;
By the main-maft, a fail, boys! then he leapt
   from his place,
And grafping his bludgeon, gave orders for
   chace.
   Derry down, &c.

Now it happen'd together fome Frenchmen
   were met,
Refolving foup-meagre and frogs to forget,
Convinc'd of their error, commanded this feaft,
To be dreft and ferv'd up in the old Englifh
   tafte.
   Derry down, &c.

At the heels of the landlord the failor appears,
And makes the room ring with three Britifh
   cheers;
Then he fits himfelf down without further
   debate,
And claps an old quid in his next neighbour's
   plate.
   Derry down, &c.

Sure nothing could equal the Frenchmen's fur-
   prize,
When they fhrugg'd up their fhoulders, and
   turn'd up their eyes;
From one dropt a ha, and the other a hem,
All gap'd at the landlord, the landlord at them.
   Derry down, &c.

One, more bold than the reft, by his brethren's
   advice,
Made a fneaking attempt to come in for a flice;
Jack, cutting his hand, quickly gave him a
   check,
Cry'd, Down with your arms, or I'll foon fweep
   the deck.
   Derry down, &c.

The landlord enrag'd, now approach'd from
   afar,
And fneaking behind, feiz'd the arms of the
   tar;
I have him, fays he; but he cou'd fay no more,
Ere he found his dull pate where his heels ftood
   before.
   Derry down, &c.

The landlord thus fprawling, the Frenchmen
   unite,
Each takes up his knife and prepares for the
   fight;
Of quarters, cries Jack, I would not have you
   think;
Strike, ftrike, you frog-eaters, ftrike, ftrike,
   or you fink.
   Derry down, &c.

So faying, he handled his trufty oak ftick,
And pour'd in his broadfides fo ftout and fo
   thick;
So well play'd his part, in a minute, that four
Were decently laid with their hoft on the floor.
   Derry down, &c.

The reft all difmay'd at their countrymen's fate,
For fear that Jack's ftick fhould alight on their
   pate,
Acknowledg'd him victor and lord of the main,
Withal humbly entreating to bury their flain.
   Derry down, &c.

Three cheers then he gave, but infifted that
   they,
For the beef, for the pudding and porter fhould
   pay:
They agreed; fo the failor reel'd off with his
   wench,
And fung as he reel'd, Down, down with the
   French.
   Derry down, &c.

SONG 422.

THE SHEPHERD'S ARTIFICE.

SURE never poor fhepherd was tortur'd like
   me,
From morning to night I could never be free;
The charms of young Phillis fo ran in my head,
I wifh'd fhe was mine, or I wifh'd myfelf dead.

Whenever I faw her, and told her my cafe,
She gave me a frown, or fhe laugh'd in my face;
Yet ftill I ador'd her, and call'd her my wife,
My paffion was fix'd, nor could end but with
   life.

I found all the offers I made her of love
Produc'd no effect, nor affection would move;
So fchem'd a contrivance her paffion to try,
And boldly refolv'd, or to conquer, or die.

'Twas fpread round the village I courted young
   Prue,
And Phillis had left her own fchemes to purfue:
This anfwer'd my wifhes, fhe foon prov'd more
   kind,
And vow'd to be true, if I'd not change my mind.

I catch'd the occafion, and fent for a prieft,
For fear fhe fhould alter, I thought it the beft;
From hence learn, ye virgins, be bleft if you can,
And never refufe the fincere honeft man.

SONG 423.

DAMON AND DOLLY; A PASTORAL BALLAD.

Written by Mr. HAWKINS.

LAST Midfummer morn, as I ftray'd thro'
    the grove,
Young Dolly I met by the way;
I told her, her charms had fubdu'd me with love,
    And caus'd her a while for to ftay.

Silly Damon, fhe cry'd, what would you be at?
    Your fooling give over, I pray;
For all your fond wooing, your cooing and chat,
    No longer fhall make me delay.

Then I prefs'd her hand clofe, faying, Can you
    deny
A favour fo trifling as this?
But ftill fhe rejected, and cry'd out, O fye!
    When I eagerly ftole a fweet kifs.

With rapture I gaz'd on her delicate charms,
    (For I could not refift it, I vow)
Then clafping her lovingly in my fond arms,
    Said fhe, I muft go to my cow.

Then away o'er the plain together we went,
    Till come to a cool river's fide,
Where we tarry'd a while, till I gain'd her
    confent
For ever to be my true bride.

Adieu, then, ye troubles and plagues of this life,
    With Dolly I fure fhall be bleft;
For when that kind Providence makes her my
    wife,
We'll lull all our cares into reft.

SONG 424.

Sung at SADLER's WELLS.

BRISK wine and women are
    The fource of all our joys;
A brimmer foftens ev'ry care,
    And beauty never cloys:
Then let us drink and love,
    While yet our hearts are gay;
Women and wine, by all approv'd,
    Are bleffings night and day.

SONG 425.

THAT man who for life is blefs'd with a wife,
    Is fure in a happy condition;
Go things how they will, fhe fticks by him ftill,
    She's comforter, friend, and phyfician.

Pray, where is the joy, to trifle and toy,
    Yet dread fome difafter from beauty?
But fweet is the blifs of a conjugal kifs,
    Where love mingles pleafure with duty.

One extravagant whore will coft a man more
Than twenty good wives that are faving;
For wives they will fpare, that their children
    may fhare,
But whores are eternally craving.

SONG 426.

HOW oft, my Clara, haft thou faid,
    (The fondnefs of the heart to prove)
That Twitcher was thy deareft friend,
    Nor wouldft thou feek another love.
And by thofe lips that fweetly fwore,
    And by thofe eyes that fhine fo bright,
I ne'er lov'd woman fo before,
    For Clara is my foul's delight.

Then let me prefs thofe ruby lips,
    And on that lovely breaft repofe;
Exhaling fragrance from thy breath,
    Fragrance that far excels the rofe.
Then let us fpend the live-long day,
    And thus the tedious night beguile;
The cares of ftate I fhall not feel,
    So Clara fing, and Clara fmile.

SONG 427.

AN HYMENEAL CANTATA.

RECITATIVE.

HENCE care and forrow, hence all jarring
    ftrife,
Let mirth abound, now Harriet is a wife;
Let difcord, enmity, and envy, ceafe,
And nought be feen but love, content, and
    peace.
And may henceforward each confenting pair
Such fatisfaction in their nuptials fhare.

AIR.

May the joyous and gay, who are prefent each
    day,
    Be ftrangers to forrowful thinking;
May ev'ry one be good-humour'd and free,
    While prudence directs us in drinking.

Let your bucks then declare, who, to fubdue the
    fair,
    News fchemes are continually trying,
How foon they are cloy'd when the object's
    enjoy'd,
    And condemn the weak fair for complying.

Then fwains learn to love, if you'd happinefs
    prove,
    Not the blooming young maiden for beauty,
But the girl who with care has avoided the fnare,
    Nor yields till commanded by duty.

Then let's fill up the glafs; may each fwain
    find his lafs,
    Like Harriet, confenting and tender;
May the fair learn to ftay till the prieft fay,
    obey,
    And ftern virtue applauds the furrender.

P

RECITATIVE.

The lovely fair, as near her lord advanc'd,
A smile upon him ravishingly glanc'd;
Conflicting passions glow within her breast,
Till potent love these sentiments exprefs'd:

AIR.

Was ever a maiden so happy as me,
  Who daily, with pleasure, can view
The man whom I chose, a foe to deceit,
  So worthy, so artless, so true!

O may, then, each fair, who to marriage
    consents,
  Be blefs'd with a husband like mine;
For when with the hand we the heart inter-
    change,
  Love then is a passion divine.

Let all those who think to be happy in life,
  This maxim for ever retain;
Tho' vice, for a time, may our reason beguile,
  The offspring of folly is pain.

But, ah! how reverse is the state of the fair,
  Whose heart is in bondage at ease!
For love is refin'd in the marriage embrace,
  And virtue is certain to please.

SONG 428.

Written by Mr. HUGHES.

CONSTANTIA, see! thy faithful slave
  Dies of the wound thy beauty gave:
Ah! gentle nymph, no longer try
From fond pursuing love to fly.

Thy pity to my love impart;
Pity my bleeding, aching heart;
Regard my sighs, and flowing tears,
And with a smile remove my fears.

A wedded wife if thou would'st be,
By sacred Hymen join'd to me,
Ere yet the western sun decline,
My hand and heart shall both be thine.

SONG 429.

LOVE AND AFFECTION.

Sung at VAUXHALL.

WHEN youth mature, to manhood grew,
  Soon beauty touch'd my heart;
From vein to vein love's lightning flew,
  With pleasing painful smart:
My bosom dear content forsook,
  And sooth'd the soft dejection;
The melting eye, the speaking look,
  Prov'd love and sweet affection.

Unus'd to arts which win the fair,
  What could a shepherd do?
And to submit to sad despair,
  Was not the way to woo.
At length I told the lovely maid,
  I hop'd she'd no objection
To talk (while round her lambkins play'd)
  Of love and sweet affection.

A blush my Chloe's cheek bedeck'd,
  A blush devoid of guile,
And what from me can you expect?
  She answer'd, with a smile.
How many nymphs have been betray'd,
  Through want of calm reflection!
Then don't my peace of mind invade
  With love and sweet affection.

Dear maid I cry'd, mistrust me not,
  In wedlock's bands let's join;
My kids, my kine, my herds, my cot,
  My soul itself, is thine.
To church I led the charming fair,
  To hymen's kind protection;
And now life's dearest joys we share,
  With love and sweet affection.

SONG 430.

Sung in the *Capricious Lovers.*

WHEN the head of poor Tummus was broke
  By Roger, who play'd at the wake,
And Kate was alarm'd at the stroke,
  And wept for poor Tummus's sake;
When his worship gave noggins of ale,
  And the liquor was charming and stout;
O these were the times to regale,
  And we footed it rarely about.

Then our partners were buxom as does,
  And we all were as happy as kings;
Each lad in his holiday cloaths,
  And the lasses in all their best things:
With merriment all the day long!
  May the feast of our Colin prove such;
Odzooks! but I'll join in the song,
  And I'll hobble about with my crutch.

SONG 431.

DAMON AND DELIA.

DAMON.

SEE, charmer, see, yon myrtle grove,
  So fragrant, fresh, and gay,
Invites my Delia, queen love,
  To hail the infant May.
Hear how the painted choirists sing
  The love-inviting strain;
The spring-clad vales with music ring;
  Have pity on my pain.

DELIA.

By Strephon's fond persuasive strain
  Poor Lucy was undone;
And, t'other eve, upon the plain,
  I, shepherd, met with one,
Who stopt me with expressive sighs,
  And cry'd, she was bereav'd
Of what young maidens mostly prize;
  That Damon had deceiv'd.

DAMON.

Why should my fair-one so much strive
  To vex her fetter'd swain!

I fwear 'tis falfe; may I not thrive
(Autumnus yield no gain)
If e'er, by flatt'ring words or arts,
I fimple maids beguile;
'Tis truth my artlefs tongue imparts,
I live in Delia's fmile.

DELIA.

Fond fhepherd, doubts I muft fuftain,
My bofom fwells with care,
Left, when I've pity'd Damon's pain,
He fhould his love forbear.

DAMON.

Sure Heav'n intended for delight
That graceful form of thine!
No, no, my maid, I cannot flight,
Nor e'er my love decline.

DELIA.

May ev'ry day your love renew!
You wife and wifer be;
Our fleecy care let's each purfue,
Both happy whilft we're free.

SONG 432.

ADVICE TO MODERN PATRIOTS.

Written by the EDITOR.

YE fage politicians, who're never content,
But always look chearlefs and glum;
Ceafe troubling your pates, for ye ne'er will
prevent
The minifter's efforts to hum.

When he brings in his bill, and gives fign for
the aid
Of thofe whom you juftly call fcum,
However contemptuoufly they are furvey'd,
All your oppofition's but hum.

Then what careth he for his country's fate,
So himfelf can procure a plum!
While he and his minions enjoy their eftate,
They laugh at the fools whom they hum.

So give o'er this ftrife, which muft always prove
vain,
And henceforth be filent and mum;
For—when they've enough—they'll be honeft
again,
But never, till then, ceafe to hum.

SONG 433.

THE HAPPY SHEPHERD.

Sung at RANELAGH.

WITH Phillis I'll trip o'er the meads,
And haften away to the plain,
Where fhepherds attend with their reeds,
To welcome my love and her fwain:
The lark is exalted in air,
The linnet fings perch'd on the fpray;
Our lambs ftand in need of our care,
Then let us not lengthen delay.

What pleafures I feel with my dear,
While gamefome young lambs are at fport,
Exceed the delights of a peer,
That fhines with fuch grandeur at court:
When Colin and Strephon go by,
They form a difguife for a while;
They fee how I'm bleft with a figh,
But envy forbids them to fmile.

Let courtiers of liberty prate,
T'enjoy it take infinite pains;
But liberty's primitive ftate
Is only enjoy'd on the plains:
With Phillis I rove to and fro,
With her my gay minutes are fpent;
'Twas Phillis firft taught me to know,
That happinefs flows from content.

SONG 434.

THE whimfical lover's a prey to all care,
 Fol derol lol, &c.
He's loft to himfelf when he fighs for the fair;
 Fol derol lol, &c.
He dreams all the day, and he wakes all the night,
His forrows are lafting, but fhort his delight.
 Fol derol lol, &c.

Let my pretty Molly go round with the toaft,
 Fol derol lol, &c.
I'm bleft if fhe's mine, and the fame if fhe's loft;
 Fol derol lol, &c.
If fhe fhould love me, I'm fure fhe'll prove true;
And if fhe fhould alter, why fo can I too,
 Fol derol lol, &c.

Shou'd fhe prove inconftant, why fhould I be fad?
 Fol derol lol, &c.
'Tis time to grow wifer, and not to run mad.
 Fol derol lol, &c.
If fhe proves conftant, fhe'll honour my love;
And the lofs of a jilt is a bleffing, by Jove.
 Fol derol lol, &c.

The lofs of a miftrefs fhall never deftroy
 Fol derol lol, &c.
The happy tranquillity which I enjoy;
 Fol derol lol, &c.
For againft all thefe evils I'll always prepare
Indiff'rence, that fovereign cure for all care.
 Fol derol lol, &c.

SONG 435.

Sung at VAUXHALL.

GENTLE gales, in pity bear
 My fighs, my tender fighs away;
To my cruel Strephon's ear
 All my foft complaints convey.

Near fome moffy fountain's fide,
 Or on fome verdant bank reclin'd,
Where bubbling ftreams in murmurs glide,
 You will the dear deluder find.

Gentle gales, in pity bear
 My fighs, my tender fighs away;
To my cruel Strephon's ear
 All my foft complaints convey.

Tell the falſe one how I mourn,
　Tell him all my pains and woes;
Tell, ah! tell him to return,
　And bring my wounded heart repoſe.

Gentle gales, in pity bear
　My ſighs, my tender ſighs away;
To my cruel Strephon's ear,
　All my ſoft complaints convey.

S O N G 436.

BLITHE COLIN.

Written by Mr. HAWKINS.

Sung at RANELAGH.

BY the ſide of the ſweet River Tay,
　Or elſe on the banks of the Tweed,
Young Colin he whiſtles all day,
　Or merrily pipes on his reed.
His mind is a ſtranger to care,
　For he is blithe, bonny, and free;
At harveſt, at wake, and at fair;
　No ſwain is ſo chearful as he.

At eve, when we dance on the green,
　How ſprightly he joins in the throng;
So pleaſing his air and his mien,
　So gaily he trips it along!
The laſſes his manners adore,
　And ſtrive his affections to gain;
When abſent, for him they deplore,
　All ſigh for the ſmiles of the ſwain.

But I am the girl to his mind,
　He choſe me above all the reſt,
And vows that to me he'll be kind,
　With me he will ever be bleſt.
The maidens all envy my bliſs,
　And tell me I'm ſimple and vain;
Yet I'm not diſpleaſed at this,
　Nor heed their contempt and diſdain.

S O N G 437.

SOMETHING NEW.

Sung at VAUXHALL.

IN all mankind's promiſcuous race,
　The ſons of error urge their chace,
　The wond'rous to purſue;
And, both in country and in town,
　The curious courtiers, cit, and clown,
　Solicit ſomething new.

The poets ſtill from nature take,
　And what is ready-made they make;
　Hiſtorians muſt be true:
How therefore ſhall we find a road,
　Thro' diſſertation, ſong, or ode,
　To give you ſomething new?

They ſay virginity is ſcarce
　As any thing in proſe or verſe;
　And ſo is honour too:
The papers of the day imply,
　No more than that we live and die,
　And pay for ſomething new.

We ſee alike the woeful dearth
　In melancholy, or in mirth;
　What, then, ſhall ladies do?
Seek virtue as th' immortal prize;
　In fine, be honeſt, and be wiſe,
　For that is ſomething new.

S O N G 438.

Sung at VAUXHALL.

YE beaux and ye wits,
　Ye courtiers and cits,
Attentive to pleaſure's gay call;
　Come, revel away,
　For this is the day;
She cries—Hark! away to Vauxhall!

Here muſic you'll find
　To enliven the mind,
That never your fancies can pall;
　Then, lads, come away,
　And laſſes be gay;
Hark—pleaſure invites to Vauxhall.

Sweet nymphs, grave or gay,
　Quite ſick of the play,
And cloy'd with each op'ra and ball;
　Come here, change the ſcene,
　Hail pleaſure's gay queen;
She cries—Hark! away to Vauxhall!

S O N G 439.

Sung in *Artaxerxes*.

TO ſigh and complain,
　Alike I diſdain,
Contented my wiſh to enjoy:
　I ſcorn to reflect
　On a lady's neglect,
Or barter my peace for a toy.

In love, as in war,
　I laugh at a ſcar;
And if my proud enemy yield,
　The joy that remains,
　Is to lead her in chains,
And glean the rich ſpoils of the field.

S O N G 440.

A MARTIAL SONG.

Written by Mr. MAYOR.

TO arms, to arms! Britannia calls;
　Awake, ye ſov'reigns of the main;
Lo! treach'ry bids the faithleſs Gauls
　Preſume upon your native reign.
Rule, Britannia; Britannia, rule the waves;
Britons never will be ſlaves.

Can free-born ſpirits ſink ſo low,
　To ſhudder at a race of ſlaves?
Will Britiſh proweſs tamely bow,
　And quit the empire of the waves?
　Rule, Britannia, &c.

Tho' folly's bafe, inglorious fway,
Thy once unclouded annals ftain;
If wifdom pointed out the way,
Thy fons their fplendor would regain.
Rule, Britannia, &c.

A Chatham, fir'd with honeft rage,
Would rouze the courage of this ifle;
Blot paft difgrace from mem'ry's page,
And make expiring commerce fmile.
Rule, Britannia, &c.

Thrice bleft the man, ordain'd to fave
Thefe nations, in this dreary hour;
To wake the flame that Heav'n firft gave,
Difpel our fears, and raife our pow'r.
Rule, Britannia, &c.

Till heaving furges ceafe to roar,
His praife fhall grace the roll of fame,
When future ages feel no more
Our prefent weaknefs, and our fhame.
Rule, Britannia; Britannia, rule the waves;
Britons never will be flaves.

SONG 441.

THE LADY'S CHOICE OF A HUSBAND.

Written by Mr. T. ADNEY.

I'D have a man of fenfe and air,
The pride of ev'ry witty fair;
Genteel in make, in ftature tall,
Polite to me, and good to all.

No powder'd, filly, flatt'ring beau,
Who of good fenfe doth nothing know:
A man of fcience, fond of books,
Who's temper's equal to his looks.

No jealous fears I'd have annoy
The pleafing profpect of our joy;
That life a fcene of love may be
To the dear youth, the world, and me.

I'd have this mild and gentle youth
Infpir'd with wifdom, grace, and truth;
And as for wealth, I'll not repine,
If he has none, I'll give him mine.

Ye gen'rous gods! I afk no more;
If fuch a man you've got in ftore,
And I'm deferving, fpeak your mind,
I'll be to him for ever join'd.

SONG 442.

Sung at MARYBONE.

A HUNTING SONG.

HARK, hark ye, how echoes the horn in the vale,
Whofe notes do fo fportingly dance on the gale,
To charm us to barter, for ignoble reft,
The joys which true pleafure can raife in the breaft:
The morning is fair, and in labour with day,
And the cry of the huntfman is, hark, hark, away:

Then wherefore defer we, one moment, our joys;
Hafte, hafte, let's away, fo to horfe, my brave boys.

What pleafure can equal the joys of the chace,
Where meaner delights to more noble give place?
While onward we prefs, and each forrow defy,
From valley to valley re-echoes the cry:
Our joys are all fterling, no forrow we fear,
We bound o'er the lawn, and look back on old care;
Forgetful of labour, we leap o'er the mounds,
Led on by the horn, and the cry of the hounds.

SONG 443.

Sung at VAUXHALL.

WHERE new-mown hay, on winding Tay,
The fweets of fpring difclofes,
As I one morning finging lay
Upon a bank of rofes,
Young Jamie, whifking o'er the mead,
By geud luck chanc'd to fpy me,
He took his bonnet off his head,
And gently fat down by me.
O my bonny Jamie, O!
I care not tho' the world fhould know
How dearly I love Jamie, O!

The fwain, tho' I right mickle prize,
Yet now I wad na ken him,
But with a frown my heart difguis'd,
And ftrave away to fend him;
But fondly he ftill nearer prefs'd,
And, at my feet down lying,
His beating heart it thump'd fa faft,
I thought the lad was dying.
O my bonny Jamie, &c.

But ftill refolving to deny,
And angry accents feigning,
I often roughly fhot him by,
With words fu' of difdaining;
He feiz'd my hand, and nearer drew,
And gently chiding a' my pride,
So fweetly did the fhepherd woo,
I, blufhing, vow'd to be his bride.
O my bonny Jamie, O!
I care not tho' the world fhould know
How dearly I love Jamie, O!

SONG 444.

WHEN Calliope and Clio to Britain's rude ifle
Perchance once a vifiting came,
All then was confufion, till they deign'd to fmile,
And hoift here the ftandard of fame.

In procefs of time, by the mufes grand aid,
Our ifland extended her fway
O'er empires and kingdoms; no land ever made
Of commerce and arts fuch difplay.

At length, full determin'd to fix their abode
In England, the mufes agreed;

For the fo'l here was good, and whenever they
    fow'd
It was certain to propagate feed.

Thus favour'd, we'll fpurn at the fcroyls of
    the age,
  And their impotent boaftings defpife;
For envy, and rancour, what ills they prefage,
  On themfelves are moft certain to rife.

SONG 445.

RURAL PROSPECT.

Written by Mr. LEMOINE.

NOW gilded groves, with verdure clad,
  Reflect bright Phœbus' golden beams,
While his celeftial glories flame
  Down the tranflucent filver ftreams.
Lo! as Aurora onward moves,
  His fleecy flocks the fhepherd-fwain
Drives from their folds in jovial glee,
  And whitens all the verdant plain.

In yonder gay, enamell'd mead,
  The ftarling plumes his golden wings,
Then tow'ring up the azure height,
  He mounts fublime, and foaring fings.
Nymph of the wave, fweet Naïad hear,
  While thy clear water's bank along,
With careless fteps I pleafing ftray,
  And warble forth my youthful fong.

Here could I ever, ever rove,
  And quit the world's contentious fcene;
What joy, with innocence and truth,
  To wrap me in your charming green!
But fate and fortune, adverfe, call,
  And fnatch me to the bufy throng;
Adieu, then! rural fweets, adieu!
  And ceafe, thou dear, deluding fong.

SONG 446.

CONTENTMENT.

Written by Mr. MAVOR.

SEQUESTER'D far from public life,
  From giddy mirth, and noify ftrife;
From headftrong paffions, vain defires;
From envy, pride, and guilty fires;
From cares and fears for ever free,
O, fweet Contentment, let me live with thee.

Thine are the joys that never fail;
Thine is the placid, conftant gale,
That bids us fmile at frequent fhocks
Of dang'rous fyrts, and latent rocks;
And fince I crave thy fmiles a'one,
Come, in my breaft, erect thy lucid throne.

Golconda's gems, and flaming mines,
Where, far from day, the di'mond fhines;
Peruvian mountains richeft ore,
And treafure of the golden fhore,
Afford no blifs, devoid of thee,
At beft more fair, more fplendid mifery.

The palace deckt with regal ftate;
The vain parade of all the great;
The title penfion, or the gown,
The ftar, the garter, or the crown,
Without you as a conftant gueft,
Leave their poffeffors joylefs and unbleft.

What's thy delight, Contentment, fay;
With what condition wilt thou ftay?
If grandeur often wooes in vain,
Wilt thou adorn the rural plain?
Wilt thou vouchfafe to blefs the cot
Where poverty obtains it's ftill unenvy'd lot?

'Tis here I fee thy fplendor's beam;
'Tis here thou roll ft thy cleareft ftream;
'Tis here thou fheddeft, in difguife,
The pureft joys beneath the fkies;
And from thy lib'ral hand here flow
Such fweets as fceptr'd monarchs feldom know.

Come, then, inftruct me how to fteer
Thro' fmiling fortune, and fevere:
With thee the turf-built cot would pleafe,
The flow'ry banks, and fhady trees;
And for thy fmiles, thou nymph divine,
I'd high purfuits, without a figh, refign.

SONG 447.

Sung in the *Prodigal Son.*

GREAT God, while fuppliant thus we bend,
  Thy kind, thy gracious hearing lend
  To this our fervent pray'r!
O may our fire's remaining day
Enjoy a foft, a calm decay,
  His eve ferenely fair!

But if difeafe, with venom'd dart,
Or forrow, wound the rev'rend heart
  Of thofe who gave us breath;
Let us their deftin'd anguifh fhare,
Prevent or dry each painful tear,
  And fmoothe the bed of death.

CHORUS.

What dear delight the duties bring,
  Wherein thus daily we engage:
From filial love what comforts fpring,
  To warm the heart of fhiv'ring age!

SONG 448.

A TRIP O'ER THE GREEN; A PASTORAL.

Written by Mr. HAWKINS.

ONE day, o'er the green as I tript it along,
  A gentle young fhepherd pafs'd by;
He play'd on his pipe, and fo fweet was his fong,
  He made my poor heart for to figh.

He called me back to fit by him a while,
  The fwain I could fcarcely deny;
So fweetly he look'd, and he gave me a fmile,
  Which caus'd me ftill more for to figh.

Then ftraight he came to me, and proffer'd a kifs,
  At which I feem'd modeft and fhy;

Yet I vow in my heart I was pleafed at this,
 Though he made me to flutter and figh.

He told me he lov'd me, and fomething befide,
 Which I muft not repeat, by the bye,
For fear the young fhepherd my conduct fhould
 chide,
 And make me for ever to figh.

He promis'd to take me next week to the fair,
 And many fine things he will buy,
Both rofes and ribbands to ftick in my hair;
 Then who'll be fo fhewy as I?

And if that the fwain fhould make me his wife,
 To pleafe him all means I will try;
I'll ever be faithful, and love him for life,
 And virtuous until that I die.

SONG 449.

THE TRAIN BANDS; A CANTATA.

RECITATIVE.

ABOUT the warm feafon when farmers reap
 corn,
A feather each citizen claps on his horn;
With the thoughts of a mufter his fpirits abound,
And without fear he fteers to th' Artillery
 Ground:
There he fees all the regiment, the colonel and
 captain,
Red cloaths and big looks ingenioufly wrapt in.
Commanders with age bent, a very fad thing,
Who ftumble and hobble like pigs in a ftring;
And after an hour is wafted, or near,
To know right from left, and the front from
 the rear;
With abundance of buftle they're jumbled to-
 gether,
The cobler and porter, the beau and his feather;
Some ftagg'ring with drink, and fome hobbling
 with corns,
And fcratching their heads as if groping for
 horns;
At length the commander for filence roars
 out,
And then thus addreffes the whimfical rout.

AIR.

Take notice of what you're about,
 All other thoughts defpife;
A foldier never fhould he out,
 But know his exercife.
A man that would acquire fame,
 Shou'd much in arms delight;
To get an everlafting name,
 He fhould fhine forth in fight.

RECITATIVE.

This faid, then the drummers beat an alarm,
And throughout the field they cry, Arm—arm
 —arm!
Then in two parts divided, both father and
 brother,
To fight, like true Englifhmen, one againft
 t'other;

Then, thus the command is, to rank and to
 file,
With looks fo important, would make a dog
 fmile.

AIR.

Make ready, my boys,
 And well ram your powder;
'Twill make the more noife,
 And found much the louder.

RECITATIVE.

The captain then holding his cane up on high,
Cries, Fire, my lads, and let your wads fly;
But pops down his noddle almoft to the grafs,
For fear that a bullet fhould fly in his face;
Or left the fierce flame, that admits no re-
 ftraining,
Should burn his fine wig, kept on purpofe for
 training:
Then their drums and their mufquets at once
 ceafe to rattle,
And thus is concluded the bloodilefs battle:
The fight being ended, the power is o'er,
And the chief now but counfels, who order'd
 before.

AIR.

My lads, you've done well;
 In fight you excel,
And are heroes in wars and alarms;
 Pray, go home to your wives,
 Thofe who've not loft their lives,
And revel and bafk in their arms.

SONG 450.

Sung in the Sorcerer.

DAMON.

CAST, my love, thine eyes around,
 See the fportive lambkins play;
Nature daily decks the ground,
 All in honour of the May:
Like the fparrow and the dove,
Liften to the voice of love.

FLORELLA.

Damon, thou haft found me long
 Lift'ning to thy foothing tale;
And thy foft, perfuafive tongue,
 Often held me in the dale;
Take, oh! Damon, while I live,
All which virtue ought to give.

DAMON.

Not the verdure of the grove,
 Not the garden's faireft flow'r;
Nor the meads where lovers rove,
 Tempted by the vernal hour;
Can delight thy Damon's eye,
If Florella is not by.

FLORELLA.

Not the water's gentle fall,
 By the bank with poplars crown'd,

Not the feather'd fongfters all,
  Nor the flute's melodious found,
Can delight Florella's ear,
If her Damon is not near.

BOTH.

Let us love, and let us live
  Like the chearful feafon gay;
Banifh care, and let us give
  Tribute to the fragrant May:
Like the fparrow and the dove,
  Liften to the voice of love.

SONG 451.

CRUEL CUPID; A RONDEAU.

Sung at VAUXHALL.

CRUEL Cupid! why diftrefs me?
  Why with fighs my bofom fill?
Come, fond urchin, to imprefs me,
  Make my flutt'ring heart lie ftill.

Force me not to pine and languifh
  For a falfe and fickle fwain,
Who, triumphing o'er my anguifh,
  Leaves me thus in grief and pain.

Virgins, be not too believing,
  Shun the vile, inconftant fex;
Man was born to be deceiving,
  Foolifh women to perplex.

SONG 452.

Written by Mr. MAVOR.

BEFORE the morn's empurpling light
  Has chac'd the fombre fhades of night,
My reftlefs thoughts to Nancy rove,
And fancy paints the maid I love.

When from the chambers of the Eaft,
In all his mildeft glories dreft,
The beauteous rifing-fun I fee,
I think his beams lefs fair than fhe.

The flow'ry vefture of the fields,
The flaming gems rich India yields,
Are far lefs grateful to my eye
Than when my deareft maid is nigh.

The fragrant rofe's crimfon dyes
Fade at the luftre of her eyes;
And as o'er banks of flow'rs fhe treads,
They feel her charms, and droop their heads.

Ye great, ambitious, and ye vain,
Poffefs your wifhes, and your pain;

All other pleafures I refign,
Be deareft Nancy only mine.

Bleft with her love, I would defy
Malignant fate, and envy fly;
And pafs thro' life without a care,
A figh, a murmur, or a fear.

SONG 453.

SUMMER.

Written by Mr. LEMOINE.

ALL nature looks gay,
  While birds on each fpray
Re-echo fweet harmony round;
  The lily and rofe
  Their beauties difclofe,
And daifies enamel the ground.

The meadows look green,
  No forrows are feen,
Each garden's enraptur'd with joy;
  Bright murmuring rills,
  That circle the hills,
Yield pleafures that never can cloy.

The fnowy-fleec'd lambs,
  Befide of their dams,
Pafs merrily all the glad day;
  While hufbandmen fweat
  By the wonderful heat
Of Phœbus's powerful ray.

And tho' the fpring's fled,
  We've fummer inftead,
With charms that enliven the foul:
  So nothing but mirth
  Inhabits our earth,
From latitude—nought, to the pole.

SONG 454.

Written Mr. GARRICK.

Sung in Epilogue to the *Clandeftine Marriage.*

I Hate all their nonfenfe,
  Their Shakefpeares and Johnfons,
Their plays, and their playhoufe, and bards:
  'Tis finging, not faying;
  A fig for all playing,
But playing, as we do, at cards.

I love to fee Jonas,
Am pleas'd, too, with Comus;
Each well the fpectator rewards:
  So clever, fo neat, in
  Their tricks, and their cheating,
Like them we would fain deal our cards.

SONG 455.

DORCHESTER-BEER.

Written by the EDITOR; and occasioned by his drinking some extraordinary fine Ale with his Friend J. MORRIS, Esq. brewed by Mr. BOWER of Dorchester.

IN these troublesome times, when each
    mortal complains,
Some praise to the man is most certainly due,
Who, while he finds out a relief for their pains,
Supplies all his patients with good liquor too:
Then attend to my song, and I'll make it appear,
A specifick for all is in Dorchester-beer.

Would our ministry drink it, instead of French
    wine,
    The blessed effects we should quickly per-
    ceive;
It would sharpen their senses, their spirits refine,
And make those—who now laugh at their
    folly—to grieve.
No Frenchman would dare at our councils to
    sneer,
If the statesmen drank nothing but Dorchester-
    beer.

But should they (for statesmen are obstinate
    things)
Neglect to comply with the wish of my muse,
Nor regard a true Briton who honestly sings,
Our soldiers and sailors will never refuse:
And, believe me, from France we have little
    to fear,
Let these but have plenty of Dorchester-beer.

E'en our brethren across the Atlantick, could
    they
    But drink of this liquor, would soon be
    content:

And quicker by half, I will venture to say,
    Our parliament might have fulfill'd their
    intent,
If, instead of commissioners, tedious and dear,
    They had sent out a cargo of Dorchester-beer.

Then let each worthy Briton, who wishes for
    peace
    With America's sons, fill his glass to the
    brim,
And drink—May our civil commotions soon
    cease,
    And war with French perfidy instant begin:
May our friends never want, nor our foes e'er
    come near,
    The pride of Old England, good Dorchester-
    beer!

SONG 456.

THE ROVER CHAINED.

Written by Mr. MAVOR.

GREAT Love! I own thy pow'r supreme,
    My mind has felt the dart;
No more the transitory flame
    Plays lambent round my heart.

Bright Nancy's charms the bosom fire,
    That erst was wont to rove;
And sense and beauty now conspire
    To light an ardent love.

Then wonder not to hear me vow
    That I can change no more;
Since she has all Heav'n can bestow,
    Or sighing swains adore.

Thus nature, foe to flatt'ry's strain,
    Instructs the busy bee
To range the produce of the plain,
    And ev'ry shrub and tree;

Q

Till lighting on the bloomy rose,
  Where each sweet essence joins,
(Like me) the warmest wish she shows,
  To live where beauty shines.

SONG 457.

Sung at VAUXHALL.

WHEN last we parted on the plain,
  Fond Damon seem'd full lothe to go;
He kiss'd, and said, That soon again
  He'd come, and wou'd not leave me so;
For that, says he, the time is near,
  And then, my love, I do design,
    It is the best day in the year,
    To come and be your Valentine.

I wish'd the tedious hours to fly,
  And long'd the look'd-for day to see;
And as the time then grew so nigh,
  How blest, thought I, will Nancy be!
The morning came, and at my door
  I heard a noise, that said, Incline
For once, dear girl, if never more,
  To rise and be my Valentine.

A thousand fears disturb'd my mind,
  'Twas Thyrsis there, in Damon's stead!
I thought my youth was quite unkind,
  Nor knew what shou'd be done or said.
I hop'd it could not be a sin;
  In spite to Damon, now not mine,
I let the kinder Thyrsis in,
  And was that shepherd's Valentine.

Nor what I did I now repent,
  For fickle Damon, soon as light,
To Lucy on that morning went,
  Nor has been since from out her sight;
And Thyrsis, late but half-lov'd swain,
  Is now both all and only mine;
I bless the time, that once was pain,
  He came to be my Valentine.

SONG 458.

Sung at RANELAGH.

THE eye that beams with lambent light;
  The crimson cheek, that glads the sight,
    The shape, the mien, the air;
With these, to soothe man's ruder breast,
With these, to be by blessing blest,
    The gods adorn the fair.

Hence each poetic genius sings;
Sweet beauty tunes th' embosom'd strings,
    And wakes th' enraptur'd soul.
The magic pow'r of form and face,
Ordain'd the gentler sex to grace,
    Resounds from pole to pole.

But shall not charms so honour'd last?
No; soon as youth's short summer's past,
    They're veil'd in time's disguise.
Thus blushing Flora's darling flow'r,
That scents the aromatic bow'r,
    Buds, bursts to bloom, and dies.

Then, ah, how vain is female pride!
Shall she that's crown'd with sense confide
    In such uncertain pow'r?
No, she reveres the milder way,
Reserv'd, tho' free; tho' modest, gay;
    And blooms to life's last hour.

Do thou, my fair-one, in whose mind
Each social moral, virtue's join'd,
    The nymph of sense appear.
Then, when the charms of youth are o'er,
The wise will Celia still adore;
    Thou'lt still be lovely here.

SONG 459.

IF 'tis joy to wound a lover,
  How much more to give him ease;
When his passion we discover,
  Oh, how pleasing 'tis to please!

This is doubly to encharm him;
  Makes him proud to be a slave;
What can more our worth inform him,
  Than to heal the wounds we gave?

Thus the warrior fam'd in story,
  Leading captive thro' the field,
Justly merits double glory,
  Gently treating those that yield.

SONG 460.

Written by a YOUNG GENTLEMAN, late of Westminster School.

FOR thee, whose warm tenderness loves
  At the sound of my pleasures to glow;
Or, when sorrow's mild influence moves,
  Can melt in the softness of woe;
Where the horrors of winter may spring,
  As o'er mountains we tremble along,
Shall friendship her offering bring,
  And chear the rude path with her song!

How sweet the reflections of peace,
  I and friendship those wishes engage!
How pleasing to think on the ease,
  The social retirement of age!
To the seats which my Shenstone has plann'd,
  Each wish of my bosom shall move;
A flow'r ne'er bloom'd from his hand,
  But for friendship, for virtue, and love.

Here let me retire for awhile;
  But should fortune hence snatch me away,
Unhurt, 'mid the desart I'll smile,
  Nor the blush of repining betray;
Soft friendship my footsteps shall guide,
  And teach me some hamlet to chuse;
And health, rosy maid, by my side,
  Shall breathe the pure air to my muse.

Here spring her first tribute shall pay,
  Here summers' first beauties combine;
While mirth thro' our vallies shall play,
  Or smile from the boughs of our vines.
While thou, for whose pleasure I raise
  Each sweet which retirement can give,

Beſtow the lov'd mite of thy praiſe,
Content 'mid ſuch beauties to live.

But hence, from theſe emblems of joy,
Unconſcious while virtue may rove,
Should death his *mild* powers employ,
And catch the laſt ſound of my love;
'Tis thine, on the grave of thy friend,
Affection's fond tribute to rear;
O'er the ſpot ſhalt thou eagerly bend,
And raiſe the young flow'r with a tear.

SONG 461.

THE INCONSTANT SWAIN.

Sung at RANELAGH.

BENEATH this grove, this ſilent ſhade,
  Come, Damon, to the gentle maid;
What other nymph would love like me?
For, oh, thou'rt all inconſtancy!

You us'd to talk of love and bliſs,
And often ſigh'd my lips to kiſs;
But roving now is ſweeter glee,
For thou art all inconſtancy.

Here fragrant flow'rets ſweetly ſpring,
The feather'd choir in concert ſing;
Yet vain is what I hear and ſee,
Since Damon's all inconſtancy.

The am'rous doves now bill and coo,
And ſo, falſe Damon, ſo can you;
But can't like them contented be,
Thy ſole delight's inconſtancy.

Ye ſimple fair! believe not man,
They all proceed on Damon's plan;
Then from the ſex your hearts keep free,
And love, like them, inconſtancy.

SONG 462.

A RONDEAU.

Sung at VAUXHALL.

SHEPHERD, ceaſe your ſoft complaining,
  I've a heart that ſcorns diſdaining:
I no baſhful meanings want,
All that virtue aſks I'll grant;
Downcaſt looks, and frequent ſighing,
Diſtant awe, and vows of dying,
All are ſenſeleſs. Who'd believe
He would die, who ſtill may live?

SONG 463.

BY a cool fountain's flowery ſide,
  The bright Celinda lay;
Her looks increas'd the ſummer's pride;
  Her eyes the bloom of day.

The roſes bluſh'd with deeper red,
  To ſee their charms outdone;
The lilies ſunk beneath their bed,
  To ſee ſuch rival's ſhown.

Quick through the air, to his retreat,
  A bee induſtrious flew;

Prepar'd to rifle ev'ry ſweet,
  And ſip the balmy dew.

Drawn by the fragrance of her breath,
  Her roſy lips he found;
Where he in tranſports met his death,
  And dropt upon the ground.

Enjoy, bleſt bee! enjoy thy fate,
  Nor at thy fall repine;
Each god would quit his bliſsful ſtate,
  To ſhare a joy like thine.

SONG 464.

Sung at VAUXHALL.

WHAT is he gone? and can it be?
  And is ſhe then more fair than me?
The ſight of her might give me pain;
Bring her not near me, fickle ſwain!
And ſince that you can leave me ſo,
Go get you gone, for ever go.

Oh, I in rage would madly tear
This gaudy ribband from my hair;
Theſe hated gifts I'd have him take;
I'll wear no baubles for his ſake;
I ſcorn the gifts and hands untrue;
For her they well enough may do.

How near was I, when, with a kiſs,
He aſk'd my heart to anſwer yes!
To hear him at the altar ſay
Vows he'd have broke the ſooneſt day!
There he may love and take his fill,
And ſwear to her juſt what he will.

A rival's power I now defy;
She may be bleſt, and ſo will I;
Before 'tis long I'm ſure to find,
A ſwain more ſuited to my mind;
Then farewel, Florio, now, for good,
I would not have you if I could.

SONG 465.

A FREE MASON'S SONG.

WHEN a lodge of free-maſons
  Are cloath'd in their aprons,
In order to make a new brother,
  With firm hearts and clean hands,
  They repair to their ſtands,
And juſtly ſupport one another,

  Truſty brother, take care,
  Of eve-droppers beware,
'Tis a juſt and a ſolemn occaſion;
  Give the word and the blow,
  That workmen may know,
One aſks to be made a free-maſon.

  The maſter ſtands due,
  And his officers too,
While the craftſmen are plying their ſtation:
  The apprentices ſtand,
  Right for the command,
Of a free and an accepted maſon.

  Now traverſe the ground,
  As in duty you're bound,

And revere the authentic oration
    That leads to the way,
    And proves the firſt ray,
Of the light of an accepted maſon.

    Here's words, and here's ſigns,
    Here's problems and lines,
And here's room, too, for deep ſpeculation;
    Here virtue and truth
    Are taught to the youth,
When firſt he's call'd up to a maſon.

    Hieroglyphics ſhine bright,
    And here light reverts light
On the rules and the tools of vocation:
    We work and we ſing,
    The craft and the king;
'Tis both duty and choice in a maſon.

    What is ſaid or is done,
    Is here truly laid down,
In this form of our high inſtallation;
    Yet I challenge all men
    To know what I mean,
Unleſs he's an accepted maſon.

    The ladies claim right
    To come to our light,
Since the apron, they ſay, is their bearing;
    Can they ſubject their will,
    Can they keep their tongues ſtill,
And let talking be chang'd into hearing?

    This difficult taſk
    Is the leaſt we can aſk
To ſecure us on ſundry occaſions;
    When with this they comply,
    Our utmoſt we'll try,
To raiſe lodges for lady free-maſons.

    Till this can be done,
    Muſt each brother be mum,
Though the fair-one ſhould wheedle or teaze on:
    Be juſt, true, and kind,
    But ſtill bear in mind,
At all times you are a free-maſon.

SONG 466.

ON THE TAKING OF LOUISBOURG.

STAND round, my brave boys! let us ſing
    and rejoice,
We dread neither dangers nor fears,
Cape Breton's our own, as ſure as a gun,
    And Boſcawen's the braveſt of tars.

Tho' the ſea ran ſo high we cou'd hardly get nigh,
    And the ſurf made a terrible roar,
We determin'd to land, though oppos'd from the
        ſtrand;
    And we boldly went bump upon ſhore.

Soon their light-houſe we took, and their co-
        lours we ſtruck,
    And our red Engliſh croſs on it heighten'd;
From their batt'ries they run, Britiſh vengeance
        to ſhun,
    For the monſieurs were damnably frighten'd.

Their ſhips of the line ſtrove to baulk our deſign,
    But into the harbour we row'd;

We damn'd their hot matches, ſoon clapp'd down
        their hatches,
    Burnt one, and out t'other we tow'd.

Then the governor ſent, to ſurrender, content
    To ſave from deſtruction the town;
What he aſk'd us we granted, we had what we
        wanted,
    And Louiſbourg all was our own.

I never could laugh at a ſhow ſo by half,
    As to ſee their lank ſoldiers and ſailors;
By Jove, my friend Will, I thought then, and
        think ſtill,
    They were nothing but journeymen taylors.

Such glorious ſucceſs all our wrongs muſt redreſs,
    And the French on their marrow-bones bring;
Now let's have a dance, with your partners ad-
        vance,
    And ſo God bleſs great George, our good
        king.

SONG 467.

YE gods! that round fair Celia wait,
    From her bright eyes to bring our fate,
Bear to the nymph my ſofteſt ſighs,
And tell her, her adorer dies;
But if that won't her pity move,
And ſhe, proud thing, diſdains to love,
Then let her know, 'tis all a lye,
For haughty Strephon ſcorns to die.

SONG 468.

OH, lovely Celia! heav'nly maid!
    Kind, gentle, fair, and free;
In all thy ſex's charms array'd,
    How few are form'd like thee?
This image always fills my mind,
    The theme of ev'ry ſong;
I'm fix'd to thee alone, I find,
    But aſk not for how long.

The fair, in gen'ral I've admir'd,
    Have long been falſe and true;
And when the laſt my fancy tir'd,
    It wander'd round to you.
Then while I can, I'll be ſincere,
    As turtles to their mates;
This moment's your's and mine, my dear!
    The next, you know, is fate's.

SONG 469.

THE KIND LASS.

TO court me young Colin came many a mile,
    And oft by my ſide he has ſat;
His meaning I often requeſted to know,
    And wonder'd what he would be at.
To gain me he ſaid many pretty ſoft things,
    Deſcribing the height of his paſſion;
When often I've bid him to hold his fool's
        tongue,
    Tho'—faith—'twas againſt inclination.

I cou'd not help laughing fometimes, I declare,
When he fwore that he lov'd beyond meafure;
He'd kifs me, and—fighing—he'd kifs me again,
Protefting I was his whole pleafure:
When I bid him forbear—my heart it faid—no,
'Twas not in my heart to deny;
And when he requefted, if I'd be his wife,
That moment—I thought I fhou'd—die.

The girl that fays no, never meant it as fo,
Tho' feemingly prudifh or fly;
She may fay what fhe will—but cannot difown
That no—the word—yes—does imply.
Oft times as he walk'd he would tell a love-tale,
And vow, that for me he fhould die;
But rather than fuch a mifchance fhould e'er hap,
I thought I'd much better comply.

My heart all the time, how it play'd pit-a-pat,
The minute he urg'd his requeft!
And, if to be teaz'd—I thought any more,
It would, to the purpofe—be beft.
To the church in the village next morning we went,
All nonfenfe being over and done,
The prieft at the altar united our hands,
And Colin and I were made one.

SONG 470.

OH, how vain is ev'ry blefling,
How infipid all our joys,
Life how little worth poffefling,
But when love it's time employs!

Love, the pureft, nobleft pleafure,
That the gods on earth beftow,
Adding wealth to ev'ry treafure,
Taking pain from ev'ry woe.

SONG 471.

AN ODE.

Sung at RANELAGH.

LET the philofophic wife
Preach up rules the gay defpife:
Let the hoary-bearded fage,
Cenfure follies of the age;
Yet while brifk the vital tide,
Pleafure, thou fhalt be my guide,
Live, oh, goddefs! live with me,
All in dear variety.

Dwell thou, love, within my breaft,
Juft enough to make me bleft;
Let thy fweets inceffant fpring,
But protect me from the fting;
Be the paffion unconfin'd,
Under no reftraint the mind;
But like birds, as fond and free,
Pleas'd with dear variety.

Keep, oh, Plutus! all thy wealth,
Give me competence and health:
Care furrounds the mifer's hoard,
Pain attends the fpendthrift's board.

Bacchus, in thy rofy bowl,
Let me flake my thirfty foul;
But let reafon wait on thee,
Reafon prompts variety.

Life on wings of joy fhou'd hafte;
Gloomy thoughts the minutes wafte;
We fhou'd banifh care and fear,
Fate predeftines all things here.
Hail to friendfhip, beauty, wine,
Thefe make tranfient life divine;
May they ever live with me,
All in dear variety.

SONG 472.

Sung at VAUXHALL.

YOUNG Jockey, who teaz'd me a twelve-month or more,
Now bolder is grown than was mortal before;
He whifpers fuch things as no virgin fhould hear,
And he preffes my lips with a warmth I can't bear.

With ftories of love he would foften my mind,
And his eyes fpeak a temper to mifchief inclin'd;
But I vow not a moment I'll truft him alone,
And when next he grows rude I will bid him be gone.

Of honour and truth not a word has he fpoke,
And his actions declare he thinks virtue a joke:
He fhall find his miftake, if he ventures to try:
For, than yield on fuch terms, oh! I rather would die.

With no creature befide he fuch freedom dare take;
Yet the handfome and witty he quits for my fake:
But how can I think that he loves me the beft?
Or how can I love him who'd break all my reft?

Oh! Jockey, reform, nor be foolifh again,
Left you lofe a fond heart you fhall never regain:
If you change your behaviour, and to church chufe to go,
I'll forgive all that's paft, and will never fay no.

SONG 473.

Sung at VAUXHALL.

LONG, long I defpair'd a young fhepherd to find,
Nor proud of his merit, nor falfe as the wind;
But at laft I have got a dear lad to my mind;
Oh! I never can part with my Willy:
We hied to the altar laft Midfummer-day;
I blufh'd all the while, and fcarce knew what to fay;
But I vow'd (I remember) to love and obey:
Can I do any lefs by my Willy?

His breath is as fragrant as frefh morning air;
His face than the rofe is more ruddy I fwear;
And his kiffes as fweet—oh! beyond all compare!
There is not fuch a lad as my Willy.

With him none pretends or to pipe or to play,
But what tender foft things does the fhepherd not
   fay!
With eafe, I am fure, he might fteal hearts
   away:
But I'll never diftruft thee, dear Willy.

When I droop'd all in pain, and hung down my
   head,
How kindly he watch'd me! what tears did he
   fhed!
He ne'er left me a moment till ficknefs was fled:
Can I ever forget thee, dear Willy?

Should death from my fight tear the fhepherd
   fo true,
Let him take, if he chufes, then, me away too;
For why fhould I tarry, or what could I do,
Should I lofe fuch a lad as my Willy?

SONG 474.

SAY, lovely peace, that grac'd our ifle,
   Why you withdraw th' indulgent fmile?
Is it, you fly the fons of fame,
That they the pride of France may tame?
   For Mars is rouz'd by war's alarms,
   And calls the Britons forth to arms.

Our chiefs, renown'd upon the main,
Once more in arms fhine forth again,
Whofe fteady courage dares oppofe
And ftem the pow'r of Gallic foes:
   For Mars, &c.

What ftate but does it's fate deplore,
Where'er the Britifh thunders roar?
All, all muft in fubjection bow;
And to Britannia's fons 'tis due:
   For Mars, &c.

As Rome of old her terrors hurld,
And prov'd the miftrefs of the world,
The globe itfelf muft fubject be
To Albion's fons, who rule the fea:
   For Mars, &c.

Arife, arife to war's great call;
Prepare to meet th' audacious Gaul;
And in return for all your toils,
Return with victory and fpoils:
   For Mars is rouz'd by war's alarms,
   And calls the Britons forth to arms.

SONG 475.
ON HUMAN LIFE.

SINCE all mankind to happinefs
   Lay fome fantaftic claim,
'Tis ftrange, among fo great a crowd,
   That all fhould mifs their aim.

How were I bleft, (the Peafant cries)
   Had empire been my fhare!—
Curft be this grandeur, (fays the Prince)
   The fource of all my care!

As when fome craggy cliff, from far,
   With pleafure we furvey,
And, with the diftant profpect fir'd,
   Straight thither make our way;

But find, at length, with pains arriv'd,
   It's tempting glory ceas'd;
By defart barrennefs convinc'd
   The diftance only pleas'd.

Thus our o'er heated fancies rove
   In all affairs of life:
Her whom a miftrefs we adore,
   We naufeate when a wife.

I'll, to be happy, be content,
   Nor break with care my fleep:
Blifs, like a fhadow, run or ftand,
   The felf-fame diftance keeps.

SONG 476.

FORGIVE, fair creature, form'd to pleafe,
   Forgive a wond'ring youth's defire:
Thofe charms, thofe virtues, when he fees,
   How can he fee, and not admire!

While each the other ftill improves;
   The faireft face, the nobleft mind;
Not with the proverb, he that loves,
   But he that loves you not, is blind.

SONG 477.
Sung in the Quaker.

WHILE the lads of the village fhall mer-
   rily, ah!
Sound the tabors, I'll hand thee along;
And I fay unto thee, that verily, ah!
   Thou and I will be firft in the throng.
   While the lads, &c.

Juft then, when the fwain who laft e'en won the
   dow'r,
With his mates fhall the fports have begun,
When the gay voice of gladnefs refounds from
   each bow'r,
And thou long'ft in thy heart to make one.
   While the lads, &c.

Thofe joys which are harmlefs, what mortal
   can blame?
'Tis my maxim, that youth fhould be free;
And to prove that my words and my deeds are
   the fame,
   Believe me, thou'lt prefently fee.
   While the lads, &c.

SONG 478.

WHAT beauteous fcenes enchant my fight!
   How clofely yonder vine
Does round that elm's fupporting height
   It's wanton ringlets twine!
That elm (no more a barren fhade)
   Is with it's clufters crown'd;
And that fair vine, without it's aid,
   Had crept along the ground.

Let this, my fair-one, move thy heart
   Connubial joys to prove;
Yet mark what care and age impart,
   Nor thoughtlefs rufh on love:

'now thy own b'ifs, and joy to hear
Vertumnus loves thy charms,
'he youthful god that rules the year,
And keeps thy groves from harms.

While fome with fhort-liv'd paffions glow,
His love remains the fame;
On him alone thy heart beftow,
And cool his conftant flame:
o fhall no froft's untimely pow'r
Deform the blooming fpring;
o fhall thy trees, from blafts fecure,
Their wonted tribute bring.

SONG 479.

Sung at SADLER's WELLS.

YOUNG Strephon, a fhepherd, the pride of
the plain,
Each day is attempting my kindnefs to gain:
He takes all occafions his flame to renew;
I always reply, that his courting won't do.

He fpares no rich prefents to make me more
kind,
And exhaufts in my praife all the wit of his
mind:
I fay, I'm engag'd, and I wifh him to go;
He afks me fo oft till I rudely fay, No.

To Thyrfis, laft Valentine's day, the dear youth'
I tell him I plighted my faith and my truth;
That wealth cannot peace and contentment be-
ftow,
And my heart is another's——fo beg he will
go.

That love is not purchas'd with titles and gold,
And the heart that is honeft can never be fold;
That I figh not for grandeur, but look down on
fhow;
And to Thyrfis muft haften, nor anfwer him No.

He hears me, and, trembling all over, replies,
If his fuit I prefer not, he inftantly dies:
He gives me his hand, and will force me to go;
I pity his fuff'ring, but boldly fay, No.

I try to avoid him, in hopes of fweet peace;
He haunts me each moment to make me fay Yes:
But, to-morrow, ye fair ones, with Thyrfis I go,
And truft me, at church, that I will not fay,
No.

SONG 430.

YOUNG COLIN.

YOUNG Colin was the bonnieft fwain,
That ever pip'd on flow'ry plain,
Or danc'd upon the lee:
The wanton kid, in gamefome round,
That frolicks o'er the flow'ry ground,
Was not fo blithe as he.

Beneath the oak in yonder vale,
You'd think you heard the nightingale,
Whene'er be rais'd his voice:

But, ah! the youth was all deceit,
His vows, his oaths, were all a cheat,
And choice fucceeded choice.

The maidens fung, in willow groves,
Of Colin's falfe and perjur'd loves;
Here Jenny told her woes:
And Moggy's tears increas'd the brook,
Whofe cheeks like dying lilies look,
That once out-blufh'd the rofe.

Unhappy fair, my words believe,
So fhall no fwain your hopes deceive,
And leave you to defpair:
Ere he difclofe his fickle mind,
Change firft yourfelves, for, ah! you'll find
Falfe Colins every where.

SONG 481.

Written by SHAKESPEARE.

ORPHEUS, with his lute, made trees,
And the mountain tops that freeze,
Bow themfelves when he did fing;
To his mufic, plants and flowers,
Ever fprung, as fun and fhowers
There had made a lafting fpring.

Ev'ry 'thing that heard him play,
E'en the billows of the fea,
Hung their heads, and then lay by;
In fweet mufic is fuch art,
Killing care, or grief of heart,
Fall afleep, or hearing die.

SONG 482.

THE nightingale, who tunes
Her warbling notes fo fweet,
Midft flow'rs ne'er prefumes
To fix her mournful feat.

Melodioufly fhe fings,
While hawthorns pierce her breaft;
Her voice fweet echo rings;
And nature lulls to reft.

'Tis thus the love-fick maid
In penfive voice complains,
Seeks out the lonely fhade,
To tell her endlefs pains.

While there fhe breathes her mind,
The verdant hills around,
By purling riv'lets twin'd,
Reverberate the found.

SONG 483.

BID me, when forty winters more
Have furrow'd deep my pallid brow;
When from my head, a fcanty ftore,
Lankly the wither'd treffes flow:
When the warm tide, that bold and ftrong
Now rolls impetuous on, and free,
Languid and flow fcarce creeps along,
Then bid me court fobriety.

Nature, who form'd the varied scene,
Of rage and calm, of frost and fire,
Unerring guide, could only mean
That age should reason—youth desire.
Shall then that rebel man, presume
  (Inverting nature's law) to seize
The dues of age in youth's high bloom,
  And join impossibilities?

No!—let me waste the frolic May
In wanton joys, and wild excess;
In revel sport, and laughter gay,
And mirth, and rosy chearfulness.
Woman, the soul of all delights,
And wine, the aid of love, be near;
All charms me that to joy incites,
And ev'ry she, that's kind, is fair.

SONG 484.

'TIS now the noon of gloomy night,
  When awful silence reigns;
And Luna darts her borrow'd light
  Along the enamell'd plains.

In homely cots, the sleeping swains
Forget the toils of day;
No longer sport in rustic games;
No lambkins skip and play.

But I, alas! a stranger grown
To comfort and repose,
In vain to Phebe make my moan,
And tell my heart-felt woes.

In that cold tomb my lover lies,
  (A youth so good and just)
There, deaf to all my mournful cries,
He moulders into dust.

SONG 485.

WOULD you wish o'er a maid to prevail,
  In sighs you your mind must impart;
You must tell her some pretty love-tale,
  And sing what you feel at your heart.

When in pity, to love she's inclin'd,
  And fondly believes all you say,
'Sure embrace her while she's in the mind:
  There's danger in longer delay.

O how happy could I be with you,
  United in wedlock's soft chain;
All the day we'd our pleasures pursue,
  And revel it over the plain.

Would the fates only grant me but this,
  All the cares of high life I'd defy;
And, while thus we enjoy'd the true bliss,
  How happy my Dicky and I!

SONG 486.
Sung in *Almena*.

WHEN beauty on the lover's soul
  Imprints it's first and fairest charms,
It soon does reason's force controul,
And ev'ry passion quite disarms.

'Tis beauty triumphs o'er the brave,
  'As ev'ry feature blooms divine ;
'Tis beauty makes the king a slave,
  When in an angel's form, like thine.

SONG 487.

MY roving heart has oft, with pride,
  Dissolv'd love's silken chains;
The wanton deity defy'd,
  And scorn'd his sharpest pains.
But from thy form, resistless, stream
  Such charms as must controul;
In thee the fairest features beam,
  The noblest, brightest soul.

Pleas'd in thy converse all the day,
  Life's sand unheeded runs;
With thee I'd hail the rising ray,
  And talk down summer's suns.
Our love's congenial still the same,
  With equal force shall shine,
No cloy'd desires shall damp the flame
  Which friendship will refine.

SONG 488.

Sung at VAUXHALL.

TENDER virgins, shun deceivers,
  Who with base seducing arts,
When they find you fond believers,
  Triumph o'er unguarded hearts.
If a fickle swain pursue you,
  O! beware his subtle wiles;
All his aim is to undo ye,
  Ruin lurks beneath his smiles.
Let the youth whose constant passion
  Scorns the meanness of deceit,
Warm'd with mutual inclination,
  Render all your joys compleat.

SONG 489.

LORD WILLOUGHBY; AN OLD BALLAD.

THE fifteenth day of July,
  With glistering spear and shield,
A famous fight in Flanders
  Was foughten in the field:
The most courageous officers
  Were English captains three;
But the bravest man in battle
  Was brave Lord Wi loughby.

The next was Captain Norris,
  A valiant man was he:
The other Captain Turner,
  From field wou'd never flee.
With fifteen hundred fighting men,
  Alas! there were no more,
They fought with fourteen thousand, then,
  Upon the bloody shore.

Stand to it, noble pikemen,
  And look you round about:

Mr MATTOCKS as Apollo in MIDAS

Ah, happy Hours how fleeting Song 490

Published as the Act directs Augt 1.1778

And fhoot you right, you bow-men,
And we will keep them out:
You mufquet and calliver-men,
Do you prove true to me,
I'll be the foremoft man in fight,
Says brave Lord Willoughby.

And then the bloody enemy
They fiercely did affail,
And fought it out moft furioufly,
Not doubting to prevail;
The wounded men on both fides fell,
Moft pitious for to fee,
Yet nothing could the courage quell
Of brave Lord Willoughby.

For feven hours to all men's view
This fight endureo fore,
Until our men fo feeble grew
That they could fight no more;
And then upon dead horfes
Full favourly they eat,
And drank the puddle water,
They could no better get.

When they had fed fo freely,
They kneeled on the ground,
And praifed God devoutly
For the favour they had found ;
And beating up their colours,
The fight they did renew,
And turning tow'rds the Spaniards,
A thoufand more they flew.

The fharp fteel-pointed arrows,
And bullets thick did fly;
Then did our valiant foldiers
Charge en moft furioufly;
Which made the Spaniards waver,
They thought it beft to flee ;
They fear'd the ftout behaviour
Of brave Lord Willoughby.

Then quoth the Spanifh general,
Come let us march away,
I fear we fhall be fpoiled all
If here we longer ftay;
For yonder comes Lord Willoughby
With courage fierce amain,
He will not give one inch of way
For all the devils in hell.

And then the fearful enemy
Was quickly put to flight,
Our men purfu'd couragioufly,
And caught their forces quite;
But at laft they gave a fhout,
Which echoed through the fky,
God, and St. George for England !
The conquerors did cry.

This news was brought to England
With all the fpeed might be,
And foon our gracious queen was told
Of this fame victory :
O this is brave Lord Willoughby,
My love that ever won,
Of all the lords of honour
'Tis he great deeds hath done.

To th' foldiers that were maimed,
And wounded in the fray,
The queen allow'd a penfion
Of fifteen pence a day,
And from all cofts and charges
She quit and fet them free ;
And this fhe did all for the fake
Of brave Lord Willoughby.

Then courage, noble Englifhmen,
And never be difmay'd;
If that we be but one to ten,
We will not be afraid
To fight with foreign enemies,
And fet our nation free:
And thus I end the bloody bout
Of brave Lord Willoughby.

SONG 490.
Sung in *Midas.*

AH, happy hours, how fleeting
Ye danc'd on down away;
When, my foft vows repeating,
At Daphne's feet I lay!
But from her charms when funder'd,
As Midas frowns prefage;
Each hour will feem an hundred,
Each day appear an age.

SONG 491.
Sung at VAUXHALL.

NO longer let whimfical fongfters compare
The merits of wine with the charms of the
fair ;
I appeal to the men to determine between
A tun-belly'd Bacchus and beauty's fair queen

The pleafures of drinking henceforth I refign,
For tho' there is mirth, yet there's madnefs in
wine :
Then let not falfe fparkles our fenfes beguile,
'Tis the mention of Chloe that makes the glafs
fmile.

Her beauties with rapture my fenfes infpire,
And the more I behold her, the more I admire !
But the charms of her temper and mind I adore!
Thefe virtues fhall blefs me when beauty's no
more.

How happy our days when with love we engage !
'Tis the tranfport of youth; 'tis the comfort
of age:
But what are the joys of the bottle or bowl ?
Wine tickles the tafte, love enraptures the foul!

A fot, as he riots in liquor, will cry,
The longer I drink, the more thirfty am I.
From this fair confeffion 'tis plain, my good
friend,
You're a toper eternal, and drink to no end.

Your big-belly'd bottle may ravifh your eye,
But how foolifh you look when your bottle is
dry !
R

From woman, dear woman, sweet pleasure must
　　spring;
Nay, the stoicks must own it, she is the best thing.

Yet some praises to wine we may justly afford;
For a time it will make one as great as a lord:
But woman, for ever, gives transport to man;
And I'll love the dear sex—aye, as long as I can.

SONG 492.

Sung in the *Golden Pippin.*

IF I have some—little—beauty—
　Can I help it?—no, not I—
Some good luck, too—'tis my duty
　Gifts so precious to apply.
Nature—fortune—gave 'em freely,
And I'll use 'em—quite genteelly.
　If the smarts of the sky
　Cringe, ogle, and sigh,
　Whene'er I pass by;
　　And cry,
　　Look y' there!
　　What an air!
　　Gods, how fair!
　　　Pray, why
　(To feed your starch'd pride)
　Must I go and hide,
　Till you're made a bride?
　　Who, I?
　No, no—If I do, may I die.

SONG 493.

Sung in the *Jovial Crew.*

NO woman her envy can smother,
　Though never so vain of her charms;
If a beauty she spies in another,
　The pride of her heart it alarms.

New conquests she still must be making,
　Or fancies her power grows less;
Her poor little heart is still aching,
　At sight of another's success.

By nature design'd, in love to mankind,
　That different beauties should move,
Still pleas'd to ordain, none ever should reign
　Sole monarch in empire of love.

Then learn to be wise, new triumphs despise,
　And leave to your neighbours their due;
If one cannot please, you'll find by degrees,
　You'll not be contented with two;
No, no, you'll not be contented with two.

SONG 494.

Sung at VAUXHALL.

YOUNG Phillis one morning a maying
　would go;
When saunt'ring among the sweet meads to
　and fro,
In vain did the cowslips her fair hand invite,
Nor daisies nor daffodils gave her delight:

Her heart with the throbbings of passion did
　move;
Each bird on the spray could have told her 'twas
　love.

At length she grew weary, and sat by a brook,
Where Strephon, the shepherd, was baiting
　his hook:
Unnotic'd he saw her, and heard her complain;
His heart was inflam'd to allay her soft pain.
The swain had led many a lass to the grove,
And he (wicked rogue!) thought that Phillis
　wou'd love.

Howe'er, as her mind was by innocence drest,
'Twas plain that fair virtue was lodg'd in her
　breast:
Her beauty was much, but her modesty more,
Which Strephon perceiv'd, and began to adore;
He knelt at her feet with a garland he wove,
And Phillis consented to make him her love.

SONG 495.

Sung at RANELAGH.

NOW the woodland choirists sing,
　Beauty takes her radiant sphere,
Love adorns the smiling spring,
　Love and beauty gild the year:
Seize the minutes as they fly,
Jocund hours and festive round;
Innocence, with virgin eye,
　Comes with rural chaplets crown'd.

Awful virtue keeps her state
　In the cot, or on the throne;
Liberty enjoys her mate,
　As fair honour holds the zone:
Love and beauty, on the wing,
　Sweep the globe, and conquer all;
Poet, hero, sage, and king,
　At their shrine submissive fall.

Where should honour love to dwell,
　But in freedom's happy isle?
Virtue here enjoys a cell
　More than in a tyrant's smile:
Where should beauty fix her reign,
　But on love that pow'r defies?
Innocence shall crown the scene
　Where ambition droops and dies.

SONG 496.

Sung in the *Conscious Lovers.*

IF love's a sweet passion, how can it torment?
　If bitter, O tell me whence comes my con-
　　tent?
Since I suffer with pleasure, why should I com-
　plain,
Or grieve at my fate, since I know 'tis in vain?
Yet so pleasing the pain is, so soft is the dart,
That at once it both wounds me and tickles my
　heart.

I grasp her hand gently, look languishing down,
And by passionate silence I make my love known;

But, oh! how I'm bleſt when ſo kind ſhe does
  prove,
By ſome willing miſtake to diſcover her love;
When, in ſtriving to hide, ſhe reveals all her
  flame,
And our eyes tell each other what neither dare
  name!

How pleaſing is beauty! how ſweet are the
  charms!
How delightful embraces! how peaceful her
  arms!
Sure there's nothing ſo eaſy as learning to love;
'Tis taught us on earth, and by all things above:
And to beauty's bright ſtandard all heroes muſt
  yield,
For 'tis beauty that conquers, and keeps the fair
  field.

SONG 497.

Sung in *King Henry the Eighth.*

LOVE'S the tyrant of the heart,
  Full of miſchief, full of woe;
All his joys are mix'd with ſmart,
Thorns beneath his roſes grow;
And, ſerpent-like, he ſtings the breaſt
Where he's harbour'd and careſs'd.

SONG 498.

Sung at VAUXHALL.

TO the conſcious groves I hie me,
  Where I late was blithe and gay;
Try to fancy Colin nigh me,
  So to paſs the hours away.

But can ſcenes like thoſe delight me,
  When my ſwain's no longer there!
Hill, nor dale, nor ſtream invite me,
  Now no more they're worth my care.

Come thyſelf, without delaying,
  In thoſe ſhades I find no eaſe;
But with thee, whilſt fondly ſtraying,
  Ev'ry place is ſure to pleaſe.

SONG 499.

ENGLISH ALE.

Sung at SADLER'S WELLS.

THE truths that I ſing none deny me,
  They're truths that muſt ever prevail;
Ye poor dogs of France, we defy ye,
  By the force of our Engliſh good ale.

The tricks ye attempt, but in vain are,
  They are what we expected, and ſtale;
Your troops, and your fleets, our diſdain are,
  By the force of our Engliſh good ale.

When Beſs, that brave queen, rul'd the nation,
  'Twas Spain's great Armada did fail;
She dealt to the Dons tribulation,
  By the force of our Engliſh good ale.

And thus we will ſerve them for ever,
  Tho' their loads on our necks they'd entail;
There's none like our people, ſo clever,
  By the force of our Engliſh good ale.

Free-born, we ſupport our defender,
  To our ſons we hand down the detail;
Defie the de'il, pope, and pretender,
  By the force of our Engliſh good ale.

SONG 500.

Sung at VAUXHALL.

MAIDENS, let your lovers languiſh,
  If you'd have them conſtant prove;
Doubts and fears, and ſighs and anguiſh,
  Are the chains that faſten love.

Jockey woo'd, and I conſented,
  Soon as e'er I heard his tale:
He with conqueſt quite contented,
  Boaſting, rov'd around the vale.

Now he doats on ſcornful Molly,
  Who rejects him with diſdain:
Love's a ſtrange bewitching folly,
  Never pleas'd without ſome pain.

SONG 501.

THE INVITATION.

COME, Colin, pride of rural ſwains,
  O come and bleſs thy native plains;
The daiſies ſpring, the beeches bud,
The ſongſters warble in the wood.

Come, Colin, haſte, O haſte away,
Your ſmiles will make the village gay;
When you return, the vernal breeze
Will wake the buds, and fan the trees.

Oh! come and ſee the violets ſpring,
The meadows laugh, the linnets ſing;
Your eyes our joyleſs hearts can chear,
O haſte! and make us happy here.

SONG 502.

ONE ſummer eve, as Nancy fair,
  Sat ſpinning in the ſhade,
While ſoaring ſky-larks ſhook the air
  In warbling o'er her head;
In tender cooes the pigeons woo'd,
  (Love's impulſe all muſt feel)
She ſung, but ſtill her work purſu'd,
  And turn'd her ſpinning-wheel.

While thus I work with rock and reel,
  So life by time is ſpun;
And as runs round my ſpinning-wheel,
  The world turns up and down.
Some rich to-day, to-morrow low,
  While I no changes feel,
But get my bread by ſweat of brow,
  And turn my ſpinning-wheel.

R 2

From me let men and women too
  This home-spun lesson learn,
Not mind what other people do,
  But eat the bread they earn :
If none were fed, were that to be,
  But what deserv'd a meal,
Some ladies, then, as well as me,
  Must turn the spinning-wheel.

The rural toast, with sweetest tone,
  Thus sung her witless strain,
When o'er the lawn limp'd gammer Joan,
  And brought home Nance's swain :
Come, cries the dame, Nance, here's thy
  spouse ;
  Away throw rock and reel.
Blithe Nancy, with the bonny news,
  O'erset her spinning-wheel.

SONG 503.

Written by Mr. LOCKMAN.

Sung at MARYBONE.

'GAINST the destructive wiles of man,
  Your hearts, ye fair-ones guard ;
Their only study's to trepan,
  And play a trickster's card :
With strange delight, poor girls they slight,
  Amuse, cajole, belye :
Hence, girls ! beware—look sharp—take care ;
  For men are wond'rous sly.

That Proteus man, like him of old,
  A thousand forms will take ;
His venal soul is all for gold,
  A crocodile or snake.
See his dire thread ! this spider spread
  To catch the female fly :
    Hence, girls ! &c.

A porcupine, with rage inspir'd,
  At nymphs he darts his quills ;
A basilisk, by frenzy fir'd,
  His glance by poison kills :
With fraudful arts he steals their hearts,
  Then throws the baubles by :
    Hence, girls ! &c.

Was the whole race of man to meet
  In one wide-spreading plain,
Of constancy, of faith to treat,
  And virtue's spotless train ;
To find a youth renown'd for truth,
  Whole ages we might try :
Hence, girls ! beware—look sharp—take care ;
  For men are wond'rous sly.

SONG 504.

THE SHEPHERDESS.

I Seek my shepherd, gone astray ;
  He left our cot the other day ;
Tell me, ye gentle nymphs and swains,
Pass'd the dear rebel through your plains ?
Oh ! whither, whither must I roam,
To find, and charm the wand'rer home ?

Sports he upon the shaven green,
Or joys he in the mountain scene ?
Leads he his flocks along the mead,
Or does he seek the cooler shade ?
Oh ! teach a wretched nymph the way
To find her lover gone astray.

To paint, ye maids, my truant swain ;
A manly softness crowns his mien ;
Adonis was not half so fair ;
And when he talks, 'tis heav'n to hear !
But, oh ! the soothing poison shun ;
To listen is to be undone.

He'll swear no time shall quench his flame,
To me the perjur'd swore the same ;
Too fondly loving to be wife,
Who gave my heart an easy prize,
And when he tun'd his syren voice,
Listen'd, and was undone by choice.

But fated now, he shuns the kiss
He counted once his greatest bliss ;
Whilst I with tender passions burn,
And pant and die his return.
Oh ! whither, whither shall I rove,
Again to find my straying love ?

SONG 505.

HOPE; AN ANACREONTIC.

Written by Mr. MAVOR.

FILL, O goddess ! fill my breast ;
  Rise on brightest colours drest,
And with thy image make me blest ;

Fairest of celestial birth,
Enliv'ner of the sons of earth,
Source of flowing joy and mirth,

Enraptur'd let me hear the song,
Warbl'd from thy syren tongue ;
Painting pleasure ever young.

Soul of bliss ! O deign to smile ;
Thou can'st fable cares beguile,
And vanquish misery and toil.

When disappointment hovers round,
When malice vents the poison'd sound,
Erect thy crest, and heal my wound.

'Tis thine, to chear the face of woe,
To bid the tears forget to flow,
And, blust'ring, adverse blasts to blow.

When ill-requited lovers pour
Their wailing to the midnight hour,
Thy balm is prevalent to cure.

Tho' Chloe fairer than the skies,
With angry frowns should meet our sighs,
Thou canst insure us half our prize.

O come, bright Hope ! possess my soul ;
For ever reign without controul,
And animate and warm the whole.

Devoid of thee, all teems with gloom ;
'Tis thou that giv'st to bear each doom,
In hoary age, and youth's gay bloom.

With thee on wings fublime we foar,
To feek th' irremeable fhore;
And dare futurity explore.

SONG 506.

A SCOTCH BALLAD.

WHEN trees did bud, and fields were green,
    And flow'rs were fair to fee;
When Mary was compleat fifteen,
    And love laugh'd in her eye;
Blithe Jockey's looks her heart did move
    To fpeak her mind thus free:
Gang down the burn, my gentle love,
    And foon I'll follow thee.

Now Jockey did each lad furpafs
    That dwelt on this burn fide;
And Mary was a bonny lafs,
    Juft meet to be a bride:
Her cheeks were rofy red and white,
    Her eyes were azure blue,
Her looks were like Aurora bright,
    Her lips like dropping dew.

What pafs'd, I guefs, was harmlefs play,
    And nothing, fure, unmeet!
For, ganging home, I heard them fay
    They lik'd a walk fo fweet:
His cheek to her's he fondly laid;
    She cry'd, Sweet love, he true;
And when a wife, as now a maid,
    To death I'll follow you.

SONG 507.

A SCOTCH BALLAD.

AT fetting day and rifing morn,
    With foul that ftill fhall love thee,
I'll afk of heav'n thy fafe return,
    With all that can improve thee:
I'll vifit oft the birken bufh,
    Where firft you kindly told me
Sweet tales of love, and hid my blufh,
    Whilft round thou didft enfold me.

To all our haunts thou didft repair,
    By green-wood, fhaw, or fountain;
Or where the fummer's day I'd fhare
    With you upon yon mountain:
There will I tell the trees and flow'rs,
    With thoughts unfeign'd and tender;
By vows you're mine, my love is yours,
    My heart, which cannot wander.

SONG 508.

ANACREON, ON HIMSELF.

WHEN I drain the rofy bowl,
    Joy exhilarates my foul;
To the nine I raife my fong,
    Ever fair, and ever young.
When null cups my cares difpel,
    Sober cou'te' then farewel;
Let the winds, that murmur, fweep
All my forrows to the deep.

When I drink dull time away;
Jolly Bacchus, ever gay,
Leads me to delightful bow'rs,
Full of fragrance, full of flow'rs:
While I quaff the fparkling wine,
And my locks with rofes twine,
Then I praife life's rural fcene,
Sweet, fequefter'd, and ferene.

When I drink the bowl profound,
Richeft fragrance flowing round,
And fome lovely nymph detain,
Venus then infpires the ftrain;
When from goblets deep and wide,
I exhauft the gen'rous tide,
All my foul unbends—I play,
Gamefome with the young and gay.

SONG 509.

Sung in the Chaplet.

YOU fay, at your feet that I wept in defpair,
    And vow'd that no angel was ever fo fair:
How could you believe all the nonfenfe I fpoke!
What know we of angels?—I meant it in joke.

I next ftand indicted for fwearing to love,
And nothing but death fhould my paffion remove:
I have lik'd you a twelvemonth, a calendar year;
And not yet contented!—Have confcience, my
    dear.

SONG 510.

THE MEN WILL ROMANCE.

WHEN I enter'd my teens, and threw play-
        things afide,
I conceiv'd myfelf woman, and fit for a bride;
By the men I was flatter'd, my pride to enhance;
For the maids will believe, and the men will
    romance!

They fwore that my eyes the bright di'mond
        excell'd,
Such a face, and fuch treffes, fure ne'er were
    beheld!
That to gaze on my neck was all rapture and
    trance!
Oh! the maids will believe, and the men will
    romance.

Young Polydore faw me one night at the ball,
And fwore to my charms he a conqueft muft
    fall;
On his knees he intreated my hand for a dance:
Ah! the maids will believe, and the men will
    romance.

He conducted me home, when the paftime was
        o'er,
And declar'd he ne'er faw fo much beauty be-
    fore;
He ogled and figh'd, as he faw me advance:
Ah! the maids will believe, and the men will
    romance.

Then day after day I his company had:
At length he declar'd all his flame to my dad;
But my father lov'd money, and would not ad-
vance;
And reply'd to my lover, Young men will ro-
mance.

But tho' my papa would not give us a shilling,
My Polydore swore he to wed me was willing:
So to church we both went, and at night had
a dance,
And, believe me, my Polydore did not romance.

SONG 511.

A CANTATA.

AIR.

WHILE others barter ease for state,
And fondly aim at growing great,
Let me, (with rosy chaplets crown'd)
Stretch'd on the flower-enamel'd ground,
The grape's nectareous juices quaff,
Alternate sing, and love, and laugh.
Already see the purple juice
Resplendent o'er my cheek diffuse
A second youth!—Again, the bowl
With warm desires inflames my soul.

RECITATIVE.

Quickly! ah, quickly! must I leave
The joys which wine and beauty give;
Soon must I quit my wonted mirth,
And mingle with my parent earth,
Where kings, divested of their state,
With slaves sustain a common fate.

AIR.

Let, then, the present hour be mine,
Blest in the joys of love and wine:
Come, ye virgin throng, advance,
And mingle in the sprightly dance:
To the lyre's enchanting sound
Nimbly tread the blithsome round;
While the genial bowl inspires
Soft delight and gay desires.

SONG 512.

THE FORLORN SHEPHERD; A PASTORAL.

Written by Mr. C. GRAHAM.

HOW blest were my moments, how soft did
they glide,
The seasons how sweet did they pass!
When peace smil'd upon me, and close by my
side
Sat Hebe my favourite lass!

The poets all tell us that Venus is fair,
That Pallas has grace in her mien;
Their words are but fiction, and light as the air,
But Hebe's perfections I've seen.

Assist me, rememb'rance, to paint the sweet
maid,
The traits of fair Hebe display;

Whose beauty surpast all the nymphs of the
shade,
The morn she was queen of the May.

A garland of roses, besprinkled with dew,
Around her bright forehead was bound;
While busy-wing'd zephyrs, to fan the nymph
flew,
And wafted sweet odours around.

Her beautiful tresses, as black as a sloe,
Her fine falling shoulders did deck;
And formed a contrast, that sweetly did shew
The delicate white of her neck!

Her eyes spoke a meekness, and dignity too,
That scorn'd to coquet or beguile;
As virtue was always the object in view,
She wore a beneficent smile.

Her cheeks—but ah! were a poet to write,
He'd talk of the roses new-blown;
To tell you they blush'd and enraptur'd the sight,
Enough of description is shewn.

Such was my dear Hebe, and oh! what delight
Her delicate answers convey'd,
When ever I prest her my toils to requite,
And render me blest, in the shade !

Oft times, to amuse, as we tend'd our sheep,
Some well-chosen song I'd rehearse;
If virtue was wounded, my charmer wou'd weep,
For Hebe delighted in verse.

Thus blest with her presence, no sorrows I
knew,
Her love all my labours beguil'd;
E'n Pan seem'd delighted such raptures to view,
And sylvan simplicity smil'd !

How short liv'd and transient, alas! was my joy,
Fate bid me these blisses forego ;
And told me that pleasures unmixt with alloy,
Portended a period of woe.

The fatal prediction extorted a sigh,
A sigh which I strove to suppress;
But Hebe perceiv'd it, and instant did cry,
What motive can cause your distress!

'Twas then I dissembl'd, and feigned a smile,
(Determin'd my sorrows to hide)
Ah! shou'd you, (said I) your fond Damon be-
guile!
Now tell me the cause that I sigh'd?

Th' evasion succeeded, the nymph seemed
pleas'd,
The incense accepts at her shrine;
And now for a moment my bosom was eas'd,
For Hebe declar'd she'd be mine!

Her innocent blandishments stole on my soul,
And banish'd reflection the while;
For fate, when she means human bliss to con-
troul,
Begins the attack with a smile.

For ah! fatal eve! (I remember it still)
As late I return'd from the fold,
By the verge of a stream, at the foot of a hill,
Where revel the fishes of gold;

I faw, by the light of the moon's gentle-ray,
My fair-one reclin'd on the grass;
The luftre that erft her fair cheeks did difplay
Did rife and alternately pafs.

I rais'd her (for who wou'd the office refrain)
And homewards the nymph I convey'd,
But oh! how it tortur'd my bofom with pain
When thus to her fhepherd fhe faid:

For this gentle office (I think 'tis the laft
I e'er from thy hand fhall receive)
I thank thee!—and as to the joys that are paft,
I pray thee, fond fwain, do not grieve!

I fee (but why fhou'd I fharpen thy grief!)
The menacing afpect of death!
It is not in mortals to grant me relief,
Or lengthen the date of my breath!

Lov'd fhepherd! let this feeble effort fuffice,
Accept my laft final farewel!—
Her meek, gentle fpirit, now fled to the fkies,
Where truth and fincerity dwell.

Now penfive and fad, at the clofe of each day,
To her filent grave I repair;
And cull the fweet flow'rets, as onward I ftray,
To ftrew round the tomb of my fair.

SONG 513.

Sung in *Thomas and Sally.*

LIFE'S a garden, rich in treafure,
  Bury'd like the feeds in earth:
There lie joy, contentment, pleafure;
  But 'tis love muft give them birth.

That warm fun it's aid denying,
  We no happinefs can tafte;
But in cold obftruction lying,
  Life is all one barren wafte.

SONG 514.

A SCOTCH BALLAD.

YE gales that gently wave the fea,
  And pleafe the canny boat-man,
Bear me frae hence, or bring to me
  My brave, my bonny Scot-man:
    In haly hands
    We join'd our hands,
  Yet may not this difcover,
    While parents rate
    A large eftate
  Before a faithfu' lover.

But I loor chufe in Highland glens
  To herd the kid and goat man,
Ere I cou'd for fic little enos
  Refufe my bonny Scot-man.
    Wae worth the man
    Wha firft began
  The bafe ungenerous fafhion,
    Frae greedy views
    Love's art to ufe,
  While ftrangers to it's paffion.

Frae foreign fields, my lovely youth,
  Hafte to thy longing laffie,
Who pants to prefs thy bawmy mouth,
  And in her bofom hawfe thee.
    Love gi'es the word,
    Then hafte on board,
  Fair winds and tenty boat-man,
    Waft o'er, waft o'er,
    Frae yonder fhore,
  My blyth, my bonny Scot-man.

SONG 515.

Sung in the *Capricious Lovers.*

GO, feek fome nymph of humbler lot,
  To fhare thy board, and deck thy cot;
With joy I fly the fimple youth,
Who holds me light, or doubts my truth.

Thy breaft, for love too wanton grown,
Shall mourn it's peace and pleafure flown;
Nor fhall my faith reward a fwain,
Who doubts my love, or thinks me vain.

SONG 516.

THE SANDMAN; A CANTATA.

Written by Mr. HAWKINS.

RECITATIVE.

I Am a poor lad, and mean's my calling;
  From morn till night I am a bawling:
Through ftreet, through lanes, and fquares
    I pafs;
My treafure all on one poor afs:
My conftant theme, where'er I go,
Is, Maids, do ye want fand? Sand ho!

AIR.

Though I am a poor fandman, I care not a jot
  For all the fine folks in the nation;
While I can get money to buy a full pot,
  I'm the happieft man in my ftation.

    What's riches and treafure,
    Or all the gay pleafure,
  Where happinefs does not unite;
    'Tis nought but a juggle,
    A mere bubble bubble
  Of pain and perplexity quite.

RECITATIVE.

Now my fong's done, a tale I'll tell,
Which fure will pleafe you all full well:
One day, as paffing through the ftreet,
I black-ey'd Sufan chanc'd to meet,
Ah, deareft Sam! (to me fhe cried)
When fhall I be thy own true bride?
Faith Sue, (quoth I) I'd rather tarry;
For hang me if I think to marry.
She call'd me, then, ungrateful wretch,
And faid the devil would me fetch:
But for all this I did not care;
I drove away, and left her there.

AIR.

For who in their wits wou'd be plagu'd with
a wife?
To be teiz'd and tormented for ever;
They'll rid you as faft as they can of your life,
And are not contented—no, never.

They're fuch a difafter,
They ftick like a plaifter
That's faften'd upon a man's back;
And what is ftill worfe,
Ah! that is the curfe,
They have fuch a confounded clack.
Oh! lack!
They have fuch a confounded clack.

Then fince this is the cafe of having a wife,
Let me ever, ye gods, live a fingle life.

SONG 517.

Sung in the *Summer's Tale.*

WHILE on earth's foft lap defcending,
Lightly falls the feather'd fnow;
Nature, awfully attending,
Each rude wind forbids to blow.

White and pure awhile appearing,
Earth her virgin mantle wears;
Soon the fickle feafon veering,
Her deluded bofom bares.

Thus my foolifh heart believing,
Liften'd to his artful tongue;
All his vows of love receiving,
On each flatt'ring accent hung.

Fondly, for a time, miftaken,
Love and joy conceal'd my fate;
Now, alas! at length forfaken,
Sad experience comes too late.

SONG 518.

STREPHON OF THE HILL.

LET others Damon's praife rehearfe,
Or Colin's, at their will;
I mean to fing, in ruftic verfe,
Young Strephon of the hill.

As once I fat beneath a fhade,
Befide a purling rill;
Who fhou'd my folitude invade,
But Strephon of the hill!

He tapt my fhoulder, fnatch'd a kifs,
I cou'd not take it ill;
For nothing, fure, is done amifs
By Strephon of the hill.

Confent, O lovely maid! (he cry'd)
Nor aim thy fwain to kill:
Confent this day to be the bride
Of Strephon of the hill.

Obferve the doves on yonder fpray,
See how they fit and bill;
So fweet your time fhall pafs away
With Strephon of the hill.

We went to church with hearty glee,
O love, propitious ftill!
May ev'ry nymph be bleft, like me
With Strephon of the hill.

SONG 519.

A PRETTY WEEK'S WORK.

Written by Mr. NICHOLLS.

ON Monday, young Colin, who liv'd in the
dale,
Came to me when milking, and carry'd my
pail;
He faid that he well had examin'd his mind,
He'd wed me on Wednefday, if I was inclin'd;
And vow'd, when we came to the willow-deck'd
brook,
If I doubted his truth, he'd fwear on the book.

To know if my lover wou'd keep to his vow,
On Tuefday, the while he was bufy at plow,
I ran to the cot of old Dorcas below,
And begg'd fhe wou'd tell me the thing I wou'd
know;
I gave her a fixpence I'd fav'd from my youth,
And promis'd another to come at the truth.

Her fpectacles quickly fhe took from her fide,
Examin'd my hand, afk'd me queftions befide;
Then told me fhe faw, by a fpark in my eye,
If Colin was willing, 'twas beft to comply:
Then faid, Child do this, left your wifhes are
crofs'd,
For in matters of love, no time's to be loft.

On Wednefday he came dizen'd out in his beft,
He gave me a pofey to ftick in my breaft;
Then fweetly he kifs'd me, and told me the time,
And faid, Let us hafte ere the village bells chime.
But I, filly I, fure the worft of my kind!
Reply'd with a fneer, Sir, I've alter'd my mind.

At this, with refentment becoming the fwain,
He turn'd from a fool, and went off with difdain;
As foon as he left me, I thought on my fate,
And the words of old Dorcas, but ah! 'twas
too late!
I ran to the vale, fearch'd the hamlets around,
To find out my fwain, but no Colin I found.

On Thurfday, fo foon as the lark ftruck my ears
I travers'd the meads in purfuit of my dear;
Sing on, pretty lark, (to the warbler I cry'd)
Thou'rt happy, becaufe thou art true to thy
bride:
But alas! all endeavours were idle and vain!
Not one on the meadows knew aught of my
fwain.

When Friday was come I grew fick of my lot;
I ran to the vale, and enquir'd at each cot;
But fuccefslefs, alas! were all efforts to me,
No tidings I heard, nor no Colin cou'd fee:
'Twas Saturday, now, and the fearch I renew'd,
As lucklefs as ever, the fearch I purfu'd.

On Sunday I wander'd diftracted till noon,
When the bells 'gan a peal, delightful in tune;

I ftopt the firft perfon I met in my way,
And afked the caufe of their being fo gay;
Who told me, this morning young Colin had
been
Wedded to beautiful Doll of the green.

That inftant I ran to the green willow'd brook,
Where Colin had fwore to be true on a book;
My garters I bound to the fturdieft bough,
And had acted, ye virgins, I cannot tell how!
If reafon had not interpos'd with her aid,
And bade me defift, for a filly young maid.

Ye maidens who hear me, ne'er act fuch a part,
Nor reject the true fwain who'd yield you his
heart;
Comply when he's kind, for I've known to
my coft,
In matters of love there's no time to be loft.
Do this, and no caufe in your bofom fhall lurk,
To make you repent of a pretty week's work.

SONG 520.

Sung at VAUXHALL.

WOULD you a female heart infpire
With tender paffion, warm defire,
Employ each foothing art:
The god of love all force difdains,
He only leads, in pleafing chains,
The kind confenting heart.

SONG 521.

A MAN TO MY MIND.

Written by Mr. CUNNINGHAM.

SINCE wedlock's in vogue, and ftale virgins
defpis'd,
To all batchelors greeting, thefe lines are pre-
mis'd;
I'm a maid that would marry—ah! could I
but find
(I care not for fortune) a man to my mind!

Not the fair-weather fop, fond of fafhion and
drefs;
Not the 'fquire, who can relifh no joys but
the chace;
Nor the free-thinking rake, whom no morals
can bind:
Neither this—that—nor t'other's the man to
my mind.

Not the ruby-fac'd fot, who topes world without end;
Nor the drone, who can't relifh his bottle and
friend;
Nor the fool, that's too fond; nor the churl
that's unkind:
Neither this—that—nor t'other's the man to
my mind.

Not the wretch with full bags, without breeding or merit;
Nor the flafh, that's all fury without any fpirit;
Nor the fine mafter fribble, the fcorn of mankind!
Neither this—that—nor t'other's the man to
my mind.

But the youth whom good-fenfe and good-
nature infpire;
Whom the brave muft efteem, and the fair
fhould admire;
In whofe heart love and truth are with honour
conjoin'd:
This, this, and no other's the man to my mind.

SONG 522.

Sung in the Wedding Ring. —

OF woman to tell you my mind,
And I fpeak from th' experience I've had,
Not two out of fifty you'll find,
Be they daughters or wives,
But are plagues of our lives,
And enough to make any man mad.

The wrong and the right
Being fet in their fight,
They're fure to take hold of the wrong;
They'll cajole and they'll whimper,
They'll whine and they'll fnivel,
They'll coax, and they'll fimper—
In fhort, they're the devil;
And fo there's an end of my fong.

SONG 523.

Sung in Artaxerxes.

WHEN real joy we mifs,
'Tis fome degree of blifs
To reap ideal pleafure,
And dream of hidden treafure.

The foldier dreams of wars,
And conquers without fcars;
The failor, in his fleep,
With fafety ploughs the deep.

So I, through fancy's aid,
Enjoy my heav'nly maid;
And, bleft with thee and love,
Am greater far than Jove.

SONG 524.

ON SPRING AND SHEPHERDS BLISS;
A PASTORAL.

Written by Mr. HAWKINS.

HOW fweet the frefhing gales of fpring!
Each blufhing morn how gay!
The tuneful lark begins to fing,
As foon as dawn of day.

Then next Aurora's golden ray
Comes glancing o'er the plains;
To hail the warblers plaintive lay,
And rouze the fturdy fwains;

S

Who from their cots to toil repair,
  Regardlefs of all ftrife ;
Unknowing, and unknown to care,
  Is fure the fhepherds life.

He toils, he carols, all the day ;
  At eve, then home he bends ;
Charm'd with birds on every fpray,
  As to his cottage tends.

His cottage teems with infants dear,
  That's wholefome, clean, and neat ;
His wife—his bed—his all is there,
  To make his joys compleat.

With thefe he fits a welcome gueft,
  So happy and fo gay ;
Till twilight points the hour of reft,
  Then they it's call obey.

SONG 525.

Sung in *Almena*.

THE golden radiance of the fun,
  Mild glancing thro' the cedar bow'rs,
Renews the glories of the day :
The beauteous fcene's again begun,
  Which nature frefhens and empowers,
And ev'ry bird exalts his lay.

Sweet is the prime of florid June,
  Sweet are the meadows as they fmile,
And fweet the rural minftrel's fong ;
But fweeter is the mind in tune,
  Sweeter the heart unknown to guile,
And fweeter where the virtues throng.

SONG 526.

THE TOAST ; A CATCH.

Written by Mr. CUNNINGHAM.

GIVE the toaft, my good fellow, be jovial
  and gay,
And let the brifk moments pafs jocund away !
Here's the King——take your bumpers, my
  brave Britifh fouls,
Who guards your fair freedom fhould crown
  your full bowls.
Let him live—long and happy—fee Lewis
  brought down ;
And tafte all the comforts, no cares, of a crown.

SONG 527.

TO DELIA.

Written by Mr. HAWKINS.

MY mufe infpire me to impart
  In humble ardent ftrain,
To tell the anguifh of my heart
  To her that gives me pain.

'Tis Delia is the lovely maid ;
  Alas ! thou charming fair,
Behold thy Damon fecks thy aid,
  To eafe his pain and care.

For thou alone can give relief,
  Or anguifh moft fevere ;
Thy matchlefs charms are all my grief,
  Until you prove fincere.

SONG 528.

THE EVENING WALK.

Written by Mr. MAVOR.

THE weftern fun with mildeft ray
  Illumes the gilded view ;
Fled are the hours of fultry day,
  And nature calls on you :

On you, my dear, cool zephyrs wait,
  And ev'ry rich perfume ;
The flow'rs fhall blow beneath your feet,
  And fairer tints affume.

From ev'ry bloomy, verdant fpray,
  The chorifters fhall fing ;
For 'tis your luftre makes the day,
  And where you walk 'tis fpring.

Yet know, your luftre too muft fade,
  As flow'rs beneath the fun ;
And wrinkles fhall that face pervade
  Which has me captive won :

Then, mindful, hear a lover's claim,
  Nor let me long purfue ;
But mingle in a mutual flame,
  And death fhall find us true.

SONG 529.

Sung in the *Golden Pippin*.

LET heroes delight in the toils of the war,
  In maims, blood, and bruifes, and blows ;
Not a fword, but a fword-knot rejoices the fair :
  And what are rough foldiers to beaux ?
Away then with laurels ! come beauty and love,
  And filence the trumpet and drum ;
Let me with foft myrtle my brows bear inwove,
  And tenderly combat at home.

SONG 530.

KITTY ; OR, THE FEMALE PHAETON.

Written by Mr. PRIOR.

Sung at VAUXHALL.

FAIR Kitty, beautiful and young,
  And wild as colt untam'd,
Befpoke the fair from whence fhe fprung,
  With little rage inflam'd ;
Inflam'd with rage at fad reftraint
  Which wife mamma ordain'd,
And forely vex'd to play the faint,
  While wit and beauty reign'd.

Muft Lady Jenny frifk about,
  And vifit with her coufins ?
At balls muft fhe make all the rout,
  And bring home hearts by dozens !

What has she better, pray, than I,
What hidden charms to boast;
That all mankind for her should die,
While I am scarce a toast?

Dear, dear mamma, for once let me,
Unchain'd, my fortune try;
I'll have my earl as well as she,
Or know the reason why!
Fond love prevail'd, mamma gave way;
Kitty, at heart's desire,
Obtain'd the chariot for a day,
And set the world on fire.

SONG 531.

THE GROVE.

Written by Mr. MAVOR.

TING'D with the beams of dying day,
A glowing purple decks each spray,
And flames upon the trees;
While Cynthia rising, thro' the shade,
In silver robes, unveils her head,
Triumphing o'er the seas.

Now not a zephyr fans the leaves;
No bending blast the reed perceives;
But silence on her throne
Seems to reprefs each noisy found,
And echo listen to refound
No voice but ours alone.

The mossy banks, with leaves o'erspread,
Th' embow'ring trees above our heads,
A richer scene display,
Than all the elegance of state,
The tinsell'd grandeur of the great,
Or foppery of the gay.

In this delightful shady grove,
Sacred to solitude and love,
For ever could I range;
With Cælia dear to smile around,
And think I trod Elysian ground,
Nor wish a happier change.

SONG 532.

THE FAITHLESS SHEPHERD; A PASTORAL.

Written by Mr. HAWKINS.

RECLIN'D in a vernal alcove,
Sat Sylvia, bemoaning her fate;
For Strephon had slighted her love,
And chang'd all his fondness to hate.
Ah! why am I doom'd thus to mourn!
(Exclaim'd the sweet maid with a sigh;)
How hard is my case to be borne!
What mortal's so wretched as I!

Oh! Strephon, thou cause of my grief,
Cease, cease, cruel swain, to torment!
Ah! give your poor Sylvia relief,
And fill her sad soul with content.

Remember, that once you was kind,
No shepherd excell'd you in mien;
But now you're as false as the wind,
And your love is converted to spleen.

Yet oft' you have vow'd on the plain,
You'd ever be constant and free;
Nay, more, you were wont to explain,
But still you are faithless to me.
By the side of the sweet silver stream,
That glides through yon neighbouring vale;
Ah! there you first made me your theme,
And I listen'd with joy to your tale.

But now what a change do I find!
Nor solace nor comfort I know;
Since thou art to me so unkind,
I'm wretched wherever I go.
For woe in my breast is replete.
Should death, then, my fortune betide;
Oh! tell each kind swain that you meet,
'Twas doating on thee that I dy'd.

Thus spoke the dear nymph, in soft strains,
While silent the birds hopp'd the spray;
In solitude still she remains,
And pines all her hours away.
Ye fair, that adorn this bright isle,
Be guarded against such a snare;
On man be not eager to smile,
Lest the fate of poor Sylvia ye share.

SONG 533.

Written by Dr. PARNELL.

WHEN thy beauty appears,
In it's graces and airs,
All bright as an angel new dropt from the sky;
At distance I gaze, and am aw'd by my fears,
So strangely you dazzle my eye.

But when, without art,
Your kind thoughts you impart,
When your love runs in blushes thro' ev'ry vein;
When it darts from your eyes, when it pants
in your heart,
Then I know you're a woman again.

There's a passion and pride
In our sex, (she reply'd)
And thus, might I gratify both, I would do:
Still an angel appear to each lover beside,
But still be a woman to you.

SONG 534.

Written by AMBROSE PHILIPS, Esq.

BLEST as th' immortal gods is he,
The youth who fondly sits by thee,
And hears and sees thee, all the while,
Softly speak, and sweetly smile.

'Twas this bereav'd my soul of rest,
And rais'd such tumults in my breast;
For while I gaz'd, in transport tost,
My breath was gone, my voice was lost;
S 2

My bôfom glow'd; the fubtle flame
Ran quick thro' all my vital frame;
O'er my dim eyes a darknefs hung,
My ears with hollow murmurs rung.

In dewy damps my limbs were chill'd,
My blood with gentle horrors thrill'd,
My feeble pulfe forgot to play,
I fainted, funk, and dy'd away!

SONG 535.

ANGELIC fair, beneath yon pine,
  On graffy verdure let's recline,
  And like the morn be gay:
See how Aurora fmiles on fpring,
See how the larks arife and fing,
  To hail the infant day.

Mufic fhall wake the morn—the day
Shall roll unheeded as we play
  In wiles, impell'd by love:
When weary, we fhall deign to reft
Alternate on each other's breaft,
  While Cupid guards the grove.

What prince can boaft more happinefs
Than I (poffeffing thee) poffefs?
  All care is banifh'd hence.
Say, mortals, who our deeds defpife,
In what fuperior pleafure lies,
  —Than love and innocence?

SONG 536.

Sung in the *Wedding Ring.*

WHEN firft the youth his fears forfook,
  And that he lov'd I fondly heard,
What fweetnefs was in ev'ry look!
What eloquence in ev'ry word!

From her whole ftore, to make me blefs'd,
  Did fortune bid me chufe;
How gladly would I all the reft
  For love and him refufe.

SONG 537.

A CANTATA.

Sung at RANELAGH.

RECITATIVE.

AS Delia, bleft with ev'ry grace,
  Invok'd foft mufic's needlefs aid;
Compleatly conquer'd by her face,
  Thus gentle Strephon, fmiling faid.

AIR.

Where partial nature may deny
  The pow'r of beauty's melting glance,
Bet tedious labour toil and try
  To fwell the fong, or form the dance;

But let your charms alone fuffice,
  And truft the mufic of your eyes.

RECITATIVE.

Damon, who chanc'd to overhear,
  Thus fpoke, as he approach'd more near:
He flatters, do not truft the fwain,
  But liften to my honeft ftrain.

AIR.

Wonders are told of beauty's pow'r,
  Nor faintly warms the tuneful lay;
Your voice and perfon ev'ry hour
  By dozens fteal our hearts away:
Then how trifling is the prize,
Since fops have ears, and fools have eyes!

Ah! lovely nymph, indeed to blefs,
  Select the worthieft fwain you've won;
Who, prizing found and colour lefs,
  Admires you for your fenfe alone;
Then leave all little arts behind,
And ftudy to improve the mind.

SONG 538.

Written by Mr. MAVOR.

VENUS, queen of Paphos' grove;
  Cupid, god of ardent love!
All your charms and darts I feel;
Wound no more, but learn to heal.

Pure emotions fire my breaft;
Sordid paffions are at reft:
Love immortal only reins,
Give it's fweets, without it's pains.

SONG 539.

Sung at SADLER'S WELLS.

WHAT a blockhead is he that's afraid to
    die poor!
We came into the world with our fkins and no
    more:
So the matter is plain, he that worfhip; his pelf,
Is a thief to mankind, and a dupe to himfelf.

I'll have women and wine, I'll have horfes and
    hounds,
And my tafte in all fhapes fhall be rul'd by no
    bounds:
  For the matter is plain, &c.

'Tis a fmatch of them all muft afford the true
    joy,
In an olio of fports that the heart cannot cloy:
  For the matter is plain, &c.

If a mifer you prove, the whole world wifh you
    dead,
And your wife and your fon pluck the prop from
    your head:
  So the matter is plain, &c.

Let me live, then, thro' life, well-belov'd and
  at eafe,
My cafh fhall provide me whatever I pleafe:
For the matter is plain, he that worfhips his pelf,
Is a thief to mankind, and a dupe to himfelf.

SONG 540.

Sung in *Harlequin's Invafion.*

COME, chear up, my lads, 'tis to glory we
  fteer,
To add fomething new to this wonderful year:
To honour we call you, not prefs you like flaves;
For who are fo free as we fons of the waves?
Heart of oak are our fhips, heart of oak are our
  men;
    We always are ready,
    Steady, boys, fteady;
We'll fight, and we'll conquer, again and again.

We ne'er fee our foes, but we wifh them to ftay;
They never fee us, but they wifh us away:
If they run, why we follow, and run them afhore;
For if they won't fight us, what can we do more!
  Heart of oak, &c.

They fwear they'll invade us, thefe terrible foes,
They frighten our women, our children, and
  beaux;
But fhould their flat-bottoms in darknefs get
  o'er,
Still Britons they'll find to receive them on fhore.
  Heart of oak, &c.

We'll ftill make them run, and we'll ftill make
  them fweat,
In fpite of the devil, and Bruffels Gazette:
Then chear up, my lads, with one voice let us
  fing,
Our foldiers, our failors, our ftatefmen, and
  king.
Heart of oak are our fhips, heart of oak are our
  men;
    We always are ready,
    Steady, boys, fteady;
We'll fight, and we'll conquer, again and again.

SONG 541.

THAT I might not be plagu'd with the non-
  fenfe of men,
I promis'd my mother, again and again,
To fay as fhe bids me wherever I go,
And to all that they afk, or would have, tell
  'em No.

I really believe I have frighten'd a fcore;
They'll want to be with me, I warrant, no more:
And I own I'm not forry for ferving them fo;
Were the fame thing to do, I again fhould fay,
  No.

For a fhepherd I like, with more courage and
  art,
Won't let me alone, tho' I bid him depart;

Such queftions he puts fince I anfwer him fo,
That he makes me mean Yes, tho' my words
  are ftill No.

He afk'd, did I hate him, or think him too plain?
(Let me die if he is not a clever young fwain)
Should he venture a kifs, if I from him would
  go?
Then he prefs'd my young lips, while I blufh'd,
  and faid No.

He afk'd, if my heart to another was gone;
If I'd have him to leave me, or ceafe to love on?
If I meant my life long to anfwer him fo?
I faulter'd, and figh'd, and reply'd to him, No.

This morning an end to his courtfhip he made:
Will Phillis live longer a virgin? he faid;
If I prefs you to church, will you fcruple to go?
In a hearty good-humour, I anfwer'd, No, no.

SONG 542.

Sung in *Comus.*

BY the gaily-circling glafs
  We can fee how minutes pafs;
By the hollow cafk are told
How the waning night grows old.

Soon, too foon, the bufy day
Drives us from our fport and play:
What have we with day to do?
Sons of care, 'twas made for you.

SONG 543.

Sung in *Hob in the Well.*

A Rogue that is hired
  To do what's required,
And ne'er ftick at honour or confcience,
  To compafs his ends,
  Will deftroy his beft friends;
For a villain's fure friendfhip is nonfenfe.

  Yet ftill he may laugh,
  Well affur'd he is fafe,
And defpife all attempts to accufe him;
  For his patron oft-times
  Promoting his crimes,
Muft (for felf-prefervation) excufe him.

SONG 544.

THE HAPPY MEETING.

Sung at RANELAGH.

AS Jamie gay, gang'd blithe his way,
  Along the banks of Tweed;
A bonny lafs, as ever was,
  Came tripping o'er the mead:
The hearty fwain, untaught to feign,
  The buxom nymph furvey'd:
And full of glee, as lad could be,
  Befpake the pretty maid.

Dear laffy, tell, why by thine fel
 Thou hait'ly wand'reft here?
My ewes, fhe cry'd, are ftraying wide;
 Canft tell me, laddy, where?
To town ife hie, he made reply,
 Some muckle fport to fee;
But thou'rt fo fweet, fo trim and neat,
 Ife feek the ewes with thee.

She gin her hand, nor made a ftand,
 But lik'd the youth's intent;
O'er hill and dale, o'er plain and vale,
 Right merrily they went:
The birds fang fweet the pair to greet,
And flowers bloom'd around;
 And as they walk'd, of love they talk'd,
And joys which lovers crown'd.

And now the fun had rofe to noon,
 (The zenith of his pow'r)
When to a fhade their fteps they made,
 To pafs the mid-day hour:
The bonny lad raw'd in his plaid
 The lafs who fcorn'd to frown;
She foon forgot the ewes fhe faught,
 And he to gang to town.

SONG 545.
Written by Mr. LEMOINE.

COME hafte, my Phillis, hafte away
 To yonder verdant grove,
Where birds fing fweetly on each fpray
 The melodies of love.
Where frifky lambkins fport and play
 Around the flow'ry green;
Drefs'd in dame nature's bright array,
 Which yields a lovely fcene.

Where the clear murm'ring rivers run,
 In foft and coiling ftreams,
Secluded from the fcorching fun,
 And Colin writes his themes.
O! there my fair-one, let us rove,
 And tafte the fweets of life;
Like turtle-doves let's always love,
 And banifh care and ftrife.

SONG 546.
Written by Dr. PARNELL.

THIRSIS, a young and am'rous fwain,
 Saw two, the beauties of the plain,
 Who both his heart fubdue:
Gay Celia's eyes were dazzling fair;
Sabina's eafy fhape and air
 With fofter magick drew.

He haunts the ftream, he haunts the grove,
Lives in a fond romance of love,
 And feems for each to die;
Till each a little fpiteful grown,
Sabina Celia s fhape ran down,
 And fhe Sabina's eye.

Their envy made the fhepherd find
Thofe eyes which love could only blind;
 So fat the lover free:

No more he haunts the grove or ftream,
Nor with a true-love knot and name
 Engraves a wounded tree.

Ah Celia! (fly Sabina cry'd)
Tho' neither love, we're both deny'd;
Now, to fupport the fex's pride,
 Let either fix the dart.
Poor girl! (fays Celia) fay no more:
For fhou'd the fwain but one adore,
That fpite which broke his chains before,
 Would break the other's heart.

SONG 547.
MISS SPARROW.

LET nightingales boaft of their voice, or
 their mien,
And parrots take pride in their habit of green;
The peacock for beauty admir'd may be,
But none like the Sparrow can truly pleafe me.

With innocent mirth how fhe chirps all day
 long,
And eafy good-nature adds grace to her fong!
No care to difturb her, but quite full of glee,
She will ever delight and truly pleafe me.

While clofely confin'd, fhe repines not, like
 thofe
Whofe pride and ambition affect their repofe;
But happily bleft with content, fhe is free:
Such is the fweet bird that doth truly pleafe me.

The limner with fkill may attempt to difplay,
With flattering pencil, the fprightly and gay;
In feathers tho' fine, and delightful to fee,
Like the form of the mind they can never
 pleafe me.

Then let me conclude, from what I have faid,
With juftice and candour—by fancy not led—
Of all the gay birds I ever did fee,
None, yet, like the Sparrow, can truly pleafe me.

SONG 548.
Written by Mr. BOOTH.

SWEET are the charms of her I love,
 More fragrant than the damafk rofe,
Soft as the down of turtle dove,
 Gentle as winds when Zephyr blows;
Refrefhing as defcending rains
To fun-burnt climes and thirfty plains.

True as the needle to the pole,
 Or as the dial to the fun,
Conftant as gliding waters roll;
 Whofe fwelling tides obey the moon;
From every other charmer free,
My life and love fhall follow thee.

The lamb the flow'ry thyme devours,
 The dam the tender kid purfues,
Sweet Philomel, in fhady bowers
 Of verdant fpring, her notes renews;
All follow what they moft admire,
As I purfue my foul's defire.

Nature muſt change her beauteous face,
  And vary as the ſeaſons riſe;
As winter to the ſpring gives place,
  Summer th' approach of autumn flies:
No change on love the ſeaſons bring,
Love only knows perpetual ſpring.

Devouring time, with ſtealing pace,
  Makes lofty oaks and cedars bow;
And marble towers, and walls of braſs,
  In his rude march he levels low:
But time, deſtroying far and wide,
Love from the ſoul can ne'er divide.

Death only with his cruel dart
  The gentle godhead can remove,
And drive him from the bleeding heart,
  To mingle with the bleſt above;
Where, known to all his kindred train,
He finds a laſting reſt from pain.

Love, and his ſiſter fair, the ſoul,
  Twin-born, from heaven together came:
Love will the univerſe controu'l,
  When dying ſeaſons loſe their name;
Divine abodes ſhall own his pow'r,
When time and death ſhall be no more.

SONG 549.

CUPID, god of pleaſing anguiſh,
  Teach the enamour'd ſwain to languiſh,
  Teach him fierce deſires to know.
Heroes would be loſt in ſtory,
Did not love inſpire their glory,
  Love does all that's great below.

SONG 550.

Written when his preſent MAJESTY was
Prince of Wales.

GOD bleſs our young prince, and endow
  him with grace,
In fit time to ſupply his brave grandfather's
  place;
Make his tutors and ſervants both faithful
  and clever,
And his youth from all evil examples deliver.
  Derry down, down, down, derry down.

From nurſes and goſſips, who nothing ſo dread
As that over-much learning ſhould burden his
  head;
Who for teaching a prince how to reaſon and
  ſpeak,
Prefer a French novel to Latin and Greek.
  Derry down, &c.

From Jeſuit hiſtorians, (to tyranny civil)
Who declare Engliſh freedom the work of the
  devil;
Who prove William a villain, if James is a fool,
And that force is our king's only title to rule.
  Derry down, &c.

From philoſophers deep, who think hell but a
  notion,
And virtue and vice only matter and motion;

Bid the bible feed moths on my grandfather's
  ſhelf,
And by algebra ſhew how the world made itſelf.
  Derry down, &c.

From the nice men of faſhion, who not for
  their life
Would tread on your toe—tho' they lie with
  your wife;
Who Papiſts and Proteſtants count much the
  ſame,
And ſit down with ſtrict honour to play the
  whole game.
  Derry down, &c.

From grave politicians, who ſhrug and who
  wink,
But have no time to ſpeak, ſo profoundly they
  think,
Who, whilſt ſcandals are carry'd, demurely
  ſtand by,
And enjoy the effects of another man's lye.
  Derry down, &c.

So God bleſs the prince, let each honeſt boy ſing,
Make him firſt a good man, and in time a good
  king;
Make him wiſe and religious, and noble and
  chaſte,
And ſend him inſtructors no worſe than the
  laſt.
  Derry down, down, down, derry down.

SONG 551.

Written by BEN JOHNSON.

STILL to be neat, ſtill to be dreſt,
  As you were going to a feaſt;
Still to be powder'd, ſtill perfum'd:
Lady, it is to be preſum'd,
Though art's hid cauſes are not found,
All is not ſweet, all is not ſound.

Give me a look, give me a face,
That makes ſimplicity a grace;
Robe looſely flowing, hair as free:
Such ſweet neglect more taketh me,
Than all th' adu'teries of art:
They ſtrike mine eyes, but not my heart.

SONG 552.

SUMMER.

Written by Mr. LEMOINE.

NOW nature's beauties bloom around,
  Sweet violets paint the velvet ground;
Perfumes abundant lade each gale,
And float along the vernal dale.

The friſky lambkins wanton play,
  In luſcious paſtures, time away;
And limpid ſtreams harmonious glide,
With ſilver cignets in their tide.

The ermin'd lilies dreſs'd in light,
And blooming roſes red and white,

With painted tulips, myrtles green,
Affift to heighten grandeur's fcene.

The fields all gay, in glory blaze,
Affifted by bright Phœbus' rays;
Whofe beams refulgent now appear,
And early bid the morning fteer.

The ftarling, blackbird, and the thrufh,
Enraptur'd chant on ev'ry bufh:
High-pois'd in air the lark, too, fings,
While cleaving fpace with nervous wings.

Yet all the beauties here I paint,
Without the fair-ones, feem but faint;
For they with prattle gild our hours,
And are by far the brighteft flow'rs.

SONG 553.

WHILST I gaze on Chloe, trembling,
　　Straight her eyes my fate declare;
When fhe fmiles, I fear diffembling,
　　When fhe frowns, I then defpair.

Jealous of fome rival lover,
　　If a wandering look fhe gives;
Fain I would refolve to leave her,
　　But can fooner ceafe to live.

Why fhould I conceal my paffion,
　　Or the torments I endure?
I'll difclofe my inclination;
　　Aweful diftance yields no cure.

Sure it is not in her nature,
　　To be cruel to her flave;
She is too divine a creature,
　　To deftroy what fhe can fave.

Happy's he whofe inclination
　　Warms but with a gentle heat;
Never mounts to raging paffion:
　　Love's a torment, if too great.

When the ftorm is once blown over,
　　Soon the ocean quiet grows;
But a conftant, faithful lover,
　　Seldom meets with true repofe.

SONG 554.

Written by Mr. W—LL—s.

HOW happy was I,
　　When Delia was by;
Her prefence rejoiced my heart;
　　No troubles I knew,
　　My cares were but few,
Till the time I from Delia did part.

　　Then how fad the reverfe!
　　With pain I rehearfe
The difquiets my mind undergoes;
　　Time moves flowly on,
　　Content I have none;
Oh! feel for, and pity my woes.

　　My fair will be juft,
　　I can't her miftruft,
Her promife is binding I'm fure;

Then why fo lament?
For fhame, be content
For the prefent, her abfence endure.

The time fhortly will be,
When I Delia fhall fee,
And with her in wedlock be join'd;
　　Then how happy my ftate,
　　I'll not envy the great,
But enjoy, with my fair, peace of mind.

I covet not wealth,
But a good fhare of health,
For myfelf and the girl I adore:
　　We'll live at our eafe,
　　And do as we pleafe;
Ye gods! what can mortals wifh more.

SONG 555.

THE INVITATION.

Written by Mr. T. B.

'TIS done, I've rais'd a rural bow'r
　　Deep in the twilight fhade:
There blooms full many a lovely flow'r;
　　Ah! wou'd they never fade.

Come, then, my Lucy, hafte away,
　　And nature's manfion view;
Screen'd from the fun's too piercing ray,
　　Each flowret blooms for you.

At your command, thy fhepherd ftrove
　　To deck the fhady green:
You faid the fpot was form'd for love;
　　I heard, and bleft the fcene.

Ah! let it not be bleft in vain;
　　But there reward my truth:
Repay thy conftant Harry's pain
　　With innocence and truth.

SONG 556.

Written by Mr. LEMOINE.

HOW fair is my love,
　　As kind as the dove;
Her temper both lively and gay:
　　The lily, and rofe,
　　Upon her cheeks blows,
To give her the fplendour of May.

Her fhape, and her mien,
　　Proclaim her the queen
Of beauty, of virtue, and truth;
　　Her eyes are like jet,
　　Her teeth neatly fet:
Ye gods! in the prime of her youth.

Her voice, like the thrufh,
　　That fings on the bufh,
When meadows look blooming and gay;
　　Each nymph and each fwain,
　　That dance on the plain,
Are charm'd with my Phyllis's lay.

MISS ABRAMS as Silvia in CYMON

Oh, why should we sorrow who never knew Sin

Song 557

Published by J. Bew Aug.t 1.st 1778

She cries, Don't repine,
I foon fhall be thine,
And eafe thy fond bofom of ftrife;
In pleafure's fweet bow'r
We'll pafs ev'ry hour,
While nature fupplies us with life.

SONG 557.

Sung in *Cymon.*

O Why fhould we forrow, who never knew fin!
Let fmiles of content fhew our rapture
within:
This love has fo rais'd me, I now tread in air!
He's fure fent from Heav'n to lighten my care!

Each fhepherdefs views me with fcorn and dif-
dain!
Each fhepherd purfues me, but all is in vain:
No more will I forrow, no longer defpair,
He's fure fent from Heav'n to lighten my care!

SONG 558.

Written by Mr. CAREY.

FROM the court to the cottage convey me
away,
For I'm weary of grandeur, and what they
call gay;
Where pride without meafure,
And pomp without pleafure,
Make life in a circle of hurry decay.

Far remote, and retir'd, from the noife of the
town,
I'll exchange my brocade for a plain ruffet gown:
My friends fhall be few,
But well chofen, and true,
And fweet recreation our evenings fhall crown.

With a rural repaft, a rich banquet to me,
On a moffy green turf, near fome fhady old tree;
The river's clear brink
Shall afford me my drink,
And temp'rance my friendly phyfician fhall be.

Ever calm and ferene, with contentment ftill
bleft,
Not too giddy joy, or with forrow depreft,
I'll neither invoke,
Nor repine at death's ftroke,
But retire from the world as I wou'd to my reft.

SONG 559.

NOW rofes bloffom, meads are fhorn,
And gently waves the verdant corn;
The fky is brightly blue, and hark!
How fweetly fings the rifing lark:
Come, come, my Molly, fleep no more,
Awake to love, and converfe dear;
When tempefts thunder on the fhore,
You'll vainly wifh the fummer near.

Inhale the breeze that fans the flower,
Which fweeter back thy lips fhall pour;

O could I breathe no gale but this,
And make my life one lengthen'd kifs!
Then grafp my arm, and let us hie
To yon grotefquely hanging grove;
Upon it's fhaggy brow I fpy
A cottage, form'd for us and love.

Not more yon fky-clad mountain's fpire
The wand'ring clouds beneath admire,
Than village fwains my conftant love,
Their vulgar flames fo far above.
But who, when lufcious grapes depend,
From thorny brake would berries pull?
And where fuch charms as thine tranfcend,
The paffion's young, though years be full.

Up heav'n's high fteep day's dazzling ftar
Behind has left the Eaft afar;
The bees, from flowery hill and plain,
Rich fun-exalted juices drain;
Let us, my fair-one, ufe, as they,
The favours granted from above;
Draw bleffings from our fhort-liv'd day;
Man's true purfuit is peace and love.

SONG 560.

ANACREONTIC.

BACCHUS, Jove's delightful boy,
Gen'rous god of wine and joy,
Still exhilarates my foul
With the raptures of the bowl.

Then with feather'd feet I bound,
Dancing in a feftive round;
Then I feel, in fparkling wine,
Tranfports delicate, divine.

Then the fprightly mufic warms;
Song delights, and beauty charms!
Debonaire, and light, and gay,
Thus I dance the hours away.

SONG 561.

Written by the EDITOR.

YE fhepherds, fo jocund and gay,
O liften awhile to my ftrain!
And while you attend to the lay,
Find out fome relief for my pain.

Not the lofs of my fheep do I mourn,
No lambkin has ftray'd from my field;
Nor does Corydon fit, thus, forlorn,
For bleffings that riches could yield.

Ah, no! were his grief but for thefe,
Your fports might foon banifh his cares;
But tell me what paftime can eafe
The fwain who both loves and defpairs!

While Phillis, too beautiful maid,
Regards not poor Corydon's fighs;
In vain he folicits your aid,
Tho' ableft of men to advife.

Nay, droop not with pity for me,
Nor hang down your heads in defpair;

T

Too well your opinion I see,
  And read what you wish to declare.

In absence, alone, ye would say,
  I must hope for a cure of my smart;
But how can the shepherd e'er stray
  From the image that dwells in his heart!

Then grieve me not more with your care
  For a wretch who for ever must weep;
But leave me, the prey of despair,
  While each of you tends on his sheep.

But mine, when you've seen me laid low,
  (Fulfil me this latest request)
To beautiful Phillis bestow;
  And, oh! may she ever be blest!

SONG 562.

SINCE beauty's the object we all do pursue,
Let us try the dear charmer to find,
  Whose virtue and truth
  Adds a lustre to youth,
And where sweetness and constancy's join'd.

In enjoyment like this, ye who know, speak
  the bliss
That's found where two hearts do unite;
  Where the lass whom we love,
  Will our wishes approve,
And sincerely that love will requite.

Say, what joy or delight that's on earth can
  compare
To the mutual endearments of love!
  Then to pleasures refin'd
  Let's all be resign'd,
And blush where we cannot improve.

And ye, O ye fair! the just pride of our isle,
Fam'd for beauty, good-nature, and dress,
  May ye ever be true
  To the man who loves you,
And with tenderness strive him to bless.

SONG 563.

LOVE AND INNOCENCE.

Written by Mr. NICHOLLS.

RECITATIVE.

WHERE two tall elms their verdant boughs
  entwin'd,
To form a shade some spreading hazels join'd,
'Twas there, to pass in sweets the sultry hours,
Young Damon hung the woodland's fairest
  flow'rs;
And when intensely beam'd the mid-day heat,
He led his Phillis to the cool retreat;
Where grew the cuckoo-bud, and daffodil,
With wild thyme sweet, that loves the moss-
  clad hill.
No eye to see, no ear to hear their chat,
Low on the velvet-grass the lovers sat:
Let not foul envy think they meant offence,
No more they knew, but Love and Innocence.
With gentle accents trembling on his tongue,
Thus to the maid he lov'd the shepherd sung:

AIR.

Whilst shelter'd from the beams of noon,
  Your ewes and lambkins rest,
Dear Phillis, grant the promis'd boon,
  And make your Damon blest.

The thrush no more shall wake the plain;
  The lark, at rising day,
Forget to give his chearing strain,
  When spring leads up the May:

These clover-vales shall bloom no more,
  No verdure dress the grove;
Yon stream forsake it's rushy shore,
  When I deceive my love.

RECITATIVE.

No more he meant, than on her breast to lie,
To dream of joys the realms of bliss supply.
The blushing maid, of virtue's sacred train,
Repuls'd his love, and thus address'd her swain:

AIR.

Far o'er the mead a shepherd dwells,
  All silver is his beard;
Note what the hoary hermit tells,
  There's truth in ev'ry word.

Last eve I ran across the vale,
  Swift as the swallow flies;
His cot obtain'd, I told my tale,
  And begg'd him to advise.

Beware (he said) our ruder race,
  For youth is fraught with art;
And he who wears the fairest face,
  Oft wants a gentle heart.

Hapless for life's the luckless fair,
  If such she's doom'd to wed;
'Twere better death should save her care,
  Upon her bridal bed.

Such were his words; and, O my swain!
  Should you prove insincere,
Phillis must thro' her life complain,
  And often drop a tear.

RECITATIVE.

The ardent lover heard the maid's surprize;
Then thus, enraptur'd, to her plaint replies:

AIR.

Pluck wild suspicion from your mind;
  Once rooted, 'twill encrease,
And soon the bitter fruits you'll find
  Destructive to your peace.

Think better, sweet, of one that's true,
  Believe my heart your own;
For were a thousand maids in view,
  I'd take but you alone.

This boon I ask of Heav'n to give:
  In some sequester'd home,
With you in wedlock's bonds to live,
  Without a thought to roam.

From grey-ey'd morn till stilly eve,
  From eve till rising day,
No joy without thee I'd receive,
  Without thee ne'er be gay.

Be thou but mine, with rofy health,
Let dear content be by;
The reſt I'll leave the fons of wealth,
Without a ſingle ſigh.

RECITATIVE.

Thus ſang the youth, whoſe breaſt was ho-
nour's throne,
Whoſe mind ſimplicity had made her own;
Till, far afield, the tinkling village bells
Call'd ſportive echo from her grots and cells.
They left the grove, unto the dance they ſped;
Revel'd till eve, and the next morn were wed.

AIR.

Now love and fond wiſhes concur
To make them the talk of the plain;
The maids take example from her,
And the ſhepherds all copy the ſwain.

Where e'er ſuch examples are ſhown,
Who of wedlock can ever repent;
Where conſtancy governs the throne,
The ſubjects are ſure of content.

RECITATIVE.

To ſeek no more, let lovers learn from hence,
Till hymen wills, than Love and Innocence.

SONG 564.

LOVE, thou'rt the beſt of human joys,
Our chiefeſt happineſs below!
All other pleaſures are but toys;
Muſic without thee is but noiſe,
Beauty but an empty ſhow.

Heav'n, that knew beſt what man cou'd move,
And raiſe his thoughts above the brute;
Said, Let him be, and let him love.
That only muſt his ſoul improve,
Howe'er philoſophers diſpute.

SONG 565.

INVOCATION TO HEALTH.

SWEETEST health, of roſy hue,
Brighteſt daughter of the ſky,
Haſte, and bid thoſe ſkies adieu,
And to Cornelia's boſom fly!
Haſte thee, nymph, ah! haſte along,
Come and liſten to my ſong:
'Tis for you I tune my lay;
Faireſt virgin, haſte away.

Wherefore, goddeſs, haſt thou fled,
Whence ſo ſweetly thou didſt reſt;
In ſo calm, ſo ſoft a bed,
With content, thy ſiſter, bleſt.
Come, ah! come, and with thee bring
Drops from Lethe's ſoothing ſpring;
Balm from Tempe's fragrant vales,
Nectar which the gods regales.

Goddeſs come! and on her breaſt
Shed thy healing influence;

Let no cares that ſpot moleſt,
Drive all pain and ſorrow thence.
Why delay'ſt thou, goddeſs, ſay?
Virtue calls thee, come away;
Fly'ſt thou from that heav'nly cell,
Where virtue's ſelf delights to dwell?

Haſte thee, faireſt, pr'ythee haſte,
Nor to quit one heaven fear;
Hie thee to Cornelia's breaſt,
Thou wilt make a heaven there.

SONG 566.

ANACREONTIC SOCIETY.

Written by RALPH TOMLINSON, Eſq.

TO Anacreon, in Heav'n, where he ſat in
full glee,
A few ſons of harmony ſent a petition,
That he their inſpirer and patron would be;
When this anſwer arriv'd from the jolly old
Grecian—
Voice, fiddle, and flute,
No longer be mute,
I'll lend ye my name, and inſpire ye to boot:
And, beſides, I'll inſtruct ye, like me, to intwine
The myrtle of Venus with Bacchus's vine.

The news through Olympus immediately flew;
When old Thunder pretended to give him-
ſelf airs—
If theſe mortals are ſuffer'd their ſcheme to
purſue,
The devil a goddeſs will ſtay above ſtairs.
Hark! already they cry,
In tranſports of joy,
A fig for Parnaſſus! to Rowley's we'll fly;
And there, my good fellows, we'll learn to
intwine
The myrtle of Venus with Bacchus's vine.

The yellow-hair'd god, and his nine fuſty
maids,
To the hill of old Lud will incontinent flee,
Idalia will boaſt but of tenantleſs ſhades,
And the biforked hill a mere deſart will be.
My thunder, no fear on't,
Will ſoon do it's errand,
And, dam'me! I'll ſwinge the ringleaders,
I warrant.
I'll trim the young dogs, for thus daring to twine
The myrtle of Venus with Bacchus's vine.

Apollo roſe up; and ſaid, Pr'ythee ne'er quarrel,
Good king of the gods, with my vot'ries
below:
Your thunder is uſeleſs—then, ſhewing his
laurel,
Cry'd, Sic evitabile fulmen, you know!
Then over each head
My laurels I'll ſpread;
So my ſons from your crackers no miſchief
ſhall dread,
Whilſt ſnug in their club-room, they jovially
twine
The myrtle of Venus with Bacchus's vine.

Next Momus got up, with his rifible phiz,
And fwore with Apollo he'd chearfully join—
The full tide of harmony ftill fhall be his,
But the fong, and the catch, and the laugh
    fhall be mine:
        Then, Jove, be not jealous
        Of thefe honeft fellows.
Cry'd Jove, We relent, fince the truth you
    now tell us;
And fwear, by Old Styx, that they long fhall
    intwine
The myrtle of Venus with Bacchus's vine.

Ye fons of Anacreon, then, join hand in hand;
Preferve unanimity, friendfhip, and love!
'Tis your's to fupport what's fo happily plann'd;
You've the fanction of gods, and the fiat
    of Jove.
        While thus we agree,
        Our toaft let it be.
May our club flourifh happy, united, and free!
And long may the fons of Anacreon intwine
The myrtle of Venus with Bacchus's vine.

SONG 567.

OH, Hymen, propitious, receive in thy train
    A pair unfeduc'd by the felfifh and vain!
Whom neither ambition nor int'reft draws,
But love, cordial fubject, fubmits to thy laws!

Our fouls for the fweets of thy union prepare,
And grant us thy bliffes, unblended with care:
Let mutual compliance endear all our days,
And friendfhip grow ftronger as paffion decays.

SONG 568.

THE SHEPHERD COMFORTED.

AS Cynthia late, within the grove,
    Bemoan'd his too fuccefslefs love,
And eas'd (retir'd) his fecret pain,
The god of love, who wander'd near,
Chanc'd his complaint to overhear,
And thus addrefs'd the fwain :

Rife, filly fhepherd, rife, (he cry'd;)
It feems you're eafily deny'd,
Becaufe the charming nymph is coy :
The tongue may learn to fpeak with art;
But would you know the fair-one's heart,
Confult it in her eye!

'Tis in that mirrour of her foul,
The fecrets of her bofom roll,
    Reveal'd, without difguife, to view;
For, Cynthia, take it for a truth,
You only are the favour'd youth,
And Lydia loves but you!

No more my altars then upbraid,
Nor thus invoke my needlefs aid!
Since faithful I have done my part:
Thy own perform with like addrefs,
She foon fhall yield, thy arms to blefs,
And ye thee all her heart! .

So fpoke, fincere, the friendly god,
When ftraight along the flow'ry road,
    The nymph with languid beauty mov'd ;
The fwain with joy the moment feiz'd,
She heard his tender vows well pleas'd,
And all his wifh approv'd.

With grateful pride, and gladfome air,
To Hymen's fhrine he led the fair!
    And made the lafting blifs fecure.
Let maids no more falfe coldnefs feign,
Let faithful fwains no more complain,
    But boldly afk a cure!

SONG 569.

Written by Mr. NICHOLLS.

SWEET Flora, revifit our ifle,
    Come quickly, and lead up the May,
For, ah! how I fuffer the while
Soft Zeph'rus and thou art away.
Now howls the North wind round my cot;
    My cot by the ftream's frozen fide :
Ah! left I grow fick of my lot,
    Bid the rigorous feafon fubfide.

From the elder-tree melt the pale fnow,
    'Tis time fhe had put forth her green;
Again bid the rivulet flow,
    And with primrofes brighten the fcene :
New robe the tall king of the grove;
    Bid the birch and the poplar look gay;
Bid the eglantine form an alcove,
    And dog-rofes blufh on the fpray.

Again bid the hawthorn-tree charm,
    That the bee may replenifh her hive;
That the finch may he fhelter'd from harm,
    And her neftlings in fafety furvive.
Bid the hornbeam it's foliage untwine,
    To harbour the innocent dove,
Where (fafe from the ruftick's oefign)
    She may rear her calm offspring of love.

Bid Zephyr diffufe his foft gale,
    That my fheep on the hare-bells may feed ;
Wake the vi'let that fleeps in the vale,
    With the cowflips which droop in the mead.
Let the furze yield it's bloffoms of gold ;
    Bid the tanfy perfume the ftill glade ;
Let the wild thyme it's flow'rets unfold,
    And fweet-briar fpring in the fhade.

Bid the clover in fragrancy yield ;
    Bid the mower refurbifh his fcythe ;
Bid the pea-bloffoms garnifh the field,
    That my Phebe may gather a tythe,
Of the faireft that blew on the plain,
    Of the fweeteft that fpring in the grove,
To wreath, gentle goddefs, thy fane,
    For thou art the mother of love.

SONG 570.

FAR fwifter than light my love flies,
    In queft of a happier clime,
See yonder he fteers through the fkies,
    And fmiles on the wreck of old time.

Since I here on earth ftill remain,
A ftranger to comfort and reft,
At once I will end all my pain——
This dagger I'll fheath in my breaft.

SONG 571.

THE PATIENT COUNTESS; AN OLD
BALLAD.

IMPATIENCE changeth fmoak to flame,
But jealoufy is hell:
Some wives by patience have reduc'd
Ill hufbands to live well;
As did the lady of an earl,
Of whom I now fhall tell.

An earl there was had wedded, lov'd;
Was lov'd, and lived long
Full true to his fair countefs; yet
At laft he did her wrong.

Once hunted he until the chace,
Long fafting, and the heat,
Did houfe him in a peakifh grange
Within a foreft great.

Where known and welcom'd (as the place
And perfons might afford)
Brown bread, whig, bacon, curds and milk,
Were fet him on the board.

A cufhion made of lifts, a ftool
Half-backed with a hoop,
Were brought him, and he fitteth down
Befide a forry coup.

The poor old couple wifh'd their bread
Were wheat, their whig were perry,
Their bacon beef, their milk and curds
Were cream, to make him merry.

Mean-while (in ruffet neatly clad,
With linen white as fwan,
Herfelf more white, fave rofy where
The ruddy colour ran;

Whom naked nature, not the aids
Of art made to excel)
The good man's daughter ftirs to fee
That all were feat and well;
The earl did mark her, and admire
Such beauty there to dwell.

Yet falls he to their homely fare,
And held him at a feaft:
But as his hunger flaked, fo
An amorous heat increas'd.

When this repaft was paft, and thanks,
And welcome too; he faid
Unto his hoft and hoftefs, in
The hearing of the maid.

Ye know (quo'h he) that I am lord
Of this, and many towns;
I alfo know that you be poor,
And I can fpare you pounds.

So will I, fo ye will confent,
That yonder lafs and I
May bargain for her love; at leaft,
Do give me leave to try.

Who needs to know it? nay, who dares
Into my doings pry?

Firft they mifdike, yet at the length
For lucre were mifled;
And then the gamefome earl did woo
The damfel for his bed.

He took her in his arms, as yet
So coy'fh to be kifs'd,
As maids that know themfelves belov'd,
And yieldingly refift.

In few, his offers were fo large
She laftly did confent;
With whom he lodged all that night,
And early home he went.

He took occafion oftentimes
In fuch a fort to hunt,
Whom when his lady often mifs'd,
Contrary to his wont,

And laftly was informed of
His amorous haunt elfewhere;
It griev'd her not a little, though
She feem'd it well to bear.

And thus fhe reafons with herfelf:
Some fault, perhaps, in me;
Somewhat is done, that fo he doth;
Alas! what may it be?

How may I win him to himfelf?
He is a man, and men
Have imperfections; it behoves
Me pardon nature then.

To check him were to make him check,
Although he now were chafte:
A man controuled of his wife,
To her makes leffer hafte.

If duty then, or dalliance, may
Prevail to alter him;
I will be dutiful, and make
Myfelf for daliiance trim.

So was fhe, and fo lovingly
Did entertain her lord,
As fairer, or more faultlefs, none
Could be, for bed or board.

Yet ftill he loves his leiman, and
Did ftill purfue that game,
Sufpecting nothing lefs, than that
His lady knew the fame:
Wherefore, to make him know fhe knew,
She this device did frame.

When long fhe had been wrong'd, and fought
The forefaid means in vain,
She rideth to the fimple grange
But with a flender train.

She lighteth, entereth, greets them well,
And then did look about her:
The guilty houfhold knowing her,
Did wifh themfelves without her;
Yet, for fhe looked merrily,
The lefs they did mifdoubt her.

When fhe had feen the beauteous wench
(Then blufhing fairnefs fairer)

Such beauty made the countefs bold
Them both excus'd the rather.

Who would not bite at fuch a bait?
Thought fhe: and who, (though lothe)
So poor a wench, but gold might tempt?
Sweet errors lead them both.

Scarce one in twenty that had bragg'd
Of proffer'd gold deny'd,
Or of fuch yielding beauty bauik'd,
But, ten to one, had ly'd.

Thus, thought fhe; and fhe thus declares
Her caufe of coming thither:
My lord, oft hunting in thefe parts,
Through travel, night, or weather,

Hath often lodged in your houfe;
I thank you for the fame:
For why—it doth him jolly eafe
To lie fo near his game.

But, for you have not furniture
Befeeming fuch a gueft,
I bring his own, and come myfelf
To fee his lodging dreft.

With that two fumpters were difcharg'd,
In which were hangings brave,
Silk coverings, curtains, carpets, plate,
And all fuch turn fhould have.

When all was handfomely difpos'd,
She prays them to have care
That nothing hap in their default,
That might his health impair.

And, damfel, (quoth fhe) for it feems
This houfhold is but three;
And for thy parents age, that this
Shall chiefly reft on thee;

Do me that good, elfe, would to God
He hither come no more.
So took fhe horfe, and ere fhe went
Beftowed gold good ftore.

Full little thought the county that
His countefs had done fo;
Who, now return'd from far affairs,
Did to his fweetheart go.

No fooner fat he foot within
The late deformed cote,
But that the formal change of things
His wond'ring eyes did note.

But when he knew thofe goods to be
His proper goods; though late,
Scarce taking leave, he home returns
The matter to debate.

The countefs was abed, and he
With her his lodging took;
Sir, welcome home (quoth fhe) this night
For you I did not look.

Then did he queftion her of fuch
His ftuff beftowed fo.
Forfooth, (quoth fhe) becaufe I did
Your love and lodging know:

Your love to be a proper wench,
Your lodging nothing lefs;

I held it for your health, the houfe
More decently to drefs.

Well, wot I, notwithftanding her,
Your lordfhip loveth me;
And greater hope to hold you fuch
By quiet, than brawls, you fee.

Then for my duty, your delight,
And to retain your favour,
All done I did, and patiently
Expect your wonted 'haviour.

Her patience, wit, and anfwer, wrought
His gentle tears to fall:
When (kiffing her a fcore of times)
Amend, fweet wife, I fhall.
He faid, and did it; fo each wife
Her hufband may recal.

SONG 572.
Sung at SADLER's WELLS.
RECITATIVE.

TO yonder beech's friendly fhade
Repair, my Aura, lovely maid;
And while our lambkins frolic make,
Thy fhepherd's treafure fmiling take.

AIR.

Were to my wifh thy temples bound,
How India's gems fhould blaze around!
Yet wifhes are but idle breath;
Accept, in lieu, a rofy wreath.

Had I proud Perfia at my beck,
What gaudy robes my fair fhould deck!
But as it is, vouchfafe to wear
What once enwrapt my fleecy care.

Of burnifh'd gold, or filver fair,
Thofe feet of thine fhould fandals bear:
But all I have to offer now,
The hide of Dao, thy fav'rite cow.

Said Aura—Sandals, robes, and crowns,
Are flender proofs 'gainft fortune's frowns;
We've health and eafe—Is heaven fcant?
Here, take my hand—we've all we want.

SONG 573.

RESOLV'D, as her poet, of Celia to fing,
For emblems of beauty I fearch'd thro' the
fpring;
To flowers foft blooming compar'd the fweet
maid,
But flowers, tho' blooming, at ev'ning may
fade.
Of funfhine and breezes I next thought to write,
Of breezes fo calm, and of funfhine fo bright;
But thefe with my fair no refemblance will hold,
For the fun fets at night, and breezes grow cold,

The clouds of mild evening array'd in pale blue,
While the fun-beams behind them peep'd glit-
tering through,
Tho' to rival her charms they can never arife,
Yet methought they look'd fomething like
Celia's fweet eyes;

These beauties are tranfient; but Celia's will
   laft,
When fpring, and when fummer, and autumn,
   are paft;
For fenfe and good-humour no feafon difarms,
And the foul of my Celia enlivens her charms.

At length, on a fruit-tree a bloffom I found,
Which beauty difplay'd, and fhed fragrance
   around,
I then thought the mufes had fmil'd on my
   pray'r:
This bloffom, I cry'd, will refemble my fair;
Thefe colours fo gay, and united fo well,
This delicate texture, and ravifhing fmell,
Be her perfon's dear emblem: but where fhall
   I find,
In nature, a beauty that equals her mind?

This bloffom, now pleafing, at fummer's gay
   call
Muft languifh at firft, and muft afterwards fall;
But behind it the fruit, it's fucceffor, fhall rife,
By nature difrob'd of it's beauteous difguife:
So Celia, when youth, that gay bloffom, is o'er,
By her virtues improv'd, fhall engage me the
   more;
Shall recal ev'ry beauty that brighten'd her
   prime,
When her merit is ripen'd by love and by time.

SONG 574.

Sung at MARYBONE.

THE lark's fhrill note awakes the morn,
   The breezes wave the ripen'd corn;
The yellow-harveft, free from fpoil,
Rewards the happy farmers toil;
The flowing bowl fucceeds the flail,
O'er which he tells the jocund tale.

SONG 575.

VALENTINE'S-DAY.

WHEN blufhes dy'd the cheek of morn,
   And dew-drops gliften'd on the thorn;
When fky-larks tun'd their carrols fweet,
To hail the god of light and heat;
Philander, from his downy bed,
To fair Lifetta's chamber fped,
Crying—Awake, fweet love of mine,
I'm come to be thy Valentine.

Soft love, that balmy fleep denies,
Had long unveil'd her brilliant eyes,
Which (that a kifs fhe might obtain)
She artfully had clos'd again:
He funk, thus caught in beauty's trap,
Like Phœbus into Thetis' lap,
And near forgot that his defign
Was but to be her Valentine.

She, ftarting, cry'd—I am undone;
Philander, charming youth, be gone!
For this time, to your vows fincere,
Make virtue, not your love, appear:

No fleep has clos'd thefe watchful eyes,
(Forgive the fimple fond difguife;)
To gen'rous thoughts your heart incline,
And be my faithful Valentine.

The brutal paffion fudden fled,
Fair honour govern'd in it's ftead,
And both agreed, ere fetting fun,
To join two virtuous hearts in one;
Their beauteous offspring foon did prove
The fweet effects of mutual love;
And, from that hour to life's decline,
She blefs'd the day of Valentine.

SONG 576.

Sung in the Serenata of Solomon.

TOGETHER let us range the fields
   Impearled with the morning dew,
Or view the fruit the vineyard yields,
   Or the apple's cluft'ring bough;
There, in clofe-embower'd fhades,
   Impervious to the noon-tide ray,
By tinkling rills, on rofy beds,
   We'll love the fultry hours away.

SONG 577.

JEALOUSY.

JEALOUSY, be gone, and leave me;
   From my bofom, ah! remove:
While thou ftay'ft thou doft but grieve me;
   Hence, thou foe to facred love!
Whilft by thee the heart's directed,
   All things double faces wear;
Chloe, in thy glafs reflected,
   Seems as falfe as fhe is fair.

Harmlefs looks and flight expreffions,
   Where love's eye no meaning reads,
To fome rival are confeffions
   Of a heart that for him bleeds.
Cruel fpy! that ne'er difcovers
   What may eafe the frantic mind;
Hence, nor blaft the blifs of lovers:
   Leave us happy, leave us blind.

SONG 578.

THE LOVER'S PETITION.

FAIRER than the op'ning lilies,
   Sweeter than the morning rofe,
Are the blooming charms of Phillis;
   Richer fweets does fhe difclofe.
Long fecure from Cupid's pow'r,
   Soft repofe had lull'd my breaft,
Till in one fhort fatal hour,
   She depriv'd my foul of reft.

Cupid, god of pleafing anguifh,
   From whofe fhafts I bleed and burn!
Teach, O! teach the maid to languifh!
   Strike fair Phillis in her turn.

From that torment in her breaft,
Soon to pity fhe'll incline,
And, to give her bofom reft,
Kindly heal the wound in mine.

SONG 579.

Sung in the *Sheep-Shearing.*

COME, come, my good fhepherds, our
flocks we muft fhear ;
In your holiday fuits, with your laffes appear :
The happieft folks are the guiltlefs and free ;
And who are fo guiltlefs, fo happy as we ?

We harbour no paffions by luxury taught ;
We practife no arts with hypocrify fraught :
What we think in our hearts, you may read in
our eyes ;
For, knowing no falfhood, we need no difguife.

That giant, ambition, we never can dread,
Our roofs are too low for fo lofty a head :
Content and fweet chearfulnefs open our door ;
They fmile with the fimple, and feed with
the poor.

When love has poffefs'd us, that love we
reveal,
Like the flocks that we feed, are the paffions
we feel ;
So harmlefs and fimple we fport and we play,
And leave to fine folks to deceive and betray.

SONG 580.

Written by Mr. NICHOLLS.

WHEN our ifle was in bloom, and all nature
look'd gay,
The queen of foft wifhes, and Bacchus, one day,
Were met round the board, with a flafk of the
beft,
Where wit, in good-humour, was fat as a gueft,
Till Bacchus prefum'd on the pow'r of his vine,
And Venus retorted, No power's like mine ;
I humble the tyrant, I conquer the brave,
Give fenfe to the clown, and relief to the flave.

The mightieft of kings, tho' the proudeft he be,
Quits his throne, and bows down in homage
to me :
To me, upon earth, fweeter off'rings arife
Than to Jove, or to any one elfe of the fkies.
To me all his wifhes the lover imparts,
And gratefully owns me the goddefs of hearts :
Wall'd cities to me their ftrong gates have
unbarr'd ;
To me all the world bears implicit regard.

'Tis granted, (faid Bacchus) but what of all
this ?
'Tis only to idle, to fondle and kifs,
To figh at the feet of the fair, and implore ;
The juice of my goblet does twenty times more :
'Twill quiet the wife, when the vixen is fhrill,
And often does more than a medical pill ;

'Tis a balm to the bofom with trouble opprefs'd,
Gives life to the dull, and infirmity reft.

Bright Venus grew warm, and forbad him to
fpeak ;
Her eyes were inflam'd, and vermilion'd her
cheek.
That pow'r (faid the goddefs) you prize above
mine,
'Tis true, turn'd the friends of Ulyffes to fwine.
To deeds moft unworthy your vot'ries have
ftoop'd,
Priefts, fages, and monarchs, by you have been
dup'd ;
The vile you make worfe, and the dull you
make fad,
In fhort, you're the pow'r to do all that is bad.

The gods faw the furies were lodg'd in her
breaft,
So begg'd for awhile fhe'd give o'er the conteft.
But Venus, determin'd his godfhip to vex,
Still fhew'd what it was to contend with the fex;
Talk'd much of his pranks, and faid this with
abufe,
Fell poifon lurks under the fweets of your juice.
To the tongue of the goddefs in vain he reply'd,
Till heav'n-born Reafon came down to decide.

Unable to bear her approach, folly fled
Along the wide path, worn by error's rude
tread ;
The vices, in terror, flew fwiftly away,
As fhadows of night from the prefence of day ;
Whilft dulnefs ftole off, fo much fweetnefs to
fhun,
As dew from the rofe, when it's kifs'd by the
fun ;
The mother of love, with each heart-chearing
grace,
Forfook her fod feat, and to Reafon gave place.

Her afpect was mild as an infant's new born,
And as chearing to all as the beams of the morn.
Give o'er, (faid the cherub) let Reafon define
The diff'rence 'twixt love and the pow'rs of
the vine.
Bright parent of nature, fo pow'rful are you,
You give harmony birth, and exiftence renew :
The world without you'd be a ftation of pain ;
Without you we might fay, it is chaos again.

Delight of the gods ! when with reafon combin'd,
Like gods you infpire and enlighten the mind ;
You humble the proudeft, the fage you confute,
Melt the flint of old age, and the breaft of the
brute ;
Teeming with love, the rude wave fpeaks thy
worth ;
The air owns thy pow'r, and the bofom of
earth :
All, all, mighty love, thy foft precepts efteem ;
Or below, or above, thou'rt acknowledg'd fu-
preme.

Difconcerted, young Bacchus arofe from the
plain ;
For Reafon (he faid) was both partial and vain.

Be ftill, (faid the honey-tongu'd deity) pray,
For Reafon has fomething for Bacchus to fay:
The juice of the bunch, if by Reafon apply'd,
Enraptures the heart, and makes forrow fubfide;
Gives fpirits to mirth, more than titles or wealth,
Warms the tide of the veins, and's produc-
tive of health.

The god bow'd to Reafon, with looks of efteem;
Told Venus 'twas true, and he own'd her
fupreme;
He kift her rofe lips with immortal delight,
And commended the queen for fupporting her
right.
Then (clafping the balm-breathing fair in his
arms)
He cry'd, 'Twas dull to contend with fuch
charms;
Thus Bacchus henceforward fhall fpeak of thy
worth,
Venus governs the fkies and the children of
earth.

She mounted her car, with a troop of young
loves,
And powder'd with daifies our meads and our
groves.
The god grafp'd his Thyrfis, and caught up
his reins,
Then drove his young pardels, well-pleas'd,
o'er the plains:
Be fertile the land (faid the pow'r, as he drove)
May it's fons prefs the vine, and it's maids be
all love;
On their cheeks may the rofe with the lily
conjoin,
And Reafon endow them with graces divine!

Written by Mr. GAY.

DAPHNIS ftood penfive in the fhade,
With arms acrofs, and head reclin'd;
Pale looks accus'd the cruel maid,
And fighs reliev'd his love-fick mind:
His tuneful pipe all broken lay,
Looks, fighs, and actions feem'd to fay,
My Chloe is unkind.

Why ring the woods with warbling throats?
Ye larks, ye linnets, ceafe your ftrains;
I faintly hear, in your fweet notes,
My Chloe's voice, that wakes my pains:
Yet why fhould you your fong forbear?
Your mates delight your fong to hear,
But Chloe mine difdains.

As thus he melancholy ftood,
Dejected as the lonely dove,
Sweet founds broke gently through the wood.
I feel the found; my heart-ftrings move:
'Twas not the nightingale that fung;
No, 'tis my Chloe's fweeter tongue;
Hark, hark, what fays my love!

How foolifh is the nymph, (fhe cries,)
Who trifles with her lover's pain!

Nature ftill fpeaks in woman's eyes,
Our artful lips were made to feign.
O Daphnis, Daphnis, 'twas my pride,
'Twas not my heart thy love deny'd,
Come back, dear youth, again.

As t'other day my hand he felz'd,
My blood, with thrilling motion flew;
Sudden I put on looks difpleas'd,
And hafty from his hold withdrew.
'Twas fear alone, thou fimple fwain!
Then hadft thou preft my hand again,
My heart had yielded too!

'Tis true, the tuneful reed I blam'd,
That fwell'd thy lip and rofy cheek;
Think not thy fkill in fong defam'd,
That lip fhould other pleafures feek:
Much, much thy mufic I approve;
Yet break thy pipe, for more I love,
Much more, to hear thee fpeak.

My heart forebodes that I'm betray'd,
Daphnis I fear is ever gone;
Laft night with Delia's dog he play'd,
Love by fuch trifles firft comes on.
Now, now, dear fhepherd, come away,
My tongue would now my heart obey,
Ah, Chloe, thou art won!

The youth ftepp'd forth with hafty pace,
And found where wifhing Chloe lay;
Shame fudden lighten'd in her face,
Confus'd, fhe knew not what to fay.
At laft, in broken words, fhe cry'd,
To-morrow you in vain had try'd,
But I am loft to-day!

IN ancient times, when England's fame
Throughout the world was fpread,
Proud Gallia trembled at our name,
And hid her humble head.

The Britifh lion greatly frown'd,
And fhook his horrid mien;
While thofe who fear'd him fkulk'd around,
And dreaded to be feen.

But now, behold what fate ordain'd!
Nations our influence mock,
The Britifh lion lies enchain'd,
While crows the Gallic cock!

WHEN mutual paffions fire the mind,
Whate'er the latent caufe;
From nature we are apt to fly,
And violate her laws.

Friends, brethren, enemies will prove,
And violate each tie;
Which ought to link 'em faft in love,
And ftrengthen liberty.

Then arts and commerce are no more,
Religion fails to bind;

U

And every facred bond is loft
Which holds the human mind. .

But ere the fatal hour is come,
Which ratifies defpair,
Let either feek the other's weal,
And wifh away her care.

Let Britain yield that fhe is wrong,
America not right ;
So may the conteft quickly end,
And end this bloody fight.

SONG 584.

Sung in the Sheep-Shearing.

LAWN as white as driven fnow,
Cyprus, black as e'er was crow ;
Gloves, as fweet as damafk rofes,
Mafks for faces and the nofes,
Bugle bracelets, necklace amber,
Perfume for a lady's chamber ;
Gold in coifs, and ftomachers,
For my lads to give their dears ;
Pins, and-poaking fticks of fteel ;
What maids lack from head to heel :
    Come buy of me ; come buy, come buy,
    Buy lads, or elfe your laffes cry.

SONG 585.

THE COMFORTS OF HOPE.

LOVELY maid, now ceafe to languifh,
    Yield not thus thy mind to woe ;
Look behind the clouds of anguifh,
    · Chearing beams of comfort glow.

Let enliv'ning Hope elate thee,
    Hope that points to fairer fkies ;
Think the tranfient ills that wait thee,
    Are but bleffings in difguife.

Be-not by diftrefs dejected ;
    Shrink not from affliction's hand:
Falfehood is from truth detected
    By the kind enchantrefs wand.

Sage inftructrefs, fhe fhall train thee ;
    Steady virtue teach thy heart ;
Sharp, but fhort-liv'd pains, await thee ;
    Endlefs bleffings to impart.

SONG 586.

THE RAINBOW.

WHAT various colours deck the bow
    That cafual ftreaks the fky !
What various tints of beauty glow
    Beneath my Chloe's eye !

The happy mixture forms the grace
    Which beauty calls her own,
And in the fky, or in the face,
    It's radiance muft be known.

Heav'n's pictur'd arch awhile outfpread,
    Attracts the wond'ring fight ;

But foon the cafual gloom is fled,
    Illufive, from our fight.

Thus, lovely Chloe, 'tis with thee,
    Thy beauties now are gay ;
Yet, ere thou read'ft thefe lines, may flee,
    And vanifh far away.

Then let one moral be impreft
    To laft till time fhall fade ;
The tints that glow within the breaft
    Immortalize the maid !

SONG 587.

THE WOODBINE ALCOVE.

WITH Phillis I fought out the woodbine
    alcove,
    And prefs'd the dear maid to my breaft ;
I fpoke in her ear half the tale of my love,
    And I bid her imagine the reft.

Lord, Sir ! (faid the damfel, and blufhing fhe
    fpoke,)
    I know not what 'tis you would fay :
I am told that you men with us virgins will
    joke ;
    Are you now, or in earneft, or play ?

In earneft, my dear, (I with rapture replied ;)
    Your blifs fhall I feek throughout life :
Permit me to-morrow to call you my bride,
    And you'll fee, how I'll boaft of my wife.

The damfel confented, the bargain was made !
    Our life is the picture of love ;
And I ftill blefs the moment I got the dear
    maid
    To confent, in the woodbine alcove.

SONG 588.

AN OLD BALLAD.

MY mind to me a kingdom is ;
    Such perfect joy therein I find,
As far exceeds all earthly blifs
    That God or Nature hath affign'd :
Tho' much I want, that moft would have,
Yet ftill my mind forbids to crave.

Content I live, this is my ftay ;
    I feek no more than may fuffice :
I prefs to bear no haughty fway ;
    Look what I lack my mind fupplies.
Lo ! thus I triumph like a king,
Content with that my mind doth bring.

I fee how plenty furfeits oft,
    And hafty climbers foeneft fall ;
I fee that fuch as fit aloft,
    Mifhap doth threaten moft of all :
Thefe get with toil, and keep with fear ;
Such cares my mind could never bear.

No princely pomp, nor wealthy ftore,
    No force to win the victory,

No wily wit to falve a fore,
  No fhape to win a lover's eye :
To none of thefe I yield, as thrall ;
  For why—my mind defpifeth all.

Some have too much, yet ftill they crave,
  I little have, yet feek no more :
They are but poor, tho' much they have,
  And I am rich with little ftore :
They poor, I rich; they beg, I give ;
They lack, I lend; they pine, I live.

I laugh not at another's lofs,
  I grudge not at another's gain ;
No worldly wave my mind can tofs,
  I brook what is another's bane.
I fear no foe, nor fawn on friend ;
I loath not life, nor dread mine end.

My wealth is health and perfect eafe ;
  My confcience clear my chief defence :
I never feek by bribes to pleafe,
  Nor by defert to give offence.
Thus do I live, thus will I die ;
Would all did fo, as well as I !

SONG 589.

SAID Colin to Daphne, one day, as they fat
  Amufing each other with innocent chat,
I've courted you long, but you ftill difapprove,
Tho' ev'ry affurance you have of my love.

Dear Colin, complain not, (was Daphne's reply ;)
No reafon you have, fo your conduct deny ;
I've Simpkin forfaken for you, I declare ;
Dear Colin, I pray, be not fo full of care.

Convinced I am, deareft Daphne, (he cry'd ;)
You have reafon, indeed, at my conduct to chide :
To the church let us go, and there end all ftrife ;
And make me once happy to call you my wife.

SONG 590.

A MARTIAL SONG.

COME, ye lads who wifh to fhine
  Bright in future ftory !
Hafte to arms, and form the line
  That leads to martial glory !
Charge the mufquet, point the lance,
  Brave the worft of dangers;
Tell the bluft'ring fons of France
  That we to fear are ftrangers.

Britain, when the lion's rouz'd,
  And her flag is rearing,
Always finds her fons difpos'd

Honour for the brave to fhare
  Is the nobleft booty ;
Guard your coaft, protect the fair,
  For that's a Briton's duty.

What if Spain, to take their parts,
  Form a bafe alliance ;
All unite, and Englifh hearts
  May bid the world defiance.
Beat the drum, the trumpet found,
  Manly and united ;
Danger face, maintain your ground,
  And fee your country righted !

SONG 591.

THE SEA-FIGHT; A CATCH.

Written by Capt. THOMPSON.

Sung at VAUXHALL.

BOATSWAIN! pipe up, all hands hoy !
  Turn out, ev'ry man and boy !
    Make fail, give chace,
    Then fplice main brace !
A gallant fhip ! my boys, fhe's French !
In grog and flip here's to each wench.
    Loof, boys, higher ;
    Stand by—fire !
She ftrikes ! fhe ftrikes ! our's is the day.
A glorious prize !—belay, belay !

SONG 592.

AS the fnow in vallies lying,
  Phœbus his warm beams applying,
    Soon diffolves and runs away ;
So the beauties, fo the graces,
Of the moft bewitching faces,
    At approaching age decay.

As a tyrant, when degraded,
Is defpis'd, and is upbraided
  By the flaves he once controul'd ;
So the nymph, if none could move her,
Is contemn'd by ev'ry lover,
  When her charms are growing old.

Melancholy looks, and whining,
Grieving, quarrelling, and pining,
  Are th' effects your rigours move ;
Soft careffes, amorous glances,
Melting fighs, tranfporting trances ;
  Are the bleft effects of love.

Fair-ones, while your beauty's blooming,
Ufe your time, left age refuming
  What your youth profufely lends,
You are robb'd of all your glories,
And condemn'd to tell old ftories
  To your unbelieving friends.

Endlefs pains the mifer takes
To increafe his heaps of money;
Lab'ring bees his pattern makes,
Yet he fears to tafte his honey.

Views with aching eyes his ftore,
Trembling, left he chance to lofe it;
Pining ftill for want of more,
Tho' the wretch wants pow'r to ufe it.
Celia thus, with endlefs arts,
Spends her days, her charms improving,
Lab'ring ftill to conquer hearts,
Yet ne'er taftes the fweets of loving.

Views with pride her fhape and face,
Fancying ftill fhe's under twenty;
Age brings wrinkles on apace,
While fhe ftarves with all her plenty.
Soon or late they both will find,
Time, their idol, from them fever;
He muft leave his gold behind,
Lock'd within his grave for ever.

Celia's fate will ftill be worfe,
When her fading charms deceive her;
Vain defire will be her curfe,
When no mortal will relieve her.
Celia, hoard thy charms no more,
Beauty's like the mifer's treafure,
Tafte a little of thy ftore;
What is beauty without pleafure?

SONG 594.

Sung in *Buxom Joan*.

THE thund'ring drums did beat to battle,
And murm'ring cannons, too, did rattle:
The enemy fiercely affail'd,
And death with it's horrors prevail'd.
    Heavy moans,
    Dying groans,
Cou'd be heard 'midft the loudeft alarms!
    I fought for your fake,
    Made the enemy quake,
And with conqueft return to your arms.

SONG 595.

Written by Sir JOHN SUCKLING.

'TIS now, fince I fat down before
    That foolifh fort, a heart,
(Time ftrangely fpent) a year and more,
    And ftill I did my part.

Made my approaches, from her hand
    Unto her lip did rife,
And did already underftand
    The language of her eyes.

Proceeded on with no lefs art,
    My tongue was engineer;
I thought to undermine the heart,
    By whifp'ring in the ear.

When this did nothing, I brought down
    Great cannon oaths, and fhot
A thoufand thoufand in the town,
    And ftill it yielded not.

I then refolv'd to ftarve the place,
    By cutting off all kiffes,
Praifing and gazing on her face,
    And all fuch little bliffes.

To draw her out, and from her ftrength,
    I drew all batteries in;
And brought myfelf to lie, at length,
    As if no fiege had been.

When I had done what man could do,
    And thought the place my own,
The enemy lay quiet too,
    And fmil'd at all was done.

I fent to know from whence and where
    Thefe hopes, and this relief?
A fpy inform'd, honour was there,
    And did command in chief.

March, march, (quoth I) the word ftraight give,
    Let's lofe no time, but leave her;
That giant upon air will live,
    And hold it out for ever.

To fuch a place our camp remove
    As will no fiege abide:
I hate a fool that ftarves her love
    Only to feed her pride.

SONG 596.

IN tuneful numbers let me tell
    The inward joys I find,
Now, freed from care, I know full well
    My lov'd Prudentia's kind!

Her charms, nor lefs her virtue, fhew
    Each beauty of the mind;
And few among the fex I know,
    Poffefs a heart fo kind.

Bafe adulation's fawning fons,
    The drofs of all mankind,
While in her thoughts difcernment runs,
    Will never find her kind.

Once, haply, in a bleft abode,
    With her, and fuch, confign'd,
On fancy's pleafing wings I rode,
    And found my charmer kind.

Can fordid wealth or grandeur bring
    Thofe pleafures of the mind,
Which flow from that delightful fpring,
    A fair-one true and kind?

In friendfhip's focial band, 'tis true,
    A fund of joys I find;
But what are fuch, when plac'd in view,
    To thofe of nobler kind!

SONG 597.

MARY AMBREE; AN OLD BALLAD.

WHEN captains courageous, whom death
    could not daunt,
Did march to the fiege of the city of Gaunt,
They mufter'd the foldiers by two and by three,
And foremoft in battle was Mary Ambree.

When brave Sir John Major was flain in her
 fight,
Who was her true lover, her joy, and delight,
Becaufe he was flain moft treacheroufly,
Then vow'd to revenge him Mary Ambree.

She clothed herfelf from the top to the toe,
In buff of the braveft, moft feemly to fhow;
A fair fhirt of mail then flipped on fhe;
Was not this a brave bonny lafs, Mary Ambree?

A helmet of proof fhe ftraight did provide,
A ftrong arming fword fhe girt by her fide,
On her hand a goodly fair gauntlet had fhe;
Was not this a brave bonny lafs, Mary Ambree?

Then took fhe her fword and her target in hand,
Bidding all fuch as would, be of her band:
To wait on her perfon came thoufand and three;
Was not this a brave bonny lafs, Mary Ambree?

Then cry'd out her foldiers, and thus they did
 fay,
So well thou becomeft this gallant array,
Thy heart and thy weapons fo well do agree,
No maiden was ever like Mary Ambree.

She cheared her foldiers that foughten for life,
With ancient and ftandard, with drum and with
 fife;
With brave clanging trumpets, that founded fo
 free;
Was not this a brave bonny lafs, Mary Ambree?

Before I will fee the worft of you all
To come into danger of death, or of thrall,
This hand and this life I will venture fo free;
Was not this a brave bonny lafs, Mary Ambree?

She led up her foldiers in battle array,
'Gainft three times their number, by break of
 the day;
Seven hours in fkirmifh continued fhe;
Was not this a brave bonny lafs, Mary Ambree?

She filled the fkies with the fmoke of her fhot,
And her enemies bodies with bullets fo hot;
For one of her own men a fcore killed fhe:
Was not this a brave bonny lafs, Mary Ambree?

And when her falfe gunner, to fpoil her intent,
Away all her pellets and powder had fpent,
Straight with her keen weapon fhe flafht him
 in three:
Was not this a brave bonny lafs, Mary Ambree?

Being falfely betray'd, for lucre of hire,
At length fhe was forced to make a retire;
Then her foldiers into a ftrong caftle drew fhe:
Was not this a brave bonny lafs, Mary Ambree?

Her foes they befet her on every fide,
As thinking clofe fiege fhe could never abide:
To beat down her walls they did all decree;
But ftoutly defy'd them brave Mary Ambree.

Then took fhe her fword and her target in hand,
And mounting the walls all undaunted did ftand,
There daring the captains to match any three:
O what a brave captain was Mary Ambree!

Now fay, Englifh captain, what wouldeft thou
 give
To ranfom thyfelf, which elfe muft not live?
Come, yield thyfelf quickly, or flain thou muft
 be.
Then fmiled fweetly fair Mary Ambree.

Ye captains courageous, of valour fo bold,
Whom think you, before you, you now do be-
 hold?—
A knight, Sir, of England, and captain fo free,
Who fhortly with us a prifoner muft be.

No captain of England; behold in your fight
Two breafts in my bofom, and therefore no
 knight:
No knight, Sirs, of England, nor captain you
 fee,
But a poor fimple maiden, call'd Mary Ambree.

But art thou a woman, as thou doft declare,
Whofe valour hath prov'd fo undaunted in war?
If England doth yield fuch brave maidens as
 thee,
Full well may they conquer, fair Mary Ambree.

The prince of Great Parma heard of her renown,
Who long had advanced for England's fair
 crown;
He woo'd her and fued her his miftrefs to be,
And offer'd rich prefents to Mary Ambree:

But this virtuous maiden defpifed them all.
I'll ne'er fell my honour for purple nor pall:
A maiden of England, Sir, never will be
The whore of a monarch, quoth Mary Ambree.

Then to her own country fhe back did return,
Still holding the foes of fair England in fcorn:
Therefore, Englifh captains of ev'ry degree,
Sing forth the brave valours of Mary Ambree.

SONG 598.

Written by Mrs. BARBAULD.

WHEN gentle Celia firft I knew,
 A breaft fo good, fo kind, fo true,
 Reafon and tafte approv'd;
Pleas'd to indulge fo pure a flame,
I call'd it by too foft a name,
 And fondly thought I lov'd.

Till Chloris came, with fad furprize
I felt the lightning of her eyes
 Thro' all my fenfes run;
All glowing with refiftlefs charms,
She fill'd my breaft with new alarms,
 I faw, and was undone.

O Celia! dear unhappy maid,
Forbear the weaknefs to upbraid,
 Which ought your fcorn to move:

I know this beauty falfe and vain,
I know fhe triumphs in my pain,
    Yet ftill I feel I love.

Thy gentle fmiles no more can pleafe,
Nor can thy fofteft friendfhip eafe
    The torments I endure;
Think what that wounded breaft muft feel
Which truth and kindnefs cannot heal,
    Nor e'en thy pity cure.

Oft fhall I curfe my iron chain,
And wifh again thy milder reign
    With long and vain regret;
All that I can, to thee I give,
And could I ftill to reafon live
    I were thy captive yet.

But paffion's wild, impetuous fea,
Hurries me far from peace and thee,
    'Twere vain to ftruggle more:
Thus the poor failor flumbering lies,
While fwelling tides around him rife,
    And pufh his bark from fhore.

In vain he fpreads his helplefs arms,
His pitying friends with fond alarms
    In vain deplore his ftate;
Still far and farther from the coaft,
On the high furge his bark is toft,
    And foundering yields to fate.

SONG 599.

Sung at VAUXHALL.

ROUSE Britain's warlike throng,
    Sound the trumpet, ftrike the lyre,
Let martial note and fong
    Martial order re-infpire.

Peace, to Britain ever dear,
    All her charms awhile forgoes;
Britons will no longer bear
    Infults from difdainful foes.

Sound the trumpets! found again!
    Britain claims the martial ftrain.

See bright honour rear it's head,
    And, while glory leads the band,
Awful war, with folemn tread,
    Stalks majeftic thro' the land.

SONG 600.

Sung at RANELAGH.

TO eafe his heart, and own his flame,
    Blithe Jockey to young Jenny came;
But, tho' fhe lik'd him paffing weel,
    She carelefs turn'd her fpinning-wheel.

Her milk-white hand he did extol,
    And prais'd her fingers long and fmall:
Unufual joy her heart did feel,
    But ftill fhe turn'd her fpinning-wheel.

Then round about her flender waift,
    He clafp'd his arms, and her embrac'd:
To kifs her hand he down did kneel;
    But yet fhe turn'd her fpinning-wheel.

With gentle voice fhe bid him rife;
    He blefs'd her neck, her lips, and eyes:
Her fondnefs fhe could fcarce conceal;
    Yet ftill fhe turn'd her fpinning-wheel.

Till, bolder grown, fo clofe he prefs'd,
    His wanton thought fhe quickly guefs'd;
Then pufh'd him from her rock and reel,
    And angry turn'd her fpinning-wheel.

At laft, when fhe began to chide,
    He fwore he meant her for his bride:
'Twas then her love fhe did reveal,
    And flung away her fpinning-wheel.

SONG 601.

WHEN once I with Phillida ftray'd,
    Where rivers run murmuring by,
I heard the foft vows that fhe made;
    What twain was fo happy as I?
My breaft was a ftranger to care,
    For my wealth by her kiffes I told;
I thought myfelf richer, by far,
    Than he that had mountains of gold.

But now I am poor and undone,
    Her vows have prov'd empty and vain;
The kiffes I once thought my own,
    Are beftow'd on a happier fwain:
But ceafe, gentle fhepherd, to deem
    Her vows fhall be conftant and true;
They're as falfe as a Midfummer dream,
    As fickle as Midfummer dew.

O, Phillis, fo fickle and fair,
    Why did you my love then approve?
Had you frown'd on my fuit, thro' defpair
    I foon had forgotten to love:
You fmil'd, and your fmiles were fo fweet,
    You fpoke, and your words were fo kind,
I could not fufpect the deceit,
    But gave my loofe fails to the wind.

When tempefts the ocean deform,
    And billows fo mountainous roar,
The pilot, fecur'd from the ftorm,
    Ne'er ventures his bark from the fhore;
As foon as foft breezes arife,
    And fmiles the falfe face of the fea,
His heart he too credulous tries,
    And, failing, is fhipwreck'd like me.

SONG 602.

LABOUR IN VAIN.

IN purfuit of fome lambs from my flocks that
    had ftray'd,
One morning I rang'd o'er the plain;
But, alas! after all my refearches were made,
    I perceiv'd that my labour was vain.

At length, growing hopelefs my lambs to reftore,
    I refolv'd to return back again;
It was ufelefs, I thought, to feek after them more,
    Since I found that my labour was vain.

On this my return, pretty Phebe I faw,
    And to love her I could not refrain;
To folicit a kifs, I approach'd her with awe,
    But fhe told me my labour was vain.

But, Phebe, (I cry'd,) to my fuit lend an ear,
And let me no longer complain.
She reply'd, with a frown, and an aspect severe,
Young Colin, your labour's in vain.

Then I eagerly clasp'd her quite close to my
breast,
And kifs'd her, and kifs'd her again ; ·
O, Colin, (she cry'd,) if you're rude, I protest
That your labour shall still be in vain.

At length, by entreaties, by kisses, and vows,
Compassion she took on my pain;
She now has consented to make me her spouse,
So no longer I labour in vain.

SONG 603.

THE HEROIC FAIR.

AWAY with soft sighs! for our danger alarms!
Our country folicits our smiles to it's aid;
Let our beauty inspirit it's vot ries to arms,
And heroes alone win the hearts of the maid.

Last month, my dear Colin, with tear-swim-
ming eyes,
Prefs'd my hand, while he look'd a whole
volume of woe;
E'en then (for my heart never wore a difguise)
If you love me, said I, go and conquer the foe.

Go and rush to the fight, go and conquer the foe;
Securing your country's, fecure your own blifs:
Love shall nerve your bold arm, love shall prof-
per each blow,
And the ruin of France shall fecure you a kifs.

Go, then! He obey'd, refolv'd not to stay,
But prefs'd my lips first; how else could we
part?
I sigh'd him success, as the youth went away;
For his worth had fecur'd ev'ry with of my
heart.

If by my example my sex was infpir'd,
No nation would dare to provoke British rage;
Our swains with true courage would always be
fir'd,
And our smiles create heroes in every age.

SONG 604.

Written by Mr. WRIGHTEN.

Sung at VAUXHALL.

SOUND the fife—beat the drum——to my
standard repair,
All ye lads who will conquer or die ;
At request of my sex, as a captain I'm here,
The men's courage and valour to try:
'Tis your king and your country now call for
your aid,
And the ladies command you to go;
By me they announce it, and you, who're afraid,
Or refuse, our vengeance shall know.

Then first to the single—these things I declare,
(So each maiden moft firmly decrees,)

Not a kifs will be granted, by black, brown, or
fair;
Not an ogle, a sigh, or a squeeze.
To the married—if they but look glum, or say,
No,
Should the monfieur dare bluster or huff,
We've determined, nem. con. that their fore-
heads shall shew—
A word to the wife is enough.

These punishments we've in terrorem pro-
claim'd;
But still, should your courage be lacking,
As our dernier refcrt, this refolve shall be nam'd,
Which, egad! will foon fend you all packing.
We'll the breeches affume——'pon my honour
'tis true!—
So determine, maids, widows, and wives;
First we'll march——beat the French——then
march back, and beat you——
Aye, and wear 'em the rest of our lives.

SONG 605.

Sung in *Buxom Joan*.

'TIS for landmen to prate,
Such trifling I hate,
To wheedle and cajole is their plan:·
For a licence let's haste,
We have no time to waste ;
'Tis actions that best speak the man.

I'm a rough, honest tar,
Just landed from far ;
My heart cannot change like the weather;
As the needle 'tis true,
And points only to you ;
Let the parfon, then, splice us together.

SONG 606.

Written by Dr. WATTS.

SAY, mighty love, and teach my fong,
To whom thy sweetest joys belong,
And who the happy pairs ;
Whose yielding hearts, and joining hands,
Find bleffings twisted with their bands,
To foften all their cares?

Not the wild herd of nymphs and fwains,
That thoughtlefs fly into the chains,
As custom leads the way:
If there be blifs without defign,
Ivies and oaks may grow and twine,
And be as bleft as they.

Not fordid fouls of earthly mould,
When drawn by kindred charms of gold
.To dull embraces move:
So two rich mountains of Peru
May rush to wealthy marriage too,
And make a world of love.

Not the mad tribe that hell infpires
With wanton flames ; those raging fires
The purer blifs deftroy:
On Ætna's top let furies wed,
And sheets of lightning drefs the bed,
T' improve the burning joy.

Nor the dull pairs whose marble forms
None of the melting passions warms,
  Can mingle hearts and hands:
Logs of green wood, that quench the coals,
Are marry'd just like stoick souls,
  With osiers for their bands.

Not minds of melancholy strain,
Still silent, or that still complain,
  Can the dear bondage bless:
As well may heavenly concerts spring
From two old lutes with ne'er a string,
  Or none besides the bass.

Nor can the soft enchantments hold
Two jarring souls of angry mould,
  The rugged and the keen:
Samson's young foxes might as well
In bands of chearful wedlock dwell,
  With firebrands ty'd between.

Nor let the cruel fetters bind
A gentle to a savage mind;
  For love abhors the fight:
Loose the fierce tyger from the deer,
For native rage and native fear
  Rise and forbid delight.

Two kindest souls alone must meet,
'Tis friendship makes the bondage sweet,
  And feeds their mutual loves:
Bright Venus on her rolling throne
Is drawn by gentlest birds alone,
  And Cupids yoke the doves.

SONG 607.

NO nymph that trips the verdant plains
  With Sally can compare;
She wins the hearts of all the swains,
  And rivals all the fair:

The beams of Sol delight and clear,
  While summer seasons roll;
But Sally's smiles can all the year
  Give pleasure to the soul.

When from the east the morning ray
  Illumes the world below,
Her presence bids the god of day
  With emulation glow:
Fresh beauties deck the painted ground,
  Birds sweeter notes prepare;
The playful lambkins skip around,
  And hail the sister fair.

The lark but strains his livid throat,
  To bid the maid rejoice,
And mimicks, while he swells his note,
  The sweetness of her voice:
The fanning zephyrs round her play,
  While Flora she'll perfume,
And ev'ry flow'ret seems to say,
  I but for Sally bloom.

The am'rous youths her charms proclaim
  From morn to eve their tale;
Her beauty and unspotted fame
  Make vocal ev'ry vale,
The stream meandring thro' the mead,
  Her echo'd name conveys;
And ev'ry voice, and ev'ry reed,
  Is tun'd to Sally's praise.

No more shall blithsome lass or swain
  To mirthful wake resort,
Nor ev'ry May-morn on the plain
  Advance in rural sport;
No more shall gush the purling rill,
  Nor music wake the grove,
Nor flocks look snow-like on the hill,
  When I forget to love.

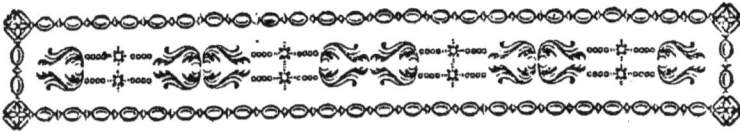

THE
VOCAL MAGAZINE.

NUMBER V.

SONG 608.

Written by Dr. BYRON.

MY time, O ye mufes! was happily fpent,
　　When Phebe went with me wherever
　　I went;
Ten thoufand foft pleafures I felt in my breaft;
Sure never fond fhepherd like Colin was bleft!
But now fhe is gone, and has left me behind,
What a marvellous change on a fudden I find!
When things were as fine as could poffibly be;
I thought 'twas the fpring, but, alas! it was fhe.

With fuch a companion to tend a few fheep,
To rife up and play, or to lie down and fleep;
I was fo good-humour'd, fo chearful and gay,
My heart was as light as a feather all day.
But now I fo crofs and fo peevifh am grown,
So ftrangely uneafy as never was known;
My fair-one is gone, and my joys are all drown'd,
And my heart, I am fure, weighs more than
　　a pound.

The fountain that wont to run fweetly along,
And dance to foft murmurs the pebbles among,
Thou know'ft, little Cupid, if Phebe was there,
'Twas pleafure to look at, 'twas mufick to hear:
But now fhe is abfent, I walk by it's fide,
And ftill as it murmurs, do nothing but chide;
Muft you be fo chearful, while I go in pain!
Peace there with your bubbling, and hear me
　　complain!

When my lambkins around me would often-
　　times play,
And when Phebe and I were as joyful as they,
How pleafant their fporting, how happy the
　　time,
When fpring, love, and beauty, were all in
　　their prime!
But now in their frolicks when by me they
　　pafs,
I fling at their fleeces an handful of grafs:

Be ftill, then, I cry, for it makes me quite mad,
To fee you fo merry, while I am fo fad.

My dog I was ever well pleafed to fee,
Come wagging his tail to my fair-one and me;
And Phebe was pleas'd too, and to my dog faid,
Come hither, poor fellow; and patted his head.
But now, when he's fawning, I with a four look,
Cry, Sirrah! and give him a blow with my crook:
And I'll give him another; for why fhould not
　　Tray
Be as dull as his mafter, when Phebe's away?

When walking with Phebe, what fights have I
　　feen!
How fair was the flower, how frefh was the
　　green!
What a lovely appearance the trees and the
　　fhade,
The corn-fields and hedges, and ev'ry thing
　　made!
But fince fhe has left me, though all are ftill
　　there,
They none of them now fo delightful appear;
'Twas nought but the magick, I find, of her
　　eyes,
Made fo many beautiful profpects arife.

Sweet mufick went with us both all the wood
　　thro',
The lark, linnet, throftle, and nightingale too;
Winds over us whifper'd, flocks by us did bleat,
And chirp went the grafhopper under our feet:
But now fhe is abfent, tho' ftill they fing on,
The woods are but lonely, the melody's gone;
Her voice in the concert, as now I have found,
Gave ev'ry thing elfe it's agreeable found.

Rofe, what is become of thy delicate hue?
And where is the violet's beautiful blue?
Does aught of it's fweetnefs the bloffoms be-
　　guile?
That meadow, thofe daifies, why do they not
　　fmile?

X

Ah! rivals! I fee what it was that you dreft
And made yourfelves fine for; a place in her
  breaft:
You put on your colours to pleafure her eye,
To be pluck'd by her hand, on her bofom to die.

How flowly time creeps, till my Phebe return,
While amidft the foft Zephyr's cool breezes I
  burn;
Methinks, if I knew whereabout he would
  tread,
I could breathe on his wings, and 'twould melt
  down the lead.

Fly fwifter, ye minutes, bring hither my dear,
And reft fo much longer for't, when fhe is here.
Ah! Colin! old time is fo full of delay,
Nor will budge one foot fafter, for all thou
  canft fay.

Will no pitying power that hears me complain,
Or cure my difquiet, or foften my pain?
To be cur'd, thou muft, Colin, thy paffion
  remove:
But what fwain is fo filly to live without love?
No, deity, bid the dear nymph to return,
For ne'er was poor fh pherd fo fadly furlorn.
Ah! what fhall I do! I fhall die with defpair!
Take heed, all ye fwains, how ye love one fo
  fair.

SONG 609.

Written by AMBROSE PHILIPS, Efq.

ON Belvidera's bofom lying,
  Withing, panting, fighing, dying;
The cold regardlefs maid to move
  With unavailing prayers I fue;
You firft have taught me how to love,
  Ah! teach me to be happy too.

But fhe, alas! unkindly wife,
To all my fighs and tears replies,
  'Tis every prudent maid's concern:
Her lover's fondnefs to improve;
If to be happy you fhould learn,
  You quickly would forget to love.

SONG 610.

AH! why muft words my flame reveal?
  Why needs my Damon bid me tell
What all my actions prove?
A blufh whene'er I meet his eye,
Whene'er I hear his name a figh,
  Betrays my fecret love.

In all their fports upon the plain,
Mine eyes ftill fix'd on him remain,
  And him alone approve;
The reft unheeded dance or play,
From all he fteals my praife away,
  And can he doubt my love?

Whene'er we meet, my looks confefs
The joys that all my foul poffefs,
  And every care remove:

Still, ftill too fhort appears his ftay,
The moments fly too faft away,
  Too faft for my fond love.

Does any fpeak in Damon's praife,
So pleas'd am I with all he fays,
  I ev'ry word approve;
But is he blam'd, although in jeft,
I feel refentment fire my breaft,
  Alas! becaufe I love.

But ah! what tortures tear my heart,
When I fufpect his looks impart
  The leaft defire to rove!
I hate the maid that gives me pain,
Yet him to hate I ftrive in vain,
  For ah! that hate is love.

Then afk not words, but read mine eyes,
Believe my blufhes, truft my fighs,
  My paffion thefe will prove;
Words oft deceive, and fpring from art,
The true expreffions of my heart
  To Damon, muft be love.

SONG 611.

SHAKESPEARE'S GARLAND.

LET beauty with the fun arife,
  To Shakefpeare tribute pay;
With heavenly fmiles and fpeaking eyes,
  Give grace and luftre to the day.

Each fmile fhe gives protects his name,
  What face fhall dare to frown?
Not envy's felf can blaft the fame
  Which beauty deigns to crown.

SONG 612.

THE LASS OF PEATY'S MILL.

THE lafs of Peaty's mill,
  So bonny, blithe, and gay,
In fpight of all my fkill,
  Hath ftole my heart away.
When tedding of the hay
  Bare-headed on the green,
Love 'midft her locks did play,
  And wanton'd in her een.

Her arms, white, round, and fmooth,
  Breafts rifing in their dawn;
To age it would give youth,
  To prefs 'em with his hand.
Thro' all my fpirits ran
  An extafy of blifs,
When I fuch fweetnefs fand
  Wrapt in a balmy kifs.

Without the help of art,
  Like flow'rs which grace the wild,
She did her fweets impart,
  Whene'er fhe fpoke or fmil'd,
Her looks they were fo mild,
  Free from affected pride,

She me to love beguil'd,
I wish'd her for my bride.

O had I all that wealth
Hoptoun's high mountains fill,
Insur'd long life and health,
And pleasures at my will;
I'd promise and fulfil,
That none but bonny she,
The lass of Peaty's mill,
Shou'd share the same wi' me.

The thoughts of past pleasure and truth,
The best of all blessings below.

Those traces for ever will last,
Which sickness nor time can remove;
For when youth and beauty are past,
Old age brings the winter of love.
A friendship insensibly grows,
By reviews of such raptures as these;
The current of fondness still flows,
Which decrepid old age cannot freeze.

SONG 613.
Written by Mr. PRIOR.

IF wine and music have the pow'r
To ease the sickness of the soul,
Let Phœbus every thing explore,
And Bacchus fill the sprightly bowl.
Let them their friendly aid employ
To make my Chloe's absence light,
And seek for pleasure, to destroy
The sorrows of this live-long night.

But she to-morrow will return ;
Venus, be thou to-morrow great,
Thy myrtles strew, thy odours burn,
And meet thy fav'rite nymph in state.
Kind goddess, to no other pow'rs
Let us to-morrow's blessings own ;
The darling loves shall guide the hours,
And all the day be thine alone.

SONG 614.

DEAR Chloe, whilst thus, beyond measure,
You treat me with doubts and disdain;
You rob all your youth of it's pleasure,
And hoard up an old age of pain:
Your maxim, that love is still founded
On charms that will quickly decay,
You'll find to be very ill grounded
When once you it's dictates obey.

The passion from beauty first drawn,
Your kindness will vastly improve ;
Soft smiles and gay looks are the dawn,
Fruition's the sun-shine of love.
And tho' the bright beams of your eyes
Should be clouded, that now are so gay,
And darkness possess all the skies,
We ne'er can forget it was day.

Old Darby, with Joan by his side,
You've often regarded with wonder;
He's dropsical, she is sore-ey'd,
Yet they're ever uneasy asunder;
Together they totter about,
Or sit in the sun at the door,
And at night when old Darby's pot's out,
His Joan will not smoak a whiff more.

No beauty or wit they possess,
Their several failings to smother;
Then what are the charms, can you guess,
That make 'em so fond of each other?
'Tis the pleasing remembrance of youth,
The endearments that love did bestow,

SONG 615.
Written by Lord LYTTELTON.

WHEN Delia on the plain appears,
Aw'd by a thousand tender fears,
I would approach, but dare not move;
Tell me, my heart, if this be love.

Whene'er she speaks, my ravish'd ear
No other voice but her's can hear,
No other wit but her's approve ;
Tell me, my heart, if this be love?

If she some other swain commend,
Tho' I was once his fondest friend,
His instant enemy I prove;
Tell me, my heart, if this be love?

When she is absent, I no more
Delight in all that pleas'd before,
The clearest spring, the shadiest grove;
Tell me, my heart, if this be love ?

When, fond of power, of beauty vain,
Her nets she spread for ev'ry swain,
I strove to hate, but vainly strove;
Tell me, my heart, if this be love?

SONG 616.
Written by Dr. GOLDSMITH.

TURN, gentle hermit of the dale,
And guide my lonely way,
To where yon taper chears the vale
With hospitable ray.

For here forlorn and lost I tread,
With fainting steps and slow:
Where wilds, immeasurably spread,
Seem lengthening as I go.

Forbear, my son, (the hermit cries,)
To tempt the dangerous gloom ;
For yonder phantom only flies
To lure thee to thy doom.

Here to the houseless child of want,
My door is open still ;
And tho' my portion is but scant,
I give it with good will.

Then turn to-night, and freely share
Whate'er my cell bestows;
My rushy couch, and frugal fare,
My blessing and repose.

No flocks that range the valley free,
To slaughter I condemn:

X 2

Taught by that Power that pities me,
I learn to pity them.

But from the mountain's graffy fide,
A guiltlefs feaft I bring;
A fcrip with herbs and fruits fupply'd,
And water from the fpring.

Then, pilgrim, turn, thy cares forego,
For earth-born cares are wrong :
Man wants but little here below,
Nor wants that little long.

Soft as the dew from heav'n defcends,
His gentle accents fell :
The modeft ftranger lowly bends,
And follows to the cell.

Far in a wildernefs obfcure
The lonely manfion lay;
A refuge to the neighbouring poor,
And ftranger led aftray.

No ftores beneath it's humble thatch
Requir'd a mafter's care;
The wicket opening with a latch,
Receiv'd the harmlefs pair.

And now when bufy crowds retire
To revels or to reft,
The hermit trimm'd his little fire,
And chear'd his penfive gueft:

And fpread his vegetable ftore,
And gaily preft, and fmil'd;
And fkill'd in legendary lore,
The ling'ring hours beguil'd.

Around in fympathetic mirth
It's tricks the kitten tries;
The cricket chirrups on the hearth;
The crackling faggot flies.

But nothing could a charm impart
To foothe the ftranger's woe;
For grief was heavy at his heart,
And tears began to flow.

His rifing cares the hermit 'fpy'd,
With anfwering cares oppreft :
And whence, unhappy youth, (he cry'd,)
The forrows of thy breaft ?

From better habitations fpurn'd,
Reluctant doft thou rove;
Or grieve for friendfhip unreturn'd,
Or unregarded love ?

Alas! the joys that fortune brings,
Are trifling, and decay;
And thofe that prize the paltry things,
More trifling ftill than they.

And what is friendfhip but a name,
A charm that lulls to fleep;
A fhade that follows wealth or fame,
But leaves the wretch to weep?

And love is ftill an emptier found,
The modern fair-one's jeft :
On earth unfeen, or only found
To warm the turtle's neft.

For fhame, fond youth; thy forrows hufh,
And fpurn the fex, (he faid:)

But while he fpoke, a rifing blufh
His love-lorn gueft betray'd.

Surpriz'd ! he fees new beauties rife,
Swift mantling to the view;
Like colours o'er the morning fkies,
As bright, as tranfient too.

The bafhful look, the rifing breaft,
Alternate fpread alarms :
The lovely ftranger ftands confeft
A maid in all her charms.

And, ah ! forgive a ftranger rude,
A wretch forlorn, (fhe cry'd;)
Whofe feet unhallow'd thus intrude
Where heaven and you refide.

But let a maid thy pity fhare,
Whom love has taught to ftray;
Who feeks for reft, but finds defpair
Companion of her way.

My father liv'd befide the Tyne,
A wealthy lord was he;
And all his wealth was mark'd for mine,
He had but only me.

To win me from his tender arms
Unnumber'd fuitors came:
Who prais'd me for imputed charms,
And felt or feign'd a flame.

Each hour the mercenary crowd,
With richeft prefents ftrove:
Among the reft young Edwin bow'd,
But never talk'd of love.

In humble, fimpleft habit clad,
No wealth nor power had he;
Wifdom and worth were all he had,
But thefe were all to me.

The bloffom opening to the day,
The dews of heaven refin'd,
Could nought of purity difplay,
To emulate his mind.

The dew, the bloffom on the tree,
With charms inconftant fhine;
Their charms were his, but woe is me,
Their conftancy was mine !

For ftill I try'd each fickle art,
Importunate and vain;
And while his paffion touch'd my heart,
I triumph'd in his pain.

Till quite dejected with my fcorn,
He left me to my pride;
And fought a folitude forlorn,
In fecret, where he died.

But mine the forrow, mine the fault,
And well my life fhall pay;
I'll feek the folitude he fought,
And ftretch me where he lay.

And there forlorn, defpairing, hid,
I'll lay me down and die;
'Twas fo for me that Edwin did,
And fo for him will I.

Forbid it, Heaven ! the hermit cry'd,
And clafp'd her to his breaft:

The wond'ring fair-one turn'd to chide ;
'Twas Edwin's felf that preft.

Turn, Angelina, ever dear,
My charmer, turn to fee,
Thy own, thy long-loft Edwin here,
Reftor'd to love and thee.

Thus let me hold thee to my heart;
And ev'ry care refign :
And fhall we never, never part,
My life—my all that's mine ?

No, never from this hour to part;
We'll live and love fo true,
The figh that rends thy conftant heart
Shall break thy Edwin's too.

SONG 617.

Sung in the *Golden Pippin.*

WITH your wife, Sir, ne'er difpute,
Lady of the manor fhe;
Due to hei the choiceft fruit,
Due to her the branch and tree:
And you know fhe'll have her right;
Yes, Sir, morning, noon, and night.

SONG 618.

OTHERS falfe tongues can you believe,
Yet not my truer fpeaking eyes ?
Men's tongues love teaches to deceive,
But with his looks no lover lyes.

The lefs I boaft my real flame,
The more my paffion truth befpeaks ;
Not what the tongue, but eyes proclaim,
Love's infidel a convert makes.

For lovers, like profeffing friends,
Are more believ'd, the lefs they fay ;
Who more our artful fpeeches minds
Than looks, does her own faith betray.

Believe not my loud rivals, then,
Whilft they to thee fuch love profefs ;
True love is, like true courage, feen
But more, as we pretend to't lefs.

SONG 619.

ETRICK BANKS; A SCOTCH BALLAD.

ON Etrick banks, in a fummer's night,
At glowming when the fheep drave hame,
I met my laffy, braw and tight,
Came wading, barefoot, a'her lane:
My heart grew light, I ran, I flang
My arms about her lily neck,
And kifs'd and clap'd her there fou lang;
My words they were na mony feck.

I faid, My laffy, will ye go
To the highland hills, the Earfe to learn;
I'll baith gi'e thee a cow and ewe,
When ye come to the brig of Earn.
At Leith auld meal comes in, ne'er fafh,
And herrings at the Broomy Law;

Chear up your heart, my bony lafs,
There's gear to win we never faw.

All day when we have wrought enough,
When winter, frofts, and fnaw begin;
Soon as the fun gaes weft the loch,
At night when you fit down to fpin,
I'll fcrew my pipes, and play a fpring:
And thus the weary night we'll end,
Till the tender kid and lamb-time bring
Our pleafant fummer back again.

Syne when the trees are in their bloom,
And gowans glent o'er ilka field,
I'll meet my lafs amang the broom,
And lead you to my fummer fhield.
Then far frae a' their fcornfu' din,
That make the kindly hearts their fport;
We'll laugh and kifs, and dance and fing,
And gar the langeft day feem fhort.

SONG 620.

Written by AMBROSE PHILIPS, Efq.

BOAST not, miftaken fwain, thy art
To pleafe my partial eyes;
The charms that have fubdu'd my heart,
Another may defpife.

Thy face is to my humour made,
Another it may fright ;
Perhaps, by fome fond whim betray'd,
In oddnefs I delight.

Vain youth, to your confufion know,
'Tis to my love's excefs
You all your fancied beauties owe,
Which fade as that grows lefs.

For your own fake, if not for mine,
You fhould preferve my fire,
Since you, my fwain, no more will fhine,
When I no more admire.

By me, indeed, you are allow'd
The wonder of your kind ;
But be not of my judgment proud,
Whom love has render'd blind.

SONG 621.

SAY, lovely dream, where could'ft thou find
Shades to counterfeit that face,
Colours of this glorious kind
Come not from any mortal place !

In heaven itfelf thou, fure, wert dreft
With that angel-like difguife ;
Thus deluded am I bleft,
And fee my joy with clofed eyes.

But ah ! this image is too kind,
To be other than a dream ;
Cruel Sachariffa's mind
Ne'er put on that fweet extreme.

Fair dream, if thou intend'ft me grace,
Change that heavenly face of thine:
Paint defpis'd love in thy face,
And make it to appear like mine.

Pale, wan, and meagre let it look,
  With a pity-moving shape ;
Such as wander by the brook
  Of Lethe, or from graves escape.

Then to that matchless nymph appear,
  In whose shape thou shinest so,
Softly in her sleeping ear,
  With humble words express my woe.

Perhaps, from greatness, state, or pride,
  Thus surprized, she may fall :
Sleep does disproportion hide,
  And death resembling equals all.

SONG 622.

MY love was fickle once, and changing,
  Nor e'er would settle in my heart,
From beauty still to beauty ranging,
  In every face I found a dart.

'Twas first a charming shape enslav'd me,
  An eye then gave the fatal stroke ;
Till by her wit Corinna sav'd me,
  And all my former fetters broke.

But now a long and lasting anguish
  For Belvidera I endure ;
Hourly I sigh, and hourly languish,
  Nor hope to find the wonted cure :

For here the false, inconstant lover,
  After a thousand beauties shown,
Does new surprising charms discover,
  And finds variety in one.

SONG 623.

NOT, Celia, that I juster am,
  Or truer than the rest ;
For I would change each hour, like them,
  Were it my interest.

But I'm so fix'd alone to thee
  By every thought I have,
That should you now my heart set free,
  'Twould be again your slave.

All that in woman is ador'd,
  In thy dear self I find ;
For the whole sex can but afford
  The handsome, and the kind.

Not to my virtue, but thy power,
  This constancy is due,
When change itself can give no more
  'Tis easy to be true.

SONG 624.

TEN years, like Troy, my stubborn heart
  Withstood th' assault of fond desire :
But now, alas! I feel a smart,
  Poor I, like Troy, am set on fire.

With care we may a pile secure,
  And from all common sparks defend :
But oh ! who can a house secure,
  When the celestial flames descend.!

Thus was I safe, till from your eyes
  Destructive fires are brightly given :
Ah ! who can shun the warm surprize,
  When, lo ! the lightning comes from heav'n.

SONG 625.

Written by Mr. Concanon.

I Love thee, by heavens, I cannot say more,
  Then set not my passion a cooling,
If thou yield'st not at once, I must e'en give
    thee o er,
  For I'm but a novice at fooling.

What my love wants in words, it shall make up
    in deeds;
  Then why should we waste time in fluff,
    child ?
A performance, you wot well, a promise ex-
    ceeds,
  And a word to the wise is enough, child.

I know how to love, and to make that love
    known,
  But I hate all protesting and arguing:
Had a goddess my heart, she shou'd e'en lie
    alone,
  If she made many words to a bargain.

I'm a quaker in love, and but barely affirm,
  Whate'er my fond eyes have been saying:
Pr'ythee, be thou so too; seek for no better
    term,
  But e'en throw thy yea or thy nay in.

I cannot bear love, like a chancery suit,
  The age of a patriarch depending;
Then pluck up a spirit, no longer be mute,
  Give it, one way or other, an ending.

Long courtship's the vice of phlegmatick fools,
  Like the grace of fanatical sinners ;
Where the stomachs are lost, and the victuals
    grow cool,
  Before men sit down to their dinners.

SONG 626.

IN Chloris all soft charms agree,
  Enchanting humour, pow'rful wit,
Beauty from affectation free,
  And for eternal empire fit.
Where'er she goes, love waits her eyes,
  The women envy, men adore ;
Tho' did she less the triumphs prize,
  She would deserve the conquest more.

But vanity so much prevails,
  She begs what none else would deny her,
Makes such advances with her eyes,
  The hope she gives prevents desire :
Catches at every trifling heart,
  Grows warm with ev'ry glimm'ring flame;
The common prey so deads her dart,
  It scarce can pierce a noble game.

I could lie ages at her feet,
　Adore her carelefs of my pain,
With tender vows her rigours meet,
　Defpair, love on, and not complain ;
My paſſion, from all change fecure,
　No favours raife, no frown controuls ;
I any torment can endure,
　But hoping with a crowd of fools.

SONG 627.

IT is not, Celia, in our power
　To fay how long our love will laſt ;
It may be we, within this hour,
May lofe the joys we now do tafte :
The bleſſed, that immortal be,
From change of love are only free.

Then fince we mortal lovers are,
Aſk not how long our love will laſt ;
　But while it does, let us take care
Each minute be with pleaſure paſt :
Were it not madnefs to deny
To live, becaufe we're fure to die ?

SONG 628.

Written by Mr. CONGREVE.

FAIR Amoret is gone aftray,
　Purfue, and feek her, ev'ry lover ;
I'll tell the figns by which you may
　The wand'ring ſhepherdefs difcover.

Coquet and coy at once her air,
　Both ftudy'd, tho' both feem neglected,
Carelefs ſhe is with artful care,
　Affecting to feem unaffected.

With ſkill her eyes dart every glance,
　Yet change fo foon you'd ne'er fufpect 'em;
For ſhe'd perfuade they wound by chance,
　Tho' certain aim and art direct 'em.

She likes herfelf, yet others hates
　For that which in herfelf ſhe prizes ;
And, while ſhe laughs at them, forgets
　She is the thing that ſhe defpifes.

SONG 629.

SINCE you will needs my heart poffefs,
　'Tis juſt to you I fiſt confefs
　The faults to which 'tis given ;
It is to change much more inclin'd
Than woman, or the fea, or wind,
　Or aught that's under heaven.

Nor will I hide from you this truth,
It has been from it's very youth
　A moſt egregious ranger :
And fince from me 't has often fled,
With whom it was both born and bred,
　'Twill fcarce ſtay with a ſtranger.

The black, the fair, the gay, the fad,
(Which often made me fear 'twas mad)
　With one kind look could win it :

So nat'rally it loves to range,
That it has left fuccefs for change,
　And, what's worfe, glories in it.

Oft, when I have been laid to reſt,
'Twould make me act like one poffeſt,
　For ſtill 'twill keep a pother;
And tho' you only I efteem,
Yet it will make me, in a dream,
　Court and enjoy another.

And now, if you are not afraid,
After thefe truths that I have faid,
　To take this arrant rover,
Be not difpleas'd if I proteſt,
I think the heart within your breaſt
　Will prove juſt fuch another.

SONG 630.

AS archers and fidlers, who cunningly know
　The way to procure themfelves merit,
Will always provide them two ſtrings to a bow,
　And follow their bufinefs with fpirit.

So likewife the provident damfel ſhould do,
　Who'd make the beſt ufe of her beauty ;
If the mark ſhe would hit, or her leſſons pafs
　thro',
　Two lovers muſt ſtill be on duty.

Thus arm'd againſt chance, and fecure of fupply,
　So far our revenge we may carry ;
Ore fpark for our fport we may jilt and fet by,
　And t'other, poor foul ! we may marry.

SONG 631.

FROM native ſtalk the Provence rofe,
　I pluckt with green attire;
But oh ! upon it's graces hung
　A fultus to defire.

A vile deftroying, preying worm,
　Who ſhelter'd in the leaf,
Had robb'd me of the priſtine joy,
　And prov'd the lucky thief.

So beauteous nymphs too oft are found
　The vileſt men to truſt ;
While conſtant lovers plead in vain,
　And die for being juſt.

SONG 632.

THE night was ſtill, the air ferene,
　Fann'd by a foutheru breeze ;
The glimm'ring moon might juſt be feen,
　Reflecting thro' the trees.

The bubbling water's conſtant courfe,
　From off th' adjacent hill,
Was mournful eccho's laſt refource,
　All nature was fo ſtill.

The conſtant ſhepherd fought this ſhade,
　By forrow fore oppreſs'd ;
Clofe by a fountain's margin laid,
　His pain he thus exprefs'd.

Ah, wretched youth! why didft thou love,
  Or hope to meet fuccefs;
Or think the fair would conftant prove,
  Thy blooming hopes to blefs?

Find me the rofe on barren fands;
  The lily 'midft the rocks;
The grape in wide deferted lands;
  A wolf to guard the flocks.

Thofe you, alas! will fooner gain,
  And will more eafy find,
Than meet with aught but cold difdain
  In faithlefs womankind.

Riches alone now win the fair,
  Merit they quite defpife;
The conftant lover, thro' defpair,
  Becaufe not wealthy, dies.

SONG 633.

Written by Mr. CONGREVE.

CYNTHIA frowns whene'er I woo her,
  Yet fhe's vex'd if I give over;
Much fhe fears I fhould undo her,
  But much more to lofe her lover:
Thus in doubting fhe refufes,
And not winning, thus fhe lofes.

Pr'ythee, Cynthia, look behind you,
  Age and wrinkles will o'ertake you,
Then, too late, defire will find you,
  When the power does forfake you.
Think, oh! think, the fad condition,
To be paft, yet wifh fruition.

SONG 634.

A SCOTCH BALLAD.

THE laft time I came o'er the moor,
  I left my love behind me;
Ye powers! what pain do I endure,
  When foft ideas mind me?
Soon as the ruddy morn difplay'd
  The beaming day enfuing,
I met betimes my lovely maid,
  In fit retreat for wooing.

Beneath the cooling fhade we lay,
  Gazing and chaftly fporting;
We kifs'd and promis'd time away,
  Till night fpread her black curtain.
I pitied all beneath the fkies,
  Ev'n kings, when fhe was nigh me;
In raptures I beheld her eyes,
  Which could but ill deny me.

Shou'd I be call'd where canons roar,
  Where mortal fteel may wound me;
Or caft upon fome foreign fhore,
  Where dangers may furround me:
Yet hopes again to fee my love,
  To feaft on glowing kiffes,
Shall make my cares at diftance move,
  In profpect of fuch blifles.

In all my foul there's not one place
  To let a rival enter:
Since fhe excels in ev'ry grace,
  In her my love fhall center.
Sooner the feas fhall ceafe to flow,
  Their waves the Alps fhall cover;
On Greenland ice fhall rofes grow,
  Before I ceafe to love her.

The next time I go o'er the moor,
  She fhall a lover find me;
And that my faith is firm and pure,
  Tho' I left her behind me;
Then Hymen's facred bonds fhall chain
  My heart to her fair bofom;
There, while my being does remain,
  My love more frefh fhall bloffom.

SONG 635.

WHEN Molly fmiles beneath her cow,
  I feel my heart I can't tell how;
When Molly is on Sunday dreft,
On Sundays I can take no reft.

What can I do on working-days?
I leave my work on her to gaze.
What fhall I fay? at fermons I
Forget the text, when Molly's by.

Good mafter curate, teach me how
To mind your preaching and my plough;
And if for this you'll raife a fpell,
A good fat goofe fhall thank you well.

SONG 636.

Written by Mr. CONCANON.

THE lafs that would know how to manage
  a man,
Let her liften and learn it from me,
His courage to quell, or his heart to trepan,
  As the time and occafion agree.

The girl that has beauty, tho' fmall be her wit,
  May wheedle the clown or the beau,
The rake may repel, or may draw in the cit,
  By the ufe of that pretty word No.

When powder'd toupees around are in chat,
  Each ftriving his paffion to fhew;
With kifs me, and love me, my dear, and all
  that,
Let her anfwer to all be, O no.

When a dofe is contriv'd to lay virtue afleep,
  A prefent, a treat, or a ball,
She ftill muft refufe, if her empire fhe'll keep,
  And No be her anfwer to all.

But when Mr. Dapperwit offers his hand,
  Her partner in wedlock to go;
A houfe and a coach, and a jointure in land,
  She's an idiot, if then fhe fays No.

Mr DOD as Linco, in CYMON.

When Peace here was reigning

Song 637

Published as the Act directs Sep.1.1778.

But if she's attack'd by a youth full of charms,
 Whose courtship proclaims him a man;
When press'd to his bosom, and clasp'd in his
  arms,
 Then let her say no, if she can.

S O N G 637.

Sung in *Cymon.*

WHEN peace here was reigning,
 And love without waining,
Or care or complaining,
Base passions disdaining;
 This, this was my way,
 With my pipe and my tabor
I laugh'd down the day,
 Nor envy'd the joys of my neighbour.

Now sad transformation
Runs thro' the whole nation;
Peace, love, recreation,
All chang'd to vexation;
 This, this is my way,
 With my pipe and my tabor
I laugh down the day,
 And pity the cares of my neighbour.

While all are designing,
Their friends undermining,
Reviling, repining,
To mischief inclining;
 This, this is my way,
 With my pipe and my tabor
I laugh down the day,
 And pity the cares of my neighbour.

S O N G 638.

Written by Mr. CONGREVE.

LOVE's but the frailty of the mind,
 When 'tis not with ambition join'd;
A sickly flame, which, if not fed, expires,
And feeding, wastes in self-consuming fires.

'Tis not to wound a wanton boy,
 Or amorous youth, that gives the joy;
But 'tis the glory to have pierc'd a swain,
For whom inferior beauties sigh'd in vain.

Then I alone the conquest prize,
 When I insult a rival's eyes;
If there's delight in love, 'tis when I see
The heart which others bleed for, bleed for me.

S O N G 639.

THE LINNET; A PASTORAL.
Written by Mr. HAWKINS.

AS passing by a shady grove,
 I heard a linnet sing,
Whose sweetly plaintive voice of love
 Proclaim'd the chearful spring.

His pretty accents seem'd to flow
 As if he knew no pain;
His downy throat he tun'd so sweet,
 It echo'd o'er the plain.

Ah! happy warbler, (I reply'd,)
 Contented thus to be;
'Tis only harmony and love
 Can be compar'd to thee.

Thus perch'd upon the spray ye stand,
 The monarch of the shade;
And even sip ambrosial sweets,
 That glow from ev'ry glade.

Did man possess but half thy bliss,
 How joyful might he be!
But man was never form'd for this,
 'Tis only joy for thee.

Then farewel, pretty bird, (I said,)
 Pursue thy plaintive tale,
And let thy tuneful accents spread
 All o'er the fragrant vale.

S O N G 640.

THE man who for life
 Is plagu'd with a wife,
Is sure in a wretched condition;
 Go things how they will,
 She sticks by him still,
And death is his only physician.
 Poor man, &c.

To trifle and toy,
 May give a man joy,
When passion's promoted by beauty?
 But where is the bliss
 Of a conjugal kiss,
When passion is prompted by duty.
 Poor man, &c.

The dog when possess'd
 Of mutton the best,
A bone he may leave at his pleasure;
 But if to his tail
 'Tis ty'd, without fail
He is harrass'd and plagu'd beyond measure.
 Poor cur, &c.

S O N G 641.

ASK not the cause why sullen spring
 So long delays her flowers to bear;
Why warbling birds forget to sing,
 And winter storms invert the year:
Chloris is gone, and fate provides
To make it spring where she resides.

Chloris is gone, the cruel fair;
 She cast not back her pitying eye,
But left her lover in despair,
 To sigh, to languish, and to die:
Ah! how can those fair eyes endure
To give the wounds they will not cure!

Great god of love, why hast thou made
 A face that can all hearts command,
That all religions can invade,
 And change the laws of ev'ry land?
Where thou had'st plac'd such pow'r before,
Thou should'st have made her mercy more.

Y

When Chloris to the temple comes,
Adoring crowds before her fall;
She can reſtore the dead from tombs,
And ev'ry life but mine recal:
I only am by love deſign'd
To be the victim for mankind.

SONG 642.

Sung in *As you Like it.*

BLOW, blow, thou winter wind,
Thou art not ſo unkind
As man's ingratitude;
Thy tooth is not ſo keen,
Becauſe thou art not ſeen,
Altho' thy breath be rude.

Freeze, freeze, thou bitter ſky,
Thou canſt not bite ſo nigh
As benefits forgot;
Tho' thou the waters warp,
Thy ſting is not ſo ſharp,
As friend remembered not.

SONG 643.

STREPHON AND COLIN.

STREPHON.

HAVE you not ſeen the morning ſun
Peep over yonder hill?
Then you have ſeen my Chloe's charms,
At beſt, but painted ill.

COLIN.

Have you not ſeen a butterfly,
With colours bright and gay?
Then you have ſeen a thing leſs fine
Than Molly cloath'd in grey.

STREPHON.

The roſe, you'll ſay, of all the field,
Can boaſt the lovelieſt hue;
But, to compare with Chloe's cheeks,
It wants the lily too.

As I ſat by her on the plain,
And talk'd the hours away,
She breath'd ſo ſweet, I thought myſelf
In fields of new mow'd hay.

COLIN.

Not the ſweet breath, that's breath'd from cows,
With Molly's can compare;
And when ſhe ſings, the liſtening ſwains
Stand ſilent round to hear.

She ſaid, as we were walking once
Along the ſhady grove,
There's none but Colin Molly loves,
And will for ever love.

STREPHON.

Believe not, friend, a woman's word,
Or you are much to blame;
For t'other night, behind the elms,
She ſwore to me the ſame.

COLIN.

Yet I'll believe your Chloe's word,
As on my breaſt ſhe laid—
This Strephon is ſo dull a clown,
He'll think me ſtill a maid.

SONG 644.

FAIREST iſle, all iſles excelling,
Seat of pleaſure and of love,
Venus here will chuſe her dwelling,
And forſake her Cyprian grove;
Cupid, from his favourite nation,
Care and envy will remove,
Jealouſy that poiſons paſſion,
And deſpair that dies for love.

Gentle murmurs, ſweet complaining,
Sighs that blow the fire of love,
Soft repulſes, kind diſdaining,
Shall be all the pains you prove.
Ev'ry ſwain ſhall pay his duty,
Grateful ev'ry nymph ſhall prove,
And, as theſe excel in beauty,
Thoſe ſhall be renown'd for love.

SONG 645.

Sung at VAUXHALL.

SHALL I, waſting in deſpair,
Die becauſe a woman's fair?
Shall my cheeks look pale with care,
'Cauſe another's roſy are?
Be ſhe fairer than the day,
Or the flow'ry meads in May;
Yet if ſhe think not well of me,
What care I how fair ſhe be.

Shall a woman's goodneſs move
Me to periſh for her love;
Or, her worthy merits known,
Make me quite forget my own?
Be ſhe with that goodneſs bleſt,
As may merit name the beſt;
Yet if ſhe be not ſuch to me,
What care I how good ſhe be.

Be ſhe good, or kind, or fair,
I will never more deſpair;
If ſhe love me, this believe,
I will die ere ſhe ſhall grieve;
If ſhe ſlight me when I woo,
I will ſcorn, and let her go:
So if ſhe be not fit for me,
What care I for whom ſhe be?

SONG 646.

YE virgin powers defend my heart
From amorous looks and ſmiles;
From ſaucy love, or nicer art,
Which moſt our ſex beguiles.

From ſighs and vows, and awful fears,
That do to pity move;
From ſpeaking ſilence, and from tears,
Thoſe ſprings that water love.

But if thro' paſſion I grow blind,
    Let honour be my guide ;
And when frail nature ſeems inclin'd,
    There place a guard of pride.

An heart, whoſe flames are ſeen, tho' pure,
    Needs every virtue's aid ;
And ſhe who thinks herſelf ſecure,
    The ſooneſt is betray'd.

SONG 647.

Written by Mr. DRYDEN.

GO tell Amyntas, gentle ſwain,
    I cannot die, nor dare complain ;
Thy tuneful voice with numbers join,
    Thy words will more prevail than mine.

To ſouls oppreſs'd, and dumb with grief,
    The gods ordain this kind relief,
That muſick ſh•u'd in ſound convey
    What dying lovers dare not ſay.

A ſigh or tear perhaps we'd give,
    But love or pity cannot live ;
Tell her, that hearts for hearts were made,
    And love with love is only paid.

Tell her my pains ſo faſt increaſe,
    That ſoon they will be paſt redreſs !
For ah ! the wretch that ſpeechleſs lies,
    Attends but death to cloſe his eyes.

SONG 648.

LOVE's a dream of mighty treaſure,
    Which in fancy we poſſeſs ;
In the folly lies the pleaſure,
    Wiſdom always makes it leſs.

When we think, by paſſion heated,
    We a goddeſs have in chace,
Like Ixïon we are cheated,
    And a gaudy cloud embrace.

Happy only is the lover,
    Whom his miſtreſs well deceives ;
Seeking nothing to diſcover,
    He contented lives at eaſe.

But the wretch that would be knowing
    What the fair-one would diſguiſe,
Labours for his own undoing,
    Changing happy to be wiſe.

SONG 649.

Written by Mr. H——.

IN Lincoln Fields there lives a laſs,
    Who for a beauty fain would paſs,
And once I thought her ſo, alas !
    But now the caſe is alter'd ;
For ſhe to me has prov'd unkind,
    Her vows were nothing more than wind,
And now, ye gods ! no charms I find
    In pretty Betſy Norton.

A lady's maid, oh ! ſhe would be,
To make her lady's ſlops and tea,
Or elſe to dreſs her rough toupee,
    With all the ſkill ſhe can, Sir ;
Now John, the footman, is her ſwain,
And him ſhe never will give pain ;
Yet me ſhe treats with cold diſdain,
    Ah ! cruel Betſy Norton.

Though oft together we have ſtray'd,
And many times have toy'd and play'd ;
But, oh ! thou falſe, deceiving maid,
    To love, and then to ſlight me !
Was ever ſuch a trick as this,
To rob me of ſuch heav'nly bliſs,
That I experienced from each kiſs
    Of the ſweet Betſy Norton.

But now, my deareſt girl, farewel,
No more my tender tale I'll tell,
But where you go I wiſh you well,
    My little dainty doxey.
May you enjoy content of mind,
And ev'ry other bleſſing find ;
But ſince you are to me unkind,
    Adieu, ſweet Betſy Norton !

SONG 650.

WHEN bright Aurelia tript the plain,
    How chearful then were ſeen
The looks of ev'ry jolly ſwain,
That ſtrove Aurelia's heart to gain,
    With gambols on the green ?

Their ſports were innocent and gay,
    Mixt with a manly air,
They'd ſing and dance, and pipe and play,
Each ſtrove to pleaſe ſome different way,
    This dear enchanting fair.

Th' ambitious ſtrife ſhe did admire,
    And equally approve,
Till Phaon's tuneful voice and lyre,
With ſofteſt muſic, did inſpire
    Her ſoul to generous love.

Their wonted ſports the reſt declin'd,
    Their arts prov'd all in vain ;
Aurelia's conſtant now they find,
The more they languiſh and repin'd
    The more ſhe loves the ſwain.

SONG 651.

MY goddeſs, Lydia, heavenly fair,
    As lily ſweet, as ſoft as air,
Let looſe thy treſſes, ſpread thy charms,
    And to my love give freſh alarms.

O ! let me gaze on theſe bright eyes,
Tho' ſacred lightning from them flies ;
Shew me that ſoft, that modeſt grace,
Which paints with charming red thy face.

Give me ambroſia in a kiſs,
That I may rival Jove in bliſs ;
That I may mix my ſoul with thine,
And make the pleaſure all divine.

O hide thy bofom's killing white,
(The milky way is not fo bright)
Left you my ravifh'd foul opprefs
With beauty's pomp and fweet excefs.

Why draw'ft thou from the purple flood
Of my kind heart the vital blood?
Thou art all over endlefs charms;
O take me dying to thy arms.

SONG 652.

WHY we love, and why we hate,
   Is not granted us to know:
Random chance, or wilful fate,
   Guides the fhaft from Cupid's bow.

If on me Zelinda frown,
   'Tis madnefs all in me to grieve;
Since her will is not her own,
   Why fhould I uneafy live?

If I for Zelinda die,
   Deaf to poor Mizella's cries,
Afk not me the reafon why,
   Seek the riddle in the fkies.

SONG 653.

AS I faw fair Chloe walk alone,
   The feather'd fnow came foftly down,
Like Jove defcending from his tower,
To court her in a filver fhower:
The wanton flakes flew to her breafts,
As little birds into their nefts;
But being overcome with whitenefs there,
For grief diffolv'd into a tear;
Thence flowing down her garments hem,
To deck her, froze into a gem.

SONG 654.
Written by the Earl of DORSET.

MAY the ambitious ever find
   Succefs in crowds and noife,
While gentle love does fill my mind
   With filent, real joys.

May knaves and fools grow rich and great,
   And all the world think them wife,
While I lie at my Nanny's feet,
   And all the world defpife.

Let conquering kings new triumphs raife,
   And melt in court delights:
Her eyes can give much brighter days,
   Her arms much fofter nights.

SONG 655.

SELINDA, fure's the brightest thing
   That decks the earth, or breathes our air;
Mild are her looks like opening fpring,
   And like the blooming fummer fair.

But then her wit's fo very fmall,
   That all her charms appear to lie,

Like glaring colours on a wall,
   And ftrike no farther than the eye.

Our eyes luxurioufly fhe treats,
   Our ears are abfent from the feaft,
One fenfe is furfeited with fweets,
   Starv'd or difgufted are the reft.

So have I feen, with afpect bright,
   And taudry pride, a tulip fwell,
Blooming and beauteous to the fight,
   Dull and infipid to the fmell.

SONG 656.

YE gentle gales that fan the air,
   And wanton in the fhady grove,
Oh! whifper to my abfent fair,
   My fecret pain and endlefs love.

When at the fultry heat of day
   She'll feek fome fhady cool retreat,
Throw fpicy odours in her way,
   And fcatter rofes at her feet.

And when fhe fees their colours fade,
   And all their pride neglected lie,
Let that inftruct the charming maid,
   That fweets not gather'd timely die.

And when fhe lays her down to reft,
   Let fome aufpicious virgin fhew
Who 'tis that love's Camilla beft,
   And what for her I'd undergo.

SONG 657.

SHE that would gain a conftant lover,
   Muft at a diftance keep the flave,
Nor by a look her heart difcover;
   Men fhould but guefs the thoughts we have.

Whilft they're in doubt, their flame increafes;
   And all attendance they will pay:
When we're poffefs'd their tranfport ceafes,
   And vows, like vapours, fleet away.

SONG 658.
A FREE-MASON'S SONG.
Written by Mr. CUNNINGHAM.

LET mafonry, from pole to pole,
   Her facred laws expand;
Far as the mighty waters roll,
   To wafh remoteft land!

That virtue has not left mankind,
   Her focial maxims prove;
For ftamp'd upon the mafon's mind
   Are unity and love.

Afcending to her native fky,
   Let mafonry increafe;
A glorious pillar rais'd on high,
   Integrity it's bafe.

Peace adds to olive-boughs entwin'd,
An emblematic dove;
As stamp'd upon the mason's mind
Are unity and love.

SONG 659.

Written by Mr. SHENSTONE.

YES, Fulvia is like Venus fair,
Has all her bloom, and shape, and air;
But still, to perfect every grace,
She wants—the smile upon her face.

The crown majestic Juno wore,
And Cynthia's brow the crescent bore,
A helmet mark'd Minerva's mien;
But smiles distinguish'd beauty's queen.

Her train was form'd of smiles and loves,
Her chariot drawn by gentlest doves,
And from her zone the nymph may find
'Tis beauty's province to be kind.

Then smile, my fair; and all whose aim
Aspires to paint the Cyprian dame,
Or bid her breathe in living stone,
Shall take their forms from you alone.

SONG 660.

A BACCHANALIAN SONG.

Sung at VAUXHALL.

COME, come, my companions, be jocund
and gay,
Forget ev'ry care, and drive spleen far away,
No doubts for to-morrow our bliss shall controul,
But ev'ry dull thought shall be drown'd in the
bowl.

Nor wealth, nor ambition, those plagues of the
great,
Our joy shall depress, or imbitter our state;
He's king for to-night who reigns highest in
mith,
And he that laughs most is possess'd of most
worth.

The miser sits plodding from morning till night,
And places in gold all his hopes and delight,
Our pleasures are greater and nobler's our crime,
He robs but poor mortals, whilst we cheat old
time.

The fool who sits gazing all night at the skies,
And fancies himself to be wonderous wise,
Was he here would confess his pursuits had been
vain,
For he ne'er saw a star shine like sparkling
Champaign.

The hermit, grown sick of this world's cares and
strife,
Makes solitude his *summum bonum* of life,
But could he once meet such a frolicksome
throng,
He'd quit his dull cave, and would join in our
song.

Wou'd the learned physician, so formal and
grave,
Who twenty destroys for each one he can save,
But alter his plan, and good liquor prescribe,
No man but would doat on the physical tribe.

When you're low take the doctor which I re-
commend,
Who'll not tire you with talk, but will prove
your best friend;
He's very well known, and one of great fame,
A rosy-cheek'd fellow, and Port is his name.

Let the bowl and the bottle go briskly about,
For others are ready when these are drank out;
In mirth and good-humour our bumpers we'll
drink,
Since thoughts bring but plagues 'tis a folly to
think.

SONG 661.

Written by Capt. THOMPSON.

Sung at VAUXHALL.

CUPID, god of love and joy,
Wanton rosy-winged boy,
Guard her heart from all alarms,
Bring her deck'd in all her charms,
Blushing, panting, to my arms.

All the heaven I ask below,
Is to use thy darts and bow,
Could I have them in my pow'r,
One sweet smiling happy hour,
One sweet woman I'd secure.

She's the first which Venus made,
With her graces full array'd;
When she treads the velvet ground
We feel the zone with which she's bound,
All is paradise around.

SONG 662.

AMPHITRYON; A CANTATA.

Sung at VAUXHALL.

RECITATIVE.

AMPHITRYON and his bride, a godlike
pair,
He brave as Mars, and she as Venus fair,
On thrones of gold, in purple triumph plac'd,
With matchless splendor held the nuptial feast;
Whilst the high roof with loud applauses rung,
Enraptur'd thus the happy hero sung.

AIR.

Was mighty Jove descending,
With all his wrath divine,
Enrag'd at my pretending
To call this charmer mine;
His shafts of bolted thunder,
With boldness I'd deride,
Not Heav'n itself can sunder,
The hearts that love has ty'd.

RECITATIVE, *accompanied.*

The thund'rer heard, he look'd with vengeance
  down,
Till beauty's glance difarm'd his awful frown;
The magic impulfe of Almena's eyes,
Compell'd the conqu'ring god to quit the fkies;
He feign'd the hufband's form, poffefs'd her
  charms,
And punifh'd his prefumption in her arms.

AIR.

He deferves fublimeft pleafure,
  Who reveals it not when won;
Beauty's like the mifer's treafure,
  Boaft it, and the fool's undone.

Learn by this, unguarded lover,
  When your fecret fighs prevail,
Not to let your tongue difcover
  Raptures that it fhould conceal.

SONG 663.

OH! wouldft thou know what facred charms
  This deftin'd heart of mine alarms,
What kind of nymph the heav'ns decree,
The maid that's made for love and me!

Who joys to hear the figh fincere,
Who melts to fee the tender tear,
From each ungen'rous paffion free;
Be fuch the maid that's made for me.

Whofe heart with gen'rous friendfhip glows,
Who feels the bleffings fhe beftows,
Gentle to all, but kind to me;
Be fuch the maid that's made for me.

Whofe fimple thoughts, devoid of art,
Are all the natives of her heart;
A gentle train, from falfhood free;
Be fuch the maid that's made for me.

Avaunt! ye light coquettes, retire,
Where flatt'ring fops around admire;
Unmov'd, your tinfell'd charms I fee,
More genuine beauties are for me.

SONG 664.

TO DELIA.

SOFT, pleafing pains, unknown before,
  My beating bofom feels,
When I behold the blifsful bow'r
  Where deareft Delia dwells.
That way I daily drive my flock;
  Ah! happy, happy vale!
There look, and wifh; and while I look,
  My fighs increafe the gale.

Sometimes at midnight I do ftray
  Beneath th' inclement fkies,
And there my true devotion pay
  To Delia's fleep-feal'd eyes:
So pious pilgrims nightly roam,
  With tedious travel faint,
To kifs alone the clay-cold tomb
  Of fome lov'd fav'rite faint.

O tell, ye fhades, that fold my fair,
  And all my blifs contain,
Ah! why fhould ye thofe bleffings fhare
  For which I figh in vain?
But let me not at fate repine,
  And thus my grief impart:
She's not your tenant—fhe is mine;
  Her manfion is my heart.

SONG 665.

Sung in the Oratorio of *Jofeph.*

WHAT's fweeter than the new-blown rofe,
  Or breezes from the new-mown clofe?
What's fweeter than an April morn,
Or May-day's filver, fragrant thorn?
What than Arabia's fpicy grove?
Oh! fweeter far the breath of love.

SONG 666.

CONTENTMENT.

O True content! fecure from harms,
  What's all the world without thy charms,
  Which ftill allure to reft?
Compar'd therewith, all earthly joys
Are empty, fading, trifling toys:
  In thee mankind is bleft.

Bereft of thee, no monarchs have
Such pleafure as the meaneft flave
  To whom thou giv'ft relief;
Tho' fubjects fhew profound refpect,
Nor duty wilfully neglect,
  Thy abfence caufes grief.

Come, then, thou pleafing beauty bright!
Refide with me both day and night,
  Difplay thy lovely charms;
Be thou diffus'd within my breaft,
And let me ftill fecurely reft
  Infolded in thy arms.

Thro' all the various fcenes of life,
Preferve me free from envious ftrife,
  On Heav'n ftill to rely
For true protecting aid; and when
Time terminates in death, oh! then
  To thee, O Heav'n! to fly.

SONG 667.

Sung at VAUXHALL.

TOO long a giddy wand'ring youth,
  From fair to fair I rov'd;
To ev'ry nymph I vow'd my truth,
  Tho' all alike I lov'd;
Yet, when the joy I wifh'd was paft,
  My truth appear'd a jeft:
But, truft me, I'm convinc'd at laft
  That conftancy is beft.

Like other fools, at female wiles
  'Twas my delight to rail;
Their fighs, their vows, their tears, their fmiles,
  Were falfe, I thought, and frail:

But, by reflection's bright'ning pow'r,
I fee their worth contest;
That man cannot enough adore,
That conſtancy is beſt.

The roving heart at beauty's fight
May glow with fond deſire;
Yet, tho' poſſeſſion yield delight,
It damps the lawleſs fire:
But love's celeſtial, faithful flames,
Still catch from breaſt to breaſt;
While ev'ry home-felt joy proclaims
That conſtancy is beſt.

No ſolid blifs from change refults,
No real raptures flow;
But, fix'd to one, the ſoul exults,
And taſtes of Heav'n below.
With love, on ev'ry gen'rous mind,
Is truth's fair form impreſt;
And reaſon dictates to mankind,
That conſtancy is beſt.

SONG 668.

RECITATIVE.

AS in a penſive form Myrtilla ſat,
Revolving on the will of fate,
A ſprightly youth, devoid of care,
Advanc'd, and thus addreſs'd the fair.

AIR.

Thou vernal bloom of beauty's tree,
I'm come to buy a heart of thee:
With tranſport I receiv'd the tale,
That ſuch a gem was up for ſale.
Could I command the ſtarry train,
For thee I'd give it back again;
And, if I could, to make thee mine,
The univerſe ſhould all be thine.

Go hence, (the maid with ſoftneſs cries;)
Merit the beſt deſerves the prize:
The tale you've heard was falſely told;
Myrtilla's heart can ne'er be ſold.

SONG 669.

LOVE REWARDED.

WITH Phœbus I often aroſe,
To feaſt on the charms of the ſpring,
The fragrance to ſmell of the roſe,
Or liſten to hear the birds fing:
When linnets exalted their ſtrains,
The muſic enchanted my ear;
My eyes too were bleſs'd on the plains,
With various ſweet blooms of the year.

When Chloe ſhone ſmiling ſo gay,
I there fix'd the ſcene of delight;
My thoughts ſhe engroſs'd all the day,
I ſaw her in dreams all the night:
Still muſing on Chloe I walk'd,
My harveſt no more in my thought:
Of nothing but Chloe I talk'd;
Her ſmiles were the harveſt I ſought.

No longer the warblers could pleaſe;
No longer the roſes look'd gay;
For muſic, and ſweetneſs, and eaſe,
Were loſt, if my love was away:
I tun'd to her beauties my lays,
I ſtudy'd each art that could move;
She took the kind tribute of praiſe,
And paid it with fondneſs and love.

SONG 670.

Sung in the *Accompliſhed Maid*.

WHILE her charms my thoughts employ,
All is rapture, all is joy;
When ſhe ſpeaks, how ſweet to hear;
Modeſt, graceful, and ſincere;
In her lovely ſhape and face,
Center ev'ry charm and grace;
Sure never nymph was half ſo fair.

Not the idle, giddy, vain,
Nor the wanton flirting train,
Did my cautious heart enſnare?
Not their artful ſubtle wiles,
Nor their ſoft deluding ſmiles,
Charming Fanny triumphs there.

SONG 671.

SYLVIA, wilt thou waſte thy prime,
Stranger to the joys of love?
Thou haſt youth, and that's the time
Every minute to improve:
Round thee wilt thou never hear
Little wanton girls and boys
Sweetly ſounding in thy ear,
Infants' prate and mothers' joys?

Only view that little dove,
Softly cooing to his mate;
As a farther proof of love,
See her for his kiſſes wait:
Hark! that charming nightingale,
As he flies from ſpray to ſpray,
Sweetly tunes an am'rous tale,
I love, I love, he ſtrives to ſay.

Could I to thy ſoul reveal
But the leaſt, the thouſandth part
Of thoſe pleaſures lovers feel
In a mutual change of heart;
Then repenting, wouldſt thou ſay,
Virgin tears, from hence remove,
All the time is thrown away,
That we do not ſpend in love.

SONG 672.

DEFEND my heart, ye virgin pow'rs,
From am'rous looks and ſmiles,
And ſhield me in my gayer hours,
From love's deſtructive wiles:
In vain let ſighs and melting tears
Employ their moving art,
Nor may deluſive oaths and pray'rs
E'er triumph o'er my heart.

My calm content and virtuous joys
May envy ne'er moleſt,
Nor let ambitious rhoughts ariſe
Within my peaceful breaſt;
Yet may there ſuch a decent ſtate,
Such unaffected pride,
As love and awe at once create,
My words and actions guide.

Let others, fond of empty praiſe,
Each wanton art diſplay,
While ſops and fools in raptures gaze,
And ſigh their ſouls away:
Far other dictates I purſue,
(My bliſs in virtue plac'd)
And ſeek to pleaſe the wiſer few,
Who real worth can taſte.

SONG 673.

FREE from confinement and ſtrife,
I'll plow thro' the ocean of life,
To ſeek new delights,
Where beauty invites,
But ne'er be confin'd to a wife.
The man that is free,
Like a veſſel at ſea,
After conqueſt and plunder may roam:
But when either confin'd
By wife or by wind,
Tho' for glory deſign'd,
No advantage they find,
But rot in the harbour at home.

SONG 674.

JENNY OF THE GREEN.

WHILE others ſtrip the new-fall'n ſnows,
And ſteal it's fragrance from the roſe,
To dreſs their fancy's queen;
Fain would I ſing, but words are faint,
All muſic's powers too weak to paint
My Jenny of the green.

Beneath this elm, beſide this ſtream,
How oft I've tun'd the fav'rite theme,
And told my tale unſeen!
While, faithful in the lover's cauſe,
The winds would murmur ſoft applauſe
To Jenny of the green.

With joy my ſoul reviews the day,
When, deck'd in all the pride of May,
She hail'd the ſylvan ſcene;
Then ev'ry nymph that hop'd to pleaſe,
Firſt ſtrove to catch the grace and eaſe
Of Jenny of the green.

Then, deaf to ev'ry rival's ſigh,
On me ſhe caſt her partial eye,
Nor ſcorn'd my humble mien:
The fragrant myrtle-wreath I wear,
That day adorn'd the lovely hair
Of Jenny of the green.

Through all the fairy-land of love,
I'll ſeek my pretty wand'ring dove,

The pride of gay fifteen;
Tho' now ſhe treads ſome diſtant plain,
Tho' far apart, I'll meet again,
My Jenny of the green.

But thou, old time, till that bleſt night
That brings her back with ſpeedy flight,
Melt down the hours between;
And when we meet, the loſs repay,
On loit'ring wing prolong my ſtay
With Jenny of the green.

SONG 675.

I Strove, but in vain,
To chaſe away pain,
Which had taken deep root in my heart;
My reſt me forſook;
Betray'd in my look,
What I felt from ſly Cupid's keen dart.

SONG 676.

RETIREMENT.

FAREWEL, the ſmoaky town! adieu
Each rude and ſenſual joy;
Gay, fleeting pleaſures, all untrue,
That in poſſeſſion cloy.

Far from the garniſh'd ſcene I'll fly,
Where folly keeps her court,
To wholeſome, ſound philoſophy,
And harmleſs rural ſport.

How happy is the humble cell,
How bleſt the deep retreat,
Where ſorrow's billows never ſwell,
Nor paſſion's tempeſts beat!

But ſafely through the ſea of life,
Calm reaſon wafts us o'er,
Free from ambition, noiſe, and ſtrife,
To death's eternal ſhore.

SONG 677.

Sung at VAUXHALL.

SINCE Jenny thinks mean her heart's love
to deny,
And Peggy's uneaſy when Harry's not by;
I will own, without bluſhing, were all the
world by,
That Willy's the lad, the lad for me.

He brought me a wreath which his hand did
compoſe,
Where the dale-loving lily was twin'd with the
roſe;
Young myrtle in ſprigs did the border incloſe.
And Willy's the lad, the lad for me.

By myrtle, ſaid he, is my paſſion expreſs'd;
The roſe, like your lips, in vermilion is dreſs'd:
And the lily, for whiteneſs, would vie with
your breaſt.
And Willy's the lad, the lad for me.

These ribbands of mine were his gifts àt the
fair,
My mother look'd crofs, and cry'd, Fanny be-
ware!
But d'ye think I regard her? Not I, I declare.
And Willy's the lad, the lad for me.

Beneath a tall beech, and reclin'd on his crook,
I faw my young fhepherd; how fweet was his
look!
He afk'd for one kifs, but an hundred he took.
And Willy's the lad, the lad for me.

Then what can I do, O inftruct me, ye maids!
When a lover fo kindly, fo warmly invades,
Whofe filence as much as his language perfuades?
And Willy's the lad, the lad for me.

SONG 678.

THE POWER OF NATURE.

WHERE virtue encircles the fair,
There lilies and rofes are vain;
Each bloffom muft drop with defpair,
Where innocence takes up her reign:
No gaudy embellifhing arts
The fair-one need call to her aid,
Who kindly by nature imparts
The graces that nature has made.

The fwain who has fenfe muft defpife
Each coquettifh art to enfnare;
If timely ye'd wifh to be wife,
Attend to my counfel, ye fair;
Let virgins whom nature has bleft,
Her fovereign dictates obey;
For beauties by nature exprefs
Are beauties that never decay.

SONG 679.

FANNY'S CHARMS.

WHAT tho' the bloom of fpring is gone,
And nature feels decay;
Tho' winter now her garb puts on;
And cafts a gloom on day:
Tho' filent ftands the lazy hill,
And mute the fylvan throng;
Yet Fanny's charms, unfading ftill;
Shall flourifh in my fong.

Tho' now no more on funny plains
The fhepherds tend their care,
And each, in emulating ftrains,
Forgets to praife his fair;
Tho' unfrequented ev'ry fhade
That catch'd the vernal breeze,
Yet Fanny's fmiles (enchanting maid!)
Can charm me more than thefe.

When fpring, in varied beauty dreft,
Does all it's fweets difclofe,
Compare the lily to her breaft,
And to her lips the rofe:
Her breaft the lily's white outvies,
Tho' whiteft of the vale,

And to her lips (in Damon's eyes)
The reddeft rofe looks pale.

No more fhall flow'rs bedeck the meads,
Or birds frequent the fpray;
Or larks forfake their dewy beds,
And hail the dawning day:
No more on yonder mountain's brow
Shall bleating lambkins rove,
And fhe no more prove fair or true,
When I forget to love.

SONG 680.

MISS BROWN.

DEAR Madam, excufe
So artlefs a mufe,
That endeavours your beauties to paint;
The fault is not mine,
For tho' you're divine,
My power to praife you is faint.

If the goddefs of love
E'er ftepp'd from above
To vifit the groves upon earth;
I think it quite plain,
You was one of her train,
Or at leaft it was there you had birth.

Let thofe of more fkill,
Paint beauties that kill,
And arm their bright eyes with a frown;
But I, for my part,
Such beauties defert
To fing the good-natur'd Mifs Brown.

SONG 681.

HERE attend all ye fwains,
And ye nymphs of the plains,
Quit your flocks and your herds for a while;
Hither quickly repair,
In our mirth a part fhare,
And each lafs her love meet with a fmile.

Hark, the drum Hymen beats!
Hark, how echo repeats
The fweet found, as it flies fwift away!
O'er hills, and o'er dales,
Ev'ry ear it affails,
And mocks their long, tedious delay.

O! how happy is he,
That contented can be,
To enjoy the beft treafure of life;
All he'd wifh e'er to gain,
He'll be fure to obtain,
In a prudent and fenfible wife.

Should the rover pretend,
That thefe joys will foon end,
And that love will expire with the moon;
Mark how pain and difeafe
The lewd libertine feize,
Ere he reaches the height of life's noon.

But how wretched indeed,
He whom fate has decreed
From the arms of his fair-one to part;

Z

All endeavours are vain
To affuage the fharp pain
Which is felt in a love-troubled heart.

Though life's bufy fcene
May oft help to ferene
And difperfe the dark clouds of defpair;
Yet when night's filent noon
Helps to add to it's gloom,
Who can fay what the mind fuffers there?

Hafte this day to employ,
Thus devoted to joy,
And with innocent mirth let's abound;
Thus in chorus we'll fing,
While the foreft fhall ring
With the burthen of mufic's foft found.

May all prefent attain
A life free from pain,
Ever ftrangers to difcord or ftrife;
May the fingle foon find,
In the maiden that's kind,
The joys of an amiable wife!

SONG 682.

FEMALE ADVICE.

PURSUING beauty, men defcry
    The diftant fhore, and long to prove,
Still richer in variety,
    The treafures of the land of love.

We women, like weak Indians, ftand,
    Inviting from our golden coaft
The wand'ring rovers to our land;
    But fhe who trades with them is loft.

With humble vows they firft begin,
    Stealing unfeen, into the heart;
But, by poffeffion fettled in,
    They quickly act another part.

For beads and baubles we refign,
    In ignorance, our fhining ftore,
Difcover nature's richeft mine,
    And yet the tyrants will have more.

Ye fair, take heed, forbear to try
    How men can court, or you be won;
For love is but difcovery,
    When that is made the pleafure's done.

SONG 683.

THE fun in virgin luftre fhone,
    May-morning put it's beauties on;
The warblers fung in livelier ftrains,
And fweeter flow'rets deck'd the plains;
When love, a foft intruding gueft,
That long had dealt in Damon's breaft,
Now whifper'd to the nymph, Away!
For this is nature's holiday.

The tender impulfe wing'd his hafte;
The painted mead he inftant pafs'd,
And foon the happy cot he gain'd,
Where beauty flept, and filence reign'd:
Awake, my fair! (the fhepherd cries)
To new-born pleafure ope thine eyes;

Arife, my Sylvia! hail the May,
For this is nature's holiday.

Forth came the maid, in beauty bright
As Phœbus in meridian light,
Entranc'd in rapture, all confefs'd,
The fhepherd clafp's her to his breaft;
Then gazing with a fpeaking eye,
He fnatch'd a kifs, and heav'd a figh;
A melting figh, and feem'd to fay,
Confider youth's our holiday.

Ah, foft, (fhe faid) for pity's fake!
What, kifs one ere I'm well awake?
For this fo early came you here?
And hail you thus the rifing year?
Sweet innocence! forbear to chide,
We'll hafte to joy, (the fwain reply'd;)
In pleafure's flow'ry fields we'll ftray,
And this fhall be love's holiday.

A crimfon glow warm'd o'er her cheek,
She look'd the things fhe dar'd not fpeak;
Confent own'd nature's foft command,
And Damon feiz'd her trembling hand:
His dancing heart in tranfports play'd,
To church he led the blufhing maid;
Then blefs'd the happy morn of May,
And now their life's all holiday.

SONG 684.

Sung at RANELAGH.

THE fragrant lily of the vale,
    So elegantly fair,
Whofe fweets perfume the fanning gale,
    To Chloe I compare;
What tho' on earth it lowly grows,
    And ftrives it's head to hide!
It's fweetnefs far outvies the rofe,
    That flaunts with fo much pride.

The coftly tulip owes it's hue
    To many a gaudy ftain,
In this we view the virgin white
    Of innocence remain:
See how the curious florift's hand
    Uprears it's humble head,
And to preferve the charming flow'r,
    Tranfplants it to his bed.

There while it fheds it's fweets around,
    How fhines each modeft grace!
Enraptur'd, how it's owner ftands
    To view it's lovely face!
But pray, my Chloe, now obferve
    The inference of my tale,
May I the florift be, and thou
    The lily of the vale.

SONG 685.

Sung in the *Capricious Lovers*.

WHEN vapours o'er the meadows die,
    And morning ftreaks the purple fky,
I wake to love with jocund glee,
To think on him who doats on me.

When eve embrowns the verdant grove,
And Philomel laments her love,

Each figh I breathe my love reveals,
And tells the pangs my bosom feels.

With secret pleasure I survey
The frolic birds in amorous play,
While fondest cares my heart employ,
Which flutters, leaps, and beats for joy.

SONG 686.

RETIREMENT.

Written by Mr. NICHOLLS.

FROM London's smoaky, fœtid air,
The seat of traffic and of care,
    Take me, ye rural pow'rs;
With you, in your sequester'd ways,
Where peace, that rose-lip'd cherub strays,
    I'd pass the fleeting hours.

What tho' with you no balls invite,
Or painted beauties catch the fight,
    Yet nature has supply'd
Far, far more lasting joys than these,
Sweet vocal birds on flow'ring trees,
    The cool meand'ring tide;

The rosy maid, the jocund swains,
The silver flocks on verdant plains,
    The unobstructed breeze;
The crystal spring, the babbling rill,
Gay prospects as we mount the hill,
    With solitude and ease;

The furze-blown heath, the fragrant thorn,
And ample fields of rising corn,
    The farmer's promis'd wealth;
But more than all, what's seldom found
In dissipation's vicious round,
    Vivacity and health.

While those whom London's walls immure,
Rheumaticks, colds, catarrhs endure,
    With all Pandora's store;
From these I'd fly to halesome plains,
And never wish, whilst life remains,
    To see the city more.

SONG 687.

THE NYMPH OF THE THAMES.

Sung at VAUXHALL.

FULL of dreams of bright beauties, and
    fond to explore
A new world of such charms as I'd ne'er seen
    before,
I travell'd all nations, and wak'd from my
    dreams,
And found that no nymphs were like those of
    the Thames.

On the banks of the Seine I was pleas'd to survey
Such crowds of fair nymphs all so merry and gay;
But then they were merry and gay to extremes,
And no nymphs cou'd I find like the nymphs
    of the Thames.

Then I travers'd each mountain, each river
    and plain,
But my labour, alas! was all labour in vain.
O Tyber! O Po! why so fam'd are your streams,
Since no nymphs can you boast like the nymphs
    of the Thames.

But of Italy's merit and fame to say true,
And give, as 'tis fit, ev'ry nation it's due,
Each fair, like a Syren, with music inflames;
But what is a song to the nymphs of the
    Thames?

As for Germany, there I was struck with surprise;
What the belles want in beauty they make up
    in size;
And 'tis just with their nymphs as it is with
    the streams,
You've a tun on the Rhine for a quart on the
    Thames.

Then ye youths of Great Britain, on wand'ring
    so keen,
To feed your fond fancies with beauties unseen,
Go enquire of the sun, and he'll tell you his
    beams
Ne'er shone on such nymphs as the nymphs of
    the Thames.

SONG 688.

THE ROSE-BUD.

SWEET bud! to Laura's bosom go,
    And live beneath her eye;
There, in the sun of beauty blow,
    Or taste of heaven and die.

Sweet earnest of the blooming year!
    Whose dawning beauties speak
The budding blush of summer near,
    The summer on her cheek!

Best emblem of the nymph I love,
    Resembling beauty's morn,
To Laura's bosom haste, and prove
One rose without a thorn.

SONG 689.

Written by Mr. HAWKINS.

LOVELY Flavia, list, I pray,
    To yon warbler on the spray;
Hear, my fair, his matin tale,
Charming as the vernal gale.

View the fields all smiling round;
See the flow'rets deck the ground;
And the frisky lambkins stray,
With their dams in wanton play.

See the shepherd pensive sit,
Making of a home-spun net;
With his bottle near at hand,
His mastiff too, at his command.

How contented is his state!
He envy's not the rich and great;

Free from forrows, free from pain,
Is the fhepherd on the plain.

Except his Daphne proves unkind,
Then difconceited is his mind ;
Till fhe refolves to prove more true,
Then all his cares fhe doth fubdue.

SONG 690.
A SONNET.

BE hufh'd, ye fweet birds, and forbear your
        fhrill notes,
Nor deign fuch a clamour to keep ;
But ftop a few moments, and reft your foft
        throats,
    For here lies a goddefs afleep!

Keep off, ye pert flies, from the cheek of my
        fair,
    And let her contentedly lay ;
For, if you prefume to alight on her face,
    " You'll wake her as fure as 'tis day !"

Ye gods ! fend young Cupids to 'bide at her feet,
    Let the Graces adorn her fweet head !
Let the pleafanteft dreams make her flumbers
        complete,
    And angels keep guard o'er her head.

SONG 691.
LOVE.

HOW fweet a torment 'tis to love!
    And ah ! how pleafant is the pain !
I would not, if i could, remove,
    And now put off the amorous chain.
Tho' Chloris' eyes do give me laws,
    And me of liberty beguile,
I, like a martyr, love my caufe,
    And on my fair tormentor fmile !

SONG 692.
ARTLESS LOVE.
Written by Mr. W—LL—S.

LOVE's a pleafing noble paffion,
    Kindly fent us from above ;
And tho' growing out of fafhion,
    What can equal artlefs love ?

What tho' moderns difregard it,
    I like them will never prove :
Diffimulation !—I difcard it ;
    Nought can pleafe like artlefs love.

When a lover fues for favour,
    And with oaths would pity move,
Truft not, Delia, fuch behaviour,
    'Tis devoid of artlefs love.

'Tis defign'd but to deceive you,
    When he fwears to pow'rs above ;
Of your peace he would bereave you,
    Think not, then, 'tis artlefs love.

When a lover mildly proffers
    You his hand—his truth to prove,
Then, you may accept his offers,
    For they come from artlefs love.

What on earth can give fuch pleafure !
    What fo foon our cares remove !
What can be fo great a treafure
    As fincere and artlefs love !

SONG 693.

OF Leinfter, fam'd for maidens fair,
    Bright Lucy was the grace ;
Nor e'er did Liffy's limpid ftream
    Reflect a fairer face.

Till lucklefs love and pining care
    Impair'd her rofy hue,
Her coral lips, her damafk cheeks,
    And eyes of gloffy blue.

Oh ! have you feen the lily pale
    When beating rains defcend ?
So droop'd this flow-confuming maid,
    Her life now near it's end.

By Lucy warn'd, of flatt'ring fwains
    Take heed, ye eafy fair !
Of vengeance due to broken vows,
    Ye perjur'd fwains, beware !

Three times, all in the dead of night,
    A bell was heard to ring ;
And fhrieking at her window thrice,
    The raven flapp'd her wing.

Too well the love-lorn maiden knew
    The folemn-boding found,
And thus in dying words befpoke
    The maidens weeping round.

I hear a voice you cannot hear,
    Which fays I muft not ftay ;
I fee a hand you cannot fee,
    Which beckons me away.

By a falfe heart, and broken vows,
    In early youth I die :
Was I to blame, becaufe the bride
    Is twice as rich as I ?

Ah, Colin, give not her thy vows,
    Vows due to me alone !
Nor thou, fond maid, receive his kifs,
    And think him all thy own !

To-morrow in the church to wed
    Impatient both prepare :
But know, fond maid, and know, falfe man,
    That Lucy will be there.

Then bear my corfe, ye comrades dear,
    The bridegroom blithe to meet ;
He in his wedding-trim fo gay,
    I in my winding-fheet !

She fpoke, and dy'd—her corfe was borne,
    The bridegroom blithe to meet ;
He in his wedding-trim fo gay,
    She in her winding-fheet.

Oh ! what were perjur'd Colin's thoughts !
    How were thofe nuptials kept !

The bride-men flock'd round Lucy dead,
And all the village wept.

Compaffion, fhame, remorfe, defpair,
At once his bofo.n fwell:
The damps of death bedew'd his brows,
He fhook, he groan'd, he fell.

From the vain bride, a bride no more,
The varying crimfon fled;
When, ftretch'd befide her rival's corfe,
She faw her hufband dead.

He to his Lucy's new-made grave,
Convey'd by trembling fwains,
One mold with her, beneath one tod,
For ever now remains.

Oft at this place the conftant hind
And plighted maid are feen:
With garlands gay, and true-love knots
They deck the facred green.

But, fwain forfworn, whoe'er thou art,
This hallow'd fpot forbear!
Remember Colin's dreadful fate,
And fear to meet him there.

SONG 694.

Written by Mr. NICHOLLS.

WITH Phebe, wherever I go,
The gay ones thus fing of my love:
On her cheek what a delicate glow!
Hark! fhe fpeaks like a feraph above.

See her eyes, how delightful they feem!
Brighter far than the brighteft of fpars!
When they deign on poor mortals to beam,
'Fore heaven they rival the ftars!

The red coral imported from far,
The rich balfam the honey-bee fips,
It were folly for us to compare
To the colour and tafte of her lips!

That fhe merits thefe praifes, I own;
That her form is compleatly defign'd,
Will, I think, be refuted by none;
But fhe wants the rare gifts of the mind.

What are eyes, lips, or cheeks, or a mien!
What is all that the fchools can impart!
What's the fineft complexion e'er feen!
If the graces are not in the heart!

Lovely Phebe, henceforward be wife,
Ah! rr'ythee coquette it no more,
Or your fhepherd will furely defpife,
Tho' the fops of the town may adore.

SONG 695.

Written by Mr. LEMOINE.

FAREWEL, ye love-enchanting fhades,
And ev'ry vernal grove;
Adieu, ye moffy woods and glades,
Your paths no more I rove!

No orient blufhes now arife,
To tinge the fpangled dawn;

No foaring pinions reach the fkies,
To hail the infant dawn.

The fhepherd now his crook forfakes,
His pipes and fleecy care;
No mattins warble from the brakes,
Or rend the gloomy air.

Fair Phillis, hear the direful truth,
To nature's laws attend;
Triumph not o'er thy gen'rous youth,
Or mourn the fatal end.

Depend not on thy fading charms,
Or their united pow'r;
Refign them to Amintor's arms,
And blefs the happy hour.

Then fhall life's fpring glide on ferene,
No ruffling tempeft reign;
So fhall you prove love's happy queen,
And blefs a faithful fwain.

SONG 696.

THE DIMPLE.

SILVIA the young, the fair, the gay,
A verdant bow'r inclos'd;
The little wanton, tir'd with play,
In downy fleep repos'd.

A bloom fo like the peach's hue,
Her glowing cheeks exprefs'd,
A bird, deluded, eager flew,
And feiz'd the lufcious feaft.

Ah! lucky fpoil, tho' rude th' alarm,
And Sylvia weeping rofe,
Since to the wound it's fmiling form
That killing dimple owes.

SONG 697.

THE fun was funk beneath the hill,
The weftern clouds were lin'd with gold,
Clear was the fky, the wind was ftill,
The flocks were penn'd within the fold;
When in the filence of the grove
Poor Damon thus defpair'd of love.

Who feeks to pluck the fragrant rofe
From the hard rock or ouzy beach;
Who from each weed that barren grows,
Expects the grape or downy peach;
With equal faith may hope to find
The truth of love in womankind.

No herds have I, no fleecy care,
No fields that wave with golden grain,
No pailures green, or gardens fair,
A woman's venal heart to gain;
Then all in vain my fighs muft prove,
Whofe whole eftate, alas! is love.

How wretched is the faithful youth,
Since women's hearts are bought and fold;
They afk no vows of facred truth,
Whene'er they figh, they figh for gold.
Gold can the frowns of fcorn remove;
But I am fcorn'd—who have but love.

To buy the gems of India's coast
　What wealth, what riches would fuffice?
Yet India's fhore fhould never boaft
　The luftre of thy rival eyes;
For there the world too cheap muft prove;
Can I then buy—who have but love!

Then, Mary, fince nor gems nor ore
　Can with thy brighter felf compare,
Be juft as fair, and value more
　Than gems or ore, a heart fincere:
Let treafure meaner beauties move;
Who pays thy worth, muft pay in love.

SONG 698.

THE ENAMOURED SHEPHERDESS.

Written by Mr. HAWKINS.

THAT little rogue Cupid, I vow,
　Is playing fuch tricks with my heart,
I flutter—I cannot tell how,
　Yet feel the fharp pangs of his dart.
What cruel, ungenerous fwain,
　Could fend this fond urchin to me,
Whofe heart was a ftranger to pain,
　And e'er rov'd as free as a bee.

But now my poor fenfes are gone,
　My fpirits are fled from me quite,
And I'm a poor maiden forlorn,
　No reft can I take day or night.
How happy, ah! once, fure, was I!
　So chearfully rofe in the morn,
But now am addicted to figh
　For him that I treated with fcorn.

Young Caledon muft be the fwain,
　None like him appears to my view;
He caught my fond heart on the plain,
　Ah! fhepherd, I'm wretched for you:
Oh! come then, dear youth, and be kind,
　No longer difdainful I'll be,
But harbour content in my mind,
　And think upon no one but thee.

SONG 699.

THE BACCHANALIAN; A CANTATA.

RECITATIVE.

AS in a tavern toping Lewis drank
　The fparkling juice, in company with
　　Frank;
Tell me, quoth he, can man in joy abound;
For where, unlefs in wine, is pleafure found?

AIR.

Then leave off all thinking,
There's pleafure in drinking,
　That none but a buck can define;
For the bottle and glafs
I prefer to a lafs,
　And would fell the whole fex for good wine.

Oh! could I with eafe
My palate but pleafe,
　Ye gods! how in claret I'd roll;

With a quantum of claret,
　Content in my garret,
　　I'd enjoy both my bottle and bowl.

Then talk not of whoring,
Of ranting, of roaring,
　And kicking a duft up at night;
For I will maintain,
All pleafure is pain,
　Where the bottle procures not delight.

Then replenifh the glafs,
Who denies is an afs,
　The bottle, the flafk, and the bowl;
But he who right thinks,
And like myfelf drinks,
　I pronounce him a buck and a foul.

SONG 700.

CEASE, dear charmer, thus to vex thee,
　Conftant, lo! thy fwain appears;
Let not groundlefs fears perplex thee,
　Faithfulnefs to thee he fwears.
　　Ceafe thy trouble, ceafe thy pain,
　　Never will we part again;
　　Then let calm content and reft
　　Poffefs again thy peaceful breaft.

From thy tender bofom banifh
　All thofe vain tormenting fears;
See, the clouds of forrow vanifh,
　And the fun of joy appears:
　　Thy trial now, fair maid, is o'er,
　　Ne'er fhall thou know forrow more;
　　But together will we prove
　　The joys of conftancy and love.

Now in Hymen's bands united,
　We a happy pair will prove;
Loving each, and each delighted,
　Tafte the joys of truth and love:
　　Then in peace our days fhall flow,
　　Sorrow will we never know;
　　But refign'd to Heav'n's decrees,
　　Live in happinefs and eafe.

SONG 701.

THE HARVEST MORNING; WITH THE SONG OF CORYDON.

Written by Mr. NICHOLLS.

HARK! the fhrill clarion of the diftant vale
　Gladly proclaims the ruddy-rifing day;
Sloth faintly hears the rude, unwelcome tale,
　Juft yawns, then fnores the halefome prime
　　away.

Whilft we, my Phebe, at his call arife,
　Fond as the lark to greet yon glorious blaze,
And as it tints with gold the eaftern fkies,
　Pour forth in fong the great Creator's praife.

See how the hills are burnifh'd by it's beams,
　Each fcene infpires me with a warmth divine:
The mifer wrapt (elate) in golden dreams,
　Feels not in fancy blifs to equal mine.

Hail! genial fovereign of the day!
Dear to the reapers of yon yellow vale,
Who, as they ſtrive beneath thy foſt'ring ray,
Beguile their toil with many a jocund tale.

THE SONG OF CORYDON.

Let fine lordlings in ſplendor remain,
Proud precedency's follow'd by ſtrife;
Still let me a few acres maintain,
And ſtill culture the bleſſings of life:
Onr rural enjoyments no ſtings leave behind,
But courts oft infect both the body and mind.

Me not all their bright circles can pleaſe
Like my reapers fo buſy below;
Like the pippens of gold on my trees,
Or the produce my hop-grounds beſtow:
Their mountains of wealth oft the worthleſs
defend,
Whilſt mine is employ'd for the poor and my
friend.

Let them boaſt of their hangings fo gay,
Of their trappings befpangled with gold;
My py'd meadows more charms can diſplay,
Theſe fern-hills brighter far to behold:
Too oft gaudy dreſs is the villain's difguiſe,
Whilſt virtue in weeds begs the means to ſuffice.

Let them boaſt of their beauties divine,
It were beſt they'd their beauties reclaim,
(But for truth, I would blot out the line)
Baſe incontinence ſullies their fame.
More happy, O Phebe! is Corydon's lot,
With virtue, contentment, and thee, in a cot.

To his ſlaves let the garter-deck'd peer
Roaſt what credulous maids he has won,
They'll ſmile at his vicious career,
And they'll ſmile ſhould they ſee him undone.
Our ruſtics are ſtrangers to flatt'ry and art,
What comes from their lips is the fruit of the
heart.

Lovely virtue again would revive,
O my Phebe! could greatneſs fav this?
Science, commerce, and Britons would thrive,
And our iſle be a garden of bliſs.
For truth upon greatneſs, ah! who can depend!
Full often they'll promiſe, but rarely befriend.

But no more—it becomes not a ſwain
To reflect on the ways of the great;
May we thrive with the reſt of the plain,
And be virtuous, whatever's our fate:
May plenty, my Phebe, return with the ſpring,
And great folks, in virtue, go copy their king.

SONG 702.

WHEN Fanny to woman is growing apace,
The roſe-bud beginning to blow in her face,
For mamma's wiſe precepts ſhe cares not a jot,
Her heart pants for ſomething—ſhe cannot
tell what.

No ſooner the wanton her freedom obtains,
When among the gay youth a tyrant ſhe reigns,
And finding her beauty fuch power has got,
Her heart pants for ſomething—ſhe cannot
tell what.

Tho' all day in ſplendor ſhe flaunts it about,
At court, park and play, the ridotto and rout;
Tho' flatter'd, and envy'd, ſhe pines at her lot,
Her heart pants for ſomething—ſhe cannot
tell what.

A touch of the hand, or a glance of the eye,
From him ſhe likes beſt, makes her ready to die;
Not knowing 'tis Cupid his arrow has ſhot,
Her heart pants for ſomething—ſhe cannot
tell what.

Ye fair take advice, and be bleſs'd while you may,
Each look, word and action, your wiſhes betray;
Give eaſe to your hearts by the conjugal knot,
Tho' they pant e'er fo much—you will foon
know for what.

SONG 703.

BENEATH a cool ſhade, by the ſide of a
ſtream,
Thus breath'd a fond ſhepherd, his Kitty his
theme:
Thy beauties comparing, my deareſt, (faid he,)
There's nothing in nature fo lovely as thee.

Tho' diſtance divides us, I view thy dear face,
And wander, in tranſport, o'er every grace;
Now, now I behold thee, ſweet ſmiling and
pretty;
Oh, gods! you've made nothing fo fair as my
Kitty.

Come, lovely idea, come fill my fond arms!
And whilſt in ſoft raptures I gaze on thy charms,
The beautiful objects which round me ariſe,
Shall yield to thoſe beauties that live in thine
eyes.

Now Flora the meads and the groves does adorn
With flowers and bloſſoms on every thorn;
But look on my Kitty! there ſweetly does blow
A ſpring of more beauties than Flora can ſhow.

See, fee how that roſe there adorns the gay
buſh,
And proud of it's colour, would vie with her
bluſh.
Vain boaſter! thy beauties ſhall quickly decay,
She bluſhes—and fee how it withers away.

Obſerve that fair lily, the pride of the vale,
In whiteneſs unrival'd, now droop and look
pale;
It ſickens, and changes it's beautiful hue,
And bows down it's head in ſubmiſſion to you.

The zephyrs that fan me beneath the cool
ſhade,
When panting with heat on the ground I am
laid,

Are lefs grateful and fweet than the heav'nly
 air
That breathes from her lips, when fhe whifpers—my dear.

I hear the gay lark as he mounts to the fkies,
How fweet are his notes! how delightful his
 voice!
Go dwell in the air, little warbler, go!
I have mufick enough while my Kitty's below.

With pleafure I watch the induftrious bee,
Extracting her fweets from each flower and tree:
Ah, fools! thus to labour to keep you alive;
Fly, fly to her lips, and at once fill your hive.

See there, on the top of that oak, how the doves
Sit brooding each other, and cooing their loves!
Our loves are thus tender, thus mutual our joy,
When folded on each other's bofom we lie.

It glads me to fee how the pretty young lambs
Are fondled, and cherifh'd, and lov'd by their
 dams:
The lambs are lefs pretty, my deareft, than
 thee;
Their dams are lefs fond, nor fo tender as me.

As I gaze on the river, that fmoothly glides by,
Thus even and fweet is her temper, I cry;
Thus clear is her mind, thus calm and ferene;
And virtues, like gems, at the bottom are feen.

Here various flowers ftill paint the gay fcene,
And as fome fade and die, others bud and look
 green;
The charms of my Kitty are conftant as they;
Her virtues will bloom as her beauties decay.

But in vain I compare her; here's nothing fo
 bright,
And darknefs approaches to hinder my fight;
To bed I will haften, and there all her charms,
In fofter ideas, I'll bring to my arms.

SONG 704.

BEAUTY and mufick charm the foul,
 Tho' feparate in the fair;
What mortal can their pow'r controul,
 When Heav'n has join'd them there?

What needed, then, my Cælia's art,
 To fing or touch the lyre?
Your charms before had won my heart,
 'Twas adding flame to fire.

SONG 705.
AUTUMN.
Written by Mr. LEMOINE.

THE fummer's gay, delightful fcene,
 With all it's pleafing charms,
It's golden groves, and polifh'd green,
 Will fink in winter's arms.

Come then, Eliza, let us rove,
 'Midft nature's richeft ftore;
Thofe bounties feize, and feaft like Jove,
 And nature's works explore.

Catch nature's beauties as they roll,
 While mutual paffions charm;
Content fhall harmonize the foul,
 And ev'ry pain difarm.

Then when ftern winter fhakes the world,
 And rapid lightnings fly,
When nature's in confufion hurl'd,
 We'll ev'ry care defy.

SONG 706.

OUR glaffes, waiter, once again fupply,
 Bring t'other dozen, broach the cellar dry;
Let not vacuity the board difgrace,
But with rich claret fill the horrid fpace!
 Potent juice, that rules the earth,
 Infpirer of wit and mirth,
 Source of joys that ne'er decay,
  Ever bubbling,
  Never troubling,
 Always fparkling, brifk and gay!
 Recruit my goblet to the brink,
 I'll fing thy praifes while I drink.

SONG 707.
TO-MORROW.
Written by Mr. NICHOLLS.

WHAT my good fire bequeath'd, when of
 age I poffefs'd,
Then I laugh'd at dull precepts, I drank, and
 I drefs'd;
 A ftranger was I unto forrow:
As wind fpreads the duft, fo my gold fled be-
 fore me,
My fellows pretended to love and adore me;
I never once thought of to-morrow.

The good rules of my grannam entirely forgot,
I was firft at confufion, the beft at a plot,
 And oft wrought the innocent forrow:
The bold miftrefs, the virgin, to me were the
 fame,
Tho' repulfed to-day, 'twas to me lawful game,
If, perchance, they prefented to-morrow.

To mafks, balls, and plays, I would frequently
 treat;
My companions commended a fpirit fo great,
 And oft condefcended to borrow;
Like a lad of high mettle, I lov'd to be free,
I lent them my money and credit with glee,
 And ne'er loft a thought on to-morrow.

The girls of the town fhar'd my bounty profufe;
The tavern-men bow'd as I pafs'd to their
 ftews;
 On this I reflect with much forrow:

MISS BROWN as Daphne in MIDAS

He's as light a Lad to see to.

Song 708

Published as the Act directs, Sep 1 1778.

Oh! could I regain what I've fquander'd on thefe,
My purfe would be full, and my bofom at eafe,
With contentment in ftore for to-morrow.

At the cock-pit and turf I've been often carefs'd
By the high-titled knave with a ftar at his breaft;
Their meannefs has brought me to forrow.
The juftice and curate have fed at mv board,
But now not a dinner thefe harpies afford;
O had I ta'en care for to-morrow.

Ye rakes take the hint, for dame fortune is blind;
Give o'er your purfuits while the deity's kind,
In truth 'twill preferve you from forrow:
The wretches who help you to fquander away,
Will fmile on your folly, and greet you to-day,
But pafs you unnotic'd to-morrow.

S O N G   708.

Sung in *Midas*.

HE's as tight a lad to fee to,
  As e'er ftept in leather fhoe,
And, what's better, he'll love me too,
  And to him I'll prove true blue.

Tho' my fifter cafts a hawk's eye,
  I defy what fhe can do;
He o'erlook'd the little doxy,
  I'm the girl he means to woo.

Hither I ftole out to meet him;
  He'll, no doubt, my fteps purfue:
If the youth prove true, I'll fit him;
  If he's falfe—I'll fit him too.

S O N G   709.

Written by the EDITOR.

AS late the celeftials together were met,
  Invited by Mars to partake of a wet
  Before his defcent from the fkies,
Jolly Bacchus, who fcarce had recover'd from fleep,
Occafion'd by drinking o'er night rather deep,
  Spoke thus as he open'd his eyes.

What fracas has happen'd, good Mars let me know,
Since I've been afleep, 'mongft our vot'ries below,
  That you muft repair to their aid?
I thought that Britannia had fent 'crofs the water
Such terms as could ne'er be refus'd by her daughter,
  And peace all the univerfe fway'd.

So would fhe, indeed, (cry'd the great god of war)
But France has contriv'd the wifh'd union to mar,
  That bafe and ungenerous foe;
Who perfuading the girl to rejoct ev'ry offer
Minerva prevail'd on her mother to proffer,
  To punifh the infult I go.

And determin'd I am, (by the love which I bear
To war, and the goddefs of beauty, I fwear)
  Before my return to the fkies,
Such flaughter this treacherous people fhall know,
My generous Britons, tho' juftly their foe,
  Will beg me to pity their cries.

Since this is the cafe, (reply'd Bacchus) I pray,
To England repair, without farther delay,
  And at once crufh the pow'r of France—
Ganymede, fill the glaffes—but, ere you depart,
Let's all drink Succefs to each true Britifh heart,
  That burns 'gainft the French to advance.

S O N G   710.

THE man who with a gentle heart
  In life ferene fteals through his part,
Needs not the villain's bufy art
  To pile his gold on gold;
Which tho' fecur'd in iron cheft,
Still burns within his tortur'd breaft,
By day and night exiling reft
  From him whofe mind is fold.

If he can boaft a quiet mind,
Domeftic bleffings he fhall find
Under the roof that keeps out wind,
  And all the weather's harm.
The fpear that glows in honour's field;
The fword that fkilful warriours wield;
Nor yet Achilles' well-wrought fhield,
  Need he wifh fuch to arm.

Place me far diftant from thofe plains,
Where ftands no cot, where pipe no fwains,
Where blow bleak winds, where fall the rains,
  And breathes a dang'rous air.
Place me, O Bacchus, near fome cafk,
For ever forc'd to fill my flafk;
With pleafure I'll renew my tafk,
  And blefs my daily care.

S O N G   711.

YOUNG Damon and Chloe were mutually fond,
  They kifs'd and they toy'd all the day;
Kind Hymen confented to finifh the reft,
  And join them for ever and aye.
Some fiend interfer'd, and the rites were delay'd,
  By a circumftance few would fuppofe;
For thoughtlefs young Damon one day as he play'd,
  Prefented to Kitty—a rofe.

Alarm'd at the gift, Chloe rated the youth,
  Fill'd with jealoufy, rage, and difdain;
She call'd him falfe-hearted, perfidious and bafe,
  And inftant'y quitted the plain.
He endeavour'd his innocence vainly to prove,
  No words could her paffion compofe:
Such prefents, fhe faid, were fure emblems of love,
  And Kitty accepted—the rofe.

A a

To the church, or the wake, or wherever she
 went,
He follow'd in hopes of relief;
Obdurate the fair, and regardless beheld
The type of his penitence—grief.
Tho' seldom, if ever, she deign'd a reply,
'Twas only to add to his woes!
No art shall e'er win me again to comply;
Remember, young Damon, the—rose.

For ever refus'd, when he knew that his heart
To Chloe was virtuous and true,
He thought 'twas too much; so neglected
 the fair,
Another more kind to pursue.
This treatment at length so afflicted the maid,
She sought him her mind to compose;
He gladly consented, and soon they were wed,
And Chloe ne'er thinks of—the rose.

SONG 712.

DORINDA was youthful, and blooming as
 May,
Would dance, and would sing, and would frolic,
 and play;
Yet some how or other, it came so to pass,
In secret she often was heard cry Alas!

Her companions in vain did the meaning ex-
 plore,
She promis'd, indeed, she would do so no more;
Yet her promise was frail, and as brittle as glass,
For immediately after she cry'd out Alas!

In secret to sigh, as old gossips declare,
Is an evident sign of some terrible care,
And in time will destroy e'en a form strong
 as brass;
Yet Dorinda continu'd to sigh out Alas!

Her friends and acquaintance convey'd the news
 round,
That Dorinda was sick, but of what was not
 found;
That certainly flesh was no more than the grass,
And Dorinda would certainly die of Alas!

Young Damon, a shepherd, that liv'd in the
 place,
Who by accident heard of her terrible case:
Determin'd to try if it might come to pass,
And ventur'd himself for the cure of Alas!

He kiss her, he press'd her, he vow'd and he
 sigh'd,
And shortly prevail'd on her to be his bride:
This circumstance only has alter'd the case,
And Dorinda is cur'd from sighing Alas!

SONG 713.

BEFORE I saw Clarinda's face
My heart was blithe and gay,
Free as the wind, or feather'd race
That hop from spray to spray.

But now dejected I appear,
Clarinda proves unkind,
I sighing drop the silent tear,
But no relief can find.

In plaintive notes my tale rehearse;
When I the fair have found;
On ev'ry tree appears my verse
That to her praise resounds.

But the ungrateful shuns my sight,
My faithful love disdains;
My vows and tears her scorn excite,
Another happy reigns.

Ah, Thyrsis, though my looks betray
I envy your success;
Yet love to friendship shall give way,
I cannot wish it less.

SONG 714.

SWEET Sally to suffer ordains me,
To languish, to sigh and despair;
By her looks, I perceive she disdains me;
So cruel she is, tho' so fair:
What fate is as wretched as mine is,
If Sally my love does neglect!
And tho' in my eyes she divine is,
Yet to gain her I ne'er can expect.

If from Sally a smile I discover,
It softens my present distress;
Tho' I fear she is loving another,
Yet still I'm in hopes of success:
But when I reflect at my leisure,
I perceive my endeavours are vain;
For how can I gain that blest pleasure
The gods for themselves do ordain.

Was to me, then, my Sally but giv'n,
Oh! what would my pleasure destroy!
For nothing on earth, nor in heav'n,
Could equal that moment of joy:
For since I have known the dear creature,
This reason I have for my fears;
Sweet Sally's a goddess in feature,
Tho' she but a woman appears.

SONG 715.

CUPID DROWN'D.

YE rosy-fac'd sons of the rich purple juice,
Attend to the carrol I now shall produce;
What subject so noble to chaunt o'er our bowls,
As that which we know will make happy our
 souls.

To make me in love, and appear like an ass,
And kneel at the feet of each proud forward lass,
The goddess of beauty has long strove in vain,
For love while I've liquor shall ne'er give me
 pain.

At length quite enrag'd that a mortal like me
Should laugh at her power and yet remain free,
The urchin young Cupid she bade quickly fly,
And never return till he made me comply.

The youth left Olympus to old England he came,
Discover'd my haunts, chose a dart, took his aim;
But 'ere he had time to pursue his design,
I plung'd him headlong in a hogshead of wine.

And now there's an end of that troublesome boy,
The pleasures of wine we may freely enjoy;
Let Sol round the globe roll as fast as he will,
The bottle and glass shall keep up with him still.

SONG 716.

Written by Mr. W—LL—S.

LOVELY nymph! oh, cease to grieve me;
   Cease to wound my tender heart;
For your frowns—you may believe me—
   Prove the cause of all my smart.

Deign! O Sylvia, to reward me;
   With compassion view your swain;
Do not cruelly discard me;
   Quickly ease me of my pain.

Would you, Sylvia, would you render
   Your adorer greatly blest;
Of his heart accept the tender,
   Then you'll see his tortur'd breast.

SONG 717.

A NAVAL CANTATA.

Written by Mr. MAVOR.

RECITATIVE.

'TWAS night—and Luna, 'midst her glow-
      ing train,
Reflective play'd upon the azure main,
As late I wander'd on the shelly shore,
Where not a gale inspir'd the wavy roar;
Where silence seem'd her awful court to keep,
And ocean to partake oblivious sleep;—
When lo! before my fear-astonish'd eyes,
I saw a form of angel brightness rise:
Fair as the goddess of the briny flood,
Supported by a spear, upright she stood:
Around her feet the nereids joy'd to play,
And waves, as she advanc'd, to form a way.
Her port majestic, soon, and pensive smile,
Betray'd the Genius of Britannia's isle:
O'ercome with awe, I press'd the humble ground;
When thus she spoke, in heav'nly breathing
      found,
And bade me learn the strains, and tell the world
      around.

AIR.

Awake! my sons, to empire born,
   Shake off despondency and fear;
'Tis yours to make the treach'rous mourn,
   That oft have drawn my briny tear.
      Again the British flag unfurl,
      Destruction on proud Gallia hurl,
      And strike with dread the distant world,

Have I not seen your navy ride
   Triumphant o'er the boundless main,
Confess'd the terror and the pride
   Of all that cut the liquid plain?
      Again the British flag, &c.

And will you less exert your sway,
   When glory calls, and ardent fame!
Say, can my sons mistake the way,
   When rouz'd by Keppel's honour'd name!
      Again the British flag, &c.

Tho' laurell'd Hawke, and Bristol, bear
   No ensigns on the foaming tide,
Some valiant heroes still prepare
   To spread your awful thunder wide.
      Again the British flag, &c.

'Tis Heav'n that orders Britain's race
   To check each vain aspiring foe;
To raise th'oppress'd, with manly grace,
   And soothe the wrinkled face of woe,
      Again the British flag, &c.

Then haste, O haste! and bid your arms
   Their flaming terrors shed afar;
Harrass each foe with fierce alarms,
   And give a loose to crimson war,
      Again the British flag, &c.

'Tis fell necessity commands;
   You stand upon the verge of fate:
And future times will curse the hands
   That for Britannia fought too late.
      Again the British flag, &c.

Tho' peace, with olive-branches crown'd,
   Long hover'd o'er this happy isle,
She sinks—she sinks—in tumults drown'd,
   And bids you think of warlike toil.
      Again the British flag, &c.

For peace and war my sons are fit,
   In arts and arms they shine the same;
And time will raise another PITT,
   To add fresh fewel to their flame.
      Again the British flag, &c.

Know! he that in his country's cause
   Th'infernal sword of treachery braves,
Tho' doom'd to fate, shall gain applause
   While Britain sees encircling waves.
      Again the British flag, &c.

The sculptur'd monument shall tell
   The martial prowess of his arm;
And emblems pointing how he fell,
   Shall youth with emulation warm.
      Again the British flag, &c.

RECITATIVE.

She said—the curling waves began to flow,
To lash the rocks, and whiten into snow;
Around her each Cerulean goddess throngs,
While vows for Britain breath'd from num'-
      rous tongues.
And swift this order echo'd round the shore;
Britannia rule the waves, till time shall be no
      more.

AIR.

Then nobly keep your charter giv'n,
Ye race to freedom dear !
The fiat of all-potent Heav'n
May well difpel your fear.

Tho' factions fhake your empire wide,
By fatal rigour fown ;
You ftill may ftem the adverfe tide,
And call the world your own.

If prudence would direct your pow'r,
And reafon fway the ftate ;
Your valour might the world fecure,
And yield to nought but fate.

SONG 718.

THE PORTRAIT.

Written by Mr. LEMOINE.

WHILE others, on pleafure's foft bofom
    reclin'd,
Seek rapt'rous joys to obtain ;
Let me picture happinefs far more refin'd,
Where beauty and innocence reign.

My Laura's the fpot where thofe jewels unite,
In her ev'ry virtue's difplay'd ;
Peace, order, and harmony, ftrongly invite
All eyes to adore the fair maid.

Tho' angelic beauties encircle her face;
Tho' her eyes are the index of love ;
Tho' her delicate features difplay ev'ry grace,
And her fhape would an anchorite move :

Tho' more than enchantment poffeffes her voice;
Tho' her tongue foft perfuafion can boaft ;
Tho' her outward perfections make nature
    rejoice,
And pale envy confume to a ghoft :

Yet her mental attractions no pen can unfold,
No tongue can her virtues difplay ;
Defcription, tho' glowing, feems lifelefs and
    cold,
And fails her leaft worth to difplay.

Good-humour eternally reigns o'er her mind,
Which brightens the charms of her face;
Whilft wit, void of malice, by reafon refin'd,
Enlivens each perfonal grace.

SONG 719.

VARIETY.

Written by Mr. R. DAWRE.

SOULS who in gay circles move,
    While from fcene to fcene ye rove,
Seeking pleafure, look on me,
Source of blifs, Variety.

See bright Phœbus, how he fhines!
No one fpot his beam confines ;
Round the world his courfers flee,
Seeking dear Variety.

Be the wretch with gold poffeft;
Let the fot with wine be bleft ;
Laurell'd let ambition be,
Give me dear Variety.

Would you lafting pleafures tafte,
Such as ne'er can cloy nor wafte ;
From folly, care, and difcord, free;
Seek them in Variety.

All ye powers of joy and mirth,
Bring your choiceft treafures forth ;
Mufic, fong, and dance, and glee,
Blended with Variety.

But when love demands the theme,
Then I quite avert my fcheme ;
Nancy's heart's enough for me,
Tho' my name's Variety.

SONG 720.

RING the bell, and fill the bowl,
Wine infpires the jovial fong ;
Care fhall never dare controul,
    While liquor can our mirth prolong.

Come, ye youths, who figh and pine
For fome filly fickle fair ;
Come, and drown in fparkling wine,
All your folly, all your care.

Ye wretches on whom fortune frowns,
Whom duns and creditors befet,
Good ftore of wine will troubles drown,
Come drink yourfelves quite out of debt.

Ye hufbands who have fcolding wives,
Come here, and leave the fhrews at home ;
With Comus lead more happy lives,
Come, hafte away, O! pr'ythee, come.

SONG 721.

WHILST I am caroufing to chear up my foul,
    Oh ! how I triumph to fee a full bowl !
    This is the treafure,
    The only pleafure,
The bleffing that makes me rejoice and fing.
    Thus while I am drinking,
    Free from dull thinking,
Then I am greater than the greateft king.

SONG 722.

MY Sylvia is the blitheft lafs
    That ever trod the downy grafs,
    Or grac'd the rural plain ;
Her modeft air, and gentle mien,
More fweet, more fair, than beauty's queen,
Are prais'd by ev'ry fwain.

Her fparkling eyes, like diamonds bright;
Each winning charm does there unite
    With features fair and gay ;
Her voice is fofter than the thrufh,
That fweetly warbles on the bufh,
    And hails return of day.

Her breath exceeds the balmy gales,
Whose fragrance sweetens all the vales,
Where sweets with sweets combine;
Her cheeks the roses far excel,
Such virtues in her bosom dwell,
As make her all divine.

Each rising morn I press'd the fair
To listen to my fervent prayer,
A pray'r devoid of art:
With pleasing smiles she sooth'd my pains;
And Sylvia, now, in triumph reigns
The goddess of my heart.

SONG 723.

A HUNTING SONG.

ROUZE, rouze, jolly sportsmen, the hounds
  are all out,
The chase is began, I declare;
Come, up too and horse, let us follow the rout,
  And join in the chace of the hare.
Hark! hark! don't you hear, they are now in
  the vale;
The horn, how melodious it sounds!
Poor puss in a fright, how she strives to prevail,
And fly from the cry of the hounds!

Tho' up to the hills and mountains she scales,
  Whose tops seem to join in the sky;
We mount in the air, like a kite in a gale,
  And follow the hounds in full cry.
Tho' into the cople, she for refuge there flies,
  We kill her, 'tis twenty the odds;
While echo surrounds us with hooting and
  cries,
  We seem to converse with the gods.

Our freedom with conscience is never alarm'd,
  We are strangers to envy and strife;
When blest with a wife, we return to her arms;
  Sport sweetens the conjugal life.
Our days pass away in a scene of delight
  Which kings and their courtiers ne'er taste;
In pleasures of love we revel all night,
  Next morning return to the chace.

SONG 724.

IN PRAISE OF WOMEN.

THE lily, and the blushing rose,
  To many give delight;
But not a flow'r on earth that grows,
  Is half so bright a sight,
    As lovely women,
    Charming women,
    Pleasing, teizing,
    Heav'nly women.

Pray what makes cowards brave and bold,
  Or what gave poets birth?
Or what makes people fond of gold,
  Or pleasure dwell on earth?
    But lovely women, &c.

When men are sore oppress'd with grief,
  And roam in search of peace;
There's nought can give such sure relief,
  And make their torments cease.
    Such pow'r have women, &c.

Then, since the fair give such delight,
  Aloud resound their praise;
For who can view 'the glorious sight,
  And not their voices raise,
    To lovely women, &c.

SONG 725.

PORTER WILL; A CANTATA.

RECITATIVE.

AS porter Will along St. Paul's did move,
  Depress'd with weighty load, but more by
  love,
By chance the fair Ceriffa there he found,
Crying her fine heart-cherries, round and found,
Will, joyous, instant pitch'd, then straight
  caress'd her,
And leaning o'er the barrow, thus address'd her:

AIR.

Thy lips are cherries, sweeter far
Than those which in the barrow are;
With such a store of charms, 'tis well
You may have stolen hearts to sell.
Mine, dear Ceriffa, too, you know,
You stole it from me long ago;
And now I stoop to ask of thee,
To give it back, or marry me.

RECITATIVE.

Ceriffa archly leering as he spake,
While all the cherry blushed on her cheek,
The mellowest fruit, unnotic'd cull'd apace,
And sent like thunder at his doleful face;
Then grasp'd her barrow, trundled soft along,
And looking round at Will, triumphant sung.

AIR.

Shall I, possess'd of all these charms,
Sleep nightly in a porter's arms!
M' ambitious soul detests such scum,
And sighs for conquests yet to come.
Fair youths my sov'reign power shall feel!
Ten thousand hearts I daily steal,
And beauteous nymphs shall envious see
Crown'd heads and dukes submit to me.

SONG 726.

RETURN'D, return'd the season of delight!
  Most welcome to the long-deluded sight!
The earth and sky, conspire to chear the soul,
And grateful joy salutes and crowns the whole.

Love calls, love calls, and Hymen leads the
  way;
The ruddy youth and maiden chaste obey:
The silken band of holy friendship tie,
And healthful raise a beauteous progeny.

Roll on, roll on, thou lively, nimble flood,
Of wanton spirits gay, and youthful blood;
Th' impatient lover ne'er shall know remorse,
If truth and honour guide his rapid course.

Strike up, strike up, add music to the feast,
Where love presides, and friendship is a guest;
Subservient music, friendship, wit, and wine,
To the bright pow'rs of female face divine.

SONG 727.

NANNY blushes when I won her,
And, with kindly-chiding eyes,
Faintly says I shall undo her,
Faintly, O forbear, she cries;
But her breasts when I am pressing,
When to her's my lips I join,
Warm'd, she seems to taste the blessing,
And her kisses answer mine.

SONG 728.

Written by E. Y.

MEN high in power, tho' darlings of mankind,
The rural, calm delights, but seldom find;
By day and night so many cares intrude,
They rarely share the sweets of solitude.
And when they seem retir'd from grand affairs,
Their inward thoughts are seldom free from
cares:
For being of so high a sphere possess'd,
They are, at once, both envy'd and caress'd.

But men of fortune, in a lower sphere,
Pleasure, content, and peace, serenely share;
No fawning suitors on their rising wait,
No injur'd poor stand mourning at their gate,
No piercing sighs nor blasted hopes are heard,
No close designs to ruin them are fear'd;
Freed from the troubles that the great molest,
They live in peace, and are the truly blest.

SONG 729.

SIR LANCELOT DU LAKE;

AN OLD BALLAD.

WHEN Arthur first in court began,
And was approved king,
By force of arms great victories wan,
And conquest home did bring:

Then into England straight he came
With fifty good and able
Knights, that resorted unto him,
And were of his round-table:

And he had justs and turnaments,
Whereto were many prest;
Wherein some knights did them excel,
And far surmount the rest.

But one Sir Lancelot du Lake,
Who was approved well,
He for his deeds and feats of arms,
All others did excel,

When he had rested him awhile,
In play, and game, and sport,
He said he would go prove himself
In some advent'rous sort.

He armed rode in forest wide,
And met a damsel fair,
Who told him of adventures great,
Whereto he gave good ear.

Such would I find, quoth Lancelot;
For that cause came I hither.
Thou seemst, quoth she, a knight full good,
And I will bring thee thither.

Whereas a mighty knight doth dwell,
That now is of great fame;
Therefore tell me what wight thou art,
And what may be thy name.

My name is Lancelot du Lake.
Quoth she, It likes me then;
Here dwells a knight who never was
Yet match'd with any man;

Who has in prison threescore knights
And four, that he did wound:
Knights of King Arthur's court they be,
And of his table round.

She brought him to a river side,
And also to a tree;
Whereon a copper bason hung,
And many shields to see.

He struck so hard, the bason broke;
And Tarquin soon he spy'd:
Who drove a horse before him fast,
Whereon a knight lay ty'd.

Sir Knight, then said Sir Lancelot,
Bring me that horse-load hither,
And lay him down, and let him rest;
We'll try our force together:

For, as I understand, thou hast,
So far as thou art able,
Done great despite and shame unto
The knights of the round-table,

If thou be of the table round,
Quoth Tarquin speedily,
Both thee and all thy fellowship
I utterly defy.

That's over much, quoth Lancelot;
Defend thee by and by.
They set their spears unto their steeds,
And each at other fly.

They couch'd their spears, (their horses ran
As though there had been thunder)
And struck them each amidst their shields,
Wherewith they broke in sunder.

Their horses backs brake under them,
The knights were both astound:
To avoid their horses they made haste,
And light upon the ground.

They took them to their shields full fast,
Their swords they drew out then,
With mighty strokes most eagerly
Each at the other ran;

They wounded were, and bled full fore,
For breath they both did ftand ;
And leaning on their fwords awhile,
Quoth Tarquin, Hold thy hand,

And tell to me what I fhall afk.
Say on, quoth Lancelot, tho'.
Thou art, quoth Tarquin, the beft knight
That ever I know !

And like a knight, that I did hate ;
So that thou be not he,
I will deliver all the reft,
And eke accord with thee.

That is well faid, quoth Lancelot ;
But fince it muft be fo,
What knight is that thou hateft thus ;
I pray thee to me fhow ?

His name is Lancelot du Lake,
He flew my brother dear ;
Him I fufpect of all the reft ;
I would I had him here !

Thy wifh thou haft, but yet unknown,
I am Lancelot du Lake,
Now knight of Arthur's table round ;
King Haud's fon of Schuwake ;

And I defire thee do thy worft.
Ho, ho, quoth Tarquin tho',
One of us two fhall end our lives
Before that we do go.

If thou be Lancelot du Lake,
Then welcome fhalt thou be ;
Wherefore fee thou thyfelf defend,
For now defy I thee.

They buckled then together fo,
Like unto wild boars rufhing,
And with their fwords and fhields they ran
At one another flafhing !

The ground befprinkled was with blood ;
Tarquin began to yield ;
For he gave back for wearinefs,
And low did bear his fhield.

This foon Sir Lancelot efpy'd,
He leapt upon him then,
He pull'd him down upon his knee,
And rufhing off his helm,

Forthwith he ftruck his neck in two ;
And, when he had fo done,
From prifon threefcore knights and four
Deliver'd every one.

SONG 730.

THO' envious old age age feems in part to
impare me,
And makes me the fport of the wanton and
gay ;
Brifk wine fhall recruit, as life's winter fhall
wear me,
And I ftill have a heart to do what I may.

Then, Venus, beftow me fome damfel of beauty,
As Bacchus fhall lend me a cherifhing glafs ;

To Selena the Great they fhall both pay their
duty,
We'll firft clafp the bottle, and then clafp
the lafs ;
The bottle and lafs,
The lafs and the bottle ;
We'll firft clafp the bottle, and then clafp
the lafs.

SONG 731.

PLUTUS, vain is all your vaunting,
Wit muft life with blifs fupply ;
Gold, alas! fhould wit be wanting,
Would not find a joy to buy.
Wit, alone, creates the bleffing
Which exchang'd for gold you fhare ;
Sterling gold, alone, poffeffing,
What has man but gloom and care?

Wit, of ev'ry art devifer,
Ev'ry paffion can controul ;
Can to pity move the mifer,
Can with mirth dilate the foul.
Gold itfelf, on wit depending,
Thence derives it's utmoft power ;
Folly all profufely fpending,
Folly hoarding all, is poor.

SONG 732.

WHILE on my Colin's knee I fit,
Lur'd by thy voice, charm'd with thy wit,
My panting heart true meafure beats,
And gladly ev'ry figh repeats :
I figh with joy, that thou may'ft fee
I fympathize in all with thee.

No matter how the ice was broke,
Or whether you or I firft fpoke ;
Who only barter love for love,
The nicenefs of the paffion prove ;
For oft ingratitude we give,
And fometimes gen'roufly receive.

Leveil'd by love, let neither try,
To fix fuperiority ;
Since all the kind, the fond conteft,
Of whether you or I love beft,
Like heedlefs touching a wrong key,
But jars the found of harmony.

SONG 733.

THE month of September
I well fhall remember,
On account of the flames and the fire,
With which Juliet the nun,
Full of frolic and fun,
Singe'd the heart of the am'rous friar.

The force of her kiffes,
And melting careffes,
I'll with pleafure and extafy own ;
For moft certain it is,
That one balmy kifs
From her lips, would enliven a ftone.

Then be filent, ye fools,
Who by mufty dull rules,
Pretend your fierce paffions to tame;
For without the bleft aid
Of a kind-hearted maid,
Life is nothing but forrow and pain.

SONG 734.

CHEVAUX DE FRIZE CAPS.

NO longer let war be ufurp'd by the men,
Nor let them campaign it again and again;
For the ladies have robb'd em, and now, when
they pleafe,
Can fight with their weapons, the Chevaux de
Frize.

No longer it's needful to follow commanders,
To America, Germany, France, or to Flanders;
Walk but the Mall, and each nymph that one
fees,
Can teach us the ufe of the Chevaux de Frize.

By the maxim of armies, indeed, we muft own,
They've been hitherto us'd as defenfive alone ;
But the ladies, not govern'd by maxims like
thefe,
Both attack and defend with their Chevaux de
Frize.

Befides, in the field, it muft not be forgot,
Thefe warlike machines were fix'd on the fpot;
But the ladies (fo little their practice agrees)
All carry about them their Chevaux de Frize.

Thus fatally arm'd at all points to annoy;
Before, or behind, on each fide they deftroy:
No fafe-guard in diftance; they kill us with
eafe,
If we dare but to look at their Chevaux de Frize.

SONG 735.

A HUNTING CANTATA.

Sung at MARYBONE.

RECITATIVE.

AWAK'D by the horn, like the fpring, deckt
in green,
Betimes in the morning the hunters are feen ;
With joy on each brow they enliven the place,
And impatiently wait to join in the chace.

AIR.

From his clofe covert rouz'd, the ftag fwiftly
flies, ·
As the arrow that's fhot from the bow;
O'er rivers and mountains all danger defies,
And fears nothing but man, his worft foe.

RECITATIVE.

Now they trace him thro' the copfe,
Panting, ftruggling—fee! he drops:
Hark ! rude clamours rend the fkies,
While the dappled victim dies.

AIR.

Thus Britain's fons, in Harry's reign,
Purfu'd the trembling Gaul,
Thro' ftreams of blood, o'er hills of flain,
And triumph'd at his fall.

CHORUS.

Now hoftile foes alarm; arm, arm, Britannia,
arm.

RECITATIVE.

Then away to the field, 'tis great George gives
the word,
Quit the horn for the trumpet, the whip for
the fword;
Like our valiant fore-fathers, ftern death let
us face,
And be glorious in war as we are in the chace.

SONG 736.

THE AGED LOVER RENOUNCETH LOVE ;

AN OLD BALLAD.

I Lothe that I did love,
In youth that I thought fweet,
As time requires; for my behove
Methinks they are not meet.

My lufts they do me leave,
My fancies all are fled;
And tract of time begins to weave
Grey hairs upon my head.

For age with ftealing fteps,
Hath claw'd me with his crutch,
And lufty youth away he leaps,
As there had been none fuch.

My mufe doth not delight
Me, as fhe did before;
My hand and pen are not in plight,
As they have been of yore.

For reafon me denies
All youthly idle rime;
And day by day to me fhe cries,
Leave off thefe toys in time.

The wrinkles in my brow,
The furrows in my face,
Say, Limping age will lodge him now,
Where youth muft give him place.

The harbinger of death,
To me I fee him ride;
The cough, the cold, the gafping breath,
Doth bid me to provide

A pikeaxe and a fpade,
And eke a fhrouding fheet,
A houfe of clay for to be made
For fuch a gueft moft meet. ·

Methinks I hear the clerk,
That knolls the careful knell,
And bids me leave my weary work.
Ere nature me compel.

My keepers knit the knot,
That youth. doth laugh to fcorn,

Of me that shall be clean forgot,
　As I had ne'er been born.

Thus must I youth give up,
　Whose badge I long did wear:
To them I yield the wanton cup,
　That better may it bear.

Lo here the bared skull;
　By whose bald sign I know,
That stooping age away shall pull
　What youthful years did sow.

For beauty with her band,
　These crooked cares had wrought,
And shipp'd me into the land
　From whence I first was brought.

And ye that bide behind,
　Have ye none other trust?
As ye of clay were cast by kind,
　So shall ye turn to dust.

SONG 737.

COME, thou rosy dimpled boy,
　Source of every heart-felt joy;
Leave the blissful bow'rs awhile,
Paphos, and the Cyprian isle;
Visit Britain's rocky shore,
Britons, too, thy pow'r adore;
Britons, hardy, bold and free,
Own thy laws, and yield to thee:
Source of ev'ry heart-felt joy,
Come, thou rosy dimpled boy.

Haste to Sylvia, haste away,
This is thine and Hymen's day;
Bid her thy soft bandage wear,
Bid her for love's rites prepare;
Let the nymphs, with many a flow'r,
Deck the sacred nuptial bow'r,
Thither lead the lovely fair,
And let Hymen, too, be there:
This is thine and Hymen's day;
Haste to Sylvia, haste away.

Only while we love we live,
Love alone can pleasure give;
Pow'r, and pomp, and tinsel state,
Idle pageants of the great;
Crowns and sceptres, envy'd things,
And the pride of Eastern kings,
Are but childish, empty toys,
When compar'd to love's sweet joys.
Love alone can pleasure give;
Only while we love we live.

SONG 738.

A SCOTCH BALLAD.

Sung at VAUXHALL.

ALL on the pleasant banks of Tweed,
　Young Jockey won my heart;
None tun'd so sweet his oaten reed,
　None sung with so much art:
　　His skilful tale,
　　Did soon prevail

To make me fondly love him;
　But now he hies,
　Nor hears my cries,
I wou'd I ne'er had seen him.

When first we met, the bonny swain
　Of aought but love could say:
Oh! give (he cry'd) my heart again,
　You've stole my heart away;
　　Or else incline,
　　To give me thine,
And I'll together join 'em:
　My faithful heart
　Will never part.
Ah! why did I believe him!

Not now my slighted face he knows,
　His soon-forgotten dear;
To a wealthier lass o'erjoy'd he goes,
　To breathe his falshood there:
　　Mistaken Kate,
　　The swain's a cheat,
Not for a moment trust him:
　For shining gold,
　He's bought and sold,
I wou'd I had not seen him.

SONG 739.

A HUNTING SONG.

Sung at VAUXHALL.

TO chace o'er the plain the fox or the hare,
　Such pleasure no sport can e'er bring;
It banishes sorrow, and drives away care,
　And makes us more blest than a king:
Whenever we hear the sound of the horn,
　Our hearts are transported with joy;
We rise and embrace, with the earliest dawn,
　A pastime that never can cloy.

O'er furrows and hills our game we pursue,
　No danger our breast can invade;
The hounds in full cry our joys will renew,
　And increase the pleasures display'd;
The freedom our conscience never alarms,
　We live free from envy and strife;
If blest with a spouse return to her arms,
　Sports, sweetness, and conjugal life.

The courtier who toils o'er matters of state,
　Can ne'er such a happiness know;
The grandeur and pomp enjoy'd by the great,
　Can ne'er such a comfort bestow:
Our days pass away in scenes of delight,
　Our pleasure's ne'er taken amiss:
We hunt all the day, and revel all night;
　What joy can be greater than this?

SONG 740.

BRITANNIA; A CANTATA.

RECITATIVE.

WHEN discord ceas'd, and bloody broils no
　more
In war destructive shook this happy shore;
When carnage ceas'd, and death refus'd to
　stain
With British blood the dreadful martial plain;

Britannia rofe, and with a graceful fmile,
In gentle accents, thus addrefs'd her ifle.

AIR.

Ye Britons, what nation but England can fing,
    In freedom we rife ev'ry day ;
In freedom we fleep, and are bleft with a king
    'Tis a pleafure in all to obey :
    Then, my children, encreafe
    The fweet bleffings of peace,
Let trumpets in melody join ;
    While truth fhall proclaim
    George's virtues and fame,
Which on record for ever will fhine.

RECITATIVE.

The found feraphic reach'd the royal ear,
And gazing crowds the heav'nly accents hear ;
Reviving joy returns in ev'ry breaft,
War difappear'd, and peace the kingdom bleft ;
The happy ifle no greater bleffing feeks.
The monarch rifes, and thus nobly fpeaks :

AIR.

Britannia, be affur'd, I pride to fee
Myfelf the monarch of a people free ;
Happy to govern o'er this blifsful ifle,
Where bleffings on my fubjects ever fmile ;
As long as I the royal fceptre bear,
My country's good fhall be my greateft care ;
May peace continue, nor my people know
The cafual griefs which from Bellona flow ;
Firm to Britannia's caufe my arms fhall fleep,
As long as England's foes their treaties keep ;
But if my lion is induc'd to roar,
Deftruction hovers round the Gallic fhore.

SONG 741.

Sung in ALFRED.

AS calms fucceed when ftorms are paft,
    And ftill the raging main ;
So love will have it's hour at laft,
    And borrow fweets from pain.

No more I'll fhun the face of day,
    Within thefe fhades to mourn ;
All joys with Alfred fled away,
    All meet in his return.

SONG 742.

Sung at VAUXHALL.

YOUNG Strephon, the artlefs, the dangerous fwain,
My love and efteem has attempted to gain ;
With the fame wicked arts he foeft had betray'd,
He thought to feduce one more innocent maid :
But appriz'd of his pow'r, of my weaknefs aware,
I baffled his fcheme, and avoided the fnare ;
For virtue I love, and was taught in my dawn,
When I gather'd the rofe, to beware of the thorn.

His tears I neglected, his oaths I defpis'd,
For his heart by thofe tears, by thofe oaths he difguis'd ;

What prefents he brought me I chofe to decline,
(The prodigal bounty of art and defign :)
He coax'd and he flatter'd, but flatter'd in vain,
And practis'd each art on my weaknefs to gain ;
Protected by prudence, I laugh'd him to fcorn,
Tho' I fancy'd the rofe, yet I dreaded the thorn.

He wantonly boafted what nymphs he had won,
What credulous beauties his arts had undone ;
He fwore that his faith fhould inviolate be,
That his heart and thofe fair-ones were victims to me :
I told him thofe victims and faith I'd defpife,
And from fuch examples would learn to be wife ;
That I never would proftitute virtue to fcorn,
Or fmell at the rofe to be hurt by the thorn.

Was the perjur'd betrayer afham'd of his guilt,
Was his paffion on virtue, not wantonnefs, built ;
Was his heart as fincere as his oaths are profane,
I could fancy (I own, I could fancy) the fwain :
But experience has taught me 'tis dang'rous to truft,
And folly to think he can ever be juft :
So I'll ftifle my flame, and reject him with fcorn ;
Left I grafp at the rofe, and be hurt by the thorn.

SONG 743.

Sung at SADLER's WELLS.

GOOD mother, if you pleafe, you may
    Place others to obferve my way ;
Or be yourfelf the watchful fpy,
And keep me ever in your eye :
Unlefs the will itfelf reftrain,
The care of others is in vain ;
And if myfelf I do not keep,
Inftead of watching, you may fleep.

When you forbid what love infpires,
Forbidding, you but fan it's fires ;
Reftraint does appetite enrage,
And youth may prove too ftrong for age :
Then leave me unconfin'd and free,
With prudence for my lock and key ;
For if myfelf I do not keep,
Inftead of watching, all may eep.

SONG 744.

RETIR'D from the crowd, in a calm, filent fpot,
Pallas, Freedom, Aftræa, together were got,
From the noife of the boifterous gods far remov'd,
To relate why the people they'd left they once lov'd.

Sage Pallas obferv'd, that the wifh of her heart,
Was to make them fuperior in arms and in art :
That, thro' Pitt, fhe advis'd them to do what was right ;
But her plans (by her form'd) they had treated with flight.

Fair Freedom next faid, On that long favour'd
   fhore,
I once thought to have fettled, till time was
   no more ;
But, in Wilkes, they refus'd to fubmit to my
   reign :
So, rejected, I fled, with each blifs in my train.

Stern Juftice declar'd, while they practis'd
   her laws,
Thro' the univerfe round fhe fupported their
   caufe ;
But, indignant, fhe lately had left them with
   pain,
For her favourite Pratt had advis'd them in vain.

Britannia, (tho' fad, yet majeftic,) appear'd,
And thus her fons fuit for her children preferr'd :
Return, my dear fifters ! oh would you return !.
No more they'd reject you, no longer I'd mourn !

In vain, fays ftern Juftice ; your pray'r comes
   too late;
'Tis determin'd by Jove, and enrolled by fate,
That we ne'er muft return, (fo 'tis weak to
   difpute)
Whilft you, or your fons, cherifh ** and **.

SONG 745.

A BALLAD FOR THE YEAR 1758.

LAST year all the cry
   Was, that taxes ran high,
And the revenue funk by foul play;
   That our fleets were defeated,
   Our armies ill-treated,
And commerce quite gone to decay.

   Port Mahon we had loft,
   And our fleets on the coaft
Paraded, but dare not attack ;
   That they went with a fhow
   Of a terrible blow,
But return'd moft inglorioufly back.

   For the fcourge of our foes,
   A Pitt then arofe,
Th' afferter of liberty's caufe ;
   Corruption then fled,
   Nor could vice fhew her head,
For virtue was guarded by laws.

   The trumpet of fame,
   Then founded the name
Of Howe; to Gallia he paft,
   And bid her prepare
   Such a clarion to hear
That the bulwarks fhould fhake at the blaft.

   Nor warn'd he in vain,
   For France once again
Felt the force of a maritime pow'r;
   Britifh hearts were employ'd,
   French ftrength was deftroy'd,
And her conquefts were talk'd of no more.

Bofcawen went forth,
   And far in the north
Spread the glories of Britain's fair ifle:
   Old Neptune and Mars
   Grant fuccefs to the tars,
And the heavens propitioufly fmile.

   Cape Breton's our own,
   Frontenac is o'erthrown,
And Senegal glorioufly won;
   Commerce lends us it's aid,
   And now flourifhes trade,
Whilft that of our foes is undone.

   No more we complain
   We are flaves, to maintain
Troops ufelefs, and fhips unemploy'd ;
   Heart and hand we combine,
   With our leaders to join,
Till our enemies all are deftroy'd.

   May our forces abroad,
   Still continue a rod,
To fcourge lawlefs ambition and pride ;
   And may patriot zeal,
   For our country's weal,
At home in our councils prefide.

   Then let each honeft heart,
   Before we depart,
Fill a glafs to the toaft I propofe ;
   May the fifty and nine,
   With the laft year combine,
To humble the pride of our foes.

SONG 746.

CAN the fhepherds and nymphs of the grove
   Condemn me for dropping a tear ;
Or lamenting aloud as I rove,
   Since Sufan no longer is here ?

My flocks, if at random they ftray,
   What wonder, fince fhe's from the plain ?
Her hand they were wont to obey,
   She rul'd both the fheep and he fwain.

SONG 747.

Sung at MARYBONE.

WELL, if I continue but in the fame mind,
   I never fhall wed, I proteft,
There's fomething fo fhocking in all the male
   kind,
   That bad my thoughts pictur'd the beft.

The nymphs would perfuade, and talk till they
   vex,
   Love's lure to catch youth in the prime;
Why if one muft like the oppofite fex,
   I think feventeen the right time.

They tell it as ftrange, I fhould be fo annoy'd
   At men who were meant for our good ;
But what's in one's nature we cannot avoid,
   I'd be in the mode if I cou'd.

The fhepherds all wonder that from them I fly,
   If feen o'er the plain as I go:

Why ftill let them wonder at diftance, fay I,
The men fhould be always kept fo.

Young Colin declares my averfion's a joke,
And thinks in my heart to fucceed;
For woman, he fays, never thought as fhe fpoke:
He's mighty obliging, indeed!

He caught me juft now, and it came in his head,
To kifs me, but from him I tore;
Yet really believe, had he done as he faid,
He could not have frighten'd me more.

I hope that fuch freedoms he'll ne'er again ufe,
My fix'd refolution to try;
For oh! I am certain I fhall not refufe——
I mean, that I fhall not comply.

SONG 748.

PRAY don't fleep or think,
But give us fome drink,
For 'faith I'm moft plaguily dry;
Wine chears up the foul,
Then fill up the bowl,
For ere long you all know we muft die.

Yefterday's gone,
This day is our own,
To-morrow we never may fee;
Thought caufes us fmart,
And eats up the heart,
Then let us be jovial and free.

The world is a cheat,
With a face counterfeit,
And freedom and mirth difcommends;
But here we may quaff,
Speak our thoughts, fing, and laugh,
For all here are mafons and friends.

SONG 749.

IN PRAISE OF FOLLY.

Written at Bath, by Mr. MAVOR.

RECITATIVE.

COME, Folly! thou goddefs whom mortals
adore,
O let none in vain your affiftance implore:
I'm no courtier, yet look with a fmile of ap-
plaufe,
For, believe me, I'm ready to honour your caufe.

Tho' under your banners great kings you may
boaft,
And ftatefmen in endlefs abfurdities toft;
I defy them to fhew more affection than I,
Were my fphere but enlarg'd—to permit me
to fly.

AIR.

The youth that fighs, and waftes his prime
In courtfhip, love, and trouble,
Beneath thy ftandard fpends his time,
And catches at thy bubble.

If Chloe frown, behold defpair
Surrounds his fteps, and taints the air;
But if fhe fmile with fictious leer,
He quick becomes thy charioteer.

Thus, whether merry, whether fad,
He rides upon thy airy pad;
Whether grave, or melancholy,
Still he's thine, enchanting Folly.

RECITATIVE.

Thou conftant attendant on wealth and on ftatefᵣ
On the vain and the proud, the ambitious and
great!
At thy fhrine what a number of fuppliants ftand,
Turn'd this way, and that, at the word of com-
mand!

AIR.

'Tis to thee, O Folly dear,
We owe that wealth is fpread;
Thy arts e'en mifers can engage
Thy flow'ry paths to tread.

Would fplendid Bath's luxurious feats
Exift, devoid of thee?
Ah, no! her fprings might ftill bathe hogs,
And Dawfon lofe his fee.

Plac'd on the pinnacle of ftate,
Thy fav'rites thou canft fave;
Canft alter the decrees of fate,
And bid the Gaul be brave.

RECITATIVE.

Thou, O thou moft lafting of all human things,
Who ftill canft befriend us, tho' riches have
wings!
Tho' reafon forfake us, and honours decay!
Let thy vot'ries ne'er harbour a doubt of thy
ftay.

SONG 750.

WHERE fhall I feek my fav'rite maid,
In valley, mead, or grove?
Or tell me, does the myrtle fhade
Inclofe the fair I love?

Or does fhe feek the fhady bower,
Or haunt the filent glade,
Where fhe has oft, at ev'ning hour,
With love and Damon ftray'd?

Or does fhe doubt my ardent love,
And feek fome other fwain;
And leave her bleating flock to rove,
Neglected, o'er the plain?

But oh! forbear, my panting breaft,
Forbear thefe vain alarms;
For fee! the fair-one deigns to reft
In fleep's foft, folding arms.

Be hufh'd awhile, ye warb'ing choir,
Your tuneful notes forbear;

In peace, ye limpid ſtreams, retire,
  Nor wake the ſleeping fair.

Ye flow'rets, that on yonder mound
  Such beauteous tints diſcloſe,
Expand your fragrancies around,
  To ſweeten her repoſe.

Ye gentle dreams, by fancy made,
  Awhile engage the fair;
And be each pleaſing ſcene diſplay'd
  To diſſipate her care.

Then deign to make the paſſion known,
  That rages in my breaſt;
That, waking, ſhe her love may own,
  And make her Damon bleſs'd.

SONG 751.

CORYDON.

To the Memory of SPRANGER BARRY, Eſq. Comedian.

Written by Mr. HAWKINS.

SINCE Barry's ſoft accents are now heard
  no more,
The muſe that ador'd them for him will deplore;
His praiſe will ſhe ſing, for, ye gods, how it ſpread!
With laurels the muſes e'er crowned his head.

What beauties he ſhew'd us in each tragic part,
Such beauties as melted and pierc'd the cold
  heart;
How eaſy and graceful the ſtage he would tread;
Then why ſhould not laurels be plac'd on his
  head.

In comedy, too, how he charm'd in each ſcene!
So pleaſing his manners, ſo ſweet was his mien;
That here no diſpraiſes he e'er had to dread,
Whilſt laurels of honour ſurrounded his head.

Then weep, all ye Nine, for your favourite ſwain,
All join in a chorus of ſome ſolemn ſtrain;
For tho' from this world the dear Corydon's fled,
Forget not the laurels ye plac'd on his head.

SONG 752.

DEAR Sylvia, hear thy faithful ſwain,
  And eaſe his tortur'd breaſt;
Ah, hear an artleſs youth complain,
  And ſet his heart to reſt!

That virtue which illumes thy mind,
  That ſenſe devoid of art;
That innocence with ſweetneſs join'd,
  Does captivate his heart.

Thou dear invader of my breaſt,
  How long muſt I repine!
How long with grief be ſore oppreſs'd,
  Ere I can call thee mine!

O deign to hear the vows I ſwear,
  And all my fears remove;
Relieve me, then, from ſad deſpair,
  And bleſs me with thy love.

The northern winds ſhall ceaſe to blow,
  And dark ſhall be the ſkies;
The purling ſtreams ſhall ceaſe to flow,
  And Sol forget to riſe;

No more the meads ſhall gay appear,
  Nor ſhepherds grace the grove;
If e'er my vows prove inſincere,
  Or I forſake my love.

SONG 753.

THE HAPPY MILKMAN.

Written by Mr. HAWKINS.

AS Joe with his pails went a milking one
  morn,
Young Sally he ſaw ſitting under a thorn:
Amaz'd at her beauty, her ſhape, and her mien,
He vow'd ſhe was lovely, and thought her a
  queen.

Thus ſaying, he haſten'd up cloſe to the maid;
Then laid down his yoke, and intreated her aid:
So ſweetly he preſs'd her, ſo ſweet play'd his part,
That, would you ſuppoſe it? he won her fond
  heart.

At firſt ſhe look'd modeſt, and ſeem'd to reſiſt,
And cry'd, Do not teize me; I will not be kiſs'd.
But he his perſuaſions ſo ſweely apply'd,
She kindly conſented ſhe would be his bride.

Then ſtraight to the church they both tript it
  ſo free,
Where they were united by Hymen's decree;
And now are as chearful as birds on the ſpray:
No monarch's more bleſt, nor ſo happy as they.

SONG 754.

Written by Mr. R. DAWES.

WHY ſleeps my ſoul! My love, ariſe!
  Heav'n now wakes with all it's eyes;
All nature's up to gaze on you,
Her ſole delight and glory too:
Awake to hear thy lover's lay;
Ariſe, my fair, and come away.

The ſilent moon full-orb'd now reigns,
And ſilver ſhews the hills and plains,
That fragrant yield their rich perfume;
Conſpiring, all invite to come;
Then why, my love, is this delay!
Ariſe, my fair, and come away.

The flowers ſend forth their choiceſt ſweets,
No ſun diſturbs with ſultry heats;
Theſe, alone, are hours to prove
All the joys of peace and love.
No longer, then, my bliſs delay;
But riſe, my fair, and come away.

For, Nancy, when thou art not near,
In vain do all theſe ſweets appear;

No pow'rful charms can they impart,
To please the sense, or ease my heart:
In pity, then, no longer stay;
But rise, my fair, and come away.

SONG 755.

Written by Mr. LEMOINE.

'TWAS near a purling river side,
　Where bending willows kiss the tide;
Young Chloe sat, with head reclin'd,
On flowery banks, oppress'd in mind.

Her bosom heav'd with throbbing sighs,
The tears ran trickling from her eyes;
Her face reflected with despair,
And ev'ry groan re-echo'd care.

Till grief at last gave such a stroke,
Her eye-lids clos'd, her heart-strings broke.
Yet, ere she dy'd, in solemn tone,
She spoke these words without a groan:

Farewel, ye meads; farewel, ye bow'rs;
Translucid streams, and fragrant flow'rs:
Colin and earthly joys adieu,
No longer I can stay with you.

SONG 756.

WITHOUT thinking on't, I gain'd Thyrsis's heart,
　As one evening we danc'd on the lee;
Without thinking on't, the youth, on his part,
　Alas! made a conquest of me.

Then, Cupid, take care of this ticklish affair,
　Nor leave poor Pastora in thrall;
Lest the swain should forget, and break off as we met,
　Without thinking of it at all.

SONG 757.

Sung at VAUXHALL.

'TIS a twelvemonth ago, nay perhaps they are twain,
Since Thyrsis neglected the nymphs of the plain,
And would tempt me to walk the gay meadows along,
To hear a soft tale, or to sing him a song.

What at first was but friendship, soon grew to a flame,
In my heart it was love, in the youth's 'twas the same;
From each other we sought not our passion to hide,
But who should love most was our contest and pride.

But prudence soon whisper'd us, Love not too well,
For envy has eyes, and a tongue that will tell;

And a flame, without fortune's rich gifts on it's side,
The grave ones will scorn, and a mother must chide.

Afraid of rebuke, he his visits forbore,
And we promis'd to think of each other no more,
But to tarry with patience a season more kind;
So I put the dear shepherd quite out of my mind.

But love breaks the fences I vainly had made,
Grows deaf to all censure, and will be repaid;
If we sigh for each other, ah! quit not your care;
Condemn the god Cupid, but bless the fond pair.

SONG 758.

A RECRUITING SONG.

Sung at SADLER'S WELLS.

COME, volunteers, come
　To the head of the drum,
And all you can muster along with you bring;
Leave masters and mothers,
And fathers, and brothers;
Nor think of a duty, but that to your king.

Thou'rt active, young neighbour,
　Then throw off thy labour,
And swop thy base pillow for bed of renown;
Dick, Harry, and Hugh,
Won't you do so too?
A guinea I'll give you, d'y'see, and a crown.

Good linen, and cloaths,
　With hats, shoes, and hose,
For a gentleman soldier fit every thing;
To my quarters then come,
Beer, brandy, and rum,
Swig your bellies full—God save the king.

SONG 759.

THE BANKS OF THE DEE.

TRUE bliss in retirement can only be found;
　In vain we shall seek it in pleasure's dull round;
The truth of this maxim Philander could see,
When the vot'ry of Cupid was modishly free.

He often resolv'd to retire from the crowd,
Quite pall'd with it's pleasures, so empty and loud;
And oft he relaps'd, thro' a whim to be free,
But at last was reform'd by the Banks of the Dee.

From noise and false pleasures, he quickly withdrew,
To taste of the solid, the lasting, and true:
Grew fond of retirement, nor car'd but for three;
A friend, and a book, and the Banks of the Dee.

His fortune was eafy, his manner polite,
He read a great deal, and at times he could write;
Unmov'd by ambition, contented and free,
He often fung thus, on the Banks of the Dee.

The monarch, ftill jealous of plots and defigns,
Who fighs at his heart while in fplendor he
    fhines,
With pity I trace through the irkfome Levee,
And blefs my kind ftars for the Banks of the Dee.

The mifer, how wretched, amidft all his ftore !
What he has, he can't tafte, yet he fighs to have
    more ;
While I with a little am happy and free,
In a pleafing retreat on the Banks of the Dee.

Let Tom, without paffion, ftill figh for the fair,
Affect their foft manner, and mimick their air,
Supply them with fcandal o'er green and bohea,
Give me a retreat on the Banks of the Dee.

No duns to moleft me, no cares to harrafs,
In pleafing fucceffion the moments will pafs ;
At peace with the world, contented and free,
I'll live and I'll die on the Banks of the Dee.

SONG 760.

Written by J. B.

WHEN merit is fterling that claims our
    attention,
    The object we eagerly wifh to purfue ;
Like a magnet poffefs'd of fuperior attraction,
We wifh to be grac'd with it's influence too:
From a hope to be bleft with fuch powers to
    pleafe,
    As are found in the lafs on whofe virtues
    I'll dwell ;
And truft me you'll not find another, with eafe,
    Whofe charms can compare to the charms
    of my Nell.

O! aid me, kind truth, to paint her perfections,
    To give ev'ry virtue it's infinite due ;
To fpeak of the many and namelefs attractions,
No language invented yet ever could do :
Our thoughts may fuppofe a moft delicate mind,
    Our reafon ideas that fuit very well ;
But thefe far deficient in power I find,
    To declare all the charms of my lovely dear
    Nell.

Her mind, fo replete with virtue's endearments,
    Not prudifh, but affable, lively, and gay;
And chearful, tho' arm'd with proper difcern-
    ments
    To quafh ev'ry hope that fhou'd mean to be-
    tray.
Her friendfhip fo great, has been ever fincere,
    And her pride it is only in truth to excel ;
Examples like her's may her fex ftill revere,
    And endeavour to vie with my lovely dear
    Nell !

O! may fhe be kept, by kind Heav'n's direction,
    Secure, to the ultimate hour of life ;
And thankful remain for fuch tender protection,
    An ornament both to the virgin and wife !
May her conftancy blefs the fond youth of her
    heart,
    And he in return ftrive in love to excel !
May he prove that his aim is, alone, to impart
    A life of good humour to pleafe my dear Nell !

SONG 761.

Sung at VAUXHALL.

TOO late for redrefs, and too foon for my eafe,
    I faw you, I lov'd, and I wifh'd I could
    pleafe;
Reflection ftood ftill, while I fancy'd your eyes
Read the language of mine, and reply'd to my
    fighs ?
Thus cheated by hope, I unheeded went on,
And judg'd of your heart by the throbs of my
    own :
Delufive, fond hope, feem'd at laft to perfuade
That friendfhip, that kindnefs, with love was
    repaid.
But, alas! all is chang'd, and with anguifh I find
Words and looks prove but civil, which once
    I thought kind;
Idea no longer it's fuccour will lend,
To form the fond lover, or fix the firm friend:
Then hufh, my poor heart, and no longer com-
    plain,
Thy honour, thy virtue, pronounce it is vain ;
Thy thoughts fwell to crimes ; drive this love
    from thy breaft,
Perform well thy duty, let fate do the reft.

SONG 762.

CYMON AND IPHIGENIA; A CANTATA.

RECITATIVE.

NEAR a thick grove, whofe deep embow'r-
    ing fhade
Seem'd moft for love and contemplation made,
A cryftal ftream with gentle murmurs flows,
Whofe flow'ry banks are form'd for foft repofe :
Thither, retir'd from Phœbus' fultry ray,
And lull'd in fleep, fair Iphigenia lay.
Cymon, a clown, who never dreamt of love,
By chance was ftumping to the neighb'ring
    grove ;
He trudg'd along, unknowing what he fought,
And whiftled as he went, for want of thought:
But when he firft beheld the fleeping maid,
He gap'd—he ftar'd—her lovely form furvey'd:
And while with artlefs voice he fweetly fung,
Beauty and nature thus inform'd his tongue.

AIR.

The ftream that glides in murmurs by,
    Whofe glaffy bofom fhews the fky,
    Compleats the rural fcene ;
But in thy bofom, charming maid,
All heav'n itfelf is fure difplay'd,
    Too lovely Iphigene.

Recitative.

She wakes, and ftarts—poor Cymon trembling
ftands ;
Down falls the ftaff from his unnerved hands :
Bright excellence, faid he, difpel all fear ;
Where honour's prefent, fure no danger's near.
Half-rais'd, with gentle accent, fhe replies,
Oh, Cymon ! if 'tis you, I need not rife ;
Thy honeft heart no wrong can entertain :
Purfue thy way, and let me fleep again.
The clown, tranfported, was not filent long,
But thus with extafy purfu'd his fong :

Air.

Thy jetty locks, that carelefs break,
In wanton ringlets, down thy neck ;
    Thy love-infpiring mien ;
Thy fwelling bofom, fkin of fnow,
And taper fhape, inchant me fo,
    I die for Iphigene.

Recitative.

Amaz'd, fhe liftens, nor can trace from whence
The former clod is thus infpir'd with fenfe :
She gazes—finds him comely, tall, and ftraight,
And thinks he might improve his aukward gait ;
Bids him be fecret, and next day attend,
At the fame hour, to meet his faithful friend.
Thus mighty love could teach a clown to plead ;
And nature's language fureft will fucceed.

Air.

Love's pure and facred fire,
Kindling gentle, chafte defire ;
Love can rage itfelf controul,
And elevate the human foul :
Depriv'd of that our wretched ftate
Had made our lives of too long date ;
But bleft with beauty, and with love,
We tafte what angels do above.

SONG 763.
Sung at RANELAGH.

YE true honeft Britons, who love your own
    land,
    Whofe fires were fo brave, fo victorious, and
        free,
Who always beat France when they took her
    in hand,
    Come join, honeft Britons, in chorus with me,

Let us fing our own treafures, Old England's
    good chear,
The profits and pleafures of ftout Britifh beer ;
Your wine-tipling, dram-fipping fellows re-
    treat,
But your beer-drinking Britons can never be
    beat.

The French, with their vineyards, are meagre
    and pale ;
They drink of the fqueezings of half-ripen'd
    fruit ;
But we, who have hop-grounds to mellow our
    ale,
    Are rofy, and plump, and have freedom to
        boot.
Let us fing, &c.

Should the French dare invade, thus arm'd
    with our poles,
    We'll bang their bare ribs, make their lan-
        tern jaws ring ;
For your beef-eating, beer-drinking Britons,
    are fouls
Who will fhed their laft drop for their coun-
    try and king.
Let us fings, &c.

SONG 764.
Sung at VAUXHALL.

WHEN firft by fond Damon Flavella was
    feen,
He flightly regarded her air and her mien,
The charms of her mind he alone did com-
    mend,
Nor warm as a lover, but cool as a friend ;
From friendfhip, not paffion, his raptures did
    move,
And he boafted his heart was a ftranger to love.

New charms he difcover'd, as more fhe was
    known ;
Her face grew a wonder, her tafte was his own,
Her manners were gentle, her fenfe was refin'd,
And ev'ry dear virtue beam'd forth in her mind :
Still, ftill for the fanction of friendfhip he
    ftrove,
Till a figh gave the omen, and fhew'd it was
    love.

Now, proud to be conquer'd, he fighs for the
    fair,
Grows dull to all pleafure, but being with her,
He's mute, till his heart-ftrings are ready to
    break ;
For fear of offending forbids him to fpeak ;
And wanders a willing example to prove
That friendfhip with woman is fifter to love.

A lover thus conquer'd can ne'er give offence ;
Not a dupe to her fmiles, but a flave to her fenfe ;
His paffion nor wrinkles nor age can allay,
Since founded on that which can never decay ;
And time, that fhall beauty's fhort empire re-
    move,
Increafing her reafon, increafes his love,

THE

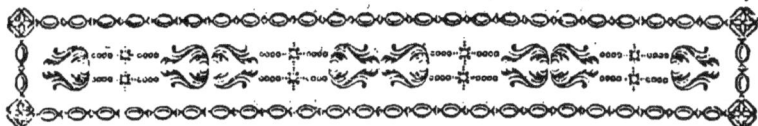

VOCAL MAGAZINE.

NUMBER VI.

SONG 765.

A NAVAL ODE.

Written by Mr. HEYWOOD.

CEASE, ye tinkling cymbals! ceafe!
  Ye lighter ftrains be ftill!
Now let the trumpet's fhrill alarms,
With never-dying glory's charms,
And hate of Bourbon's treach'rous race,
  Each free-born bofom fill.

Hence green-ey'd envy, pallid fear;
Hence treachery, with friendly air;
  And difcord, with Gorgonian front:
To Gallia's fruitlefs coaft repair;
Go fix your hateful dwelling there;
  Ye hell-born crew, avaunt!

Let fhouts triumphant fill the fky,
While yet each generous breaft beats high,
  And thirft of glory warms:
Let every craggy rock around,
From diftant fhore to fhore rebound,
'Till Heaven's blue arch ring back the found,
  To arms! to arms! to arms!

Now Britons, now your glorious crofs difplay,
Let concord now unite each heart and hand;
So fhall you ftill with Neptune rule the fea,
While Gallia trembles on her frighted ftrand.

What tho' Chatham he no more,
Heroes ftill we have in ftore,
  For council form'd, or field:
Still Shelburne, uncorrupt, remains;
And ftill victorious Keppel reigns;
  Their country's fword and fhield.

Hark! on Gallia's diftant fhore,
I hear the murd'ring cannon roar
  Tremendous o'er the fea:
'Tis warlike Keppel's fiery foul
Now bids Britannia's thunders roll,
  And wipes her ftains away.

Conqueft crown thee, matchlefs chief,
  Glory hover round thee ftill;
Far be from thee every grief,
  Every pain, and every ill:
Honour'd may'ft thou live, and long,
  (Bourbon trembling from afar;)
Glorious theme of future fong,
  Britain's thunder-bolt of war.

But lo! I fee th' approaching navy move;
  Mark on the deck the godlike chief appears;
Fierce and refiftlefs as the bolt of Jove,
  Hardy and honeft as the fword he wears;
And lo! before him, o'er the bounding tide,
High in their fhells, the fea-green Nereids ride;
Beneath their cars the foaming billows roar;
And thus the virgins fing, flow moving to the
  fhore:

Hail, virtuous brother, hail!
  May thy glories never fail;
Nor in time of war, or peace,
  Thy full tide of fame decreafe:
Still may Conqueft's golden wing,
  Round thy head her radiance fling;
Till at length death's friendly hand
  Bring thee this our mild command:
Brother, bid the world farewel;
  Come, and with thy fifters dwell.
For of more than mortal race,
We thy lineage well can trace:
Proteus oft the tale hath told,
How, within a cavern old,
On a fummer's fultry day,
Screen'd from Phœbus' rays he lay;
When Neptune with Britannia came,
There to quench his ardent flame;
For oft the god his irkfome pain
Had told the nymph, but told in vain;
Till chancing on the falt-fea fhore
He faw her, feiz'd, and thither bore;
There on a bed of fea-weed laid,
He prefs'd the coy, confenting maid;

C c

Then bade the charmer name her want,
And ftraight he would her wifhes grant.
The forlorn goddefs rofe, and figh'd,
And, fighing, to the god reply'd : -

Grant, (nor let me afk in vain)
Grant me the empire of the main.

She fpoke, and blufh'd ; the love-fick god
Confents, and gave the fealing nod.

When now nine changing moons were o'er,
The goddefs on the falt-fea fhore,
Within the fatal cavern laid,
Implor'd divine Lucina's aid.

Soon Neptune, from his wat'ry bed,
O'er-heard thy cries, and thither fped ;
Then in his arms he rais'd and preft
Thee, fcar'd and trembling, to his breaft.

Go now, my fon, (he faid) obey;
Go, take the empire of the fea:
So I refign to thee the waves;
Go, make Britannia's foes her flaves;
Go, conquer in thy mother's right,
And be a fecond Mars in fight.

The godhead faid; and, ere he left the ftrand,
Refign'd his trident to thy infant hand!

So fung the blue-ey'd fift-rs of the main,
Melodious, o'er the wide Cerulean wafte;
Before them Triton founds his twifted fhell,
The cliffs and cavern'd rocks rebellow to
the blaft.

High on a rock reclin'd,
Black louring o'er the fea,
Her plumage dancing in the wind,
Divine Britannia lay.

Soon as the chief fhe fpies,
Approaching o'er the tide,
Joy burft irradiate from her eyes ;
And hail, my fon! fhe cry'd.

Welcome, mighty conqueror,
Welcome to thy native fhore;
Lo, in many a mazy round,
Peace and plenty trip the ground,
By thee again reftor'd ;
Whilft fair freedom, hand in hand
With Neptune, guards our facred ftrand,
And hails thy conqu'ring fword.

Still o'er yon detefted band,
Stretch thy unrefifted hand,
And all their boafts defy ;
Let them but thy face behold,
(As at immortal Talbot's old)
They tremble, and they fly.

For ne'er to mix in war's alarms,
Or join the direful clang of arms,
Was form'd that treach'rous race ;
No patriot flames their bofom warms,
Nor publick virtues grace.

Singing, dancing, whining, fighing,
All the arts that they purfue ;
Treach'ry, fawning, cringing, lying,
All the godlike deeds they do.

Go, the faithlefs race chaftifing,
Let them foon their folly rue ;
Go, each toil, each pain defpifing;
'Tis thy country bids thee go.

Thus to her fon the heav'nly goddefs fpoke,
And fhook her glitt'ring jav'lin in the air ;
Then to the fhore her hafty courfe fhe took,
Dire war and conqueft following in the rear.

Fame faw the train, and o'er the murm'ring
waves
High-rais'd her trump, and fpread the news
around ;
And foon, too foon, the fated land of flaves
Heard the tremendous blaft, and trembled
at the found!

SONG 766.

AN OLD BRITON'S COMPLAINT.

Written by the EDITOR.

POOR England! how hard is thy lot,
That once waft the pride of the world!
Thy honours are all gone to pot,
And thy commerce far diftant is hurl'd!

The French and the Spaniards unite,
While Dutchmen (by ftealth) aid their caufe,
And Britons may now bid good night
To their trade, to their freedom, and laws.

How diff'rent in good Befs's days,
When Englifhmen valiant and ftout,
Had the rafcals e'en thought of fuch ways,
Would quickly have knock'd them about!

But then, ftead of coffee and tea,
They liv'd upon beef and ftrong beer;
And, believe me, we yet had been free,
If we'd ftuck to the fame honeft chear.

For tea was the caufe, we well know,
Of our prefent unhappy difpute ;
And America feels all her woe
Proceeded from that fatal root.

Then let us, ere yet 'tis too late,
Abandon this dangerous leaf;
And refolve with no woman to mate,
Who'll not change it for ale and good beef.

So fhall we, as formerly, find
The world will a Briton revere;
Nor dare any treaty unbind
With a people in arms they muft fear.

Our men will all then be robuft,
And our women all free from the fpleen ;
While each to the other'll be juft,
And liberty heighten the fcene.

SONG 767.

WHEN firft Vaneffa's bhooming face
Surpriz'd my dazzled fight ;
I wifh'd, I figh'd, view'd ev'ry grace
With wonder and delight.

In fuch an heav'nly form, I cry'd,
Sure all perfections meet!
I thought her conftant, free from pride,
Fair, virtuous, and difcreet.

But foon my judgment falfe I find,
Pride fwell'd her fcornful breaft;
Say was fhe conftant?—as the wind:
But was fhe not the reft?

Can godlike virtue be her guide,
Who turns with every wind?
Or can difcretion reign, where pride
Unbounded fways the mind?

Can fhe lay claim to beauty's pow'r,
Whofe face is all her boaft?
Alas! Vaneffa is no more:
As foon as found fhe's loft.

Ixïon thus his arms had caft
Around his fleeting fair;
His fancy'd Juno prov'd, at laft,
Delufive, empty air.

SONG 767.

A Good repute, a virtuous name,
Philofophers fet forth,
As the unerring path to fame,
If fame confifts in worth.

This precious ointment, gently fhed,
O'er mental ill prevails;
And where the fragrant med'cine's fpread,
It animates and heals.

Yet hard it is to ufe it right,
Tho' beautiful to view;
It fhines diftinguifhingly bright,
How tranfitory too!

Like glafs it glitters, foon 'tis crackt,
Irreparably frail;
All moralifts allow the fact,
So I apply the tale.

When things inanimate cou'd fpeak,
Fire once agreed with Water,
A friendly jaunt one day to take,
But where, 'tis no great matter.

It happen'd that, the day before
Each left their different ftation,
They chofe a third, worth twenty more,
And that was Reputation.

The three companions now reflect,
If chance fhou'd once divide 'em,
How each their letters might direct,
Or who fhou'd fureft guide 'em.

Says Water, Friends, you'll hear my name,
Tho' loft upon a mountain;
Enquire at any murm'ring ftream,
Or feek me in a fountain:

Sometimes from deep cafcades I pour,
Thro' meadows gently glide;
I drop a dew, defcend a fhower,
Or thunder in a tide:

Where marfhes ftagnate, bogs extend,
Green reeds and rufhy fods,
Direct a path to meet your friend;
A path the bulrufh nods.

Your reftlefs make (quoth Fire) I know,
Juft like your parent ocean;
I love to rove as well as you,
My life confifts in motion:

In poets all my marks you'll fee,
Since fmoak and flafh reveal me;
Sufpect me always near Nat. Lee,
E'en Blackmore can't conceal me.

In Milton's page I glow, by art,
One flame intenfe and even;
In Shakefpeare's blaze a fudden ftart,
Like lightning flafh'd from heaven:

In many more, as well as they,
Thro' various forms I fhift;
I'm gently lambent while a Gay,
But brighteft when a Swift:

From fmoak fure tidings you may get,
It can't fubfift without me;
Or find me, like fome fond coquet,
With fifty fparks about me.

The beft of flaves I'm call'd by men,
When bound in proper durance;
But if I once do mifchief, then
I'm heard of at th' Infurance.

Alas! poor Reputation cry'd,
How happy in each other!
Such fignal marks muft furely guide
Each ftragg'ler to his brother.

'Tis I, alone, muft be undone,
Such ill has fate defign'd me;
If I be loft, 'tis ten to one,
You never more will find me.

SONG 768.
Sung at the NONSENSICAL CLUB.

ALL whimfical people, come hither,
And chufe a nonfenfical ftrain;
For who'd be a wit in hot weather,
T'indanger the lofs of his brain?

'Tis nonfenfe we fing, and we deal in,
And generoufly dole it abroad;
And if common-fenfe chance to fteal in,
We kick the precife rafcal out.

Whereof, forafmuch, notwithftanding,
Moreover, to wit, furthermore,
Sure never were words fo commanding,
So fweetly adapted before.

Th' are free from reftraint, or we rattle,
Unflav'd by no precepts nor rules;
Whilft thofe who in form prittle prattle,
Are nothing but fenfible fools.

Should nonfenfe from human kind fever,
What numbers muft ftraight away run!
The beau pick his teeth muft for ever,
The chatt'ring coquet be undone.

The bards would have little to write on,
The lawyers have little to fay,
The criticks would nought have to bite on,
The non-cons not know how to pray.

Befides, for a plague wit is fent ye,
It's owners for ever are poor;
Whilft nonfenfe is vefted with plenty,
Whereof you may fee now therefore.

S O N G   769.

ANACREONTIC.

THE mufes once intent on play
Young Cupid roving caught,
With flow'ry wreaths they ty'd his hands,
And bound, to beauty brought.

Fond Venus ranges all the plain
To feek her little joy,
And foon a pow'rful ranfom brings
To free th' imprifon'd boy.

But tho' releas'd, the captive god
Refus'd to quit his chains,
And ftill to beauty's gentle fway
A willing flave remains.

S O N G   770.

THoughtlefs of all, but love and you,
From place to place I range,
But ftill no happinefs I know,
Nor pleafure by the change.

The murm'ring ftream, the fruitful field,
The plain, the fhady grove,
Alike to me, no pleafure yield,
When abfent from my love.

Yet if my Delia but appears,
How chang'd is all the fcene!
Nature a gayer livery wears;
And I forget my pain.

The murm'ring ftream, the fruitful field,
The plain, the fhady grove,
Alike to me, all pleafure yield,
When bleft with her I love.

S O N G   771.

A Wit and captain ftrove, Sir,
To gain a lady's love, Sir;
And warm in competition,
Each pleafed his condition,
To pleafe his miftrefs moft.
The bravo, like a warrior,
Thought he by ftorm fhou'd carry her,
And fwore he'd guard her perfon
From danger and afperfion,
And fhe fhou'd be his toaft.

The poet foftly told her,
That tho' he was no foldier,

He'd make her fame eternal,
In Magazine or Journal,
And fing away her cares.
The lady then reflecting
Whofe parts were moft affecting,
Thought fpark of tuneful merit
Outweigh'd the bluft'ring fpirit,
And thus her mind declares.

My honour wants no Hector
To be it's ftern protector;
No Myrmidon to frighten,
But Phaön to delight in;
So, captain, march along.
'Tis gentle wit and breeding,
Is worth a lady's healing;
No hopes our hearts of gaining,
Without firft entertaining;
So let me have a fong.

But juft then in the nick, Sir,
A fquire of filver quick, Sir,
With gold-knot on his rapier,
Who well cou'd cut a caper,
Now play'd before her eyes.
His air and drefs fo taking,
Without the pains of fpeaking,
This moft engaging youngfter
By far outfhone the fongfter,
And danc'd off with the prize.

S O N G   772.

WHEN the dear caufe of all my pain
Is abfent from my fight,
Mufic, and books, and friends, in vain
Attempt to give delight.

So, tho' a thoufand ftars by night
Heav'n's canopy adorn,
If the fair moon's fuperior light
Be wanting, ftill we mourn.

S O N G   773.

HARRY AND MARY.

Sung at VAUXHALL.

NEAR a hawthorn, I met on the plain
Young Mully, the ev'ning was ftarry;
I talk'd in ftrong terms of my pain,
Tho' I never intended to marry.
Her modeft demeanor was fuch,
More than half it prevail'd over Harry;
I love her, I own, very much,
'Tis true, but I never fhall marry.

My companions all loudly complain,
With them that I now never tarry;
They have found out the caufe of my pain,
And fancy at laft I fhall marry:
Believe me, they know not my heart;
This face I much longer can carry;
I can bear a vaft deal of love's fmart,
But I ne'er fhall be tempted to marry.

But 'tis long fince I faw the dear maid,
With Cupid for life muft I parry!
Of Hymen I'm not much afraid,
But furely I'd better not marry:
Do I fee her amongft this gay throng,
Then what will become of poor Harry?
By paffion I'm hurry'd along,
Then take me, I'm ready to marry.

SONG 774.

JESSY; OR, APRIL DAY.

Sung at VAUXHALL.

WHILE the bee flies from bloffom to bloffom, and fips,
And my Jeffy looks buxom and gay;
Let me hang on her neck, and tafte from her lips,
All the fweets of an April day.

The fhepherd his flock, the ruftic his plough,
The farmer with joy views his hay,
And Jeffy, my charmer, when milking her cow,
Sings the fweets of an April day.

Like fnow-drops with innocent fweetnefs array'd,
As blithfome and chearful as May,
My Jeffy, the pride of all the gay mead,
Sung the fweets of an April day.

Remember, dear Jeffy, and ufe well your pow'r,
Your rofe-buds then pluck while you may;
And guiltlefs enjoy all the fweets of this hour,
For youth's but an April day.

SONG 775.

THE RETREAT; A PASTORAL.

Written by Mr. NICHOLLS.

WITH Phillis I ftray'd to a new-mantled grove,
Where blue-bells emitted their fweet;
Where birds in full concert delightfully ftrove
To gladden the peaceful retreat.
On a feat rais'd by nature, befprinkl'd with flow'rs,
We fat ourfelves under a fhade;
When thus, in foft ftrains, to divert the young hours,
Began my dear innocent maid.

How bounteous is nature; how wond'rous her plan!
This copfe, but a moon or two paft,
Prefented no object attractive to man,
But, murmuring, fhrunk from the blaft:

See now (what a change!) ten thoufand gay fweets
Enamel the new-mantled fpray;
The breeze foftly kiffes each cheek that it meets,
And whifpers, How charming is May!

Wherever I turn me, fo great's my furprize,
Enraptur'd I'm forced to fing,
No pow'r can be equal to that which fupplies
The beauties which wait upon fpring!
On the bloom of that wildling, behold the gay bees,
There lately a honey-dew fell;
Now fee how they fcud thro' the neighbouring trees!
Each flies to replenifh his cell.

T'obferve their ftrict order, what blifs to the wife!
If but inftinct, how nearly ally'd
To reafon, the faireft-born child of the fkies,
Whom we boaft was but fent for our guide!
In funfhine they toil 'gainft the feafon's extreme,
When winter rolls floods from it's urn;
A leffon proud man, who's acknowledg'd fupreme,
Would not be degraded to learn.

Behold yonder oak, with what majefty plac'd
On the brow of that flow-rifing hill;
How clofe by the woodbine that poplar's embrac'd,
Which mantles the prattling rill!
And hark! how delightful the choir of this grove;
That nightingale, note him, how fweet!
All this, my dear fwain, is a language of love,
Which never yet harbour'd deceit.

That finch on the rofe-bufh, how tuneful his tongue!
What kindnefs he fhews to his mate!
See, fee! how together they cherifh their young:
Such charms upon conftancy wait.
Ah, Damon, if Phillis could once have her will,
Thefe trees fhould bloom fweet all the year;
Thefe birds fuch gay fonnets for ever fhould trill,
And no more gloomy winter appear.

But foon as brown harveft has yielded it's ftore,
Thefe beauties which ravifh the fight,
Muft fly from our ifle, and be heard of no more
Till May comes again to delight! —
Sweet Phillis my bofom with rapture poffefs'd,
I gaz'd, and fo great was the charm,
My cheek unawares was reclin'd on her breaft,
And her waift was entwin'd by my arm.

Such freedom offended, fhe bade me beware,
For envy (fhe faid) might be near;
And fcandal, who never fhews things as they are,
Who delights in the figh and the tear.

I thought it but reason; I bade her not fear:
Said nought that was ill fhould befal;
I lov'd her too well to give caufe for a tear,
To bitter her honey with gall.

From the daify-deck'd fod then together we
rofe,
O'er the meadows I led her along;
Grac'd my lay with the truth' fhe was pleas'd
to difclofe,
And I gave it the ruftical throng.

SONG 776.

JENNY is a charming creature,
R ch in all the gifts of nature;
Had fhe thofe of fortune too,
Powder'd flaves wou'd then attend her,
She might figh in ftate and fplendour,
With a wretchednefs in view.

But fince Jenny has no dower,
Some poor bee fhall fip the flower,
Butterflies ftill foar above;
Corydon with joy fhall take her,
And fhall reap, from one fmall acre,
More content than landlords prove.

Since, gallants, 'tis gold muft win ye,
And the moft deferving Jenny
Wants the reconciling pence;
Call not fortune blind, nor Cupid;
Sparks are felfifh, falfe and ftupid,
Merit is above their fenfe.

SONG 777.

THE LOVER'S STREAM.

Sung at VAUXHALL.

FLOW, murm'ring river, flow;
Whilft on thy borders grow
Gay Flora's richeft pride:
And fince thy bounty feeds
The neighb'ring verdant meads,
In ceafelefs tinklings glide.

Upon thy whifp'ring ftream,
May faithful lovers dream,
Whilft fings the humming-bee:
Or let th' impaffion'd fwain
Moft fweetly there complain,
Or pipe in tuneful glee.

Upon thy banks I'll ftray,
To lull my cares away,
There fhun the noontide beam:
Fair quiet here I find,
This foothes my thoughtful mind;
I thank thee, gentle ftream.

SONG 778.

THO' to others fome fairer than Delia may be,
Yet none are fo fair, or fo lovely to me,
So free is each motion, fo charming each grace,
Such good-humour and fweetnefs appear in her
face.

Such wit and vivacity fhine in her eyes,
That whilft I gaze on her, I'm loft in furprize.
But, ye gods! when fhe fpeaks I admire no
more,
But fall at her feet, and her wifdom adore.

Such, fuch is my Delia, and Venus would be
Not fo charming, fo fair, nor fo lovely to me,
And if Heaven fo kind to my prayers fhall prove,
That as I love her, fo fhe alfo may love;
The reft I will leave with the gods, and require
No more; fince in her, I have all I defire.
Nor nobles will envy, nor kings in their power;
Nor afk for a world, fince in her I have more.

SONG 779.

THE FOX-CHACE; AN ODE.

Written by Mr. NICHOLLS.

RECITATIVE.

HARK! from that cottage by the filent
ftream,
How fweet the fwallow greets the rifing gleam
Of light, that dawns upon the eaftern hill,
Tipping with grey the fails of yonder mill;
And hark! from the farm below the watchful
cock
Warns the dull fhepherd to unfold his flock;
His hurdled flocks the frefh'ning breeze inhale,
And bleat for freedom, and the clover vale.
See! how away the fevering clouds are driven,
How gay already feems the face of heaven!
Thofe ruddy ftreaks foretel the fun is near
To drink the dew, and glad our hemifphere.
O! did the fons of diffipation know
What calm delights from early-rifing flow,
They'd leave (with us) their down, and in the
fields
Imbibe the health that frefh Aurora yields.

AIR.

Now indolence fnores upon pillows of down,
Now infirmity, guilt, and difeafe,
Envy the gentle repofe of the clown,
And in vain beg the bleffing of eafe:
Whilft we honeft fellows, who follow the chace,
Of fuch troubles are never poffefs'd,
The banner of health is difplay'd in each face,
To fhew Peace holds the fort of the breaft.

Can the flaves of a court, can the mifer fay this?
Or the wretches who feed on diftrefs?
O! may fuch ne'er tafte of our rational blifs,
Till, like us, they difdain to opprefs.

RECITATIVE.

See! to the copfe how the dogs fcud along,
They've found out the drag of the foe;
And hark! how the huntfmen ride fhouting
along,
He's now in the cover below.

Let's follow the cry, he'll soon be in view;
See! yonder he sculks o'er the glade;
Spur your coursers, my lads, and briskly pursue;
Or's craft will our vengeance evade.

AIR.

The shepherd with joy views the chace,
His lambs the vile traitor would fleece;
The farmer, delighted, beholds his disgrace,
And thinks on his turkies and geese.

The maids of the hamlet look gay;
The dames, o'er a noggin of ale,
Tell what poultry of late was his prey,
And wish the staunch pack may prevail.

In quest of the fleet-footed foe,
As the hunters fly over the plain,
Ev'ry breast feels a rap urous glow,
Ev'ry tongue trills the jocular strain.

RECITATIVE.

Far from the east had roll'd the glorious sun,
And through each well-known haunt the fox
    had run;
The stream he'd past, and the vast mountain's
    height,
Seeking the dell where darkling brakes invite:
There strove to earth, but strove to earth in
    vain,
He breaks the covert, tries the lawns again;
But, as he fled, the crafty spoiler found,
Fleeting behind, the never-fault'ring hound:
Weary at length, he views the wide-mouth
    throng,
And drags in pain his mired brush along;
Now spent, he falls, rolling his haggard eves;
And, savage like, he wounds, and snarling dies.
Eager to view, the shouting train surround;
Hills, woods, and rocks, reverberate the found.

AIR.

Whilst the huntsman exults to hunters around,
And holds up the strong-scented prize;
Elated with conquest, each staunch mettled
    hound,
Sends a clam'rous peal to the skies;

The deep sound of the horn, borne afar on the
    gale,
Calls the sportsmen thrown out, to the pack;
They meet round the spoil—t their coursers
    don't fail,
Then away, to regale, they ride chearfully
    back.

RECITATIVE.

Such are the manly pleasures of the chace,
Which kings of old were eager to embrace:
Whilst o'er the champaign ran the courtly crew,
The cheek was garnish'd with a roseat hue;
Then no pale Ganymede disgrac'd the court,
And he was honour'd who most lov'd the sport;
No brooding malice there assail'd the breast,
To cloud the brow, or poison mental rest.
Oh! glorious sport, which can at once impart
Health to the veins, and quiet to the heart.

AIR.

Our fathers of old lov'd the sport,
Our nobles rejoic'd in the chace;
They fled the intrigues of a court,
The heart-chearing toil to embrace.

Their offspring was ruddy and stout,
Curst lux'ry was yet in the bud;
They scarce knew the pangs of the gout,
Activity phyfick'd the blood.

A fribble they seldom could meet;
But now how revers'd is the scene!
The creature's in every street
Erecting his butterfly mien.

Could our ancestors rise from their graves,
At sight of the gay-spangled train,
They'd fly the degenerate slaves,
And wish to be bury'd again.

May such never taste of our joy,
We hunters disclaim the whole race;
Whilst time over tea they destroy,
We're lost in the charms of the chace.

CHORUS.

All you who would follow the musical horn,
Go early to bed, and salute the young morn.
Our sports shall secure you the bosom's repose,
And your cheek in old age wear the tint of
    the rose;
Your nerves shall be strong, and feel, e'en in
    decay,
The raptures enjoy'd by the young and the gay.
Then hither come you who'd live long in good
    health,
A blessing the wise much esteem before wealth.

SONG 780.

LAVINIA; A PASTORAL.

WHY steals from my bosom the sigh?
    Why fix'd is my gaze on the ground?
Come, give me my pipe, and I'll try
    To banish my cares with the sound.

Erewhile were it's notes of accord
    With the smile of the flow'r-footed muse;
Ah! why, by it's master implor'd,
    Shou'd it now the gay carrol refuse?

'Twas taught by Lavinia's sweet smile,
    In the mirth-loving chorus to join:
Ah, me! how unweeting the while!
    Lavinia—can never be mine!

Another, more happy, the maid
    By fortune is destin'd to bless;
Tho' the hope has forsook that betray'd,
    Yet why shou'd I love her the less?

Her beauties are bright as the morn,
    With rapture I counted them o'er;
Such virtues those beauties adorn,
    I knew her, and prais'd them no more.

I term'd her no goddess of love,
    I call'd not her beauty divine:
These far other passions may prove,
    But they could not be figures of mine.

It ne'er was apparell'd with art,
  On words it could never rely;
It reign'd in the throb of my heart,
  It gleam'd in the glance of my eye.

Oh, fool! in the circle to shine
  That fashion's gay daughters approve,
You must speak as the fashions incline;
  Alas! are there fashions in love?

Yet sure they are simple who prize
  The tongue that is smooth to deceive;
Yet sure she had sense to despise
  The tinsel that folly may weave.

When I talk'd, I have seen her recline
  With an aspect so pensively sweet;
Tho' I spoke what the shepherds opine,
  A fop were asham'd to repeat.

She is soft as the dew-drops that fall
  From the lip of the sweet-scented pea;
Perhaps, when she smil'd upon all,
  I have thought that she smil'd upon me.

But why of her charms should I tell?
  Ah, me! whom her charms have undone!
Yet I love the reflection too well,
  The painful reflection to shun.

Ye souls of more delicate kind,
  Who feast not on pleasure alone,
Who wear the soft sense of the mind,
  To the sons of the world still unknown;

Ye know, tho' I cannot express,
  Why I foolishly doat on my pain;
Nor will ye believe it the less,
  That I have not the skill to complain.

I lean on my hand with a sigh,
  My friends the soft sadness condemn;
Yet, methinks, tho' I cannot tell why,
  I should hate to be merry like them.

When I walk'd in the pride of the dawn,
  Methought all the region look'd bright:
Has sweetness forsaken the lawn?
  For, methinks, I grow sad at the sight.

When I stood by the stream, I have thought
  There was mirth in the gurgling soft sound;
But now 'tis a sorrowful note,
  And the banks are all gloomy around!

I have laugh'd at the jest of a friend;
  Now they laugh and I know not the cause,
Tho' I seem with my looks to attend,
  How silly! I ask what it was.

They sing the sweet song of the May,
  They sing it with mirth and with glee;
Sure I once thought the sonnet was gay,
  But now 'tis all sadness to me.

Oh! give me the dubious light
  That gleams thro' the quivering shade;
Oh! give me the horrors of night,
  By gloom and by silence array'd!

Let me walk where the soft-rising wave
  Has pictur'd the moon on it's breast;
Let me walk where the new-cover'd grave
  Allows the pale lover to rest!

When shall I in it's peaceable womb
  Be laid with my sorrows asleep!
Should Lavinia but chance on my tomb—
  I could die if I thought she would weep.

Perhaps, if the souls of the just
  Revisit these mansions of care,
It may be my favourite trust,
  To watch o'er the fate of the fair.

Perhaps the soft thought of her breast
  With rapture more favour'd to warm;
Perhaps, if with sorrow oppress'd,
  Her sorrow with patience to arm.

Then! then! in the tenderest part
  May I whisper, Poor Colin was true;
And mark if a heave of her heart
  The thought of her Colin pursue.

SONG 781.

BANISH'D by your severe command,
  I make an awful, sad retreat,
To some more hospitable land;
  But shall I then my fair forget?

No, there I'll charm the list'ning throng,
  With repetitions of your name;
My passion tell in plaintive song,
  And sadly pensive soothe my flame.

With inbred sighs, the grateful swains
  My tale will beg me to renew;
Sweetly appeas'd, beguile their pains,
  Transported when I speak of you.

But should some curious youth demand,
  Why from my beauteous theme I stray?
With what confusion should I stand!
  What wou'd my charmer have me say?

SONG 782.

Occasioned by a young Gentleman's declining
to write, after having read the Works of
POPE and SWIFT.

AMINTOR, how canst thou refuse
  To grant me so small a request;
Why urge you the want of Pope's muse,
  Or the Doctor's poetical zest?
I vow, tho' their numbers are sweet,
  And ev'ry sentence divine;
Tho' their value I reckon so great,
  No less would I set upon thine.

Would'st thou sing of the plain or the grove,
  Or lament some unfortunate maid,
The muses, fair daughters of Jove,
  With raptures would readily aid.
What tho' they at first may seem coy,
  'Tis but to be closer pursu'd;
They, like other nymphs, will comply,
  When once they are heartily woo'd.

Will nought thy ambition suffice,
  But the laurel thy temples to grace?
If still thou resolve to despise
  All but the superlative place;

Mr VERNON, as Cymon, in CYMON V.

"What exquisite Pleasure!"

Song 783

Published by J.Bew. Oct 1778.

Yet think how the criticks in town
  Misjudge of poetical fire;
From the skies should Apollo come down,
  They'd carp at his heavenly lyre.

If the blind Grecian poet they praise,
  'Tis to shew you their skill in the tongue,
Despising Pope's beautiful lays,
  And swearing his version is wrong:
But had not that bard of renown
  Their ignorance deign'd to inform,
Of Homer no more they'd have known,
  Than if he had never been born.

For me, I disdain to regard
  What these trifling censurers say;
If such are deny'd their reward,
  Hope I to speed better than they?
Le : my friends but approve of my strains,
  Vouchsafing a smile on my song;
Then I'm overpaid for my pains,
  Nor value an ill-natur'd tongue.

SONG 783.

Sung in *Cymon*.

WHAT exquisite pleasure
  This sweet treasure
From me they shall never
    Sever;
  In thee, in thee,
  My charmer I see:
I'll sigh, and caress thee,
I'll kiss thee, and press thee,
Thus, thus, to my bosom, for ever and ever.

SONG 784.

THE FORSAKEN MAID.

YOUNG Chloe, once the gayest maid
  That tript upon the plain,
Upon a shady bank was laid,
  There to lament her pain.

The laughing Cupids left her eyes,
  Her hand supports her head:
Her tuneful voice was drown'd in sighs,
  Her ev'ry charm was fled.

The little birds sung from on high,
  And strain'd their warbling throats;
Yet she regardless seem'd to lie,
  Nor harken'd to their notes.

A purling stream ran murm'ring by,
  In pity to her pain;
Sad echo, who stood list'ning nigh,
  Return'd each sigh again.

Heart-rending sighs, flown from her breast,
  Make way for some sad words;
Her flutt'ring heart, now more at rest,
  Some little ease affords.

Ye warbling choirs, your music cease!
  The love-sick Chloe said;
Thou bubbling brook! a moment's peace,
  And hear a wretched maid!

Ah! cruel Strephon, faithless youth!
  Thou dear ungrateful swain!
Thus to reward my love and truth,
  And leave me to complain.

I range the groves through ev'ry part,
  In hopes to ease my care;
But ah!-'tis grounded in my heart,
  Your dear idea's there.

Each tender whisper that I hear,
  Each soft, deceiving noise,
I tremble betwixt hope and fear,
  And think 'tis Strephon's voice.

But Strephon thinks no more of me,
  His heart's too full of joys;
He's found a more deserving she,
  Who all his thoughts employs.

SONG 785.

THE INFALLIBLE DOCTOR.

ADVISE your friend, grave man of art,
  I find a strange, unusual smart,
'Tis here—fierce symptoms at my heart.
                              Discover

'Tis pleasure, pain, a mix'd degree,
My pulse examine, here's your fee;
What think you can my sickness be?
                              A lover.

A lover!—'tis my case, too sure!
O ease me straight—I'll not endure;
Prescribe, I'll follow close the cure.
                              Take hope.

But if she (spite of speech or pen)
Prove coy, or false with other men,
Ah, doctor!—what expedient then?
                              A rope.

SONG 786.

AS lately, at a rural fair,
  I ey'd around the beauties there,
With top-knots red, and green, and blue,
How comic was the motley crew!

The farmer's daughter baulk'd her cows,
  To buy of gingerbread a spouse;
And kitchen Malkin pinn'd her hood,
  To meet her spark of flesh and blood.

The country lady cheapen'd toys,
  And ballad-finger strain'd her voice;
Plebeian dames join nymphs of birth,
  As grass and flow'rs enamel earth.

The country ladies seem'd to me
  Too much to mimic quality;
And milk-maids charms, and aukward ways,
  Could not my nicer fancy please.

But when I turn'd, and look'd again,
  I spy'd Miss Jenny in the train,
In blooming youth and beauty gay,
  As fresh as any queen of May.

D d

Of graceful mien, and high-born race,
Yet humble as the village lafs;
Like fome defert which crowns the feaft,
And makes amends for all the reft.

In orchard fo the faunt'ring youth
Surveys the fruit with gaping mouth,
Where many an apple meets his tafte,
Which he rejects with fputt'ring hafte.

But when he views the Cath'rine pear,
Of tempting form, and colours rare;
The lufcious bait to reach he fkips,
And longs to have it at his lips.

SONG 787.

CUPID, thou waggifh, artful boy,
  What have I done t' excite thy hate?
Oh! ever arm'd with cruelty,
  Thus to precipitate my fate.

I faw, I lov'd, I am undone,
  She at each vifit feems more coy,
You Urchin! fneering at my moan,
  Half promife blifs, and half deny.

The wound you gave, admits no cure,
  Till time has thaw'd her frozen heart,
Jenny can life or death enfure,
  Jenny! my foul's far dearer part.

With equal force once twang the bow,
  Transfix the charmer, let her bleed;
The feeds of love fecurely fow,
  And clear the foil of ev'ry weed.

Were I, thro' fome fierce tyrant's hate,
  Condemn'd to racks, the fmiling fair
Cou'd blunt the keeneft dart of fate,
  And from the dying chace defpair.

If pray'rs and tears are ftill in vain,
  Think not (proud chit) I dread your pow'r;
Know, that to truckle I difdain,
  Or fhrink, tho' all thy thunders roar.

If I muft die, the ftroke begin,
  For I'm a man unus'd to fear;
By Jenny's hand wreck all thy fpleen,
  I die content, to die by her.

SONG 788.

ON A PIPE OF TOBACCO.

PRETTY tube of mighty power,
  Charmer of an idle hour,
Object of my hot defire,
Lip of wax, and eye of fire;
And thy fnowy, taper waift,
With my finger gently brac'd,
And thy lovely, fwelling creft,
With my bended ftopper preft,
And the fweeteft blifs of bliffes
Breathing from thy balmy kiffes;
Happy thrice and thrice again,
Happieft he of happy men,
Who, when again the night returns,
When again the taper burns,

When again the crickets gay,
(Little crickets full of play)
Can afford his tube to feed
With the fragrant Indian weed;
Pleafure for a nofe divine,
Incenfe of the god of wine;
Happy thrice and thrice again,
Happieft he of happy men.

SONG 789.

PLACINDA.

WHEN Placinda's beauties appear,
  How enchanting then is her air!
Such a fine fhape and fize,
Such lips, and teeth, and eyes!
So many pointed darts who can bear!

Then her temper, fo good, and fo fweet!
Such her carriage and elegant wit;
  Whate'er fhe does or fays
  We all in tranfports gaze,
Like young fquires in the opera-pit.

But to cut off all hopes of retreat,
There's Eliza to captivate;
  The mighty Hercules
  With two fuch foes as thefe
Muft have look'd for a total defeat.

SONG 790.

COX-HEATH CAMP.

Written by THOMAS HASTINGS.

COME, brave Britons, advance; let us face
  the proud foe!
To Cox-Heath, my bold lads, to the camp let
  us go:
Frefh glory to win, let's go forth to the wars;
For Britannia's bold fons are the offspring of
  Mars.
  While Britons are free, and our country us
  calls,
  We fearlefs will fight, boys,
  Maintain George's right, boys,
  And like Britons of old, we will conquer
  the Gauls.

Should the fons of falfe France, now our force
  to withftand,
Surround us by fea, or approach us by land,
We undaunted will meet them, and make them
  retire,
Or fink them beneath, if they dare ftand our
  fire.
  While Britons are free, &c.

Tho' into our borders they come five to one,
Regardlefs we'll face them, with fword, and
  with gun:
We fight for our freedom, we fight for our King,
And the proud Gallic flaves to his feet we will
  bring.
  While Britons are free, &c.

Recal we what Edward at Creſſy once won,
And the thouſands were cruſh'd by his conquer-
ing ſon;
When five times ten thouſand in battle were
ſlain,
And each Briton his man took alive on the plain.
While Britons are free, &c.

So fam'd Henry reap'd glory on Agincourt's
field,
When firſt the French lilies bedeck'd his bright
ſhield;
Lo! fearleſs his files up to Paris advance,
And ſons of this iſland did rule over France.
While Britons are free, &c.

Let the deeds of our heroes now Britons inſpire,
Now let each glowing breaſt catch the flame of
his fire;
The ſoul of great Marlb'rough, the ſoul of fam'd
Stair,
Call their ſons forth to war, and their glories to
ſhare.
While Britons are free, and our country us
calls,
We fearleſs will fight, boys,
Maintain George's right, boys,
And like Britons of old, we will conquer
the Gauls.

SONG 791.

AGAIN in ruſtic weeds array'd,
A ſimple ſwain, a ſimple maid;
O'er rural ſcenes with joy we'll rove,
By dimpling brook, or cooling grove.

The birds ſhall ſtrain their little throats,
And warble wild their merry notes;
Whilſt we converſe beneath the ſhade,
A happy ſwain and happy maid.

Thy hands ſhall pluck, to grace my bow'r,
The luſcious fruit, the fragrant flow'r;
Whilſt joys ſhall bleſs, for ever new,
Thy Phebe kind, my Colin true.

SONG 792.

LOVE NO NOUN-SUBSTANTIVE.

WHAT tho' my love has got no pelf,
She is a good fortune of herſelf,
With a vaſt ſtock of pow'rful charms;
Of ſtature tall, and graceful mien,
Good ſenſe withal, and temper ſerene:
With a form fitted to bleſs my arms.
Two dove-like eyes, two ivory rows,
And, like the eagle, riſing noſe;
And when her hand I think upon,
And fingers like the wax-work ſhown,
Oh! then my heart beats thick with alarms.

Thus inclination drives me to,
But prudence tells me 'twill never do.
Naked love will quickly catch cold;

And ſomething more muſt now be ſaid,
Than four bare legs in one little bed,
Notwithſtanding ſtrange ſtories of old;
That love indeed may laugh awhile,
And warm himſelf in Delia's ſmile,
But without means muſt ſoon expire:
There muſt be coal to feed the fire;
I mean, good ſtore of ſilver and gold.

SONG 793.

THE THUNDER-STORM.

Written by Mr. NICHOLLS.

THE ponderous cloud was black and low,
And ſail'd majeſtically ſlow,
Red lightning ſcorch'd the ground;
Tremendous, now, the thunder rolls,
As if it would have riv'd the poles,
And torrents pour around.

No ſhelter nigh, to ſhield my head,
Along the champaign ſwift I fled,
Before the opening ſkies;
Till from the weſt a gale aroſe,
Diſpers'd the cloud, the welkin glows,
And vernal ſweets ariſe.

Creation ſeem'd as new awake,
From every dingle, buſh, and brake,
E'en from the very ſod;
The feather'd race their throats eſſay,
Who ſhall ſalute, in ſongs moſt gay,
The wonder-working God.

Aſham'd, that thoſe of leaſt eſteem
Should praiſe the Pow'r alone ſupreme,
I crav'd to be forgiven:
Straight, like the little grateful throng,
I, in an unaffected ſong,
Addreſs'd my voice to Heaven.

SONG 794.

RETIREMENT.

Written by Mr. J WRENCH.

IMMORTAL powers, convey me where
No tumultuous throngs appear;
Far from flatt'ry, far from care,
Let me breathe the rural air.

Bear me to ſome ſhady grove,
Bleſt retreat of peace and love;
Where, ſecure, the warbling choir
From the buſy world retire.

Where nature's beauties deck the ground,
Thouſand beauteous flowers abound:
Still, to make the ſcene more fair,
Let lovely Delia meet me there.

Delia's preſence will improve
The vernal beauty of the grove;
Give each flower a pleaſing dye,
Brighter azure to the ſky.

Venus, to complete my joy,
Hither ſend thy ſportive boy;

And, in this propitious hour,
Let my Delia own his power.

Rofeate health, fair peace, gay pleafure,
Happinefs, and balmy leifure;
When my Delia's heart poffeffing,
Ever bleft, and ever bleffing.

SONG 795.

A ROUNDELAY.

WHILE thefe clofe walls thy beauties hide,
Immur'd within this guarded grove,
On the clear ftream's oppofing fide
The mufe fhail wail my hopelefs love.

My love!—which nothing can outvie,
Which never fhall a period know;
Ye breezes, tell her as ye fly;
Ye waters, bear it as ye flow.

And tho' (by adverfe friends confin'd)
The yielding fair I vainly crave;
O bring her murmurs, gentle wind,
Her image, ev'ry ebbing wave!

Yet, oh! ye winds, her fighs conceal;
Nor you, ye waves, reflect her face;
Left Æolus my paffion feel,
And Neptune fue for her embrace.

Small need ye fhou'd her accents bear,
Or to my view her form impart,
Whofe voice dwells ever on my ear,
Whofe image ever in my heart.

SONG 796.

THE COUNTRY WEDDING.

ALL you that e'er tafted of Swanfal-Hall beer,
Or ever cry'd roaft-meat for having been
there;
To crown your good chear, pray accept of a catch,
Now Harry and Betty have ftruck up a match.
Derry down, down; down, derry down.

As things may fall out which nobody would
guefs,
So it happens that Harry fhould fall in with Befs;
May they prove to each other a mutual relief!
To their plenty of carrots, I wifh 'em much beef.
Derry down, &c.

She had a great talent at roaft-meal and boil'd,
And feldom it was that her pudding was fpoil'd;
Renown'd, too, for dumpling, and dripping-pan
fop,
At handling a difh-clout, and twirling a mop.
Derry down, &c.

To kitchen-ftuff only her thoughts did afpire,
Yet wit fhe'd enough to keep out of the fire;
And tho' in fome things fhe were fhort of the
fox,
'Tis faid, fhe has twenty good pounds in her box.
Derry down, &c.

Now we've told you the bride's rare defert and
eftate,
'Tis fit that the bridegroom's good parts we
relate;
As honeft a ploughman as e'er held a plough,
As trufty a carter as e'er cry'd, Gee-ho.
Derry down, &c.

So lovingly he with his cattle agreed,
That feldom a lafh for his whip he did need:
When a man is fo gentle and kind to his horfe,
His wife may expect that he'll not ufe her worfe.
Derry down, &c.

With induftry he has collected the pence,
In thirty good pounds there's a great deal of
fenfe;
And tho' he fufpected ne'er was of a plot,
None yet in good-humour e'er call'd him a fot.
Derry down, &c.

For brewing we hardly fhall meet with his
fellow,
His beer was well hopt, clear, fubftantial, and
mellow;
He brew'd the good liquor, fhe made the good
cake,
And as they have brew'd even fo let 'em bake.
Derry down, &c.

Your fhoes he can cobble, fhe mend your old
clothes,
And both are ingenious at darning of hofe:
Then fince he has gotten the length of her foot,
As they make their own bed, fo pray let 'em
go to't.
Derry down, &c.

Bid the laffes and lads to the merry brown bowl,
Whilft rafhers of bacon fhall fmoak on the coal :
Then Roger and Bridget, and Robin and Nan,
Hit 'em each on the nofe, with the hofe, if
ye can.
Derry down, &c.

May her wheel and his plough be fo happily fped,
With the beft in the parifh to hold up their head:
May he load his own waggon with butter and
cheefe,
Whilft fhe rides to market with turkies and
geefe.
Derry down, &c.

May he be a churchwarden, and yet come to
church,
Nor when in his office take on him too much :
May fhe meet due refpect, without fcolding or
ftrife,
And live to drink tea with the minifter's wife.
Derry down, &c.

Rejoice ye good fellows that love a good bit,
To fee thus united the tap and the fpit;
For as bread is the ftaff of man's life, fo you
know
Good drink is the fwitch makes it merrily go.
Derry down, &c.

Then drink to good neighbourhood, plenty, and
   peace,
That our taxes may leffen, and weddings increafe;
Let the high and the low, like good fubjects,
   agree,
Till the courtiers for fhame grow as honcft as we.
   Derry down, &c.

Let conjugal love he the pride of each fwain,
Till true-hearted maids have no caufe to com-
   plain;
To the church pay her dues, to their majeflies
   honour,
And homage and rent to the lord of the manor.
   Derry down, down; down, derry down.

SONG 797.

Written by Mr. HAWKINS.

TO fpeak, my mufe, fweet Charlotte's praife,
   And all her charms explore;
How far beyond thy feeble lays,
   On themes like thefe to foar!

In her is ev'ry grace combin'd,
   Divefted of all art;
An angel's form, with fenfe refin'd
   To captivate the heart!

A temper open, mild and free,
   A heart replete with truth;
In her we ev'ry virtue fee,
   Refplendent with her youth.

Thrice happy he who gains the maid,
   For wedlock to incline;
But happier I, could it be faid
   That Heav'n had ftamp'd her mine!

SONG 798.

Sung in the Honeft Yorkfhireman.

COME hither my country fquire,
   Take friendly inftructions rrom me:
     The lords fhall adm're
     Thy tafte in attire,
   The ladies fhall languifh for thee.
Such flaunting, gallanting, and jaunting,
   And frolicking thou fhalt fee,
     Thou ne'er, like a clown,
     Shall quit London's fweet town,
   To live in thine own country.

A fkimming-difh hat provide,
With little more brim than lace:
     Nine hairs on a fide,
     To a pigtail tv'd,
Will fet off thy jolly broad face,
   Such flaunting, &c.

Go get thee a footman's frock,
A cudgel quite up to thy nofe;
     Then frize like a fhock,
     And plaifter thy black,
And buckle thy fhoes at thy toes.
   Such flaunting, &c.

A brace of ladies fair
To pleafure thee fhall ftrive;
     In a chaife and pair
     They fhall take the air,
And thou on the box fhalt drive.
   Such flaunting, &c.

Convert thy acres to cafh,
And faw thy timber down;
     Who'd keep fuch trafh,
     And not cut a flafh,
Or enjoy the delights of the town?
   Such flaunting, gallanting, and jaunting,
     And frolicking thou fhalt fee,
     Thou ne'er, like a clown,
     Shall quit London's fweet town,
   To live in thine own country.

SONG 799.

PASTORA.

Written by Mr. NICHOLLS.

ALONE, by the fide of a murmuring rill,
   That lav'd the gay foot of a primrofy hill,
Paftora beneath a broad pop'lar was laid,
When Damon in extafy enter'd the fhade.

He blefs'd the kind ftar that directed him there,
And vow'd on his knees fhe had long been his
   care;
He figh'd, and he fwore by the pow'rs over head,
If fhe'd blefs him to-day, to-morrow he'd wed.

She heard his falfe vows, fhe believ'd his foft
   tale—
Ah! virgins, ne'er venture alone to the vale!
Leaft you, like Paftora, fhould mourn all the
   year
For a bloffom which only a virgin can bear!

O'er the maids of the hamlet, the hill and the
   dale,
And the maids of the town, may my precepts
   prevail!
May the fwain who'd deceive them his vices
   repent,
And the bofom of Damon defpair of content!

Alas! cruel rake, may his fields wear the blight,
May his vines never bear the juice of delight!
I could wifh, (but 'tis pity his lambkins fhould
   bleed)
Some rover would ravage his fold for the deed.

SONG 800.

Written by Mr. MAVOR.

THOU fetting fun, that calls my fair
   To take the cool and ev'ning air,
With joy I hail thy lateft rays,
That fhew me where my Chloe ftrays.

O, let no clouds obfcure the fkies,
Or noxious exhalations rife!
But may fweet flow'rs uprear their heads,
And rofe bloffom, where fhe treads.

Let ev'ry tenant of the grove,
Remind her youthful heart of love;
And ev'ry breeze convey a figh,
And whifper 'tis for her I die.

O! fweet, tormenting love, I feel
Thy wound, which reafon cannot heal:
Thy fire, conceal'd within my breaft,
Deprives my flutt'ring heart of reft.

At ev'ry glance of Chloe's eyes,
My boafted réfolution flies:
And ftill I'm diffident to name
My inward racks, and fecret flame.

While Philomela fad complains,
And pours out all her plaintive ftrains;
I likewife mourn, in lays fincere
As ever reach'd a female ear.

Thou fon of Venus, hear my pray'r,
And with thy dart transfix my fair;
With her fond fwain, O! make her prove
The lafting blifs of ardent love.

SONG 801.

AH! bright Belinda, hither fly,
And fuch a light difcover,
As may the abfent fun fupply,
And chear the drooping lover.

Arife, my day, with fpeed arife,
And all my forrows banifh;
Before the fun of thy bright eyes
All gloomy terrors vanifh.

No longer let me figh in vain,
And curfe the hoarded treafure:
Why fhould you love to give us pain,
When you were made for pleafure?

The petty pow'rs of hell deftroy,
To fave's the pride of Heaven;
To you the firft, if you prove coy,
If kind, the laft is given.

The choice then fure's not hard to make
Betwixt the good and evil;
Which title had you rather take,
My goddefs, or my devil?

SONG 802.

THE DESPAIRING LOVER.

Written by Mr. HAWKINS.

YE fhepherds adhere to my woe,
And pity the anguifh I bear;
Oh! did ye my forrows but know,
Ye furely would grant me a tear:
My Phillis, that gladden'd the plain,
And formerly gave fuch delight;
Has left me to languifh in pain,
And banifh'd me quite from her fight.

Ah! once fhe was mild as the dove,
No nymph was more faithful and free;
And I thought her the goddefs of love,
So fweetly fhe fmil'd upon me:

Together, in grove or in mead,
Delighted we travers'd along;
While around us the herds were at feed,
Or we heard the fweet warblers fong.

But now I am fad and forlorn,
My pleafure and paftime are o'er;
For Phillis rejeéts me with fcorn,
And never will think on me more.
I met her one day in the dale,
And tenderly told her my care;
But oh! fhe rejeéted my tale,
And bade me go droop and defpair.

She told me that I was unkind,
Yet, truft me, I fcarce can tell why;
And hop'd that fome fwain fhe fhould find
That never would caufe her to figh.
With wonder I gaz'd at the maid,
For to her I was ever fincere;
Yet fhe frown'd at whatever I faid,
So faithlefs, alas! was my dear.

Oh! think, cruel maid, I reply'd,
What vows you have proffer'd to me!
Then why am I fcorn'd and deny'd,
While thus I'm diftraéted for thee?
Remember, one eve in the grove,
With freedom you valu'd my truth;
In tears you then plighted your love,
And ftrongly regarded my youth.

Then why will you leave me to weep,
Nor pity the anguifh I find?
Will Phillis her cruelty keep?
Ah! will fhe be ever unkind?
Awhile, oh! refleét on my woe;
Your malice no longer invoke;
I'm wretched you furely muft know,
And die with fo fatal a ftroke.

'Twas thus I unbofom'd my grief,
Though fruitlefs I found was my plea;
For ftill fhe ne'er gave me relief,
Nor longer will fmile upon me:
Then, fhepherds, fo rural and gay,
Since my charmer will never be won,
Oh! give a kind ear to my lay,
And pity a youth that's undone.

SONG 803.

THAT all men are beggars, we plainly may
fee,
For beggars there are of ev'ry degree,
Tho' none are fo blefs'd or fo happy as we,
Which nobody can deny, deny; which no-
body can deny.

The tradefman he begs that his wares you
would buy,
Then begs you'd believe the price is not high,
And fwears 'tis his trade, when he tells you
a lye
Which nobody can deny, &c.

The lawyer he begs that you'd give him a fee,
Tho' he reads not your brief, or regards not
your plea,

But advises your foe how to get a decree.
Which nobody can deny, &c.

The courtier he begs for a pension or place,
A ribband or title, or smile from his grace,
'Tis due to his merit, 'tis writ in his face.
Which nobody can deny, &c.

But if, by mishap, he should chance to get none,
He begs you'd believe that the nation's undone;
There's but one honest man, and himself is
that one.
Which nobody dare deny, &c.

The fair-one she labours whole mornings at
home,
New charms to create, and much paint to con-
sume,
Yet begs you'd believe 'tis her natural bloom.
Which nobody should deny, &c.

The courtier he begs the dear nymph to comply:
She begs he'd be gone; yet with languishing eye
Still begs he would stay, for a maid she can't die,
Which none but a fool can deny, deny; which
none but a fool can deny.

SONG 804.

AH! how vainly mortals treasure
Hopes of happiness and pleasure,
Hard and doubtful to obtain:
By what standards false we measure!
Still pursuing ways to ruin,
Seeking bliss, and finding pain.

SONG 805.

QUOTH Strephon to Flora, Your charms
I adore,
You're witty, you're pretty, you're pleasing all
o'er;
Your lips are like rubies, your cheeks like the
rose,
And your breath far more sweet than Arabia
blows:
But tho' charming, alas! your delight is to teize:
Yet all she reply'd, was, Sir, just as you please.

Oh! think, he return'd, of the pains I endure,
And as you 're the cause, O extend me the cure;
My passion's so strong, that my rest I forsake,
And a paleness o'erspreads, now, my once rosy
cheek;
No longer be coy, then, but give me some ease:
Yet she careless reply'd still, Sir, just as you
please.

Enrag'd that she paid him no greater regard,
When his passion he knew was deserving reward;
He boldly advancing, saluted the fair,
And vow'd that such treatment no longer he'd
bear.
No longer declar'd he would sue on his knees:
Yet she careless reply'd still, Sir, just as you
please.

Then seizing her hand, he straight led her along,
While she careless ne'er said he was right or was
wrong:
He took her to church, and there made her his
wife,
And vow'd he would love her as long as he'd
life:
No longer she thinks that his passion can teize,
Tho' she answers him still, Sir, 'tis just as you
please.

SONG 806.

TO FELICIA.

Written by Mr. HAWKINS.

THY plaintive pipe, Felicia, flows,
Like Philomela's in the shade;
My heart with ardent rapture glows
At thy enchanting serenade.

Doth melody to thee belong!
In thee my fair it doth reside;
The tuneful accents of thy tongue
Shall ever be thy shepherd's pride.

Euterpe's child, dear maid, thou art,
And softest soother of my care;
Thy accents strike like Cupid's dart,
Thou sweetly-charming, lovely fair.

Then fill thy Damon's heart with bliss,
Ah! let him hear thy melting strain;
Deny him not a boon like this,
Come chear your slave, and chear the plain.

So doubly tune thy vocal tale,
And rid me of corroding strife;
Oh! let me on thy charms regale,
And make thy shepherd blest for life.

SONG 807.

CELADON; A CANTATA.

RECITATIVE.

BENEATH a beech's spreading shade,
The youthful Celadon was laid,
His pipe lay careless by his side,
His flock had wander'd far and wide;
With fault'ring voice, and languid eyes,
And hands uplifted to the skies,
He sung—and quick the groves around
Return'd the soul-dissolving sound.

AIR.

Ye pow'rs who rule this earthly ball,
Who hear us whensoe'er we call,
Attend my prayer, my grief remove,
Or haughty Delia touch with love;
Let her heart
But feel love's smart,
Forlorn like me, in some lonely grove.

Let tears swell her eyes,
Let her bosom heave sighs!

Let her heart crack with pain,
Till like me she complain,
And like me, unrelented, she dies.

RECITATIVE.

By chance the nymph, to seek a favourite lamb,
Which stray'd that very morning from it's dam,
Behind the shady tree arriv'd, and heard
The very prayer that he to Heav'n preferr'd;
Fear shook her mind, and pity touch'd her breast,
And thus her love to Celadon expiest.

AIR.

Cease, fond shepherd, thy upbraiding,
Call thy rash petition back,
Pity now my breast invading,
Forbids to keep thee on the rack.

Love can ne'er be won by railing,
But by kindness is begot;
Here let's cancel each past failing,
All my folly be forgot.

Take my hand, a slave to Hymen,
I resign me to thy arms.
Prudes, avaunt! I think no crime in,
To such love to yield my charms.

SONG 808.

THE CHOICE OF A FRIEND.

Written by Mr. NICHOLLS.

ERE Phœbus from Aries directs his faint
   beams,
To melt the pale snow and the ice on the
   streams,
This boon (with submission) great Jove, I
   require;
May I ne'er want good chear, nor a friend by
   my fire!
If my purse should prove light, and my cellar
   be dry,
May I ne'er want a patron to deal a supply!
So Ben sung of old, his petition was heard,
And relief from the hand of good Falkland
   appear'd.

In chusing that friend, Pallas, thou be my guide;
O! shield me from folly, from ign'rance, and
   pride;
From the wretch who will smile in your face,
   whilst his heart
Is the source of deceit, and the store-house
   of art;
From the cold flinty bosom, that ne'er heav'd
   a sigh
When the sorrowful wreck of oppression was by.
I ask not such trifles, Minerva, as these;
Thy ne'er meet my eye, but they rob me of ease.

I ask not the Atheist (bright author of bliss)
Of all that's obnoxious, defend me from this;
Nor the gloomy fanatick, conventicle thing,
From whose errors a thousand absurdities spring;
I ask not the fribble, averse to the bowl,
Let the trifle, o'er tea, with his Chloe condole;

I ask not the man to opinion a slave,
Nor volatile rattle, nor one who's too grave.

I ask not the gamester, the sot, nor the fool;
Nor he who's to party or faction a tool:
The man, mighty pow'r, I would chuse for
   my friend,
Should be one on whose faith I could always
   depend;
Who'll not favour the cause that he knows is
   not right,
Nor will flatter an ass to be reckon'd polite;
Who dares to be honest when times are the worst;
Such a one could I meet with, my friendship
   I'd trust.

His mind I'd have fraught with a store of
   good sense;
Well read, and his manners be free from offence:
His tongue should the dictates of virtue obey,
And reason reclaim him whenever astray.
If such I could meet, I would constantly strive,
Untainted to keep the dear blessing alive;
And when thou shalt bid me relinquish my
   breath,
I'd chearfully smile upon friendship in death.

SONG 809.

OF all the things beneath the sun,
   To love's the greatest curse:
If one's deny'd, then he's undone;
   If not, 'tis ten times worse.
Poor Adam, by his wife, 'tis known,
   Was trick'd some years ago;
But Adam was not trick'd alone,
   For all his sons were so.

Lovers the strangest fools are made,
   When they their nymphs pursue,
Which they will ne'er believe, till wed,
   But then—alas! 'tis true:
They beg, they pray, and they adore,
   Till weary'd out of life;
And pray, what's all this trouble for?
   Why, truly, for a wife.

How odd a thing's a whining sot,
   Who sighs in greatest need,
For that which, soon as ever got,
   Does make him sigh indeed!
Each maid's an angel whilst she's woo'd,
   But when the wooing's done,
The wife, instead of flesh and blood,
   Proves nothing but a bone.

Ills, more or less, in human life,
   No mortal man can shun;
But when a man has got a wife,
   He has them all in one.
The liver of Prometheus
   A gnawing vulture fed;
A fable, that the thing was thus,
   The poor old man was wed.

A wife, all men of learning know,
   Was Tantalus's curse;
The apples which did tempt him so,
   Were nought but a divorce.

Let no fool dream, that to his fhare
  A better wife will fall ;
They're all the fame, faith, to a hair,
  For they are women all.

When firft the fenfelefs empty nokes
  With wooing does begin,
Far better he might beg the ftocks
  That they would let him in.
Yet for a lover you may fay,
  He wears no cheating phiz;
Tho' others looks do oft betray,
  He looks like what he is.

More joys a glafs of wine doth give
  (Wife take him that gainfays)
Than all the wenches, fprung from Eve,
  Ere gave in all their days.
But come, to lovers here's a glafs,
  God-wot, they need no curfe!
Each wifhes he may wed his lafs;
  No foul can wifh him worfe.

SONG 810.

Written by DEAN SWIFT.

SAYS my uncle, I pray now difcover
  What has been the caufe of your woes,
That you pine and you whine like a lover?
  I've feen Molly Mogg of the Rofe!

O nephew! your grief is but folly,
  In town you may find better prog;
Half a crown there will get you a Molly,
  A Molly much better than Mogg.

The fchool-boy's delight is a play-day,
  The fchool-mafter's joy is to flog;
A fop's the delight of a lady,
  But mine is in fweet Molly Mogg.

Will o' Wifp leads the trav'ler a-gadding
  Thro' ditch, and thro' quagmire and bog ;
But no light can e'er fet me a-madding,
  But the eyes of my fweet Molly Mogg.

For guineas in other men's breeches
  Your gamefters will prum and will cog;
But I envy them none of their riches,
  So I pawn my fweet Molly Mogg.

The heart that's half-wounded is ranging,
  It here and there leaps like a fog;
But my heart can never be changing,
  'Tis fo fixed on fweet Molly Mogg.

I know that by wits 'tis recited,
  That women, at beft, are a clog;
But I'm not fo eafily frighted
  From loving my fweet Molly Mogg.

A letter when I am inditing,
  Comes Cupid, and gives me a jog,
And I fill all my paper with writing
  Of nothing but fweet Molly Mogg.

I feel I'm in love to diftraction,
  My fenfes are loft in a fog;
And in nothing can find fatisfaction,
  But in thoughts of my fweet Molly Mogg.

If I would not give up the three graces,
  I wifh I were hang'd like a dog, .
And at court all the drawing-room faces,
  For a glance at my fweet Molly Mogg.

For thofe faces want nature and fpirit,
  And feem as cut out of a log;
Juno, Venus, and Pallas's merit
  Unite in my fweet Molly Mogg.

Were Virgil alive with his Phillis,
  And writing another Eclogue,
Both his Phillis and fair Amaryllis
  He'd give for my fweet Molly Mogg.

When Molly comes up with the liquor,
  Then jealoufy fets me a-gog;
To be fure fhe's a bit for the vicar,
  And fo I fhall lofe Molly Mogg.

SONG 811.

THE FORSAKEN MAID; A CANTATA.

Written by Mr. HAWKINS.

RECITATIVE.

AH! whither fhall I fly to find relief?
  Is there no cure for wretchednefs and grief?
My deareft Dorilas has prov'd untrue,
And what, alas! muft haplefs Sylvia do?
Fool that I was to truft perfidious man,
Whofe falfe diffembling love our hearts trapan!
Ah! then they leave us in a wretched ftate!
Ye nymphs, take warning, ere it is too late.

AIR.

How fevere is my affliction,
  Thus to wander in defpair;
Gods, give ear to my direction!
  Ceafe, ah! ceafe a maiden's care.

Did the youth know how I languifh,
  He would furely give relief;
Turn again, and eafe my anguifh;
  Succour my diftrefs and grief.

SONG 812.

THE charms of Florimel
  No force of time or art
Shall fever from my heart;
But ever to the world I'll tell
  The charms of beauteous Florimel.

Each rock and funny hill,
  The flow'ry meads and groves,
  Shall fay Myrtillo loves;
And echo fhall be taught to tell
  The charms of beauteous Florimel.

Each tree within the vale,
  That on it's banks doth wear
  The triumphs of my fair,
To future times in verfe fhall tell
  The charms of beauteous Florimel.
      E e

Each brook and purling rill,
Shall on it's bubbling stream
Convey the virgin's name;
And, as it rolls, in murmurs tell
The charms of beauteous Florimel.

The sylvan gods, that dwell
Amidst this sacred grove,
Shall wonder at my love;
While ev'ry sound conspires to tell
The charms of beauteous Florimel.

SONG 813.

Written by Mr. D. BEST.

WHEN shrubs did bloffom, fields were green,
And ev'ry thing was gay,
All nature reap'd the fruits of spring,
And hail'd the welcome May;
The little birds quite lively were,
They tun'd their downy throats,
The lark high-foaring in the air,
With chearful, pleasing notes;

The bleating sheep were heard around,
The lambs did skip and play,
In fportive innocence combin'd
To hail the welcome May;
When Nancy fair attended was
By her adoring fwain:
With fparkling eyes, and tender looks,
He told to her his pain.

He faid, that he could take no reft
Without she would relent.
With blushes that adorn'd her cheek,
The fair-one gave consent.
To Hymen's altar they repair'd,
Where love did join their hands;
And now they live fecure from harm,
In wedlock's happy bands.

SONG 814.

HASTE! sweet nymph, the eve invites,
Jocund let us tread the dale;
There to blend in sweet delights,
The soft caress and tender tale.
Free from guile, devoid of art,
Are thy shepherd's simple ways;
My fond lips shall speak my heart,
While I tell Meliffa's praife.

Hark! the bird on yonder spray,
Chanting out it's warbling notes;
Pouring in sweet melody,
Music from it's little throat.
It's wild lays are unconfin'd,
Ev'ry stranger drinks the stream;
Thou shalt all possess my mind,
Be thy Corin's only theme.

See! the flock, thy shepherd's store,
All in fnowy fleeces dreft,
Let me wash them more and more,
Ne'er can match thy virgin breast.

Lambkins fportive all around,
Looking fweet fimplicity,
In their bofoms is not found
Th' innucence which dwells in thee.

See the ivy, how it twines
Round the oak—it's tendrils clue;
Thus Meliffa! were you mine,
My fond arms should circle you.—
The maiden fmil'd, no more delay'd,
Gave her hand with joy and glee;
Through the dell we fondly ftray'd,
Conftant, happy, blithe, and free.

SONG 815.

GREAT Jove, in merry mood, once faid,
Enthron'd on high Olympus fitting,
He'd form one lovely mortal maid,
With all the female graces fitting:
His fpoufe, ill-natur'd Juno, wept,
While Venus, lovely creature, laugh'd;
But Jove his promife fairly kept,
And nam'd the fair-one, Nancy Taft.

SONG 816.

YOUNG Polly was the blitheft maid
That tript it o'er the plain;
But now to cruel grief's betray'd,
By Damon's cold difdain.
And till of late, was always free
To fing the charms of liberty.

Each love-taught shepherd ftrove to tell
His paffion in the glade,
And vow'd her beauty did excel
Bright Venus, faireft maid.
But Polly ftill continu'd free
To fing the charms of liberty.

Till Damon, with his fleecy care,
By chance pafs'd by that way;
She faw—fhe lov'd—Ah! haplefs fair,
No longer is fhe gay;
Nor can fhe boaft of being free
To fing the charms of liberty.

For now, dejected and forlorn,
The nymph is left to rove;
With Philomel, at eve and morn,
To moan her hopelefs love.
And Polly, now, no longer free,
Laments the lofs of liberty.

SONG 817.

Written by W. C——

LET coxcombs boaft of painted belles,
Whofe cheeks with rofes vie;
Their pleafing bloom will foon be o'er,
Will wither, pine, and die.

Yet, ere that rofy feafon's gone,
Or we time's patience try;
Ye powers divine, a lover hear,
He fues for Betfey Guy.

To win this fair, this fav'rite maid,
I'll each endearment try:
Say, will a faithful heart enchant
My lovely Betsey Guy?

As oft with her I cross the mead,
See, see! (the virgins cry)
How happy youthful Colin seems,
Since blest with Betsey Guy.

The shepherds all admire the maid,
The nymphs to please her try;
Ask for the pride of Chelmer's banks,
They point to Betsey Guy.

Matilda's Polydore was blest;
Yet not so blest as I,
When walking round yon flow'ry mead
With pretty Betsey Guy.

Let kings enjoy that pomp and state
For which vain mortals sigh;
Content I'd in a desert live
With charming Betsey Guy.

No other bliss on earth I ask,
With her I'd live and die;
Ye gods! take all your favours back,
Or give me Betsey Guy.

SONG 818.

THE PLAINTIVE SWAIN.

To the Memory of Mr. JOHN CUNNINGHAM.

Written by Mr, HAWKINS.

HE said—on the banks, by the stream,
He had pip'd for the shepherds too long;
But oh! how delightful his theme,
For innocence brighten'd his song:
Then how could he wish to rehearse
Such lessons so lofty and wide?
When Phillis was fond of his verse,
And nature sat down by his side?

Ah! Colin, how cou'd you mistake
Till Pan bid you stick to your strain?
Could you leave the white swans on the lake,
Or quit the delights of the plain?
Oh! no, honest Colin, you found
No flame like your Phillis's praise;
And poets came creeping around,
To listen, and envy your lays.

But vain were their efforts to try
To copy thy soft-soothing strains;
Their skill they were wont to deny,
As a wretched reward for their pains:
Yes, Colin, thy music was sweet,
With melody glided along;
While primroses bloom'd at thy feet,
And shepherds stood by in a throng.

The nymphs, too, came flocking the while,
From their cots where they dwelt in the dale!
And each of them seemed to smile
At the joys they receiv'd from the tale;

But now you have bid them adieu!
Death has seiz'd you a victim away;
While in sorrow they languish for you,
And weep wheresoever they stray.

SONG 819.

Written by Mr. NICHOLLS.

LOVELY Maria, skilful maid,
Whene'er you touch the tuneful chords,
To speak the rapture that's convey'd,
Is not within the force of words.

Whene'er you turn Admetus o'er,
And tune your Handel's *Spera si*;
We think on worldly things no more,
Our thoughts are fixt above the sky.

Nor do you charm our race alone,
You tempt (at hand) the gentle dove;
Who sits attentive to each tone,
Then flies, and fills his cote with love.

The surly cur that keeps thy door,
When you essay those pow'rs so sweet,
Bays at the passing clown no more,
But fawns and frolicks at his feet.

Thus, like Cecilia, sacred fair,
And Orpheus, mighty with the lute,
You ease the human soul of care,
And melt the bosom of the brute.

Go on, dear maid, tune Handel's strains;
Since such soft charms around thee wait;
To turn our thoughts from these low plains,
And fit us for a better state.

SONG 820.

A WELCH LOVE-SONG.

SOME sing Molly Mogg of the Rose,
And call her the Oakingham Pelle;
Whilst others do serses compose
On peautiful Molly Lepelie.

Put of all the young firgins so fair,
Which Pritain's crete monarchy owns;
In peauty there's none to compare
With hur charming tear Gwinifrid Shones.

Unenviet the splentit contition
Of princes that sit upon thrones:
The highest of all hur ampition
Ifs the lose of fair Gwinifrid Shones.

Pold mortals the clohe will search ofer
For cold and for tiamond stones;
Put hur can more treasure tiscofer
In peautiful Gwinifrid Shones.

From the piggest crete mountain in Pritain
Hur would fenture the preaking hur pones,
So that the soft lap hur might sit on
Of peautiful Gwinifrid Shones.

Not the nightingale's pitiful note
Can expreß how poor Shenkin bemoans
His fate, when in places remote
Hur is absent from Gwinifrid Shones.

Hur lofe ifs than honey far fweeter,
　And hur is no Shenkin ap drones;
Put hur would lapour in profe and in metre,
　To praife hur tear Gwinifrid Shones.

As the harp of Saint Tavit furpaffes
　The pagpipes poor tweetles and crones;
So Lepelle, Molly Mogg, and all laffes,
　Are excell'd by hur Gwinifrid Shones.

SONG 821.

DESPAIR.

Written by Mr. MAVOR.

WHY fhines the moon with filver ray,
　Amid her ftarry fplendors gay!
Why trills the nightingale her note,
And ftrains her fweet mellifluous throat!
Why breathes the incenfe of the grove,
On me, a flave to care and love!

Now fnowy bloffoms clothe the year,
In verdant vefture meads appear ;
Favonian gales, and tepid fhow'rs,
Revive the gaudy, fmiling flow'rs;
All nature wantons in her bloom,
While I, alone, bewail my doom.

Ye deeply-piercing frofts return,
And freeze each Naïad in her urn;
The tender bloffoms tear away,
Deform the fields, unleaf the fpray;
And O! if able, chill this flame,
That burns my heart, and mars my frame;
Ront out the feeds of am'rous fire,
And quench both fear and fond defire.

But ah! in vain I beg your aid,
My heart your rigour can't pervade;
Like Hecla, 'midft eternal fnows,
With unextinguifh'd heat it glows.

What can I pray! where turn my eyes!
Ye howling winds infuriate rife!
With tenfold rage impetuous fweep
The furrow'd bofom of the deep ;
Let fpiry trees from land be torn,
And on your winged furges borne;
That in the aggravated roar,
My fatal lofs I may deplore;
Unheeded blend my frantic voice,
With gen'ral fhrieks, and hideous noife.

SONG 822.

COME, my faireft, learn of me,
　Learn to give and take the blifs;
Come, my love, here's none but we;
　I'll inftruct thee how to kifs.

Why turn from me that dear face?
Why that blufh, and downcaft eye?
Come, come, meet my fond embrace,
And the mutual rapture try.

Throw thy lovely twining arms
　Round my neck, or round my waift;
And whilft I devour thy charms,
　Let me clofely be embrac'd;

Then when foft ideas rife,
　And the gay defires grow ftrong ;
Let them fparkle in thy eyes,
　Let them murmur from thy tongue.

To my breaft with rapture cling,
　Look with tranfport on my face;
Kifs me, prefs me, ev'ry thing
　To endear the fond embrace.

Ev'ry tender name of love,
　In foft whifpers let me hear;
And let fpeaking nature prove
　Ev'ry extafy fincere.

SONG 823.

A GOOD-FELLOW'S WILL.

SHOULD I die by the force of good wine,
　'Tis my will, when I fall, that a tun be my
　　fhrine;
　And for the age to come,
　Engrave this ftory on my tomb:
Here lies a body once fo brave,
Who with drinking made his grave.

Since thus to die will purchafe fame,
And raife an everlafting name,
　Drink, drink away, and dare to be nobly
　　interr'd:
　　Let mifers and flaves
　　Sneak into their graves,
　And rot in a dirty church-yard.

SONG 824.

Written by the EARL of DORSET,

AT noon, on a fultry fummer's day,
　The brighter lady of the May,
Young Chloris, innocent and gay,
　Sat knotting in a fhade.

Each flender finger play'd it's part
With fuch activity and art,
As would inflame a youthful heart,
　And warm the moft decay'd.

Her fav'rite fwain by chance came by,
He faw no anger in her eye;
Yet when the bafhful boy drew nigh,
　She would have feem'd afraid.

She let her ivory needle fall,
And hurl'd away the twifted ball:
But ftraight gave Strephon fuch a call,
　As wou'd have rais'd the dead.

Dear gentle youth, is't none but thee?
With innocence I dare be free :
By fo much truth and modefty
　No nymph was e'er betray'd.

Come, lean thy head upon my lap,
While thy fmooth cheeks I ftroke and clap,
Thou may'ft fecurely take a nap :
　Which he, poor fool! obey'd.

She faw him yawn, and heard him fnore;
And found him faft afleep all o'er:
She figh'd, and could endure no more,
　But ftarting up, fhe faid,

Such virtue fhall rewarded be;
For this thy dull fidelity,
I'll truft thee with my flocks, not me:
  Purfue thy grazing trade.

Go, milk thy goats, and fhear thy fheep,
And watch all night thy flocks to keep;
Thou fhalt no more be lull'd afleep
  By me, miftaken maid.

SONG 825.

WHY, cruel creature, why fo bent
  To vex a tender heart?
To gold and title you relent,
  Love throws in vain his dart.

Let glitt'ring fools in courts be great,
  For pay let armies move;
Beauty fhou'd have no other bait,
  But gentle vows and love.

If on thofe endlefs charms you lay
  The value that's their due;
Kings are themfelves too poor to pay,
  A thoufand worlds too few.

But if a paffion without vice,
  Without difguife or art,
Ah, Celia! if true love's your price,
  Behold it in my heart.

SONG 826.

DAMON AND DELIA; A PASTORAL.

Written by Mr. D. BEST.

DAMON.

HOW bright in the morn are Aurora's gay
    beams,
When juft peeping behind yonder hill!
How tranfient the luftre, how bright to behold!
But my Delia furpaffes them ftill.

DELIA.

What's beauty, how vain, the mere tints of a
    fkin!
And the maid yet more vain, to her coft,
That's proud of the favour ordain'd her by fate,
When virtue, dear virtue, is loft!

How artful each fwain the weak maid to be-
    tray,
Who with patience will hear the foft tale!
To diffemble and flatter by nature they're taught,
And the paffion will ever prevail.

DAMON.

And does my dear Delia fufpect my fond heart,
And rail at the faults of my fex!
'Tis all the mere tale of fome artful old maid,
Who has ftrove my fair maid to perplex.

Let my Delia doubt that the ftars afford light,
And believe the fun deftin'd to be
For ever confin'd to one part of the globe,
  But ne'er doubt my fincerity.

DELIA.

How unarm'd my weak fex 'gainft your arts
  are prepar'd;
Ah! how eafy and apt to believe!
By falfhood they're often entic'd to a fnare,
  With promifes meant to deceive.

Forbear, honeft Damon, defpife the bafe art,
  Nor ftrive a weak maid to betray;
Rafh vows are repented whenever they're made,
  And promifes fly with the day.

If virtue's ftern rule we but once difobey,
  And fwerve from the pattern of truth;
We're blam'd for complying, by all your bafe
    fex,
  And cenfur'd by ev'ry falfe youth.

DAMON.

Believe me, coy maid, that my vows are as true
  As the fun to the courfe of the day;
And if Delia fhould farther fufpect my fond
    heart,
  I'm ready to anfwer, Obey.

DELIA.

Since Damon is faithful, ye nymphs, I'll be
    kind,
  And blefs, if I can, the dear youth;
What pleafure fo great, as to anfwer, Obey;
  And yield, when commanded by truth.

DAMON.

What fays my dear Delia, to-morrow let's hafte,
  Where Hymen our hands fhall unite?

DELIA.

Ye gods, I'll with rapture the fummons obey,
  And anfwer the prieft with delight!

BOTH.

Ye gods, I'll with rapture the fummons obey,
  And anfwer the prieft with delight!

SONG 827.

WAS love a fweet paffion, how bleft fhould
    I be;
No mortal could e'er be fo happy as me!
But O it torments me, it tortures my breaft;
It rifles my fenfes, it robs me of reft!

Long time I've been captive to Chloe's bright
    eyes;
Her bloom and her beauty firft gave the furprize;

But foon as I found, by the pride of her heart,
That her bloom and her beauty were govern'd
   by art,

I then took my leave of this prodigal dame.
And ftrove all I could to extinguifh the flame;
But ftill on my thoughts her fweet converfe re-
   mains:
So love is a burden, and heavy the chains.

Then hear, O ye youths, and this maxim pur-
   fue;
Let beauty ne'er fway you, nor pride e'er fub-
   due:
But place your affections where virtue remains;
Then love will be pleafing, and eafy the chains.

SONG 828.

Written by Mr. LEMOINE.

THE fprightly eye, the rofy cheek,
   The dimpled chin, and look fo meek,
A namelefs grace and air;
The ruby lip in fweetnefs dreft,
The foftly-fwelling angel breaft;
   All thefe adorn my fair.

See what unnumber'd beauties rove
Around each feature of my love,
   And fire my rapt'rous foul!
Ten thoufand fweets her looks difclofe,
At ev'ry glance my bofom glows,
   And yields to love's controul.

Juft heav'ns! why gave ye charms like thefe,
With ev'ry grateful art to pleafe,
   To one whom rigid fate,
Permits me not to tell my pain,
But makes me fear the cold difdain
   Of her I wifh my mate.

Curfe on the fordid thirft of gold!
When tend'reft paffions all are fold
   To win the world's applaufe;
When, for defire, and love, and joy,
Low int'reft fhall it's pow'rs employ,
   And gain th' ignoble caufe.

SONG 829.

WHILE harmony's echo refounds
   In the vallies where innocence reigns,
Where health and contentment abounds,
   And the birds charm the hills and the plains;
How delightful the fweets that are known!
   When retirement it's pleafures difplays,
Ev'ry blefling below, we muft own,
   Is center'd in that happy way.

Tho' mufic the favage may charm,
   And difperfe dreary thoughts from the mind;
'Tis retirement alone can difarm,
   And reftrain the grand foe of mankind;
For contentment thofe joys will refine
   Which peace and retirement doth bring,

When a current of pleafures combine
   To flow from fo pleafing a fpring.

Fame, honour, and grandeur defpife,
   If pleafures innate we purfue;
No bleflings will truly fuffice
   By coveting all in our view;
With friendfhip's few fons let me dwell
   In a homely retreat, to enjoy;
In vain pomp I would never excel,
   For that muft contentment deftroy.

SONG 830.

WHAT pleafure I feel when fequefter'd from
   town,
Where nought but confufion and difcord is
   known!
Blefs'd with health and contentment, no mor-
   tal I fear;
I'm more happy than thofe who have thoufands
   a year.
If perchance a dark cloud hovers over the day,
At night with good ale it will vanifh away.

Tho' meanly, to great ones, my cottage may
   feem,
Sufficient for me that it's decent and clean:
Without the vain fhow of an elegant manfion,
Unnotic'd I'll pafs thro' the world's wide ex-
   panfion.
   If perchance, &c.

By various delights which no forrow can bring,
My body's relaxed from autumn to fpring;
Retrofpecting with pleafure the years which
   are gone,
I look for enjoyment in thofe yet to come.
   If perchance, &c.

When age has o'er-reach'd me, and mirth is no
   more,
And time hath allow'd me to run out fourfcore;
I'll fet down contented, of Providence crave
That I may in quiet go down to my grave.
For I heed not the thoughts of my laft gloomy
   day;
While my confcience is clear 'twill vanifh away.

SONG 831.

A GRATEFUL EFFUSION.

Written by Mr. NICHOLLS.

WHEN I behold, at vernal tide,
   The halefome herbage fpring,
Note how the tree's with leaves fupply'd,
   My fancy takes the wing;

Grateful I meet the April fhower;
   Chearful, at rifing day,
I trace the lawns, and kifs the flowers
   Which make the feafon gay.

Sweet lark, (I cry) fhall you, untaught,
   Praife with thy feeble voice;
And I, a creature blefs'd with thought,
   Be backward to rejoice!

No, by the name of gratitude,
  In loftier strains I'd sing,
To Him whose kindness has renew'd
  The life-inspiring spring!

Who bids the bows with bloom to team,
  Sweet fruits that bloom to yield;
Who deal's, in f mmer-time, the stream,
  To chear the harvest-field;

Who, when the harvest time is past,
  Gives us a golden store,
And kindly makes the plenty last
  Till summer brings us more!

Him will I praise, above all pow'rs,
  Without whose bounteous will,
Spring could not deck the dale with flow'rs,
  Nor harvest cloths the hill.

SONG 832.

MOTHERS, thro' too much pride or love,
  Ne'er fail of inclination
To breed their children far above
  The level of their station.
The farmer to the dancing-school
  Must send his aukward daughter,
To spend what he should give the fool,
  To match her well hereafter.

So when the wench by am'rous sighs
  Declares she's ripe and ready,
In minuet and in boree lies
  The fortune of my lady.
Thus bred, the wanton clumsey lass
  A working life despises,
And rather chusing to be base,
  She falls before she rises.

When if the hoyden had been bred
  To th' ladle and the needle,
She would not then have been misled,
  To ogle, kiss, and wheedle.
Wherefore those parents act awry,
  And in the main deceive 'em,
Who breed their children proudly high,
  Yet little have to give 'em.

SONG 833.
Sung in Comus.

ON ev'ry hill, in ev'ry grove,
  Along the margin of each stream,
Dear conscious scenes of former love,
  I mourn, and Damon is my theme.
The hills, the groves, the streams remain,
But Damon there I seek in vain.

Now to the mossy cave I fly,
  Where to my swain I oft have sung,
Well pleas'd the browzing goats to spy,
  As o'er the airy steep they hung.
The mossy cave, the goats remain,
But Damon there I seek in vain.

Now thro' the trembling vale I pass,
  And sigh to see the well-known shade,

I weep, and kiss the bended grass,
  Where love and Damon fondly play'd.
The vale, the shade, the grass remain,
But Damon there I seek in vain.

From hill, from dale, each charm is fled,
  Groves, flocks, and fountains please no more,
Each flower in pity droops it's head,
  All nature does my loss deplore.
All, all reproach the faithless swain,
Yet Damon still I seek in vain.

SONG 834.
FLORA AND LUCINDA; A PASTORAL.
Written by Mr. MAVOR.
RECITATIVE.

ON Avon's bank, beneath the beechen shade,
  Two beauteous maids in pensive mood
    were laid;
Each mourn'd the absence of her faithful swain,
And cast her longing eyes o'er all the plain:
But no fond Damon blest his Flora's eyes;
Or young Alexis stopt Lucinda's sighs.
At length, to chase the tedious hours away,
By turns they tune their throats, by turns
    they play;
While the charm'd river check'd it's flowing
    waves,
And crept on slowly thro' the meads it laves.
Eager to hear, their flocks around them throng,
While love and music thus inform'd their
    tongue.

FLORA.

Ye innocent flocks that feed all around,
  You may ramble and stray where you please;
And think yourselves happy, you feel not the
    wound
  That robs me of comfort and ease.

O Damon! come quickly, and pity the lass
  Who dies at your tedious delay;
'Tis your presence that sweetly can make my
    time pass,
  'Tis your absence that brings my dismay.

Did you know the keen anguish and pains
    that I feel,
  The tortures and racks of my breast;
Tho' your heart were as hard as the flint or
    the steel,
  You would hasten to soothe me to rest.

LUCINDA.

Now fair is the bloom on the trees,
  Now bright are the tints of the flow'rs;
Now gentle the breath of the breeze,
  And the eglantine sweet after show'rs.

Now May in it's beauty appears,
  The choristers chant thro' the air;
But e'en music's now harsh to my ears,
  And nature herself is not fair.

If you afk what can make me think fo—
'Tis becaufe my Alexis is gone;
'Tis his abfence that makes my tears flow,
While I feed thefe few lambkins alone.

RECITATIVE.

Advancing flowly o'er th' adjacent vale,
By chance their fhepherds came, to hear
their tale;
Charm'd into filence, 'midft th' embowring
fhade,
Whofe boughs thick-waving mantl'd o'er their
head,
They laid them down to liften to the ftrains
That eas'd them of their cares, their fears,
and pains.
Thofe ftrains now finifh'd, love condemn'd
their ftay;
Each to his miftrefs wings his rapid way,
And clafp'd her in his arms.—Fair maids,
they faid,
In truth and neat fimplicity array'd;
Your fears difmifs, your anxious doubts give o'er;
Your fhepherds are return'd, to part no more.
No more to part, fince chance has now reveal'd
The feelings of your breafts, fo long conceal'd;
No more to part, fince love's foft fway you own,
And deign our ardent vows at length to crown.
Let fafhion treat with fcorn the virgin's fighs,
Her love-dejected looks, and flowing eyes;
Or ufe her paffion to compleat her fhame,
And wreck it's honour for a tranfient flame.
Such arts there are; but we thofe arts difdain,
For innocence and truth abjure their reign.
Then, oh! fair maids, in Hymen make us bleft,
And mutual love fhall always fire the breaft.
The fwains thus fpoke, the blufhing maids
comply'd;
And liv'd with pleafure, with compofure dy'd.

AIR.

From hence, ye tender virgins, learn
To blefs the gen'rous heart;
Treat not the paffion with difdain,
Nor play the coquette's part.

The fouls that Heav'n has form'd to twine
In love's delightful bands,
Will never give each other grief,
But join their hearts and hands.

SONG 835.

Sung at VAUXHALL.

HOW pleafing's my Damon, how charming
his face!
Adorn'd with fweet fmiles, and bedeck'd with
each grace!
His manners are gentle, engaging, and free;
And what is ftill better, the fhepherd loves me.

Tho' plaintive his fong, it drives forrow away;
To hear his fweet voice I could liften all day;
I always am happy when Damon I fee;
I love the young fhepherd, becaufe he loves me.

T'other day, as I fat beneath a green fhade,
He pres'd my hand gently, and call'd me dear
maid:
His words, and his looks, and his actions agree,
And I love the dear fhepherd, becaufe he
loves me.

The morn now invites, to the fhade I'll repair,
And furely my Damon will follow me there.
Should he urge his fond fuit, we fhall quickly
agree;
I'll marry my fhepherd becaufe he loves me.

SONG 836.

Written by the Earl of DORSET.

PHILLIS, for fhame, let us improve,
A thoufand different ways,
Thofe few fhort moments, fnatch'd by love,
From many tedious days.

If you want courage to defpife
The cenfures of the grave;
For all thofe tyrants of your eyes,
Your heart is but a flave.

My love is full of noble pride;
Nor can it e'er fubmit
To let that fop, difcretion, ride
In triumph over it.

Falfe friends I have, as well as you,
That daily counfel me,
Fame and ambition to purfue,
And leave off loving thee:

But when the leaft regard I fhow
To fools who thus advife,
May I be dull enough to grow
Moft miferably wife.

SONG 837.

BLUE-EY'D NANCY.

Sung at VAUXHALL.

THE flow'r of females, beauty's queen!
Who fees thee fure muft prize thee;
Tho' thou art dreft in robes but mean,
Yet thefe cannot difguife thee:
Thy graceful air, and modeft look,
Strike ev'ry fhepherd's fancy O;
Thou'rt match for fquire, for lord, or duke,
My lovely blue-ey'd Nancy O.

Oh! were I but fome fhepherd fwain,
To feed my flocks befide thee,
To tend my fheep upon the plain,
In milking to abide thee;
I'd think myfelf a happier man,
With thee to pleafe my fancy O,
Than he that hugs his thoufands ten,
Had I my blue-ey'd Nancy O.

Then I'd defpife th' imperial throne,
And ftatefmen's dang'rous ftations;
I'd be no king, I'd wear no crown,
And fmile at conqu'ring nations;

Mrs WEICHSEL, at VAUXHALL.

O'er the Seas my Love is sailing.
Song 841

Publish'd by J Bew Oct 1778

Might I poſſeſs, and ſtill careſs,
    This laſs that ſtrikes my fancy O!
For theſe are joys, and ſtill look leſs,
    Compar'd with blue-ey'd Nancy O.

SONG 838.

Sung at VAUXHALL.

TO Flora's fragrant bower,
    My dear ſhepherd, haſte away:
Hark! Zeph'rus fans each flow'r,
Shakes the dew-drops from each ſpray.

Cupid leads the hours along,
    Chearful ſpring bedecks the grove:
The lark with her early ſong
Joins the milkmaid's tales of love.

SONG 839.

Written by the EDITOR.

SINCE you, my fair, demand the lay,
    Tho' rude your ſhepherd's voice,
He ſurely cannot diſobey
    The object of his choice.

But ſlight not, deareſt maid, the love
    Thy faithful Strephon bears,
Becauſe you needs muſt diſapprove
    The ſtrain which meets your ears.

No ſkill has he to reach the heart
    With muſic's pow'rful charm;
Nor wiſhes to poſſeſs an art
    That reaſon might diſarm.

As from the heart his numbers flow,
    Tho' harſh may be the ſound;
O liſten to his plaintive woe,
    And heal the faithful wound!

So may your kind requeſt procure
    Thy ever conſtant ſwain,
For all his pangs a ſpeedy cure,
    And he not ſing in vain.

SONG 840.

A CANTATA.

Sung at VAUXHALL.

RECITATIVE.

THE pendant foreſt ſeem'd to nod,
    In drowſy fetters bound;
And fairy elves in circles trod
    The daiſy-painted ground;
When Daphne ſought the conſcious grove,
    Of ſlighted vows to tell;
And thus, to ſoothe neglected love,
    Invok'd ſad Philomel.

AIR.

Hither, ſweet nightingale, in haſte,
    Direct thy hov'ring wing;
The vernal green's a dreary waſte,
    Till thou vouchſafe to ſing.

So thrilling ſweet thy numbers flow,
    Thy warbling ſong diſtreſs,
The tear that tells the lover's woe
    Falls cold upon my breaſt.

To hear ſad Philomel complain,
    Will ſoften my deſpair;
Then quickly ſwell thy melting ſtrain,
    And ſoothe a lover's care.

SONG 841.

A SCOTCH RONDEAU.

Sung at VAUXHALL.

O'ER the ſeas my love is ſailing,
    Gently blow, ye Eaſtern gales;
Love his dear approach is hailing,
Flies to view the ſwelling ſails.

O'er the ocean whilſt he's roving,
    Who has brav'd the ſultry clime,
I endure the pain of loving,
    I grow ſick of thought and time.

Sea-nymphs all the while are playing,
    Guard his veſſel ſafe from harms;
But no more ſhall he be ſtaying,
    Damon's port ſhall be my arms.

SONG 842.

THE MILKMAID.

Written by Mr. THOMSON.

'TWAS at the cool and fragrant hour
    When ev'ning ſteals upon the ſky,
That Lucy ſought a woodbine grove,
    And Colin taught the grove to ſigh:
The ſweeteſt damſel ſhe on all the plains,
The ſofteſt lover he of all the ſwains.

He took her by the lily-hand,
    Which oft had made the milk look pale;
Her cheeks with modeſt roſes glow'd,
    As thus he breath'd his tender tale:
The liſt'ning ſtreams awhile forgot to flow,
The doves to murmur, and the breeze to blow.

O ſmile, my love! thy ſimply ſmiles
    Shall lengthen on the ſetting ray.
Thus let us paſs the hours in bliſs,
    Thus ſweetly languiſh life away:
Thus ſigh our ſouls into each other's breaſt,
As true as turtles, and as turtles bleſt!

So may thy cows for ever crown
    With floods of milk thy brimming pail!
So may thy cheeſe all cheeſe ſurpaſs,
    And may thy butter never fail:
Then may each village round this truth declare,
That Lucy is the faireſt of the fair.

Thy lips with ſtreams of honey flow,
    And beauteous ſwell with healing dews;
More ſweets are blended in thy breath,
    Than all thy father's fields diffuſe:
The thouſan-flow're adorn each blooming field,
Thy lovely cheeks more blooming beauties yield.

F f

Too long my erring eyes had rov'd
 On city dames in scarlet dress;
And scorn'd the charmful village maid,
 In innocence and grogram bless.
Since Lucy's native graces fill'd my fight,
The painted city dames no more delight.

The living purple, when you blush,
 Outglows the scarlet's deepest dye;
No diamonds tremble on thy hair,
 But brighter sparkle in thine eye:
Not e'er is found, on all the British plain,
So fair a maid, and eke so kind a swain.

The tuneful linnet's warbling notes
 Are grateful to the shepherd-twain;
To drooping plants, and thirsty fields,
 The silver drops of kindly rain;
To blossoms dews, as blossoms to the bee;
And thou, my Lucy, only art to me.

But mark, my love, yon Western clouds,
 With liquid gold they seem to burn;
The ev'ning star will soon appear,
 And overflow his silver urn.
Soft stillness now approaching shades invite,
To taste the balmy blessings of the night.

Yet ere we part one boon I crave,
 One tender boon! nor this deny;
O promise that you still will love!
 O promise this, or else I die!
Death else my only remedy must prove;
I'll cease to live, whene'er you cease to love!

She sigh'd, and blush'd a sweet consent;
 Joyous he thank'd her on his knee,
And warmly press'd her virgin lip:
 Was ever youth so blest as he!
The moon, to light the lovers homeward, rose,
And Philomela lull'd them to repose.

SONG 843.

THE VICAR OF BRAY.

IN good King Charles's golden days,
 When loyalty had no harm in't,
A zealous high-church man I was,
 And so I got preferment:
To teach my flock I never mist,
 Kings are by God appointed,
And those are damn'd that do resist,
 And touch the Lord's anointed.
  And this is law, I will maintain
   Until my dying day, Sir;
  That whatsoever king shall reign,
   I will be vicar of Bray, Sir.

When royal James obtain'd the throne,
 And pop'ry came in fashion,
The penal laws I hooted down,
 And read the declaration:
The church of Rome I found would fit
 Full well my constitution,
And had become a Jesuit,
 But for the Revolution.
  And this is law, &c.

When William was our king declar'd,
 To ease this nation's grievance;

With this new wind about I steer'd,
 And swore to him allegiance;
Old principles I did revoke,
 Set conscience at a distance,
Passive-obedience was a joke,
 And pish was non-resistance.
  And this is law, &c.

When gracious Anne ascends the throne,
 The church of England's glory,
Another face of things was seen,
 And I became a tory:
Occasional conformists base,
 I damn'd their moderation,
And thought the church in danger was
 By such prevarication.
  And this is law, &c.

When George in pudding-time came o'er,
 And moderate men look'd big, Sir,
I turn'd a cat in pan once more,
 And then became a whig, Sir;
And so preferment I procur'd
 By our new faith's defender;
And always every day abjur'd
 The pope and the pretender.
  And this is law, &c.

Th' illustrious house of Hanover,
 And protestant succession,
To these I do allegiance swear,
 While they can keep possession;
For by my faith and loyalty
 I never more will faulter,
And George my lawful king shall be,
 Until the times shall alter.
  And this is law, I will maintain
   Until my dying day, Sir;
  That whatsoever king shall reign,
   I will be vicar of Bray, Sir.

SONG 844.

Sung at RANELAGH.

WHEN first my dear laddie gade to the
 green hill,
And I at ewe-milking first show'd my young
 skill;
To bear the milk bowie nae pain gave to me,
So at eve I was bless with thy piping and thee:
For aye as I milk'd, and aye as I sang,
My yellow-hair'd laddie shall be my good man.

When corn-riggs wav'd yellow, and blue he-
 ther-bells
Bloom'd bonny on moorland, or sweet rising
 fells;
Nae birns, briers, or brakens, gave trouble
 to me,
So I eat the sweet berries when gather'd by thee:
For aye as I walk'd, and aye as I sang,
My yellow-hair'd laddie shall be my good man.

When you ran, or you wrestled, or putted the
 stane,
And came off the victor, my heart was aye fain;

Give me still all these pleasures, my study
shall be
To make myself better and sweeter for thee:
For aye as I wedded, and aye as I sang,
My yellow-hair'd laddie shall be my good man.

SONG 845.

Sung at VAUXHALL.

DEAR smiling Kitty's to my mind,
  She ev'ry way can please me ;
Good bumour'd, faithful, fond, and kind;
  She never tries to teize me.
At home, abroad, by light or day,
  The same engaging creature;
She lets me ever have my way,
  With joy I always meet her.

To vex or harm a girl so good,
  Would be a shame and pity ;
I would not injure, if I could,
  My ever smiling Kitty.
To rove abroad from fair to fair,
  No longer is my passion ;
One, only one, is all my care,
  Too' more is now the fashion:

No art's vermilion has she shewn,
  She is the child of nature ;
Her face, her shape, is all her own,
  And ev'ry other feature.
From folly, spite, and cunning free,
  She s lively, gay, and witty ;
Her like I ne'er expect to see ;
  I'll live and die with Kitty.

SONG 846.

CHEVY-CHACE; AN OLD BALLAD.

GOD prosper long our noble king,
  Our lives and safeties all;
A woeful hunting once there did
  In Chevy-Chace befal ;

To drive the deer with hound and horn,
  Earl Percy took his way;
The child may rue that is unborn,
  The hunting of that day.

The stout Earl of Northumberland
  A vow to God did make,
His pleasure in the Scottish woods
  Three summer's days to take;

The chiefest harts in Chevy-Chace
  To kill and bear away.
These tidings to Earl Douglas came,
  In Scotland where he lay;

Who sent Earl Percy present word,
  He would prevent his sport :
The English Earl, not fearing this,
  Did to the woods resort,

With fifteen hundred bow-men bold,
  All chosen men of might,
Who knew full well in time of need
  To aim their shafts aright.

The gallant greyhounds swiftly ran,
  To chase the fallow deer :
On Monday they began to hunt,
  Ere day-light did appear ;

And long before high noon they had
  An hundred fat bucks slain;
Then having din'd, the drovers went
  To rouze them up again.

The bow-men muster'd on the hills,
  Well able to endure;
Their backsides all, with special care,
  That day were guarded sure.

The hounds ran swiftly through the woods,
  The nimble deer to take,
And with their cries the hills and dales
  An echo shrill did make.

Lord Percy to the quarry went,
  To view the slaughter'd deer;
Quoth he, Earl Douglas promised
  This day to meet me here :

But if I thought he would not come,
  No longer would I stay.
With that, a brave young gentleman
  Thus to the Earl did say:

Lo. yonder doth Earl Douglas come,
  His men in armour bright;
Full twenty hundred Scottish spears
  All marching in our sight;

All men of pleasant Tivydale,
  Fast by the river Tweed.
Then cease your sport, Earl Percy said,
  And take your bows with speed :

And now with me, my countrymen,
  Your courage forth advance ;
For never was there champion yet,
  In Scotland or in France,

That ever did on horseback come,
  But if my hap it were,
I durst encounter man for man,
  With him to break a spear.

Earl Douglas on a milk-white steed,
  Most like a baron bold,
Rode foremost of his company,
  Whose armour shone like gold.

Show me, said he, whose men you be,
  That hunt so boldly here;
That, without my consent, do chase
  And kill my fallow deer?

The man that first did answer make,
  Was noble Percy he;
Who said, We list not to declare,
  Nor shew whose men we be :

Yet will we spend our dearest blood,
  Thy chiefest harts to slay.
Then Douglas swore a solemn oath,
  And thus in rage did say,

Ere thus I will out-braved be,
  One of us two shall die;
I know thee well, an Earl thou art;
  Lord Percy, so am I.

But truft me, Percy, pity it were,
  And great offence to kill
Any of thefe our harmlefs men,
  For they have done no ill.

Let thou and I the battle try,
  And fet our men afide.
Accurs'd be he, Lord Percy faid,
  By whom this is denied.

Then ftept a gallant fquire forth,
  Witherington was his name,
Who faid, I would not have it told
  To Henry our king for fhame,

That e'er my captain fought on foot,
  And I ftood looking on.
You be two Earls, faid Witherington,
  And I a fquire alone;

Yet I will do the beft I may,
  While I have power to ftand;
While I have pow'r to wield my fword,
  I'll fight with heart and hand.

Our Englifh archers bent their bows,
  Their hearts were good and true;
At the firft flight of arrows fent,
  Full threefcore Scots they flew.

To drive the deer with hound and horn,
  Earl Douglas had the bent;
Two captains mov'd with mickle pride,
  Their fpears to fhivers went.

They clos'd full faft on every fide,
  No flacknefs there was found;
And many a gallant gentleman
  Lay gafping on the ground.

O Chrift! it was a grief to fee,
  And likewife for to hear,
The cries of men lying in their gore,
  And fcattered here and there.

At laft thefe two ftout Earls did meet,
  Like captains of great might:
As lions wou'd, they laid on load,
  And made a cruel fight:

They fought until they both did fweat,
  With fwords of temper'd fteel;
Until the blood, like drops of rain,
  They trickling down did feel.

Yield thee, Lord Percy, Douglas faid;
  In faith I will thee bring,
Where thou fhalt high advanced be
  By James our Scottifh king:

Thy ranfom I will freely give,
  And thus report of thee,
Thou art the moft courageous knight
  That ever I did fee.

No, Douglas, quoth Earl Percy then,
  Thy proffer I do fcorn;
I will not yield to any Scot
  That ever yet was born.

With that, there came an arrow keen
  Out of an Englifh bow,
Which ftruck Earl Douglas to the heart,
  A deep and deadly blow:

Who never fpoke more words than thefe,
  Fight on, my merry men all;
For why, my life is at an end;
  Lord Percy fees my fall.

Then leaving life, Earl Percy took
  The dead man by the hand;
And faid, Earl Douglas, for thy life
  Would I had loft my land!

O Chrift! my very heart doth bleed
  With forrow for thy fake;
For fure, a more renowned knight
  Mifchance did never take.

A knight amongft the Scots there was,
  Which faw Earl Douglas die,
Who ftraight in wrath did vow revenge
  Upon the Lord Percy:

Sir Hugh Mountgomery was he call'd,
  Who, with a fpear moft bright,
Well mounted on a gallant fteed,
  Ran fiercely through the fight;

And paft the Englifh archers all,
  Without all dread or fear;
And thro' Earl Percy's body then
  He thruft his hateful fpear:

With fuch a vehement force and might
  He did his body gore,
The fpear went through the other fide
  A large cloth-yard, and more.

So thus did both thefe nobles die,
  Whofe courage none could ftain:
An Englifh archer then perceiv'd
  The noble Earl was flain;

He had a bow bent in his hand,
  Made of a trufty tree;
An arrow of a cloth-yard long
  Up to the head drew he:

Againft Sir Hugh Mountgomery,
  So right the fhaft he fet,
The grey goofe-wing that was thereon,
  In his heart's blood was wet.

This fight did laft from break of day,
  Till fetting of the fun;
For when they rung the evening-bell,
  The battle fcarce was done.

With brave Earl Percy, there was flain
  Sir John of Egerton,
Sir Robert Ratcliff, and Sir John,
  Sir James that bold baron:

And with Sir George and ftout Sir James,
  Both knights of good account,
Good Sir Ralph Raby there was flain,
  Whofe prowefs did furmount.

For Witherington needs muft I wail,
  As one in doleful dumps;
For when his legs were fmitten off,
  He fought upon his ftumps.

And with Earl Douglas, there was flain
  Sir Hugh Mountgomery;
Sir Charles Murray, that from the field
  One foot would never flee.

Sir Charles Murray, of Ratcliff, too,
His fifter's fon was he;
Sir David Lamb, fo well efteem'd,
Yet faved could not be.

And the Lord Maxwell in like cafe
Did with Earl Douglas die:
Of twenty hundred Scottifh peers,
Scarce fifty-five did fly.

Of fifteen hundred Englifhmen,
Went home but fifty-three;
The reft were flain in Chevy-Chafe,
Under the green-wood tree.

Next day did many widows come,
Their hufbands to bewail;
They wafh'd their wounds in brinifh tears,
But all would not prevail.

Their bodies bath'd in purple gore,
They bare with them away;
They kifs'd them dead a thoufand times,
When they were clad in clay.

This news was brought to Edinburgh,
Where Scotland's king did reign,
That brave Earl Douglas fuddenly
Was with an arrow flain:

O heavy news, King James did fay,
Scotland can witnefs be,
I have not any captain more
Of fuch account as he.

Like tidings to King Henry came,
Within as fhort a fpace,
That Percy of Northumberland
Was flain in Chevy-Chafe:

Now God be with him, faid our king,
Sith 'twill no better be;
I truft I have, within my realm,
Five hundred good as he:

Yet fhall not Scot nor Scotland fay,
But I will vengeance take;
I'll be revenged on them all,
For brave Earl Percy's fake.

This vow full well the king perform'd
After, at Humbledown;
In one day, fifty knights were flain,
With lords of great renown:

And of the reft, of fmall account,
Did many thoufands die.
Thus endeth the hunting of Chevy-Chafe,
Made by the Earl Percy.

God fave the king, and blefs this land
In plenty, joy, and peace;
And grant henceforth, that foul debate
'Twixt noblemen may ceafe.

SONG 847.

Written by the CURATE of CRAMAN.

YE fhepherds and nymphs of the plain,
Your paftimes a moment forego,
And kindly attend to my ftrain;
Your pity will foften my woe!

Ye vallies, where often I've ftray'd,
To tafte the mild breath of the morn,
And rapur'd have met my chafte maid,
I leave you, no more to return.

Sweet echo! no more from thy bed
I'll roufe thee to hail the new day;
Some happier fwain in my ftead
Shall wake thee when I'm far away:
And you, the fad caufe of my woe,
My parents, who know all my plaint,
Who force me reluctant to go,
Forbear when I'm gone to lament.

But you, who can nature controul,
And check the foft pulfe of the heart,
Can ftifle the voice of the foul,
And hear of my death without fmart.
Oh, Laura! a name ever dear,
Which once could difpel ev'ry care,
Now heaveft the heart-throbbing tear,
And wring'ft my fad foul with defpair.

By vows and by love you are mine,
O ever adorable maid!
But tyranny bids me refign,
And tyranny muft be obey'd.
When far from thy fame I am drove,
I'll tell the deaf waves of our wrong;
Each gale fhall figh deep with our love,
Till hoary death filence my tongue.

SONG 848.

A PASTORAL DIALOGUE.

Written by Mr. LEMOINE.

DAMON.

SWEET Silvia, let's rove
To yonder green grove,
Where mufic exerts all it's pow'rs;
There linnet and thrufh,
Make vocal each bufh,
And fields bear a garland of flow'rs:
There daifies and vi'lets in fplendor appear,
Surrounded with beauties to diffipate care.

SILVIA.

To go I'm inclin'd,
Tho' a tim'rous mind
Forebodes many dangers there be;
Yet Damon's a youth,
Whofe bofom beats truth,
And fuch can't with ruin agree:
On virtue and honour he builds all his fame,
And they fhall procure him a lafting good name.

DAMON.

Thy praifes, fond maid,
Let rofers degrade,
To gain them, unfully'd, I'll try;
Together let s go,
Regardlefs of woe,
No danger attends while I'm nigh:
Sad fpectres, unrefting, forfake the green grove;
It's tenants, my fair-one, are emblems of love.

SILVIA.

Your words are like charms,
They foothe away harms,
So go, I'm determin'd, and will;
(Nor danger I'll fear,
If Damon is near;)
But hear the foft flow of yon rill !
O grant that our tempers as fmoothly may flow,
Our lives ever after difturb'd not by woe.

DAMON.

Hence, hence, ye vain fears,
Sighs, fobbings, and tears,
Ye can't with my Silvia agree;
Nor ftrive to moleft,
Her bofom beats reft,
Befides a mind eafy and free:
Like the dove to her mate; oh! ever be true:
A fig for vaft riches ! I care not for you.

SILVIA.

The fparrow and dove
Are emblems of love,
Like them I'll be conftant and kind;
From Phœbus's rife,
To his leaving the fkles,
Our lambkins at pafture I'll mind:
To increafe our fmall ftore, induftrious I'll prove,
And ftudy, fond youth, to deferve all thy love.

BOTH.

Ye nymphs and ye fwains,
Come dance on the plains,
While meadows look blooming and gay;
Sweet Silvia is true,
And Damon's fo too,
Each breaft feels the glowing of May !
To church let us go, defpifing all care,
For none are fo happy as thofe who go there.

SONG 849.

OLD Saturn, that drone of a god,
And father of all the divine,
Still govern'd the world with a nod,
Yet fancy'd brifk women and wine ;
And when he was whimfical grown,
By fipping his plentiful bowl,
Then frankly the truth he'wou'd own,
That a wench was the joy of his foul.

Great Jupiter, like his old dad,
To love and a bottle inclin'd,
When mellow was conftantly glad
To find a plump girl to his mind;
And then, as the ftory is told,
He'd conjure himfelf in her arms,
As once in a fhower of gold
He rifled fair Danäe's charms.

Stern Mars, the great god of the field,
All day tho' delighting in blood,
At night his fierce godfhip would yield
To beauty, and wine that was good :

With nectar he'd cherifh his heart,
And raife up his wanton defires;
Then to Venus, his darling, impart
The warmth of his amorous fires.

Apollo, the patron of bays,
Full goblets would merri y drain,
And fing forth poetical lays,
When the fumes had got into his brain;
But full as he whimfical grew,
By top'ng the juice of the vine,
To Parnaffus daily he flew,
To kifs all the mufical nine.

Sly Mercury too, like the reft,
Made wenching and wine his delight;
And thought himfelf perfectly bleft
With a bottle and miftrefs at night:
No wonder debauches he lov'd,
And cheating his pleafure he made,
For the gods have ev'ry one prov'd,
That pimping was always his trade.

Plump Bacchus, that tun-belly'd fot,
His thirft could but feldom allay,
Till aftride o'er a hogfhead he got,
And drank all the liquor away:
As long as upright he could fit,
He'd bawl for the finifhing glafs;
When drunk, then the veffel would quit;
And reel to his fav'rite lafs.

SONG 850.

Written by Sir JOHN SUCKLING.

HONEST lover, whofoever,
If in all thy love there ever
Was one wav'ring thought; if thy flame
Were not ftill even, ftill the fame:
Know this,
Thou lov'ft amifs;
And to love true,
Thou muft begin again, and love anew.

If when fhe appears i' th' room,
Thou doft not quake, and art ftruck dumb;
And in ftriv'ng this to cover,
Doft not fpeak thy words twice over:
Know this,
Thou lov'ft amifs;
And to love true,
Thou muft begin again, and love anew.

If fondly thou doft not miftake,
And all defects for graces take ;
Perfwad'ft thyfelf that jefts are broken,
When fhe hath little or nothing fpoken:
Know this,
Thou lov'ft amifs;
And to love true,
Thou muft begin again, and love anew.

If when thou appear'ft to be within,
Thou lett'ft not men afk and afk again;
And when thou anfwer'ft, if it be
To what was afk'd thee properly:
Know this,
Thou lov'ft amifs;
And to love true,
Thou muft begin again, and love anew.

If when thy ſtomach calls to eat,
Thou cutt'ſt not fingers 'ſtead of meat,
And with much gazing on her face
Doſt not riſe hungry from the place:
    Know this,
    Thou lov'ſt amiſs;
    And to love true,
Thou muſt begin again, and love anew.

If by this thou doſt diſcover
That thou art no perfect lover,
And deſiring to love true,
Thou doſt begin to love anew:
    Know this,
    Thou lov'it amiſs;
    And to love true,
Thou muſt begin again, and love anew.

SONG 851.

YE winds, to whom Colin complains
   In ditties ſo ſad and ſo ſweet,
Believe me, the ſhepherd but reigns
He's wretched, to ſhew he has wit,
No charmer like Colin can move,
   And this is ſome pretty new art:
Ah! Colin's a juggler in love,
   And likes to play tricks with my heart.

When he will, he can ſigh and look pale,
   Seem doleful and alter his face,
Can tremble, and breathe out his tale;
   Ah! Colin has every pace.
The willow my rover prefers
   To the breaſts where he once begg'd to lie;
And the ſtreams that he ſwells with his tears,
   Are rivals belov'd more than I.

His head my fond boſom would bear,
   And my heart would ſoon beat him to reſt;
Let the ſwain that is ſlighted deſpair,
   But Colin is only in jeſt.
No death the deceiver deſigns,
   Let the maid that is ruin'd deſpair;
For Colin but dies in his lines,
   And gives himſelf that modiſh air.

Can ſhepherds, bred far from the court,
   So wittily talk of their flame?
But Colin makes paſſion his ſport;
   Beware of ſo fatal a game.
My voice of no muſic can boaſt,
   Nor my perſon of aught that is fine;
But Colin may find, to his coſt,
   A face that is fairer than mine.

Ah! then will I break my lov'd crook,
   To thee I'll bequeath all my ſheep;
And die in the much-favour'd brook,
   Where thou but pretendeſt to weep.
Then mourn the ſad fate that you gave,
   In ſonnets ſo ſmooth and divine;
Perhaps I may riſe from my grave,
   To hear ſuch ſoft muſic as thine.

Of the violet, daiſy, and roſe,
   The heart's-eaſe, the lily, and pink,
Let thy fingers a garland compoſe,
   And crown'd by the rivulet's brink:

How oft, my dear ſwain, did I ſwear,
   How much my fond ſoul did admire
Thy verſes, thy ſhape, and thy air,
   Tho' deck'd in thy rural attire!

Your ſheep-hook you rul'd with ſuch art,
   That all your ſmall ſubjects obey'd;
And ſtill you reign'd king of this heart,
   Whoſe paſſion you falſely upbraid.
How often, my ſwain, have I ſaid,
   That thy arms were a palace to me;
And how well I could live in a ſhade,
   Tho' adorned with nothing but thee?

Oh! what are the ſparks of the town,
   Tho' never ſo fine and ſo gay?
I freely would leave beds of down,
   For thy meat, and a bed of new hay.
Then, Colin, return once again,
   Again make me happy in love;
Let me find thee a faithful, true ſwain,
   And as conſtant a nymph I will prove.

SONG 852.

Written by the Earl of DORSET.

TO all you ladies now at land
   We men at ſea indite;
But firſt would have you underſtand
   How hard it is to write;
The muſes now, and Neptune too,
We muſt implore to write to you.

For tho' the muſes ſhould prove kind,
   And fill our empty brain,
Yet if rough Neptune rouze the wind,
   To wave the azure main;
Our paper, pen, and ink, and we,
Roll up and down our ſhips at ſea.

Then if we write not by each poſt,
   Think not we are unkind,
Nor yet conclude our ſhips are loſt
   By Dutchmen, or by wind;
Our tears we'll ſend a ſpeedier way,
The tide ſhall bring them twice a day.

The king, with wonder and ſurprize,
   Will ſwear the ſeas grow bold,
Becauſe the tides will higher riſe
   Than e'er they did of old:
But let him know, it is our tears
Bring floods of grief to Whitehall-ſtairs.

Shou'd foggy Opdam chance to know
   Our ſad and diſmal ſtory,
The Dutch would ſcorn ſo weak a foe,
   And quit their fort at Goree;
For what reſiſtance can they find
From men who've left their hearts behind?

Let wind and weather do it's worſt,
   Be you to us but kind,
Let Dutchmen vapour, Spaniards curſe,
   No ſorrow we ſhall find;
'Tis then no matter how things go,
Or who's our friend, or who's our foe.

To paſs our tedious hours away,
   We throw a merry main;
Or elſe at ſerious Ombre play;

But why should we in vain,
Each other's ruin thus pursue?
We were undone when we left you!

But now our fears tempestuous grow,
And cast our hopes away,
Whilst you, regardless of our woe,
Sit careless at a play;
Perhaps permit some happier man
To kiss your hand, or flirt your fan.

When any mournful tune you hear,
That dies in ev'ry note,
As if it sigh'd with each man's care,
For being so remote;
Think then how often love we've made
To you, when all those tunes were play'd.

In justice you cannot refuse
To think of our distress,
When we for hopes of honour, lose
Our certain happiness;
All these designs are but to prove
Ourselves more worthy of your love.

And now we've told you all our loves,
And likewise all our fears;
In hopes this declaration moves
Some pity from your tears;
Let's hear of no inconstancy,
We have too much of that at sea.

SONG 853.

O'ER the bowl we'll laugh and sing;
Melancholy, hence away!
Ring, ring, the bowl is empty;
Fill it landlord, let's be gay.
Rouse, ye genial sons of mirth!
Now's the time to baffle care;
Tho' we're mortal now on earth,
Let us fancy heaven here.

Happiness alone pursue;
Where is more than dwells in wine!
Each full bumper gives a new
Pleasure to the theme divine.
Why should man, with sorrow pining,
Lose a life of joy and ease,
When his bliss is still refining
In sublime delights like these.

SONG 854.

THE HARP OF ÆOLUS.

Written by Mr. LEMOINE.

SWEET Zephyr, leave th' enamell'd plain,
And hither wave thy gentle wing;
Would'st thou out-rival Orpheus' strain,
O haste, and touch this trembling string.

The balmy-breathing pow'r obeys,
'Tis his my slender harp to claim;
He comes, and o'er it's bosom plays,
And rapture wakes the slender frame!

The tender melting notes of love,
The soul in soothing murmurs steal;

Low as the languor-breathing dove,
That lonesome cooes her plaintive tale.

Hark! what sounds of pleasing pain,
Deep as some bleeding lovers lay;
Sad as the cygnets moving strain,
When on the shore she dies away.

A nobler gale now sweeps the wire,
The hollow frame responsive rings;
Loud as when angels strike the lyre,
Sweet as the heav'nly chorus sings.

And hark! the numbers roll along,
Majestically, smooth, and clear;
Like Philomel's enchanting song,
The notes mellifluous pierce the ear.

Thus, as the varying accents flow,
Each passion feels th' accordant found;
This lifts the soul, that sinks it low;
We seem to tread on fairy ground.

SONG 855.

Written by the CURATE of CRAMAN.

WHEN sculptur'd urns, and storied tombs,
And animated busts;
When regal palaces and stately domes,
Shall drop to native dust;

When solid rocks, and mountains vast,
Shall fall immense, and rise no more;
When seas profound shall roar their last,
And naked leave the vanish'd shore:

Benevolence shall still remain,
In yon empirium raise it's head,
When earth, and stars, and sun, are fled,
And ev'ry project vain.

SONG 856.

Written by Mr. LEMOINE.

O Sweet content,
Were thou but sent
To us on Britain's isle;
Our feuds wou'd cease,
Our trade increase,
And plenty 'round us smile:
No more our funds oppress'd with wars,
Or soldiers wear rebellion's scars.

Thy heav'nly rays,
Permit always,
To soothe each British breast;
Nor hate, nor pain,
Within them reign,
But calmness, love, and rest:
Be thund'ring cannons heard no more,
But peace resound from shore to shore.

Make envy flee,
With massacre,
To dwell in foreign spheres;
Let Britons be
From discord free,
Nor shed oppression's tears:

But all be mild, and all serene,
Pay homage both to king and queen.

Then happy shall
Live great and small,
Beneath great George's pow'r;
With bowl and glass,
The minutes pass,
Would thou but join each hour:
'Tis thee content, who art the gate below,
Which shuts out strife and heart-corroding woe.

SONG 857.

On the taking of MONTREAL, by General
AMHERST, in the Year 1760.

I Fill not the glass
To some favourite lass,
A hero engrosses my lays;
Thy trumpet, O fame!
His deeds shall proclaim,
And spread round the globe Amherst's praise.

Thro' woods, and o'er lakes,
His progress he takes,
With Montreal full in his eye;
The French wou'd in vain,
Or Indians, restrain
His troops, who to victory fly.

Cape Breton's our own,
Gallia's fishery's o'erthrown,
Chief nursery of her marine;
Invasion, that joke,
Will thence end in smoke,
And Britain still reign ocean's queen.

The Indians and we
Shall henceforth agree,
Thus our manufactures advance;
Our foes, to their cost,
See their rich fur-trade lost,
Great blow to the commerce of France.

Triumphant, with pride,
O'er ocean we ride,
Not a single attempt now miscarries;
To our ravish'd eyes,
Cressy, Agincourt rise,
And the days of our Edwards and Harry's.

Just George! O for thee,
The fates did decree,
A reign will eternally shine;
The fam'd conquests told,
In our annals of old,
Are already equall'd in thine.

O'erwhelm'd with sad fears,
See Gallia in tears
The loss of Montreal bemoan;
The French are undone,
And now Canada's won,
Britannia shall there fix her throne.

But hark! Heav'n-born peace
Bids war's horrors cease,
And lo! where the goddess descends!
Her charms all adore,
Human blood streams no more,
And foes long contending are friends.

SONG 858.

Sung in the *Provok'd Wife*.

AS tippling John was jogging on,
Upon a riot-night;
With tott'ring pace, and fiery face,
Suspicious of high flight:
The guards, who took him by his look,
For some chief fire-brand,
Ask'd, whence he came; what was his name?
Who are you? stand, friend, stand.

I am going home; from meeting come.
Ay, says one, that's the case;
Some meeting he has burnt, you see
The flame's still in his face.
John thought 'twas time to purge the crime;
And said, 'twas his intent,
For to assuage his thirsty rage;
That meeting 'twas he meant,

Come, friend, be plain, you trifle in vain,
Says one; pray, let us know,
That we may find how you're inclin'd,
Are you high-church, or low?
John said to that, I'll tell you what,
To end debates and strife;
All I can say, this is the way
I steer my course of life.

I ne'er to Bow, nor Burgess go,
To steeple-house, nor hall;
The brisk har-bell best suits my zeal,
With, Gentlemen, d'ye call?
Now judge, am I low-church, or high?
From tavern or the steeple,
Whose merry toll exalts the soul,
And makes us high-flown people.

The guards came on, and look'd at John,
With countenance most pleasant:
By whisper round, they all soon found,
He was no dang'rous peasant:
So while John stood, the best he cou'd,
Expecting their decision;
Pox on't, says one, let him be gone,
He's of our own religion.

SONG 859.

Written in the Year 1760.

HARK, hark! the drum sounds,
The echo rebounds,
And bids us for fighting prepare;
Then let us advance,
And conquer all France,
For with Britons no troops can compare;
G g

Refentment's great call,
To Englifhmen all,
Cries loudly to recompence wrong;
The voice let's obey,
And rife with the day,
For glory to us fhall belong.

When in a juft caufe,
And liberty's laws,
With vigour our fpirits let's chear;
Our fwords drawn in hand,
We'll ufe at command,
And fhew we are ftrangers to fear.

Let enemies boaft
Of ftorming our coaft,
Whofe veffels in harbour do lie;
We wifh them all out,
To bang them about,
Then we'll vanquifh, brave boys, or we'll die.

Crown-Point, Senegal,
And Gaudaloupe's fall,
Enrichments to England do bring;
But France poor is grown,
And their fubjects muft moan,
While Quebec's brave conqueft we'll fing.

SONG 860.

Written by Mr. LEMOINE.

ANCIENT fages loudly fpeak
   In praife of Adam's ale;
Yet all their notions feem too weak,
   They can't with me prevail.

My joys all center in a bowl,
   Brimful of faucy grog;
And when it's out, I loudly bawl,
   Come, fill it up, you dog!

My leifure hours I freely fpend,
   Without a grain of fenfe;
I crack a joke with ev'ry friend,
   And thus I ufe my pence.

SONG 861.

THE CHAISE-MARINE.

MY deareft life, were thou my wife,
   How happy fhould I be!
And all my care, in peace and war,
   Should be to pleafure thee.
When up and down, from town to town,
   We jolly foldiers rove;
Then you, my queen, in chaife-marine,
   Shall move like queen of love.

Your love I'd prize beyond the fkies,
   Beyond the fpoils of war;
Would'ft thou agree to follow me,
   In humble baggage-car.
For happinefs, tho' in diftrefs,
   In foldiers wives is feen;
And pride in coach has more reproach
   Than love in chaife-marine.

Oh! do not hold your love in gold,
   Nor fet your heart on gain;
Behold the great, with all their ftate,
   Their lives are care and pain.
In houfe or tent, I pay no rent,
   Nor care nor trouble fee;
But ev'ry day I get my pay,
   And fpend it merrily.

Love not thofe knaves, great fortune's flaves,
   Who lead ignoble lives:
Nor deign to fmile on men fo vile,
   Who fight none but their wives.
For Britain's right and you we fight,
   And ev'ry ill defy;
Should but the fair reward our care,
   With love and conftancy.

If fighs, nor groans, nor tender moans,
   Can win your harden'd heart;
Let love in arms, with all his charms,
   Then take a foldier's part.
With fife and drum the foldiers come,
   And all the pomp of war;
Then don't think mean of chaife-marine,
   'Tis love's triumphant car.

SONG 862.

THE KENNEL-RAKER.

Sung at SADLER'S WELLS.

THO' I fweep to and fro old iron to find,
   Brafs, pins, rufty nails, they are all to my
   mind;
Yet I wear a found heart, true to great George
   our king,
And tho' ragged and poor, with clear confcience
   can fing:
Tho' I fweep to and fro, yet I'd have you to
   know,
There are fweepers in high-life as well as in low.

The ftatefman he fweeps in his coffers the blunt,
That fhou'd pay the poor foldiers who honour
   do hunt;
The action, tho' dirty, he cares not a ftraw,
So he gets but the ready, the rabble may jaw.
   Tho' I fweep, &c.

I'm told, that the parfon, for I never go
To hear a man preach what he'll never ftick to;
'Tis all for the fweepings he tips ye the cant,
You might pray by yourfelves elfe, depend Sirs
   upon't.
   Tho' I fweep, &c.

One fweeps you from this life, you cannot tell
   where,
And to what place you go to the doctor don't care;
So he brings in his bill, your long purfes to
   broach,
Then he laughs in his fleeve as he rides in his
   coach.
   Tho' I fweep, &c.

But honefty's beft, in what ftation we are,
For the grand fweeper death we can fooner pre-
pare;
Your ftatefman, your parfon, your phyfic, and
law,
When death takes a fweep, are no more than
a chiw.
Tho' I fweep to and fro, yet I'd have you to
know,
There are fweepers in high-life as well as in low.

SONG 863.

IN ftory we're told,
How our monarchs of old,
O'er France fpread their royal domain;
But no annals can fhow
Their pride laid fo low,
As when brave George the Second did reign,
Brave boys.

Of Roman and Greek,
Let fame no more fpeak,
How their arms the old world did fubdue;
Thro' the nations around,
Let our trumpets now found,
How Britons have conquer'd the new
Brave boys.

Eaft, Weft, North, and South,
Our cannon's loud mouth
Shall the rights of our monarch maintain;
On America's ftrand
Amherft limits the land,
Bofcawen gives law on the main,
Brave boys.

Each port and each town
We ftill make our own,
Cape-Breton, Crown-Point, Niagar;
Guadaloupe, Senegal,
Quebec's mighty fail,
Shall prove we've no equal in war,
Brave boys.

Tho' Conflans did boaft
To conquer our coaft,
Our thunder foon made monfieur mute;
Brave Hawke wing'd his way,
Then bounc'd on his prey,
And gave him an English falute,
Brave boys.

At Minden, you know,
How we conquer'd the foe,
While homeward their army now fteals;
Tho' (they cry'd) Britifh bands
Are too hard for our hands,
Begar we can beat them in heels,
Morblieu!

While our heroes from home
For laurels now roam,
Shou'd the flat-bottom boats but appear;
Our militia fhall fhow,
No wooden-fhoe foe
Can with freemen in battle compare,
Brave boys.

Our fortunes and lives,
Our children and wives,
To defend is the time now, or never;
Then let each volunteer
To the drum-head repair;
King George and Old England for ever,
Brave boys.

SONG 864.

Sung at RANELAGH.

FLY, fly to yon vale, other paftimes purfue,
My eyes and my tongue have determin'd
thy fate;
This face and this fhape are not deftin'd for you,
And former difdain is now turn'd into hate.

SONG 865.

FEATHER'D FELICITY.

Written by Mr. LEMOINE.

TWO milk-white doves upon a bough
Sat courting t'other day;
Enraptur'd with each other's vow,
Time fweetly ftole away.

Foft'ring zephyrs gently blew,
To fan their foft defires;
While Phœbus bright upon them threw
The warmth of heav'nly fires.

With kiffes fweet the male careft
The pride of nature's art;
While fhe, all fondnefs, heav'd the breaft
That clos'd a truth-fraught heart.

No mundane cares within them dwelt,
To gall the fleeting hour:
Both own'd the happinefs they felt
Arofe from Cupid's pow'r.

SONG 866.

THE SPINNING-WHEEL.

Sung at MARYBONE.

YOUNG Colin fifhing near the mill,
Saw Sally underneath the hill,
Whofe heart love's tender power could feel;
Dear maid! th' enraptur'd fhepherd cries,
I fee love fporting in thy eyes.
But ftill fhe turn'd her fpinning-wheel.

Thy cheeks, fays he, like peaches bloom,
Thy breath is like the fpring's perfume,
On thy fweet lips my love I'll feal;
Yon ftately fwans, fo white and fleek,
Are like to Sally's breaft and neck!
But ftill fhe turn'd her fpinning-wheel.

Tho', fair-one, beauty's tranfient power
Fades like the new-blown gaudy flower,
Not fo where virtue loves to dwell;

C g 2

For where sweet modesty appears,
We never see the vale of years.
　　She smil'd, and stopp'd her spinning-wheel.

The pomp of state, the pride of wealth,
Says she, I scorn for peace and health,
　　Where honest labour earns her meal:
Who tells the flatterer's common tale,
Can never o'er my heart prevail,
　　And make me leave my spinning-wheel.

The swain who loves the virtuous mind,
Alone can make young Sally kind;
　　For him I'll toil, I'll spin and reel.
It is the voice, (says he) of love,
Come hasten to the church above!
　　She blush'd, and left her spinning-wheel.

SONG 867.

WHEN first I saw my Delia's face,
　　Adorn'd with every bloom and grace
　　That love and youth could bring:
Such sweetness too in all her form,
I thought her one celestial born,
　　And took her for the Spring.

Each day a charm was added more,
Musick and language swell'd the store,
　　With all the force of reason:
And yet so frolick and so gay,
Deck'd with the opening sweets of May,
　　She look'd—the Summer season.

Admiring crowds around her press,
But none the happy he could guess.
　　Unwish'd her beauties caught them:
I urg'd my passion in her ear,
Of love, she said, she could not hear;
　　And yet seem'd ripe as Autumn.

The rose, not gather'd in it's prime,
Will fade and fall in little time !
　　So I began to hint her?
Her cheeks confess a summer glow;
But, ah! her breast of driven snow
　　Conceals a heart of Winter.

SONG 868.

THE GOOD-FELLOW.

Sung at VAUXHALL.

DISTANT hie thee, carping care,
　　From the spot where I do dwell;
Rigid mortals, come not there,
Frowns, begone to hermit's cell;
But let me live the life of souls,
With laughter, love, and flowing bowls.

Miser, with thy paltry pelf
I give 'gainst thee my hate it's scope;
　Wretch that liv'st but for thyself,
With heart of rust that cannot ope:
Fly, bird of night, from sun and souls,
That love and laugh o'er flowing bowls.

Who can let the pensive go,
Or the eye that drops a tear,

And not weed their minds of woe,
May not, dare not peep in here :
Who can't be friends, can ne'er be souls,
Nor e'er shall quaff our flowing bowls.

Joys on joys, O let me taste;
Health and mirth dwell in my gate,
　　While with ease my sand doth waste,
Whilst I bless the book of fate :
Then let me live the life of souls,
With laughter, love, and flowing bowls.

SONG 869.

Sung at RANELAGH.

YOU say she's fair; 'tis no such matter,
　　'Tis not her glass, but you that flatter;
And few that beauty e'er can spy,
Which strikes the partial lover's eye.

Phebe, my council pray approve ;
Think heav'n for a good man's love :
All markets will not pay your price,
So strike the bargain in a trice.

SONG 870.

Sung at VAUXHALL.

SINCE they trac'd me alone with a swain
　　to the grove,
Each tongue in the village proclaims I'm in
　　love ;
With a laugh they point at us, as passing along,
And Colin and Nell are their jest and their song.

Suspicion long whisper'd it over the green,
But Scandal now tells what she never has seen ?
Wherever we wander, yet faster she flies,
What we do, or we say, she reflects with her
　　lies.

How we trip all by moonlight to love-haunted
　　bow'rs ;
How we toy and we kiss at the sweet gliding
　　hours :
All this, and yet more, if she will she may name,
For we meet without crime, and we part with-
　　out shame.

I own that I love him, he's so to my mind,
And waits with impatience till fortune's more
　　kind;
I still will love on till our fate's to be blest,
And the talk may be louder, it shan't break
　　our rest.

Let malice her tongue and her eyes all employ,
And envy do all to embitter our joy;
The time that is coming shall soften the past,
And crown the gay nymph and her Colin at last.

SONG 871.

FREE from envy, strife, and sorrow,
　　Jealous doubts and heart-felt fears ;
Free from thoughts of what to-morrow
　　May o'er-charge the soul with cares.

By me plays the stream meandring,
Slowly as it's waters glide ;
And in gentle murmurs wand'ring,
Lulls to downy rest my pride.

Here I walk in meditation,
Pond'ring on sublunar things ;
From the silent soft persuasion,
Which from virtue's basis springs,

Here in midnight's gloomy terror,
I enjoy the silent night ;
Darkness shews the soul her error,
And darkness leads to inward light.

Near me ancient ruins falling,
From the time-shook castle's brow ;
Once the greatest seats installing,
Where are all their honours now ?

Silent as the gloomy graves are,
Now the mansions once so loud ;
Still and quiet now the brave are,
Fled the horrors of a crowd.

What, says truth, are pomp and riches,
Gilded baits to folly lent !
Honour which the soul bewitches,
When obtain'd we may repent.

This was once the seat of plunder,
Blood of heroes stain'd the floor ;
Heroes nature's pride and wonder,
Heroes heard of now no more.

Owls and ravens haunt the buildings,
Sending gloomy dread to all ;
Yellow moss the summit yielding,
Pellitory decks the wall.

Time with rapid speed still wanders,
Journies on an even pace ;
Fame of greatest actions squanders,
And ever perpetrates disgrace.

Sigh not, then, for pomp or glory ;
What avails a hero's name !
Future times may tell your story,
To your then disgrace and shame.

Chuse some humble cot as this is,
In sweet philosophic ease ;
With dame nature's frugal blisses,
Live in joy, and die in peace.

SONG 872.

A SCOTCH BALLAD.

Sung at VAUXHALL.

WHEN Jemmy first began to love,
He was the gayest swain
That ever yet a flock had drove,
Or danc'd upon the plain :
'Twas then that I, wae's my poor heart,
My freedom threw away,
And finding sweets in ev'ry smart,
I could not say him nay ;
And ever when he talk'd of love,
He would his eyes decline ;
And every sigh a heart would move,
Gwid faith, and why not mine ?

He'd press my hand, and kiss it oft,
In silence spoke his flame ;
And while he treated me thus soft,
I thought him not to blame.

Sometimes to feed my flocks with him,
My Jemmy would invite me,
Where he the softest songs wou'd sing,
On purpose to delight me ;
And Jemmy ev'ry grace display'd,
Which were enough, I trow,
To conquer any princely maid,
So he did me, I vow.
But now for Jemmy I must mourn,
Who to the wars must go ;
His sheep-hook to a sword must turn,
Alack ! what shall I do ?
His bag-pipe into warlike sounds
Must now exchanged be ;
Instead of bracelets fearful sounds,
Then what becomes of me ?

SONG 873.

Sung at VAUXHALL.

WHEN I see my Strephon languish,
With his tender love opprest,
When I see his pain and anguish,
Pity moves my tender breast.

Strephon's plain and humble nature
Mov'd me first to hear his tale ;
Strephon's truth, by ev'ry creature,
Is proclaim'd thro' all the vale.

I love, and am belov'd again ;
No more shall Strephon sigh in vain !
I've try'd his faith, and find it true,
And all my coyness bid adieu.

SONG 874.

THE MYRTLE AND ROSE.

Sung at VAUXHALL.

AT once I'm in love with two nymphs that
are fair,
And to sweets in my garden these nymphs I
compare ;
Nor can shrub nor can blossom be better than
those,
And Jenny's my myrtle, and Chloe's my rose.

My Chloe is fond all her charms to display ;
With the rose in her cheek, she to all would
be gay ;
On all paler beauties she looks down with pride,
And can bear not a flow'ret to grow by her side.

She thinks not how quickly these charms will
expire,
That with May they first came, and with summer retire ;
That pride, so soon over, is foolish and vain,
And love, built on beauty, can't hold with a
swain.

But Jenny, my myrtle, ne'er changes her face,
No season nor age can her features displace ;

She covets no praiſe, nor with envy is ſtung,
She always is pleas'd, and is pleaſing and young.

Then, Chloe, I ſudden muſt make my retreat,
Thy roſe is too blooming, too ſhort-liv'd and
    ſweet;
But Jenny, thy myrtle is laſting and green,
And all the year thro' thou the ſame ſtill art ſeen.

SONG 875.

NANCY OF THE VALE.

RECITATIVE.

THE Weſtern ſky was purpled o'er,
    With every pleaſing ray,
And flocks reviving felt no more
    The ſultry heats of day;
When from a hazel's artleſs bow'r,
    Soft warbled Strephon's tongue;
He bleſt the day, he bleſt the hour,
    While Nancy's charms he ſung.

AIR.

Let fops with ſickle falſehoods range
    The paths of wanton love,
While weeping maids lament the change,
    And ſadden ev'ry grove;
But endleſs bleſſings crown the day
    I ſaw fair Eſham's dale,
And ev'ry bleſſing find it's way
    To Nancy of the Vale.

Far in the winding vale retir'd,
    This peerleſs bud I found,
And ſhad'wing rocks and woods conſpir'd
    To fence her beauties round:
That nature in ſo lone a cell
    Should form a nymph ſo ſweet,
Or fortune to her ſecret cell,
    Conduct my wand'ring feet!

Gay lordlings ſought her for their bride,
    But ſhe would ne'er incline;
Prove to your equals true, ſhe cry'd,
    As I will prove to mine;
'Tis Strephon on the mountain's brow
    Has won my right good will;
To him I gave my plighted vow,
    With him I'll climb the hill.

Struck with her charms and gentle truth,
    I claſp'd the conſtant fair;
To her alone I gave my youth,
    And vow'd my future care.
And when this vow ſhall faithleſs prove,
    Or I thoſe charms forego;
The ſtream that ſaw our tender love,
    That ſtream ſhall ceaſe to flow.

SONG 876.

Sung at VAUXHALL.

WHEN Fanny I ſaw, as I tripp'd o'er the
    green,
Fair, blooming, artleſs, and kind,
Fond love in her eyes, wit and ſenſe in her
    mien,
And warmneſs with modeſty join'd;

With ſudden amazement I ſtood,
    Faſt rivetted down to the place;
Her delicate ſhape, eaſy motion I view'd,
    And wand'red o'er every grace.

Ye gods! what luxuriance of beauty! I cry;
    What raptures muſt dwell in her arms!
On her lips I could feaſt, on her breaſt I could
    O! Fanny how ſweet are thy charms! [die;

Whilſt thus in idea my paſſion I fed,
    Soft tranſports my ſenſes invade;
Young Damon ſtepp'd up, with the ſubſtance
    he fled,
And left me to kiſs the dear ſhade.

SONG 877.

THE COQUETTE RECLAIM'D.

Sung at VAUXHALL.

THE ſtory goes, 'That ſiſter Bet,
    Reſolv'd to play the field coquette,
    Amongſt the ruſtic breed:
But tir'd of flirting on the green,
She cry'd, Who'd live, to live unſeen?
    Not I, not I, indeed.

Away ſhe flies, leaves ev'ry ſquire,
To tell his tale by winter fire,
    While hearts like cherries bleed:
But what's all this to I? ſays ſhe;
A rural life won't do for me,
    It won't, it won't, indeed.

Give me the Park to flaunt about,
The play-houſe, Ranelagh, and route.—
    But how did this ſucceed?
Admir'd by lords, ſhe loſt her fame,
On ev'ry window glar'd her name,
    'Tis true, 'tis true, indeed.

At length ſhe ſought the ſlighted plain,
Grew a good girl, careſs'd her ſwain,
    And ſoon they were agreed:
Will you not love me now? he ſays,
O yes! the longeſt nights and days,
    I'll love, I'll love, indeed.

SONG 878.

DIANA AND CUPID; A CANTATA.

Sung at VAUXHALL.

RECITATIVE.

AS Dian and her hunting train
    Once rov'd to try the woods and plain,
Poor Cupid faſt aſleep they found,
His bows and arrows on the ground.
Well pleas'd to find his godſhip there,
She thus commands her liſt'ning fair:

AIR.

Break, break with ſpeed, each pointed dart!
    For if he wakes he'll ſurely turn our foe;
'Tis his to wound the tender heart,
    His only joy's to give us woe.

Now fhall we fafely trace the plain,
And haunt the river, lawn and grove;
His arrows broke, his pow'r is vain;
You now may fafely laugh at love.

RECITATIVE.

When now, too late, the god awoke,
Saw Dian and her fav'rites by;
The fatal mifchief thus he fpoke,
Whilft malice fparkled from each eye.

AIR.

Tho' Cupid is vanquifh'd to-day,
Believe not my empire is o'er,
To Venus I'll hie me away,
She'll arm me as well as before.
Oh, Dian! what nymph of the train
Is fafe when I aim the fore dart!
I'm mad with the wrongs I fuftain,
Then, goddefs, take care of thy heart.

SONG 879.

THE ROSE.

Written by Mr. LEMOINE.

WHAT fate attends the blufhing rofe,
How fwift it's beauty flies!
Sweet fcents at morn it does difclofe,
Ere eve it fades and dies.

O think, dear Julia, on thy charms,
They, like the rofe, will fade;
Then hafte, enchantrefs, to my arms,
Thou fweet and lovely maid.

Thy beauty, like a fragrant flow'r,
Juft emblem of the rofe;
Whofe longeft fpace is but an hour,
Ere all it's fplendors clofe.

Then hafte, dear Julia, hafte away
Unto that happy land,
Where joy and mirth reign all the day,
And Cupid bears command.

SONG 880.

Sung in *Twelfth - Night*.

HOW imperfect is expreffion,
Some emotions to impart!
When we mean a foft confeffion,
And yet feek to hide the heart!
When our bofoms, all complying,
With delicious tumults fwell,
And beat what broken, falt'ring, dying
Language would, but cannot tell.

Deep confufion's rofy terror,
Quite expreffive paints my cheek.
Afk no more—behold your error;
Blufhes eloquently fpeak.
What tho' filent is my anguifh,
Or breath'd only to the air;
Mark my eyes, and as they languifh,
Read what yours have written there.

O, that you could once conceive me!
Once my heart's ftrong feelings view!
Love has nought more fond, believe me;
Friendfhip nothing half fo true.
From you I am wild defpairing,
With you fpeechlefs as I touch;
This is all that bears declaring,
And perhaps declares too much.

SONG 881.

THE VIRGIN MONITOR.

Sung at VAUXHALL.

YE virgins of Britain, who wifely attend
The dictates of reafon, who value a friend,
Come lift to my counfel, and mark what I fay;
Ye damfels beware of the dangers of May.

Tho' guarded by virtue's all-foftering hand;
Tho' modefty lend you her magical wand;
Tho' innocence deck you with fpotlefs array,
Ye damfels beware of the dangers of May.

When firft the gay beauties of nature appear,
And Phœbus' bright fmile chears the juvenile
    year;
When the birds chant their amorous notes from
    each fpray,
Ye damfels beware of the dangers of May.

Should Flora propofe you the vernal delight,
Her delicate paintings exhibit to fight;
In her meadows and fields fhould you frolic and
    play,
Beware, O beware of the dangers of May.

When the blood brifkly flows, the all-eloquent
    eyes
Reveal ev'ry fecret the heart would difguife;
The bofom quick-panting with force teems to
    fay,
'Tis hard to refift all the dangers of May.

Should an amorous youth, this foft fcene to
    improve,
With ardour implore the reward of his love;
If Hymen attend you, his dictates obey,
For wedlock removes all the dangers of May.

SONG 882.

THE HUMOROUS LASS.

Sung at VAUXHALL.

SMART Doll of the green, who lov'd mirth
    as her life,
By many a fwain was requefted to wife;
Her figure was graceful, and comely her face,
Yet in her affections no man had ta'en place:
The fquire of the vill took it into his head,
That he by great proffers could win her to bed;
But all his fine artifice Dolly thro' law,
And bawk'd the poor fquire with a hearty
    ha! ha!

Next Hodge of the vale all his flame did impart,
Who knew nothing more than a plough or a
  cart;
With aukward addrefs he made a ftrange fufs,
Turn'd his hat o'er his thumb, and begg'd for
  a bufs.
The lout fetch'd a figh, and cry'd, 'Deed Doll
  'tis true,
Ife love the moft woundely, i'faith, girl, I do;
But fhe flapp'd his fool's chaps and bid him
  withdraw,
So fent him away, while fhe loud laugh'd ha! ha!

The next was a fellow fo fmart and fo fpruce,
Who caper'd and fung, 'mong the girls play'd
  the deuce,
And poor Doll thought to ferve as the reft,
But fhe was too fharp, and of him made a jeft.
Quoth Doll, I'll ne'er wed till I meet with a man!
Much lefs let a fop my affections trapan;
And faid, fuch a thing fhe before never faw,
But hop'd he'd excufe it, and laugh'd out
  ha! ha!

With the ladies, I know, 'tis a primitive rule,
Much better be plagu'd with a knave than a
  fool;
And others, again, this opinion impart,
Their eyes they will pleafe if they torture their
  heart.
From thefe I diffent, but approve of the plan
That Dolly laid down, till you meet with your
  man;
Then your hands and your hearts may unite
  without flaw,
And your conjugal ftate be one fcene of ha! ha!

SONG 883.

Sung in the *Election.*

AH! let it ne'er with truth be faid,
  That public virtue droops her head,
That Englifh faith fhould lucklefs prove,
Or crofs one Englifh virgin's love.

If in my Sally's youthful heart,
  Her Richard e'er may claim a part,
This happy hour fhall fmiling prove,
That honour firmly fixes love.

SONG 884.

Sung at MARYBONE.

DEAREST Kitty, kind and fair,
  Tell me when, and tell we where,
Tell thy fond and faithful fwain,
When we thus fhall meet again?
When fhall Strephon fondly fee
Beauties only found in thee?

Kifs thee, prefs thee, toy and play,
All the happy live-long day:
Deareft Kitty, kind and fair,
Tell me when, and tell we where?

All the happy day, 'tis true,
Blefs'd but only when with you;
Nightly Strephon fighs alone,
Sighs till Hymen makes us one.
Tell me, then, and eafe my pain,
Tell thy fond and faithful fwain,
When the prieft fhall kindly join
Kitty's trembling hand to mine?
Deareft Kitty! kind and fair,
Tell me when?—I care not where.

SONG 885.

ANACREONTIC.

Sung at VAUXHALL.

YOU know that our ancient philofophers held,
  There is nothing in beauty, or honour, or
    gold;
That blifs in externals no mortal can find;
And in truth, my good friends, I am quite of
  their mind.

What makes a man happy, I never can doubt;
'Tis fomething within him, and nothing without;
This fomething, they faid, was the fource of
  content,
And whate'er they call'd it, 'twas wine that
  they meant.

Without us, Indeed, it is not worth a pin;
But, ye gods! how divine if we get it within;
'Tis then, of all bleffings, the flourifhing root,
And in fpite of the world, we can gather the
  fruit.

When the bottle is wanting, the foul is depreft,
And beauty can kindle no flame in the breaft;
But with wine at our hearts we are always in
  love,
We can fing like the linnet, and bill like the
  dove.

The richeft and greateft are poor and repine,
If with gold and with grandeur you give them
  no wine;
But wine to the peafant or flave if you bring,
He's as rich as a Jew, and as great as a king.
With wine at my heart, I am happy and free,
Externals without it are nothing to me;
Come fill, and this truth from a bumper you'll
  know,
That wine is, of bleffings, the bleffing below.

THE

VOCAL MAGAZINE.

NUMBER VII.

SONG 885.

Written by Mr. ROWE.

AS on a fummer's day,
    In the green-wood fhade I lay;
    The maid that I lov'd,
    As her fancy mov'd,
Came walking forth that way.

And as fhe paffed by,
With a fcornfu' glance of her eyes
    What a fhame, queth fhe;
    For a fwain muft it be,
Like a lazy loon for to lie!

And doft thou nothing heed
What Pan, our god, has decreed;
    What a prize to-day
    Shall be given away
To the fweeteft fhepherd's reed?

There's not a fingle fwain
Of all this fruitful plain,
    But with hopes and fears,
    Now bufily prepares
The bonny boon to gain.

Shall another maiden fhine
In brighter array than thine?
    Up, up, duli fwain,
    Tune thy pipe once again;
And make the garland mine.

Alas! my love, I cried,
What avails this courtly pride?
    Since thy dear defert
    Is written in my heart,
What is all the world befide?

To me thou art more gay,
In this homely ruffet grey,
    Than the nymphs of our green,
    So trim and fo fheen,
Or the brighteft queen of May.

What tho' my fortune frown,
And deny thee a filken gown;
    My own dear maid,
    Be content with this fhade,
And a fhepherd all thy own.

SONG 886.

LET milkfops, in love, whine and cant if
        they will,
While merrily we of good wine take our fill;
A frown often fits on the brow of your lafs,
But nought but a fmile's ever feen in a glafs,
    Derry down, down, down derry down.

No jealoufy e'er fhall our bofoms inflame,
Our miftiefs is common, and claret her name;
There's for wine no occafion to quarrel or
        brawl,
For if we all lov't, there's enough for us all.
    Derry down, &c.

Then be merry, companions, the bottle pufh
        round,
No miftrefs like this under heaven is found:
If there's not enough here, friends, you foon
        fhall have more,
For where this bottle came from there's plenty
        in ftore.
    Derry down, down, down derry down.

SONG 887.

ANACREONTIC.

CROWN'D with rofes, let us quaff
    The gen'rous liquor, jeft and laugh;
Let our laffes dance around,
To the cittern's fportive found,
Each a Thyrfie in her hand;
Let the boys, too, join the band;
One fhall fing, and one fhall play,
All fhall merry be, and gay.

H h

Cupid, with his golden hair,
Ever young, and ever fair;
Bacchus, sprightly god and gay;
Venus, queen of love and May:
These our choir shall join and bring
With them everlasting spring;
Beauty, mirth, and wine, and love,
Ev'ry sorrow shall remove.

SONG 888.

Sung at VAUXHALL.

YE beaux and ye belles pray attend to my song,
'Tis new, I assure you, and will not be long.
From the camp I'm arriv'd, that scene of de-
light,
Where they romp, sing, and dance, all the day
and the night.
To the camp then all repair,
Gallant swains, and blooming fair;
Gaily laughing, let us tramp
To the merry, merry camp.

Well, who could have thought that war was so
charming!
Nothing there's in it that can be alarming;
Nor Margate, nor Bath, nor the fam'd Tun-
bridge Wells,
Like the camp all our sorrow so sweetly dispels.
To the camp, &c.

With parsons, squires, clowns, there is such
intrusion,
The camp is a type, sure, of Babel's confusion;
There hautboys and trumpets, brisk fifes and
bassoons,
Both charm you and stun you with fifty old
tunes.
To the camp, &c.

E'en Cupid, gay Cupid, to Coxheath is come,
For love he's recruiting with fife and with drum!
A thousand sweet damsels he has in his train,
A heart he now offers each martial young swain.
To the camp then all repair,
Gallant swains, and blooming fair;
Gaily laughing, let us tramp
To the merry, merry camp.

SONG 889.

IN the bloom of her youth, shall it ever be
said,
That a lass so engaging e'er dy'd an old maid,
Oh! no—I'm determin'd to get me a mate,
For wedlock I'm told's an agreeable state;
Of suitors, I'm sure, I've at least half a score,
Who swear that they love me, and sigh and
adore;
Dull cits, country squires, prating barristers,
beaux;
But I needs must confess, that I like none of
those.

I'm a bale of rich goods, so the citizen swore,
And look ten *per cent.* better each day than
before;

The squire, with a kiss, bawls to cover; swears
zounds,
But he fancies me more than his kennel of
hounds;
The lawyer his suit he with modesty press'd,
That for him I'd decree, and eject all the rest.
While the beau talk'd of nothing but fashion
and clothes.
Can you blame me, ye fair, if I like none of
those?

Some friends would persuade me to marry a fool,
For women, they say, are desirous to rule;
But as that is a pow'r which I never will use,
I'll tell you what sort of a man I would chuse;
A youth with some sense and good-nature com-
bin'd,
Just too learn'd for a dunce, not too wise to
be kind;
Where I'm wrong, just with spirit to gently
oppose:
Why, I needs must confess, I should like
those.

SONG 890.

ODE IN HONOUR OF THE ANTIGALLICANS.

AS liberty, from out the sky,
Held o'er our isle her scepter'd hand;
Griev'd was the goddess, breath'd a sigh,
And thus bespoke the sinking land:
Shame, inglorious race! grow wise,
And Antigallicans arise.

In ancient time, your sires renown'd,
With honest heart, and surly face,
Fought well their battles, gain'd their ground,
And scorn'd the puny Gallic race:
Shame, inglorious sons! grow wise,
And Antigallicans arise.

No fopp'ries then were ap'd from France;
Their language was as plain as dress:
Think on their honours, Oh! advance,
And Heav'n shall your endeavours bless!
Hence victorious reign, and wise,
And Antigallicans arise.

Ye sacred few! who boast the name,
Whose bosoms burn with patriot fire!
Hail, friends of freedom! dear to fame,
And grac'd with all that gods admire.
You're transcendent great and wise,
Who Antigallicans arise.

'Tis yours to bid fair science smile,
To welcome commerce to our shore;
Teach arts to flourish round the isle,
And Britain to itself restore:
You're transcendent great and wise,
Who Antigallicans arise.

Again shou'd curst rebellion glow,
Or bold invasion spread it's wing,
Then arm'd revengeful, on the foe,
To save their country and their king,
All-courageous, gen'rous, wise,
The Antigallicans shall rise.

And when this globe shall melt away,
The temples sink, the columns fall,
Then shall, distinguish'd as the day,
The beams of glory crown them all:
And imperial, in the skies,
The Antigallicans shall rise.

SONG 891.

A Taylor there was, and he liv'd in a garret,
Who ne'er in his days tasted champaign or
claret;
With high soups, or ragouts, he never was fed,
But cabbage, believe me, was his daily bread.
Derry down, &c.

His work he pursu'd without any repining,
When blest with a pint of three-threads for his
lining;
Till Cupid, whose arrows most cruelly treat us,
With a sempstress's bodkin destroy'd his quietus:
Derry down, &c.

No longer a birth-night affords any pleasure,
His patterns lie scatter'd, in tatters his measure:
His bill he contrives not with items to swell;
Silk, twist, tape, and buckram, he wishes in hell.
Derry down, &c.

Cupid pitying his case, at length flew to his aid,
And help'd him to fine-draw the hole he had
made;
He bade him be bold, and not stand like a mute,
And never give out, till he'd finish'd his suit.
Derry down, &c.

He visits the sempstress, with aukward addrefs,
Protests on her kindness hung his happiness:
But she scornfully sneer'd at his speeches and
wheedle;
For she, lack-a-day! was as sharp as a needle.
Derry down, &c.

He told her on hon'rable terms he was come,
And begg'd he might soon be inform'd of his
doom;
Unless she'd consent to be shortly his wife,
The fates sheais wou'd soon snip off his rem-
nant of life.
Derry down, &c.

D'ye think, cry'd the sempstress, I'll take for
a spouse,
One whom no one esteems at three skips of a
louse;
Advance in your favour whatever you can,
A taylor is but the ninth part of a man.
Derry down, &c.

The taylor proceeded with lying, intreating,
And making such speeches as scarce bear re-
peating:
A woman unmarry'd was useless, he said,
Was just like a needle without any thread.
Derry down, &c.

When the priest shou'd have tack'd them toge-
ther, he cry'd,
For her palate, when dainty, he'd nicely provide;
Tho' to turkies and capons he cou'd not aspire,
She might always be sure of a goose at the fire.
Derry down, &c.

As she work'd, he commended her fingers so
nimble!
And swore that her eyes were more bright than
her thimble.
Though small was his wit, he so acted his part,
That I know not how 'twas, but he cabbag'd
her heart.
Derry down, &c.

Away, hand in hand, to the chapel they went,
Nor appear'd in her visage the least discontent;
None but death could the conjugal knot have
unty'd,
For cross-legg'd together they work'd till they
dy'd.
Derry down, &c.

SONG 892.

A CANTATA.

Sung at RANELAGH.

RECITATIVE.

OFT I've implor'd the gods in vain,
And pray'd till I've been weary,
For once I'll try my wish to gain
Of Oberon the fairy.

AIR.

Sweet airy being, wanton sprite,
That lurks in woods unseen,
Or oft, by Cynthia's silver light,
Trips gaily o'er the green;
If e'er thy pitying heart was mov'd
As ancient stories tell,
And for th' Athenian maid that lov'd
Thou fought'st a wond'rous spell,
O deign once more t'exert thy pow'r,
Haply some herb or tree,
Sov'reign as juice of Western flow'r,
Conceals a balm for me.

RECITATIVE.

Ah! haste, and shed the sacred balm,
My shatter'd nerves new string;
And for my guest serenely calm
The nymph indiff'rence bring.
At her approach see fear, pale fear,
And expectation fly!
And disappointment in the rear,
That blasts the promis'd joy.
The tear that pity taught to flow,
The eye shall then disown;
The heart that griev'd for other's woe,
Shall then scarce feel it's own;
And wounds that now each moment bleed,
Each moment then shall close;
And tranquil days shall then succeed
To nights of calm repose.

AIR.

O fairy elf, but grant me this,
This one kind comfort send;
And so may never-fading bliss,
Thy flow'ry paths attend.

So may the glow-worm's glittering light
Thy tiny footsteps lead
To some new region of delight
Unknown to mortal tread,

And be thy acorn goblet fill'd
With heaven's ambrofial dew,
From fweeteft, frefheft flow'rs diftill'd,
That fhed frefh fweets for you.

And what of life remains for me
I'll pafs in fober eafe;
Half-pleas'd, contented will I be,
Content but half to pleafe.

SONG 893.

ANACREONTIC.

WITHIN a cool and pleafant fhade,
By myrtles and by poplars made,
I fit where rofes round me twine,
And laughing Cupid brings me wine;
His loofely-flowing garments ty'd
With reeds pluck'd from the river-fide.
The moments fwiftly fly, I feel,
Quick-whirling like a chariot-wheel;
And when a few fleet years are paft,
Life gone, we turn to duft at laft.
Say, why fhould we anoint the dead,
Or why fweet flow'rs around them fpread;
Why pour libations on their tomb!
'Tis liquor wafted; rather come,
And pour on me the ointment; bring
The rofe, and all the flow'rs that fpring
Around us wild; and bring to me
A lafs that's pretty, kind, and free;
For I'm refolv'd, before I go
To Plutus, and the realms below,
To caft my ev'ry care away,
Laugh and be happy while I may.

SONG 894.

CUPID'S ARROW.

Sung at VAUXHALL.

AS Chloe ply'd her needle's art,
A purple drop the fpear
Made from her heedlefs finger ftart,
And from her eyes a tear.

Ah! might but Chloe, from her fmart,
Be taught for mine to feel;
Mine caus'd by Cupid's piercing dart,
More fharp to me than fteel.

Then I her needle wou'd adore,
Love's arrow it fhou'd be;
Endu'd with fuch a fubtle pow'r,
To reach her heart for me.

SONG 895.

Sung at VAUXHALL.

ALEXIS, a pretty young fwain,
To court me comes many a mile;
I bid him make hafte back again,
Tho' I wifh him to ftay a great while:
With all by which love is expreft,
He ftudies my heart to beguile;
I wifh him fuccefs, I proteft,
But I tell him he'll wait a great while.

He brought me a nofegay to-day,
And vow'd 'twas more pleafure than toil;
I took it I fafely can fay,
And I let him not afk a great while:
He begg'd me to grant him a kifs
So earneft, he made me to fmile;
Have done! I cry'd; fie, 'tis amifs!
But I wifh'd it to laft a great while.

He tells me I ought to be kind,
That time all my beauties will fpoil;
I crofs him, tho' quite of his mind,
For I love him to talk a great while:
I think fuch fweet things he has faid,
My coynefs at laft he will fpoil;
And when he once afks me to wed,
Oh! I'll not live a maid a great while.

SONG 896.

A HUNTING SONG.

Sung at MARYBONE.

WHEN the morning peeps forth, and the
zephyr's cool gale
Carries fragrance and health over mountain
and dale;
Up, ye nymphs and ye fwains, and together
we'll rove
Up hill, and down valley, by thicket and grove;
Then follow with me, where the welkin refounds
With the notes of the horn, and the cry of
the hounds.

Let the wretched be flaves to ambition and
wealth,
All the bleffings I afk, is the bleffing of health;
So fhall innocence felf give a warrant to joys,
No envy difturbs, no dependence deftroys,
Then follow, &c.

O'er hills, dales and woodlands, with raptures
we roam,
Yet returning ftill find the dear pleafures at
home;
Where the chearful good-humour gives honefty
grace,
And the heart fpeaks content in the fmiles of
the face.
Then follow with me, where the welkin refounds
With the notes of the horn, and the cry of
the hounds.

SONG 897.

WILLIAM AND SUSAN.

'TWAS in his veffel failing,
When gentle breezes blew,
Sweet William lay bewailing
The fate of lovely Sue:
All on his bed extended
The faithful failor lay,
His grief was never ended,
He mourn'd her night and day.

Juſt at the midnight hour
  A gentle voice he hears,
And at his cabin-door
  The black-ey'd maid appears;
All pale ſhe look'd, tho' ſmiling,
  And dreſs'd in ſpotleſs white,
Like ſome bright cloud a ſailing
  When Cynthia ſmiles at night.

Why mourns my faithful lover?
  The damſel viſion ſaid;
Who hath the ſea croſs'd over
  To tell thee I was dead?
What tongue the fatal ſtory
  Unto thine ear convey'd?
And why art thou ſo ſorry
  To loſe a ſilly maid?

None brought the hapleſs meſſage,
  The weeping lover ſaid;
None came the tedious paſſage
  To tell me thou wert dead:
But fancy, ever teeming,
  The fatal ſtory told;
At midnight I was dreaming
  I ſaw thee dead and cold.

Then from my ſleep I ſtarted,
  And thus in anguiſh cry'd,
Why were we ever parted?
  Ah! why has Suſan dy'd?
Since then my wretched boſom
  No peace or comfort knew;
And now, like a full bloſſom,
  I'll drop and die with you.

SONG 898.

ALEXIS, a ſhepherd, young, conſtant, and kind,
Has often declar'd I'm the nymph to his mind;
I think he's ſincere, and he will not deceive,
But they tell me a maid ſhould with caution
    believe.

He brought me this roſe that you ſee in my
    breaſt,
He begg'd me to take it, and ſigh'd out the reſt;
I cou'd not do leſs than the favour receive,
And he thinks it now ſweeter, I really believe.

This flow'ret, he cry'd, reads a leſſon to you;
How bright and how lovely it ſeems to the view!
'Twou'd fade if not pluck'd, as your ſenſe muſt
    conceive.
I was forc'd to deny what I really believe.

My flocks he attends; if they ſtray from the
    plain,
Alexis is ſure ev'ry ſheep to regain;
Then begs a dear kiſs for his labour I'll give,
And I ne'er ſhall refuſe him, I really believe.

He plays on his pipe while he watches my eyes,
To read the ſoft wiſhes we're taught to diſguiſe;
And tells me ſweet ſtories from morning to eve;
Then he ſwears that he loves, which I really
    believe.

An old maid I once was determin'd to die,
But that was before I'd this ſwain in my eye;
And as ſoon as he aſks me his pain to relieve,
With joy I ſhall wed him, I really believe.

SONG 899.

THE DUST-CART; A CANTATA.

RECITATIVE.

AS tink'ring Tom the ſtreets his trade did
    cry,
He ſaw his lovely Sylvia paſſing by;
In duſt-cart high advanc'd, the nymph was
    plac'd,
With the rich cinders round her lovely waiſt:
Tom with uplifted hands th' occaſion bleſt;
And thus, in ſoothing ſtrains, the maid addreſt.

AIR.

O Sylvia, while you drive your cart,
To pick up duſt, you ſteal our hearts,
You take our duſt, and ſteal our hearts:
That mine is gone, alas! is true,
And dwells among the duſt with you,
And dwells among the duſt with you:
Ah! lovely Sylvia, eaſe my pain;
Give me my heart you ſtole again.
Give me my heart, out of your cart;
Give me my heart you ſtole again.

RECITATIVE.

Sylvia, advanc'd above the rabble rout,
Exulting roll'd her ſparkling eyes about;
She heav'd her ſwelling breaſt, as black as ſloe,
And look'd diſdain on little folks below:
To Tom ſhe nodded, as the cart drew on,
And then, reſolv'd to ſpeak, ſhe cry'd, Stop,
    John.

AIR.

Shall I, who ride above the reſt,
  Be by a paltry crowd oppreſt;
Ambition now my ſoul does fire,
  The youths ſhall languiſh and admire;
And ev'ry girl, with anxious heart,
  Shall long to ride in my duſt-cart.

SONG 900.

ONE morning very early, one morning in the
    ſpring,
I heard a maid in Bedlam who mournfully did
    ſing,
Her chains ſhe rattled on her hands, while
    ſweetly thus ſung ſhe,
I love my love, becauſe I know my love loves me.

O cruel were his parents, who ſent my love to ſea,
And cruel, cruel was the ſhip that bore my love
    from me;
Yet I love his parents, ſince they're his, altho'
    they've ruin'd me,
And I love my love, becauſe I know my love
    loves me.

O fhould it pleafe the pitying pow'rs to call
me to the fky,
I'd claim a guardian angel's charge around my
love to fly;
To guard him from all dangers how happy
fhould I be!
For I love my love, becaufe I know my love
loves me.

I'll make a ftrawy garland, I'll make it won-
d'rous fine,
With rofes, lilies, daifies, I'll mix the eglantine;
And I'll prefent it to my love when he returns
from fea,
For I love my love, becaufe I know my love
loves me.

Oh, if I were a little bird to build upon his
breaft,
Or if I were a nightingale to fing my love to
reft!
To gaze upon his lovely eyes all my reward
fhould be;
For I love my love, becaufe I know my love
loves me.

Oh, if I were an eagle, to foar into the fky!
I'd gaze around with piercing eyes where I may
love might fpy;
But ah! unhappy maiden, that love you ne'er
fhall fee,
Yet I love my love, becaufe I know my love
loves me.

SONG 901.

ASSIST me ev'ry tuneful bard,
Oh, lend me all your fkill,
In choiceft lays that I may praife,
Dear Nanny of the hill:
Sweet Nanny, dear Nanny,
Sweet Nanny of the hill.

How gay the glitt'ring beam of morn,
That gilds the cryftal rill!
But far more bright than morning light
Shines Nanny of the hill:
Dear Nanny, fhines Nanny,
Dear Nanny of the hill.

The gayeft flow'r, fo fair of late,
The ev'ning damps will kill;
But ev'ry day, more frefh and gay,
Blooms Nanny of the hill:
Sweet Nanny, blooms Nanny,
Sweet Nanny of the hill.

Old time arrefts his rapid flight,
And keeps his motion ftill,
Refolv'd to fpare a face fo fair
As Nanny's of the hill:
Dear Nanny's, fweet Nanny's,
Dear Nanny's of the hill.

To form my charmer, nature has
Exerted all her fkill,
Wit, beauty, truth, and rofy youth,
Deck Nanny of the hill:
Deck Nanny, fweet Nanny,
Dear Nanny of the hill.

And now around the feftive board
The jovial bumpers fill;
Each take his glafs to my dear lafs,
Sweet Nanny of the hill,
Dear Nanny, fweet Nanny,
Dear Nanny of the hill.

SONG 902.

Sung at VAUXHALL.

AS Chloe fat fhelter'd, and breath'd the cool
air,
While mufick awaken'd the grove;
Young Damon approach'd, and addrefs'd the
coy fair
In all the foft language of love:
But fhe was fo cruel, his fuit fhe deny'd,
And laugh'd as he told her his pain;
And while the poor fhepherd fat wooing, fhe
cry'd,
I will die a maid, my dear fwain.

O what! fays the fwain, muft thy beauty fo gay,
Perplex us at once and invite!
Embrace ev'ry rapture, left time make a prey
Of that which was meant for delight:
When age has crept round, and thy charms
wrinkled o'er,
Then all will my Chloe difdain;
But ftill all her anfwer was, Teize me no more,
I will die a maid, my dear fwain.

Young Damon protefted no other he'd prize,
His flame was fo ftrong and fincere;
Then watch'd the emotions that play'd in her
eyes,
And banifh'd his torture and fear:
My joys fhall be fecret, enraptur'd he cry'd,
Ah! Chloe, be gentle and good:
The fair-one grew fofter, and fighing reply'd,
I'd fain die a maid—if I cou'd.

SONG 903.

ARISE fweet meffenger of morn,
With thy mild beams our fkies adorn;
For long as fhepherds pipe and play,
This, this, fhall be a holiday.

See! morn appears; a rofy hue
Steals foft o'er yonder orient blue;
Soon let us meet in trim array,
And frolick out this holiday.

SONG 904.

Written by MATTHEW PRIOR.

AS Chloe came into the room t'other day,
I peevifh began, Where fo long cou'd you
ftay?
In your life-time you never regarded your hour;
You promis'd at two, but, look child! 'tis
four:

A lady's watch needs neither figures nor wheels,
'Tis enough that 'tis loaded with baubles and
    feals;
A temper fo heedlefs no mortal can bear!
Thus far I went on with a refolute air.

Lord blefs us! fays fhe, let a body but fpeak,
Here's an ugly hard rofe-bud fall'n into my
    neck;
It has hurt me, and vex'd me, to fuch a degree;
Look here! for you never believe me, pray fee!
On the left fide my breaft what a mark it has
    made!
So faying, her bofom fhe carelefs difplay'd:
That fcene of delight, I with wonder furvey'd,
And forgot ev'ry word I defign'd to have faid.

SONG 905.

HAIL, friendfhip! hail, thou heav'nly pow'r!
    To thee I tune my lay;
To thee, who giv'ft each tranquil hour,
    When hope is flown away.

Sure from the gods thou firft was fent
    To mortals here below,
That man might learn to be content,
    Nor dread the fhaft of woe.

The gen'rous heart with pity melts
    To hear each mournful tale,
With kindnefs ftrives each care to foothe,
    And friendfhip's balm prevail.

Ye powers, O grant me fuch a friend,
    To fmooth the paths of life;
Soft to the grave will I defcend,
    Without or care or ftrife.

SONG 906.

WHAT beauty does Flora difclofe!
    How fweet are her fmiles upon Tweed!
But Mary's, ftill fweeter than thofe,
    Both nature and fancy exceed.
No daify, nor fweet b'ufhing rofe,
    Nor all the gay flowers of the field,
Nor Tweed gliding gently thro' thofe,
    Such beauty and pleafure can yield.

The warblers are heard in each grove,
    The linnet, the lark, and the thrufh;
The blackbird and fweet cooing dove
    With mufic enchant ev'ry bufh.
Come let us go forth to the mead,
    Let us fee how the primrofes fpring;
We'll lodge in fome village on Tweed,
    And love while the feather'd folks fing.

How does my love pafs the long day?
    Does Mary not tend a few fheep?
Do they never carelefsly ftray,
    While happily fhe lies afleep?
If Tweed's murmurs fhould lull her to reft,
    Kind nature indulging my blifs,
To relieve the foft pains of my breaft
    I'd fteal an ambrofial kifs.

'Tis fhe does the virgins excel,
    No beauty with her can compare,
Love's graces all round her do dwell,
    She's faireft where thoufands are fair.
Say, charmer, where do thy flocks ftray,
    Oh! tell me at noon where they feed:
Shall I feek them on fweet winding Tay,
    Or the pleafanter banks of the Tweed?

SONG 907.

STREPHON, when you fee me fly,
    Let not this your fear create,
Maids may be as often fhy
    Out of love as out of hate;
When from you I fly away,
It is becaufe I dare not ftay.

Did I out of hatred run,
    Lefs you'd be my pain and care;
But the youth I love, to fhun,
    Who can fuch a trial bear?
Who that fuch a fwain did fee,
Who could love and fly like me?

Cruel duty bids me go,
    Gentle love commands my ftay;
Duty's ftill to love a foe,
    Shall I this or that obey?
Duty frowns, and Cupid fmiles;
That defends, and this beguiles.

Ever by thefe chryftal ftreams
    I could fit and hear thee figh,
Ravifh'd with thefe pleafing dreams,
    O 'tis worfe than death to fly:
But the danger is fo great,
Fear gives wings inftead of hate.

Strephon, if you love me, leave me,
    If you ftay I am undone;
Oh! with eafe you may deceive me,
    Pr'ythee charming fwain be gone.
Heav'n decrees that we fhould part;
That has my vows, but you my heart.

SONG 908.
SOLITUDE.

HAIL, thou fource of thought divine!
    Aweful folitude be mine:
Let me, from the world fecluded,
By no glitt'ring joys deluded,
Earthly pleafures all defpife,
Hoping for eternal joys.

Let me wander o'er thy plains,
Where perpetual filence reigns;
Whilft I, at the clofe of even,
View the blue befpangl'd heaven;
Let me then my God adore,
Mark his works, and own his pow'r.

When the blufhing morn has fpread
Dewy fragrance o'er the mead;
When the newly-rifen fun
Has his daily tafk begun;
Teach me then, in tuneful lays,
To chant my great Creator's praife,

When my peaceful life is fpent,
Free from care and difcontent,
Let me, O my God! when thou
Call'ft me from this world below,
With hope of heav'nly pleafures bleft,
In gentle flumbers fink to reft.

SONG 909.

BALLY SPELLING.

ALL you that wou'd refine your blood,
　As pure as fam'd Lewellin,
By waters clear, come ev'ry year,
　And drink at Bally Spelling:
If fpots, or itch, the fkin enrich
　With rubies paft the telling,
'Twill clear the fkin, before you've been
　A month at Bally Spelling.

If lady's cheek be green as leek,
　When fhe comes from her dwelling;
The kindling rofe within it glows,
　When fhe's at Bally Spelling:
The footy brown, who comes to town,
　Grows here as fair as Helen;
Then back fhe goes, to kill the beaux,
　By dint of Bally Spelling.

Our ladies are as frefh and fair
　As Rofs, or bright Dunkelling;
And Mars might make a fair miftake,
　Was he at Bally Spelling:
We men fubmit, as they think fit,
　And here is no rebelling;
The reafon's plain, the ladies reign;
　They're queens at Bally Spelling.

By matchlefs charms, unconquer'd arms,
　They have the pow'r of quelling
Such defp'rate foes, as dare oppofe
　Their pow'r at Bally Spelling:
Cold water turns to fire, and burns,
　I know, becaufe I fell in
A ftream that came from one bright dame,
　Who drank at Bally Spelling.

Fine beaus advance, equipt for dance,
　And bring their Anne or Nell in,
With fo much grace, I'm fure no place
　Can vie with Bally Spelling:
No politics, no fubtle tricks,
　No man his country felling;
We eat, we drink, we never think
　Of thefe at Bally Spelling.

The troubled in mind, the puff'd with wind,
　Do all come here pell-mell in;
And they are fure to work their cure,
　By drinking Bally Spelling:
If dropfy fills you to the gills,
　From chin to toe tho' fwelling;
Pour in, pour out, you cannot doubt
　A cure at Bally Spelling.

Death throws no darts thro' all thefe parts,
　No fexton's here a knelling;
Come, judge, and try, you'll never die,
　And live at Bally Spelling;

Except you feel dart's tipt with fteel,
　Which here are ev'ry belle in;
When from their eyes fweet ruin flies,
　We die at Bally Spelling.

Good chear, fweet air, much joy, no care,
　Your fight, your tafte, your fmelling,
Your ears, your touch, tranfporteth much;
　Each day, at Bally Spelling:
Within this ground, we all fleep found,
　No noify dogs are yelling,
Except you wake for Celia's fake,
　All night, at Bally Spelling.

Here all you fee, both he and fhe,
　No lady keeps her cell in;
But all partake the mirth we make,
　Who drink at Bally Spelling:
My rhimes are gone; I think I've none,
　Unlefs I fhould bring Hell in;
But fince I'm here, to Heav'n fo near,
　I can't at Bally Spelling.

SONG 910.

ROBIN HOOD.

AS blithe as the linnet fings in the green wood,
　So blithe we'll wake the morn;
And, thro' the wide foreft of merry Sherwood,
　We'll wind the bugle born.

The fheriff attempts to take bold Robin Hood;
　Bold Robin difdains to fly;
Let him come when he will, we'll in merry
　Sherwood,
Or vanquifh, boys, or die.

Our hearts they are ftout, and our bows they
　are good,
　As well their mafters know;
They're cut in the foreft of merry Sherwood,
　And ne'er will fpare a foe.

Our arrows fhall drink of the fallow-deers blood;
　We'll hunt them o'er the plain;
And thro' the wide foreft of merry Sherwood,
　No fhaft fhall fly in vain.

Brave Scarlet and John, who were never fubdu'd,
　Gave each his hand fo bold;
We'll reign thro' the foreft of merry Sherwood;
　What fay, my hearts of gold!

SONG 911.

ATTEND, ye ever-tuneful fwains,
　That in melodious, foothing ftrains,
　Of Chloe fing, or Phillis;
Tho' weak my fkill, tho' rude my verfe,
Upbraid me not, while I rehearfe
　The charms of Polly Willis.

Tho' languid I, and poor in thought,
No fimile fhall here be brought
　From rofes, pinks, or lilies;

Miss Thornton, at Vauxhall.

I'll pass no dull, inglorious Life.

Song 914

Published by J. Bew, Nov.ʳ 1, 1778.

Some meaner beauties they may hit;
But sure no simile can fit:
   The charms of Polly Willis.

A simile to match her hair,
Her lovely forehead, high and fair,
   Beyond my greatest skill is;
How then, ye gods! can be express'd
The eyes, the lips, the heaving breast,
   Of charming Polly Willis.

She's not like Venus on the flood,
Or as she once on Ida stood,
   Nor mortal Amaryllis:
Frame all that's lovely, bright, and fair,
Of pleasing shape, and killing air,
   And that is Polly Willis.

Tho' time her charms may wear away,
(All beauty must in time decay)
   Yet in her pow'r there still is
A charm which shall her life endure;
I mean, the spotless mind and pure
   Of charming Polly Willis.

SONG 912.

THE ROSE.

Written by Mr. CUNNINGHAM.

SWEET object of the Zephyr's kiss,
  Come, Rose!—come courted to my bow'r!
Queen of the banks! the garden's bliss!
  Come! and abash my tawdry flow'r!

Why call us to revokeless doom?
  (With grief the op'ning buds reply;)
Not suffer'd to extend our bloom;
  Scarce born, alas! before we die!

Man having pass'd appointed years,
  (Ours are but days)—the scene must close!
And when fate's messenger appears,
  What is he? but—a with'ring rose!

SONG 913.

AS Celadon once from his cottage did stray,
  To court his dear Jug on a hillock of hay,
What awkward confusion opprest the poor swain,
When thus he deliver'd his passion in vain!

O joy of my heart! and delight of my eyes!
Sweet Jug, 'tis for thee faithful Celadon dies;
My pipe I've forsaken, tho' reckon'd so sweet,
And sleeping or waking, thy name I repeat.

When swains to an alehouse by force do me lug,
Instead of a pitcher, I call for a jug;
And sure you can't chide at repeating your name,
When the nightingale ev'ry night does the same.

Sweet Jug, he a hundred times o'er does repeat,
Which makes people say that his voice is so
   sweet:
Ah! why dost thou laugh at my sorrowful tale?
Too well I'm assur'd that my words won't pre-
   vail;

For Roger the thatcher possesses thy breast,
As he at our last harvest-supper confest.
I own it, says Jug; he has gotten my heart;
His long curling hair looks so pretty and smart;

His eyes are so black, and his cheeks are so red,
They prevail more with me than all you have
   said:
Tho' you court me, and kiss me, and do all you
   can,
'Twill signify nothing, for Roger's the man.

SONG 914.

THE SOGER LASSIE; A SCOTCH BALLAD,

Sung at VAUXHALL.

I'LL pass no dull, inglorious life,
  At home I will not tarry;
I like the drum and martial fife,
  I'll to the camp with Harry.
The peaceful pipe, and rustic play,
  No longer is my passion;
If Harry goes, I will not stay,
  For war is now the fashion.

Your Jean will not be left behind,
  My heart's to fear a stranger;
High seas and rocks I'll never mind,
  I laugh at toil and danger.
I hope he will not tell me, nay,
  Nor fancy I'm unsteady;
If glory calls my swain away,
  Love bids me to be ready.

To other lands, from pleasant Tweed,
  With him I must be flying;
For shady grove, and painted mead,
  Your Jenny won't be crying.
Till tumult's o'er, adieu to all,
  Not long I hope to tarry;
I hear the drum's enliv'ning call,
  I must be gone with Harry.

SONG 915.

AT the foot of a hill, in a neat lonely cot,
  To die an old maid I'm afraid is my lot;
Not a man but my father e'er seen in the place:
Think how hard my condition, and pity my
   case.

Young Willy, the pride of the plains, I adore;
He's handsome, good-humour'd, has riches in
   store:
But I'm a poor damsel, of parentage base;
Think how hard my condition, and pity my
   case.

My mother once caught us alone in the dark,
She chid me, and forc'd me away from my
   spark;
Then talk'd much of sorrow, of shame and
   disgrace:
Think how hard my condition, and pity my
   case.

Such a ftrange alteration has feiz'd me of late,
Like a turtle I mourn all the day for my mate;
At night in my dreams his bleft image I trace:
Think how hard my condition, anc pity my
    cafe.

Whene'er I think on him, I figh and look pale;
My mother fhe afks me, what is it I ail:
My rural companions all look in iny face,
And in friendly compaffion they pity my cafe.

Oh, Hymen! be kind, and give ear to my fighs,
Reftore my young fhepherd once more to my
    eyes;
The dear nuptial moment with joy I'll embrace,
And maidens fhall envy, not pity my cafe.

SONG 916.

Sung at VAUXHALL.

I Have ferioufly weigh'd it, and find it but juft,
    That a wife makes a man either bleffed or
    curft;
I declare I will marry, ah! can I but find,
Mark me well, ye young laffes, the maid to my
    mind.

Not the pert little Mifs who advice will defpife,
Nor the girl who's fo foolifh to think herfelf
    wife,
Nor fhe who to all men alike would prove kind;
Not one of thefe three is the maid to my mind.

Not the prude who in public will never be free,
Yet in private a toying for ever will be,
Nor coquette that's too forward, nor jilt that's
    unkind;
Not one of thefe three is the maid to my mind.

Nor fhe who for pleafure her hufband will flight,
Nor the pofitive dame, who thinks always fhe's
    right,
Nor fhe who a dupe to the fafhion's inclin'd;
Not one of thefe three is the maid to my mind.

But the fair with good-nature and carriage gen-
    teel,
Who her hufband can love and no fecrets reveal,
In whofe breaft I may virtue and modefty find;
This, this, and this only's the maid to my mind.

SONG 917.

THE MYRTLE AND ROSE.

Sung at VAUXHALL.

AT once I'm in love with two nymphs that
    are fair,
And to fweets in my garden thefe nymphs I
    compare;
Nor can fhrub, nor can bloffom, be better than
    thofe;
And Jenny's my myrtle, and Chloe's my rofe.

My Chloe is fond all her charms to difplay;
With the rofe in her cheek, fhe to all would be
    gay;
On all paler beauties fhe looks down with pride,
And can bear not a flow'ret to grow by her fide.

She thinks not how quickly thefe charms will
    expire,
That with May they firft came, and with fum-
    mer retire:
That pride, fo foon over, is foolifh and vain,
And love, built on beauty, can't hold with a
    fwain.

But Jenny, my myrtle, ne'er changes her face,
No feafon nor age can her features difplace;
She covets no praife, nor with envy is ftung,
She always is pleas'd, and is pleafing and young.

Then, Chloe, I fudden muft make my retreat,
Thy rofe is too blooming, too fhort-liv'd and
    fweet;
But Jenny, thy myrtle is lafting and green,
And all the year thro' thou the fame ftill art
    feen.

SONG 918.

THE HONEY-MOON.

AS May in all her youthful drefs,
    So gay my love did once appear;
A fpring of charms adorn'd her face,
    The rofe and lily flourifh'd there:
Thus, while th' enjoyment was but young,
    Each night new pleafures did create;
Ambrofial words dropp'd from her tongue
    And am'rous Cupids round did wait.

But, as the fun to weft declines,
    The eaftern fky does colder grow,
And all his radiant looks refigns
    To the pale moon that rules below;
So love, while in her blooming hour,
    My Chloe was all kind and gay;
But when poffeffion nipp'd that flow'r,
    Her charms, like autumn, droop'd away.

SONG 919.

SOMETHING THAT'S UNSEEN.

'TWAS not Belinda's face, tho' fair,
    Her arched brow, or auburn hair,
    Her fweetly graceful mien;
Nor yet her cheeks eternal glow,
That firft difturb'd my reft—Ah! no,
    'Twas fomething that's unfeen.

The fweets her fairy form that deck,
The grace that moulds her taper neck,
    Her bofom foft and fheen,
That proudly mocks December's fnow,
Not all my heart could win—Ah! no;
    I die for what's unfeen.

You tell me, and you tell me true,
Her scarlet lip, her eyes of blue,
 The velvet of her skin:
But these disturb not me—Ah! no;
The force of these full well I know;
 I sigh for what's unseen.

What tho' her charms are heavenly bright,
The endless source of sweet delight,
 The envy of a queen!
The vulgar see them and adore;
My bosom bleeds for something more;
 The something that's unseen.

'Tis that, whose peerless mystic charms
Give me a thousand fond alarms,
 And pleases all mankind;
Whose beams divine would gild a court,
Give splendour to a crown—In short,
 That something is—her mind.

SONG 920.

THE SPORTSMAN.

HARK! the loud-tuning horn bids the sports-
 man prepare,
 And the hounds wooe him forth to the lawn;
The huntsman proclaims that the morning is
 fair,
 And Aurora with red streaks the dawn.

With pleasure he hearkens the heart-soothing
 chear,
 Shakes Morpheus and slumber away;
While joyful he starts, and with speed doth ap-
 pear
 The foremost to welcome the day.

With the horn's jolly clangor he quickens the
 chace,
 And fills all the vale with his joys;
While his pleasure, full glowing, enlivens his
 face,
 And the hounds in full concert rejoice.

From the sportsman, ye drones, you may learn
 how to live,
 Exempted from pain or disease;
He'll shew, that the fields and the meadows
 will give
 That health which you barter for ease.

SONG 921.

THE sages of old,
 In prophecy told,
The cause of a nation's undoing;
 But our new English breed
 No prophecies need,
For each one here seeks his own ruin.

 With grumbling and jars,
 We promote civil wars,
And preach up false tenets to many;

We snarl and we bite,
 We rail and we fight
For religion, yet no man has any.

 Then him let's commend,
 That's true to his friend,
And the church and the senate would settle;
 Who delights not in blood,
 But draws when he shou'd,
And bravely stands brunt to the bottle.

 Who rails not at kings,
 Nor politick things,
Nor treason will speak when he's mellow;
 But takes a full glass
 To his country's success;
This, this is an honest brave fellow.

SONG 922.

A SCOTCH BALLAD.

Sung at MARYBONE.

YE verdant woods, and crystal streams,
 By whose enamell'd side
I shar'd the sun's refreshing beams,
 While Jockey was my guide:
No more their shades or murmurs please
 Poor Sylvia's love-sick mind;
No rural streams can give me ease,
 Since Jockey proves unkind.

Come, gloomy eve, and veil the sky
 With clouds of darkest hue;
Wither, ye plants—ye flow'rets die!
 Unchear'd with balmy dew.
Ye wildly-warbling birds, no more
 Your songs can soothe my mind;
My hours of joy, alas! are o'er,
 Since Jockey proves unkind.

I'll hie me to some dreary grove,
 For sighing sorrow made,
Where nought but plaintive strains of love
 Resound through ev'ry shade;
Where the sad turtle's melting grief
 With Philomela's join'd,
Alone shall yield my heart relief,
 Since Jockey proves unkind.

Be warn'd by Sylvia's fate, ye maids,
 And shun the soft deceit,
Tho' love's own eloquence persuades,
 'Tis all a dang'rous cheat.
Fly quickly, fly the faithless swain,
 His treacherous arts despise;
So shall you live exempt from pain,
 While hapless Sylvia dies.

SONG 923.

BENEATH a bower of blooming May,
 Young Damon all complaining lay,
 Of Chloe's cold disdain;
In vain the flowers adorn'd the mead,
Neglected lay his crook and reed;
 His flocks forsake the plain.

Whither, he cries, ye happy hours,
That gaily frolick'd round thefe bowers,
   Ah! whither take your flight?
Will Chloe deign no more to hear
The ardent vows, the fighs finceie?
   That gave fo much delight.

Ye rapt'rous joys, that fir'd my breaft,
When by no jealous fears opprefs'd,
   Of happier rival's claim;
Where are ye fled! for ever gone,
Tho' ardours in my bofom burn;
   My paffion ftill the fame.

The modeft blufh, the down-caft look,
Whene'er i of my paffion fpoke,
   Did ev'ry fear annoy;
Chearful I tun'd my pipe all day,
My flocks delighted, fought their play;
   All nature fmil'd with joy.

Defpair now only racks my mind,
My Chloe now no more is kind,
   But flights my ardent vows:
The fmiles fhe once beftow'd on me,
The vows, that conftant fhe would be,
   On Colin now beftows.

Careful I'll fhun my fellow fwains;
Their youthful fports, their rural games,
   Can yield delight no more:
Retired to the fhady grove,
That has my artlefs tales of love,
   So often echo'd o'er;

(But now the fad reverfe muft know,
And only echo to my woe,
   Since Chloe's prov'd untrue;)
Alone I'll feek the once-blefs'd fhade,
Where arm in arm we oft have ftray'd,
   Till death my pains fubdue.

SONG 924.

HAROLD AND EMMA; A CANTATA.

RECITATIVE.

IN yonder grove, where Cyprefs fpreads it's
   gloom,
In thofe dark fhades no happy lovers ftray;
See, where in tears the wretched Emma moans
Her Harold's abfence, and his too hard fate;
Doom'd from her arms in diftant climes to roam,
And tempt the fatal fhaft in war's alarms,
While with fufpence and doubtful fears opprefs'd,
Sad Emma wakes the grove with fad complaint,
And likeft Philomel the woods among,
She thus, in fweeteft accents, tunes her fong.

AIR.

If thy too cruel bow be bent,
   Stern fate! to wound my Harold's heart,
O! change for once thy dire intent,
   Or in my bofom plunge the dart;
The happy means fo may I prove,
To fave my lord, my life and love.

RECITATIVE.

Thus funk in deep diftrefs, the beauteous Emma
   mourn'd;
When founds of triumph ftruck her lift'ning
   ear;
Nearer they drew, and fung of Harold's fame.
As when the fun obfcur'd by envious clouds,
Breaks thro' the gloom, and brightens all around,
So chang'd the fcene where lovely Emma griev'd,
When crown'd with honour the brave youth
   fhe found.
And when hereafter to this grove fhe ftray'd,
And heard the turtles from the cyprefs bough,
For none but happy lovers, fure, fhe faid,
This fweet fequefter'd fcene was ever made.

AIR.

Tune, Philomel, a happy ftrain,
   And charm the lift'ning grove:
My Harold fafe from war's alarms,
   Returns to blefs his love.
Take thy fad breaft from off the thorn,
   Nor mourn the woods among;
But from the rofe and woodbine fhade,
   Pour forth th' enraptur'd fong:
Ye flow'ring fhrubs, your odours fpread,
   Wanton on Zephyr's wing,
And ev'ry fweet, and ev'ry charm,
   To happy Emma bring.

SONG 925.

Written by Mr. HASTINGS.

WHEN firft the tow'ring mountains rofe,
   When fudden fprang the lafting hills,
The rifing ftreams their pearly courfes chofe,
   And fang in wild, meand'ring rills.
Raife Britannia! Britannia raife the fong!
Still freedom's fire pervade thy tongue

'Twas then on Albion's new-form'd fhore,
   Her guardian angel tun'd the lay,
Heaven's firm decree thus to explore,
   He fung the page of George's day.
Raife Britannia! &c.

Go forth along the pathlefs main;
   Thy future fons lead forth to war—
Return with glory in thy train,
   And wand'ring peace bring home from far.
Raife Britannia! &c.

Tho' faction as the billows rage,
   Beyond the wide Atlantic main,
Thy guardian ftill from age to age,
   Shall facred freedom's caufe maintain.
Raife Britannia! &c.

Thy countlefs fons, born to be free,
   No gloomy tyrant e'er fhall rule;
The weftern world fhall bend to thee,
   And reafon raging, paffion cool.
Raife Britannia! &c.

The hateful hydra lately fprung,
   Shall yield to George's milder fway,

Soft peace again infpire each gen'rous tongue,
Bright glory crown his future day.
Raife Britannia! &c.

While waves thy beauteous coafts fhall lave,
And ancient ocean round thee flow,
Thy dauntlefs fons fhall ftill be brave;
No walls of brafs could guard thee fo!
Raife Britannia! Britannia raife the fong!
Still freedom's fire pervade thy tongue.

SONG 926.

Sung at VAUXHALL.

AS on Tay's banks I wander'd in fearch of
my fair,
How fmooth was the ftream! and how foft was
the air!
To nothing but thee fuch a fcene I compare;
And thee it refembles, dear Jenny.

The deep cryftal wave was a type of thy face,
(I thought it fo clear it might ferve for thy glafs,)
And the curls, if there were, for thy dimples
might pafs:
I vow'd 'twas the picture of Jenny.

Methought it took in all the charms of thy
mind,
To virtue, to love, and to pity inclin'd,
The tender, foft paffions that feel no rude wind;
For calm is the bofom of Jenny.

All pleas'd with the profpect, I wifh'd the bright
maid
Cou'd have feen her dear felf in this mirror dif-
play'd;
'Twas like her when laft the dear girl I furvey'd:
Like none it cou'd be but my Jenny.

But fudden a tempeft, I ne'er faw before,
Made the billows arife, and the fea foam and
roar;
I thought that I fcarcely was fafe on the fhore:
Ah, me! even then it was Jenny.

The fame dreadful fight, when to fpleen you're
inclin'd,
When to me you are crofs, and to others are
kind:
But never, dear girl, raife this ftorm in your
mind;
'Twill kill me, believe me, dear Jenny.

SONG 927.

Sung at VAUXHALL.

AS Thyrfis, reclin'd by her fide he lov'd beft,
With a figh her foft hand to his bofom he
preft,
While his paffion he breath'd in the grove;
As the bird to his neft ftill returns for repofe,
As back to the fountain the conftant ftream
flows,
So true and unchang'd is my love.

If e'er this heart roves or revolts from it's chains,
May Ceres, in rage, quit the vallies and plains;
May Pan his protection deny!
In vain wou'd young Phillis and Laura be kind;
On the lips of another no rapture I find;
With thee as I've liv'd, fo I'll die.

More ftill had he fwore, but the queen of the
May,
Young Jenny the wanton, by chance pafs'd that
way,
And fought fweet repofe in the fhade;
With forrow, young lovers, I tell the fad tale,
The lafs was alluring, the fhepherd was frail,
And forgot ev'ry vow he had made.

To comfort the nymph, and her lofs to fupply,
In the form of Alexis young Cupid drew nigh;
Of fhepherds the envy and pride;
Ah! blame not the maid, if o'ercome by his truth,
Her hand and her heart fhe beftow'd on the
youth;
And the next morn beheld her his bride.

Learn rather from Sylvia's example, ye fair,
That a pleafing revenge fhou'd take place of
defpair.
Give forrow and care to the wind:
If faithful the fwain, to his paffion be true;
If falfe, feek redrefs from a lover that's new,
And pay each inconftant in kind.

SONG 928.

FAIR is the fwan, the ermine white,
And fair the lily of the vale;
The moon refplendent queen of night,
And fnows that drive before the gale;
In fairnefs thefe the reft excel;
But fairer is my Ifabel.

Sweet is the vi'let, fweet the rofe,
And fweet the morning breath of May;
Carnations rich their fweets difclofe,
And the fweet winding woodbines ftray:
In fweetnefs thefe the reft excel;
But fweeter is my Ifabel.

Conftant the poets call the dove,
And am'rous they the fparrow call;
Fond is the fky-lark of his love,
And fond the feather'd warblers all:
In fondnefs thefe the reft excel;
But fonder I of Ifabel.

SONG 929.

ANACREON'S DREAM.

AS I on purple tap'ftry lay,
And flept the tedious night away,
Well warm'd within
With fparkling wine,
I feem'd with virgins brifk as May
To dance, and fing, and wanton play.

The fhepherds all together flew,
And envious glanc'd, and look'd afkew;

And ev'ry fwain
Upon the plain
Both envy'd and reproach'd me too,
That I with virgins had to do.

An am'rous kifs I would have ta'en;
But, waking, found my hopes were vain;
   Then curs'd the day,
   Whofe glaring ray
Bereav'd me of fo fweet a pain;
And ftrove to fleep and dream again.

SONG 930.

MYRTILLA.

Sung at RANELAGH.

YE chearful virgins, have ye feen
   My fair Myrtilla pafs the green,
   To rofe or jefs'mine bow'r?
Where does fhe feek the woodbine fhade?
For fure ye know the blooming maid,
   Sweet as the May-born flow'r.

Her cheeks are like the maiden rofe,
Join'd with the lily as it grows,
   Where each in fweetnefs vies:
Like dew-drops glitt'ring in the morn,
When Phœbus gilds the flow'ring thorn,
   Health fparkles in her eyes.

Her fong is like the linnet's lay,
That warbles chearful on the fpray
   To hail the vernal beam:
Her heart is blither than her fong;
Her paffions gently move along,
   Like the fmooth-gliding ftream.

SONG 931.

COLIN AND PHEBE.

Sung at RANELAGH.

WHERE the jeffamine fweetens the bow'r,
   And cowflips adorn the gay green,
The rofes, refrefh'd by the fhow'r,
   Contribute to brighten the fcene;
In a cottage, retir'd, there live
   Young Colin and Phebe the fair;
The bleffings each other receive
   In mutual enjoyments they fhare;
And the lads and the laffes, that dwell on the plain,
Sing in praife of fair Phebe, and Colin her fwain.

The fweets of contentment fupply
   The fplendor and grandeur of pride;
No wants can the fhepherd annoy,
   While bleft with his beautiful bride;
He wifhes no greater delight
   Than to tend on the lambkins by day,
And return to his Phebe at night,
   His innocent toil to repay;
And the lads tell the laffes, in hopes to prevail,
They're as conftant as Colin who lives in the dale.

If delighted her lover appears,
   The fair-one partakes of his blifs;
If dejected, fhe foothes all his cares,
   And heals all his pains with a kifs;
She defpifes the artful deceit
   That is practis'd in city and court;
Thinks happinefs no where compleat,
   But where fhepherds and nymphs do refort:
And the lads tell the laffes they die in defpair,
Unlefs they are kind as Phebe the fair.

Ye youths, who're accuftom'd to rove,
   And each innocent fair-one betray,
No longer be faithlefs in love,
   The dictates of honour obey;
Ye nymphs, who with beauty are bleft,
   With virtue improve ev'ry grace;
The charms of the mind, when poffeft,
   Will dignify thofe of the face;
And ye lads and ye laffes, whom Hymen has join'd,
Like Colin be conftant, like Phebe be kind.

SONG 932.

AS t'other day o'er the green meadow I paft,
   A fwain overtook me, and held my hand faft;
Then cry'd, My dear Lucy, thou caufe of my care,
How long muft thy faithful young Thyrfis defpair?
To crown my foft wifhes, no longer be fhy!
But frowning, I anfwer'd, Oh! fie, fhepherd, fie.

He told me his paffion, like time fhould endure,
That beauty, which kindled his flame, would fecure;
That all my fweet charms were for pleafure defign'd,
And youth was the feafon to love and be kind.
Lord what cou'd I fay! I could hardly deny,
And faintly I utter'd, Oh! fie, fhepherd! fie.

He fwore with a kifs that he could not refrain,
I told him 'twas rude, but he kifs'd me again;
My conduct, ye fair-ones, in queftion ne'er call,
Nor think I did wrong, I did nothing at all:
Refolv'd to refift, yet inclin'd to comply,
Now guefs, if I ftill faid, Oh, fie, Shepherd, fie.

SONG 933.

WHERE is pleafure? tell me where;
   What can touch my foul with joy?
All around this fpacious fphere,
   Let my mufe her fearch employ.
Honour, let thy chariot roll,
   Deck'd with titles, pageant arms,
Thou may'ft pleafe th' ambitious foul;
   But for me thou haft no charms.

Wealth, thy fhining ftores produce,
Heap'd in golden mountains rife,
Thee let fenfelefs mifers chufe,
Thou can'ft ne'er allure mine eyes:
Only Delia, lovely fair!
Can the precious boon beftow;
Give me, ye pow'rs, O give me her!
She is all I afk below.

SONG 934.

Sung in the *Wives Revenged.*

OUR wives at home, your hufband gone,
To them leave care and thinking;
While gaily we the hours pafs on
In laughing and in drinking.

The real joys of love are fhar'd
By thofe who are difcreeteft;
And here's his health who firft declar'd
Stol'n pleafures are the fweeteft.

SONG 935.

Written by Mr. DAWRE.

YE fongfters from ev'ry tree,
And all that inhabit the grove,
Come, liften a moment to me,
Whilft I fing in the praife of my love.
How bleft and how happy's your ftate!
You can bafk in the beams of her eyes;
But, alas! fad to tell, cruel fate
To me the dear bleffing denies.

Ye lambkins who play at her feet,
And enjoy her fweet fmiles all the day,
I fhould think my blifs more than complete
In her prefence one moment to ftay:
Thofe beauties are hid from your eyes,
As bleating around her you ftand;
Ye feel no emotions arife
While contented ye feed from her hand.

In her all the graces do meet,
In her all the virtues combine,
With all that is lovely or fweet,
And all that is reckon'd divine.
Oh! would fhe but imile on my lays,
'Twould more than compenfate my pain;
Ye poets contend for the bays,
Such trifles as thefe I difdain.

SONG 936.

THE MILITIA MARCH.

Sung at VAUXHALL.

HARK! the loud drum;
Hark the fhrill trumpet founds to arms;
Come, Britons! come:
Prepar'd for war's alarms,
Whilft in array we ftand,
What Frenchman dares to land?
Sure in th' attempt to meet his doom;
A leaden death, or a wat'ry tomb.

The Briton brave,
On land or wave,
Will invaders defy;
Will repulfe them, or die,
And fcorns to live a flave.

Recal the days
When bravely your forefathers fought;
When, crown'd with praife,
They martial glory fought.
Bid their high deeds infpire!
Bid Magna Charta fire!
Greatly they labour'd for our good;
All forms of tranny withftood.
Thefe we defy:
On our own ftrength rely.
What Briton fo bafe,
Wou'd his country difgrace,
And from his colours fly?

Now party fpite
No more our meafures will oppofe;
For all unite
'Gainft our infulting foes.
All then in chorus fing,
Long live our gracious king!
Fill to George the fparkling bowl;
Hand it round, each loyal foul.
Rife patriot fame!
Thy glories proclaim:
Who his fword boldly draws
In his country's caufe,
Will win a deathlefs name.

SONG 937.

WOU'D you the charming queen of love
Invite with you to dwell,
No want your poverty fhou'd prove,
No ftate your riches tell:

Both her and happinefs to hold,
A middle ftate muft pleafe;
They fhun the houfe that fhines with gold,
And that which fhines with greafe.

SONG 938.

MY father and mother (what ail them!)
Pretend I'm too young to be wed;
They expect, but in troth I fhall fail them,
That I finifh my chairs and my bed.

Provided our minds are but cherry,
Wooden chairs wo'not argue a glove,
Any bed will hold me and my deary,
The main chance in wedlock is love.

My father, when afk'd if he'd lend us
An horfe to the parfon to ride:
In a wheel-barrow offer'd to fend us,
And John for the footman befide.

Wou'd we never had afk'd him! for whip it,
To the church, tho' two miles and a half;
Twice as far 'twere a pleafure to trip it,
But then how the people wou'd laugh!

The neighbours are nettled moſt ſadly :
  Was e'er ſuch a forward, bold thing !
Sure girl never acted ſo madly !
  Thro' the pariſh theſe backbitings ring.

Yet I will be married to-morrow,
  And charming young Harry's the man:
My brother's blind nag we can borrow,
  And he may prevent us that can.

Not waiting for parents conſenting,
  My brother took Nell of the green;
Yet both far enough from repenting,
  Now live like a king and a queen.

Pray, when will your gay things of London
  Produce ſuch a ſtrapper as Nell ?
Their wives by their huſbands are undone,
  As Saturday's newſpapers tell.

Poll Barnley ſaid, over and over,
  I ſoon ſhou'd be left in the lurch :
For Harry ſhe knew was a rover,
  And never wou'd venture to church.

And I know the ſorrows that wound her !
  He courted her once he confeſt;
With another too great when he found her,
  He bid her take them ſhe lik'd beſt.

But all that are like her, or wou'd be,
  May learn from my Harry and me,
If maids would be maids while they ſhou'd be,
  How faithful their ſweethearts wou'd be.

My mother ſays, cloathing and feeding,
  Will ſoon make me ſick of a brat;
But, tho' I grow ſick in my breeding,
  I care not a farthing for that:

For, if I'm not hugely miſtaken,
  We can by the ſweat of our brow,
Stick a hog once a year for fat bacon,
  And all the year round keep a cow.

I value no dainties a button,
  Coarſe food will our ſtomachs allay :
If we can't get beef, veal, or mutton,
  A chine and a pudding we may.

A fig for your richeſt brocading;
  In lindſey there's nothing that's baſe :
Your finery ſoon ſets a fading;
  My dowlaſs will ſtand beyond lace.

I envy not wealth to the miſer,
  Nor wou'd I be plagu'd with his ſtore :
To eat all and wear all is wiſer;
  Enough muſt be better than more.

So nothing ſhall tempt me from Harry,
  For he is as true as the ſun :
Eve with Adam was order'd to marry;
  This world it ſhould end as begun.

S O N G 939.

Sung in the *Wives Revenged.*

MASTER Jenkins ſmok'd his pipe,
  And ſwore he'd ne'er be married,
But 'gainſt each huſband threw ſome wipe,
  Or dry jeſt drolly carried.

Maſter Jenkins thought a wife
  The greateſt mortal evil,
And ſwore to lead a huſband's life
  Muſt be the very devil.

Maſter Jenkins ſmok'd his pipe
  At home, content, and married,
Regardleſs of each ſneer or wipe,
  Or dry jeſt drolly carried :
Maſter Jenkins ſwore a wife
  Was not ſo great an evil ;
And any but a huſband's life
  Was now the very devil.

Maſter Jepkins ſmok'd his pipe,
  And had been ſome months married ;
Severely now he felt each wipe,
  For horns the poor man carried :
Maſter Jenkins curs'd his wife,
  And ſwore of ſuch an evil,
To get well quit he'd part with life,
  Or ſend her to the devil.

S O N G 940.

IN young Aſtrea's ſparkling eye,
  Reſiſtleſs love has fixt his throne;
A thouſand lovers bleeding lie
For her, with wounds they fear to own :
While the coy beauty ſpeeds her flight,
  To diſtant groves, from whence ſhe came ;
So lightning vaniſhes from ſight,
  But leaves the foreſt in a flame.

S O N G 941.

ONE ev'ning good-humour met wit as a gueſt,
  By friendſhip invited, to ſhare at a feaſt ;
Their liquor was claret, and love was their hoſt,
And harmony garniſh'd each double-meant toaſt.

But while, like true bucks, they enjoy'd their
  deſign,
(For the joys of a buck lie in love, wit, and
  wine)
Surpriz'd, they all heard at the door a loud
  knock,
And the watchman hoarſe bellow'd, 'twas paſt
  twelve o'clock.

They nimbly ran down, the diſturbing dog found,
Then up ſtairs they dragg'd the impertinent
  bound ;
But when come to the light, how much they
  were pleas'd,
To ſee 'twas the grey glutton, Time, they had
  ſeiz'd!

His glaſs, as a lanthorn, his ſcythe as a pole,
His ſingle lock dangling all down his ſmooth
  ſcull.
My friends, (cry'd he, coughing) I thought fit
  to knock,
And bid you be gone, for 'tis paſt twelve o'clock.

Cry'd the venom-tooth'd favage, On this advice fix,
Tho' nature ftrikes twelve, folly ftill points at fix.
He longer had preach'd, but no longer they'd hear it,
So they hid him at once in a hogfhead of claret.

That is right, cry'd out wit; while we're yet in our prime,
There's nothing like claret for killing of time:
Huzza! cry'd out love; now no more he will knock,
Nor impertinent tell us, 'Tis paft twelve o'clock.

Now time is no more, nor no more can forbid us,
Love and wit of that troublefome gueft has well rid us;
But fhou'd he be wanted for any defign,
Henceforth he'll be found in a hogfhead of wine.

SONG 942.

Sung at VAUXHALL.

YOUNG Thyrfis, ye fhepherds, is gone;
I look all around for the fwain:
He's fled, and joy with him is flown;
He leaves me to forrow and pain.
Where is it I madly wou'd rove?
Can ye tell me what's left worth my ftay?
Too late I perceive it was love
All the while led my fancy aftray.

What avails if I tarry behind,
Now my heart he has ftole quite away?
No comfort on earth fhall I find,
No reft or by night or by day.
When he fung, oh! I liften'd with glee:
When he fmil'd, how I languifh'd and figh'd!
Ne'er thought I the moment to fee,
Than to fee I cou'd wifh to have died.

But who is it comes o'er the green?
'Tis Thyrfis, the dear, wifh'd-for youth;
Not death e'er fhall part us, I ween,
For than death is much ftronger his truth.
The mufe faw them meet in the grove;
Saw the maid and the fhepherd all bleft:
He vow'd to be true to his love;
She dares not to whifper the reft.

SONG 943.

THE DESPAIRING SHEPHERD.

BENEATH a cooling fhade
Young Strephon fought relief:
The flow'rs around his head
Pin'd, confcious of his grief.

Fond, foolifh wretch, (he cry'd)
I love, and yet defpair;
Purfue, tho' ftill deny'd
By the too-cruel fair.

The courtier afks a place;
The failor tempts the fea;
The mifer begs increafe;
Love only governs me.

Not honour, wealth, or fame,
Can like foft tranfports move;
On earth 'tis blifs fupreme,
And heav'n is but to love.

SONG 944.

Sung at RANELAGH,

TO take in good part the fqueeze of the hand,
That language of lovers who dare not demand;
And when with another, as clofe and as dear,
You've made him believe his happinefs near;
Then to tell him a tale of a cock and a bull,
That you meant no fuch thing, but was playing the fool.

The tread on the toe, to admit, and be free,
And ftraight to rep'y with the toe repartee;
To exprefs with your eyes your inward defires,
And thus with full hopes to kindle his fires;
Then to tell him a tale, &c.

When he wants to difclofe what he dares not reveal;
When he looks very filly, and means a great deal;
When he thinks (if e'er thinking fhou'd enter his brain)
You'll now grant his wifh, the eafe of his pain;
Then to tell him a tale, &c.

To let him, enraptur'd, proceed on to blifs;
To fuffer the fnatch or the theft of a kifs;
When coynefs retreating unwillingly flies;
When fighs anfwer murmurs, and eyes talk to eyes;
Then to tell him a tale of a cock and a bull,
That you meant no fuch thing, but was playing the fool.

SONG 945.

THE PARTING.

THE rifing fun thro' all the grove
Diffus'd a gladfome ray;
My Lucy fmil'd, and talk'd of love,
And ev'ry thing look'd gay:
But oh! the fatal hour was come
That forc'd me from my dear;
My Lucy then, through grief was dumb,
Or fpoke but by a tear.

Now far from her and blifs I roam,
All nature wears a change;
The azure fky feems wrapt in gloom,
And ev'ry place looks ftrange:
Thofe flow'ry fields, this verdant fcene,
Yon larks that tow'ring fing,

K k

With fad contraft increafe my fpleen,
And make me loath the fpring.

My books, that wont to foothe my mind,
No longer now can pleafe ;
There only thofe amufements find
That have a mind at eafe :
Nay, life itfelf is taftelefs grown,
From Lucy whilft I ftray ;
Sick of the world, I mufe along,
And figh the live-long day.

SONG 946.

FAIR CHLOE.

COME, all ye young fpirits of lively addrefs,
Ye arts that can joy and good-humour ex-
prefs ;
Come, all the foft numbers that Ovid has writ,
To fweeten my language, infpire my wit ;
For thefe are all wanting, my flame to declare,
Since Chloe, tho' pretty, is witty as fair.

With flatt'ry attempt not her bofom to move ;
She'll fee thro' the fraud, and perceive it from
love :
Her wit is fo ready, her judgment fo clear,
With a look fhe difcovers the falfe from fincere.
'Tis wifdom and truth, then, my flame muft
declare,
Since Chloe, tho' pretty, is witty as fair.

SONG 947.

WOULD you obtain the gentle fair,
Affume a French, fantaftic air ;
Oft, when the gen'rous Briton fails,
A foppifh foreigner prevails.

You muft teach her to dance,
As the mode is in France,
And make the beft ufe of your feet ;
Cock your hat with a grace,
All be-brazen your face,
And drefs moft affectedly neat.

Then bow down like a beau,
Hop and turn out your toe,
Lead Mifs by the hand, and leer at her ;
Draw your glove with an air,
At your white ftockings ftare,
And fimper, and ogle, and flatter.

Walk the figure of eight,
With your rump ftiff and ftraight,
Then turn her with delicate eafe ;
Bow again very low,
Your good-breeding to fhew,
And Miffy you'll perfectly pleafe.

If thefe fteps you purfue,
You will foon bring her too,
And rifle the child of her charms ;

Her poor heart will heave high,
And fhe'll languifh and figh,
And caper quite into your arms.

SONG 948.

THE RACE.

IF from the luftre of the fun
To catch your fleeting fhade you run,
In vain is all your hafte, Sir ;
But if your feet reverfe the race,
The fugitive will urge the chace,
And follow you as faft, Sir.

Thus, if at any time, as now,
Some fcornful Flavia you purfue,
In hopes to overtake her ;
Be fure you ne'er too eager be,
But look upon't as cold as fhe,
And feemingly forfake her.

So I and Phillis, t'other day,
Were courfing round a cock of hay,
Whilft I cou'd ne'er o'erget her :
But when I found I ran in vain,
Quite tir'd, I turn'd me back again ;
And, flying from her, met her.

SONG 949.

THO' form'd by the tendereft care of young
love,
A wonderful clufter of charms you appear ;
So fweet no May morning, fo gentle no dove,
The rofe not fo blooming, the lily fo fair ;
Yet nothing fhall make me fubmit to your chain,
For free I was born, and free will remain.

Tho' the di'mond was foil'd when match'd with
your eyes ;
Tho' ermine and fnow were difgrac'd by your
fkin ;
Tho' your foul too was lovely, noble, and wife,
All luftre without, and all fweetnefs within ;
Yet nothing, &c.

Tho' your hair, black as jet, with beautiful
twine
Down your fhoulders in ringlets wantonly
flow'd ;
Your fhape was perfection, your air was divine,
You fpoke like an angel, and mov'd like a
god ;
Yet nothing fhall make me fubmit to your chain,
For free I was born, and free will remain.

SONG 950.

DEAR Madam, old Homer, an honeft, blind
bard,
Has told us (and who need difpute the man's
word ?)
To withftand the fweet Syren's deluding, foft
ftrain,
How weak ev'ry art was, all efforts how vain.

To the charms of the voice thofe of beauty
  were join'd,
(How pow'rful, when fingle! refiftlefs, combin'd)
And, living in ocean fome dreadful fharp rocks
  on,
Whole heaps of poor tars were allur'd to deftruction.

For, foon as their fweet-flowing accents were
  heard,
Plum againft the rough rocks the mad mari-
  ners fteer'd:
Thus, like a poor bird, by the charmer de-
  coy'd,
The veffel was fplit, and the failors deftroy'd.

Now, Madam, believe, for 'tis certainly true,
Juft, juft fuch a terrible creature are you:
You act to perfection the Syren's fell part:
We are drawn by your charms, and the rock is
  your heart.

But fince, cruel fair, 'tis in vain to deplore,
Or repine at what thoufands have fuffer'd be-
  fore,
I fubmit; but, oh l grant this laft boon to your
  flave,
As I die by your heart, be your bofom my grave.

SONG 951.

Sung at VAUXHALL.

LOVE, thou bane of foft content;
  Love, thou inaufpicious gueft;
Say, fay, oh! why thy fhaft was fent
  To this once peaceful breaft?
Sweet, at firft, I thought the paffion,
  Fancy ftill new joys could fee;
Now how fad an alteration,
  Damon flies from love and me.

Thus Sylvia, in the confcious grove,
  All fweetly plaintive mourn'd,
When Damon chanc'd that way to rove,
  And to the nymph return'd:
He figh'd repentant at her feet,
  She fmil'd upon the fwain;
And each fond heart refponfive beat
  To love and joy again.

SONG 952.

Written by Mr. HAMILTON.

GO plaintive founds! and to the fair
  My fecret wounds impart,
Tell all I hope, tell all I fear,
  Each motion in my heart.

But fhe, methinks, is lift'ning now
  To fome enchanting ftrain;
The fmile that triumphs o er her brow
  Seems not to heed my pain.

Yes, plaintive founds! yet, yet delay,
  Howe'er my love repine;
Let that gay minute pafs away,
  The next perhaps is thine.

Yes, plaintive founds! no longer croft,
  Your grief fhall foon be o'er;
Her cheek, undimpled now, has loft
  The fmile it lately wore.

Yes, plaintive founds! fhe now is yours,
  'Tis now your time to move;
Effay to foften all her powers,
  And be that foftnefs, love.

Ceafe, plaintive founds! your tafk is done;
  That anxious tender air
Proves o'er her heart the conqueft won;
  I fee you melting there.

Return, ye fmiles, return again,
  Return each fprightly grace;
I yield up to your charming reign
  All that enchanting face.

I take no outward fhew amifs,
  Rove where you will, her eyes;
Still let her fmiles each fhepherd blefs,
  So fhe but hear my fighs.

SONG 953.

Written by the Earl of DORSET.

LET the ambitious favour find
  In courts and empty noife,
Whilft greater love does fill my mind
  With filent real joys.

Let fools and knaves grow rich and great,
  And the world think 'em wife,
Whilft I lie dying at her feet,
  And all that world defpife.

Let conquering kings new trophies raife,
  And melt in court delights,
Her eyes can give me brighter days,
  Her arms much fofter nights.

SONG 954.

AS the Thames' filent ftream crept penfive
  along,
And the winds murmur'd folemn the willows
  among;
On a green turf complaining, a fwain lay reclin'd,
And wept to the river, and figh'd to the wind.

In vain, he cry'd, nature has waken'd the
  fpring,
In vain blooms the vi'let, the nightingales fing:
To an ear full of forrow no beauties appear,
Each zephyr's a figh, and each dew-drop's a
  tear.

In vain my Selinda has graces to move
The faireft to envy, the wifeft to love;
Her prefence no more gives delight to the eye,
Since without her to live, is more pain than
  to die.

Oh! that Somnus his pinions wou'd over me
    spread,
And paint but her image in dreams in her stead;
The beautiful vision wou'd soften my pain :
But sleep's a relief I solicit in vain.

The wretch thus, like me, his heart loaden
    with care,
Is deluded by hope, and undone by despair;
His pain ever waking, denies him repose,
And the moments but vary to vary his woes.

SONG 955.

HERO AND LEANDER; AN OLD BALLAD.

LEANDER on the bay
    Of Hellespont all naked stood;
Impatient of delay,
    He leap'd into the fatal flood :
        The raging seas,
        Whom none can please,
'Gainst him their malice show ;
        The heavens lour'd,
        The rain down pour'd,
And loud the winds did blow.

Then casting round his eyes,
    Thus of his fate he did complain,
Ye cruel rocks and skies!
    Ye stormy winds, and angry main !
        What 'tis to miss
        The lover's bliss,
    Alas! ye do not know ;
        Make me your wreck
        As I come back,
    But spare me as I go.

Lo! yonder stands the tower
    Where my beloved Hero lies,
And this the appointed hour
    Which sets to watch her longing eyes.
        To his fond suit
        The gods were mute;
    The billows answer, No :
        Up to the skies
        The surges rise,
    But sunk the youth as low.

Meanwhile the wishing maid,
    Divided 'twixt her care and love,
Now does his stay upbraid;
    Now dreads he shou'd the passage prove :
        O fate! said she,
        Nor Heaven, nor thee,
    Our vows shall e'er divide.
        I'd leap this wall,
        Cou'd I but fall
    By my Leander's side.

At length the rising sun
    Did to her sight reveal, too late,
That Hero was undone;
    Not by Leander's fault, but fate.
        Said she, I'll shew,
        Tho' we are two,
    Our loves were ever one :
        This proof I'll give,
        I will not live,
    Nor shall he die alone.

Down from the wall she leapt
    Into the raging seas to him,
Courting each wave she met,
    To teach her weary'd arms to swim.
        The sea-gods wept,
        Nor longer kept
    Her from her lover's side.
        When join'd at last,
        She grasp'd him fast,
    Then sigh'd, embrac'd, and died.

SONG 956.

WE all to conquering beauty bow,
    It's pleasing power admire ;
But I ne'er knew a face till now,
    That cou'd like yours inspire :
Now I may say I've met with one
    Amazes all mankind ;
And, like men gazing on the sun,
    With too much light am blind.

Soft as the tender moving sighs,
    When longing lovers meet ;
Like the divining prophets wise,
    Like new-blown roses sweet ;
Modest, yet gay ; reserv'd, yet free;
    Each happy night a bride ;
A mien like awful majesty,
    And yet no spark of pride.

The patriarch, to win a wife,
    Chaste, beautiful and young,
Serv'd fourteen years a painful life,
    And never thought it long :
Ah! were you to reward such care,
    And life so long would stay,
Not fourteen, but four hundred years,
    Would seem but as one day.

SONG 957.

WHEN the bright god of day
    Drove westward his ray,
And the ev'ning was charming and clear,
    The swallows amain
    Nimbly skim o'er the plain,
And our shadows like giants appear.

In a jessamine bower,
    When the bean was in flower,
And zephyrs breath'd odours around,
    Lov'd Celia she sat
    With her song and spinnet,
And she charm'd all the grove with her sound.

Rosy bowers she sung,
    Whilst the harmony rung,
And the birds they all flutt'ring arrive,
    The industrious bees
    From the flowers and trees,
Gently hum with their sweets to their hive.

The gay god of love,
    As he flew o'er the grove,
By zephyrs conducted along;
    As she touch'd on the strings,
    He beat time with his wings,
And echo repeated the song.

O ye mortals! beware
How you venture too near,
Love doubly is armed to wound;
Your fate you can't shun,
For you're surely undone,
If you rashly approach near the sound.

SONG 958.

AN OLD SCOTCH BALLAD.

THERE came a ghost to Marg'ret's door,
With many a grievous groan,
And ay he tirled at the pin,
But answer made she none.

Is that my father Philip?
Or is't my brother John?
Or is't my true love Willy
_ From Scotland new come home?

'Tis not thy father Philip,
Nor yet thy brother John;
But 'tis thy true love Willy
From Scotland new come home.

O sweet Marg'ret! O dear Marg'ret!
I pray thee speak to me;
Give me my faith and troth, Marg'ret,
As I gave it to thee.

Thy faith and troth thou's never get,
Nor yet will I thee lend,
Till that thou come within my bower,
And kiss my cheek and chin.

If I shou'd come within thy bower,
I am no earthly man;
And shou'd I kiss thy rosy lips,
Thy days will not be lang.

O sweet Marg'ret! O dear Marg'ret!
I pray thee speak to me;
Give me my faith and troth, Marg'ret,
As I gave it to thee.

Thy faith and troth thou's never get,
Nor yet will I thee lend,
Till you take me to yon kirk-yard,
And wed me with a ring.

My bones are buried in yon kirk-yard,
Afar beyond the sea;
And it is but my spirit, Marg'ret,
That's now speaking to thee.

She stretch'd out her lily-white hand,
And for to do her best,
Hae there's your faith and troth, Willy,
God send your soul good rest.

Now she has kilted her robes of green
A piece below her knee,
And aw the live-lang winter night
The dead corpse follow'd she.

Is there any room at your head, Willy?
Or any room at your feet?
Or any room at your side, Willy,
Wherein that I may creep?

There's no room at my head, Marg'ret;
There's no room at my feet;
There's no room at my side, Marg'ret,
My coffin's made so meet.

Then up and crew the red, red cock,
And up then crew the grey;
'Tis time, 'tis time, my dear Marg'ret,
That you were going away.

No more the ghost to Marg'ret said,
But, with a grievous groan,
He vanish'd in a cloud of mist,
And left her all alone.

O stay, my only true love, stay,
The constant Marg'ret cry'd;
Wan grew her cheeks, she clos'd her een,
Stretch'd her soft limbs, and dy'd.

SONG 959.

CELIA, too late you wou'd repent:
The offering all your store,
Is now but like a pardon sent
To one that's dead before.

While at the first you cruel prov'd,
And grant the bliss too late,
You hindred me of one I lov'd,
To give me one I hate.

I thought you innocent as fair,
When first my court I made;
But when your falshoods plain appear,
My love no longer stay'd.

Your bounty of these favours shown,
Whose worth you first deface,
Is melting valu'd medals down,
And giving us the brass.

O! since the thing we beg's a toy,
That's priz'd by love alone,
Why cannot women grant the joy,
Before the love is gone?

SONG 960.

UNGRATEFUL NANNY.

DID ever swain a nymph adore,
As I ungrateful Nanny do?
Was ever shepherd's heart so sore,
Or ever broken heart so true?
My cheeks are swell'd with tears, but she
Has never wet a cheek for me.

If Nanny call'd, did e'er I stay,
Or linger when she bid me run?
She only had the word to say,
And all she wish'd was quickly done.
I always think of her, but she
Does ne'er bestow a thought on me.

To let her cows my clover taste,
Have I not rose by break of day!
Did ever Nanny's heifers fast,
If Robin in his barn had hay!
Tho' to my fields they welcome were,
I ne'er was welcome yet to her.

If ever Nanny loft a fheep,
  I chearfully did give her two;
And I her lambs did fafely keep
  Within my folds in froft and fnow:
Have they not there from cold been free?
But Nanny ftill is cold to me.

When Nanny to the well did come,
  'Twas I that did her pitchers fill;
Full as they were, I brought them home:
  Her corn I carried to the mill;
My back did bear the fack, but fhe
Will never bear a fight of me.

To Nanny's poultry oats I gave,
  I'm fure they always had the beft;
Within this week her pigeons have
  Eat up a peck of peafe at leaft:
Her little pigeons kifs, but fhe
Will never take a kifs from me.

Muft Robin always Nanny woo,
  And Nanny ftill on Robin frown;
Alas, poor wretch! what fhall I do,
  If Nanny does not love me foon!
If no relief to me fhe'll bring,
I'll hang me in her apron-ftring.

S O N G 961.

YES, all the world will fure agree,
  He who's fecur'd of having thee
Will be entirely bleft;
But 'twere in me too great a wrong,
To make one who has been fo long
  My queen, my flave at laft.

Nor ought thefe things to be confin'd,
That were for public good defign'd:
  Cou'd we, in foolifh pride,
Make the fun always with us ftay,
'Twou'd burn our corn and grafs away,
  To ftarve the world befide.

Let not the thoughts of parting, fright
Two fouls which paffion does unite;
  For while our love does laft,
Neither will ftrive to go away;
And why the devil fhould we ftay,
  When once that love is paft!

S O N G 962.

YOU that love mirth, attend to my fong,
  A moment you never can better employ.
Sawny and Teague were trudging along,
  A bonny Scots lad, and an Irifh dear-joy;
They neither before had feen a windmill,
  Nor had they heard ever of any fuch name:
    As they were a walking,
    And merrily talking,
  At laft by mere chance to a windmill they
    came.

Haha! cries Sawny, what do ye ca' that?
  To tell the right name o't I am at a lofs.
Teague very readily anfwer'd the Scot,
  Indeed I believe it's fhaint Patrick's crofs.

Says Sawny, Ye'll find yourfel meikle mif-
    taken,
  For it is Saint Andrew's crofs I can fwear;
    For there is his bonnet,
    And tartans hang on it,
  The plaid and the trews our apoftle did wear.

Nay, o' my fhoul joy, thou telleft all lees,
  For that I will fhwear is fhaint Patrick's coat;
I fhee't him in Ireland buying the freeze,
  And that I'm fhure ifh the fhame that he
    bought;
And he is a fhaint mufh better than ever
  Made either the covenantfh fholemn or
    league:
    For o' my fhalwafhion,
    He was my relafhion,
  And had a great kindnefh for honefht poor
    Teague.

Wherefore, fays Teague, I will, by my fhoul,
  Lay down my napfhack, and take out my
    beads,
And under this holy crofs' fet I will fall,
  And fhay pater nofhter, and fhome of our
    creeds.
So Teague began with humble devotion,
  To kneel down before St. Patrick's crofs;
    The wind fell a blowing,
    And fet it a-going,
  And it gave our dear-joy a terrible tofs.

Sawny tehee'd, to fee how poor Teague
  Lay fcratching his ears, and roll'd on the grafs,
Swearing, it was furely the de'il's whirly-gig,
  And none (he roar'd out) of St. Patrick's
    crofs:
But ifh it indeed, cries he in a paffion,
  The crofs of our fhaint that has crofht me
    fo fore;
    Upo' my falwafhion,
    This fhall be a cawfhion,
  To truft to St. Patrick's kindnefs no more.

Sawny to Teague then merrily cry'd,
  This patron of yours is a very fad loon,
To hit you fic a fair thump on the hide,
  For kneeling before him, and feeking a
    boon:
Let me advife ye to ferve our St. Andrew,
  He, by my faul, was a fpecial gude man;
    For fince your St. Patrick
    Has ferv'd ye fic a trick,
  I'd fee him hung up e'er I ferv'd him again.

S O N G 963.

FEMALE WOOING.

DEAR Colin, prevent my warm blufhes,
  How can I fpeak without pain?
My eyes have oft told you their wifhes,
  Why can't you the meaning explain?

My paffion wou'd lofe by expreffion,
  And you too might cruelly blame;
Then pray don't expect a confeffion
  Of what is too tender to name.

Since yours is the province of fpeaking,
  How can you expect it from me?
Our wifhes fhou'd be in our keeping,
  Till you tell us what they fhou'd be.

Then quickly why don't you difcover?
  Did your heart feel fuch tortures as mine,
I need not tell over and over
  What I in my bofom confine.

SONG 964.

COLIN'S REPLY.

GOOD Madam, when ladies are willing,
  A man muft needs look like a fool;
For me, I wou'd not give a fhilling
  For one that does love without rule.

At leaft you fhou'd wait for our offers,
  Not fnatch like old maids in defpair:
Had you liv'd to thefe years without proffers,
  Your fighs were all fpent in the air.

You fhou'd leave us to guefs by your blufhing,
  And not tell the matter fo plain;
'Tis ours to be writing and pufhing,
  And yours to affect a difdain.

But you're in a terrible taking,
  By all the fond oglings I fee;
The fruit that can fall without fhaking,
  Indeed, is too mellow for me.

SONG 965.

THE RIVAL.

OF all the torment, all the care,
  By which our lives are curft,
Of all the forrows that we bear,
  A rival is the worft.
By partners in another kind
  Afflictions eafier grow,
In love alone we hate to find
  Companions in our woe.

Silvia, for all the griefs you fee
  Arifing in my breaft,
I beg not that you'd pity me,
  Would you but flight the reft.
Howe'er fevere your rigours are,
  Alone with them I'd cope,
I can endure my own defpair,
  But not another's hope.

SONG 966.

THE TOPERS.

MY friend and I,
  We drank gallon-pots
  Full of fack up to the brim;
I drank to my friend,
  And he drank his pot,
So we put about the whim:
Three bottles and a quart
We fwallow'd down our throat,

(But hang fuch puny fips as thefe;)
We laid us all along,
With our mouths unto the bung,
  And tipp'd whole hogfheads off with eafe.

I heard of a fop
  That drank whole tankards,
  Stil'd himfelf the prince of fots:
But I fay now, hang
  Such filly drunkards,
  Melt their flaggons, break their pots.
My friend and I did join
For a cellar full of wine,
  And we drank the vintner out of door;
We drank it all up
In a morning, at a fup,
  And greedily rov'd about for more.

My friend to me
  Did make this motion,
  Let us to the vintage fkip:
Then we embark'd
  Upon the ocean,
  Where we found a Spanifh fhip
Deed laden with wine,
Which was fuperfine,
  The failors fwore five hundred tun;
We drank it all at fea,
E'er we came unto the key,
  And the merchant fwore he was quite undone.

My friend, not having
  Quench'd his thirft,
  Said, Let's to the vineyards hafte:
Straight then we fail'd
  To the Canaries,
  Which afforded juft a tafte;
From thence unto the Rhine,
Where we drunk up all the wine,
  Till Bacchus cry'd, Hold, ye fots, or you die;
And fwore he never found,
In his univerfal round,
  Such thirfty fouls as my friend and I.

Out fie! cries one,
  What a beaft he makes him,
  He can neither ftand nor go!
Out you beaft, you,
  You're much miftaken,
  When e'er knew you a beaft drink fo?
'Tis when we drink the leaft,
That we drink moft like a beaft;
  But when we caroufe it fix in hand;
'Tis then, and only then,
That we drink the moft like men,
  When we drink till we can neither go nor
  ftand.

SONG 967.

Written by the Duke of BUCKINGHAM.

FROM all uneafy paffions free,
  Revenge, ambition, jealoufy,
Contented, I had been too bleft
If love and you had let me reft:
  Yet that dull life I now defpife,
  Safe from your eyes
I fear'd no griefs, but then I found no joys.

Amidft a thoufand kind defires,
Which beauty moves, and love infpires,
Such pangs I feel of tender fear,
No heart fo foft as mine can bear.
Yet I'll defy the worft of harms,
   Such are your charms,
'Tis worth a life to die within your arms.

SONG 968.

OFT on the troubled ocean's face
  Loud ftormy winds arife;
The murmuring furges fwell apace,
  And clouds obfcure the fkies :

But when the tempeft's rage is o'er,
  Soft breezes fmooth the main;
The billows ceafe to lafh the fhore,
  And all is calm again.

Not fo in fond and amorous fouls
  If tyrant love once reigns,
There one eternal tempeft rolls
  And yields unceafing pains.

SONG 969.

THE graces and the wandering loves
  Are fled to diftant plains,
To chace the fawns, or in the groves
  To wound admiring fwains:
With their bright miftrefs there they ftray,
Who turns her carelefs eyes
From daily victories; yet each day
Beholds new triumphs in her way,
And conquers as fhe flies.

But fee! implor'd by moving prayers
  To change the lover's pain;
Venus her harnefs'd doves prepares,
  And brings the fair again.
Proud mortals who this maid purfue,
Think you fhe'll e'er refign?
Ceafe, fools, your wifhes to renew,
Till fhe grows flefh and blood like you,
  Or you like her divine.

SONG 970.

PHILLIS; A PASTORAL.

HOW dear is my Phillis to me,
  Whofe innocence equals the dove;
As fweet as the rofe to the bee?
  In prefence the goddefs of love:
But what is a beautiful face,
  Tho' more than a Venus refin'd;
Compar'd to the beauties which grace,
  The Pallas in Phillis's mind.

Whene'er my dear charmer appears,
  The fwains gaze in raptures around;
The fun with more brilliancy chears,
  Frefh flow'rets bedapple the ground:

Gay Flora may fpread her perfumes,
  And fcent with her odours the air;
Yet never a flow'ret that blooms
  Is fo fweet as the breath of my fair.

The warblers exult and rejoice
  As thro' the green vallies we ftray,
And mimic their notes from her voice,
  In melody fweeter than they:
Ye fhepherds, with envy not hear,
  Nor at my good fortune repine;
For Phillis fo charming, fo dear,
  Has vow'd fhe'll for ever be mine.

SONG 971.

SWEETEST of pretty maids, let Cupid
  incline thee
T'accept of a faithful heart which now I re-
  fign thee;
Scorning all felfifh ends, regardlefs of money,
It yields only to the girl that's gen'rous and
  bonny.
    Take me, Jenny,
     Let me win you,
   While I'm in the humour;
    I implore you,
    I adore you,
  What can mortal do more;
Kifs upon't, kifs upon't, turn not fo fhyly,
There's my hand, and here's my heart, which
  never will beguile thee.

Bright are thy lovely eyes, thy fweet lips delighting,
Well polifh'd thy iv'ry neck, thy round arms
  inviting;
Oft at the milk-white churn with rapture I've
  feen them,
But oh! how I figh'd, and wifh'd my own arms
  between them!
    Take me Jenny, &c.

I've ftore of fheep, my love, and goats on the
  mountain,
And water to brew good ale, from yon chryf-
  tal fountain;
I've, too, a pretty cot, with garden and land
  to't,
But all will be doubly fweet, if you put a hand
  to't.
    Take me, Jenny,
     Let me win you,
   While I'm in the humour;
    I implore you,
    I adore you,
  What can mortal do more;
Kifs upon't, kifs upon't, turn not fo fhyly,
There's my hand, and here's my heart, which
  never will buguile thee.

SONG 972.

FAIR Hebe I left with a cautious defign,
  To efcape from her charms, and to drown
  them in wine;
I try'd it, but found, when I came to depart,
The wine in my head, and ftill love in my heart.

Mr WEBSTER as Corporal William, in the CAMP.

My Nancy Quits the Rural Plain.

Song

Published by J. Bew Nov 1 1778

I repair'd to my reason, intreated her aid,
Who paus'd on my cafe, and each circumstance weigh'd,
Then gravely pronounc'd, in return to my pray'r,
That Hebe was faireſt of all that were fair.

That's a truth (reply'd I) I've no need to be taught,
I came for your counfel to find out a fault.
If that's all (quoth reafon) return as you came,
To find fault with Hebe would forfeit my name.

What hopes then, alas! of relief from my pain,
While like lightning ſhe darts through each throbbing vein?
My fenfes furpriz'd, in her favour took arms,
And reafon confirms me a flave to her charms.

SONG 973.

EDWARD; AN ELEGIAC BALLAD.

Written by Mr. HEYWOOD.

NOW lilies and rofes were feen,
  And fragrance perfumed the air;
Now the birds carroll'd fweet on the green,
  And their mufic delighted the ear:

Now the meadows with verdure bedight
  Did their charms and their graces difplay;
Now the ſhepherds in concerts unite,
  They fing, and all nature looks gay:

All fave Edward, unhappy young fwain,
  So brifk and fo blithſome before;
With him nature's fmiles are in vain,
  For Eliza, his love, is no more.

Full oft, where yon flow-gliding brook
  Runs fweetly tinkling by,
The ſhepherd, reclin'd on his crook,
  All fad and defpairing wou'd lie.

And oft to yon fad, folemn grove,
  Unweeting the fwain wou'd repair,
To weep the fad fate of his love,
  And utter the plaint of defpair.

There, beneath the green canopy'd glade,
  Wou'd he walk, and his forrows bewail;
And ſtill as he mourn'd the fair maid,
  Fond echo wou'd mimic the tale.

Will nothing my anguifh remove!
  Ah, never thefe eyes will be dry!
Ah, never! ah, never! remurmur'd the grove;
  Ah, never! the brook wou'd reply.

When night had refum'd her fad fway,
  And Phebe illumin'd the gloom;
To Eliza's green grave wou'd he ftray,
  And fit and lament on her tomb;

There, hopelefs, his fate wou'd bewail,
  And breathe out his plaint to the air;
Still filling each paufe in his tale
  With a heart-rending figh or a tear.

Then all the night long has he lain,
  Unpity'd, unheard, and alone;

Delighting (alas, gentle fwain!)
  To drain his fad eyes on her ftone.

But Heav'n had mark'd the fad fwain,
  (Had mark'd him, and pity'd his woes)
And foon fent relief to his pain;
  For death brought his bofom repofe.

All on her green grave as he lay,
  And with anguifh opprefs'd, his fad heart
To his fighs could no longer give way;
  He felt the keen eafe-giving dart.

His death fadden'd all the gay train,
  So blithe and fo joyous erewhile;
No piping was heard on the plain,
  No face was bedeck'd with a fmile.

All pleafure was banifh'd their looks,
  And their drefs was of mournfulleſt hue;
While the ſhepherds entwined their crooks
  With garlands of rofem'ry and yew.

And ſtill as the day of his doom
  Comes round with the flow-rolling year,
The ruſtics repair to his tomb,
  And embalm his remains with a tear.

SONG 974.

SANDY.

Written by Mr. HAWKINS.

MY Sandy is the fweeteſt fwain
  That ever pip'd on Tay;
He tends the ſheep upon the plain,
  And chears me all the day.

As on a moffy bank we fat,
  Beneath a verdant ſhade,
The youth fo charm'd me with his chat,
  While on his bagpipes play'd.

He call'd me his dear life and care,
  And his own Moggy, too;
He vow'd by all that's good and fair,
  To me he will prove true.

For Sandy is a bonny fwain,
  And I'll be Sandy's wife;
Then bid adieu to care and pain,
  And fo be bleſt for life.

SONG 975.

MATRIMONIAL DEAFNESS.

TWO ears at a time are two many for ufe,
  When they're only the inlet of ſtrife;
But few they are found who, tho' wife, would refufe
  To poffefs the fair organs of life:
Yet deafnefs fometimes of advantage is found;
  Misfortunes may turn to a bleffing;
For when nonfenfe diſtracts, or when tumults furround,
  They then lofe the pow'r of diſtreffing.

Hence I wifely am taught to be deaf of one ear,
  While the other for ufe I employ;
One gate I ſhut up againſt trouble and care,
  And the other keep open for joy:

L l

When my confort begins her loud windpipe to
   clear,
With a peal would the world rend afunder,
Serenely I fit, and I cock my deaf ear,
   Unmov'd 'midft the roar of the thunder.

T'other day comes a dun, with, Good Sir! you
   well know—
   What fay you? fpeak louder a little:
You know, Sir, you borrow'd three twelve-
   months ago—
   Alas, friend! I can't hear a tittle:
You owe me ten pounds! then louder he cries;
   And repeats it as loud as he can:
I point to my ears, and lift up my eyes,
   Till he hardly can think me the man.

I, as grave as a don, cry, My hearing's quite
   loft!
   And my money, (fays he) too, I fear:
Plague on him, 'tis folly to talk to a poft!
   So he leaves me, as mad as a hare.
Thus my life, night and day, in foft indolence
   flows;
   Scolding, dunning, nor brawling I fear.
Ye marry'd men all, as ye wifh for repofe,
   Be fure to be deaf of one ear.

SONG 976.

BACCHUS TRIUMPHANT.

Sung at VAUXHALL.

TO Phillis and Chloe, and all the gay throng,
   Too long the foft lay has been rais'd;
Too long to their beauty has flow'd the vain fong,
   Too long has their beauty been prais'd:
Great Bacchus, repentant, thy pardon I afk,
   Forgivenefs I humbly implore;
If e'er for a female I quit a full cafk,
   May I never enjoy one drop more—great god;
   May I never enjoy one drop more.

Ye fops and ye fribbles, your title I own
   To fing all the charms of the fair;
Their beauties to praife is your province alone;
   Alone make their beauties your care:
For who in his fenfes that mortal can blame
   Who ftrives his own merit to raife?
For women and fops are fo nearly the fame,
   In theirs, that he fings his own praife—fweet
   Mifs;
   In theirs, that he fings his own praife.

Tho' wit, fparkling wit, fome rare females
   poffefs,
   Tho' kindnefs may add to their ftore;
Good-nature and fmiles have a bumper no lefs,
   And fparkles an hundred times more:
With virtue unfully'd adorn'd tho' fhe be,
   Tho' modefty blooms in each feature,
A bottle is not more immodeft than fhe,
   It's virtue ten thoufand times greater—dear
   boys;
   It's virtue ten thoufand times greater.

Their beauty attracting I freely confefs;
   Their fex, I muft own, has it's charms;
I own for a moment they're able to blefs,
   And melt us away in their arms:
Yet lafting the pain is, and tranfient the joy;
   The raptures are inftantly paft;
But wine, happy juice! is fure never to cloy,
   It's pleafures till doomfday fhall laft—brave
   fouls;
   It's pleafures till doomfday fhall laft.

Then adieu to their charms, to their beauties
   adieu,
   All thoughts of the fex I refign;
I fight in thy caufe, to thy int'reft am true,
   And yield me eternally thine:
And if ever, great mafter, thy colours I fly,
   If e'er like a rover I pine,
May (greateft of curfes!) my hogfhead run dry,
   Nor more be replenifh'd with wine—bleft
   wine;
   Nor more be replenifh'd with wine.

SONG 977.

Written by Mr. WELLES.

HOW happy a ftate does the lover poffefs,
   Who enjoys the fweet fmiles of his fair!
No troubles can ever his fpirits deprefs,
No cares in his mind will he ever poffefs,
   For tranquility's fure to reign there.

But how wretched his fate, who is doom'd to
   adore,
   And to doat on a nymph that's unkind:
Like a mariner wreck'd on a defolate fhore,
In vain does he wander, in vain does implore;
   No affiftance, alas! can he find.

Then from fuch a ftate, gracious Heaven, de-
   fend
   All thofe who are conftant and true;
To their tale may the fair ever kindly attend;
On each, may the bleffings of Hymen defcend!
   Tho' their number, I fear, is but few.

SONG 978.

THE ROVER.

IN all the fex fome charms I find;
   I love to try all womankind,
   The fair, the fmart, the witty:
In Cupid's fetters, moft fevere,
I languifh'd out a long, long year,
   The flave of wanton Kitty.

At length I broke the galling chain,
And fwore that love was endlefs pain,
   One conftant fcene of folly;
I vow'd no more to wear the yoke;
But foon I felt a fecond ftroke,
   And figh'd for blue-ey'd Molly.

With treſſes next of flaxen hue,
Young Jenny did my ſoul ſubdue,
   That lives in yonder valley;
Then Cupid threw another ſnare,
And caught me in the curling hair
   Of little tempting Sally.

Adorn'd with charms, tho' blithe and young,
My roving heart from bondage ſprung,
   This heart of yielding metal;
And now it wanders here and there,
By turns the prize of brown and fair,
   But never more will ſettle.

SONG 979.

Written by Mr. J. R.

HOW blithe, within my native wild,
   I trod each paſſing day!
When Sylviana fondly ſmil'd,
   And luv'd her ſhepherd's lay.

The furze, the brake, the rugged hill,
   The wild heath's yellow broom,
With her wou'd all my wiſhes fill;
   My heart ne'er felt a gloom.

But now, remote from her I love,
   The faireſt paſtures fade;
I ſeek the ſolitary grove,
   And turn it's winding ſhade.

Where gay imagination toys,
   To chear my penſive mind;
With pleaſing hopes my boſom joys,
   And paints the maiden kind.

SONG 980.

THE BROKEN CHINA.

Written by Mr. CUNNINGHAM.

SOON as the ſun began to peep,
   And gild the morning ſkies,
Young Chloe from diſorder'd ſleep
   Unveil'd her radiant eyes.

A guardian Sylph, the wanton ſprite
   That waited on her ſtill,
Had teiz'd her all the tedious night
   With viſionary ill.

Some ſhock of fate is ſurely nigh!
   Exclaim'd the tim'rous maid:
What do theſe horrid dreams imply!
   My Cupid can't be dead!

She call'd her Cupid by his name,
   In dread of ſome miſhap;
Wagging his tail, her Cupid came,
   And jump'd into her lap.

And now the beſt of brittle ware
   Her ſumptuous table grac'd:
The poliſh'd emblems of the fair,
   In beauteous order plac'd!

The kettle boil'd, and all prepar'd
   To give the morning treat;
When Dick, the country beau, appear'd;
   And bowing, took his ſeat.

Well—chatting on of that and this,
   The maid revers'd her cup;
And, tempted by the forfeit kiſs,
   The bumkin turn'd it up.

With tranſport he demands the prize;
   Right fairly it was won!
With many a frown the fair denies:
   Fond baits to draw him on!

A man muſt prove himſelf polite,
   In ſuch a caſe as this;
So Richard ſtrives with all his might
   To force the forfeit kiſs.

But as he ſtrove—Oh, dire to tell!
   (And yet with grief I muſt)
The table turn'd—the china fell,
   A heap of painted duſt!

O fatal purport of my dream!
   The fair afflicted cry'd,
Occaſion'd (I confeſs my ſhame)
   By childiſhneſs and pride!

For in a kiſs, or two, or three,
   No miſchief could be found!
Then had I been more frank and free,
   My china had been found.

SONG 981.

A LOYAL TOAST.

Written by the EDITOR.

FILL, fill your glaſſes,
   Baniſh care;
See the toaſt paſſes
   Round, and fair:
Health to the king; to his arms ſucceſs!
Bleſs his royal conſort; their offspring bleſs.

SONG 982.

Written by Mr. MAVOR.

THE bright, reſplendent orb of day,
   On mortals pours his blaze;
The balmy zephyrs kiſs the ſpray,
   And dance in endleſs maze.
Awake to ſtrains of mirth and joy,
   Of cares ſhake of the load;
'Tis beauty calls, your notes employ
   To ſing of charming Broad.

Now groves their verdant liv'ry wear,
   And flow'rs perfume the air;
Sweet May, the honour of the year,
   Appears ſupremely fair:
Now nymphs and ſwains enamour'd meet,
   And bend at Cupid's nod;
But all muſt feel the piercing eye
   Of ſweetly charming Broad.

Fair as the beams of morn ſhe ſhines,
   And wins the ſoul to love;
Happy the heart that fate entwines
   With her's, it's ſweets to prove;

Who would not leave each blooming fweet,
    And ev'ry bleſt abode;
To lie a fuppliant at her feet,
    And figh for lovely Broad.

Were mine the far-fam'd Paphian ifle,
    Or Peru's filver fhore;
The climes where flow'rs eternal fmile,
    Unknown to winter hoar;
I'd quit them all, and only pray
    To love's all-potent god,
That I might fpend my lateſt day
    With beauty's fav'rite Broad.

SONG 983.

COLIN, one day, in angry mood,
    Becauſe Myrtilla, whom he lov'd,
Laugh'd at his flame, and mock'd his fighs,
Thus fervently to Jove applies:
Oh, Jove! thou fov'reign god above,
Who know'ſt the pains of flighted love;
Hear a poor mortal's pray'r, and take
All the whole fex for pity's fake;
And then we men might live at eafe,
Secure of happinefs and peace.

Jove kindly heard, (he pray'd not twice;)
And took the women in a trice.
When Colin faw the coaſt was clear,
(For not a fingle girl was near;)
Reflecting with himfelf, 'Twas kind,
Says he, to gratify my mind;
But now my paffion's o'er, O! Jove,
Give me Myrtilla back, my love;
Let me with her on earth be bleſt,
And keep in heaven all the reſt.

SONG 984.

Sung at VAUXHALL.

YOUNG Daphne was the prettieſt maid
    The eyes of love cou'd fee;
And but one fault the charmer had,
    'Twas cruelty to me.

No fwain that e'er the nymph ador'd
    Was fonder, or was younger;
Yet, when her pity I implor'd,
    'Twas, Stay a little longer.

It chanc'd, I met the blooming fair,
    One May morn in the grove;
When Cupid whifper'd in my ear,
    Now, now's the time for love.

I clafp'd the maid; it wak'd her pride;
    What! did I mean to wrong her!
Not fo, my gentle dear, I cry'd;
    But love will ſtay no longer.

Then, kneeling at her feet, I fwore
    How much I lov'd, how well;
And that my heart, which beat for her,
    With her fhould ever dwell.

Confent ſtood fpeaking in the eye
    Of all my care's prolonger;

Yet Daphne utter'd with a figh,
    Oh! ſtay à little longer.

The conflict in her foul I faw,
    'Twixt virtue and defire:
Oh! come, (I cry'd) let Hymen's law
    Give fanction to love's fire.

Ye lovers, guefs how great my joys!
    Cou'd rapture well prove ſtronger?
When virtue fpoke in Daphne's voice,
    You now fhall ſtay no longer.

SONG 985.

THE CONTEST.

Written by Mr. LEMOINE.

I Say, if Paris was a beau,
    Yet he was not polite;
For he on Ida's top did fhow
    To two bright nymphs a flight.

Three fair-ones begg'd him to decide
    Which was the greateſt beauty;
He might have footh'd each fair-one's pride,
    And yet have done his duty.

To one he might have given fhape,
    And piercing eyes to t'other;
Then had he made a good efcape,
    And fav'd a mighty pother.

Minerva then had dwelt in peace,
    And Juno without paffion,
Had caus'd a ten years war to ceafe,
    And fav'd old Priam's nation.

Had one alone obtain'd the bays,
    And wit's bright prize have borne;
The other two throughout their days,
    The willow muſt have worn.

SONG 986.

AN ADDRESS TO THE LADIES.

Sung at RANELAGH.

YE belles, and ye flirts, and ye pert little
    things,
Who trip in this frolickfome round,
Pray tell me from whence this indecency fprings,
    The fexes at once to confound?
What means the cock'd hat, and the mafculine
    air,
    With each motion defign'd to perplex?
Bright eyes were intended to languiſh, not ſtare,
    And foftnefs the teſt of your fex—dear girls,
    And foftnefs the teſt of your fex.

The girl who on beauty depends for fupport,
    May call ev'ry art to her aid;
The bofom difplay'd, and the petticoat fhort,
    Are famples fhe gives of her trade:
But you, on whom fortune indulgently fmiles,
    And whom pride has preferv'd from the fnare,
Shou'd flily attack us, with coynefs and wiles,
    Not with open and infolent air—dear girls,
    Not with open and infolent air.

The Venus, whofe ftatue delights all mankind,
Shrinks modeftly back from the view,
And kindly fhou'd feem, by the artift defign'd,
To ferve as a model for you.
Then learn, with her beauties, to copy her air,
Nor venture too much to reveal;
Our fancies will paint what you cover with care,
And double each charm you conceal—fweet
girls,
And double each charm you conceal.

The blufhes of morn, and the mildnefs of May,
Are charms which no art can procure:
Oh! he but yourfelves, and our homage we'll
pay,
And your empire is folid and fure:
But if, Amazon-like, you attack your gallants,
And put us in fear of our lives,
You may do very well for our fifters or aunts;
Believe me, you'll never be wives—poor girls,
Believe me, you'll never be wives.

SONG 987.

Written by Mr. HEYWOOD.

COME liften, ye fair,
And the reafon declare,
('Tis a point much your anfwer behoving)
Why the words of a fcold,
As we often are told,
Are fo very pathetic and moving?

Why the reafon's foon fhewn;
Was there ever man known,
In his fenfes, would tarry to hear her?
Then there needs little proving
Her words muft be moving,
Since none who can move will ftay near her.

SONG 988.

HIGHAM HILL; A PASTORAL.

Written by Mr. NICHOLLS.

ON Higham Hill, when profpects fair
Salute the wand'ring fight,
I love to breathe the morning air,
And fleep the fummer night.
There, how charming 'tis to wake
While filver Cynthia reigns!
Whilft Philomel, from flow'ry brake,
Pours forth her love-lorn ftrains.

Then, oh! then, I love to rife,
To trace the broom-clad hill;
Whilft thro' the ftillnefs foftly flies
The whifpers of the rill.
Nor elfe is heard to interpofe
From dingle, bufh, or dale,
Save Thames, foft kiffing as he goes
The rufh-embroider'd vale.

As down the flope I traverfe then,
I fcan with curious eye
The wonders Heav'n prefents to men,
And wifh the atheift by:

His mind, howe'er impervious grown
To theologic lore,
I think, with me, he'd quickly own
A fupernat'ral pow'r.

When bus'nefs dulls the mental pow'rs,
To Higham Hill I run,
And with the breath of op'ning flow'rs
I hail the rifing fun.
Ah! how my foul revives again,
My fancy takes her flight,
My mufe refumes her wonted ftrain,
And fings with new delight!

Let the proud thing of human race,
Who, like a fummer fly,
Scuds to-day from place to place,
And muft to-morrow die;
Let him to greatnefs bend the knee,
Or heap up fordid wealth;
The top of Higham Hill for me!
There's treafur'd peace and health.

Peace and health! O, facred theme,
With all that's blifsful fraught!
The reft is but an empty dream,
Not worth a poet's thought:
May he, who ftrives for more than this,
Still turn a barren foil,
And never meet a ray of blifs
To mitigate his toil!

Bear me from hence, fome rural god,
To Higham Hill again;
The choiceft bloom that decks the fod
I'll fcatter round thy fane.
For, O! I long, at fervid noon,
To breathe the blue-bell's fweet,
To fit and hear the throftle's tune,
Where fpreading hazels meet;

Or ftray by hawthorn hedge, or rove
Adown the pathlefs way,
When ev'ry fong-bird chears his love
Beneath the bloom of May.
Till weary herds retire to reft,
Till fheep are pent in fold,
Till Phœbus leaves the ruddy weft
With tints of burnifh'd gold.

If, when I ftray to Higham Hill,
I meet the ruftic throng,
They greet me with a right good will,
And note me for my fong:
For oft at May, in rural fport,
I fpend with them the day,
And make the vices of a court
The burden of my lay.

And oft I've fang the tender ftrain,
The while the village maid
Was leaning on her fav'rite fwain,
And all her heart betray'd.
The lofty theme I ne'er effay'd,
(Let Laureats fuch rehearfe)
But wherefoe'er my fancy ftray'd,
A moral mark'd my verfe.

Their loves to me the fhepherds tell,
What fwains have faithlefs prov'd,
What maids for beauty bear the belle,
And who are leaft belov'd:

The virgins come in modeſt guiſe,
I love their plaint to hear;
'Tis joy to ſoothe their artleſs ſighs,
And ſtop the ſtarting tear.

No thorns obſtruct their path of life,
With health their farms abound;
And, foes to law and lawleſs ſtrife,
They live the zodiack round.
To me their tranquil ſtate they owe,
They all confeſs it ſtill,
And praiſe, ye ſwains, where'er they go,
The bard of Higham Hill.

SONG 989.

Written by Mr. WELLES.

WHEN Flavia is preſent, how ſwiftly time
moves!
Whole days I to minutes compare;
But when ſhe is abſent, I ſwear by our loves,
The loit'ring of time I can't bear.

In vain do I ſigh, no relief can I find;
In vain ſtrive to baniſh dull care;
For nought can give eaſe and content to my
mind,
But the preſence and ſmiles of my fair.

Then, gods! be propitious, and grant my re-
queſt;
May Flavia prove kind and ſincere;
May I with her preſence for ever be bleſt,
And enjoy the ſweet ſmiles of my dear!

In me, may the lover be loſt in the friend;
And may Flavia my efforts approve;
May we ever with friendſhip love properly blend!
Grant this! O ye Power above!

SONG 990.

MORNING.

Written by Mr. CUNNINGHAM.

IN the barn the tenant cock,
Cloſe to partlet perch'd on high,
Briſkly crows (the ſhepherd's clock!)
And proclaims the morning nigh.

Swiftly from the mountain's brow,
Shadows nurs'd by night retire;
And the peeping ſun-beam, now,
Paints with gold the village ſpire.

Philomel forſakes the thorn,
Plaintive where ſhe prates at night;
And the lark, to meet the morn,
Soars beyond the ſhepherd's ſight.

From the clay-built cottage ridge,
See the chatt'ring ſwallow ſpring;
Darting through the one-arch'd bridge,
Quick ſhe dips her dappled wing.

Trickling through the crevic'd rock,
See the ſilver ſtream diſtil

Sweet refreſhment for the flock,
When 'tis ſun-drove from the hill.

Plowmen for the promis'd corn,
Ripening o'er the banks of Tweed,
Anxious hear the huntſman's horn,
Soften'd by the ſhepherd's reed.

Sweet, oh! ſweet, the warbling throng,
On the white embloſſom'd ſpray!
All in muſic, mirth and ſong,
At the jocund dawn of day.

SONG 991.

EVENING.

Written by Mr. CUNNINGHAM.

AS the plowman homeward goes,
Plodding to the hamlet bound,
Giant-like his ſhadow grows,
Lengthen'd o'er the level ground.

The ſteer along the meadow ſtrays
Now the furrow'd taſk is done;
And the village windows blaze,
Gliſt'ning to the ſetting ſun.

Mark him from behind the hill,
Streak the purple painted ſky:
Can the pencil's mimic ſkill
Copy the reſulgent dye?

Where the riſing foreſt ſpreads
Round the time-decaying dome;
To their high-built airy beds,
See the rooks returning home!

As the lark with vary'd tune,
Carols to the ev'ning loud,
Mark the mild, reſplendent moon,
Breaking through a parted cloud!

Tripping through the ſilken graſs,
O'er the path-divided dale,
See the roſe-complexion'd laſs
With the well-pois'd milking pail.

Linnets with unnumber'd notes,
And the cuckow bird with two,
Tuning ſweet their mellow throats,
Bid the ſetting ſun adieu.

SONG 992.

INCONSTANT EDWIN.

Written by Mr. LEMOINE.

GO, perjur'd youth, thou foe to truth,
Retract the vows you ſwore;
A Proteus true I've found in you,
And ne'er can like you more.

Ungen'rous boy! made to deſtroy,
And rob me of my peace;
Awake, aſleep, pangs round me creep,
That never, never ceaſe.

Sad throbbing ſighs, tear-ſtreaming eyes,
The emblems of deſpair;

Each friend in vain (while you difdain)
Attempts to foothe my care.

But all their arts to cure my fmarts,
Inefficacious prove;
My mind's not free from flavery,
'Tis bound in chains of love.

Maria's fair, falfe man, declare,
Juft as thou didft to me;
(But maid beware his fatal fuare,
It's wrapt in perjury.)

His main delight is ftories bright,
They fteal upon our ears;
Our tempers vex, degrade the fex,
And force down floods of tears.

O! favage man, made to trepan,
And call love's pains a jeft;
O grant that I might change the figh,
For joys within my breaft!

I'd then be free from fuch as thee,
I'd fpend in mirth each hour;
My virgin heart fhould know no fmart,
But laugh at all thy pow'r.

I'll envy not the fair-one's lot,
To whom young Edwin roves;
But wifh to fee them ever be
The portraits of fond doves.

For fweet content was never meant
To wretched me below;
Yet when I die, my foul fhall fly
Beyond the reach of woe.

SONG 993.

HEBE; A PASTORAL.

To the Memory of Mifs SANDERS.

Written by Mr. HAWKINS.

COME, virgins, who dwell on the plain,
And weep with a fhepherd fincere;
Come liften, and learn from my ftrain,
Since Hebe no longer is near:
For fhe was fo modeft and meek,
What mildnefs with her could compare!
But oh! my mufe fcarcely can fpeak
The beauties that bloom'd in the fair.

Her mind was a ftranger to ftrife,
Contentment fhe valu'd fo free;
Religion fhe lov'd as her life,
For none were more pious than fhe:
Her Maker fhe e'er made her theme,
His goodnefs was glad to rehearfe;
And oft, by fome fweet winding ftream,
She echo'd his praifes in verfe.

But ah! the dear damfel is gone,
Her fongs of devotion are o'er;
And the nymphs and the fwains are forlorn,
Since Hebe, their pride, is no more:
For oh! fhe e'er taught them the way
To virtue, to honour, and truth;
And while they were fportive and gay,
She bade them reflect in their youth!

Till death with his fcythe came along,
And blighted her bloffoms fo foon;
He cut her off fhort from the throng,
When erft with the maid it was noon:
Yet calmly her breaft fhe refign'd,
For no one e'er faw her diftrefs'd;
And while on her arm fhe reclin'd,
She gently funk into reft.

Then, virgins, who frolic and play,
Regardlefs of forrow and care;
Come round, and attend to the lay,
And weep for the lofs of the fair!
Like her, oh! purfue the right way;
Like her, be religious and ftaid;
Ah! ceafe, ye gay nymphs for to ftray,
And copy the mild, matchlefs maid!

SONG 994.

Written by Mr. J. R.

HOW happy loves the youth!
(His miftrefs ever kind)
Whofe paffion's told with truth,
And innocent his mind.

Whofe bofom, free from guile,
Need no falfe arts to fcreen;
Nor no deceiving fmile
To hide the fiend within.

Whofe heart, the maiden's friend,
Where more he could obtain,
It loveth to defend,
And fcorns the cruel gain!

Whofe mind the pride difdains,
To act a rover's part;
To give the maid a pain,
Who yieldeth him her heart.

How guilelefs to embrace,
His fpotlefs wifhes move!
His ev'ry action chafte,
His paffion only love!

Tranfported to poffefs
The object of his joys;
He feeks no more to blefs,
Contented with his choice.

SONG 995.

MELANCHOLY.

Written by Mr. LEMOINE.

COME, thou queen of penfive air,
In thy fable-footed car,
By two mournful turtles drawn;
Let me meet thee on yon lawn,
With decent veftments wrapt around,
And thy brows with cyprefs bound!
Quickly come, thou fober dame,
And thy mufing poet claim.
Bear me where thou lov'ft to rove,
In the deep, dark, folemn grove;
Where on banks of velvet green,
Peace with filence ftill is feen;

And leisure at the sultry noon
On flow'ry carpet flings him down,
There, sweet queen ! I'll sing thy pleasures
In enthusiastic measures,
And sound thy praises thro' the vale,
Responsive to the hollow gale;
The murm'ring rills shall spread it round,
And grottos the wild notes rebound.

SONG 996.

THE VIGIL OF MAY.

Written by Mr. NICHOLLS.

NOW sweet is the bloom on the spray,
  How soft from the west blows the gale !
Now, charm'd with the nightingale's lay,
  The villagers haste to the dale!

Bright Dian, who silver'st the lawn,
  I'm come with the shepherds to stray,
Till your beauty's eclips'd by the dawn,
  A tribute that's due to the May.

May no wat'ry cloud hide thy face,
  For Phebe will join the gay throng;
E'en now they are flocking apace,
  Hark! the tabor, and Corydon's song!

Ah! how the shrill pipe strikes my ear!,
  How sweetly it trills with the lay!
I wish my dear Phebe was here,
  We'd hasten to welcome the May.

She surely will be on the plain!
  She promis'd, ere this, to be here;
These pleasures but sicken and pain,
  Till the mate of my bosom is near.

When I but a moment delay'd,
  She frown'd, and upbraided her swain;
Sure something's befall'n the dear maid!
  I die till I see her again.

Ah! how my poor bosom's alarm'd!
  But the fair-one, who trips yonder stile,
Has now ev'ry terror disarm'd;
  'Tis Phebe!—she comes with a smile.

But why do I keep from her arms!
  I'll fly and salute her with glee;
To my sheep has the clover less charms,
  Than the taste of her kisses to me.

SONG 997.

I'LL to some shady, cool retreat,
  Where spreading trees conspire to meet,
To hide my blush, while I repeat
  The love I bear my Colin:
Name all that's amiable in love,
My Colin amply doth improve;
The sacred truth of Heav'n above,
  Is center'd in my Colin.

Were I possess'd of monarchs lands,
Of eastern shores, or golden sands;
No one shou'd share in Hymen's bands
  With me, but lovely Colin.

With him, beneath a myrtle seat,
I'll sing, and bless my happier fate,
Than seated on a throne of state,
  With any one but Colin.

So long as Saran's glass shall run,
Or Persian's hail the rising sun,
Or till my thread of life is spun,
  So long shall I love Colin;
And when I take the parting kiss;
In death I'll chear my heart with this;
That I shall meet in future bliss,
  Again, with thee my Colin.

SONG 998.

Written by Mr. MAVOR.

COME, dearest Nancy! bless my eyes,
  And stop the flowing tear;
In you alone the magic lies,
  To animate and chear.

Not half so sweet the flow'rs display
  Their variegated hue;
Not all the bloom of smiling May
  Can charm so much as you.

Where'er you tread, the warblers sweet
  Melodious fill the grove;
And smiling nature seems to greet
  The presence of my love.

But blasted ev'ry flow'r appears,
  When you forsake these plains ;
No grove the feather'd songster chears,
  In sweet mellifluous strains.

Come, dearest Nancy! come, and stay!
  From you my joys arise;
Your face gives brightness to the day,
  And lustre to the skies.

For you I sigh, and waste my prime;
  Then haste, and let us prove,
That rolling years, and fleeting time,
  Are far too short for love.

SONG 999.

THE TEAR.

Written by the late Queen of DENMARK.

HOW prone the bosom is to sigh !
  How prone to weep, the human eye!
As thro' this painful life we steer,
This valley of the sigh and tear.

When by the heart with sorrow griev'd,
A thousand blessings are receiv'd,
With ev'ry comfort that can chear;
'Tis then bright virtue's grateful tear.

When ev'ry parting pang is o'er,
And friends long absent meet once more,
Fraught with delight, and love sincere;
'Tis then sweet friendship's joyful tear.

When two fond lovers, doom'd to part,
Feel deadly pangs invade their heart,
Torn from the object each holds dear;
'Tis then, O then! the parting tear.

When wretches, on the earth reclin'd,
Their doom of condemnation sign'd,
(The end of earthly being near;)
'Tis then soft pity's gentle tear.

If on some lovely creature's face,
Rich in proportion, colour, grace,
A pearly drop should once appear,
'Tis then the lovely, beauteous tear.

When mothers, (O! the greateful sight)
Their children view with fond delight;
Surrounded by a charge so dear,
'Tis then the fond, maternal tear.

When lovers see the beauteous maid,
To whom their fond attention's paid,
With conscious blushing sobs draw near;
'Tis then the lovely, pleading tear.

When two dear friends, of kindred mind,
By ev'ry gen'rous tie conjoin'd,
Behold their dreaded parting near,
'Tis then, O then! the bitter tear.

But when the wretch, with sins oppress'd,
Strikes in an agony his breast;
When torn with guilt, remorse, and fear;
'Tis then the best, the saving tear.

S O N G 1000.

Written by Mr. LEMOINE.

OFT had I laugh'd at female pow'r,
And slighted Venus' chain;
Then chearful sped each fleeting hour,
Unknown to eating pain:
By stoic rules severely taught
To scorn bright beauty's charms,
Sage wisdom sway'd each rising thought,
And woo'd me to her arms.

Till Sylvia, heavenly Sylvia, came,
Sweet pleasure play'd around;
Her lucid eyes shot forth a flame
That hardest hearts would wound.
O charmer, cease that ardent gaze,
Nor rob me of my rest!
Such lightning from those eyelids plays,
It burns my tortur'd breast.

Deluded swains, who, vainly proud,
Assume gay freedom's air,
And boastful scorn the prostrate crowd
That sigh before the fair!
If once fair Sylvia you should meet,
And view her heav'nly mein;
To love converted, at her feet,
You'll hug the pleasing chain.

S O N G 1001.

TELL me, Delia, charming fair,
Why I hope, or why despair?
Why I'm blest when thou art by,
Or whilst absent steals the sigh?
Ease my breast, my doubts remove;
Is it friendship? is it love?

Friendship's privilege I claim,
But I fear the lover's name;
Age and fortune both conspire
To suppress each fond desire;
Reason too, (but reason's vain)
Bids me be myself again.

Still I struggle, still pursue
Restless cares, and all for you:
Then tell me, Delia, lovely fair,
Why I hope, or why despair?
Thou canst each fond doubt remove;
Is it friendship? is it love?

S O N G 1002.

TO FLORIO.

Written by Mr. NICHOLLS.

YOU talk of your wealthy possession,
You say you're esteem'd by the fair,
And boast that your wond'rous discretion
Has baffled the efforts of care.

Sure wealth and possessions are charming!
Alike's the esteem of the fair;
The want of discretion's alarming,
And sooner or later brings care.

Yet tell me, proud boaster, if ever
(Amongst all the goods you possess)
You've exerted your earnest endeavour
To dry up the tears of distress?

Did you e'er feel a pang, when oppression
Has wounded the honest man's peace?
Did you ever for wrongs make concession?
Or ever from bondage release?

Did you ever a bounty contribute,
When poverty stood at your door?
Or ever an action exhibit
That virtue's sweet countenance bore?

If the springs of humanity never
Have flow'd o'er the brims of your eye;
If oppression has been your endeavour,
Where mis'ry demanded a sigh;

What, then, are your care and your treasure?
I'll tell you, young beau, in a trice:.
Sure signs that you're mean beyond measure,
And foils, but to set off your vice.

S O N G 1003.

THE QUEEN OF MAY.

Sung at RANELAGH.

EV'RY nymph and shepherd, bring
Tribute to the queen of May;
Rifle for her brows the spring,
Make her as the season gay;
Teach her then, from ev'ry flow'r,
How to use the fleeting hour.

Now the fair Narcissus blows,
With his sweetness now delights;
By his side the maiden rose
With her artless blush invites:
M m

Such, fo fragrant and fo gay,
Is the blooming queen of May.

Soon the fair Narciffus dies,
　Soon he drops his languid head;
From the rofe her purple flies,
　None inviting to her bed:
Such, tho' now fo fweet and gay,
Soon fhall be the queen of May.

Tho' thou art a rural queen,
　By the fuffrage of the fwains,
Beauty, like the vernal green,
　In thy fhrine not long remains:
Blefs, then, quickly blefs the youth,
Who deferves thy love and truth.

S O N G 1004.

TRUE PLEASURE.

Written by Mr. J. R.

AH! pleafure, thou idol! thee once did I
　feek,
In the heart-chearing glafs, the enliv'ning
　bowl;
Thy fhort-liv'd effufions my fancy did cheat,
And deluded my youth, and enflaved my foul.

On the breaft of the wanton I've toyed at night,
　Tranfported with rapture, encircled with
　charms;
And while my young bofom has throbb'd with
　delight,
　I thought that I clafp'd thee fecure in my
　arms.

But, ah! all deceit; for fure, on the morrow,
　As reafon return'd, and my paffions were calm,
Reflection produced contrition and forrow,
　Without a good action to prove the mind's
　balm.

Then farewel ye trifles! no longer I toy,
The pleafures I now feek, in virtue are view'd;
There no fell reflection e'er harbours to cloy,
Or confcience avenger! unwelcome intrude.

Each object delights me difplayed around,
　My heart is expanded with gladnefs and glee;
The fweets of content in my bofom abound,
　And pleafure, true pleafure! refideth with
　me.

S O N G 1005.

GAY Damon long ftudy'd my heart to obtain,
　The prettieft young fhepherd that pipes on
　the plain;
I'd hear his foft tale, then declare 'twas amifs,
And I'd often fay No, when I long'd to fay
　Yes.

Paft Valentine's day to our cottage he came,
And brought me two lambkins, to witnefs his
　flame;

Oh! take thefe (he cry'd) thou, more fair than
　their fleece!
I could hardly fay No, tho' afham'd to fay Yes.

Soon after, one morning, we fat in the grove,
He prefs'd my hand hard, and in fighs breath'd
　his love;
Then tenderly afk'd, if I'd grant him a kifs?
I defign'd to've faid No, but miftook, and faid
　Yes.

At this, with delight, his heart danc'd in his
　breaft;
Ye gods (he cry'd) Chloe will now make me
　bleft;
Come, let's to the church, and fhare conjugal
　blifs;
To prevent being teiz'd, I was forc'd to fay
　Yes.

I ne'er was fo pleas'd with a word in my life
I ne'er was fo happy as fince I'm a wife;
Then take, ye young damfels, my counfel in
　this;
You muft all die old maids, if you will not fay
　Yes.

S O N G 1006.

PHILLIS; A PASTORAL.

Written by Mr. HAWKINS.

COME hafte thee, my Phillis, I pray,
　And let us repair to the grove;
Where nightingales, chearful and gay,
　Attune their fweet accents of love:
So foft is the found of their fong,
　'Twill furely delight you, my fair;
Then hafte thee, dear charmer, along,
　And ftraight to the grove let's repair.

For fomething I have to impart,
　That labours quite hard in my breaft;
So ardent and fierce is the fmart,
　It robs me of peace and of reft:
'Tis love, that fond paffion, I fwear,
　By all that is honeft and true;
And thou art the fource of my care,
　I figh and I languifh for you.

Then come, deareft Phillis, I pray,
　And eafe all your Doriland's pain;
Ah! let him be chearful and gay,
　Nor longer implore you in vain,
But let honeft freedom invite,
　For virtue's the path I purfue;
And may happinefs ever unite
　With thofe who are conftant and true.

S O N G 1007.

Sung at VAUXHALL.

COME give your attention to what I unfold,
　The moral is true, tho' the matter is old;
My honeft confeffion's intended to prove,
How taftelefs, infipid, is life without love.

In works of old fophifts my mind I employ'd,
My bottle and friend too, by turns I enjoy'd,
I laugh'd at the fex, and prefumptuoufly ftrove
Their charms to forget, and bid farewel to love.

I toil'd and I traffick'd, grew wealthy and great,
A patriot in politicks, fond of debate;
Each paffion indulging, my doubts did remove,
They center'd in pleafure, and pleafure in love.

How weak my refolves! I confefs'd, with a
  figh,
When Phillis, fweet Phillis, tripp'd wantonly
  by;
I caught her, and mention'd a turn in the grove:
Confenting! fhe made me a convert to love.

Ye lovers of freedom, no longer complain;
We're born fellow-fubjects of beauty's foft
  chain:
My purchas'd experience this maxim will prove,
That life is not life when divided from love.

SONG 1008.

Sung at VAUXHALL.

PALÆMON lov'd Paftora,
  Paftora figh'd for Damon;
But Damon lov'd Aurora,
  Aurora young Palæmon.

Palæmon gave Paftora,
  A wreath and fhepherd's crook;
And Damon gave Aurora,
  A knot and reaping-hook.

Paftora gave to Damon,
  A cap with chaplets crown'd;
Aurora gave Palæmon,
  A pipe with hazel bound.

The cap with chaplets crown'd,
  Young Damon gave Aurora;
The pipe with hazel bound,
  Palæmon gave Paftora.

The wreath and fhepherd's crook
  Paftora gave to Damon;
The knot and reaping-hook,
  Aurora gave Palæmon.

So crofsly turn'd their prefents went,
  Their loves fo oddly varied;
That every token which was fent,
  It's true defign mifcarried.

SONG 1009.

SMILE, fmile, Britannia, fmile,
  Thy genius comes again,
To guard thy fruitful ifle,
  And thunder o'er the main:
Thy gallant fons, difdaining eafe,
Now crown thee miftrefs of the feas.

While dauntlefs they advance,
  And bid the cannons roar;
They'll fcourge the pride of France,
  And fhake th' imperial fhore:
Deriding trumpets o'er the waves,
With courage never known to flaves.

The deck diftain'd with blood,
  The bullets wing'd with fate;
The wide and reftlefs flood,
  Cannot their rage abate:
In Anfon and in Warren; wake
  The fouls of Ruffel, and of Blake.

Britons, purfue the blow,
  Like fons of freedom fight;
Convince the haughty foe,
  That you'll maintain your right:
Defiance bid to France and Spain,
Affert your empire o'er the main.

SONG 1010.

BEHOLD the fweet flowers around,
  With all the bright beauties they wear;
Yet none on the plains can be found
  So lovely as Celia is fair:
Ye warblers, come raife your fweet throats,
  No longer in filence remain;
Oh! lend a fond lover your notes,
  To foften my Celia's difdain.

Oft-times in yon flowery vale,
  I breathe my complaints in a fong;
Fair Flora attends the fad tale,
  And fweetens the borders along:
But Celia, whofe breath might perfume
  The bofom of Flora in May,
Still frowning pronounces my doom,
  Regardlefs of all I can fay.

SONG 1011.

WHEN fairies dance round on the grafs,
  And revel to night's awful noon;
O fay, will you meet me, fweet lafs,
  All by the pale light of the moon?
My paffion I feek not to fcreen,
  Then can I refufe you your boon!
I'll meet you at twelve on the green,
  All by the pale light of the moon.

The nightingale perch'd on a thorn,
  Then charms all the plains with her tune,
And glad of the abfence of morn
  Salutes the pale light of the moon:
How fweet is the jeffamine grove,
  And fweet are the rofes of June!
But fweeter ftill the language of love,
  Breath'd forth by the light of the moon.

Too flow rolls the chariot of day,
  Unwilling to grant me my boon:
Away, envious funfhine, away!
  Give place to the light of the moon.
But fay, will you never deceive,
  The lafs whom you conquer'd too foon;
And leave a foft maiden to grieve,
  Alone, by the light of the moon?

The planets shall start from their spheres,
Ere I prove so fickle a loon ;
Believe me I'll banish thy fears,
'Dear maid, by the light of the moon:
Our loves when the shepherds shall view,
To us they their pipes shall attune;
While we our soft pleasures renew,
Each night, by the light of the moon.

SONG 1012.

THE ADVICE.

Sung at VAUXHALL.

YE nymphs, who to the throne of love
With hearts submissive bow;
Who hope the mutual bliss to prove,
That crowns the nuptial vow:
Thro' caution's glass, by reason lent,
Oh! view your lovers clearly,
Nor think to wed, till that present
The man that loves you dearly.

Still blind to wisdom's ray, the rake
No social bliss allows;
And he who long has rov'd, must make
A good-for-nothing spouse:
Nor trust the fop, tho' piteous sighs
Proclaim you've touch'd him nearly;
His own sweet charms too much he'll prize,
Nor can he love you dearly.

But when with ev'ry manly grace,
A youth of soul refin'd,
Who, doating on your form and face,
Thinks brighter still your mind:
When such shall for the favour sue,
Oh! yield your hand sincerely ;
And you'll love him, and he'll love you,
To life's last moment, dearly.

SONG 1013.

THE PATRIOT FAIR.

WHEN young and artless as the lamb,
That plays about the fondling dam,
Brisk, buxom, pert, and silly;
I slighted all the manly swains,
And put my virgin-heart in chains,
For simple, smock-fac'd Billy.

But when experience came with years,
And rais'd my hopes, and quell'd my fears,
My blood was blithe and bonny;
I turn'd off ev'ry beardless youth,
And gave my love, and fix'd my truth,
On honest sturdy Johnny.

But when at wake I saw the squire,
For lace I found a new desire,
Fond to outshine my mammy;
I sigh'd for fringe, and frogs, and beaux,
And pig-tail'd wigs, and powder'd cloaths,
And silken Master Sammy.

For riches then I felt a flame,
When to my cot old Gripus came
To hold an am'rous parly ;

For music next I chanc'd to burn,
And fondly listen'd, in his turn,
To warbling, quiv'ring Charley.

At length, alike the fools and wits,
Fops, fidlers, foreigners, and cits,
All struck me by rotation:
Then learn from me, ye patriot fair,
Ne'er make one single man your care,
But sigh for all the nation.

SONG 1014.

FANNY OF THE DALE.

Written by Mr. CUNNINGHAM.

LET the declining, damask rose,
With envious grief look p le;
The summer bloom more freely glows
In Fanny of the dale.

Is there a sweet that decks the field,
Or scents the morning gale,
Can such a vernal fragrance yield,
As Fanny of the dale?

The painted belles, at court rever'd,
Look lifeless, cold, and stale :
How faint their beauties, when compar'd
With Fanny of the dale!

The willow binds Pastora's brows,
Her fond advances fail :
For Damon pours his warmest vows
To Fanny of the dale.

Might honest truth, at last, succeed,
And artless love prevail ;
Thrice happy cou'd he tune his reed
With Fanny of the dale!

SONG 1015.

NOW hear me, dear Nanny, nor treat with
disdain,
The voice of my passion, the words of my pain;
Thou dear source of all, 'tis to you I complain,
Then pr'ythee, now hear me, dear Nanny!

By all those bright charms that appear in your
face,
By those eyes far outshining bright Phœbus's
rays,
By thy bosom where dwells ev'ry virtue and
grace,
I beseech thee to hear me, dear Nanny !

By thy sweet ruby lips, where true eloquence
dwells,
Whose sweets all the sweets of fam'd Hybla
excels,
Whose accents alone all my anguish expels,
I beseech thee to hear me, dear Nanny !

By thy dearest dear self, fraught with charms
so compleat,
By all that is lovely, and all that is sweet,

By love, that now makes me to figh at your feet,
I befeech thee to hear me, dear Nanny!

By Hymen's bright torch, and by Cupid's bright flame,
By all that you love, and by all I can name,
By your fpotlefs honour, your virtue, and fame,
I befeech thee to hear me, dear Nanny!

SONG 1016.

MUTUAL LOVE.

Written by Mr. NICHOLLS.

WHERE the blithe bee her honey fips,
In cowflip dale, in vi'let fhade;
Dear Chloe, there I've kifs'd thy lips,
While no rude eye my blifs furvey'd.

Kifs, love! (you cry'd;) more kiffes give;
Thy Chloe's pleafure ftill increafe :
O could our bloom for ever live,
I'd never bid my Damon ceafe.

The tongue that fpoke your fhepherd blefs'd :
What mortal could refift fuch charms!
Thy bofom to my heart I prefs'd,
And, panting, dy'd in Chloe's arms.

SONG 1017.

A CANTATA.

Sung at MARYBONE.

CLEORA fat beneath a fhade,
Her wanton flocks forgot to play;
Then liften to the lovely maid,
While thus fhe mourns her fhepherd's ftay.

Sure time and love are both afleep,
Or Dorus would his promife keep;
Hafte, gentle fhepherd, hither move,
And we'll awake both time and love.

Dorus, wing'd with fwift defire,
Came haft'ning o'er the neighb'ring plain;
Approaching joys the maid infpire,
And thus fhe meets her panting fwain.

Fly care and anguifh far away,
While pleafures blefs this happy day;
Let ev'ry fhepherd joyful be,
And ev'ry pair as bleft as we.

SONG 1018.

DAMON AND CELIA.

Sung at VAUXHALL.

CELIA.

YES, Damon, yes, I can approve,
See all thy merit, all thy love;
But, fhipwreck'd once, I leave the fhore,
And truft the faithlefs feas no more :
Thy vows are loft, thy tears are vain,
For I can never love again,

DAMON.

And could'ft thou then, bewitching maid,
Could'ft thou be flighted, or betray'd?
Or, is it but an artful tale,
O'er Damon's paffion to prevail?
For furely thou wert born to reign,
To love, and to be lov'd again.

CELIA.

If Celia cou'd once more believe,
Damon, like Thyrfis, would deceive;
And yet, methinks, it cannot be:
There muft be faith and truth in thee;
Truft me, thy Celia feels thy pain,
And wifhes fhe cou'd love again.

DAMON.

Why, then, thofe fears that rack thy breaft?
Say that thou wilt, and I am bleft :
But, if my vows fuccefslefs prove,
Damon fhall bid adieu to love;
Like thee, refolve to quit the plain,
And never, never love again.

SONG 1019.

DAPHNE.

Written by Mr. CUNNINGHAM.

NO longer, Daphne, I admire
The graces in thine eyes;
Continu'd coynefs kills defire,
And famifh'd paffion dies.
Three tedious years I've figh'd in vain,
Nor could my vows prevail;
With all the rigours of difdain,
You fcorn'd my amorous tale.

When Celia cry'd, How fenfelefs fhe,
That has fuch vows refus'd;
Had Damon giv'n his heart to me,
It had been kinder us'd.
The man's a fool that pines and dies,
Becaufe a woman's coy :
The gentle blifs, that one denies,
A thoufand will enjoy.

Such charming words, fo void of art,
Surprizing rapture gave ;
And tho' the maid fubdu'd my heart,
It ceas'd to be a flave.
A wretch condemn'd, fhall Daphne prove;
While bleft without reftraint,
In the fweet calendar of love
My Celia ftands—a faint.

SONG 1020.

THE MAIDEN'S CHOICE.

IF ever, oh! Hymen, I add to thy tribe,
Let fuch be my partner, my mufe fhall defcribe;
Not in party too high, nor in ftature too low,
Not the leaft of a clown, nor too much of a beau.

Be his perfon genteel, and engaging his air,
His temper ftill yielding, his foul, too, fincere;
Not a dupe to his paffion 'gainft reafon to move,
But kind to the fweeteft, the paffion of love.

Let honour, commendable pride in the fex,
His actions direct, and his principles fix;
Then groundlefs fufpicion he'll never furmife,
Nor jealoufy read ev'ry glance of my eyes.

If fuch a bleft youth fhould approve my fmall
　　charms,
And no thought of int'reft his bofom alarms;
In wedlock I'll join with a mutual defire,
And prudence fhall cherifh the wavering fire.

Thus time fhall glide on, unperceiv'd in decay,
Each night fhall be blifsful, and happy each day;
Such a partner giant, Heav'n, with my pray'r
　O comply!
Or a maid let me live, and a maid let me die.

SONG 1021.

JOLLY mortals, fill your glaffes;
　　Noble deeds are done by wine;
Scorn the nymph and all her graces:
Who'd for love or beauty pine?

Look upon this bowl that's flowing,
　　And a thoufand charms you'll find,
More than Chloe when juft going,
　　In the moment to be kind!

Alexander hated thinking;
　　Drank about at council board;
Made friends, and gain'd the world by drinking,
　　More than by his conquering fword.

SONG 1022.

SPRING returns; the fauns advance,
　　Leading on the fprightly dance,
O'er the fallow, o'er the glade,
Thro' the funfhine, thro' the fhade;
　　Whilft I forlorn, and penfive ftill,
　　Sit fighing for my daffodil.

See the wanton nymphs appear,
Smiling all, as fmiles the year!
Sporting, print where'er they tread,
Daify ground, or primrofe bed.
　　Whilft I forlorn, &c.

Now the fwain with wat'ry fhoe,
Brufhes by the morning dew;
With officious love to bear
Frefh-blown cowflips to his fair.
　　Whilft I forlorn, &c.

Gentle nymphs, forfake the mead,
To my love for pity plead;

Go, ye fwains, and feek the fair,
This my laft petition bear.
　　Whilft I forlorn, &c.

Sweeteft maid, that e'er was feen,
Dance at wake, or trip the green;
See a love-fick, fighing fwain,
Hear my vows, relieve my pain;
Or with your frowns for pity kill
Too charming, cruel, daffodil.

SONG 1023.

Written by the EDITOR.

AS Bacchus and Mars once together were fit-
　　ting,
Difcourfing on fubjects their godfhips befitting;
Quoth Mars, My friend Bacchus, I ne'er could
　　divine,
Why our fav'rite ifland produces no wine,
For, fure there's no people on earth better me-
　　rit
This excellent drink of the gods to inherit.

That the Britons deferve to have plenty of wine,
Is true, (reply'd Bacchus) becaufe they are
　　thine:
And when they have wanted I gladly would
　　know,
Since I, my good friend, have difpos'd it below;
For tho' the rich cluiters their ifle don't pro-
　　duce,
I always take care to fupply them with juice.

Their neighbours, in France, Spain, and Por-
　　tugal, toil,
To make up this defect in the fam'd Britifh
　　foil:
For you know, that when Jove firft created the
　　ball,
He decreed, in each country fome error fhould
　　fall;
And who can difcover aught wanting, but this,
For England to rival e'en Heaven in blifs.

Their women as beauteous we often behold,
As if they'd been form'd in your fav'rite's mould;
And their men do in war fo much brav'ry fhew,
I have frequently taken a Briton for you:
Befides, tho' in England no vineyards appear,
Not a god 'mongft us all but can relifh their
　　beer.

'Tis true that the Gauls, who have broken
　　their truce,
May debar them awhile from fome fav'rite
　　juice:
But when on the earth you in perfon appear,
They'll fupply it again—for your prefence they
　　fear.
Then foon as our liquor is fairly drunk out,
To England repair, and their enemies rout.

Accordingly Mars clapt the bowl to his mouth,
And drank to Great Britain's friends, North,
Eaft, and South;

Then reaching his hand to old Bacchus, he
said,
For our fav'rite people, boy, ne'er be afraid:
Tho' the rich purple clusters their island can't
shew,
They shall always beat those in whose kingdoms
they grow.

SONG 1024.

Written by Mr. D. Best.

WHENE'ER I Sylvia meet, in wood or
leafy grove,
She casts my suit aside, and bids me cease to
love;
Her cheeks surpass the rose, her sparkling eyes
appear
More fierce than radiant beams from the refulgent sphere.

Her snowy bosom glows with chastity divine;
Her voice as wood-larks sweet, or syren's softer
chime;
Her nut-brown, braided locks, in waving ringlets play;
Her form and lovely mien have stole my heart
away.

Go, urchin god of love, and point your golden
dart,
To soothe my throbbing breast, and soften
Sylvia's heart;
Then lead to Hymen's shrine what banishes my
care,
And to my arms consign the fairest of the fair.

SONG 1025.

THE PRINCESS ELIZABETH.

Occasioned by a Story recorded of her when she
was a Prisoner at Woodstock, 1554.

Written by Mr. SHENSTONE.

WILL you hear how once repining
Great Eliza captive lay?
Each ambitious thought resigning,
Foe to riches, pomp, and sway?

While the nymphs and swains delighted
Tript around in all their pride;
Envying joys by others slighted,
Thus the royal maiden cry'd:

Bred on plains, or born in vallies,
Who would bid those scenes adieu?
Stranger to the arts of malice,
Who would ever courts pursue?

Malice never taught to treasure,
Censure never taught to bear:
Love is all the shepherd's pleasure;
Love is all the damsel's care.

How can they of humble station
Vainly blame the pow'rs above?
Or accuse the dispensation
Which allows them all to love?

Love like air is widely given;
Pow'r nor chance can these restrain;
Truest, noblest gifts of Heaven!
Only purest on the plain!

Peers can no such charms discover,
All in stars and garters drest,
As, on Sundays, does the lover
With his nosegay on his breast.

Pinks and roses in profusion,
Said to fade when Chloe's near:
Fops may use the same allusion;
But the shepherd is sincere.

Hark to yonder milk-maid singing
Chearly o'er the brimming pail;
Cowslips all around her springing,
Sweetly paint the golden vale.

Never yet did courtly maiden
Move so sprightly, look so fair;
Never breast with jewels laden,
Pour a song so void of care.

Would indulgent Heav'n had granted
Me some rural damsel's part!
All the empire I had wanted
Then, had been my shepherd's heart.

Then, with him, o'er hills and mountains,
Free from fetters, might I rove:
Fearless taste the chrystal fountains;
Peaceful sleep beneath the grove.

Rustics had been more forgiving;
Partial to my virgin bloom:
None had envy'd me when living;
None had triumph'd o'er my tomb.

SONG 1026.

Sung at RANELAGH.

TELL me, lasses, have you seen,
Lately wand'ring o'er the green,
Beauty's son, a little boy,
Full of frolic, mirth, and joy?
If you know his shelter, say;
He's from Venus gone astray:
Tell me, lasses, have you seen
Such a one trip o'er the green?

By these marks the god you'll know,
O'er his shoulder hangs a bow,
And a quiver fraught with darts,
Poison sure to human hearts:
Tho' he's naked, little, blind,
He can triumph o'er the mind.
Tell me, lasses, &c.

Subtle as the lightning's wound,
Is his piercing arrow found;
While the bosom'd heart it pains,
No external mark remains;
Reason's shield itself is broke,
By the unsuspected stroke.
Tell me, lasses, &c.

Oft the urchin's seen to lie
Basking in the sunny eye;
Or his destin'd prey he seeks
On the maiden's rosy cheeks:

Snowy breafts, or curling hair,
Oft conceal his pleafing fnare.
   Tell me laffes, &c.

She that the recefs reveals
Where the god himfelf conceals,
Shall a kifs receive this night
From him who is her heart's delight;
To Venus let her bring the boy,
She fhall tafte love's fweeteft joy.
   Tell me, laffes, have you feen
   Such a one trip o'er the green?

SONG 1027.

A COMICAL ODE.

Written by Mr. HEYWOOD.

COME, ev'ry bold blade, come, each honeft
   foul,
Whofe only delight upon earth is good drink-
   ing;
Come, mix your ingredients, and fill up your
   bowl,
   While I tell you a cure I've difcover'd for
     thinking:
     Come! come all to me,
     For this recipe,
It will fill all your bofoms with gladnefs and
   glee;
For fure fuch a med'cine has never been feen,
As what is compounded in this Magazine.

Tho' fome fay I fing like an owl, or an afs,
   And ftill the fame tune to each fong will be
     ringing;
Yet I care not for that, for while I have my
   glafs,
   In fpight of their fneers, and their fleers,
     I'll be finging:
     And I'd glad know his name
     Who fays I'm to blame,
Or who, in the fame cafe, would not do the
   fame!
For fure, there's no mortal on earth can re-
   ftrain,
Who, join'd to good liquor, has this Maga-
   zine.

But now let each jolly companion draw near,
   And a ferious face each of you put on;
While I tell you the names of thofe writers fo
   rare,
   Who immortal fhall be, and their names
     ne'er forgotten;
     But firft fill me high
     This glafs of brandy,
For how can I fing while my lips are fo dry!

Then tofs off your bumpers each ftanza between,
   Let the toaft be, Succefs, boys, to this Ma-
     gazine.

And firft Mr. EDITOR ftands on the roll,
   Whofe ballads fo hearty, fo jovial, and witty,
Shew he loves a brifk glafs as he loves his own
   foul;
   Then fill the old boy up a bumper for pity:
     With bottle and bowl
     Let us ply the old foul,
Till his wit, like the fun-beams, fhines thro'
   all controul;
   Till, bright as his fancy, his nofe fhall be
     feen;
   Then drink to his health, and his new Ma-
     gazine.

Next comes Mafter HAWKINS, that fighing
   young fwain,
   Of whom I fay little, becaufe, boys, between
     us,
(Tho' none of his finging can greatly complain)
   He fuits not with us jolly fons of Silenus:
     Let Strephon and Phillis
     Do juft as their will is,
Mine, mine, to be jovial and tippling ftill is;
   Yet we'll all join his pipe, or in bower or
     plain,
   To chaunt out the praifes of this Magazine.

Next comes brother NICHOLLS, a tender young
   fwain;
   And not far behind him, comes foft brother
     MAVOR;
Some think them the doves that draw Venus's
   train,
   At leaft, all allow they are high in her fa-
     vour:
     To thefe let us join
     The gentle LEMOINE;
Then toaft all their healths in a bumper of wine;
For fure fuch a trio has never been feen,
As this that enriches our new Magazine.

Now HAWKINS, now NICHOLLS, now MA-
   VOR, LEMOINE,
   Leave your fighings, your dyings, your bat-
     tles, and flaughter!
Fill, fill up your glaffes, and drink off your
   wine;
   For who can write well who drinks nothing
     but water!
     Can the lips of the Mifs,
     That you figh fo to kifs,
Be fweeter, or fofter, or redder than this!
   Then join in the chorus, with might and with
     main,
   And all drink fuccefs to this new Magazine.

Mrs *WRIGHTEN* as Fatima *in* CYMON.

Tax my Tongue, it is a Shame

Song 1029

Published by J Bew Dec 1.1778

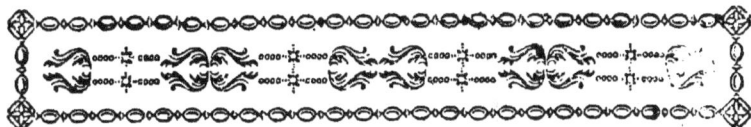

THE

VOCAL MAGAZINE.

NUMBER VIII.

SONG 1028.

ON THE TALK OF A DUTCH WAR.

Written by the EDITOR.

THAT the French far exceed us in ev'ry
    mean art,
Is a truth muſt by all be confeſt;
But, that we ſurpaſs them in true brav'ry of
    heart,
    There's a proof in each Engliſhman's breaſt.
Then let them engage whom they pleaſe on
    their ſide,
The ſons of Britannia each effort deride.

By their uſual fineſſe, tho' they've ſet on
    Mynheer,
And made Spain ſeem diſpoſed for peace,
'Tis as plain as the ſun doth at noon-tide
    appear,
    That they all mean poor England to fleece.
But, truſt me, whilſt Britain is true to herſelf,
She'll beat them united—and pocket their pelf.

Then let not, my countrymen, diſcord divide
    A people whoſe freedom and laws
Have obtain'd them that envy, from impo-
    tent pride,
    Which virtue continually draws.
Tho' nation with nation, then, 'gainſt us
    ſhould join,
We ſhall conquer them all—for our cauſe is
    divine.

SONG 1029.

Sung in Cymon.

TAX my tongue, it is a ſhame:
    Merlin, ſure, is much to blame,
Not to let it ſweetly flow.
Yet the favours of the great,
And the ſilly maiden's fate,
    Oft depend on Yes or No.

Lack-a-day!
Poor Fatima!
Stinted ſo,
    To Yes or No.

Should I want to talk or chat,
Tell Urganda this or that,
    How ſhall I about it go!
Let her aſk me what ſhe will,
I muſt keep my clapper ſtill,
    Striking only Yes or No.

Lack-a-day!
Poor Fatima!
Stinted ſo,
    To Yes or No!

SONG 1030.

FASHION; AN ADDRESS TO REASON:
A PASTORAL.

Written by Mr. NICHOLLS.

WHERE vanity governs the breaſt,
    Dear Reaſon, how rare art thou known!
She thinks thee a troubleſome gueſt,
    And bars thy approach to her throne.

To me thou art dearer than gold;
    As the bloom in the ſpring's to the bee,
As the clover in June's to my fold,
    So art thou, deareſt Reaſon, to me.

Come thou, who'rt of folly the dread,
    The kindeſt companion e'er ſent
To ſmooth the rude path we've to tread
    In our way to the vale of content!

Come, goddeſs! and lend me thy aid
    To bring back a wandering fair,
Who with Folly and Faſhion is ſtray'd
    To a manſion that's built in the air.

'Tis my Mira, the pride of my heart,
    Who ſo much was eſteem'd on the plains;

N n

Who fcorn'd the affiftance of art,
  And for neatnefs was prais'd by the fwains.

When the pole on the green pleas'd her fight,
  When fhe lov'd the ftill walk on the mead ;
When the tabor and pipe could delight,
  Ah, then fhe was charming indeed !

Her treffes, how fweet would they play
  With the breezes that wanton'd around !
Her cheeks ! of a colour more gay,
  No cheeks in the village were found.

Her breath might compare with the rofe,
  Her neck with the lily might vie !
And fweet was the converfe fhe chofe,
  When innocence lighten'd her eye.

Thofe treffes (ah ! who will believe,
  That knew her fo fweet on the dale)
No more kifs the breezes at eve,
  Or wanton at morn with the gale.

Gay Fafhion has tortur'd each curl,
  To a fhape like the cock on the mead ;
When the gay robes of nature unfurl,
  And all things are lovely indeed !

Her tongue ! which fo fweetly could tell
  Of the feafons which chequer'd the year;
Now remarks but the ways of the belle,
  Or what fops have infus'd in her ear.

That cheek, fo delightfully feen !
  That neck, fo invitingly fair !
Is alter'd, and fo is her mien,
  To en aukward, ineligant air !

When firft the fad change I efpy'd,
  I begg'd thee the caufe to exprefs;
With my wifhes you quickly comply'd,
  And wifper'd—the Demon of Drefs.

When I heard it, I wonder'd, 'tis true,
  For fhe knew that my flock was but fmall;
She knew that my acres were few,
  My int'reft much lefs than them all.

I figh, and I cannot refrain,
  Dear Reafon, in fpite of thy pow'rs;
Reflection but adds to my pain,
  And her prefence makes heavy my hours.

That prefence fo often admir'd,
  By the nymphs of fobriety's train,
Of late is moft rudely attir'd,
  With baubles both ufelefs and vain!

When I bid her confider of this,
  She anfwers me thus, with a frown !
I cannot think aught is amifs;
  I but copy the modes of the town.

In vain I endeavour to prove,
  That utility, neatnefs and grace,
May rivet the fetters of love,
  By adding new charms to the face.

In vain I endeavour to fhow,
  Without them 'tis common to find,
That pride and inconftancy too
  Soon fill the recefs of the mind.

Come goddefs ! my Mira reftore ;
  Ah ! come e're the feafon's too late ;

If fhe will not give heed to thy lore,
  May fhe fall by the arrows of fate.

If fhe doth not this fafh'on forfake,
  Thofe modes which but ferve to deceive,
The cup of affliction fhe'll take,
  When fhe finds it too late to retrieve.

Should the graces revifit her mind,
  Again we will fly to the plains;
Leave Fafhion and Folly behind,
  Who're too high for the nymphs and the
    fwains.

My heart feems to dance at the found ;
  We fure fhall be happy at laft!
The moment fhe's rational found,
  I forget all her folly that's paft.

SONG 1031.
Written by the Rev. Mr. J——.

CYPRIAN goddefs, take the lyre,
  Attune yourfelf each trembling ftring ;
My judgment guide, my fancy fire,
  While lovely Rachel's charms I fing.

Let others boaft a beauteous face,
  A fhape, a neck, a graceful air ;
Good-fenfe and prudence give her grace,
  Thefe make her more than blooming fair.

Benevolence, that heav'n-born pow'r,
  Her words and all her actions guide ;
'Tis this that claims each leifure hour,
  This conftitutes her only pride.

Ye fair-ones hence a truth confefs,
  No charms with virtue can compare ;
Be cautious when the beaux addrefs ;
  When mifery fues, his forrows fhare.

Then, like my Rachel, you will be
  Beyond the reach of flattery's lore ;
Inconftancy will bend the knee,
  And wond'ring infidels adore.

SONG 1032.
Written by Mr. DAWRE.

YE fhepherds, what words can exprefs
  The half of my anguifh and pain !
O how fhall I paint my diftrefs,
  Since Celia is fled from the plain !
She was all my fond wifhes could prize,
  My blifs's fublimeft degree :
But while fhe abfents from my eyes,
  No joy can be joyous to me.

Forlorn in the garden I tread,
  And it's beauties deftroy with my feet ;
In vain their perfumes they now fhed,
  'Twas Celia that made them fo fweet.
What balm can your odours impart,
  In your fragrance what charm can I find,
To cure the deep wound in my heart,
  Or reftore the loft peace of my mind !

Thou fiate, that fo often could eafe
The pangs I've long felt in my breaft,
You've loft ev'ry pow'r to pleafe,
Thy joys are all fled like the reft !
How oft, when my Celia was near,
With thee would I charm the dull night !
So pleas'd if fhe'd deign but to hear,
No mortal e'er felt fuch delight.

All the day now I figh out my woe,
Nor ever will ceafe to complain :
No joy fhall my hofom e'er know,
Till I fee the dear fair-one again.
Thus, Celia, while you are away,
Inceffant thy abfence I'll mourn ;
But, oh ! I fhall die if you ftay !
Return then, my charmer, return.

SONG 1033.

THE RURAL BALL.

THE gay Daddy Diddle had new ftrung his
fiddle,
And hobbled away to the Rofe,
Where he met with Tom Trot, who with
pipe and with pot,
Sat jovially painting his nofe.

There was Gregory too, and Nelly and Sue,
And Peg that match'd Billy the Tinker ;
There were Maudlin and Jerry, and Martin
the Merry,
And he with one peep, Ben the Blinker.

There was Judy his joy, for fhe lov'd the
blind boy,
(A fweet cooing couple they were)
And Martin the Merry fung hey down, down
derry,
'Caufe Fanny, his fair-one, was there.

There was bandy-legg'd Joe, almoft how came
ye fo,
And Hannah that twifts like a lizard ;
With hunch-backed Nan, and her timber-
toed Jan.
Who the juftice once took for a wizard.

Firft a chirruping cup, and old Catgut ftruck up,
And flourifh'd a tune of his own ;
But Peg haul'd aloud, fhe wou'd batter his
crown,
Unlefs he wou'd play Bobbing Joan.

Then how they did jump, huftle, buftle, and
ftump,
And jig it, and jog it, and trip it,
Till they fweat, ftunk and ftar'd, as if they'd
been fcar'd,
And about, in and out they did whip it.

Now tir'd with dancing, id eft with their
prancing,
They fat foot to foot, and did fwill ;
Till Peg, with a hiccup, a duft try'd to kick up,

'Caufe Nan was too free with her Will.
But Will, with a frown, fwore he'd ftraight
knock her down,
If fhe did not fit ftill, and be quiet ;
For that no faucy punk, becaufe mad and drunk,
Shou'd break up the ball with a riot.

That's right, faid Tom Trot ; and feizing the pot,
Here's a health to the ftrength of the na-
tion.
They pledg'd him around, all but Peg, who,
they found,
Was ready to fplit with vexation.

Mild Maudlin, quite mellow, kifs'd Jerry,
dear fellow,
Love's paffion had fcorch'd 'em to tinder ;
Grinning Greg. with fweet Sue would have
made much ado,
But the tell-tales about them did hinder.

Martin frifk'd with fair Fanny ; fays fhe,
Lor' how can ye ?
Pooh ! fee how my handkerchief's torn.
Ben leer'd at his Judey, as in a brown ftudy,
But Hannah was left all forlorn.

Nelly's Bibo, Tom Trot, was fo fond of his
pot,
Neglected, poor girl, fhe might lie ;
Not regarding her fcorn, or threats of the
horn,
He fwore he would drink till he'd die.

Now they all being muzzy, each hob and his
huzzy,
Some fung, others laugh'd, and fome cry'd ;
But Old Tap-tub then come, and foon bundled
them home,
Where we'll leave 'em till next merry tide.

SONG 1034.

WINTER.

Written by Mr. HEYWOOD.

LO! what dreary, darkfome morning,
Ufhers in the rifing day ;
Phœbus, from the weft returning,
Dimly gleams a trembling ray.

Now no more the lark, high-foaring,
Chaunts her fweetly-thrilling ftrain ;
Far away fhe haftes, exploring
Some more hofpitable plain.

Flocks of fparrows, pertly hopping,
Here and there collect a grain ;
While the fweet domeftic robin,
For the city quits the plain.

Birds of ev'ry fong and pinion,
Own ftern winter's rigid reign ;
And for fummer's foft dominion
Silent figh, but figh in vain.
Some in penfive notes repining,
On the fnow-emboffed fpray,
For their abfent partners pining,
Sigh their little lives away.

Now no more is heard refounding,
  Up yon cliff, the bufy mill;
Winter's frigid arms furrounding,
  Lock the fweetly-tinkling rill.

Lo! how all our fcenes of pleafure,
  Cloth'd in fpotlefs liveries lie,
Where nymphs and fwains, in frolick meafure,
  Tript and fung fo merrily.

Ah! how oft, at eve, refounding
  Mufick ftole from yonder hill,
Which (fickly fogs and mifts furrounding)
  Now breeds damps and vapours chill.

But hark! in yonder vale, gay moving,
  Breathes the far-refounding horn;
Whilft the jovial fportfmen roving,
  Hail, with fhouts, the rifing morn.

SONG 1035.

FHEBE TO SILVIUS.

Written by Mifs BIGGERSTAFF.

WHY will you plague me with your pain?
  You know fuch nonfenfe I difdain!
Your paffion, anguifh, tears, and fighs,
And all fuch folly, I defpife.
If I but frown, you fay, you die;
Sure frowns can never hurt a fly:
But fince my fmiles fuch bleffings prove,
I'll ever fmile at you and love.

You fay that I am all divine,
My eyes the brighteft ftars outfhine;
And I of charms have fuch a ftore,
As never girl poffefs'd before:
And when I am as mad as you,
I may believe it to be true;
But never, till that time fhall be,
Let me hear more of love or thee.

SONG 1036.

A SCOTCH CANTATA.

Written by Mr. HAWKINS.

RECITATIVE.

AS Jockey fat beneath a cyprefs fhade,
  (While breezes fported thro' each vernal
    glade)
The youth was tuning of his oaten reed,
When lovely Jenny tript along the mead;
With eager hafte to her he gladly fprang,
And thus, in foothing ftrains, moft fweetly fang.

AIR.

Oh! Jenny, did you know the pain
  That harbours in my breaft;
You ne'er would let me fue in vain,
  But make me ever bleft.
For, oh! I love you frae my heart,
  Your fhape's fo bonny fine;
Nay more, my dear, I could impart,
  If, laffy, you'll be mine.

Then let's gang down the burn, I fay,
  Or thro' yon verdant grove;
For there we'll toy, we'll kifs, and play,
  And you fhall be my love.

For I'll no longer fingle be,
  So wearied is my life;
Then, Jenny, do incline to me,
  And you fhall be my wife;
For, oh! your een, they gliften fo,
  Their charms I fcarce can teel,
But this I know, where'er I go,
  I love my Jenny weel.
Then let's gang down the burn, &c.

Young Jenny heard the fhepherd's tale,
  And promis'd to be kind;
For he fo fweetly did prevail,
  He gain'd her to his mind.
Then to the kirk fhe gave confent
  With Jockey for to fteer;
Where ftraight with joy away they went,
  And foon were wedded there.
Now down the burn, or through the grove,
  They gang fo blithe and gay;
Each forming tender tales of love
  To crown their nuptial day.

SONG 1037.

Written by Mr. TOMLINS.

PITY, come, thou gentle pow'r!
  Shd thy influence o'er my heart,
In my breaft thy bleffings pour;
  Come, to me thy gifts impart.

Never let my heart be fteel'd
  'Gainft a fellow-creature's woe;
Ne'er let mis'ry, when reveal'd,
  From my gate unaided go.

And when death fhall call me forth,
  O! may then a friend fincere,
O'er my cold corps, laid in earth,
  Gently drop the pitying tear,

SONG 1038.

Written by Mr. BEST.

YE grave, fober mortals, ye fons of old care,
  What pleafures from fadnefs can flow?
'Tis the juice of the vine that difperfes defpair,
  Which Bacchus diftributes below.

The prieft, clad in fanctity, rages and bawls,
  Exclaims againft liquor divine;
But when from the church to obey nature's calls,
  His worfhip's not quite fo fublime.

With the beft of us all he will tipple and quaff,
  And with glee will drink, riot, and fmoke;
At church and at ftate he will merrily laugh,
  While a bumper enlivens the joke.

The lover with fighs intercedes with the fair,
  In fonnets unburdens his mind;
Intreats for a fmile to difpel all his care;
  But the hard-hearted nymph's ftill unkind.

Was the bowl but the object ye lovers adore,
    Without eloquence, reason, or verse,
Great Bacchus affords you a plentiful store,
    Which we sons of old Noah disperse.

Let philosophers reason of systems divine,
    And patriots of politicks prate ;
Their reasons agree when at Bacchus's shrine,
    And a bumper dispenses their hate.

Let the soup-maigre Frenchmen who threaten
        our isle,
    Attack us whenever they please ;
Animated by wine, at their forces we'll smile,
    And with thunder their fury appease.

Let war, wit, and beauty, religion and laws,
    No longer with Bacchus contend ;
He dispels all our care, and evinces our cause,
    And Mars does our liquor defend.

SONG 1039.

TO SYLVIA.

Written by Mr. J. R.

COME, my Sylvia! come and bless
    This spot, which I have toil'd to dress
In all that charms the gazer's eye,
In ev'ry tint that wears a dye.

In peace we'll dwell, and placid ease,
We'll do whatever each shall please ;
Free as the seas our senses roll,
And speak a boundless, fluent soul.

Nor time shall waft our loves away,
Swift as the thread of life decays ;
Each gale that flits the hours along,
Shall bring fresh wreathes to deck our song:

From virtue's sweets, that never cloy ;
From rural scenes, extatic joy !
Or turn the mind-instructing page,
And learn to live a good old age.

SONG 1040.

POLITENESS.

Written by Mr. NICHOLLS.

AT Palæmon's rural retreat,
    How glad could I spend the long day,
If Mira the spot could conceit !
    But she loves amidst crowds to be gay.

She us'd to be fond of the grove,
    Of my flock and the pastoral strain ;
But now she's delighted to rove,
    And slights both my flock and her swain.

To find out the cause of the change,
    I wonder'd, but could not conceive ;
Till I found, in a manner quite strange,
    What I'm forc'd 'gainst my will to believe.

She went 'mongst the gay and the proud,
    Unknown were such circles before ;
She was struck with the airs of the crowd,
    And sure she'll have reason no more.

Quite alter'd, alas ! is our state,
    From simplicity, quiet, and health !
She'll copy the ways of the great,
    Tho' she has not their portion of wealth.

Each morn 'twas her custom to rise
    When the lark dealt his melod'ous tune ;
But now ('tis politeness, she cries !)
    She scarcely emerges till noon.

Our table was furnish'd full neat,
    There friendship oft sat with delight ;
Our meal was plain, halesome, and sweet ;
    Politeness has alter'd it quite !

Her gossips now flirt it around,
    And their tongues sound so shrill in my ear
That I would not to bear it be bound,
    For a farm of a thousand a year.

Where the tongue so incessantly goes,
    Fair character often is marr'd ;
They spare not their friends nor their foes,
    And truth has but little regard.

To convince her, I take the best pains,
    That her conduct is not in the right ;
In return, my dear Mira complains,
    I do not know what is polite.

If politeness in scandal consists,
    ('Tis my nature, ye swains, to be free)
If in wounding of truth it exists,
    Pursue it, who likes it, for me.

Let me have my rustical gear,
    With peace in my vine-circled cot ;
Good health, and a friendship sincere,
    Politeness I envy ye not.

Even thus should the pitying pow'rs
    Cause my fair-one astray to opine,
I'll sing in the grottos and bow'rs,
    Not a nymph can be equal to mine.

SONG 1041.

Written by Mr. DAWRE.

COME Phœbus, and tune thy soft lyre;
    Ye muses, come join in the song ;
While Celia the theme shall inspire,
    The fairest of all the gay throng ;
The goddess of virtue and grace,
    The queen of all beauty and charms ;
'Tis transport to gaze on her face,
    'Tis heaven to rest in her arms.

O could I charm Pluto's dull ears,
    Like Orpheus of old, with my lay,
Or with Milton soar up to the spheres,
    I then might her merits display :
While her charms I attempt to rehearse,
    A field so unbounded doth rise,
The subject's too great for my verse,
    I sink, and am lost with surprize.

Urania, my bosom inspire,
    My genius enlarge it's degrees,
To the height that my theme doth require,
    Tho' I aim not the criticks to please.

'Tis Celia, the theme of my ftrain,
 Whofe plaudits I only can prize.
Could I but her favor obtain,
 Let envy my fonnets defpife.

SONG 1042.

STREPHON AND LUCINDA; A PASTORAL.

Written by Mr. MAVOR.

STREPHON.

HARK! the birds on ev'ry-fpray
 Sweetly carrol thro' the grove;
Flow'rets all around difplay
 Scenes for harmony and love.
Fair Lucinda, come with me,
Where true love can only fee.

LUCINDA.

No, my Strephon, man's forfworn;
 To the grove I dare not go;
Scarce the rofy dimpled morn
 Bids it's tops with purple glow;
Then excufe a virgin's fear,
Tho' true love is only there.

STREPHON.

Sweet Lucinda, heav'nly fair,
 Mild as May, or dawning light,
Can my heart thus falfe appear?
 Could deceit approach thy fight?
Or a wanton wifh arife,
'Neath the chaftnefs of thofe eyes?

LUCINDA.

Gentle youth, your gen'rous tale,
 Oft has charm'd me in the grove;
I'll no more my flame conceal,
 Nor diftruft the fwain I love:
But 'tis time our flocks to feed,
And our lambs to pafture lead.

BOTH.

Thro' the pearly, glift'ning dew,
 To the fold then let us hafte;
Hear, the tender, bleating ewes,
 Long the morning herb to tafte;
And at noon, within the grove,
We'll renew our vows of love.

SONG 1043.

THE PLACEMAN.

THE patriot in the fenate burns,
 Harangues on ev'ry thing by turns;
Religion, liberty, and laws,
His much-lov'd country's facred caufe!

By place or penfion well appl'y'd,
 The premier gains him on his fide:
His country's ardent love is o'er?
The facred caufe inflames no more.

Long did my heart fecure defy
The fhafts of many a brilliant eye;

And ftill it's liberty could boaft
At eafe, while toaft reign'd after toaft.

Now, Hymen, if you wifh to gain
This heart, defended long in vain;
My penfion be Eliza's charms!
My place, for life, her faithful arms!

SONG 1044.

Written by Mr. W—LL—S.

WITH Phillis how oft have I ftray'd,
 O'er hill, dale, and in the green grove!
How pleas'd to attend the fweet maid!
To tell her how fondly I love.

My Phillis fuch charms does impart,
 Such beauties difplay to the view!
From me fhe has ftolen a heart;
 A heart that will ever prove true.

She lends a kind ear to my tale;
 With fmiles fhe my toil does reward;
And when I my paffion reveal,
 Her looks fully fpeak her regard.

What mortal more happy can be!
 What cares can my bofom alarm!
Whilft Phillis, dear girl, is fo free;
 Poffeffing each power to charm.

But fhould fhe e'er flight her fond fwain,
 And leave me her lofs to deplore,
Then, Lethe, relieve me from pain,
 And let me not think of her more.

Not think of her more—did I fay?
 How vain fuch an effort would prove!
For, long as I live, I each day
 Muft think of her charms, and ftill love.

SONG 1045.

Written by Mr. SELLEW.

TO fpeak my mind, of womankind,
 They are unfettled creatures;
I never yet, two females met
 Alike, except in features.

We ever find, that like the wind,
 They frequently are changing;
From morn till night, their chief delight,
 In fearch of folly's ranging.

They gad about, from ball to rout,
 On fcandal ever feeding;
They talk and chat, of this and that,
 To fhow their fenfe and breeding.

Puff'd up with pride—fo vain befide,
 They ne'er will wifdom learn;
And when once bent, they're fo intent,
 As foon the tide you'll turn.

Seldom pleafing, often teizing;
 Murmuring if they're tv'd;
If fui jurls, then they're furies,
 Never, never fatisfied.   •

Oh! fickle fex, no more perplex,
Nor with your follies teize us ;
Think, e'er too late, you were by fate
Intended but to pleafe us.

And not to gad, and make us mad,
Purfuing each new folly.
When once the rein, the females gain,
They'll drive us melancholy.

Learn wifdom then, ye fons of men,
Be kind, but not too civil ;
For fhould your wives, e'er guide your lives,
They'll govern like the devil.

SONG 1046.

STREPHON ; A PASTORAL BALLAD.

Written by Mr. HAWKINS.

AS Strephon was ftrolling along to the fair,
So blithefome, fo bonny, and quite debonair,
Reclin'd in a grove a young fhepherdlefs lay,
To reft her awhile from the heat of the day.

Her fheep had been ftraying wide over the plain,
And one fhe had loft, which fhe fought for
in vain,
That drove the dear damfel almoft to defpair,
For doleful fhe feem'd, and dejected her air.

In filence the fwain fat him down on a ftile,
To hear her complainings, then fpoke with a
fmile,
That rouz'd all her paffions, and thrill'd thro'
her heart;
So keen was his arrow, fo piercing his dart :

For fhe of a fudden forgot all her care,
And tripp'd it with Strephon away to the fair;
Where topknots he bought her, the beft he
could find,
Likewife a ftraw-hat, for to him fhe was kind.

Her looks were delightful, her charms were
moft fweet;
Her drefs, tho' not gaudy, was cleanly and neat;
From pride and ambition the maiden was free;
Untainted her mind, and fo virtuous was fhe.

The youth, as he view'd her, the fonder he
grew,
And vow'd he would ever be faithful and true:
He promis'd to banifh all forrow and ftrife;
And made the dear damfel, next morning, his
wife.

SONG 1047.

THE WINTER WISH.

Written by Mr. MAVOR.

STRIPT is the foliage of the trees,
No flow'rs the fields adorn ;
No more the balmy weftern breeze,
Or fweetly fmiling morn !

No more the bright Apollo fheds
His warm prolific ray ;
But chearlefs, in his car pervades
The fhort-liv'd, brumal day.

When rattling hail burfts from the fky,
And dances o'er the plain ;
When the roof echoes, tempefts fly,
And roaring winds complain ;

When fable night, with ebon wand,
Brings tedious darknefs on, ·
And bids fair Cynthia, at command,
Sit fhrouded on her throne;

Then, deareft Celia, deign to fmile,
Nor fcorn a mutual love ;
Thy fmiles the blackeft ftorms beguile,
The richeft joys improve.

With rapture while I catch the found,
That fpeaks my flame repaid,
How fwift my glowing heart will bound,
To fee my blufhing maid !

O ! be our love or lot the fame,
Thro' every fcene below ;
Be ours an unextinguifh'd flame,
When age has fhed it's fnow :

Then, whether fpring in colours gay
Adorns the genial ground,
When mufic warbles from each fpray,
And all is bloom around ;

Or whether winter's fullen wafte,
Deforms the gailefs year ;
No anxious care fhall fill my breaft,
No vifionary fear.

Calmnly ferene thro' life I'll glide,
And think each feafon kind ;
Till doom'd to fail th' eternal tide,
I leave no wifh behind.

SONG 1048.

SUMMER.

Written by Mr. BEST.

NOW the lufcious fweets are flown,
Spring's forfook her ebon throne ;
Summer now, in rich array,
Bears alone defpotic fway ;
Blufhing now, in early bloom,
Spreads around a rich perfume ;
While the gentle zephyrs play,
Boafting fweets that equal May.

Now Pomona's fweets we tafte,
Smiling at the rich repaft,
Which her labours ever yield,
Banquets, rich and nobly fill'd ;
Bright Aurora's fcorching beams,
Gild the azure flowing ftreams.
While the gentle zephyrs play,
Boafting fweets that equal May.

View the fertile hills and plains,
Where the fmiling goddefs reigns;
Ceres, ever kind and true,
Cultivates her crops for you ;

And the chearful nightingale
Warbles forth her tender tale.
  While the gentle zephyrs play,
  Boafting fweets that equal May.

SONG 1049.

By Mr. R—GB—Y.

FAREWEL all the joys which of late I
  poffeft,
When with Sylvia's bright prefence and fight
  I was bleft ;
How fwift fled the hours, undifturbed with care,
No fears durft intrude, when along with my
  fair.

Her cheeks were like rofes, her fhape like
  the pine,
Her perfon and action were furely divine ;
To her perfon alone were not graces confin'd,
Tho' lovely her body, more charming her mind.

How fhort-liv'd is beauty ! how frail is our
  ftate !
Ah, who can forefee the intentions of fate !
The rofes are wither'd, infipid they lie !
Ah, who can be fafe, when fuch beauty muft
  die !

Poffeffing her, life would have been worth my
  care,
But now 'tis a burden I fcarcely can bear :
A dungeon would pleafe me, poffeffing my fair ;
In a palace unhappy, if abfent from her.

By her looks I was chear'd, and with eager
  delight
Could gaze at her beauty, from morning till
  night :
But fince fate was cruel enough to deprive
My life of it's comfort, why fhould I furvive ?

SONG 1050.

Written by the Rev. Mr. J——.

WHEN Britain's queen, on Albion's ftrand
  Firft landed from the German main,
Neptune, the guardian of our land,
  With Naïds join'd, and fung this ftrain :

  Hail, happy ifle !
    Whofe fun has feldom feen,
  So gracious, fo
    Belov'd a queen.

Fair freedom dreads no galling chain,
  In George and Charlotte's love fecure ;
For while the laws his will reftrain,
  Her mild commands our hearts allure.

  Britons with glory,
    With glory crown the day,
  From whence fprung George
    And Charlotte's fway.

In her the power to charm is feen,
  With unaffected wit and fenfe ;
A truly great, yet humble mien,
  Effulgent truth and innocence.

And when no more thefe virtues fhine,
  Save in the bright hiftoric page,
Or in her own illuftrious line,
  Prolong'd by heav'n from age to age ;

  Still Britannia
    Her grateful voice fhall raife,
  In joyful ftrains,
    To Charlotte's praife.

SONG 1051.

Written by Mr. DAWRE.

BACCHUS, god of rofy wine,
  Shed your influence divine ;
Fill to the brim the fprightly bowl,
Nought but wine can chear the foul.

By this Alexander fought ;
By this god-like Plato thought :
This was, fure, the facred fpring,
Where the mufes us'd to fing.

Mirth by this will ever fmile,
This will ev'ry care beguile ;
Ev'ry joy and focial blifs,
Rifes hence, and moves to this.

Love may beat his foft alarms,
This excels e'en Nancy's charms :
Often frowns deform her face ;
Wine has everlafting grace.

SONG 1052.

ANACREONTIC.

Written by Mr. TOMLINS.

I Crave not Gyge's boundlefs pow'r,
  Nor wifh I for the golden ftore ;
I envy not the regal ftate
Of pompous kings, fupremely great ;
For mirth and joy alone I care,
And wreaths of rofes for my hair.
To-day I banifh ev'ry forrow,
Nor think I of the coming morrow.
While chance permits, we'll drink and laugh,
And Bacchus' gifts in goblets quaff ;
For fooner than we wifh comes death,
And ftops our drinking, and—our breath.

SONG 1053.

Written by Mr. J. R.

HOW oft, my dear Damon, we've plea-
  fingly ftray'd
'Long Medway's fweet banks, and it's hamlets around ;
E're the dew cryftal drop was exhal'd from
  the glade,
  Or the lark's fhrilly note gave to echo a
  found !

And feen the blithe fhepherd repair from his
    cot,
, To the flock his fond breaft accounted his
    · ftore ;
And he whiftled and fung, nor cared a jot ;
    His defires were crown'd, he afk'd for no
    more.

Or ken'd the rude hufbandman fpeed to his
    toil,
    With heart that was happy, contented and
    free ;
O ! how our young bofoms have ponder'd the
    while,
And cull'd fweet reflection for Damon and me !
And pity'd the wealthy, enrolled in ftate,
    That ne'er tafted joys from delights fuch as
    thefe ;
Let them fmile in their fhackles, be proud to
    be great,
    We boafted our freedom, and cherifh'd our
    eafe !

The mofly green turf, with pied daifes crown'd,
    Exceeded the carpet's moft beautiful dye;
The wild rofy thorn fcatter'd perfume around,
    Our mufick the notes from each fongfter
    hard by.
No honours to deck, nor no titles to grace,
    A heart free from guile we enclofed within;
No falfe affectation with us found a place,
    Or hypocrify's mafk our actions to fcreen.

Blooming health ftrung our nerves, and flufh'd
    on our cheeks,
    It breath'd thro' each bufh, and fang thro'
    the trees ;
While ficknefs, appall'd, from our prefence
    did creep,
    And clogg'd the high breaft with her loath-
    fome difeafe,
We purchas'd no pleafures, they flow'd free as
    air,
    From nature-deck'd beauties around us dif-
    play'd ;
No figh from our bofoms, the border of care,
    E'er pierc'd the dark grot, or e'er fullied the
    fhade.

With true patriot feelings enraptur'd we
    glow'd,
    To fee fmiling Ceres her vot'ries repay ;
And hail'd the beneficient hand that beftow'd,
    With ardour unknown to the free-thinking
    gay.
Thus trod we through life, as to manhood
    we grew,
    Nor envy'd proud grandeur her glittering
    charms ;
If Laura was conftant, Melifla but true,
    Their fmile was an audience, a palace
    their arms.

S O N G 1054.

Written by Mr. MAVOR.

THE pleafures of a lady's fmiles
    How falfe, and yet how fair !

In ev'ry charm there lies a dart,
    In ev'ry glance a fnare.
How they recal the youthful mind
    From ev'ry glorious aim,
Fill the foft breaft with racks and fears,
    And blaft the buds of fame !

Bound in the fetters of the fair,
    In vain we ftrive to move ;
In vain we form the great refolve,
    When all the foul is love.

Yet, O bright angel, fmile on me,
    Your beauties I adore ;
No other blifs I afk below ;
    Nor can the fkies give more.

S O N G 1055.

PACULUM BONI DEI.

Written by Mr. NICHOLLS.

FRIEND DRAUMA, go hafte, let a goblet
    be made
By thine hand, gentle artift, the beft of thy
    trade ;
Attend to the fhape, and 'twere beft if the fize
Refembled that cup poets feign in the fkies.
With fuch I'll invoke my good genius to free,
From all that's oppreffive, my Chloe and me.

On the foot let the vine and it's clufters ap-
    pear,
Mount it lofty, and turn it as round as a
    fphere ;
Let the filver be pure as the liquor I'd quaff,
Left my friends, as they pledge me, fhould
    fay with a laugh,
This goblet fo mighty, and fculpture fo fair,
Is no better than Sheffield or Birmingham
    ware.

Let old Mofer, that excellent prince of his
    tribe,
Enchafe on my goblet the fcenes I defcribe ;
Firft, let him mark at right angles the bowl,
And then let four circles encircle the whole ;
On thefe let the heart-chearing hop and the
    vine,
In airy alliance enclofe the defign.

In the firft fpacious round let the artift pro-
    duce
Old Falftaff, loud calling for more potent
    juice ;
Let the prince of good fellows, young Harry,
    be there,
With the reft of thofe fpirits who laugh away
    care ;
Bring Quickly and Doll too ; and, left the
    fcene droop,
Give fiery-faced Bardolph to finifh the group.

O o

In the next let the gay wives of Windfor
    appear,
Where the knight in the bafket difcovers his
    fear,
Or give (for my Shakefpear with laughter is
    ftor'd)
Where his corpulent fides feel the cudgel of
    Ford.
Or let good Sir Hugh and old Caius engage ;
Or poor lathy Slender, with lovely Ann Page.

Now under the green oaken tree lay the wight,
While fairies dance round by the moon's
    filver light ;
Or, crefted like Herne, let the amorous deer,
In fearch of his hind, in the foreft appear.
Yes, mark in his face all that lecherous fin
I've feen in the faces of Shuter and Quin.

In the laft give the fcene where bright reafon
    again
Bids the prince fcorn the knight and his riot-
    ous train.
A moral like this I would wifh to beftow ;
Such acts of difcretion to wifdom we owe :
Dear goddefs, who never takes up thy abode
Where the brute knows no bounds, or the
    fot has his load.

Abftracted from fuch fhall my goblet go round,
Till vacuum prates, with a fonorous found,
From the lees of my cafk, that my liquor is
    out ;
Then my friends muft excufe till the next
    merry bout.
My friends to enjoy's the delight of my foul ;
Then hafte ye, and thus fafhion Nicholls's
    bowl.

SONG 1056.

TO-MORROW.

Sung at VAUXHALL.

I Heed not, while life's on the wing,
    What fate or what fortune may bring,
    Nor think or of care or of forrow ;
Would you know why fo happy and gay ;
I've liv'd, my companions, to-day,
    And will wafte not a thought on to-morrow.

What pleafures already are flown,
The joys my fond heart might have known,
    I could not repeat without forrow ;
When eagerly brimm'd the brifk wine,
When Jove, half-confenting, was mine,
    A whifper came, ftay till to-morrow.

I'll live, for I'm wifer at laft,
The prefent fhall pay for the paft,
    No moment of future I'll borrow ;
The cheat now I fairly defcry ;
On to-day you muft only rely,
    Look not for a friend in to-morrow.

I'll catch ev'ry fwift-flying hour,
I'll tafte ev'ry joy in my pow'r,
    And teach you to fmile away forrow :

If love now bids beauty be kind,
If you've nectar to gladden your mind,
    Have nothing to do with to-morrow.

SONG 1057.

Sung in *Cymon.*

I Laugh, and I fing,
    I am blithefome and free,
The rogue's little fting,
It can never reach me :
    For with fal, la, la, la !
    And ha, ha, ha, ha !
    It can never reach me.

My fkin is fo tough,
Or fo blinking is he,
He can't pierce my buff,
Or he miffes poor me.
    For with fal, la, la, la !
    And ha, ha, ha, ha !
    He miffes poor me.

O, never be dull,
By the fad willow tree :
Of mirth be brimful,
And run over like me.
    For with fal, la, la, ah !
    And ha, ha, ha, ha !
    Run over like me.

SONG 1058.

AH ! Chloris, could I now but fit
    As unconcern'd as when
Your infant beauty could beget
    No happinefs nor pain !
When I this dawning did admire,
    And prais'd the coming day,
I little thought that rifing fire
    Would take my reft away.

Your charms in harmlefs childhood lay
    As metals in a mine ;
Age from no face takes more away
    Than youth conceal'd in thine :
But as your charms infenfibly
    To their perfection preft,
So love, as unperceiv'd, did fly,
    And center'd in my breaft.

My paffion with your beauty grew,
    While Cupid, at my heart,
Still as his mother favour'd you,
    Threw a new flaming dart :
Each gloried in their wanton part ;
    To make a beauty, the
Employ'd the utmoft of her art ;
    To make a lover, he.

SONG 1059.

LET poets tell of fhape and air,
    Of faces beauteous, lovely, fair,
There's nought on earth that can compare
    With half the charms of Nelly.

The lily, nor the rose so sweet,
So fair, so fragrant, nor so neat;
Nought in creation's so compleat
    As is my lovely Nelly.

How happy will that mortal be,
His days will pass from mis'ry free,
Whom gracious Heaven shall bless with thee,
    My ever-blooming Nelly.
Then, whilst those charms adorn your face,
With ev'ry blooming, youthful grace,
Remember, beauty never stays,
    When old-age comes, my Nelly.
Then take a lover to your arms,
Whom vigorous, youthful spirit warms,
Who's worthy to possess those charms
    Which now adorn my Nelly.

If such a swain you e'er can find,
Possess'd of such a form and mind,
He is by Heaven itself design'd
    To bless my charming Nelly.
That search was vain you soon would prove;
For should you thro' the whole world rove,
You'd find none worthy of the love
    Of charming, beauteous Nelly.

SONG 1060.

Sung in *Cymon*.

YOU gave me last week a young linnet,
    Shut up in a fine golden cage;
Yet how sad the poor thing was within it,
Oh, how did it flutter and rage!
    Then he mop'd and he pin'd,
    That his wings were confin'd,
Till I open'd the door of his den;
    Then so merry was he,
    And because he was free,
He came to his cage back again.

SONG 1061.

REASON A CURE FOR JEALOUSY;

A PASTORAL.

Written by Mr. NICHOLLS.

THE sweet blossoms of May gaily silver'd
    the grove,
And wherever I turned 'twas music and love;
When the maid of my bosom in converse was seen
With the smartest young shepherd that pipes
    on the green :
So soon as these tidings were told unto me,
I snatch'd up my crook, and ran over the lee;
My lambkins I left to the care of my cur,
For I car'd for no creature on earth but for her.

With the speed that the bolt from the archer's
    bow flies,
With the speed that the falcon returns with
    his prize,
I vaulted each stile I came to in my way,
And these rancorous words I determin'd to say :

Know this, thou false Phebe, I've alter'd my
    mind,
And will seek out another more constant and
    kind.
Thus murm'ring, I fled, at my fancy'd disgrace,
Till bright Reason o'ertook me, and slacken'd
    my pace.

Pry'thee hold, silly swain, said the heaven-
    born fair;
Your rage is unmanly, return to your care.
I plainly perceive for the passion's confess'd,
'Tis jealousy rifles your bosom of rest.
Can your Phebe be faithless! remember, dull
    swain,
That your absence to her's the commencement
    of pain :
Her lovers were many, rich, handsome, and
    true;
Yet she scorn'd ev'ry one for a cottage and you.

'Tis Reason commands, hence her precepts
    obey;
Who's govern'd by her, cannot easily stray;
Go, in haste seek your flocks; for your rose-
    bud of youth
Is just as you'd have her, all virtue and truth;
Her manners are charming, I'm proud to allow,
And smiling content sits with peace on her
    brow :
Hence never more think her inconstant in love,
Whose breast is as pure as the breast of a dove.

Quite convinc'd of my folly, and rid of my pain
I hasten'd away to my pastures again;
Where, under the sycamore boughs, by the
    brook,
As recumbent I lean'd on the stem of my crook;
I saw the dear maid tripping blithe o'er the plain
With a posey receiv'd from the hand of the swain.
Straight I fled to my love, and (I own it with
    pride)
Commended the gift, and the giver beside.

Ye swains, ne'er let jealousy enter the breast;
The demon's delight is to rob you of rest :
'Tis heartless to think what the jealous must
    know;
They feel all the pangs of the wretched below !
To 'scape from this fury, be gentle and gay
To the fair you esteem, and still give her her
    way :
To please her, the tenderest methods pursue;
And still think her kind, till you find her un-
    true.

SONG 1062.

Written by Mr. MALLET.

FAR in the windings of a vale,
    Fast by a sheltering wood,
The safe retreat of health and peace,
    An humble cottage stood:

There beauteous Emma flourish'd fair
    Beneath a mother's eye,

Whose only wish on earth was now
To see her blest, and die.

The softest blush that nature spreads
Gave colour to her cheek ;
Such orient colour smiles thro' heav'n
When May's sweet mornings break.

Nor let the pride of great ones scorn
This charmer of the plains ;
That sun which bids their diamond blaze,
To deck our lily deigns.

Long had she fir'd each youth with love,
Each maiden with despair ;
And tho' by all a wonder own'd,
Yet knew not she was fair.

Till Edwin came, the pride of swains,
A soul that knew no art,
And from whose eyes serenely mild,
Shone forth the feeling heart.

A mutual flame was quickly caught,
Was quickly too reveal'd ;
For neither bosom lodg'd a wish
Which virtue keeps conceal'd.

What happy hours of heartfelt bliss,
Did love on both bestow !
But bliss too mighty long to last,
Where fortune proves a foe.

His sister, who like Envy form'd,
Like her in mischief joy'd,
To work them harm, with wicked skill
Each darker art employ'd.

The father too, a sordid man,
Who love nor pity knew,
Was all unfeeling as the rock
From whence his riches grew.

Long had he seen their mutual flame,
And seen it long unmov'd ;
Then with a father's frown, at last,
He sternly disapprov'd.

In Edwin's gentle heart a war
Of differing passions strove ;
His heart which durst not disobey,
Yet could not cease to love.

Deny'd her sight, he oft behind
The spreading hawthorn crept,
To snatch a glance, to mark the spot
Where Emma walk'd and wept.

Oft too in Stanemore's wintry waste,
Beneath the moonlight shade,
In sighs to pour his soften'd soul,
The midnight mourner stray'd.

His cheeks, where love with beauty glow'd,
A deadly pale o'ercast ;
So fades the fresh rose in it's prime,
Before the northern blast.

The parents now, with late remorse,
Hung o'er his dying bed,
And weary'd heav'n with fruitless pray'rs,
And fruitless sorrows shed.

'Tis past, he cry'd ; but, if your souls
Sweet mercy yet can move,

Let these dim eyes once more behold
What they must ever love.

She came ; his cold hand softly touch'd,
And bath'd with many a tear ;
Fast falling o'er the primrose pale
So morning dews appear.

But oh ! his sister's jealous care
(A cruel sister she !)
Forbade what Emma came to say—
My Edwin, live for me.

Now homeward as she hopeless went,
The church-yard path along,
The blast blew cold, the dark owl scream'd
Her lover's fun'ral song.

Amid the falling gloom of night,
Her startling fancy found
In ev'ry bush his hovering shade,
His groan in every sound.

Alone, appall'd, thus had she pass'd
The visionary vale,
When lo ! the death-bell smote her ear,
Sad sounding in the gale.

Just then she reach'd, with trembling steps,
Her aged mother's door ;
He's gone, she cry'd, and I shall see
That angel face no more.

I feel, I feel this breaking heart
Beat high against my side !
From her white arm down sunk her head,
She shiver'd, sigh'd, and died.

SONG 1063.

Sung at VAUXHALL.

AH! why should love, with tyrant sway,
Oppress each youthful heart ;
Must all his rigid laws obey,
And feel his pointed dart!

On reason's aid in vain we call,
To break the slavish chain ;
The potent god disdains it all,
And triumphs in our pain.

SONG 1064.

Sung in *Cymon*.

IF you make it your plan,
To love but one man,
By one you are surely betray'd:
Shou'd he prove untrue,
Oh! what can you do ?
Alas! you must die an old maid.
And you too must die an old maid.

Wou'd you ne'er take a sup,
But out of one cup,
And it proves brittle ware, you can't trust
If down it shou'd tip,
Or thro' your hands slip,
O how wou'd you then quench your thirst.

If your palate to hit,
You chuse but one bit,
And that dainty tit-bit should not keep:
Then reftlefs you lie,
Pout, whimper and cry,
And go without fupper to fleep.

As your fhepherds have chofe
Two ftrings to their bows,
Shall one for each female fuffice?
Take two, three or four,
Like me take a fcore,
And then you'll be merry and wife.

SONG 1065.

THE BEE.

Written by Mr. Nicholls.

SEE, Phillidel, that bufy bee,
How fwift fhe fends from tree to tree,
To kifs the fwe teft flow'r!
Thus all the day fhe loves to roam,
At eve fhe feeks her ruftick home,
And hives a precious ftore.

'Gainft hoary winter binds the green,
When not a bud or bloffom's feen
To tempt her vagrant wing;
Contented with her precious ftore
She dwells, nor feeks the meadows more
Till Flora gives the fpring.

Not fo the drone; in funny haunts
He juft fupplies his prefent wants,
Unmindful of the hour
When black December's chilling air
Shall mock his timely want of care,
And dumb each vital pow'r.

E'en fo the youth, who thoughlefs throws
Away what Providence beftows,
Soon feels the hand of need;
Whilft thofe who carefully increafe,
Find, like the bee, in winter peace,
And pleafures fair fucceed.

SONG 1066.

THE NUN.

SURE a lafs in her bloom, at the age of nine-
teen,
Was ne'er fo diftrefs'd as of late I have been;
I know not, I vow, any harm I have done,
But my mother oft tells me fhe'll have me a
nun.

Don't you think it a pity, a girl fuch as I
Should be fentenc'd to pray, and to faft, and to
cry?
With ways fo devout I'm not like to be won,
And my heart loves a frolic too well for a nun.

To hear the men flatter, and promife and fwear,
Is a thoufand times better to me, I declare;
I can keep myfelf chafte, nor by wiles be un-
done:
Nay, befides, I'm too handfome, I think, for
a nun.

Not to love, nor be lov'd, oh! I never can bear,
Nor yield to be fent to—one cannot tell where;
To live or to die, in this cafe, were all one;
Nay, I fooner would die than be reckon'd a nun.

Perhaps, but to teize me fhe threatens me fo,
I'm fure were fhe me, fhe would ftoutly fay, No;
But if fhe's in earneft, I from her will run,
And be marry'd in fpite, that I mayn't be a nun.

SONG 1067.

WHEN firft I faw the graceful maid,
Ah! me, what meant my throbbing breaft;
Say, foft confufion, art thou love!
If love thou art, then farewel reft.

With gentle fmiles affwage the pain
Thefe gentle fmiles did firft create;
And though you may not love again,
In pity, ah! forbear to hate.

SONG 1068.

WINTER; AN ODE.

Written by Mr. Nicholls.

NOW doth bleak quarter rudely blow,
And clad in fable, fring'd with fnow,
Hoary-headed winter's come:
To pluck the rofes from the cheek,
To chap the fkin before fo fleek;
Ev'ry pliant joint to numb.

Now round the embers goffips darn,
The thatcher blithe, in well-thatch'd barn,
Whiftles to his flying flail;
Whilft Robin Red-breaft, perch'd on high,
Shelter'd from the frowning fky,
Sweetly blends his merry tale.

Now fkulking under hedges low,
With nofe and knuckles tipp'd with blue,
Lazy Dicken feeks his cows;
Whimpering for his aching toes,
Blowing fingers almoft froze,
Wifhing moft with Doll to houfe.

Whilft the alert and active fwain,
Exercifing every vein,
Skims the flide with open breaft,
His fav'rite lafs, from brake below,
Refcends the ball of filver fnow;
Jeering him fhe loves the beft.

And now beneath the houfe-leek'd thatch,
Hard tugging at her frozen latch,
Goody Goffip fhiv'ring ftands;
As o'er the ftile brifk Colin comes,
She hails the fwain with toothlefs gums,
Begging him to lend his hands.

Now in yonder clay-thatch'd cell,
Lift'ning to the difmal knell,
Poverty her head reclines;
A pallid languor wreathes her brow,
To rear her form fhe knows not how;
There fhe fits, and fadly pines.

Go, fons of wealth, while winter reigns,
Search through the hamlet, fearch the plains;

Where you find a scene of woe,
Soon a bounteous aid impart,
Re-animate the drooping heart;
   'Tis more than's mortal to beftow.

Do this, and peace fhall fure fucceed,
Reflection fhall approve the deed;
   You'll ne'er mifs the kind fupply.
How can the fordid wretch conceive,
Heaven will e'er his wants relieve
   Who can let his fellow die.

SONG 1069.

SWEET CAROLS OF LOVE.

Sung at VAUXHALL.

NOW fummer approaches dull winter recedes,
   Primrofes and vi'lets adorn ev'ry hill,
The lads and the laffes trip o'er the green meads,
   Or fit by meanders flow-murmuring rill.
While the upland, the lowland, the woodland,
   the grove,
And valley, re-echo—fweet carols of love.

While Colin with Phillis repair to the bow'r,
   To exchange a fweet kifs or plight a fond vow,
Gay Florimel gathers each odorous flow'r,
   To deck with a chaplet her fwain's youthful
   brow.

Fair Daphne at morn bids adieu to her cot,
   And feeks the cool grot or fecluded alcove;
Her Damon fhe greets at the critical fpot;
   His heart leaps for joy at the fight of his love.

When Phœbus forfakes this low region of clay,
   And finks in foft rapture on Thetis' fair breaft,
For the wearifome labour of rigorous day
   Balmy fleep has an adequate portion of reft.

SONG 1070.

TO THE NIGHTINGALE.

Written by Mr. NICHOLLS.

SAY, Philomela, fweet bird fay,
   Why 'tis you fhun the folar ray ?
Has the pale emprefs of the night
Such a rare ftore of calm delight,
That you from melody refrain
Till fhe leads up her ftarry train :
Then to her filver beams you fing
The fweeteft cadence of the fpring.

Ah! lovely warbler, quit the fhade
For penfive melancholy made :
Come whilft the meads are frefh and gay,
From lift'ning morn till fitting day,
And with thy moft melodious ftrains,
Make light the labour of the fwains;
So may the thorn, that's in thy neft,
Ne'er rankle in thy tender breaft !

When the dull fhades of night are fled,
And Phœbus fhews his radiant head,
Amidft the fweets of op'ning flow'rs,
From hills, from vales, from woods and bow'rs;

All but the moping owl, and thee,
Climb the vaft building, and the tree,
Stretch wide their throats, and warble fweet,
To hail the genial god of heat.

Come! with the gayeft choir unite,
And greet with them the fource of light!
For when thou firft effay'd thy wing,
He led thee forth to cooling fpring.
Matur'd the worm thou lov'ft fo well,
And fpread the bloffoms round thy cell :
Made thick the fhades, you haunt in June,
To fhun the fultry beams of noon.

Come, and with thy varied fong
Make glad my heart the whole day long.
O come! and, of the ruftick throng,
Should one effay to do thee wrong,
May he ne'er know that peace of mind
The fons of tendernefs can find :
May fairy elves, and dapper fprights,
Make fad his noon-day and his nights.

Thus fings a fwain who fcorns the throng!
Who'd do nor neft, nor neftlings wrong ;
Whofe will would never do offence
To helplefs, artlefs innocence ;
But would with all his might divert
The hand uplift to do thee hurt.
Then quickly to my vale defcend,
And entertain me as your friend !

SONG 1071.

FLORIZEL.

Sung at VAUXHALL.

WHEN larks forfake the flow'ry plain,
   And love's fweet numbers fwell ;
My voice fhall join their morning ftrain,
   In praife of Florizel.

Where woodbines twift their fragrant fhade,
   And noontide beams repel;
I'll reft me on the tufted mead,
   And fing of Florizel.

When moon-beams dance among the boughs,
   That lodge fweet Philomel,
I'll pour with her my tuneful vows,
   And fing of Florizel.

Were mine, ye great, your envy'd lot,
   In gilded courts to dwell ;
I'd leave them for a lonely cot,
   With love and Florizel.

SONG 1072.

Written by Mr. HAMILTON.

AH! the fhepherd's mournful fate!
   When doom'd to love, and doom'd to lan-
   guifh,
To bear the fcornful fair-one's hate,
   Nor dare difclofe his anguifh.
Yet eager looks, and dying fighs,
   My fecret foul difcover,
While rapture trembling thro' my eyes
   Reveals how much I love her.

The tender glance, the redd'ning cheek,
O'erfpread with rifing blufhes,
A thoufand various ways they fpeak
A thoufand various wifhes.

For oh! that form fo heavenly fair,
Thofe languid eyes fo fweetly fmiling!
That artlefs blufh, and modeft air,
So artfully beguiling!
Thy every look, and every grace
So charms whene'er I view thee,
Till death o'ertake me in the chace
Still will my hopes purfue thee:
Then when my tedious hours are paft
Be this laft bleffing given,
Low at thy feet to breath my laft,
And die in fight of heaven.

SONG 1073.

SURE YOU WILL NOT LEAVE ME.

Sung at VAUXHALL.

WHEN firft you woo'd me to comply,
And taught my heart to flutter,
You faid you ne'er wou'd from me fly,
As plain as tongue could utter;
That you'd be ev'ry thing that's dear,
Of joy you'd not bereave me;
I'd all to hope, and nought to fear,
Then fure you will not leave me.

Were I fo wickedly inclin'd,
I might abufe the leifure;
I know who wou'd be fond and kind,
And think attendance pleafure:
But I to honour will be true,
And never once deceive ye;
What's juft to plighted love I'll do,
Then fure you will not leave me.

Say, fay the word you will not go,
Nor cruel let me find ye,
With you all rifk and toil I'll know,
But cannot ftay behind ye.
ho' left on Tweed's or Thames' fmooth fide,
Your abfence fure would grieve me;
O what a pain it is to chide!
Sure, fure you will not leave me.

SONG 1074.

NANCY WALL.

Written by Mr. GIFFARD.

Sung at VAUXHALL.

HASTE, heavenly nine, ye mufes hafte,
At doating Strephon's call,
And blefs him with your fweeteft tafte,
To fing of Nancy Wall:
Tho' in her faultlefs form you'll find
The namelefs graces all,
Yet greater beauties deck the mind
Of lovely Nancy Wall.

How elegantly does fhe move
Along this myftic ball.

And all is grace, and all is love
In blooming Nancy Wall.
Sublimely fweet, whene'er fhe fings,
The melting accents fall;
And lift'ning Cupids clap their wings,
Applauding Nancy Wall.

A foul fo bright, a form fo fair,
For adoration call;
And reafon bids us worfhip there,
And points to Nancy Wall:
Whilft thus divine, my fears how great!
My hope how very fmall!
If he alone is bleft by fate,
Who merits Nancy Wall.

SONG 1075.

ANACREONTIC.

Written by Mr. MAVOR.

WHILE I figh'd with idle care,
For a jilting, cruel fair,
Thracia's god forbade to pine,
And prefcrib'd his rofy wine.

Quick tormenting Cupid flew,
And to love! bade adieu:
Bacchus came with jolly face,
And fupply'd his vacant place.

Ev'ry joy on earth was mine,
Social friends, and mirth and wine;
Then I fwore by Stygian Jove,
Ne'er to tafte the cares of love.

But how frail the vow that dies
At a glance of beauty's eyes!
Chloe taught me wine was vain,
And I turn'd to love again.

SONG 1076.

POLITICIANS may prate
On affairs of the ftate,
But our voices we'll join,
In the praife of good wine,
So my friends pufh the bottle about.

'Tis this makes us bold,
And will keep out the cold,
Such virtues in claret combine;
While the flafk is in view,
Our joys are ftill new,
And our cares are all drown'd in good wine.

That fellow's an afs,
Who would fneak from his glafs,
For fome infolent Chloe to whine;
Let him come no more here,
For by Bacchus I fwear,
He's not worthy to tafte of our wine.

The nectar of old,
That fo much is extoll'd,

Which the deities drink when they dine;
Let none hence deceive ye,
For if you'll believe me,
Their nectar's no more than good wine.

Those heroes so stout,
Who our enemies rout,
And to glory so much do incline;
Was the flask out of fight,
They no longer could fight,
So the praise is all due to good wine.

The poet, whose wit
Each humour can hit,
Who with rapture makes flow ev'ry line;
What tho' he may chuse
Other names for his muse,
Yet the name of the muse is good wine.

The priest so devout,
His text to help out,
Seeks relief in his cardinal fine;
After taking a sup
From a full-flowing cup,
Cries, There's nothing on earth like good wine.

To sum up my song,
That you mayn't think it long,
Tho' the subject, you'll own, is divine;
From the east to the west,
By all folks 'tis confest,
That there's nothing can equal good wine.

SONG 1077.

THE BRAES OF YARROW.

Sung at VAUXHALL.

THE sun just glancing thro' the trees
Gave light and joy to ilka grove,
And pleasure in each southern breeze,
Awaken'd hope and slumb'ring love.
When Jenny sung with hearty glee
To charm her winsome marrow,
My bonny laddie gang with me,
We'll o'er the braes of Yarrow.

Young Sandy was the blithest swain,
That ever pip'd on broomy brae:
No lass cou'd ken him free fra pain,
So graceful, kind, so fair and gay.
And Jenny sung, &c.

He kiss'd and lov'd the bonny maid,
Her sparkling een had won his heart;
No lass the youth had e'er betray'd,
No fears had she, the lad no art.
And still she sung, &c.

SONG 1078.

Written by the Rev. Dr. DE LA COUR.

Occasioned by seeing a Lady in an opposite
Window.

WHILST on forbidden fruit I gaze,
And look my heart away;
Behold my star of Venus blaze,
And rise upon the day:

Fair as the purple-blushing hours,
That paint the morning eye;
Or cheek of evening after-show'rs,
That flush the western sky.

I send a sigh with ev'ry glance,
And drop a softer tear;
Hard fate, no farther to advance,
And yet to be so near:
So Moses, from fair Pysga's height,
The land of Canaan ey'd;
Survey'd the region of delight,
He saw, came down, and dy'd.

SONG 1079.

JEMMY DAWSON.

Written by Mr. SHENSTONE.

COME listen to my mournful tale,
Ye tender hearts and lovers dear;
Nor will you scorn to heave a sigh,
Nor need you blush to shed a tear.

And thou, dear Kitty, peerless maid,
Do thou a pensive ear incline;
For thou canst weep at every woe;
And pity every plaint—but mine.

Young Dawson was a gallant boy,
A brighter never trod the plain;
And well he lov'd one charming maid,
And dearly was he lov'd again.

One tender maid, she lov'd him dear,
Of gentle blood the damsel came;
And faultless was her beauteous form,
And spotless was her virgin fame.

But cause on party's hateful strife,
That led the favour'd youth astray!
The day the rebel clans appear'd;
O, had he never seen that day!

Their colours and their sash he wore,
And in the fatal dress was found;
And now he must that death endure,
Which gives the brave the keenest wound.

How pale was then his true-love's cheek
When Jemmy's sentence reach'd her ear!
For never yet did Alpine snows
So pale, or yet so chill appear.

With fault'ring voice, she weeping said,
Oh, Dawson, monarch of my heart;
Think not thy death shall end our loves,
For thou and I will never part.

Yet might sweet mercy find a place,
And bring relief to Jemmy's woes;
O George, without a pray'r for thee,
My oraisons should never close.

The gracious prince that gave him life,
Would crown a never-dying flame;
And ev'ry tender babe I bore
Should learn to lisp the giver's name.

But tho' he should be dragg'd in scorn
To yonder ignominious tree;

He shall not want one constant friend
To share the cruel fate's decree.

O then her mourning-coach was call'd,
The sledge mov'd slowly on before ;
Tho' borne in a triumphal car,
She had not lov'd her fav'rite more.

She follow'd him, prepar'd to view
The terrible behests of law ;
And the last scene of Jemmy's woe,
With calm and stedfast eye she saw.

Distorted was that blooming face,
Which she had fondly lov'd so long ;
And stilled was that tuneful breath,
Which in her praise had sweetly sung ;

And sever'd was that beauteous neck,
Round which her arms had fondly clns'd ;
And mangled was that beauteous breast,
On which her love-sick head repos'd :

And ravish'd was that constant heart,
She did to ev'ry heart prefer ;
For though it could it's king forget.
'Twas true and loyal still to her.

Amid those unrelenting flames
She bore this constant heart to see ;
But when 'twas moulder'd into dust,
Yet, yet, she cry'd, I follow thee.

My death, my death alone can shew
The pure, the lasting love I bore ;
Accept, O heaven ! of woes like ours,
And let us, let us weep no more.

The dismal scene was o'er and past,
The lover's mournful hearse retir'd ;
The maid drew back her languid head,
And sighing forth his name, expir'd.

Tho' justice ever must prevail,
The tear my Kitty sheds is due ;
For seldom shall she hear a tale
So sad, so tender, yet so true.

SONG 1080.
THE LANDSCAPE.
Written by Mr. SHENSTONE.

HOW pleas'd within my native bowers
Erewhile I pass'd the day !
Was ever scene so deck'd with flowers ?
Were ever flowers so gay ?

How sweetly smil'd the hill, the vale,
And all the landscape round !
The river gliding down the dale,
The hill with beeches crown'd !

But now, when urg'd by tender woes
I speed to meet my dear,
That hill and stream my zeal oppose,
And check my fond career.

No more, since Daphne was my theme,
Their wonted charms I see :

Their verdant hill, and silver stream,
Divide my love and me.

SONG 1081.
THE KNIGHT AND SHEPHERD'S DAUGH-
TER; AN OLD BALLAD.

THERE was a shepherd's daughter
Came tripping on the way ;
And there by chance a knight she met,
Which caused her to stay.

Good morrow to you, beauteous maid,
These words pronounced he :
O I shall die this day, he said,
If I've not my will of thee.

The Lord forbid, the maid reply'd,
That you should wax so wode !
But for all that she could do or say,
He would not be withstood.

Sith you have had your will of me,
And put me to open shame ;
Now, if you are a courteous knight,
Tell me what is your name ?

Some do call me Jack, sweet-heart,
And some do call me Jill ;
But when I come to the king's fair court
They call me Wilful Will.

He set his foot into the stirrup,
And away then he did ride ;
She tuckt her girdle about her middle,
And ran close by his side.

But when she came to the broad water,
She set her breast and swam ;
And when she was got out again,
She took to her heels and ran.

He never was the courteous knight,
To say, Fair maid, will ye ride ?
And she was ever too loving a maid,
To say, Sir Knight abide.

When she came to the king's fair court,
She knocked at the ring ;
So ready was the king himself
To let this fair maid in.

Now Christ you save, my gracious liege,
Now Christ you save and see,
You have a knight within your court
This day hath robbed me.

What hath he robbed thee of, sweet-heart ?
Of purple or of pall ?
Or hath he took thy gay gold-ring
From off thy finger small ?

He hath not robbed me, my liege,
Of purple nor of pall :
But he hath got my maidenhead,
Which grieves me worst of all.

Now if he be a batchelor,
His body I'll give to thee ;
But if he be a married man,
High hanged he shall be.

He called down his merry men all,
By one, by two, by three;
Sir William ufed to be the firft,
But now the laft came he.

He brought her down full forty pound,
Tied up within a glove :
Fair maid, I'll give the fame to thee ;
Go, feek thee another love.

O I'll have none of your gold, fhe faid,
Nor I'll have none of your fee;
But your fair body I muft have
The king hath granted me.

Sir William ran and fetched her then
Five hundred pounds in gold,
Saying, Fair maid, take this to thee,
Thy fault will ne'er be told.

Tis not thy gold that fhall me tempt,
Thefe words then anfwered fhe,
But your own body I muft have,
The king hath granted me.

Would I had drank the water clear,
When I did drink the wine,
Rather than any fhepherd's brat
Should be a lady of mine !

Would I had drank the puddle foul,
When I did drink the ale,
Rather than ever a fhepherd's brat
Should tell me fuch a tale !

A fhepherd's brat even as I was,
You might have let me be,
I never had come to the king's fair court,
To crave any love of thee.

He fet her on a milk-white fteed,
And himfelf upon a grey ;
He hung a bugle about his neck,
And fo they rode away.

But when they came unto the place,
Where marriage rites were done,
She prov'd herfelf a duke's daughter,
And he but a fquire's fon.

Now marry me, or not, Sir Knight,
Your pleafure fhall be free ;
If you make me lady of one good town,
I'll make you lord of three.

Ah ! curfed be the gold, he faid,
If thou hadft not been true,
I fhould have forfaken my fweet love,
And have changed her for a new.

And now their hearts being linked faft,
They joined hand in hanc :
Thus he had both purfe, and perfon too,
And all at his command.

SONG 1082.

FLY care to the winds, thus I blow thee away,
I'll drown thee in wine if thou dar ft here
to ftay,
With bumpers of claret my fpirits I'll raife,
I'll laugh and I'll fing all the reft of my days.

God Bacchus this moment adopts me his fon
And infpir'd, my breaft glows with tranfports
unknown.
The fparkling liquor new vigour fupplies,
And makes the nymph kind who before was
too wife.
Then dull fober mortals be happy as me,
Two bottles of claret will make us agree,
Will open your eyes to fee Phillis's charms,
And her coynefs wafh'd down, fhe'll fly to your
arm.

SONG 1083.

ARISE, arife, great dead, for arms renown'd,
Rife from your urns, and fave your dying
ftory ;
Your deeds will be in dark oblivion drown'd,
For mighty William feizes all your glory.

Aga'n the Britifh trumpet founds,
Again Britannia bleeds ;
To glorious death, or comely wounds,
Her godlike monarch leads.

Pay us, kind fate, the debt you owe,
Celeftial minds from clay untie ;
Let coward fpirits dwell below,
And only give the brave to die.

SONG 1084.

Written by MATTHEW PRIOR.

YES, faireft proof of beauty's power,
Dear idol of my panting heart ;
Nature points this my fatal hour;
And I have liv'd ; and we muft part.

While now I take my laft adieu,
Heave thou no figh, nor fhed a tear ;
Left yet my half-clos'd eye may view
On earth an object worth it's care.

From jealoufy's tormenting ftrife
For ever be thy bofom freed ;
That nothing may difturb thy life,
Content I haften to the dead.

Yet when fome better-fated youth
Shall with his amorous parley move thee,
Reflect one moment on his truth
Who dying thus perfifts to love thee.

SONG 1085.

Written by MATTHEW PRIOR.

IN vain you tell your parting lover
You wifh fair winds may waft him over:
Alas ! what winds can happy prove,
That bear me far from what I love ?
Alas ! what dangers on the main
Can equal thofe which I fuftain
From flighted vows and cold difdain ?

Be gentle, and in pity chufe
To wifh the wildeft tempefts loofe ;

That, thrown again upon the coaft
Where firft my fhipwreck'd heart was loft,
I may once more repeat my pain,
Once more in dying notes complain
Of flighted vows and cold difdain.

SONG 1086.

THE CAUTION.

PHILIRA's charms poor Damon took;
  How eager he for billing!
When, lo! the Nymph the fwain forfook,
  To fhew her pow'r of killing:
In either eye fhe fheath'd a dart;
  He felt it, never doubt him:
Odzooks! a man were through the heart,
  Ere he cou'd look about him.

But mark the end, with fcythe fo fharp
  Time o'er the forehead ftruck her,
And all her charms began to warp;
  Then fhe was in a pucker:
She then began to rave and curfe,
  Her time fhe pafs'd no better;
Yet ftill had hopes, ere bad grew worfe,
  Some comely fwain might get her.

Philira, ev'ry lad fhe meets,
  Now makes an am'rous trial;
But each with fcorn her warmnefs treats;
  Each frowns in cold denial.
Coquettes, take warning; change your tune,
  This woeful cafe remember:
The bedfellow you flight in June,
  You'll wifh for in December.

SONG 1087.

Written by Mrs. BARBAULD.

COME here, fond youth, whoe'er thou be
  That boafts to love as well as me,
And if thy breaft have felt fo wide a wound,
  Come hither and thy flame approve;
  I'll teach thee what it is to love,
And by what marks true paffion may be found.

It is to be all bath'd in tears,
To live upon a fmile for years,
To lie whole ages at a beauty's feet;
  To kneel, to languifh, and implore,
  And ftill tho' fhe difdain, adore;
It is to do all this, and think thy fuff'rings fweet.

It is to gaze upon her eyes
With eager joy and fond furprize,
Yet temper'd with fuch chafte and awful fear
  As wretches feel who wait their doom;
  Nor muft one ruder thought prefume,
Tho' but in whifpers breath'd, to meet her ear.

It is to hope, tho' hope were loft,
Tho' heaven and earth thy paffion croft;
Tho' fhe were bright as fainted queens above,
  And thou the leaft and meaneft fwain
  That folds his flock upon the plain,
Yet if thou dar'ft not hope, thou doft not love.

It is to quench thy joy in tears,
To nurfe ftrange doubts and groundlefs fears;
If pangs of jealoufy thou haft not prov'd,
  Tho' fhe were fonder and more true
  Than any nymph old poets drew,
O never dream again that thou haft lov'd.

If when the darling maid is gone,
Thou doft not feek to be alone,
Wrapt in a pleafing trance of tender woe;
  And mufe, and fold thy languid arms,
  Feeding thy fancy on her charms,
Thou doft not love, for love is nourifh'd fo.

If any hopes thy bofom fhare,
But thofe which love has planted there,
Or any cares but his thy breaft enthrall,
  Thou never yet his power haft known;
  Love fits on a defpotic throne,
And reigns a tyrant, if he reigns at all.

Now if thou art fo loft a thing,
Here all thy tender forrows bring,
And prove whofe patience longeft can endure;
  We'll ftrive whofe fancy fhall be loft
  In dreams of fondeft paffion moft;
For if thou thus haft lov'd, oh! never hope a
  cure.

SONG 1088.

Sung at VAUXHALL.

I Like the man whofe foaring foul
  Is gen'rous and refin'd,
Whofe paffions act beneath controul,
  With love and honour join'd.
The oak, by woodbines on the plain,
  Encompafs'd and carefs'd,
Is not more fteadfaft in it's reign,
  Nor is more fweetly drefs'd.

The frothy fons of vice and fhow,
  Like fhadows, and like noife,
Have nothing in themfelves, we know,
  That fober fenfe enjoys;
But pure and conftant love endears,
  And feafts both ear and fight,
While ev'ry thing that virtue fears
  Can give no true delight.

SONG 1089.

Written by Mrs. BARBAULD.

IF ever thou didft joy to bind
  Two hearts in equal paffion joind,
O fun of Venus! hear me now,
And bid Florella blefs my vow.

If any blifs referv'd for me
Thou in the leaves of fate fhould'ft fee,
If any white propitious hour,
Pregnant with hoarded joys in ftore;

Now, now the mighty treafure give,
In her for whom alone I live;
In fterling love pay all the fum,
And I'll abfolve the fates to come.

In all the pride of full-blown charms
Yield her, relenting, to my arms;
Her bosom touch with soft desires,
And let her feel what she inspires.

But, Cupid, if thine aid be vain
The dear reluctant maid to gain,
If still with cold averted eyes
She dash my hopes, and scorn my sighs;

O grant ('tis all I ask of thee)
That I no more may change than she:
But still with duteous zeal love on,
When ev'ry gleam of hope is gone.

Leave me then alone to languish,
Think not time can heal my anguish,
Pity the woes which I endure,
But never, never grant a cure.

S O N G   1090.

SEE, the god of day appearing,
　Gilds yon eastern azure skies:
See, the flow'rs their heads are rearing,
　And from drowzy slumbers rise.

But in hopeless love's no dawning
　Of contentment's peaceful light:
Vain t'expect the chearful morning;
　All is one continued night.

'S O N G   1091.

THE EARLY HORN.

Sung at SADLER'S WELLS.

WITH early horn salute the morn
　That gilds this charming place;
With chearful cries bid echo rise,
And join the jovial chace.
　The vocal hills around,
　　The waving woods,
　　The chrystal floods,
All, all return th'enliv'ning sound.

S O N G   1092.

Sung at VAUXHALL.

YE fair, who shine thro' Britain's isle,
　And triumph o'er the heart;
Be once attentive for a while
　To what I now impart.
Would you obtain the youth you love,
The precepts of a friend approve,
　And learn the way to keep him.

As soon as Nature had decreed
　The bloom of eighteen years,
And Isabel from school is freed,
　Then beauty's force appears:

The youthful blood begins to flow;
She hopes for man, and longs to know
　The surest way to keep him.

When first the pleasing pain is felt
　Within the lover's breast;
And you by strange persuasion melt,
　Each wishing to be blest:
Be not too bold, nor yet too coy,
With prudence lure the happy boy,
　And that's the way to keep him.

At court, at ball, at park, or play,
　Assume a modest pride;
And, left your tongue your mind betray,
　In fewer words confide:
The maid, who thinks to gain a mate
By giddy chat, will find, too late,
　That's not the way to keep him.

In dressing ne'er the hours kill,
　That bane to all the sex;
Nor let the arts of dear spadille
　Your innocence perplex:
Be always decent as a bride;
By virtuous rules your reason guide;
　For that's the way to keep him.

But when the nuptial knot is fast,
　And both it's blessings share,
To make those joys for ever last,
　Of jealousy beware;
His love with kind compliance meet,
Let constancy the work complete,
　And you'll be sure to keep him.

S O N G   1093.

A HUNTING CANTATA.

Sung at VAUXHALL.

RECITATIVE.

HARK, the horn calls away;
　Come the grave, come the gay;
Wake to music that wakens the skies,
Quit the bondage of sloth, and arise.

AIR.

From the East breaks the morn,
　See the sun-beams adorn
The wild heath, and the mountains so high;
　Shrilly opes the staunch hound,
　The steed neighs to the sound,
And the floods and the vallies reply.

Our forefathers so good
　Prov'd their greatness of blood,
By encount'ring the hart and the boar;
　Ruddy health bloom'd the face,
　Age and youth urg'd the chace,
And taught woodlands and forests to roar.

Hence, of noble descent,
　Hills and wilds we frequent,
Where the bosom of nature's reveal'd;
　Though in life's busy day,
　Man of man makes a prey,
Still let ours be the prey of the field.

Mr LOWE, at SADLERS WELLS.

With early Horn salute the Morn

Song 1091

Published by J. Bow Dec 1.1778.

With the chace in full fight,
Gods! how great the delight!
How our moral fenfations refine!
Where is care, where is fear?
Like the winds, in the rear;
And the man's loft in fomething divine.

Now to horfe, my brave boys;
Lo! each pants for the joys
That anon fhall enliven the whole:
Then at eve we'll difmount,
Toils and pleafures recount,
And renew the chace over the bowl.

SONG 1094.

THE GENEROUS DISTRESS.

BLOW, ye bleak winds, around my head,
    And foothe my heart-corroding care,
Flafh round my brows, ye lightnings red,
    And blaft the laurels planted there!
But may the maid, where'er fhe be,
Think not of my diftrefs nor me.

May all the traces of our love
    Be ever blotted from her mind;
May from her breaft my vows remove,
    And no remembrance leave behind!
But may the maid, &c.

Oh! may I ne'er behold her more,
    For fhe has robb'd my foul of reft,
Wifdom's affiftance is too poor
    To calm the tempeft in my breaft!
But may the maid, &c.

Come, death! O come, thou friendly fleep,
    And with my forrows lay me low;
And fhould the gent'e virgin weep,
    Nor fharp, nor lafting be her woe:
But may fhe think, where'er fhe be,
No more of my diftrefs nor me.

SONG 1095.

NOW the happy knot is ty'd,
    Betfey is my charming bride;
Ring the bells, and fill the bowl,
Revel all without controul.
Who fo fair as lovely Bet!
Who fo bleft as Colinet!

Now adieu to maiden arts,
Angling for unguarded hearts;
Welcome Hymen's lafting joys,
Lifping, wanton, girls and boys:
Girls as fair as lovely Bet,
Boys as fweet as Colinet.

Tho' ripe fheaves of yellow corn
Now my plenteous barn adorn;
Tho' I've deck'd my myrtle-bow'rs,
With the faireft, fweeteft flow'rs:
Riper, fairer, fweeter yet,
Are the charms of lovely Bet.

Tho' on Sundays I was feen,
Drefs'd like any May-day queen;

Tho' fix fweethearts daily ftrove
To deferve thy Betfey's love:
Them I quit without regret,
All my joy's in Colinet.

Strike up, then, the ruftic lay,
Crown with fports our bridal day;
May each lad a miftrefs find,
Like my Betfey, fair and kind,
And each lafs a hufband get,
Fond and true as Colinet.

Ring the bells, and fill the bowl,
Revel all without controul.
May the fun ne'er rife or fet,
But with joy to happy Bet,
And her faithful Colinet.

SONG 1096.

ON THE ABSENCE OF MAY.

Written by Mr. CUNNINGHAM.

THE rooks in the neighb'ring grove
    For fhelter cry all the long day;
Their huts, in the branches above,
    Are cover'd no longer by May.
The birds that fo chearfully fung,
    Are filent, or plaintive each tone,
And as they chirp low to their young,
    The want of their goddefs bemoan.

No daifies on carpets of green,
    O'er nature's cold bofom are fpread;
Not a fweet-brier fprig can be feen
    To furnifh frefh wreaths for my head:
Some flow'rs indeed may be found,
    But thefe neither blooming nor gay;
The faireft ftill fleep in the ground,
    And wait for the coming of May.

December perhaps has purloin'd
    Her rich, though fantaftical gear,
With envy the month's may have join'd,
    And joftled her out of the year.
Some fhepherds, 'tis true, may repine
    To fee their lov'd gardens undreft,
But I, while my Phillida's mine,
    Shall always have May in my breaft.

SONG 1097.

PERHAPS it is not love, faid I,
    That melts my foul when Flavia's nigh:
Where wit and fenfe like her's agree,
One may be pleas'd, and yet be free.

The beauties of her polifh'd mind,
It needs no lover's eye to find;
The hermit freezing in his cell
Might wifh the gentle Flavia well.

It is not love—averfe to bear
The fervile chain that lovers wear;
Let, let me all my fears remove,
My doubts difpel—it is not love—

Oh! when did wit fo brightly fhine
In any form lefs fair than thine?

It is—it is love's fubtle fire,
And under friendfhip lurks defire.

SONG 1098.

Written by Mr. SHENSTONE.

YE gentle nymphs and generous dames,
   That rule o'er every Britifh mind ;
Be fure you foothe their amorous flames,
   Be fure your laws are not unkind.

For hard it is to wear their bloom
   In unremitting fighs away ;
To mourn the night's oppreffive gloom,
   And faintly blefs the rifing day.

And cruel 'twere a free-born fwain,
   A Britifh youth fhould vainly moan ;
Who fcornful of a tyrant's chain,
   Submits to yours, and yours alone.

No pointed fpear, nor links of fteel,
   Could e'er thofe gallant minds fubue,
Who beauty's wounds with pleafure feel,
   And boaft the fetters wrought by you.

SONG 1099.

Written by Mr. SHENSTONE.

ON every tree, in every plain,
   I trace the jovial fpring in vain !
A fickly languor veils mine eyes,
And faft my waning vigour flies.

Nor flow'ry plain, nor budding tree,
   That fmile on others, fmile on me ;
Mine eyes from death fhall court repofe,
   Nor fhed a tear before they clofe.

What blifs to me can feafons bring !
   Or, what the needlefs pride of fpring !
The cyprefs bough, that fuits the bier,
   Retains it's verdure all the year.

'Tis true, my vine fo frefh and fair,
   Might claim awhile my wonted care ;
My rural ftore fome pleafure yield ;
   So white a flock, fo green a field !

My friends, that each in kindnefs vie,
   Might well expect one parting figh ;
Might well demand one tender tear ;
   For when was Damon infincere ?

But ere I afk once more to view
   Yon fetting fun his race renew,
Inform me, fwains, my friends declare,
   Will pitying Delia join the prayer ?

SONG 1100.

THO' Chloe's out of fafhion,
   Can blufh and be fincere,
I'll toaft her in a bumper,
   If all the belles were here.

What tho' no di'monds fparkle
   Around her neck and waift ?

With ev'ry fhining virtue
   The lovely maid is grac'd.

In modeft, plain apparel,
   No patches, paint, nor airs ;
In debt alone to nature,
   An angel fhe appears.

From gay coquettes, high-finifh'd,
   My Chloe takes no rules ;
Nor envies them their conquefts,
   The hearts of all the fools.

Who wins her muft have merit,
   Such merit as her own ;
The graces all poffefling,
   Yet knows not fhe has one.

Then grant me, gracious heav'ns,
   The gifts you moft approve ;
And Chloe, charming Chloe,
   Will blefs me with her love.

SONG 1101.

Written by Mrs. BARBAULD.

AS near a weeping fpring reclin'd,
   The beauteous Araminta pin'd,
And mourn'd a falfe ungrateful youth ;
While dying echoes caught the found,
And fpread the foft complaints around
Of broken vows and alter'd truth.

An aged fhepherd heard her moan,
And thus in pity's kindeft tone
Addrefs'd the loft, defpairing maid ;
Ceafe, ceafe, unhappy fair, to grieve,
For founds, tho' fweet, can ne'er relieve
A breaking heart by love betray'd.

Why fhouldft thou wafte fuch precious fhowers,
That fall like dew on wither'd flowers
But dying paffion ne'er reftor'd ;
In beauty's empire is no mean,
And woman, either flave or queen,
Is quickly fcorn'd when not ador'd.

Thofe liquid pearls from either eye,
Which might an eaftern empire buy,
Unvalued here and fruitlefs fall ;
No art the feafon can renew
When love was young, and Damon true,
No tears a wandering heart recall.

Ceafe, ceafe to grieve, thy tears are vain,
Should thofe fair orbs in drops of rain
Vie with a weeping fouthern fky ;
For hearts o'ercome with love and grief
All nature yields but one relief ;
Die, haplefs Araminta, die.

SONG 1102.

THE FREE MASON'S GARLAND.

GOOD people, draw near,
   And the truth you fhall hear,
I fcorn to put any grimace on ;
   You've been bamm'd long enough,
With the d——d filly ftuff,
   Of a free and accepted mafon.

The dear brotherhood
(As they certainly fhould)
Their follies do put a good face on ;
Tho' 'tis nought but a gin,
To catch other fools in,
So fly is an accepted mafon.

With aprons before 'em,
For better decorum,
Of fecrets they talk, 'twou'd amaze one.
In aprons array'd
Of calves leather made,
True type——of an accepted mafon.

Their folly fo great is—
Rifum teneatis?
And their title to fuch they would blazon ;
That they'd trace from the flood,
Their rife, if they cou'd,
And make Noah——an accepted mafon.

If on houfe ne'er fo high,
A brother they fpy,
As his trowel he dext'roufly lays on,
He muft leave off his work,
And come down with a jerk,
At the fign of an accepted mafon.

They know this and that,
The devil knows what,
And themfelves they employ all their praife on:
But—this by the bye—
There's none that can lye
Like—a free and accepted mafon.

A brother one time
Being hang'd for fome crime,
All the brethren did ftupidly gaze on ;
They gave figns without end,
But—faft hung their friend—
Like a free and accepted mafon.

They tells us fine things,
How that lords, dukes, and kings,
Their myft'ries have put a good grace on ;
For their credit be't faid,
Many a fkip has been made
A free and accepted mafon.

From whence I conclude,
Tho't may feem fomewhat rude,
That no value their tribe we fhould place on ;
Since a fool, as we fee,
Of any degree.
May commence free and accepted mafon.

SONG 1103.

ASK me not how calmly I
All the cares of life defy ;
How I baffle human woes ;
Woman, woman, woman knows.

You may live and laugh, as I ;
You like me may cares defy ;
All the pangs that heart endures,
Woman, woman, woman cures.

Afk me not of empty toys,
Feats of arms, and drunken joys ;

I have pleafure more divine,
Woman, woman, woman's mine.

Raptures more than folly know,
More than fortune can beftow ;
Flowing bowls and conquer'd fields,
Woman, woman, woman yields.

Afk me not of woman's arts,
Broken vows and faithlefs hearts ;
Tell the wretch, who pines and grieves,
Woman, woman, woman lives.

All delights the heart can know,
More than folly can beftow ;
Wealth of worlds and crowns of kings,
Woman, woman, woman brings.

SONG 1104.

Written by Mr. SHENSTONE.

THE lovely Delia fmiles again !
That killing frown has left her brow :
Can fhe forgive my jealous pain,
And give me back my angry vow ?

Love is an April's doubtful day :
Awhile we fee the tempeft lour ?
Anon the radiant heav'ns furvey,
And quite forget the flitting fhow'r.

The flow'rs that hung their languid head,
Are burnifh'd by the tranfient rains ;
The vines their wonted tendrils fpread,
And double verdure gilds the plains.

The fprightly birds, that droop'd no lefs
Beneath the pow'r of rain and wind,
In every raptur'd note exprefs
The joy I feel—when thou art kind.

SONG 1105.

Sung at VAUXHALL.

MY days have been fo wondrous free,
The little birds that fly,
With carelefs eafe from tree to tree,
Were but as bleft as I.
Afk gliding waters, if a tear
Of mine increas'd their ftream ;
Or afk the gentle gales, if e'er
I lent a figh to them.

But now my former days retire,
And I'm by beauty caught ;
The tender chains of foft defire
Are fix'd upon my thought ;
And eager hope, within my breaft,
Does ev'ry doubt controul,
And lovely Nancy ftands confefs'd
The fav'rite of my foul.

Ye nightingales, ye twifting pines,
Ye fwains that haunt the grove,
Ye gentle echoes, breezy winds,
Ye clofe retreats of love ;
With all of nature, all of art,
Affift the dear defign !
O, teach a young, unpractis'd heart,
To make her ever mine.

The very thought of change I hate,
  As much as of defpair;
And hardly covet to be great
  Unlefs it be for her:
'Tis true, the paffion in my mind
  Is mix'd with foft diftrefs;
Yet, while the fair I love is kind,
  I cannot wifh it lefs.

But if fhe treats me with difdain,
  And flights my well-meant love,
Or looks with pleafure on my pain,
  A pain fhe won't remove;
Farewel, ye birds, ye lonely pines,
  Adieu to groans and fighs;
I'll leave my paffion to the winds,
  Love unreturn'd foon dies.

SONG 1106.

LET mifers ftarve over the wealth they poffefs,
  And as it grows greater ftill fancy it lefs:
Give me but my bottle, my pipe, and my glafs,
And heighten my blifs with a fweet blooming
    lafs,
        I'll defpife
        Being fo wife.
        As the wind blows,
        So the world goes;
  I'll ne'er quit my bottle until the fun rife.

Let lawyers, phyficians, and parfons pretend
That the good of mankind is their principal end;
Law, phyfic, divinity, foon would expire,
Were Bacchus and Plutus from hence to retire.
        Life, at beft,
        Is but a jeft,
        E'en a bubble,
        Noife and trouble:
  Give me but my bottle, I'll give up the reft.

Let fond, foolifh lovers, whine over the fair,
And, in love difappointed, yield up to defpair:
No fickle, coy maiden, my mind fhall perplex,
No female inconftancy me e'er fhall vex.
        Thus let me,
        Eafy and free,
        Void of all care,'
        Hope or defpair,
  Sit down to my bottle, or rove like a bee.

SONG 1107.

Sung in *Alfred.*

THE Shepherd's plain life,
  Without guilt, without ftrife,
Can only true bleffings impart:
  As nature directs,
  That blifs he expects
From health, and from quiet of heart.

  Vain grandeur and pow'r,
  Thofe joys of an hour,
Tho' mortals are toiling to find;
  Can titles or fhow
  Contentment beftow?
All happinefs dwells in the mind.

Behold the gay rofe,
  How lovely it grows,
Secure in the depth of the vale!
  Yon oak, that on high
  Afpires to the fky,
Both lightning and tempefts affail.

DUETTO.

  Then let us the fnare
  Of ambition beware,
That fource of vexation and fmart;
  And fport on the glade,
  And repofe in the fhade,
With health and with quiet of heart.

SONG 1108.

Written by Mr. SHENSTONE.

WHEN bright Roxana treads the green,
  In all the pride of drefs and mien;
Averfe to freedom, love and play,
None other beauties ftrike mine eye,
The lilies droop, the rofes die.

But when, difclaiming art, the fair
Affumes a foft engaging air;
Mild as the opening morn of May,
Familiar, friendly, free and gay:
The fcene improves, where'er fhe goes,
More fweetly fmile the pink and rofe.

O lovely maid! propitious hear,
Nor deem thy fhepherd infincere;
Pity a wild illufive flame,
That varies objects ftill the fame:
And let their very changes prove
The never-vary'd force of love.

SONG 1109.

VALENTINE'S DAY.

Written by Mr. SHENSTONE.

'TIS faid that under diftant fkies,
  Nor you the fact deny;
What firft attracts an Indian's eyes
  Becomes his deity.

Perhaps a lily, or a rofe,
  That fhares the morning's ray,
May to the waking fwain difclofe
  The regent of the day.

Perhaps a plant in yonder grove,
  Enrich'd with fragrant pow'r,
May tempt his vagrant eyes to rove,
  Where blooms the fov'reign flow'r.

Perch'd on the cedar's topmoft bough,
  And gay with gilded wings,
Perchance, the patron of his vow,
  Some artlefs linnet fings.

The fwain furveys her pleas'd, afraid,
  Then low to earth he bends;
And owns upon her friendly aid,
  His health, his life depends.

Vain futile idols, bird or flow'r,
  To tempt a votary's pray'r !—
How would his humble homage tow'r
  Should he behold my fair !

Yes—might the pagan's waking eyes
  O'er Flavia's beauty range,
He there would fix his lasting choice,
  Nor dare, nor wish to change.

SONG 1110.

THE CONSENT.

Written by Mr. CUNNINGHAM.

'TIS the birth-day of Phillis, hark how the
    birds sing,
  Their notes are remarkably sweet;
The villagers brought all the honours of spring,
  And scatter'd their pride at her feet.
With ribbands and roses her lambkins are
    crown'd,
  Awhile they respectfully stand,
Then o'er the green lawn with a frolic they
    bound,
  But first take a kiss from her hand.

'Mongst shepherds in all the gay round of the
    year,
  This, this is their principal day;
It gave Phillis birth, and pray what can appear
  More lovely, more pleasingly gay ?
Hark, hark ! how the tabor enlivens the scene,
  Ye lads with your lasses advance;
'Tis charming to sport on a daisy-dress'd green,
  And Phillis shall lead up the dance.

The sun, (and he shines in his brightest array,
  As if on this festival proud)
In order to give us a beautiful day,
  Has banish'd each travelling cloud:
The priest pass'd along, and my shepherdess
    sigh'd,
  Sweet Phillis ! I knew what she meant:
We stole from the pastimes, I made her my
    bride ;
  Her sigh was the sigh of consent.

SONG 1111.

Sung at VAUXHALL.

I See it, Mira, know it well,
  That love has reach'd your heart ;
For what your tongue denies to tell,
  Your willing eyes impart.
When Damon wrestles on the green,
  Your looks your passion prove,
For in your eyes is plainly seen
  The partial joy of love.

When Sukey gave her lily hand
  To Damon of the vale,

Say, could you then your fears command ?
  Did not your cheeks turn pale ?
Cease then, dear maid, to teize the youth,
  But plainly own your flame;
For love consists of honest truth,
  And will itself proclaim.

SONG 1112.

Sung at VAUXHALL.

ERE Phœbus shall peep on the fresh-budding
    flow'r,
  Or blue-bells are robb'd of their dew ;
Sleep on, my Maria, while I deck the bow'r,
  To make it more worthy of you.

There roses and jes'mine each other shall greet,
  And mingle to copy your hue;
The lily, to match with thy bosom so sweet,
  How faint it's resemblance to you.

With the sweets of your breath, the hedge-
    violet shall vie,
  But weakly, and pay it it's due;
The thorn shall be robb'd of the sloe for your
    eye,
  Yet nature paints nothing like you.

The leaves of the sensitive-plant must declare
  The truth of my well-belov'd she ;
Whose branch, if to touch it bold shepherds
    shall dare,
  Would shrink from all others but me.

SONG 1113.

THE FRUITLESS ENDEAVOUR.

WHEN gentle Harriot first I saw,
  Struck with a reverential awe,
I felt my bosom mov'd :
Her easy shape, her charming face;
She smil'd, and talk'd with so much grace ;
  I gaz'd, admir'd, and lov'd.

Up to the busy town I flew,
And wander'd all it's pleasures thro',
  In hopes to ease my care :
The busy town but mocks my pain,
It's gayest pleasures all are vain,
  For Harriot haunts me there.

The labours of the learned sage,
The comic clamour of the stage,
  By turns my time employ ;
I relish not the sage's lure,
The stage's humours please no more,
  For Harriot's all my joy.

Sometimes I try'd the jovial throng,
Sometimes the female train among,
  To chace her form away :
The jovial throng is noisy, rude,
Nor other females dare intrude,
  Where Harriot bears the sway.

Since, then, nor art nor learning can,
Nor company of maid or man,
  For want of thee atone;
O come, with all thy conqu'ring charms,
O come, and take me to thy arms,
  For thou art all in one.

SONG 1114.

Written by Mr. SHENSTONE.

THE fatal hours are wond'rous near,
  That from these fountains bear my dear;
A little space is giv'n, in vain;
She robs my fight, and shuns the plain.

A litle space for me to prove
My boundless flame, my endless love ;
And like the train of vulgar hours,
Invidious time that space devours.

Near yonder beech is Delia's way,
Oa that I gaze the live-long day ;
No eastern monarch's dazzling pride
Should draw my longing eyes aside.

The chief, that knows of succours nigh,
And sees his mangled legions die,
Casts not a more impatient glance,
To see the loitering aids advance.

Not more the school-boy, that expires
Far from his native home, requires
To see some friend's familiar face,
Or meet a parent's last embrace.

She comes—but ah ! what crowds of beaux
In radiant bands my fair inclose ;
Oh ! better had'st thou shunn'd the green,
Oh, Delia ! better far unseen.

Methinks, by all my tender fears,
By all my sighs, by all my tears,
I might from torture now be free—
'Tis more than death to part from thee !

SONG 1115.

THE WANDERING JEW.

WHEN as in fair Jerusalem
  Our Saviour Christ did live,
And for the sins of all the world
  His own dear life did give ;
The wicked Jews with scoffs and scorns
  Did daily him molest,
That never till he left his life,
  Our Saviour could not rest.

When they had crown'd his head with thorns,
  And scourg'd him to disgrace,
In scornful sort they led him forth,
  Unto his dying-place ;
Where thousand thousands in the street
  Beheld him pass along,
Yet not one gentle heart was there,
  That pitied this his wrong.

Both old and young reviled him,
  As in the street he went,
And nought he found but churlish taunts,
  By every one's consent :
His own dear cross he bore himself,
  A burden far too great,
Which made him in the street to faint,
  With blood and water sweat.

Being weary thus, he sought for rest,
  To ease his burden'd soul,
Upon a stone ; the which a wretch
  Did churlishly controul ;
And said, Away, thou king of Jews,
  Thou shalt not rest thee here :
Pass on ; thy execution place
  Thou seest now draw near.

And thereupon he thrust him thence ;
  At which our Saviour said,
I sure will rest, but thou shalt walk,
  And have no journey stayed.
With that this cursed shoemaker,
  For offering Christ this wrong,
Left wife and children; house and all,
  And went from thence along.

Where after he had seen the blood
  Of Jesus Christ thus shed,
And to the cross his body nail'd,
  Away with speed he fled
Without returning back again
  Unto his dwelling-place,
And wandered up and down the world,
  A runnagate most base.

No resting could he find at all,
  No ease, nor heart's content ;
No house, nor home, nor biding-place ;
  But wandering forth he went
From town to town in foreign lands,
  With grieved conscience still,
Repenting for the heinous guilt
  Of his fore-passed ill.

Thus after some few ages past
  In wandering up and down ;
He much again desired to see
  Jerusalem's renown ;
But finding it all quite destroyed,
  He wandered thence with woe,
Our Saviour's words, which he had spoke,
  To verify and show.

" I'll rest, said he, but thou shalt walk,"
  So doth this wandering Jew
From place to place, but cannot rest
  For seeing countries new ;
Declaring still the power of him,
  Whereas he comes and goes,
And of all things done in the east,
  Since Christ his death, he shows.

The world he hath still compass'd round
  And seen those nations strange,
That hearing of the name of Christ,
  Their idol gods do change ;

To whom he hath told wondrous things
Of time forepaſt, and gone,
And to the princes of the world
Declares his cauſe of moan.

Deſiring ſtill to be diſſolv'd,
And yield his mortal breath ;
But, if the Lord hath thus decreed,
He ſhall not yet ſee death.
For neither looks he old nor young,
But as he did thoſe times,
When Chriſt did ſuffer on the croſs
For mortal ſinners crimes.

He hath paſt through many a foreign place,
Arabia, Egypt, Africa,
Grecia, Syria, and great Thrace,
And throughout all Hungaria :
Where Paul and Peter preached Chriſt,
Thoſe bleſt apoſtles dear ;
There he hath told our Saviour's words,
In countries far and near.

And lately in Bohemia,
With many a German town ;
And now in Flanders, as 'tis thought,
He wandereth up and down :
Where learned men with him confer
Of thoſe his lingering days,
And wonder much to hear him tell
His journies, and his ways.

If people give this Jew an alms,
The moſt that he will take
Is not above a groat a time :
Wdich he, for Jeſus' ſake,
Will kindly give unto the poor,
And thereof make no ſpare,
Affirming ſtill that Jeſus Chriſt
Of him hath daily care.

He ne'er was ſeen to laugh nor ſmile,
But weep and make great moan ;
Lamenting ſtill his miſeries,
And days forepaſt and gone :
If he hear any one blaſpheme,
Or take God's name in vain,
He tells them that they crucify
Their Saviour Chriſt again.

If you had ſeen his death, ſaid he,
As theſe mine eyes have done,
Ten thouſand thouſand times would ye
His torments think upon :
And ſuffer for his ſake all pain
Of torments and all woe.
Theſe are his words and eke his life,
Whereas he comes or goes.

SONG 1116.
Written by Mr. SHENSTONE.

O'E R deſert plains, and ruſhy meets,
And wither'd heaths I rove ;
Where tree nor ſpire, nor cut appears,
I paſs to meet my love.

But tho' my paths were damaſk'd o'er
With beauties e'er ſo fine ;
My buſy thoughts would fly before
To fix alone—on thine.

No fir-crown'd hills cou'd give delight,
No palace pleaſe mine eye :
No pyramid's aërial height,
Where mould'ring monarchs lie.

Unmov'd, ſhould eaſtern kings advance :
Could I the pageant ſee :
Splendour might catch one ſcornful glance,
Not ſteal one thought from thee.

SONG 1117.
Written by the Earl of ROCHESTER.

M Y dear miſtreſs has a heart,
Soft as thoſe kind looks ſhe gave me,
When with love's reſiſtleſs art,
And her eyes, ſhe did enſlave me :
But her conſtancy's ſo weak,
She's ſo wild and apt to wander,
That my jealous heart would break
Should we live one day aſunder.

Melting joys about her move,
Wounding pleaſures, killing bliſſes,
She can dreſs her eyes in love,
And her lips can arm with kiſſes ;
Angels liſten when ſhe ſpeaks,
She's my delight, all mankind's wonder,
But my jealous heart would break
Should we live one day aſunder.

SONG 1118.

W HEN charming Teraminta ſings,
Each new air, new paſſion brings ;
Now I reſolve, and now I fear ;
Now I triumph, now deſpair ;
Frolic now, now faint I grow ;
Now I freeze, and now I glow.
The panting zephyrs round her play,
And trembling on her lips would ſtay ;

Now would liſten, now would kiſs,
Trembling with divided bliſs ;
Till, by her breath repuls'd, they fly,
And in luw pleaſing murmurs die.
Nor do I aſk that ſhe would give
By ſome new note, the pow'r to live ;
I would, expiring with the ſound,
Die on the lips that gave the wound.

SONG 1119.

W HILE in the bower with beauty bleſt
The lov'd Amintor lies,
While ſinking on Zelinda's breaſt
He fondly kiſs'd her eyes ;

A waking nightingale who long
Had mourn'd within the ſhade,

Sweetly renew'd her plaintive song
And warbling thro' the glade.

Melodious songstress, cried the swain,
To shades less happy go,
Or if with us thou wilt remain
Forbear thy tuneful woe.

While in Zelinda's arms I lie
To song I am not free;
On her soft bosom while I sigh
I discord find in thee.

Zelinda gives me perfect joys;
Then cease thy fond intrusion;
Be silent, music now is noise,
Variety, confusion.

SONG 1120.

ARNO'S VALE.

Written by the Duke of DORSET.

WHEN here, Lucinda, first we came,
Where Arno rolls his silver stream,
How blithe the nymphs, the swains how gay!
Content infpir'd each rural lay;
The birds in livelier concert sung,
The grapes in thicker clusters hung;
All look'd as joy could never fail
Among the sweets of Arno's Vale.

But since the good Pamelon died,
The chief of shepherds, and their pride,
Now Arno's sons must all give place
To northern men, an iron race:
The taste of pleasure now is o'er;
Thy notes, Lucinda, please no more;
The Mufes droop, the Goths prevail;
Adieu the sweets of Arno's Vale!

SONG 1121.

THE SCHOLAR'S RELAPSE.

Written by Mr. SHENSTONE.

BY the side of a grove, at the foot of a hill,
Where whisper'd the beech, and where
murmur'd the rill;
I vow'd to the mufes my time and my care,
Since nothing could win me the smiles of my
fair.

Free I rang'd like the birds, like the birds
free I sung,
And Delia's lov'd name scarce escap'd from my
tongue;
But if once a smooth accent delighted my ear,
I should wish, unawares, that my Delia might
hear.

With fairest ideas my bosom I stor'd,
Allufive to none but the nymph I ador'd!
And the more I with study my fancy refin'd,
The deeper impression she made on my mind.

So long as of nature the charms I pursue,
I still must my Delia's dear image renew:
The graces have yielded with Delia to rove,
And the mufes are all in alliance with love.

SONG 1122.

Written by NATHANIEL LEE, Efq.

HAIL to the myrtle shade,
All hail to the nymphs of the fields!
Kings would not here invade
The pleasure that virtue yields.
Beauty here opens her arms,
A To soften the languishing mind,
nd Phyllis unlocks her charms;
Ah, Phyllis! oh, why so unkind?

Phyllis, thou soul of love,
Thou joy of the neighbouring swains;
Phillis, that crowns the grove,
And Phyllis that gilds the plains;
Phyllis, that ne'er had the skill
To paint, to patch and be fine;
Yet Phyllis whose eyes can kill,
Whom nature hath made divine

Phyllis, whose charming song
Makes labour and pains a delight;
Phyllis, that makes the day young,
And shortens the live-long night;
Phillis, whose lips like May
Still laugh at the sweets they bring;
Where love never knows decay.
But sits with eternal spring.

SONG 1123.

STREPHON, when you see me fly,
Let not this your fear create,
Maids may be as often shy
Out of love as out of hate;
When from you I fly away,
It is because I dare not stay.

Did I out of hatred run
Lefs you'd be my pain and care;
But the youth I love, to shun,
Who can such a trial bear?
Who, that such a swain did see,
Who could love and fly like me?

Cruel duty bids me go,
Gentle love commands me stay;
Duty's still to love a foe,
Shall I this or that obey?
Duty frowns, and Cupid's smiles,
That defends, and this beguiles.

Ever by these crystal streams
I could fit and hear thee sigh,
Ravish'd with these pleasing dreams
O 'tis worse than death to fly:
But the danger is so great,
Fear gives wings, instead of hate.

Strephon, if you love me, leave me,
If you stay I am undone;

Oh, with ease you may deceive me,
Pry'thee charming swain be gone.
Heav'n decrees that we should part,
That has my vows, but you my heart.

SONG 1124.

Sung in *Artaxerxes.*

HOW hard is my fate,
How desp'rate my state,
When honour and virtue excite,
To suffer distress,
Contented to bless
The object in whom I delight.
Yet amidst all the woes
My soul undergoes,
Thro' virtue's too rigid decree,
I'll scorn to complain
If the force of his pain
Awaken his pity for me.

SONG 1125.

'TIS not the liquid brightness of those eyes,
That swim with pleasure and delight;
Nor those fair heavenly arches which arise
O'er each of them to shade their light;
'Tis not that hair which plays with every wind,
And loves to wanton round thy face;
Now straying o'er thy forehead, now behind
Retiring with insidious grace.

'Tis not that lovely range of teeth, as white
As new-shorn sheep, equal and fair;
Nor even that gentle smile, the heart's delight,
With which no smile could e'er compare;
'Tis not that chin so round, that neck so fine,
Those breasts that swell to meet my love;
That easy sloping waist, that form divine,
Nor aught below, nor aught above.

'Tis not the living colours over each,
By nature's finest pencil wrought,
To shame the fresh-blown rose, and blooming
peach;
And mock the happiest painter's thought:
But 'tis that gentle mind, that ardent love,
So kindly answering my desire;
That grace with which you look, and speak,
and move,
That thus have set my soul on fire.

SONG 1126.

THE ROSE-BUD.

Written by Mr. SHENSTONE.

SEE, Daphne, see, Florello cry'd,
And learn the sad effects of pride;
Yon shelter'd rose, how safe conceal'd!
How quickly blasted, when reveal'd!

The sun with warm attractive rays
Tempts it to wanton in the blaze:
A gale succeeds from eastern skies,
And all it's blushing radiance dies.

So you, my fair, of charms divine,
Will quit the plains too fond to shine
Where fame's transporting rays allure,
Tho' here more happy, more secure.

The breath of some neglected maid
Shall make you sigh you left the shade:
A breath to beauty's bloom unkind,
As to the rose an eastern wind.

The nymph reply'd—You first, my swain,
Confine your sonnets to the plain;
One envious tongue alike disarms,
You, of your wit, me, of my charms.

What is, unknown, the poet's skill?
Or what, unheard, the tuneful thrill?
What, unadmir'd, a charming mien?
Or what the rose's blush, unseen?

SONG 1127.

Sung in the *Duenna.*

HOW oft, Louisa, hast thou said
(Nor wilt thou the fond boast disown)
Thou would'st not lose Anthonio's love,
To reign the partner of a throne.

And by those lips that spoke so kind!
And by this hand I press'd to mine!
To gain a subject nation's love,
I swear I would not part with thine.

Then how, my soul, can we be poor,
Who own what kingdoms could not buy!
Of this true heart thou shalt be queen,
And, serving thee, a monarch I.

Thus uncontroul'd in mutual bliss,
And rich in love's exhaustless mine,
Do thou snatch treasures from my lips,
And I'll take kingdoms back from thine.

SONG 1128.

VARIETY IS CHARMING.

I'M in love with twenty,
I'm in love with twenty,
And could adore
As many more,
For nothing's like a plenty.
Variety is charming,
Variety is charming,
And constancy
Is not for me,
So ladies you have warning.

He that has but one love,
Looks as poor
As any boor,
Or like a man with one glove.
Variety, &c.

Not the fine regalia
Of eastern kings,
The poet sings,
But oh! the fine seraglio.
Variety, &c.

Girls grow old and ugly,
  And can't inspire
  The same desire,
As when they're young and smugly.
  Variety, &c.

Why has Cupid pinions;
  If not to fly
  Through all the sky,
And see his favourite minions.
  Variety, &c.

Love was born of beauty,
  And when she goes,
  The urchin knows,
To follow is his duty.
  Variety, &c.

SONG 1129.

WINTER.

Written by Mr. SHENSTONE.

NO more, ye warbling birds rejoice ;
  Of all that chear'd the plain,
Echo alone preserves her voice,
  And she—repeats my pain.

Were'er my love-sick limbs I lay,
  To shun the rushing wind,
It's busy murmur seems to say,
  " She never will be kind !"

The naiads, o'er their frozen urns,
  In icy chains repine ;
And each in sullen silence mourns
  Her freedom lost, like mine !

Soon will the sun's returning rays
  The chearless frost controul ;
When will relenting Delia chase
  The winter of my soul ?

SONG 1130.

THE lilies of France, and the brave English
  rose,
Could never agree, as old history shows;
But our Edwards and Henrys, those lilies have
  torn,
And in their rich standards such ensigns have
  borne ;
To shew that Old England, beneath her strong
  lance,
Has humbled the pride and the glory of France.

What would these monsieurs ! would they know
  how they ran,
Only look at the annals of glorious queen Anne:
We beat them by sea, and we beat them by land,
When Marlbrough and Russel enjoy'd the com-
  mand ;
We'll beat them again, boys, so let them ad-
  vance,
Old England despises the insults of France.

Then let the grand monarch assemble his host,
And threaten invasion to England's fair coast ;
We bid them defiance so let them come on,
Have at them, their business will quickly be
  done :
Monsieurs, we will teach you a new English
  dance,
To our Grenadiers March, which will frighten
  all France.

Let's take up our muskets, and gird on our
  swords,
And monsieurs shall find us as good as our
  words ;
Beat drums and sound trumpets, huzza to our
  king,
Then welcome Belleisle with what troops thou
  canst bring;
Huzza for Old England, whose strong-pointed
  lance,
Shall humble the pride and the glory of France.

SONG 1131.

FLY, thoughtless youth, th' enchantress fly !
  To other climes direct thy way;
Let honour's plume attract thine eye,
  Nor waste in indolence the day :
She nor regards thy sighs or tears,
She triumphs in thy jealous fears,
And would rejoice to blast the blossom of thy
  years.

Yet yonder myrtle's fragrant shade,
  Where sparkling winds the crystal rill,
Has seen this false, this cruel maid,
  Fond as her wanton lover's will :
Has seen thee on her breast reclin'd,
Has seen her arms around thee twin'd,
While with caresses sweet she woo'd thee to
  be kind.

But since no more th' inconstant fair
  Will listen to thy tender vow,
Let nobler objects claim thy care,
  And bid the faithless maid adieu.
  Adieu, false beauty ! hence no more
Catullus will thy smile implore ;
To shun thy hated charms he seeks a foreign
  shore.

Him thou wilt mourn, when sure decay
  Shall rob that form of every grace ;
And for each charm it steals away,
  Shall add a wrinkle to that face :
No lover then for thee will sigh,
Or read the glances of thine eye,
Or on thy once-lov'd breast in amorous trans-
  ports die.

Alas, Catullus ! you in vain
  Would spurn imperial beauty's sway;
Fast bound in Venus' magic chain,
  Soon will each rebel wish decay :

E'en now, fhould Lefbia hither move
In her accuftom'd looks of love,
How weak, how feeble all thy ftrong refolves
   would prove !

SONG 1132.

Written by Lord LANDSDOWN.

PREPAR'D to rail, refolv'd to part,
   When I approach the perjur'd maid,
What is it awes my timorous heart?
Why is my tongue afraid?

With the leaft glance a little kind,
   Such wond'rous power have Mira's charms,
She calms my doubts, enflaves my mind,
   And all my rage difarms.

Forgetful of her broken vows
   When gazing on that form divine,
Her injur'd vaffal trembling bows,
· Nor dares her flave repine.

SONG 1133.

DAPHNE'S VISIT.

Written by Mr. SHENSTONE.

YE birds! for whom I rear'd the grove,
   With melting lay falute my love :
My Daphne with your notes detain :
Or I have rear'd my grove in vain.

Ye flow'rs! before her footfteps rife ;
Difplay at once your brighteft dyes ;
That fhe your opening charms may fee :
Or what were all your charms to me ?

Kind zephyr! brufh each fragrant flow'r,
And fhed it's odours round my bow'r :
Or never more, O gentle wind,
Shall I, from thee, refrefhment find.

Ye ftreams ! if e'er your banks I lov'd,
If e'er your native founds improv'd,
May each foft murmur foothe my fair :
Or, oh ! 'twill deepen my defpair.

And thou, my grot ! whofe lonely bounds
The melancholy pine furrounds,
May Daphne praife thy peaceful gloom,
Or thou fhalt prove her Damon's tomb !

SONG 1134.

MAKE HAY WHILST THE SUN SHINES.

'TIS a maxim I hold, whilft I live to purfue,
   Not a thing to defer, which to-day I can do :
This piece of good counfel attend to, I pray,
For while the fun fhines is the time to make hay.

Attend the dear nymph to an arbour or grove,
In her ear gently pour the foft poifon of love :
With kiffes and preffes your rapture convey,
For while the fun fhines is the time to make hay.

If Chloe is kind, and gives ear to your plaint,
Declare your whole fentiments free from re-
   ftraint :
Enforce your petition, and make no delay, /
For while the fun fhines is the time to make hay.

But fhould you the prefent occafion let pafs,
The world may with juftice proclaim you an afs:
Then brifkly attack her, if longer you ftay,
The fun may not fhine, and you cannot make hay.

SONG 1135.

Sung in Comus.

WOULD you tafte the noon-tide air,
   To yon fragrant bow'r repair,
Were woven with the poplar bough,
The mantling vine will fhelter you.
Down each fide a fountain flows,
Tinkling, murm'ring, as it goes,
Lightly o'er the mofly ground,
Sultry Phœbus fcorching roung.

Round the languid herds, and fheep,
Stretch'd o'er funny hillocks, fleep;
While on the hyacinth and rofe,
The fair does all alone repofe :
All alone ; yet in her arms
Your breaft fhall beat to love's alarms,
Till, bleft and bleffing, you fhall own,
The joys of love are joys alone.

SONG 1136.

Written by Mr. OTWAY.

COME all ye youths whofe hearts e'er bled
   By cruel beauty's pride ;
Bring each a garland on his head,
   Let none his forrows hide :
But hand in hand around me move,
Singing the faddeft tales of love ;
And fee, when your complaints ye join,
If all your wrongs can equal mine.

The happieft mortal once was I,
   My heart no forrows knew ;
Pity the pain with which I die,
   But afk not whence it grew :
Yet if a tempting fair you find,
That's very lovely, very kind,
Tho' bright as Heaven whofe ftamp fhe bears,
Think of my fate, and fhun her fnares.

SONG 1137.

Written by Mr. SHENSTONE.

ADIEU, ye jovial youths, who join
   To plunge old care in floods of wine ;
And, as your dazzled eye-balls roll,
Difcern him ftruggling in the bowl.

Not yet is hope fo wholly flown,
Not yet is thought fo tedious grown,
But limpid ftream, and fhady tree,
Retain, as yet, fome fweets for me.

And fee, thro' yonder filent grove,
See yonder does my Daphne rove:
With pride her foot-fteps I purfue,
And bid your frantic joys adieu.

The fole confufion I admire,
Is that my Daphne's eyes infpire:
I fcorn the madnefs you approve,
And value reafon next to love.

SONG 1138.

Sung in the Reprifal.

FROM the man whom I love, tho' my heart
   I difguife,
I will freely defcribe the wretch I defpife;
And if he has fenfe but to balance a ftraw,
He will fure take a hint from the picture I draw.

A wit without fenfe, without fancy a beau,
Like a parrot he chatters, and ftruts like a
   crow;
A peacock in pride, in grimace a baboon;
In courage a hind, in conceit a gafcoon.

As a vulture rapacious, in falfhood a fox,
Inconftant as waves, and unfeeling as rocks;
As a tyger ferocious, perverfe as a hog,
In mifchief an ape, and in fawning a dog.

In a word, to fum up all his talents together,
His heart is of lead, and his brains are of
   feather:
Yet if he has but fenfe to balance a ftraw,
He will fure take a hint from the picture I
   draw.

SONG 1139.

PHILLIS, the goddefs of the plain,
   Admir'd by ev'ry youthful fwain,
Who us'd to laugh at Cupid's dart,
And fcorn each captivated heart;
To Strephon now hath giv'n her own.
And filent doth it's lofs bemoan.

Tho' now 'tis paft, there was a time,
When I lov'd her, as fhe loves him:

But when I knelt and told my pain,
With frowns fhe fent me back again,
And told me each returning day,
Wou'd help to wear t e chains away.

Since now, dear Phillis, thou art caught,
Pray ufe the precepts you have taught;
Convince me that your charms decay,
As each new hour rolls away;
Then I your dictates will purfue,
And die content as well as you.

SONG 1140.

GENTLY touch the warbling lyre,
   Chloe feems inclin'd to reft;
Fill her foul with fond defire,
   Softeft notes will footh her breaft.
Pleafing dreams affift in love,
Let them all propitious prove.

On the moffy bank fhe lies,
   (Nature's verdant velvet-bed)
Beauteous flowers meet her eyes,
   Forming pillows for her head.
Zephyrs waft their odours round,
And indulging whifpers found.

SONG 1141.

GENTLY ftir and blow the fire,
   Lay the mutton down to roaft:
Get me, quick, 'tis my defire,
   In the driping-pan a toaft,
That my hunger may remove;
Mutton is the meat I love.

On the dreffer fee it lies;
   O the charming white and red!
Finer meat ne'er met my eyes,
   On the fweeteft grafs it fed:
Swiftly make the jack go round,
Let me have it nicely brown'd.

On the table fpread the cloth,
   Let the knives be fharp and clean;
Pickles get of ev'ry fort,
   And a fallad crifp and green:
Then with fmall beer, and fparkling wine,
O, ye gods! how I fhall dine!

THE

VOCAL MAGAZINE.

NUMBER IX.

SONG 1142.

LADY ANNE BOTHWELL'S COMPLAINT.

Altered by Mr. T. B.

BALOW, my boy, lie ftill and fleep,
It grieves me fore to hear thee weep;
If thou'lt be filent, I'll be glad,
Thy mourning makes my heart full fad.
Balow, my boy, thy mother's joy,
Thy father bred me great annoy.
    Balow, my boy, &c.

Balow, my darling, fleep awbile,
And when thou wak'ft then fweetly fmile;
But fmile not as thy father did,
To cozen maids; nay, God forbid!
For in thine eye his look I fee,
The tempting look that ruin'd me.
    Balow, my boy, &c.

When he began to court my love,
And with his fugar'd words to move,
His tempting face, and flatt'ring chear,
In time to me did not appear;
But now I fee, that cruel he
Cares neither for his babe nor me.
    Balow my boy, &c.

Farewel, farewel, thou falfeft youth
That ever fwerv'd from facred truth,
Oh! may no maiden, after me,
Submit unto thy courtefy:
For, if fhe does, O! cruel thou,
Wilt her abufe, and care not how.
    Balow my boy, &c.

I was too ready to believe,
Nor thought thou ever couldft deceive:
You fwore for ever true to prove,
Thy faith unchang'd, unchang'd thy love;
But, quick as thought, the change is wrought,
Thy love's no more, thy promife nought.
    Balow my boy, &c.

I wifh I were a maid again,
From young men's flatt'ry i'd refrain,
For now unto my grief I find,
They all are perjur'd and unkind:
Bewitching charms bred all my harms,
Witnefs my babe within my arms.
    Balow my boy, &c.

A parent's fond anxiety,
My haplefs infant, hangs o'er thee.
I'll fold thee clofe within my arms,
And fondly dwell o'er all thy charms.
Then reft, my darling, free from fear,
No rude alarm can reach thee here.
    Balow, my boy, &c.

Balow, my boy, weep not for me,
Whofe greateft pain is wronging thee;
Nor, if you rife to man's eftate,
Mourn an imprudent mother's fate:
Too foon, alas! that mother finds,
With faireft tongues are falfeft minds.
    Balow, my boy, &c.

Balow, my boy, thy father's fled,
Who dragg'd perdition on my head.
Of vows and oaths forgetful, he
Preferr'd the wars to thee and me.
Who knows but there fome ftroke divine
May make him feel thy curfe and mine.
    Balow, my boy, &c.

Ah, why our curfe! perhaps now he,
Stung with remorfe, is blefling thee:
Perhaps at death; for who can tell
Whether the Judge of heaven and hell,
By fome proud foe has ftruck the blow,
And laid the dear deceiver low.
    Balow, my boy, &c.

I wifh I were within the bounds,
Where he lies fmother'd in his wounds,
Repeating, as he pants for air,
My name, whom once he call'd his fair.
    R r

O'er his pale.corfe I'd heave a figh,
While all my wrongs forgotten lie.
   Balow, my boy, &c.

Balow, my boy, I'll weep for thee ;
Too foon, alas ! thou'lt weep for me :
Thy griefs are growing to a fum,
God grant thee patience when they come !
Born to fuftain thy mother's fhame,
A haplefs fate, a baftard's name.

SONG 1143.

Written by Mrs. TAYLOR.

STREPHON has fafhion, wit and youth,
   With all things elfe that pleafe;
He nothing wants but love and truth
   To ru'n me with eafe:
But he is flint, and bears the art
   To kindle ftrong defire ;
His pow'r inflames another's heart,
   Yet he ne'er feels the fire.

O ! how it does my foul perplex,
   When I his charms recal,
To think he fhould defpife the fex,
   Or worfe, fhould love 'em all.
My wearied heart, like Noah's dove,
   Thus feeks in vain for reft;
Finding no hope to fix it's love,
   Returns into my breaft.

SONG 1144.

TELL my Strephon that I die ;
   Let echoes to each other tell,
Till the mournful accents fly
   To Strephon's ear, and all is well.

But gently breathe the fatal truth,
   And foften every hafher found,
For Strephon's fuch a tender youth,
   The fofteft words too deep will wound.

Now fountains, echoes, all be dumb ;
   For fhould I coft my fwain a tear,
I fhould repent it in my tomb,
   And grieve I bought my reft fo dear.

SONG 1145.

Written by Mr. TOMLINS.

WHAT charms does my Laura difclofe!
   What beauties her perfon adorn !
She is fweet as the new-budded rofe,
   And foft as the dew of the morn.

Her air, how engagingly fweet!
   What melody flows from her tongue !
In her all the graces have met;
   She is fair, fhe is blooming, fhe's young.

The charms of her form, tho' fo bright,
   Are excell'd by the charms of her mind ;
There fenfe and good-nature unite ;
   Politenefs and eafe are combin'd.

No frowns on her brow ever lour,
   Soft pity prefides in her breaft ;
No paffions her temper to four ;
   Her foul is for ever at reft.

As the dove fhe is harmlefs and mild,
   And like that fhe's devoid of all art ;
She is fweet fenfibility's child,
   And innocence reigns in her heart.

Ye pow'rs that prefide over love,
   With pity attend to my pray'r,
And grant that my Laura may prove
   That fhe is not lefs kind than fhe's fair.

O would fhe my paffion approve,
   Then I fhould fupremely be bleft !
All the day would I fpend with my love,
   And at night I'd repofe on her breaft.

SONG 1146.

Written by Mr. DRYDEN.

ON a bank, befide a willow,
   Heaven her covering, earth her pillow,
   Sad Aminta figh'd alone :
From the chearlefs dawn of morning,
Till the dews of night returning,
   Singing, thus fhe made her moan ;
     Hope is banifh'd,
     Joys are vanifh'd,
   Damon, my belov'd, is gone.

Time, I dare thee to difcover
Such a youth, and fuch a lover;
   Oh ! fo true, fo kind was he
Damon was the pride of nature,
Charming in his every feature.
   Damon liv'd alone for me ;
     Melting kiffes,
     Murmuring bliffes,
   Who fo liv'd and lov'd as we !

Never fhall we curfe the morning,
Never blefs the night returning,
   Sweet embraces to reftore ;
Never fhall we both lie dying,
Nature failing, love fupplying
   All the joys he drain'd before :
     Death come end me,
     To befriend me ;
   Love and Damon are no more !

SONG 1147.

Written by Mr. COLLINS.

Sung in *Cymbeline*.

TO fair Fidele's graffy tomb
   Soft maids and village hinds fhall bring
Each op'ning fweet of earlieft bloom,
   And rifle all the breathing fpring.

No wailing ghoft fhall dare appear
   To vex with fhrieks this quiet grove;
But fhepherd lads affemble here,
   And melting virgins own their love.

No wither'd witch fhall here be feen,
   No goblins lead their nightly crew ;

But female fays shall haunt the green,
And dress thy grave with pearly dew.

The red-breast oft at evening hours
Shall kindly lend his little aid,
With hoary moss, and gather'd flow'rs,
To deck the ground where thou art laid.

When howling winds and beating rain
In tempests shake the sylvan cell;
Or 'midst the chase upon the plain
The tender thought on thee shall dwell.

Each lonely scene shall thee restore,
For thee the tear be duly shed;
Belov'd, till life can charm no more,
And mourn'd, till pity's self be dead.

SONG 1148.

Written by Sir RICHARD STEELE.

FROM place to place, forlorn, I go,
With downcast eyes, a silent shade;
Forbidden to declare my woe;
To speak, till spoken to, afraid.

My inward pangs, my secret grief,
My soft consenting looks betray;
He loves, but gives me no relief;
Why speaks not he—who may?

SONG 1149.

THERE is one dark and sullen hour,
Which fate decrees our lives should know,
Else we should slight th' Almighty power,
Wrapt in the joys we find below:
'Tis past, dear Cynthia, now let frowns be gone,
A long, long penance I have done
For crimes, alas! to me unknown.

In each soft hour of silent night
Your image in my dream appears;
I grasp the soul of my delight,
Slumber in joys, but wake in tears:
Ah! faithless, charming saint, what will you do?
Let me not think I am, by you,
Lov'd less for being true.

SONG 1150.

FAIR, and soft, and gay, and young,
All charms! she play'd, she danc'd, she sung,
There was no way to 'scape the dart,
No care could guard the lover's heart.
Ah! why, cry'd I, and dropt a tear,
(Adoring, yet despairing e'er
To have her to myself alone)
Was so much sweetness made for one?

But growing bolder, in her ear
I in soft numbers told my care:
She heard, and rais'd me from her feet,
And seem'd to glow with equal heat.
Like heaven's, too mighty to express,
My joys could but be known by guess!
Ah! fool, said I, what have I done,
To wish her made for more than one?

But long I had not been in view,
Before her eyes their beams withdrew;
Ere I had reckon'd half her charms,
She sunk into another's arms.
But she that once could faithless be,
Will favour him no more than me:
He, too, will find himself undone,
And that she was not made for one.

SONG 1151.

Written by Mr. HAMILTON.

YE shepherds and nymphs that adorn the gay
plain,
Approach from your sports, and attend to my
strain;
Amongst all your number a lover so true
Was ne'er so undone with such bliss in his view.

Was ever a nymph so hard-hearted as mine?
She knows me sincere, and she sees how I pine;
She does not disdain me, nor frown in her wrath,
But calmly and mildly resigns me to death.

She calls me her friend, but her lover denies;
She smiles when I'm chearful, but hears not
my sighs.
A bosom so flinty, so gentle an air,
Inspires me with hope, and yet bids me despair.

I fall at her feet, and implore her with tears;
Her answer confounds, while her manner
endears:
When softly she tells me to hope no relief,
My trembling lips bless her, in spite of my grief.

By night, when I slumber, still haunted with
care,
I start up in anguish, and sigh for the fair:
The fair sleeps in peace, may she ever do so!
And only when dreaming imagine my woe.

Then gaze at a distance, nor farther aspire,
Nor think she could love whom she cannot
admire:
Hush all thy complaining, and dying her slave,
Commend her to heaven, thyself to the grave.

SONG 1152.

THO' cruel you seem to my pain,
And hate me because I am true;
Yet, Phyllis, you love a false swain,
Who has other nymphs in his view.

Enjoyment's a trifle to him,
To me what a heaven 'twould be!
To him but a woman you seem,
But, ah! you're an angel to me.

Those lips which he touches in haste,
To them I for ever could grow;
Still clinging around that dear waist,
Which he spans as beside him you go.

R r 2

That arm, like a lily fo white,
　Which over his fhoulders you lay,
My bofom could warm it all night,
　My lips they could prefs it all day.

Were I like a monarch to reign,
　Were graces my fubjects to be,
I'd leave them, and fly to the plain,
　To dwell in a cottage with thee.

But if I muft feel your difdain,
　If tears cannot cruelty drown;
Oh! let me not live in this pain,
　But give me my death in a frown.

SONG 1153.

ANACREONTIC.

Written by Mr. TOMLINS.

HERE am I in this world of ftrife,
　And bound to tread the path of life:
How much is paft I know, but that
Which is to come, my future fate,
Uncertain is, or when or where.
Then what have I to do with care?
Care, get thee gone, for e'er I die,
I'll laugh, and drink my goblet dry.

SONG 1154.

YOUNG I am, and yet unfkill'd
　How to make a lover yield;
How to keep, and how to gain,
When to love, and when to feign.

Take me, take me, fome of you,
While I yet am young and true;
Ere I can my foul difguife,
Heave my breafts, and roll my eyes.

Stay not till I learn the way
How to lye, and to betray;
He that has me firft, is bleft,
For I may deceive the reft.

Could I find a blooming youth
Full of love, and full of truth,
Brifk, and of a janty mien,
I fhould long to be fifteen.

SONG 1155.

Written by Sir CHARLES SEDLEY.

DAMON, if you will believe me,
　'Tis not fighing on the plain,
Song nor fonnet can relieve ye;
　Faint attempts in love are vain.

Urge but home the fair occafion,
　And be mafter of the field;
To a powerful, kind invafion,
　'Twere a madnefs not to yield.

Love gives out a large commiffion,
　Still indulgent to the brave;
But one fin of bafe omiffion
　Never woman yet forgave.

Tho' fhe vows fhe'll ne'er permit ye,
　Cries, you're rude and much to blame,
And with tears implores your pity;
　Be not merciful, for fhame.

When the fierce affault is over,
　Chloris time enough will find,
This her cruel furious lover
　Much more gentle, not fo kind.

SONG 1156.

EDWIN AND ETHELINDE.

ONE parting kifs, my Ethelinde!
　Young Edwin fault'ring cried,
I hear thy father's hafty tread,
　Nor longer muft I bide.

To-morrow eve, in yonder wood,
　Beneath the well-known tree,
Say, wilt thou meet thy own true love,
　Whofe only joy's in thee?

She clafp'd the dear-beloved youth,
　And figh'd, and dropt a tear;
Whate'er betide my only love,
　I'll furely meet thee there.

They kifs, they part; a lift'ning page
　To malice ever bent,
O'erheard their talk, and to his lord
　Reveal'd their fond intent.

The baron's brow grew dark with frowns,
　And rage diftain'd his cheek,
Heavens! fhall a vaffal fhepherd dare
　My daughter's love to feek!

But know, rafh boy, thy bold attempt
　Full forely fhalt thou rue;
Nor e'er again, ignoble maid,
　Shalt thou thy lover view.

The dews of evening faft did fall,
　And darknefs fpread apace,
When Ethelinde, with beating breaft,
　Flew to th' appointed place.

With eager eye fhe looks around,
　No Edwin there was feen:
He was not wont to break his faith,
　What can his abfence mean!

Her heart beat thick at ev'ry noife,
　Each ruftling thro' the wood;
And now fhe travers'd quick the ground,
　And now fhe lift'ning ftood.

Enliv'ning hope, and chilling fear,
　By turns her bofom fhare;
And now fhe calls upon his name,
　Now weeps in fad defpair.

Meantime the day's laft glimm'rings fled;
　And, blackening all the fky,
A hideous tempeft dreadful rofe,
　And thunders roll'd on high.

Poor Ethelinde aghaft, difmay'd,
　Beholds with wild affright
The threat'ning fky, the lonely wood,
　And horrors of the night,

mm.

Where art thou now, my Edwin dear?
Thy friendly aid I want:
Ah me! my boding heart foretels
That aid thou canst not grant.

Thus rack'd with pangs, and beat with storms,
Confus'd and lost she roves;
Now looks to heaven with earnest pray'r,
Now calls on him she loves.

At length a distant taper's ray
Struck beaming on her sight;
Thro' brakes she guides her fainting steps
Towards the welcome light.

An aged hermit peaceful dwelt
In this sequester'd wild,
Calm goodness sat upon his brow,
His words were soft and mild.

He ope'd his hospitable door,
And much admiring view'd
The tender virgin's graceful form,
Dash'd by the tempest rude.

Welcome, fair maid, whoe'er thou art,
To this warm shelter'd cell;
Here rest secure thy wearied feet,
Here peace and safety dwell.

He saw the heart-wrung starting tear,
And gently fought to know,
With kindest pity's soothing looks,
The story of her woe.

Scarce had she told her mournful tale,
When struck with dread they hear
Voices confus'd with dying groans,
The ceil approaching near.

Help, father! help, they loudly cry,
A wretch here bleeds to death;
Some cordial balsam quickly give,
To stay his parting breath.

All deadly pale they lay him down,
And gush'd with many a wound;
When, woeful sight! 'twas Edwin's self
Lay bleeding on the ground.

With frantic grief poor Ethelinde
Beside his body falls;
Lift up thine eyes, my Edwin dear,
'Tis Ethelinde that calls.

That much-lov'd found recals his life,
He lifts his closing eyes,
Then feebly murmuring out her name,
He gasps, he faints, he dies!

Stupid awhile, in dumb despair
She gaz'd on Edwin dead;
Dim grew her eyes, her lips turn'd pale,
And life's warm spirit fled.

SONG 1157.
Sung in *Comus*.

MORTALS, learn your lives to measure,
Not by length of time, but pleasure;
Now the hours invite, comply;
While you idly pause, they fly:
Blest, a nimble pace they keep,
But in torment, then they creep.

Mortals, learn your lives to measure,
Not by length of time, but pleasure;
Soon your spring must have a fall;
Losing youth, is losing all:
Then you'll ask, but none will give,
And may linger, but not live.

SONG 1158.
Written by Mr. EATON.

TELL me not I my time misspend,
'Tis time lost to reprove me;
Pursue thou thine, I have my end,
So Chloris only prize me.

Tell me not other's flocks are full,
Mine poor, let them despise thee
Who more abound in milk and wool,
So Chloris only prize me.

Tire others' easier ears with these
Unappertaining stories;
He never feels the world's disease,
Who cares not for her glories.

For pity, thou that wiser art,
Whose thoughts lie wide of mine,
Let me alone with my own heart,
And I'll ne'er envy thine.

Nor blame him, whoe'er blames my wit,
That seeks no higher prize,
Than in unenvy'd shades to sit,
And sing of Chloris' eyes.

SONG 1159.
Written by Mr. CONGREVE.

I Tell thee, Charmion, could I time retrieve,
And could again begin to love and live,
To you I should my earliest off'ring give;
I know my eyes would lead my heart to you,
And I should all my oaths and vows renew;
But, to be plain, I never would be true.

For by our weak and weary truth, I find,
Love hates to centre in a point assign'd,
But runs with joy the circle of the mind:
Then let us never chain what should be free,
But for relief of either sex agree;
Since women love to change, and so do we.

SONG 1160.
Written by Mr. ETHERIDGE.

YE happy swains whose hearts are free
From love's imperial chain,
Take warning, and be taught by me
T' avoid th' inchanting pain;
Fatal the wolves to trembling flocks,
Fierce winds to blossoms prove,
To careless seamen hidden rocks,
To human quiet love.

Fly the fair sex, if bliss you prize,
The snake's beneath the flow'r;

Who ever gaz'd on beauteous eyes
That tafted quiet more?
How faithlefs is the lover's joy!
How conſtant is their care!
The kind with falſhood do deſtroy,
The cruel with defpair.

SONG 1161.

ANACREONTIC.

Written by Mr. TOMLINS.

SOME fing of Thebans, fome of Phrygians,
  Of mighty men, who now are Stygians,
And in heroic numbers tell
How many Greeks and Trojans fell
In war before proud I'lum's town;
I fing no flaughters but my own:
'Tis not from horfe or foot I fly,
I vanquifh'd am by Chloe's eye.

SONG 1162.

YE little loves that round her wait,
  To bring me tidings of my fate,
As Celia on her pillow lies,
Ah! gently whifper—Strephon dies.

If this will not her pity move,
And the proud fair difdains to love,
Smile and fay 'Tis all a lye,
And haughty Strephon fcorns to die.

SONG 1163.

PHILANDER AND DAPHNE.

Sung at VAUXHALL.

PHILANDER.

DEAREST Daphne, turn thine eyes,
  Jocund day begins to rife;
See! the morn, with rofes crown'd,
Sprinkling dew-drops on the ground.
Love invites to yonder grove,
Where none but lovers dare to rove.
Let us hafte, make no delay;
Cupid calls, we muſt obey.

DAPHNE.

Ah, Philander! I'm afraid;
There poor Laura was betray'd
By young Strephon's fubtle wiles,
Soothing words, and artful fmiles.
Simple maids are foon undone,
When their eafy hearts are won.
Prefs me not, I muſt away,
And honour's ftrict commands obey.

PHILANDER.

Gentle Daphne, fear not you,
I'll be ever kind and true;
Think no more on Laura's fate,
View yon turtle, and his mate;
See how freely they impart
Th' impulfe of each other's heart.
Like them, my fair, let s fport and play;
Nature prompts us to obey.

DAPHNE.

Shepherd, I perceive your aim,
You and Strephon are the fame;
You like him wou'd me betray,
Shou'd I truſt to what you fay.

PHILANDER.

If Daphne doubts, let Hymen's hands
This inſtant join our willing hands.
The invitation I obey,
And love with honour will repay.

SONG 1164.

LOVE and Folly were at play,
  Both too wanton to be wife,
They fell out, and in the fray
Folly put out Cupid's eyes.

Straight the criminal was try'd,
And had this punifhment affign'd,
Folly fhould to Love be ty'd,
And condemn'd to lead the blind.

SONG 1165.

AN amorous fwain to Juno pray'd,
  And thus his fuit did move;
Give me, oh! give me the dear maid,
Or take away my love.

The goddefs thunder'd from the fkies,
And granted his requeſt;
To make him happy, made him wife,
And drove her from his breaſt.

SONG 1166.

Written by Dr. PERCY.

O Nancy, wilt thou go with me,
  Nor figh to leave the flaunting town?
Can filent glens have charms for thee,
  The lowly cot and ruffet gown?
No longer dreſt in filken fheen,
  No longer deck'd with jewels rare,
Say, canſt thou quit each courtly fcene,
  Where thou wert faireſt of the fair?

O Nancy! when thou'rt far away,
  Wilt thou not caſt a wifh behind?
Say, canſt thou face the parching ray,
  Nor fhrink before the wintry wind?
O can that foft and gentle mien
  Extremes of hardfhip learn to bear,
Nor, fad, regret each courtly fcene,
  Where thou wert faireſt of the fair?

O Nancy! canſt thou love fo true,
  Thro' perils keen with me to go;
Or when thy fwain mifhap fhall rue,
  To fhare with him the pang of woe?
Say, fhould difeafe or pain befal,
  Wilt thou affume the nurfe's care;
Nor, wiftful, thofe gay fcenes recal
  Where thou wert faireſt of the fair?

And when at laft thy love fhall die,
  Wilt thou receive his parting breath ?
Wilt thou reprefs each ftruggling figh,
  And chear with fmiles the bed of death ?
And wilt thou o'er his breathlefs clay
  Strew flowers, and drop the tender tear;
Nor then regret thofe fcenes fo gay,
  Where thou wert faireft of the fair ?

SONG 1167.

SAY not, Olinda, I defpife
  The faded glories of your face,
The languid vigour of your eyes,
  And that once-lov'd embrace.

In vain, in vain, my conftant heart
  On aged wings attempts to meet,
With wonted fpeed, thofe flames you dart,
  It faints, and flutters at your feet.

I blame not your decay of power,
  You may have pointed beauties ftill,
Tho' me, alas! they wound no more;
  You cannot hurt what cannot feel.

On youthful climes your beams difplay,
  There you may cherifh with your heat,
And rife the fun to gild their day,
  To me, benighted, when you fet.

SONG 1168.

Written by the Earl of ROCHESTER.

ALL my paft life is mine no more,
  The flying hours are gone;
Like tranfitory dreams given o'er,
  Whofe images are kept in ftore
    By memory alone.

The time that is to come, is not;
  How, then, can it be mine ?
The prefent moment's all my lot,
And that, as faft as it is got,
  Phillis, is only thine.

Then talk not of inconftancy,
  Falfe hearts, and broken vows;
If I, by miracle, can be
This live-long minute true to thee,
  'Tis all that heaven allows.

SONG 1169.

THE LASS OF THE MILL.

WHO has e'er been at Baldock muft needs
    know the mill,
At the fign of the horfe, at the foot of the hill;
Where the grave and the gay, the clown and
    the beau,
Without all diftinction promifcuofly go.

The man of the mill has a daughter fo fair,
With fo pleafing a fhape, and fo winning an air,
That once on the ever-green bank as I ftood,
I fwore fhe was Venus, juft fprung from the
    flood.

But looking again, I perceiv'd my miftake,
For Venus, tho' fair, has the look of a rake;
While nothing but virtue and modefty fill
The mere beautiful looks of the lafs of the
    mill.

Prometheus ftole fire, as the poets all fay,
To enliven that mafs which he modell'd of clay;
Had Polly been there, the beams of her eyes
Had fav'd him the trouble of robbing the fkies.

Since firft I beheld this dear lafs of the mill,
I can ne'er be at quiet, but do what I will,
All the day and all night I figh and think ftill,
I fhall die if I have not this lafs of the mill.

SONG 1170.

Written by Mr. TOMLINS.

BLEST be the man whofe bofom beats
  To hear the anxious tale of woe,
Whofe gen'rous heart with pity melts,
  And bids the tender tear to flow:

Whofe bounteous hand has wip'd the dew
  From poverty's afflicted cheek;
Whofe fearch misfortune's haunt has found,
  And eas'd diftrefs that fear'd to fpeak.

When he to fate refigns his breath,
  Regretted and rever'd by all,
Then oft, full oft, upon his tomb,
  The tear of gratitude fhall fall.

SONG 1171.

WHAT! put off with one denial,
  And not make a fecond trial ?
You might fee my eyes confenting,
All about me was relenting;
Women, oblig'd to dwell in forms,
Forgive the youth that boldly ftorms.

Lovers, when you figh and languifh,
When you tell us of your anguifh,
To the nymph you'll be more pleafing
When thofe forrows you are eafing:
We love to try how far men dare,
And never wifh the foe fhould fpare.

SONG 1172.

Written by SOAME JENYNS, Efq.

WHEN firft I fought fair Cælia's love,
  And ev'ry charm was new,
I fwore by all the gods above
  To be for ever true.

But long in vain did I adore,
  Long wept and figh'd in vain;
She ftill protefted, vow'd, and fwore
  She ne'er would eafe my pain.

At laft o'ercome, fhe made me bleft,
  And yielded all her charms;
And I forfook her when poffeft,
  And fled to others arms.

But let not this, dear Cælia, now
 To rage thy breast incline,
For why, since you forgot your vow,
 Should I remember mine ?

SONG 1173.

CORINNA cost me many a pray'r,
 Ere I her heart could gain,
But she ten thousand more should hear
 To take that heart again.

Despair I thought the greatest curse,
 But to my cost I find
Corinna's constancy still worse,
 Most cruel when too kind.

How blindly then does Cupid carve,
 How ill divide the joy ;
Who does at first his lovers starve,
 And then with plenty cloy !

SONG 1174.

SWAIN, thy hopeless passion smother,
 Perjur'd Celia loves another ;
In his arms I saw her lying,
 Panting, kissing, trembling, dying ;
There the fair deceiver swore,
 All she did to you before.

Oh! said you, when she deceives me,
 When that constant creature leaves me,
Isis' waters back shall fly,
 And leave their oozy channels dry ;
Turn, ye waters, leave your shore,
 Perjur'd Celia loves no more.

SONG 1175.

CUPID, instruct an amorous swain
 Some way to tell the nymph his pain,
 To common youths unknown ;
To talk of sighs, and flames, and darts,
Of bleeding wounds, and burning hearts,
 Are methods vulgar grown.

What need'st thou tell ! (the god reply'd)
That love the shepherd cannot hide,
 The nymph will quickly find ;
When Phœbus does his beams display,
'To tell men gravely that 'tis day,
 Is to suppose them blind.

SONG 1176.

Written by Mr. CONGREVE.

TELL me no more I am deceiv'd,
 'That Chloe's false and common ;
I always knew (at least believ'd)
 She was a very woman :
As such I lik'd, as such caress'd,
She still was constant when possess'd,
 She could do more for no man.

But oh ! her thoughts on others ran ;
 And that you think a hard thing !
Perhaps she fancy'd you the man ;
 And what care I one farthing ?
You think she's false, I'm sure she's kind,
I take her body, you her mind,
 Who has the better bargain ?

SONG 1177.

Written by Lord LANDSDOWN.

CHLOE's the wonder of her sex,
 'Tis well her heart is tender ;
How might such killing eyes perplex,
 With virtue to defend her !

But nature, graciously inclin'd,
 With liberal hand to please us,
Has to her boundless beauty join'd
 A boundless bent to ease us.

SONG 1178.

VAIN are the charms of white and red,
 Which paint the blooming fair ;
Give me the nymph whose snow is spread
 Not o'er her face, but hair.

Of smoother cheeks the winning grace
 With open force defies ;
But in the wrinkles of her face
 Cupid in ambush lies.

If naked eyes set hearts on blaze,
 And amorous warmth inspire ;
Thro' glass, who darts her pointed rays,
 Lights up a fiercer fire.

Nor rivals, nor the train of years,
 My peace or bliss destroy ;
Alive, she gives no jealous fears,
 And dead, she crowns my joy.

SONG 1179.

CHLOE brisk and gay appears,
 On purpose to invite ;
Yet, when I press her, she, in tears,—
 Denies her sole delight.

Whilst Celia, seeming shy and coy,
 To all her favours grants ;
And secretly receives that joy,
 Which others think she wants.

I would, but fear I never shall,
 With either fair agree ;
For Celia will be kind to all,
 But Chloe won't to me.

SONG 1180.

OH ! turn away those cruel eyes,
 The stars of my undoing ;
Or death, in such a bright disguise,
 May tempt a second wooing.

Punish their blindly impious pride
Who dare contemn thy glory;
It was my fall that deify'd
Thy name, and seal'd thy story.

Yet no new suff'rings can prepare
A higher praise to crown thee;
Tho' my first death proclaim thee fair,
My second will dethrone thee.

Lovers will doubt thou canst entice
No other for thy fuel;
And if thou burn one victim twice,
Think thee both poor and cruel.

SONG 1181.

IF the quick spirit of your eye,
Now languish, and anon must die;
If every sweet and every grace
Must fly from that forsaken face;
Then, Celia, let us reap our joys,
Ere time such goodly fruit destroys.

Or if that golden fleece must grow
For ever free from aged snow;
If those bright suns must know no shade,
Nor your fresh beauty ever fade;
Then, Celia, fear not to bestow
What still being gather'd, still must grow,

  Thus either time his fickle brings
  In vain, or else in vain his wings.

SONG 1182.

LATE when love I seem'd to slight,
Phillis smil'd, as well she might;
Now, said she, our throne may tremble,
Men our province now invade,
Men take up our royal trade;
Men, e'en men, do now diffemble,
In the dust our empire's laid.

Tutor'd by the wise and grave,
Lothe I was to be a slave;
Mistress founded arbitrary;
So I chose to hide my flame,
Friendship, a discreeter name;
But she scorns one jot to vary;
She will love, or nothing, claim.

Be a lover, or pretend,
Rather than the warmest friend;
Friendship of another kind is
Swedish coin of gross allay,
A cart-load will scarce defray;
Love, one grain is worth the Indies,
Only love is current pay.

SONG 1183.

Written by Mr. SHENSTONE.

YE shepherds, give ear to my lay,
And take no more heed of my sheep;
They have nothing to do but to stray,
I have nothing to do but to weep.

Yet do not my folly reprove;
She was fair—and my passion begun;
She smil'd—and I could not but love;
She is faithless—and I am undone.

Perhaps I was void of all thought;
Perhaps it was plain to foresee,
That a nymph so compleat would be sought
By a swain more engaging than me.
Ah! love ev'ry hope can inspire,
It banishes wisdom the while;
And the lip of the nymph we admire
Seems for ever adorn'd with a smile.

She is faithless, and I am undone;
Yet that witness the woes I endure,
Let reason instruct you to shun
What it cannot instruct you to cure.
Beware how ye loiter in vain
Amid nymphs of an higher degree:
It is not for me to explain
How fair and how fickle they be.

O ye woods! spread your branches apace,
To your deepest recesses I fly;
I would hide with the beasts of the chace;
I would vanish from every eye.
Yet my reed shall resound through the grove,
With the same sad complaint it begun;
How she smil'd, and I could not but love;
Was faithless, and I am undone.

SONG 1184.

A SIGH.

GENTLE air, thou breath of lovers,
Vapour from a secret fire,
Which by thee itself discovers,
Ere yet daring to aspire.

Softest note of whisper'd anguish,
Harmony's refined part;
Striking, while thou seem'st to languish,
Full upon the list'ner's heart.

Softest messenger of passion,
Stealing thro' a cloud of spies,
Which constrain the outward fashion,
Close the lips, and guard the eyes.

Shapeless sigh, we ne'er can show thee,
Form'd but to assault the ear;
Yet, ere to their cost they know thee,
Ev'ry nymph may read thee here.

SONG 1185.

Written by Mr. WALLER.

CHLORIS, yourself you so excel,
When you vouchsafe to breathe my thought,
That, like a spirit, with this spell
Of my own teaching, I am caught.

S f

The eagle's fate and mine are one,
　Which on the shaft that made him die,
Espy'd a feather of his own,
　Wherewith he us'd to soar so high.

Had Echo, with so sweet a grace,
　Narcissus' loud complaints return'd ;
Not for reflection of his face,
　But of his voice, the boy had burn'd.

SONG 1186.

WINE, wine in the morning
　　Makes us frolick and gay,
That, like eagles, we soar
　In the pride of the day ;
Gouty sots of the night
　Only find a decay.

'Tis the fun ripes the grape,
　And to drinking gives light ;
We imitate him
　When by noon we're at height ;
They steal wine, who take it
　When he's out of fight.

Boy, fill all the glasses,
　Fill them up now he shines ;
The higher he rifes,
　The more he refines ;
For wine and wit fail
　As their maker declines.

SONG 1187.

WHY, Celia, should you so much strive
　Your kindling passion to conceal ?
Your lips, tho' they denial give,
　Yet all your actions love reveal.

In vain you strive, in vain, alas !
　The charming passion to disguise ;
It glows, it blushes on your face,
　And sparkles in your swimming eyes.

Your eyes, those emblems of the heart,
　Still contradict whate'er you say ;
And tho' your lips deny the smart,
　Your eyes are more believ'd than they.

SONG 1188.

IN vain, dear Chloe, you suggest,
　That I, inconstant, have possest,
　Or lov'd a fairer she ;
Would you with ease at once be cur'd
Of all the ills you've long endur'd,
　Consult your glass and me.

If then you think that I can find
A nymph more fair, or one more kind,
　You've reason for your fears ;
But if impartial you will prove
To your own beauty, or my love,
　How needless are your tears !

If in my way I should by chance
Receive or give a wanton glance,
　I like but while I view ;

How slight the glance, how faint the kiss,
Compar'd to that substantial bliss
　Which I receive from you !

With wanton flight the curious bee
From flower to flower still wanders free,
　And where each blossom blows,
Extracts the juice from all he meets ;
But, for his quintessence of sweets,
　He ravishes the rose.

So, my fond fancy to employ
On each variety of joy,
　From nymph to nymph I roam ;
Perhaps see fifty in a day ;
These are but visits that I pay,
　For Chloe is my home.

SONG 1189.

A BACCHANALIAN SONG.

Written by Mr. HEYWOOD.

WELL met, jolly fellows, well met ;
　By this bowl you're all welcome, I swear :
See where on the table 'tis set,
　And defign'd for the grave of our care.
　　From this social convention,
　　'Twill drive all contention,
Save only who longest can drink ;
　　Then fill up your glasses,
　　And drink to your lasses,
The head-ache take him that shall shrink.

Do but look at this glass ! here, boys, hand it
　around ;
Why it sparkles like Phillis's eye ;
But 'tis better by far, boys ; for when her
　eyes wound,
　This balm to the wound will supply :
　　Then a fig for all thinking ;
　　Fill, fill, and be drinking ;
Let us drown all our cares and our sorrow :
　　Come, the toast, boys, the toast !
　　There's no time to be lost,
For our cares will return with to-morrow.

SONG 1190.

THE ATTIC FIRE.

WHEN all the Attic fire was fled,
　And all the Roman virtue dead,
　　Poor Freedom lost her seat ;
The Gothic mantle spread a night,
That damp'd fair virtue's fading light,
　　The muses lost their mate.

Where should they wander, what new shore
Has yet a laurel left in store ?
　　To this blest isle they steer ;
Soon the Parnassian choir was heard,
Soon virtue's sacred form appear'd,
　And Freedom soon was here.

The lazy monk has left his cell,
Religion rings her hallow'd bell,
　She calls thee now by me :

Hark, her sweet voice all plaintive sounds,
See, she receives a thousand wounds,
  If shielded not by thee.

SONG 1191.

HOW blest has my time been! what days
  have I known
Since wedlock's soft bondage made Jessy my
  own!
So joyful my heart is, so easy my chain,
That freedom is tasteless, and roving a pain.

Through walks grown with woodbines as often
  we stray,
Around us our boys and girls frolic and play;
How pleasing the sport is! the wanton ones see,
And borrow their looks from my Jessy and me.

To try her sweet temper, oft times I am seen
In revels all day with the nymphs of the green;
Tho' painful my absence, my doubts she be-
  guiles,
And meets me at night with compliance and
  smiles.

What tho' on her cheeks the rose loses it's hue,
Her ease and good humour bloom all the year
  through:
Time still, as he flies, adds increase to her truth,
And gives to her mind what he steals from her
  youth.

Ye shepherds so gay, who make love to ensnare,
And cheat with false vows the too credulous
  fair;
In search of true pleasure, how vainly you
  roam!
To hold it for life, you must find it at home.

SONG 1192.

HUSH, ye birds, your amorous tales,
  Purling rills in silence move!
Softly breathe, ye gentle gales,
  Lest ye wake my slumb'ring love.

O the joy beyond expression,
  That enchanting form to own!
Then to hear the soft confession,
  That her heart is mine alone.

SONG 1193.

THE FOND FAIR.

WHEN lovers for favours petition,
  Oh! then they approach with respect;
But when in our hearts they've admission,
  They treat us with scorn and neglect;
'Tis dangerous ever to try them,
  So artful are men to deceive;
'Tis safer, much safer to fly them,
  So easy are maids to believe.

O Cupid! why art thou pursuing
Such endless designs on my heart,
To make me so fond of my ruin,
And doat on the cause of my smart:
In vain do I strive to remove him;
Affection to reason is blind;
In spite of his failings I love him,
He's charming, tho' false and unkind.

SONG 1194.

MY former time, how brisk and gay,
  So blithe was I, as o'ithe could be;
But now I'm sad, ah! well-a-day,
  For my true love is gone to sea.

The lads pursue, I strive to shun,
  Their wheedling arts are lost on me;
For I to death shall love but one,
  And he, alas! is gone to sea.

As droop the flow'rs till light return,
  As mourns the dove it's absent she;
So will I droop, so will I mourn,
  Till my true love returns from sea.

SONG 1195.

IN this shady blest retreat
  I've been wishing for my dear;
Hark! I hear his welcome feet
  Tell the lovely charmer's near.

'Tis the sweet bewitching swain,
  True to love's appointed hour;
Joy and peace now smile again:
  Love! I own thy mighty power.

SONG 1196.

Sung in *Comus*.

SWEET Echo! sweetest nymph, that liv'st
  unseen
  Within thy airy cell,
By slow meander's margin green,
  And in the violet-embroider'd vale,
  Where the love-lorn nightingale
Nightly to thee her sad song mourneth well;
  Canst thou not tell me of a gentle pair,
  That likest thy Narcissus are?
    O! if you have
  Hid them in some flow'ry cave;
    Tell me but where,
Sweet queen of parley, daughter of the sphere?
So may'st thou be translated to the skies,
And give resounding grace to all heaven's
  harmonies!

SONG 1197.

THE new-flown birds the shepherds sing,
  And welcome in the May;
Come, Pastorella, now the spring
  Makes ev'ry landscape gay:
     S f 2

Wide-spreading trees their leafy shade
  O'er half the plain extend,
Or, in reflecting fountains play'd,
  Their quiv'ring branches bend.

Come, taste the season in it's prime,
  And bless the rising year;
Oh! how my soul grows sick of time,
  Till thou, my love, appear!
Then shall I pass the gladsome day,
  Warm in thy beauty's shine,
When thy dear flock shall feed and play,
  And intermix with mine.

For thee of doves a milk-white pair
  In silken bands I hold;
For thee a firstling lambkin fair
  I keep within the fold :
If milk-white doves acceptance meet,
  Or tender lambkins please,
My spotless heart without deceit,
  Be offer'd up with ease.

SONG 1198.

Sung in the *Beggar's Opera.*

VIRGINS are like the fair flow'r in it's
  luftre,
Which in the garden enamels the ground;
Near it, the bees in play flutter and cluster,
And gaudy butterflies frolick around.

But when once pluck'd, 'tis no longer alluring,
  To Covent-Garden 'tis sent as yet sweet;
There shrinks, and fades, and grows past all en-
  during;
Rots, stinks, and dies, and is trod under feet.

SONG 1199.

WHEN Flora decks the mantling bow'rs
  In elegant array,
And scatters all her op'ning flowers
  To compliment the May;

With glowing joy my bosom beats,
  I gaze delighted round,
And wish to see the various sweets
  In one rich nosegay bound.

'Tis granted; and their bloom decay'd,
  To bless my wond'ring view,
I see them all, my beauteous maid,
  I see them all in you.

SONG 1200.

ON his face the vernal rose,
  Blended with the lily, glows;
His locks are as the raven black,
In ringlets woven down his back.

His eyes with milder beauties beam,
Than billing doves beside the stream;
His youthful cheeks are beds of flow'rs,
Enripen'd by refreshing show'rs.

His lips are of the rose's hue,
Still dropping with a fragrant dew;
Tall as the cedar he appears,
And as erect his form he bears.

SONG 1201.

Sung in the *Rose.*

AH! think not to deceive me
  With flatt'ring oaths and lies,
'Tis all in vain, believe me,
  For love has piercing eyes.

A trifling present given,
  Oft binds affection fast,
And grateful woman's driven
  To give herself at last.

SONG 1202.

Sung in the *Rose.*

BRIGHT the sky, and calm the ocean,
  Now my bark will sweetly glide;
Oh! how pleasing is the motion,
  Sailing thus with wind and tide.

Hidden rocks no more beguiling,
  Swelling sails the breezes court,
Cupid at the helm sits smiling,
  And conducts me safe to port.

SONG 1203.

NATURE gave all creatures arms,
  Faithful guards from hostile harms;
Jaws the lion brood defend,
Horrid jaws that wide distend;
Horns the bull's resistless force,
Solid hoofs the vigorous horse,
Nimble feet the fearful hare,
Wings to fly the birds of air.

To the fox did wiles ordain,
The craftiest of the sylvan train;
Tufks she gave the grunting swine,
Quills the fretful porcupine;
Fins to swim the wat'ry kind,
Man the virtues of the mind;
Nature lavishing her store,
What for woman had she more!

Helpless woman, to be fair,
Beauty fell to woman's share;
Beauty, that nor wants, or fears,
Sword or flames, or shield or spears;
Beauty stronger aid affords,
Stronger far than shield or swords;
Stronger far than swords or shields,
Man himself to beauty yields.

SONG 1204.

LOVELY maid! fair beauty's pride,
  Do not thus my bliss deny;
Cease, my tender love, to chide;
  Why so cruel, Daphne, why?

Kindly to my wifh incline,
Why will Daphne faithlefs prove?
Know my foul is wholly thine,
And my heart is form'd for love.

Why, thus flight a faithful fwain,
Who to love was ever true ;
Why thus give that bofom pain,
Which fo long hath figh'd for you?

SONG 1205.

Written by Mr. DRYDEN.

A Choir of bright beauties in fpring did appear,
To chufe a May-lady to govern the year;
All the nymphs were in white, and the fhepherds in green,
The garland was giv'n, and Phillis was queen:
But Phillis refus'd it, and fighing did fay,
I'll wear not a garland while Pan is away.

While Pan and fair Syrinx are fled from our fhore,
The graces are banifh'd, and love is no more :
The foft god of pleafure, that warm'd our defires,
Has broken his bow, and extinguifh'd his fires;
And vows that himfelf and his mother will mourn,
Till Pan and fair Syrinx in triumph return.

Forbear your addreffes, and court us no more;
For we will perform what the deity fwore:
But if you dare think of deferving our charms,
Away with your fheep-hooks, and take to your arms :
The laurels and myrtles your brows fhall adorn,
When Pan, and his fon, and fair Syrinx, return.

SONG 1206.

APOLLO MAKING LOVE.

Written by Mr. TICKELL.

I Am, cry'd Apollo, when Daphne he woo'd,
And, panting for breath, the coy virgin purfu'd;
When his wifdom, in manner moft ample, expreft
The long lift of graces his godfhip poffeft.

I'm the god of fweet fong, and infpirer of lays.
Nor for lays nor fweet fong the fair fugitive ftays.
I'm the god of the harp—ftop, my faireft. In vain ;
Nor the harp, nor the harper, could fetch her again.

Ev'ry plant, ev'ry flow'r, and their virtues I know;
God of light I'm above, and of phyfic below.

At the dreadful word phyfic, the nymph fled more faft;
At the fatal word phyfic fhe doubled her hafte.

Thou fond god of wifdom, then alter thy phrafe,
Bid her view thy young bloom, and thy ravifhing rays;
Tell her lefs of thy knowledge, and more of thy charms,
And, my life for't, the damfel fhall fly to thy arms.

SONG 1207.

Written by Mr. WALLER.

PHILLIS ! why fhould we delay
Pleafures fhorter than the day?
Could we (which we never can!)
Stretch our lives beyond their fpan ;
Beauty like a fhadow flies,
And our youth before us dies.
Or would youth, and beauty, ftay,
Love hath wings, and will away.
Love hath fwifter wings than time :
Change in love to heaven does climb;
Gods, that never change their ftate,
Vary oft their love and hate.

Phillis ! to this truth we owe
All the love betwixt us two :
Let not you and I enquire,
What has been our paft defire;
On what fhepherds you have fmil'd,
Or what nymphs I have beguil'd :
Leave it to the planets, too,
What we fhall hereafter do:
For the joys we now may prove,
Take advice of prefent love.

SONG 1208

THE HAPPY SWAIN.

Written by AMBROSE PHILIPS.

HAVE ye feen the morning fky,
When the dawn prevails on high,
When, anon, fome purple ray,
Gives a fample of the day;
When, anon, the lark on wing,
Strives to foar, and ftrains to fing?

Have ye feen th' ethereal blue,
Gently fhedding filver dew,
Spangling o'er the filent green,
While the nightingale, unfeen,
To the moon and ftars full bright,
Lonefome chants the hymn of night?

Have ye feen the broider'd May,
All her fcented blooms difplay,
Breezes opening every hour,
This and that expecting flower,
While the mingling birds prolong,
From each bufh, the vernal fong?

Have ye feen the damafk rofe
Her unfully'd blufh difclofe;

Or the lily's dewy bell,
In her gloſſy white excel;
Or a garden vary'd o'er
With a thouſand glories more?

By the beauties theſe diſplay,
Morning, evening, night, or day;
By the pleaſures theſe excite,
Endleſs ſources of delight!
Judge by them the joys I find,
Since my Roſalind was kind;
Since ſhe did herſelf refign
To my vows, for ever mine.

SONG 1209.

Sung in the *Provok'd Huſband*.

OH, I'll have a huſband! ay, marry;
For why ſhould I longer tarry
Than other briſk girls have done ?
For if I ſtay, till I grow grey,
They'll call me old maid, and fuſty old jade;
So I'll no longer tarry;
But I'll have a huſband, ay, marry,
If money can buy me one.

My mother ſhe ſays I'm too coming;
And ſtill in my ears ſhe is drumming,
That I ſuch vain thoughts ſhould ſhun.
My ſiſters they cry, O fye! O fye!
But yet I can ſee, they're as coming as me;
So let me have huſbands in plenty:
I'd rather have twenty times twenty,
Than die an old maid undone.

SONG 1210.

Written by Mr. WALLER.

PEACE, babling muſe!
I dare not ſing what you indite;
Her eyes refuſe
To read the paſſion which they write:
She ſtrikes my lute, but, if it found,
Threatens to hurl it on the ground:
And I no leſs her anger dread,
Than the poor wretch that feigns him dead,
While ſome fierce lion does embrace
His breathleſs corſe, and licks his face:
Wrapt up in ſilent fear he lies,
Torn all in pieces if he cries.

SONG 1211.

Written by Sir JOHN VANBURGH.

NOT an angel dwells above
Half ſo fair as her I love;
Heaven knows how ſhe'll receive me:
If ſhe ſmiles, I'm bleſt indeed;
If ſhe frowns, I'm quickly freed;
Heaven knows ſhe ne'er can grieve me.

None can love her more than I,
Yet ſhe ne'er ſhall make me die.
If my flame can never warm her,

Other beauties I'll adore,
I ſhall never love her more,
Cruelty will ſo deform her.

SONG 1212.

Sung in the *Cuſtom of the Manor*.

WHEN the roſe is in bud, and blue violets
blow,
And the birds ſing us love-ſongs from every
bough;
When cowſlips and daiſies, and daffodils ſpread,
Adorning, perfuming the flowery mead;
Our cleanly milk-pail
Is fill'd with brown ale;
Our table, our table's the graſs :
There we ſit and and we ſing,
And we dance in a ring,
And every lad has his laſs.

When without the plough the fat oxen do low,
The lads and the laſſes a ſheep-ſhearing go;
Our ſhepherd ſhears his jolly, jolly fleece,
How much richer than that which they ſay
was in Greece !
'Tis our cloth, and our food,
And our politic blood ;
'Tis the feat which our nobles all ſit on;
'Tis a mine above ground,
Where our treaſure's all found ;
'Tis the gold and the ſilver of Britain.

SONG 1213.

SAYS Damon to Phillis, Suppoſe my fond
eyes
Reveal with what ardour I glow !
Well, what if they do ? there's no harm, ſure,
ſhe cries ;
I can but deny you, you know.

Suppoſe I ſhould aſk of thoſe lips a ſweet kiſs,
Say, would you the favour beſtow ?
Lord bleſs me! ſaid ſhe, what a queſtion is this!
I can but deny you, you know.

Suppoſe, not contented, I ſtill aſk for more ?
For pleaſure from pleaſure will grow.
Suppoſe what you will, ſhe reply'd as before,
I can but deny you, you know.

Come then, my dear love, to the woods let's
repair ?
Cry'd Damon; and offer'd to go.
No, no, (with a bluſh) anſwer'd Phillis, for
there
I could not deny you, you know.

SONG 1214.

LOVE AND CONSTANCY.

Sung at RANELAGH.

LONG time my heart had rov'd,
Inconſtant as the wind ;
Each girl I ſaw, I ſwore I lov'd,
Till one my heart confin'd.

The maid was blithe, was young and fair,
From affectation free :
No imperfection did appear,
While she look'd kind on me.

When her my pain I told,
And all my grief confefs'd,
The infolence of female pride
Her cold difdain exprefs'd ;
The beauty I efteem'd before,
Appear'd deformity ;
Each charm I thought a charm no more,
She was unkind to me.

Forbear, fond youth, no more
The fex's weaknefs fcan ;
'Twas not inconftancy, or pride,
But trial of the man :
When time had prov'd my flame fincere,
She own'd the fame to me ;
Not love alone can win the fair,
But love and conftancy.

SONG 1215.

Sung at VAUXHALL.

HARK ! the birds begin their lay,
Flowrets deck the robe of May :
See the little lambkins bound,
Playful, o'er the clover-ground ;
While the heifers fportive low
Where the yellow cowflips blow.

Now the nymphs and fwains advance
O'er the lawn in perfect dance ;
Garlands from the hawthorn bough
Grace the happy fhepherd's brow ;
While the laffes, in array,
Wait upon the queen of May.

Innocence, content and love,
Fill the meadows and the grove ;
Mirth that never wears a frown,
Health with fweetnefs all her own ;
Labour puts on pleafure's fmile,
And pale care forgets his toil.

Ah ! what pleafures fhepherds know !
Monarchs cannot fuch beftow ;
Love improves each happy hour,
Grandeur has not fuch in ftore.
Learn, ambition, learn from hence,
Happinefs is innocence.

SONG 1216.

CURE FOR THE VAPOURS.

Sung at RANELAGH.

WHY will Delia thus retire,
And languifh all her life away,
While the fighing crowd admire ?
'Tis too foon for hartfhorn-tea.

All thofe difmal looks and fretting
Cannot Damon's life reftore ;
Long ago the worms have eat him ;
You can never fee him more.

Once again confult your toilette,
In the glafs your face review ;
So much weeping foon will fpoil it,
And no fpring your charms renew.

I like you was born a woman,
Well I know what vapours mean ;
The difeafe, alas ! is common ;
Single, we have all the fpleen.

All the morals that they tell us,
Never cur'd the forrow yet :
Chufe, among the pretty fellows,
One of humour, youth and wit.

Pr'ythee hear him ev'ry morning,
At the leaft an hour or two ;
Once again at night returning :—
I believe the dofe will do.

SONG 1217.

Sung in the *Confcious Lovers*.

DOES the languid foul complain,
Virtuous love fhall chafe the pain ;
Or if love wou'd truth attend,
Honour fhou'd be virtue's friend.

Glory is not half fo fair
As bright virtue's rifing ftar ;
Female truth, with fenfe combin'd,
Wins and claims the gen'rous mind.

SONG 1218.

CELIA'S COMPLAINT.

WHAT fadnefs reigns over the plain !
How droop the fweet flowrets around !
How penfive each nymph and each fwain !
How filent each mufical found !
No more the foft lute in the bow'rs,
Beguiles the cool ev'nings away ;
Sad fighs meafure out the long hours,
Since Damon has wander'd away.

Oh ! he was our village's pride,
This change from his abfence is feen ;
'Twas he that our mufic fupply'd,
When gaily we danc'd on the green :
At fhearing, at wake, and at fair,
How jovial and frolic were we !
But now ev'ry feaft in the year
Is joylefs as joylefs can be.

Ah ! why did he venture from home,
To mix among hoftile alarms ?
No juftice oblig'd him to roam,
Or take up thofe terrible arms :
Let thofe who are cruel and rough,
Be heedlefs of life and of limb ;
The country had foldiers enough,
Nor needed one gentle like him.

Where'er the adventurer goes,
On land or the dangerous main,
Kind heaven protect him from woes,
And give him to Celia again.

Oh! give him to Celia again,
　My true love in safety restore ;
I'll cease on his breast to complain,
　From my arms he shall wander no more.

SONG 1219.

DELIA; A PASTORAL.

Sung at VAUXHALL.

THE gentle swan, with graceful pride,
　Her glossy plumage laves ;
And sailing down the silver tide,
　Divides the whisp'ring waves :
The silver tide that wand'ring flows,
　Sweet to the bird must be ;
But not so sweet, blithe Cupid knows,
　As Delia is to me.

A parent bird, in plaintive mood,
　On yonder fruit-tree sung ;
And still the pendant nest she view'd,
　That held her feather'd young :
Tho' dear to her maternal heart
　The genial brood must be ;
They're not so dear, the thousandth part,
　As Delia is to me.

The roses that my brow surround,
　Were natives of the dale ;
Scarce pluck'd, and in a garland bound,
　Before their hue grew pale :
My vital blood would thus be froze,
　If luckless torn from thee ;
For what the root is to the rose,
　My Delia is to me.

Two doves I found like new fall'n snow,
　So white the beauteous pair ;
The birds to Delia I'll bestow,
　They're like her bosom fair :
May they, of our connubial love,
　A happy omen be :
Then such fond bliss as turtles prove,
　Shall Delia share with me.

SONG 1220.

AN ANTIGALLICAN SONG.

YE sons of freedom ! hail the day
　When first our order rose ;
To chace corruption's cloud away,
　And venal arts oppose :
Grant heav'n, that o'er the nation
　Our principles may spring !
The forest preservation
　Of country and of king.

Great George, for whom our bosoms glow,
　Send all thy statesmen here ;
Thy ministers more wise shall grow ;
　All courtiers more sincere :
True honour shall inspire them,
　The Gallic race to brand,
And patriot love shall fire them
　To save this sinking land.

Tho' Spain shou'd Gallia's pride assist,
　No honest heart will fail ;
Our thunder shall their force resist ;
　The British cross prevail.
Tho' some our wrongs wou'd smother,
　Yet we'll those wrongs resent.
Here's a health to every brother,
　And to our president.

SONG 1221.

STELLA and Flavia ev'ry hour
　Do various hearts surprise !
In Stella's soul lies all her pow'r,
　And Flavia's in her eyes !

Like Britain's monarch, Stella reigns
　O'er cultivated lands !
Like eastern tyrants, Flavia deigns
　To rule o'er barren sands.

More boundless Flavia's conquests are,
　And Stella's more confin'd ;
All can discern a face that's fair,
　But few a beauteous mind !

Then boast, vain Flavia! boast thy face,
　Thy beauty's slender store !
Thy charms will every day decrease,
　Each day give Stella more.

SONG 1222.

JENNY GREY.

Sung at RANELAGH.

BRING, Phœbus, from Parnassian bow'rs,
　A chaplet of poetic flow'rs
That far out-bloom the May ;
Bring verse so smooth, and thoughts so free,
And all the muses heraldry,
　To blazon Jenny Grey.

Observe yon almond's rich perfume,
Preventing spring with early bloom,
　In ruddy tints how gay !
Thus, foremost of the blushing fair,
With such a blithsome, buxom air,
　Blooms lovely Jenny Grey.

The merry, chirping, plumy throng,
The bushes and the twigs among,
　That pipe the sylvan lay,
All hush'd at her delightful voice,
In silent extasy rejoice,
　And study Jenny Grey.

Ye balmy odour-breathing gales,
That lightly sweep the green-rob'd vales,
　And in each rose-bush play ;
I know you all, you're errant cheats,
And steal your more than nat'ral sweets
　From lovely Jenny Grey.

Pomona, and that goddess bright,
The florists and the maids delight,
　In vain their charms display ;
The luscious nectarine, juicy peach,
In richness nor in sweetness reach
　The lips of Jenny Grey.

To the sweet knot of graces three,
Th' immortal bands of bards agree
  A tuneful tax to pay ;
There yet remains a matchless worth,
There yet remains a lovelier fourth,
  And she is Jenny Grey.

SONG 1223.

A FREE-MASON'S SONG.

WE have no idle prating,
    Of either whig or tory ;
      But each agrees
      To live at ease,
And sing or tell a story.
      Fill to him,
      To the brim,
Let it round the table roll :
      The divine
      Tells us wine
Chears the body and the soul.

We're always men of pleasure,
Despising pride and party ;
      While knaves and fools,
      Prescribe us rules,
We are sincere and hearty.
    Fill to him, &c.

If an accepted Mason
Should talk of high or low church ;
      We'll set him down
      A shallow crown,
And understand him no church.
    Fill to him, &c.

The world is all in darkness;
About us they conjecture,
      But little think
      A song and drink
Succeed a Mason's lecture.
    Fill to him, &c.

Then landlord bring a hogshead,
And in the corner place it;
      Till it rebound
      With hollow sound,
Each Mason here will face it.
      Fill to him,
      To the brim,
Let it round the table roll ;
      The divine
      Tells us wine
Chears the body and the soul.

SONG 1224.

THE MIDSUMMER WISH.

Written by Dr. CROXALL.

WAFT me, some soft and cooling breeze,
    To Windsor's shady, kind retrreat;
Where sylvan scenes, wide-spreading trees,
    Repel the raging dog-star's heat :
Where tufted grass, and mossy beds,
    Afford a rural, calm repose ;
Where woodbines hang their dewy heads,
    And fragrant sweets around disclose.

Old oozy Thames, that flows fast by,
    Along the smiling valley plays,
His glossy surface chears the eye,
    And thro' the flow'ry meadows strays:
His fertile banks, with herbage green,
    His vales with golden plenty swell ;
Where'er his purer streams are seen,
    The gods of health and pleasure dwell.

Let me thy clear, thy yielding wave,
    With naked arms once more divide ;
In thee my glowing bosom lave,
    And cut the gently-rolling tide.
Lay me with damask roses crown'd,
    Beneath some osier's dusky shade ;
Where water-lilies deck the ground,
    And bubbling springs refresh the glade.

Let dear Lucinda too be there,
    With azure mantle slightly drest :
Ye nymphs, bind up her flowing hair;
    Ye zephyrs, fan her panting breast.
O haste away, fair maid, and bring
    The muse, the kindly friend to love!
To thee alone the muse shall sing,
    And warble through the vocal grove.

SONG 1225.

SOLICITUDE; A PASTORAL.

Written by Mr. SHENSTONE.

WHY will you my passion reprove,
    Why term it a folly to grieve,
Ere I tell you the charms of my love!
    She's fairer than you can believe.

With her mien she enamours the brave,
    With her wit she engages the free,
With her modesty pleases the grave ;
    She's every way pleasing to me.

When Paridel tries in the dance
    Some favour with Phillis to find,
Oh ! how with one trivial glance
    Might she ruin the peace of my mind !

In ringlets he dresses his hair,
    And his crook is bestudded around ;
And his pipe—oh ! may Phillis beware
    Of a magick there is in it's found.

Let his crook be with hyacinths bound,
    So Phillis the trophy despise !
Let his forehead with laurels be crown'd,
    So they shine not in Phillis's eyes.

The language that flows from the heart
    Is a stranger to Paridel's tongue ;
Yet may she beware of his art,
    Or sure I must envy the song.

SONG 1226.

YOU may cease to complain,
    For your suit is in vain,
All attempts you can make
But augment her disdain:

T t

She bids you give o'er
  While 'tis in your power;
For, except her esteem,
  She can grant you no more.

Her heart has been long since
  Assaulted and won,
Her truth is as lasting
  And firm as the sun;
You'll find it more easy
  Your passion to cure,
Than for ever those fruitless
  Endeavours endure

You may give this advice
  To the wretched and wise,
But a lover like me
  Will those precepts despise;
I scorn to give o'er,
  Were it still in my power;
Tho' esteem were deny'd me,
  Yet her I'll adore.

A heart that's been touch'd
  Will some sympathy bear,
'Twill lessen my sorrows,
  If she takes a share;
I'll count it more honour
  In dying her slave,
Than did her affections
  My steadiness crave.

You may tell her, I'll be
  Her true lover, tho' she
Should mankind despise
  Out of hatred to me;
'Tis mean to give o'er
  'Cause we get no reward,
She lost not her worth
  When I lost her regard.

My love on an altar
  More noble shall burn;
I still will love on
  Without hopes of return!
I'll tell her some other
  Has kindled the flame,
And I'll sigh for herself
  In a counterfeit name.

SONG 1227.

HARK, Daphne, from the hawthorn-bush
  The spotted finches sing;
In artless notes the merry thrush
  Salutes the blooming spring:
On verdant bed the vi'let lies,
  To woo the western gale;
While tow'ring lilies meet our eyes,
  Like love-sick virgins pale.

The rill that gushes o'er the shore,
  Winds murm'ring thro' the glade;
So heart-struck Thyrsis tells his moan,
  To win his clay-cold maid:
The golden sun, in fresh array,
  Flames forward on the sphere;
Around the may-pole shepherds play,
  To hail the flow'ry year.

Say, shall we taste the breezy air,
  Or wander thro' the grove;
There talk of Sylvia's wild despair,
  The prey of lawless love?
Ah, no! she cries; o'er Sylvia's fall
  Exult not, tho' 'twas just;
Dash not the sinner's name with gall,
  Nor triumph o'er her dust.

True virtue scorns to fling the dart,
  Herself above all fear;
When justice stings the guilty heart,
  She drops the gen'rous tear:
Then own, ye nymphs, this god-like truth
  Is on your hearts imprest;
On brightest patterns form your youth,
  And be for ever blest.

SONG 1228.

Sung at RANELAGH.

THE heroes preparing to finish the war,
  And bid to the camp an adieu,
Now sheathe up their swords, and rejoice, O
  ye fair!
  To think of returning to you.
With smiles, then, ye lasses, embellish your
  charms,
  Your lovers with raptures will come;
O take the brave fellows, then, close to your
  arms,
  And tenderly welcome them home.

SONG 1229.

THE MILLER'S WEDDING.

LEAVE, neighbours, your work, and to
  sport and to play,
Let the tabor strike up and the village be gay.
No day thro' the year shall more cheerful be
  seen,
For Ralph of the mill marries Sue of the green.
    I love Sue, and Sue loves me,
      And while the wind blows,
      And while the mill goes,
    Who'll be so happy, so happy as we?

Let lords and fine folks, who for wealth take a
  bride,
Be married to-day, and to-morrow be cloy'd;
My body is stout, and my heart is as sound,
And my love, like my courage, will never give
  ground.
    I love Sue, &c.

Let ladies of fashion the best jointers wed,
And prudently take the best bidders to bed;
Such signing and sealing's no part of our bliss,
We settle our hearts, and we seal with a kiss.
    I love Sue, &c.

Tho' Ralph is not courtly, nor none of your
  beaus,
Nor bounces, nor flatters, nor wears your fine
  cloaths;

In nothing he'll borrow from folks of high life
Nor e'er turn his back on his friend, or his wife.
I love Sue, &c.

While thus I am able to work at my mill,
While thou art kind, and thy tongue but lies
    still ;
Our joys shall continue, and ever be new,
And none be so happy as Ralph and his Sue.
    I love Sue, and Sue loves me,
    And while the wind blows,
    And while the mill goes,
Who'll be so happy, so happy as we ?

SONG 1230.

A PASTORAL BALLAD.

Sung at VAUXHALL.

STREPHON arose at early dawn,
    And sought as wont his fleecy care ;
His fleecy care, alas! were gone,
    Nor knew the hapless shepherd where :
In vain each hill, in vain each dale,
    Each dell, each brake he travers'd round ;
Each pathless wood and flow'ry vale,
    But not one lambkin could be found.

Cælia, he cry'd, my flocks are fled,
    How shall I e'er thy grief assuage?
How shall I chear thy drooping head,
    If poverty should mark my age ?
Said she, My love, misfortune's dart
    Is pointed, and is spent in vain ;
While I possess my shepherd's heart,
    I laugh at ills, and smile at pain.

Tho' ev'ry lambkin devious stray,
    And grace our envious neighbours folds,
Nought can thy Cælia's soul dismay,
    While Strephon to her breast she holds.
Said he, My warmest thanks, O take !
    Hence shalt thou be my only care ;
If I thy virtues e'er forsake,
    May Heav'n regardless hear my pray'r.

If from thy lovely form mine eyes
    Should swerve but in the least degree ;
Thy dear idea will arise,
    And lead the wand'rer back to thee.
Thus long they liv'd, and long they lov'd,
    As oft I've heard the story told ;
Kind Heav'n their fortitude approv'd,
    And amply fill'd the shepherd's fold.

SONG 1231.

YE woods and ye mountains unknown,
    Beneath whose pale shadows I stray ;
To the breast of my charmer alone,
    These sighs bid sweet echoes convey :
Wherever he pensively leans,
    By fountain, or hill, or in grove ;
His heart will explain what she means,
    Who sings both from sorrow and love.

More soft than the nightingale's song,
    Oh ! waft the sad sound to his ear ;

Or say, tho' divided so long,
    The friend of his bosom is near :
Then tell him what years of delight,
    Then tell him what ages of pain,
I felt while I liv'd in his sight ;
    I feel till I see him again

SONG 1232.

Written by Mr. GARRICK.

ONCE more I'll tune the vocal shell,
    To hills and dales my passion tell,
A flame which time can never quell,
    That burns for thee, my Peggy :
You, greater bards, the lyre should hit;
For say, what subject is more fit,
Than to record the sparkling wit
    And bloom of lovely Peggy?

The sun first rising in the morn,
That paints the dew-bespangled thorn,
Does not so much the day adorn,
    As does my lovely Peggy :
And when in Thetis' lap to rest,
He streaks with gold the ruddy west,
He's not so beauteous as, undrest,
    Appears my lovely Peggy.

When Zephyr on the vi'let blows,
Or breathes upon the damask rose,
It does not half the sweets disclose,
    As does my lovely Peggy :
I stole a kiss the other day,
And (trust me) nought but truth I say,
The fragrance of the blooming May
    Was not so sweet as Peggy.

Was she array'd in rustic weed,
With her the bleating flocks I'd feed,
And pipe upon the oaten reed,
    To please my lovely Peggy :
With her a cottage would delight ;
All's happy when she's in my sight;
But when she's gone, 'tis endless night;
    All's dark without my Peggy.

While bees from flow'r to flow'r still rove,
And linnets warble thro' the grove,
Or stately swans the water love,
    So long shall I love Peggy :
And when death, with his pointed dart,
Shall strike the blow that rives my heart,
My words shall be, when I depart,
    Adieu, my lovely Peggy.

SONG 1233.

COME Roger and Nell, come Simkin and
        Bell,
    Each lad with his lass hither come,
With singing and dancing, and pleasure ad-
        vancing,
    To celebrate harvest-home:
    'Tis Ceres bids play, and keep holiday,
    To celebrate harvest-home ; harvest-home,
    To celebrate harvest-home.

T t 2

Our labour is o'er, our barns in full ftore
  Now fwell with rich gifts of the land ;
Let each man then take, for his prong and his
  rake,
    His cann and his lafs in his hand :
    For Ceres, &c.

No courtier can be fo happy as we,
  In innocence, paftime, and mirth ;
While thus we caroufe, with our fweetheart or
  fpoufe,
    And rejoice o'er the fruits of the earth :
    When Ceres bids play, and keep holiday,
    To celebrate harveft-home, harveft-home,
    To celebrate harveft-home.

SONG 1234.

ON a primrofy bank, by a murmuring ftream,
  Paftora fat finging, and I was her theme ;
  Whilft charm'd with her beauty, behind a
    green bufh,
  I liften'd to hear her fweet tale with a blufh.
Of all the young fhepherds that pipe on the reed,
'Tis Damon alone I can fancy, indeed ;
  I tell him I value him not of a rufh,
  Yet furely I love him, or why do I blufh.

When I went to the grove at the top of the hill;
It was the laft May, I remember it ftill;
  He brought me a neft of young linnets quite
    flufh,
  And I the kind prefent receiv'd with a blufh.
Whenever he meets me, he'll fimper and fmile;
I feem as I did not obferve him the while,
  He offers to kifs me, I give him a pufh ;
  Why can't you be eafy! I cry with a blufh.

One Sunday he came to intreat me to walk,
'Twas down in a meadow, and love was our
  talk ;
  He call'd me his deareft—Pray, Damon, be
    hufh ;
  There's fomebody coming! I cry'd, with a
    blufh :
My mother fhe chides when I mention the
  fwain ;
Forbids me to go to the meadow again:
  But fure for his fake I will venture a brufh ;
  For love him I do, I confefs with a blufh.

Thus warbled the fair, and my heart leap'd for
  joy,
Though little fhe thought that her Damon was
  nigh;
  But chancing to fpy me behind a green bufh,
  She ended her fong, and arofe with a blufh.

SONG 1235.

A SCOTCH BALLAD,

Sung at VAUXHALL.

YOUNG Jockey fought my heart to win,
  And woo'd as lovers woo ;

I, vers'd in all our fex's art,
  Did juft as maidens do:
Whate'er he'd figh, whate'er he'd vow,
  I'd ftudy to be fhy at ;
And when he prefs'd his fate to know,
  'Twas, Pr'ythee, fool be quiet.

Month after month, of am'rous pain
  He made a mighty fufs ;
Why if, you know, one loves a fwain,
  'Tis wrong to fay one does :
He told me paffion could not live
  Without more pleafing diet;
And pray what anfwer could I give,
  But, Pr'ythee, fool, be quiet?

At length he made a bold effay,
  And like a man he cry'd,
Thy hand, my dear, this very day
  Shall Celia be my bride :
Convinc'd he would have teiz'd me ftill,
  I could not well deny it;
And now, believe me, when I will,
  I make the fool be quiet.

SONG 1236.

GOD fave great George, our king!
  Long live our noble king,
  God fave the king!
Send him victorious,
Happy and glorious,
Long to reign over us,
  God fave the king.

O Lord, our God, arife,
Scatter his enemies,
  And make them fall :
Confound their politicks,
Fruftrate their knavifh tricks ;
On him our hopes we fix;
  God fave us all.

Thy choiceft gifts in ftore,
On George be pleas'd to pour,
  Long may he reign ;
May he defend our laws,
And ever give us caufe,
To fing with heart and voice,
  God fave the king.

SONG 1237.

AS Celia in her garden ftray'd,
  Secure, nor dream'd of harm,
A bee approach'd the lovely maid,
  And refted on her arm.

The curious infect thither flew,
  To tafte the tempting bloom ;
But with a thoufand fweets in view,
  It found a fudden doom.

Her nimble hand of life bereav'd
  The darling little thing;
But firft her fnowy arm receiv'd,
  And felt the painful fting.

Once only could that fting furprize,
Once be injurious found:
Not fo the darts of Celia's eyes,
They never ceafe to wound.

Oh! would the fhort-liv'd burning fmart
The nymph to pity move,
And teach her to regard the heart
She fires with endlefs love!

SONG 1238.

TWO gods of great honour, Bacchus and
Apollo,
The one fam'd in mufic, the other in wine,
In heaven were raving, difputing, and braving,
Whofe theme was the nobleft, and trade moft
divine.

Your mufic, fays Bacchus, would ftun us and
rack us,
Did claret not foften the difcord you make;
Songs are not inviting, nor verfes delighting,
Till poets of my great influence partake.

I'm young, plump and jolly, free from me-
lancholy;
Who ever grew fat by the found of a ftring?
Rogues doom'd to a gibbet, do often contribute
To purchafe a bottle before they do fwing.

In love I am noted, by old and young courted:
A girl, when infpir'd by me, is foon won;
So great are the motions of one of my potions,
The mufes, tho' maids, I could whore ev'ry
one.

When mortals are fretted, perplex'd, or in-
debted,
To me, as a father, for fuccour they cry;
In their fad condition, I hear their petition;
A bottle relieves the opprefs'd votary.

Then leave off your tooting, your fiddling and
fluting,
Afide lay your harp, and bow down to the
flafk;
My joys they are riper than fongs from a piper;
What mufic is fweeter than founding a cafk!

Says Phœbus, This fellow is drunk fure, or
mellow,
To prize mufic lefs than wine and October;
Since thofe who love drinking are void of all
thinking,
And want fo much fenfe as to keep themfelves fober.

Thus while they were wrangling, difputing,
and jangling,
Come buxom bright Venus to end the difpute:
Says fhe, Now to eafe ye, Mars beft of all pleas'd
me,
When arm'd with a bottle, and charm'd
with a flute.

Your mufic has charm'd me, your wine has
alarm'd me,
When I have feem'd coy, and hard to be won;
When both have been moving, I could not help
loving,
And wine has compleated what mufic begun.

The gods, ftruck with wonder, declar'd by
Jove's thunder,
They'd mutually join in fupplying love's
flame:
So each in their function, mov'd on in con-
junction,
To melt with foft pleafure the amorous dame.

SONG 1239.

OBSERVE the rofe-bud ere it blows,
While the dawn glimmers o'er the fky,
Obferve it's filken leaves unfold,
As fond of day's majeftic eye!

At noon, more bold, in fulleft bloom,
It fpreads a gale of fweets around;
At eve it mourns the fetting fun,
And fheds it's honour on the ground.

So beauty's bafhful bud appears,
So blufhes in the eye of praife;
So ripens in the noon of life,
And wither'd fo in age decays.

Time is the canker-worm of youth,
It bites the bloffom as it grows,
It blafts the flow'r that blooms at full,
And rudely fheds the falling rofe.

See, beauty, fee! how love and joy
On youth's light pinions hafte away;
How fwift the moments glide along,
And age advances with delay!

Now, beauty, crop the rofe-bud now,
And catch the effence as it flies;
Let pleafure revel in it's bloom,
Let time poffefs it when it dies.

SONG 1240.

CLARISSA's charms poor Strephon ftruck;
He fain would have been billing:
But yet the fair the lad forfook,
To fhew her power of killing.

Forth from her eyes fuch beauties ftart,
They mortal man confounded:
The youths were whipp'd quite thro' the heart,
Ere they knew they were wounded.

But when old Time, with fcythe fo fharp,
Had crofs the forehead ftruck her,
And ev'ry charm began to warp,
The ftriplings all forfook her.

Oh! then the hag began to curfe,
Her time fhe pafs'd no better,
Yet ftill before that bad grew worfe,
She hope'd fome youth would take her.

But hopes are vain when beauty's gone;
　No lovers now affail her;
We never into prifon run,
　But when we like the jailor.

Then, cruel fair-ones, think how foon
　You'll this fad cafe remember;
The bedfellow you hate in June,
　Would warm you in December.

S O N G　1241.

VULCAN, contrive me fuch a cup
　As Neftor us'd of old;
Shew all thy fkill to trim it up,
　Damafk it round with gold.

Make it fo large, that fill'd with fack
　Up to the fwelling brim,
Vaft toafts on the delicious lake,
　Like fhips at fea, may fwim.

Engrave no battle on his cheek,
　With war I've nought to do;
I'm none of thofe that took Maeftricht,
　Nor Yarmouth leaguer knew.

Let it no names of planets tell,
　Fix'd ftars or conftellations;
For I am not Sir Sidrophel,
　Nor one of his relations.

But carve thereon a fpreading vine,
　Then add two lovely boys;
Their limbs in am'rous folds intwine,
　The type of future joys.

Cupid and Bacchus my faints are,
　May drink and love ftill reign;
With wine I wafh away my care,
　And then to love again.

S O N G　1242.

Written by Mr. HEYWOOD.

AS late in the meadow reclined I lay,
　I figh'd, for I'd reafon to figh;
I threw by my pipe, for I never can play,
　Except my Paftora is by.

Sure fomewhere, unweeting, the charmer has
　ftray'd,
　That nor her, nor her fheep, I have feen!
But I hardly had fpoke, e'er I faw the fweet
　maid
　Come tripping it over the green.

Ah! help me, my love, my Amintor! fhe cried,
　While a tear trickled down from her eye;
I fcarcely could credit my ears, or my eyes,
　For fhe always was bafhful and fhy.

What ails my Paftora?—Alas! fhe reply'd,
　I was fhaking fome plums from a tree,
When fomething fell into my bofom befide;
　I fhall die! for I fear 'tis a bee.

Then ftraight to my gaze fhe her bofom dif-
　play'd,
O, gods! 'twas Elizium to fee;
Half fick'ning with pleafure, the fcene I fur-
　vey'd,
　But faw neither prickle nor bee.

Yet foon all the caufe of her fears I could fee,
　'Twas Cupid, (the rogue) and no other,
Who, it feems, as he lighted to feaft on the tree,
　Miftook the fair maid for his mother.

Now ftung to the quick, when the blunder he
　knew,
He pluck'd from his quiver a dart,
Which up to the head in his paffion he drew,
　And buried it deep in her heart.

Oh, it ftings me! it ftings me! Paftora then
　cried,
　And fainted away with the pain;
Then quick to her bofom my lips I applied,
　And kifs'd them again and again.

But foon fhe recover'd, and fat on my knee,
　Then own'd 'twas a judgment divine;
A punifhment juft, for her jefting at me;
　So next Sunday fhe vows fhe'll be mine.

S O N G　1243.

Sung in the *Prefs-Gang.*

SINCE again bold defiance appears in proud
　France,
Ye ftaunch Britifh tars, let us boldly advance;
And now, in our turns, let us teach them to
　dance.
　O! the brave tars of Old England;
　And, O! the Old Englifh brave tars.

Tho' furious at firft, yet we know they'll foon
　fly O;
But brave Britifh tars, they will conquer or
　die O;
From the fhores of old Thames, to the banks
　of Ohio.
　O the brave tars, &c.

As foon as juft vengeance fhall take up her
　whip,
From the head to the ftern they will tremble
　and fkip;
For they live on *foup-maigre*, while we drink
　good flip.
　O the brave tars, &c.

Our commanders, tho' wife, will give valour
　due fcope,
As the fhip is impell'd, or reftrain'd, by a rope;
Fair caution's our helm, and our anchor is hope.
　O the brave tars, &c.

As foon as our glorious commander embarks,
In fpite of the threats of ten thoufand mo-
    narques;
We are gudgeons, they think, but they'll find
    we are fharks.
    O the brave tars, &c.

The genius of Britain behold on the deck,
And Old Englifh faith without blemifh or
    fpeck;
For either, or both, I'd venture my neck.
    O the brave tars, &c.

Behold naval glory prefents her own crown t'ye:
Come hither, brave boys, from each town and
    each county,
And joyous partake of his majefty's bounty.
    O the brave tars, &c.

No more fhall the French, with their gafco-
    nades brave ye,
But each fop in armour fhall cry out peccavi;
Sing huzza! to King George, and his brave
    royal navy.
    O! the brave tars of Old England;
    And, O! the Old Englifh brave tars.

S O N G 1244.

GO gentle breeze, that fans the grove,
    And waft in fighs a lover's woes;
Or through the blooming garden rove,
    And lodge within the damafk rofe;
To ev'ry blufhing fold made known,
That Colin's fighs exceed thy own.

Beneath her crimfon foliage lie,
    Till on my Delia's bofom bleft;
Then from thy filken covert fly,
    And plead my caufe within her breaft,
But never leave that frozen part,
Unlefs to bring me Delia's heart.

S O N G 1245.

ON the white cliffs of Albion fee Fame where
    fhe ftands,
And her fhrill-fwelling notes reach the neigh-
    bouring lands;
Of the natives free-born, and their conqueft
    fhe fings,
The happieft of men, with the greateft of kings.

George the third fhe proclaims, his vaft glory
    repeats,
His undifmay'd legions, invincible fleets;
Whom nor caftles, or rocks, can from honour
    retard,
Since e'en death for their king they with fcorn
    difregard.

O! but fee a cloud burfts, and an angel appears!
'Tis Peace, lovely virgin, diffolved in tears;
Say, Fame, cry'd the maid, is't not time to give
    o'er,
With fieges and famine, explofions and gore!

His juft right to affert, that the king amply try'd,
Nor his wifdom or ftrength can by parents
    abide;
Then no longer in rage let dread thunder be
    hurl'd,
But leave him to me, and give peace to the
    world.

'Tis done, and great George is to mercy inclin'd;
The bleft word is gone forth, for the good of
    mankind.
'Tis the act of a Briton to beat, then to fpare;
And our king is a Briton—deny it who dare.

To Hodgfon and Keppel let bumpers next fmile,
And to all our brave troops who have taken
    Belleifle;
May they meet juft reward, and with courage
    advance,
Still to humble the pride and the power of
    France.

Charge your glaffes lip high, and drink health
    to the king,
To the duke and the princefs, and make the
    air ring;
May the days of great George be all happy and
    long,
And the man be ftill right, who yet never was
    wrong.

S O N G 1246.

Sung in ARTAXERXES.

IF o'er the cruel tyrant love
    A conqueft I believ'd;
The flatt'ring error ceafe to prove,
    O let me be deceiv'd.

Forbear to fan the gentle flame
    Which love did firft create;
What was my pride is now my fhame,
    And muft be turn'd to hate.

Then call not to my wav'ring mind
    The weaknefs of my heat,
Which, ah! I feel too much inclin'd
    To take a traitor's part.

S O N G 1247.

Written by the Earl of CHESTERFIELD.

WHEN Fanny blooming fair
    Firft caught my ravifh'd fight,
Pleas'd with her fhape and air,
    I felt a ftrange delight:
Whilft eagerly I gaz'd,
    A fmiling ev'ry part,
And ev'ry feature prais'd,
    She ftole into my heart.

In her bewitching eyes
    Ten thoufand loves appear;
There Cupid bafking lies,
    His fhafts are hoarded there.

Her blooming cheeks are dy'd
With colour all their own,
Excelling tar the pride
Of rofes newly blown.

Her well-turn'd limbs confefs
The lucky hand of Jove;
Her features all exprefs
The beauteous queen of love!
What flames my nerves invade,
When I behold the breaft
Of that too-charming maid
Rife, fuing to be preft?

Venus round Fanny's waift,
Has her own Ceftus bound,
Three guardian Cupids grace,
And dance the circle round.
How happy muft he be
Who fhall her zone unlofe!
That blifs to all, but me,
May Heaven and fhe refufe!

SONG 1248.

WINTER.

Written by SHAKESPEARE.

WHEN ificles hang by the wall,
And Dick the fhepherd blows his nails;
And Tom bears logs into the hall,
And milk comes frozen home in pails;
When blood is nipt, and ways he foul,
Then nightly fings the ftaring owl,
Tu-whit! tu-whoo!
A merry note,
While greafy Joan doth keel the pot.

When all aloud the wind doth blow,
And coughing drowns the parfon's faw;
And birds fit brooding in the fnow,
And Marian's nofe looks red and raw;
When roafted crabs hifs in the bowl,
Then nightly fings the ftaring owl,
Tu-whit! tu-whoo!
A merry note,
While greafy Joan doth keel the pot.

SONG 1249.

WHEN Chloe we ply,
We fwear we fhall die,
Her eyes do our hearts fo enthrall;
But 'tis for her pelf,
And not for herfelf;
'Tis all artifice, artifice all.

The maidens are coy,
They'll pifh! and they'll fie!
And fwear if you're rude, they will call;
But whifper fo low,
You may eafily know,
'Tis all artifice, artifice all.

My dear, the wives cry,
If ever you die,
To marry again I ne'er fhall;
But in lefs than a year,
Will make it appear,
'Tis all artifice, artifice all.

In matters of ftate,
And party debate,
For church and for juftice we bawl;
But if you'll attend,
You'll find in the end,
'Tis all artifice, artifice all.

The non-cons will rant
In their pulpits, and cant,
And the honeft conformifts will maul;
In holy difguife
They lift up their eyes;
'Tis all artifice, artifice all.

The lawyers, you know,
To Weftminfter go,
And plead for their fees in the hall;
For their clients they'll wrangle,
And make fuch a jangle!
'Tis all artifice, artifice all.

The wretch that attends,
And on courtiers depends,
His fortune he'll find to be fmall;
For their actions declare,
Their words are but air;
'Tis all artifice, artifice all.

SONG 1250.

Sung in Midas.

NE'ER will I be left i'the lurch;
Ceafe your bribes and wheedling:
Till I'm made a bride i'the church
I'll keep man from meddling.
What are riches
And foft fpeeches!
Baits and fetches
To bewitch us;
When you've won us,
And undone us,
Cloy'd, you fhun us,
Frowning on us,
For our heedlefs piddling.

SONG 1251.

ONE night when all the village flept,
Myrtilla's fad defpair
The wretched fhepherd waking kept
To tell the woods his care;
Be gone (faid he) fond thoughts, be gone;
Eyes, give your forrows o'er!
Why fhould you wafte your tears for one
Who thinks on you no more?

Yet, oh! ye birds, ye flocks, ye powers!
That dwell within this grove!
Can tell how many tender hours
We here have pafs'd in love!
Yon ftars above! my cruel foes!
Can tell how fhe has fworn,
A thoufand times, that like to thofe,
Her flame fhould ever burn!

But fince fhe's loft—oh! let me have
My wifh, and quickly die;

Mrs MATTOCKS, as Nysa in MIDAS

Ne'er will I be left i' the lurch.

Song 1250

Published by J. Bew Jan 1, 1779.

In this cold bank I'll make a grave,
And there for ever lie :
Sad nightingales the watch shall keep,
And kindly here complain !—
Then down the shepherd lay to sleep,
But never rose again,

SONG 1252.

NEAR the side of a pond, at the foot of a hill,
A free hearted fellow attends on his mill;
Fresh health blooms her strong rosy hue o'er his face,
And honesty gives e'en to aukwardness grace :
Beflour'd with his meal does he labour and sing,
And regaling at night is as blest as a king :
After heartily eating, he takes a full swill
Of liquor home-brew'd, to success of the mill.

He makes no nice scruples of toll for his trade,
For that's an excise to his industry paid :
His conscience is free, and his income is clear,
And he values not those of ten thousand a year;
He's a freehold sufficient to give him a vote ;
At elections he scorns to accept of a groat ;
He hates your proud placemen; and, do what they will,
They ne'er can seduce the staunch man of the mill.

On Sunday he talks with the barber and priest,
And hopes that our statesmen do all for the best,
That the Spaniards shall ne'er interrupt our free trade,
Nor good British coin be in subsidies paid :
He fears the French navy and commerce increase,
And he wishes poor Germany still may have peace :
Tho' Old England, he knows, may have strength, and have skill,
To protect all her manors, and save his own mill.

With this honest hope he goes home to his work ;
And if water is scanty he takes up his fork,
And over the meadows he scatters his hay,
Or with the stiff plough turns up furrows of clay :
His harvest is crown'd with good English glee :,
That his country may ever be happy and free :
With his hand and his heart to King George does he fill.
May all loyal souls act the man of the mill.

SONG 1253.

SPRING.

Written by SHAKESPEARE.

WHEN dazies py'd, and violets blue,
And cuckow-buds of yellow hue,
And lady's smocks all silver white,
Do paint the meadows with delight ;

The cuckow then, on every tree,
Mocks married men, for thus sings he;
Cuckow, cuckow; O! word of fear,
Unpleasing to a married ear.

When shepherds pipe on oaten straws,
And merry larks are plowmen's clocks,
When turtles tread, and rooks and daws,
And maidens bleach their summer smocks;
The curkow then, on every tree,
Mocks married men, for thus sings he;
Cuckow, cuckow, O! word of fear,
Unpleasing to a married ear.

SONG 1254.

DECLARE, my pretty maid,
Must my fond suit miscarry ?
With you I'll toy, I'll kiss and play ;
But hang me if I marry.

Then speak your mind at once,
Nor let me longer tarry :
With you I'll toy, I'll kiss and play ;
But hang me if I marry.

Tho' charms and wit assail,
The stroke I well can parry :
I love to kiss, to toy and play ;
But do not chuse to marry.

Young Molly of the dale
Makes a mere slave of Harry ;
Because, when they had toy'd and kiss'd,
The foolish swain wou'd marry.

These fix'd resolves, my dear,
I to the grave will carry :
With you I'll toy, and kiss, and play ;
But hang me if I marry.

SONG 1255.

WHENE'ER I meet my Celia's eyes,
Sweet raptures in my bosom rise,
My feet forget to move ;
She too declines her lovely head,
Soft blushes o'er her cheeks are spread :
Sure this is mutual love !

My beating heart is wrapt in bliss,
Whene'er I steal a tender kiss,
Beneath the silent grove :
She strives to frown, and puts me by,
Yet anger dwells not in her eye;
Sure this is mutual love !

And once, O once, the dearest maid,
As on her lips my head was laid,
Some secret impulse drove ;
Me, me, her gentle arms carest,
And to her bosom closely prest ;
Sure this was mutual love !

And now, transported with her charms,
A soft desire my bosom warms,
Forbidden joys to prove ;
Trembling, for fear he should comply,
She from my arms prepares to fly,
Tho' warm'd with mutual love !

O ftay! I cry'd—let Hymen's bands
This moment tie our willing hands,
   And all thy fears remove;
A modest blush confent exprefs'd ;
And now we live, fupremely bleft,
   A life of mutual love !

SONG 1256.

DIOGENES furly and proud,
   Who fnarl'd at the Macedon youth,
Delighted in wine that was good,
Becaufe in good wine there was truth ;
But growing as poor as a Job,
Unable to purchafe a flafk,
He chofe for his manfion a tub,
   And liv'd by the fcent of the cafk,

Heraclitus ne'er would deny
   A bumper to cherifh his heart;
And when he was maudlin would cry,
   Becaufe he had empty'd his quart:
Tho' fome are fo foolifh to think,
   He wept at men's follies and vice;
'Twas only his cuftom to drink,
   Till the liquor flow'd out of his eyes.

Democritus always was glad
   To tipple and cherifh his foul;
Would laugh like a man that was mad,
   When over a good flowing bowl ;
As long as his cellar was ftor'd,
   The liquor he'd merrily quaff ;
And when he was drunk as a lord,
   At them that were fober he'd laugh.

Wife Solon, who carefully gave
   Good laws unto Athens of old,
And thought the rich Crœfus a flave
   (Tho' a king) to his coffers of gold ;
He delighted in plentiful bowls,
   But drinking much talk would decline,
Becaufe 'twas the cuftom of fools,
   To prattle much over their wine.

Old Socrates ne'er was content,
   Till a bottle had heighten'd his joys,
Who in's cups to the oracles went,
   Or he ne'er had been counted fo wife :
Late hours he moft certainly lov'd,
   Made wine the delight of his life,
Or Xantippe would never have prov'd
   Such a damnable fcold of a wife.

Grave Seneca, fam'd for his parts,
   Who tutor'd the bully of Rome,
Grew wife o'er his cups and his quarts,
   Which he drank like a mifer at home ;
And, to fhew he lov'd wine that was good,
   To the laft, (we may truly aver it)
He tinctur'd his bath with his blood,
   So fancy'd he dy'd in his claret.

Pythagoras did filence enjoin
   On his pupils who wifdom would feek ;
Becaufe he tippled good wine
   Till himfelf was unable to fpeak ;

And when he was whimfical grown
   With fipping his plentiful bowls,
By the ftrength of the juice in his crown,
   He conceiv'd tranfmigration of fouls.

Copernicus too, like the reft,
   Believ'd there was wifdom in wine,
And thought that a cup of the beft
   Made reafon the brighter to fhine ;
With wine he replenifh'd his veins,
   And made his philofophy reel ;
Then fancy'd the world, like his brains,
   Turn'd round like a chariot wheel.

Ariftotle, that mafter of arts,
   Had been but a dunce without wine,
And what we afcribe to his parts
   Is due to the juice of the vine ;
His belly, moft writers agree,
   Was as big as a watering-trough ;
He therefore leap'd into the fea,
   Becaufe he'd have liquor enough.

When Pyrrho has taken a glafs,
   He faw that no object appear'd
Exactly the fame as it was
   Before he had liquor'd his beard :
For things running round in his drink,
   Which fober he motionlefs found,
Occafion'd the fceptic to think
   There was nothing of truth to be found.

Old Plato was reckon'd divine,
   He fondly to wifdom was prone ;
But had it not been for good wine,
   His merits had never been known.
By wine we are generous made,
   It furnifhes fancy with wings,
Without it we ne'er fhould have had
   Philofophers, poets, or kings.

SONG 1257.

A Cobler there was, and he liv'd in a ftall,
   Which ferv'd him for parlour, for kitchen,
     and ball ;
No coin in his pocket, nor care in his pate,
No ambition had he, nor duns at his gate.
   Derry down, down; down, derry down.

Contented he work'd ; and he thought himfelf
     happy,
If at night he could purchafe a jug of brown
     nappy :
How he'd laugh then, and whiftle, and fing too
     moft fweet,
Saying, Juft to a hair I have made both ends
     meet.
   Derry down, down, &c.

But love, the difturber of high and of low,
That fhoots at the peafant as well as the beau ;
He fhot the poor cobler quite thro' the heart,
I wifh he had hit fome more ignoble part.
   Derry down, down, &c.

It was from a cellar this archer did play,
   Where a buxom young damfel continually lay;

Her eyes shone so bright when she rose ev'ry
   day,
That she shot the poor cobler quite over the
   way.
Derry down, down, &c.

He sung her love-songs as he sat at his work,
But she was as hard as a Jew or a Turk:
Whenever he spake she would flounce and
   would fleer,
Which put the poor cobler quite into despair.
Derry down, down, &c.

He took up his awl that he had in the world,
And to make away with himself was resolv'd;
He pierc'd thro' his body, instead of the sole,
So the cobler he dy'd, and the bell it did toll.
Derry down, down, &c.

And now, in good-will, I advise as a friend,
All coblers take warning by this cobler's end;
Keep your hearts out of love, for we find by
   what's past,
That love brings us all to an end at the last.
Derry down, down; down, derry down.

SONG 1258.

THE stone that all things turns at will
   To gold, the chymist craves;
But gold, without the chymist's skill,
   Turns all men into knaves.

The merchant wou'd the courtier cheat,
   When on his goods he lays
Too high a price—but, faith he's bit,
   For a courtier never pays.

The lawyer with a face demure,
   Hangs him who steals your pelf:
Because the good man can endure
   No robber but himself.

Betwixt the quack and highwayman,
   What diff'rence can there be?
Tho' this with pistol, that with pen,
   Both kill you for a fee.

The husband cheats his loving wife,
   And to a mistress goes;
While she, at home, to ease her life,
   Carouses with the beaus.

The tenant doth the steward nick,
   (So low this art we find)
The steward doth his lordship trick,
   My lord tricks all mankind.

One sect there is, to whose fair lot,
   No cheating arts do fall;
And those are parsons call'd, God wot—
   And so I cheat you all.

SONG 1259.

DRINK about, my dear friend,
   For, I pray, to what end
Stands useless the full-flowing bowl?

Leave your sorrows behind,
   Give your cares to the wind,
And drink to each jolly brave soul.

For Alcides the fam'd,
   Who monsters all tam'd,
And bound the stout porter of hell;
   Though immortal his line,
   Had it not been for wine,
Might, like them he conquer'd, have fell,

Though Achilles the great,
   When he fought at such rate,
He slew the great Hector of Troy;
   'Twas the grape's potent juice
   Made him wonders produce,
And Priam's whole race to destroy.

Neoptolemus, too,
   The same steps did pursue,
And trac'd the fam'd heroes of yore;
   He'd in drinking relax,
   And then Pyrrhus's acts
Were as great as his father's before.

And Ulysses the sly
   Had been drinking (for why)
When the Trojan Palladium he stole;
   For his subtle thoughts sprung,
   If e'er Ajax but sung
The charms of a sparkling full bowl.

Since in drinking we find
   There's a charm for the mind,
Let Bacchus then join in his train;
   Drink, my lads, drink about,
   Let us see the bowl out,
And once more we'll fill it again.

SONG 1260.

Sung in Perseus and Andromeda.

HOW pleasant a sailor's life passes,
   Who roams o'er the watery main!
No treasure he ever amasses,
   But chearfully spends all his gain.
We're strangers to party and faction,
   To honour and honesty true,
And would not commit a base action,
   For power or profit in view.
Then why should we quarrel for riches,
   Or any such glittering toys?
A light heart, and a thin pair of breeches,
   Goes thorough the world, brave boys.

The world is a beautiful garden,
   Enrich'd with the blessings of life.
The toiler with plenty rewarding,
   Which plenty too often breeds strife.
When terrible tempests assail us,
   And mountainous billows affright,
No grandeur or wealth can avail us,
   But skilful industry steers right.
Then why, &c.

The courtier's more subject to dangers,
   Who rules at the helm of the state,
Than we, that to politicks strangers,
   Escape the snares laid for the great.

The various bleffings of nature,
In various nations we try;
No mortals than us can be greater,
Who merrily live till we die.
Then why fhould we quarrel for riches,
Or any fuch glittering toys?
A light heart, and a thin pair of breeches,
Goes thorough the world, brave boys.

SONG 1261.

WINE, wine is alone the brifk fountain of mirth,
Whence jollity fprings, and contentment has birth;
What mortals fo happy as we who combine,
And fix our delight in the juice of the vine?
No care interrupts when the bottle's in view,
Then glafs after glafs, my boys, let us purfue.

Our laws are our own, not inforc'd by the crown,
And we ftand to them fair, till we fairly fall down;
At acts or repeals we difdain to repine,
Nor grudge any tax, but the tax on our wine:
To Cæfar and Bacchus our tribute is due,
Then glafs after glafs, my boys, let us purfue.

His worfhip fo grave here may revel and roar,
The lawyer fpeak truth, who ne'er fpoke fo before;
The parfon here, ftript of his priefthood's difguife,
And Chloe's fcorn'd lover get drunk and grow wife;
The hufband may learn here to combat the fhrew;
So glafs after glafs, my boys, let us purfue.

The chace of the bottle few accidents wait,
We feldom break necks, tho' we oft crack a pate,
If wars rife among us, they foon again ceafe,
One bumper brings truce, and another brings peace:
'Tis this way alone we life's evils fubdue;
Then glafs after glafs, my boys, let us purfue.

SONG 1262.

SOME hoift up fortune to the fkies,
Others debafe her to a bubble;
I not her frowns or favours prize,
Nor think the changling worth my trouble.

If at my door fhe chance to light,
I civilly my guest receive;
The vifit paid, I bid good night;
Nor murmur when fhe takes her leave.

Tho' profperous gales my canvas croud,
Tho' fmooth the waves, ferene the fky,
I suit not calms, they ftorms forbode,
And freak th' approaching tempeft nigh.

Then, virtue, to the helm repair,
Thou, innocence, fhalt guide the oar;
Now rage ye winds, ftorms rend the air,
My barque thus mann'd fhall gain the fhore.

SONG 1263.

MY paffion is as muftard ftrong,
I fit all fober fad,
Drunk as a piper all day long,
Or like a March-hare mad.

Round as a hoop the bumpers flow,
I drink, yet can't forget her;
For tho' as drunk as David's fow,
I love her ftill the better.

Pert as a pear-monger I'd be,
If Molly were but kind,
Cool as cucumber could fee
The reft of womankind.

Like a ftuck pig I gaping ftare,
And eye her o'er and o'er;
Lean as a rake with fighs and care,
Sleek as a moufe before.

Plump as a partridge I was known,
And foft as filk my fkin,
My cheeks as fat as butter grown,
But as a groat now thin.

I melancholy as a cat,
Am kept awake to weep;
But fhe, infenfible of that,
Sound as a top can fleep.

Hard is her heart, as flint or ftone,
She laughs to fee me pale;
And merry as a grig is grown,
And brifk as bottled-ale.

The god of love, at her approach,
Is bufy as a bee;
Hearts found as any bell or roach,
Are fmit, and figh like me.

Ah me! as thick as hops or hail
The fine men croud about her;
But foon as dead as a door-nail
Shall I be, if without her.

Straight as my leg her fhape appears,
Oh! were we join'd together,
My heart would foon be free from cares,
And lighter than a feather.

As fine as five-pence is her mien,
No drum was ever tighter;
Her glance is as a razor keen,
And not the fun is brighter.

As foft as pap her kiffes are,
Methinks I feel them yet;
Brown as a berry is her hair,
Her eyes as black as jet.

As fmooth as glafs, as white as curds,
Her pretty hand invites;
Sharp as a needle are her words,
Her wit like pepper bites.

Briſk as a body-louſe ſhe trips,
Clean as a penny dreſt,
Sweet as a roſe her face and lips,
Round as a globe her breaſt.

Full as an egg was I with glee,
And happy as a king;
Good lack ! how all men envy'd me !
She lov'd like any thing.

But falſe as hell, ſhe like the wind
Chang'd as her ſex muſt do,
Tho' ſeeming as the turtle kind,
And as the goſpel true.

If I and Molly could agree,
Let who will take Peru ;
Great as an emp'ror I ſhould be,
And richer than a Jew.

Till you grow tender as a chick,
I'm dull as a any poſt;
Let us like burrs together ſtick,
And warm as any toaſt.

You'll know me truer than a die,
And wiſh me better ſped,
Flat as a flounder when I lie,
And as a herring dead.

Sure as a gun ſhe'll drop a tear,
And ſigh, perhaps, and wiſh;
When I'm as rotten as a pear,
And mute as any fiſh.

SONG 1264.

LET a ſet of ſober aſſes
Rail againſt the joys of drinking,
While water, tea,
And milk agree,
To ſet cold brains a thinking ;
Power and wealth,
Beauty, health,
Wit and mirth in wine are crown'd :
Joys abound,
Pleaſure's found
Only where the glaſs goes round.

The ancient ſects on happineſs
All differ'd in opinion ;
But wiſer rules
Of modern ſchools,
In wine fix their dominion.
Power and wealth, &c.

Wine gives the lover vigour,
Makes glow the cheeks of beauty,
Makes poets write,
And ſoldiers fight,
And friendſhip do it's duty.
Power and wealth, &c.

Wine was the only Helicon,
Whence poets are long-liv'd ſo ;
'Twas no other main
Than briſk champaign,
Whence Venus was deriv'd too.
Power and wealth, &c.

When heav'n in Pandora's box
All kinds of ill had ſent us,

In a merry mood,
A bottle of good,
Was cork'd up, to content us.

All virtues wine is nurſe to,
Of ev'ry vice deſtroyer,
Gives dullard's wit,
Makes juſt the cit,
Truth forces from the lawyer.
Power and wealth, &c.

Wine ſets our joys a flowing,
Our care and ſorrow drowning.
Who rails at the bowl,
Is a Turk in's ſoul,
And a chriſtian ne'er ſhould own him :
Power and wealth,
Beauty, health,
Wit and mirth in wine are crown'd :
Joys abound,
Pleaſure's found
Only where the glaſs goes round.

SONG 1265.

COME, all ye jolly Bacchanals,
That love to tope good wine,
Let us offer up a hogſhead
Unto our maſter's ſhrine.
And a toping we will go, &c.

Then let us drink, and never ſhrink,
For I'll give a reaſon why ;
'Tis a great ſin to leave a houſe,
Till we've drank the cellar dry.
And a toping, &c.

In times of old I was a fool,
I drank the water clear;
But Bacchus took me from that rule,
He thought 'twas too ſevere.
And a toping, &c.

He fill'd a goblet to the brim,
And bade me take a ſup ;
But had it been a gallon pot,
By Jove I'd toſs'd it up.
And a toping, &c.

And ever ſince that happy time,
Good wine has been my chear,
Now nothing puts me in a ſwoon,
But water or ſmall-beer.
And a toping, &c.

Then let us tope about, my boys,
And never flinch, nor fly ;
But fill our ſkins brimful of wine,
And drain the bottles dry.
And a toping we will go, &c.

SONG 1266.

YES, Strephon, yes, theſe charms muſt fade,
As does the pride of May;
Such fate attends the faireſt maid,
Poor ſovereign of a day :

Warn'd by the rose's hasty fall,
I know my longest reign;
Yet, for that pow'r I can't recal,
I'll scorn to feel a pain.

Then know, false man, thy subtlest arts
Shall ne'er my soul betray,
Nor fear of what old age may bring,
Enslave my heart a day;
True, were my beauty all my boast,
Since that will pass so soon,
'Twere not amiss in you to ask,
Or me to grant the boon.

But sped with wisdom's friendly aid,
I ask no happier state;
Should Chloe live and die a maid,
Is that a curse so great?
No Strephon, no? I've yet one charm,
When all the rest are spent,
Shall of it's cares e'en age disarm
'Tis—virtue, with content.

SONG 1267.

YOUNG Dorilas, an artless swain,
And Daphne, pride of western plain,
Their flocks together drove :
Gay youth sat blooming on his face,
She no less shone with ev'ry grace;
Yet neither thought of love.

With equal joy each morn they meet ;
At mid-day, seek the same retreat,
And shelter in one grove;
At ev'ning haunt the self-same walk,
Together innocently talk,
But not a word of love.

Hence mutual friendship firmly grew,
Till heart to heart spontaneous flew, -
Like bill to bill of dove;
Both feel the flame which both conceal,
Both wish the other would reveal,
Yet neither speaks of love

She hung with rapture o'er his sense;
He doated on her innocence :
Thus each did each approve.
They vow'd, and all their vows obferv'd ;
The maid was true, the swain ne'er swerv'd,
Then ev'ry word was love.

SONG 1268.

Song in the Masque of *Alfred*.

WHEN Britain first, at Heav'n's command,
Arose from out the azure main;
This was the charter of the land,
And guardian angels sung this strain:
Rule, Britannia, Britannia rule the waves;
Britons never will be slaves.

The nations not so blest as thee,
Must, in their turns, to tyrants fall:
Whilst thou shalt flourish great and free,
The dread and envy of them all.
Rule, Britannia, &c.

Still more majestic shalt thou rise,
More dreadful from each foreign stroke ;
As the loud blast that tears the skies,
Serves but to root thy native oak.
Rule, Britannia, &c.

Thee haughty tyrants ne'er shall tame;
All their attempts to bend thee down,
Will but arouse thy gen'rous flame;
But work their woe, and thy renown.
Rule, Britannia, &c.

To thee belongs the rural reign,
Thy cities shall with commerce shine;
All thine shall be the subject main,
And ev'ry shore it circles thine.
Rule, Britannia, &c.

The muses still with freedom found,
Shall to thy happy coast repair:
Blest isle! with matchless beauty crown'd,
And manly hearts to guard the fair.
Rule, Britannia, Britannia rule the waves;
Britons never will be slaves.

SONG 1269.

TELL me no no more of pointed darts,
Of flaming eyes and bleeding hearts,
The hyperboles of love:
Be honest to yourself and me,
Speak truly what you hear and see,
And then your suit may move.

Why call me angel? why divine ?
Why must my eyes the stars outshine?
Can such deceit prevail?
For shame, forbear this common rule;
'Tis low, 'tis insult, calls me fool;
With me 'twill always fail.

Would you obtain an honest heart,
Address my nobler, better part;
Pay homage to my mind;
The passing hour brings on the day,
And beauty quickly fades away,
Nor leaves a rose behind.

Let then your open, manly sense,
The moral ornaments dispense,
And to my worth be true ;
So may your suit itself indear,
Not for the charms you say I wear,
But those I find in you.

SONG 1270.

ON tree-topt hill, or tufted green,
While yet Aurora's vest is seen;
Before the sun has left the sea,
Let the fresh morning breathe on me.

To furze-blown heath, or pasture mead,
Do thou my happy footsteps lead ;
Then shew to me the pleasing stream,
Of which, at night, so oft I dream.

At night the mazy wood I'll tread,
With autumn-leaves and dry moss spread,
And cooling fruits for thee prepare,
For sure, I think, thou wilt be there.

Till birds begin their evening fong,
With thee the time feems never long;
O let us fpeak our love that's paft,
And count how long it has to laft.

I'll fay eternally, and thou
Shalt only look as kind as now;
I afk no more, for that affords
What is not in the force of words.

SONG 1271.

SEE the purple morn arife,
　　Streak with red the blufhing fkies,
Zephyr from his balmy wing,
Shakes the fragrance of the fpring.

Winter's vigour now is paft,
Joy and raptures fmile at laft;
Swelling billows ceafe to roar,
And die along the filent fhore.

SONG 1272.

MY fhepherd is gone far away o'er the plain,
　　While in forrow behind I am forc'd to re-
main;
Tho' blue-bells and vi'lets the hedges adorn,
Tho' trees are in bloffom, and fweet blows the
thorn;
No pleafure they give me, in vain they look
gay,
There's nothing can pleafe now my Jockey's
away;
Forlorn I fit finging, and this is my ftrain,
Hafte, hafte, to my arms my dear Jockey again.

When lads and their laffes are on the green met,
They dance and they fing, they laugh and they
chat,
Contented and happy, with hearts full of glee;
I can't without envy their merriment fee:
Thofe pleafures offend me, my fhepherd's not
there,
No pleafure I relifh that Jockey don't fhare;
It makes me to figh, I from tears fcarce refrain,
And wifh my dear Jockey return'd back again.

But hope fhall fuftain me, nor will I defpair,
He promis'd he wou'd in a fortnight be here;
On fond expectation my wifhes I'll feaft,
For love my dear Jockey to Jenny will hafte:
Then farewel each care, adieu each vain figh;
Who'll then be fo bleft, or fo happy as I?
I'll fing on the meadows, and alter my ftrain,
When Jockey returns to my arms back again.

SONG 1272.

Sung in the Oratorio of *Abel*.

HOW chearful, along the gay mead,
　　The daify and cowflip appear?
The flocks, as they carefefsly feed,
Rejoice in the fpring of the year.

The myrtles that fhade the gay bow'rs,
The herbage that fprings from the fod,

Trees, plants, cooling fruits, and fweet flow'rs,
All rife to the praife of my God.

Shall man, the great mafter of all,
The only infenfible prove!
Forbid it, fair gratitude's call,
Forbid it devotion and love.

The Lord, who fuch wonders could raife,
And ftill can deftroy with a nod,
My lips fhall inceffantly praife;
My foul fhall be wrapt in my God.

SONG 1273.

STREPHON AND CHLOE; A CANTATA.

RECITATIVE.

WHILST Strephon on fair Chloe hung,
　　And gently woo'd, and fweetly fung;
The nymph in a difdainful air,
Thus, fmiling, mock'd the fhepherd's care.

AIR.

Swain, I know that you difcover
　　In my form a thoufand charms;
Can you point me out a lover
　　Worthy my encircling arms?
Boy, no more approach my beauty,
　　Till you equal merit boaft;
To adore me is a duty,
　　Thoufands witnefs to their coft.

RECITATIVE.

Stung to the heart, the redd'ning fwain,
On the vain maid retorts again:

AIR.

Foolifh creature, did each feature
Bloom beyond the pride of nature,
Artful feigning, coy, difdaining,
　　Vain coquette, deftroys them all.
Go, o'erbearing, proud, enfnaring,
Lay a thoufand fops defpairing,
Then complying, fighing, dying,
　　To fome fool a victim fall.
Nymphs like you, whilft they're deceiving,
　　Angels all in front appear;
But the fot their arts believing,
　　Finds a devil in the rear.

SONG 1274.

ATTEND all ye nymphs and ye fwains of
　　the green,
For you I have rov'd the plains round;
Whole months I've been prying, and now I
have feen
Where fmiling Content's to be found.
Come quickly with me, and I'll fhew you the
way
To the fpot where he chofe his retreat;
You muft fly from thefe plains, to be eafy and
gay,
And near him muft take up your feat.

I fought him 'mongft crowds, and in each
gaudy place,
But thofe were the manfions of care;
In the palace of greatnefs unknown was his
face,
Contentment had never been there:
I hied me to roofs that invited to joys,
Hope tempted me thither to rove;
But rude was their wit, and their pleafure was
noife,
Though they beckon'd to peace and to love.

And at laft, near a brook, to a cottage I ftray'd,
With a few fimple fheep on the green;
The rofe and the woodbine their fweetnefs dif-
play'd,
Not plenty, but health, bleft the fcene:
Good-nature appear'd, and unlatcht me the door,
Nor knew what my coming there meant;
How great my furprize! here my fearth was
all o'er,
He told me his name was Content.

But my wine neither nurfes nor babies can
bring;
And a big-belly'd bottle's a mighty good thing.

We fhorten our days when with love we engage;
It brings on difeafes, and haftens old age:
But wine from grim death can it's votaries fave,
And keep out t'other leg, when there's one in
the grave.

Perhaps, like her fex, ever falfe to their word,
She had left me to get an eftate, or a lord:
But my bumper, regarding nor title or pelf,
Will ftand by me when I can't ftand by myfelf.

Then let my dear Chloe no longer complain;
She's rid of her lover, and I of my pain:
For in wine, mighty wine, many comforts I
fpy;
Should you doubt what I fay, take a bumper,
ana try.

SONG 1275.

Sung at RANELAGH.

THE women all tell me I'm falfe to my lafs;
That I quit my poor Chloe, and ftick to
my glafs;
But to you men of reafon, my reafons I'll own;
And, if you don't like them, why—let them
alone.

Altho' I have left her, the truth I'll declare:
I believe fhe was good, and I'm fure fhe was fair;
But goodnefs and charms in a bumper I fee,
That make it as good and as charming as fhe.

My Chloe had dimples and fmiles, I muft own:
But, tho' fhe could fmile, yet in truth fhe could
frown:
But tell me, ye lovers of liquor divine,
Did you e'er fee a frown in a bumper of wine?

Her lilies and rofes were juft in their prime;
Yet lilies and rofes are conquer'd by time;
But in wine, from it's age, fuch a benefit flows,
That we like it the better, the older it grows.

They tell me, my love would in time have been
cloy'd,
And that beauty's infipid when once 'tis en-
joy'd;
But in wine I both time and enjoyment defy;
For the longer I drink, the more thirfty am I.

Let murders, and battles, and hiftory prove
The mifchiefs that wait upon rivals in love:
But in drinking, thank heav'n, no rival con-
tends;
For the more we love liquor, the more we are
friends.

She, too, might have poifon'd the joy of my life,
With nurfes and babies, and fqualling and ftrife;

SONG 1276.

AWAY to the woodlands, away!
The fhepherds are forming a ring,
To dance to the honour of May,
And welcome the pleafures of fpring.
The fhepherdefs labours a grace,
And fhines in her Sunday's array,
And bears, in the bloom of her face,
The charms and the beauties of May.

Away, to the woodlands, away,
And join with the amorous train;
'Tis treafon to labour to day,
Now Cupid and Bacchus muft reign.
With garlands of primrofes made,
And crown'd with the fweet blooming fpray,
Through woodland, and meadow, and fhade,
We'll dance to the honour of May.

SONG 1277.

THE HUMOURS OF A COUNTRY-WAKE.

Written by Mr. CUNNINGHAM.

COME laffes and lads, take leave of your dads,
And away to the maypole hie;
For every fhe has got her a he,
And a fidler ftanding by.
There's Nanny has got her Jack, and Jenny has
got her Joe,
To jig it, to jig it, to jig it, to jig it, to jig it
to and fro.

Strike up, fays Wat; agreed, fays Kate;
I pray the fidler pay;
Content, fays Hodge; and fo fays Madge;
For this is holiday:
Then every man began to foot it round about,
And every maid did jetty it, jetty it, jetty it
in and out.

You're out, fays Dick; you lye, fays Nick,
The fidler plays it falfe;
So, fays Hugh; and fo, fays Sue;
And fo, fays nimble Al'ce.
The fidler then began to play the tune again,
And every maid did trip it, did trip it, did trip
it unto the men.

Let's kifs, fays Nan; content, fays Jane;
And fo fays every fhe;
How many, fays Nat? why three, fays Matt,
For this is a maiden's fee.
But they, inftead of three, did give them half a
fcore;
The men in kindnefs did give them, did give
them, did give them as many more.

Then after an hour, they tript to a bower,
To play for ale and cakes,
And kiffes too, until they were due
The maidens held the ftakes.
The women then began to quarrel with the men,
And bid them to take their kiffes back, and
give them their own again.

Thus they fat until it was late,
And tir'd the fidler quite,
With finging and playing, without any paying,
From morning until night.
They told the fidler then, they'd pay him for
his play,
And each gave two-pence, gave two-pence,
gave two-pence and went their way.

Good night, fays Cis; good night, fays Prifs;
Good night, fays Harry to Doll;
Good night, fays John; good night, fays Joan;
Good night, fays every one.
Some ran, fome went, fome ftay'd, fome tarry'd
by the way;
Each bound themfelves, in kiffes twelve, to
meet the next holiday.

SONG 1278.

THE DANGERS OF THE SEA.

CEASE, rude Boreas, bluft'ring railer,
Lift ye landmen all to me;
Mefs-mates, hear a brother failor
Sing the dangers of the fea:
From bounding billows, firft in motion,
When the diftant whirlwinds rife,
To the tempeft troubled ocean,
When the feas contend with fkies.

Hark, the boatfwain hoarfly bawling,
By top-fail fheets, and haulyards ftand;
Down top-gallants quick be hawling,
Down your ftay-fails, hand, boys, hand!
Now it frefhens, fet the braces,
The lee top-fail fheets let go;
Luff, boys, luff, don't make wry faces,
Up your top-fails nimbly clew.

Now all you on down-beds fporting,
Fondly lock'd 'twixt beauty's arms;
Frefh enjoyments wanton courting,
Safe from all but love's alarms:

Round us roars the tempeft louder,
Think what fears our minds enthral;
Harder yet, it yet blows harder,
Now again the boatfwain calls.

The top-fail yards point to the wind, boys,
See all clear to reef each courfe;
Let the fore-fheet go, don't mind, boys,
Tho' the weather fhould be worfe:
Fore and aft the fprit-fail yard get,
Reef the mizen, fee all clear;
Hands up, each preventer brace fet,
Man the fore-yard, chear, lads, chear;

Now the dreadful thunders roaring,
Peals on peals contending clafh;
On our heads fierce rain falls pouring,
In our eyes blue lightnings flafh:
One wide water all around us,
All above but one black fky;
Different deaths at once furround us.
Hark! what means yon dreadful cry?

The fore-maft's gone! cries ev'ry tongue out,
O'er the lee, twelve feet 'bove deck;
A leak beneath the cheft-tree's fprung out,
Call all hands to clear the wreck:
Quick the laniards cut to pieces,
Come, my hearts, be ftout and bold;
Plumb the well, the leak increafes,
Four feet water's in the hold!

While o'er the fhip the wild waves beating,
We for wives or children mourn;
Alas! from hence there's no retreating,
Alas! to them there's no return:
Still the leak is gaining on us,
Both chain-pumps are choak'd below;
Heav'n have mercy here upon us,
Only He can fave us now.

On the lee-beam is the land, boys,
Let the guns o'erboard be thrown,
To the pump come ev'ry hand, boys;
See, her mizen-maft is gone:
The leak we've found, it can't pour faft,
We've lighten'd her a foot or more;
Up and rig a jury fore-maft:
She rights, fhe rights, boys, wear off fhore.

Now once more on joys we're thinking,
Since kind fortune fav'd our lives;
Come, the cann, boys, let's be drinking
To our fweethearts and our wives:
Fill it up, about fhip wheel it,
Clofe to lips the brimmer join;
Where's the tempeft now? who feels it?
None; our danger's drown'd in wine.

SONG 1279.

HAIL! Burgundy, thou juice divine!
Infpirer of my fong!
The praifes given to other wine,
To thee alone belong;
Of poignant wit and rofy charms
Thou canft the power improve;
Care of it's fting thy balm difarms,
Thou nobleft gift of Jove.

X x

Bright Phœbus on the parent vines,
 From whence thy current streams,
Sweet smiling thro' the tendril shines,
 And lavish darts his beams ;
The pregnant grape receives his fires,
 And all his force retains ;
With that same warmth our brains infpires,
 And animates our ftrains.

From thee my Chloe's radiant eye
 New sparkling beams receives ;
Her cheeks imbibe a rofier dye,
 Her beauteous bofom heaves :
Summon'd to love by thy alarms,
 O ! with what nervous heat,
Worthy the fair, we fill their arms,
 And oft our blifs repeat !

The Stoic, prone to thought intenfe,
 Thy foftnefs can unbind,
A chearful gaiety difpenfe,
 And make him tafte a friend :
His brow grows clear, he feels content,
 Forgets his penfive ftrife ;
And then concludes his time well fpent,
 In honeft focial life.

E'en beaux, thofe foft amphibious things,
 Wrapt up in felf and drefs,
Quite loft to the delight that fprings
 From fenfe, thy pow'r confefs ;
The fop, with chitty maudlin face,
 That dares but deeply drink,
Forgets his queue and ftiff grimace,
 Grows free, and feems to think.

SONG 1280.

SHEPHERDS, I have loft my love,
 Have you feen my Anna ?
Pride of ev'ry fhady grove
 Upon the banks of Banna.
I for her my home forfook,
 Near yon mifty mountain ;
Left my flock, my pipe, my crook,
 Greenwood fhade, and fountain.

Never fhall I fee them more,
 Until her returning ;
All the joys of life are o'er,
 From gladnefs chang'd to mourning.
Whither is my charmer flown ?
 Shepherds, tell me whither ?
Ah ! woe for me, perhaps fhe's gone
 For ever, and for ever.

SONG 1281.

Sung in the *School for Scandal.*

HERE's to the maid of bafhful fifteen,
 Likewife to the widow of fifty ;
Here's to the bold and extravagant quean,
 And here's to the houfewife that's thrifty.
 Let the toaft pafs,
 Drink to the lafs,
warrant fhe'll prove an excufe for the glafs.

Here's to the maiden whofe dimples we prize,
 And likewife to her that has none, Sir ;
Here's to the maid with a pair of blue eyes,
 And here is to her that's but one, Sir.
 Let the toaft pafs, &c.

Here's to the maid with a bofom of fnow,
 And to her that's as brown as a berry ;
And here's to the wife with a face full of woe,
 And here's to the girl that is merry.
 Let the toaft pafs, &c.

Let her be clumfy, or let her be flim,
 Young, or ancient, I care not a feather ;
So fill the pint bumper quite up to the brim,
 And e'en let us toaft them together.
 Let the toaft pafs,
 Drink to the lafs,
I warrant fhe'll prove an excufe for the glafs.

SONG 1282.

THE SWEET OF SWEETS.

SWEET are the banks when fpring perfumes
 The verdant plants and laughing flowers,
Fragrant the violet as it blooms,
 And fweet the bloffom after fhowers :
Sweet is the foft, the funny breeze,
 That fans the golden orange-grove ;
But oh ! how fweeter far than thefe
 The kiffes are of her I love.

Ye rofes, blufhing in your beds,
 That with your odours fcent the air ;
Ye lilies chafte, with filver heads,
 As dear Cleora's bofom fair ;
No more I court your balmy fweets,
 For I, and I alone, can prove
How fweeter, when each other meets,
 The kiffes are of her I love.

Her tempting eyes my gaze inclin'd,
 Their pleafing leffon firft I caught,
Her fenfe, her friendfhip, next confin'd
 The willing pupil fhe had taught.
Should fortune, ftooping from the fky,
 Conduct me to her bright alcove :
Yet like the turtle I fhould die,
 Denied the kifs of her I love.

SONG 1283.

Written by Mr. HAWKINS.

LET poets praife the pafture mead,
 The mofs-clad hill, the dale ;
The fhepherd piping on the reed,
 The maid with milking-pail.

The lark who foars on pinions high,
 With mellifluous note ;
The fheep, the herd, the butterfly,
 The frifky fawn, the goat.

The bubbling brook, the grot, the grove,
 The blooming flow'rs fo gay ;
The wood, the brake, the fweet alcove,
 Or fmiling dawn of day.

While I a loftier theme rehearfe,
And think on thefe no more;
But praife, in fond and faithful verfe,
The object I adore.

Her fkin is like the lily white,
Her cheeks red rofes are;
Her eyes outfhine the fun-beams light,
Her fhape moft debonair.

Her manner is mild as turtle-dove,
In ringlets flow her hair;
She looks—fhe is the queen of love,
And faireft of the fair.

Her breath like fpicy odours fweet
That fcent the eaftern clime;
Her mind, her ways, are all compleat,
And fource of all fublime.

To dwell with her through life's fhort fpace,
And view her heav'nly charms;
Are all the joys I wifh to trace,
Then die within her arms.

SONG 1284.

A PASTORAL.

Written by Mr. BEST.

MY chearful companions attend,
Ye fhepherds and nymphs of the plain,
In filence my forrows befriend,
Thofe forrows which furely are vain;
Yet gratitude claims the foft figh,
And pity fubdues my fond heart;
Compaffion now flows from my eye,
Unfeign'd, or untainted by art.

My Colin, alas! is no more
The pride and delight of each eye,
No more fhall he cherifh the poor,
No more the afflicted fupply;
How anxious to foothe the diftreft,
How eager their griefs to affwage;
Nor ever was Colin more bleft,
Than, in fondnefs, when waiting on age.

The rich and the great he defpis'd,
Nor valu'd the world for it's wealth;
'Twas wifdom and honour he priz'd,
The fource of contentment and health:
While blooming with virtue and truth,
Simplicity lifp'd on his tongue,
Vivacity fmil'd with his youth,
And the fyrens would ceafe when he fung,

No more fhall I hear his fond tale,
Beneath yonder oak in the grove;
No more fhall I blefs the foft gale,
That fann'd the recefs of my love:
See, Philomel weeps on the fpray,
No more to revifit the grove;
The fongfters no longer are gay,
But mourn the fad lofs of my love.

Adieu, ye dear fhades of my blifs,
Where Colin was conftant and true;
Where oft I've receiv'd his fond kifs;
Farewel, and for ever adieu.

Ye nymphs, my companions fo dear,
Whofe feelings my forrows opprefs,
Adieu! but forgive the fond tear
That flows from the fount of diftrefs.

Alas! the delights of the gay,
The joys of the rich and the great,
All fade as the flowers in May,
That bloom and confume with the heat.
What's life, but the offspring of care;
A fhadow, that rapidly flies,
A dream of diftrefs and defpair,
That bloffoms with hope, as it dies?

I'll hie me, where Colin is laid,
And there, undifturb'd will I weep;
Till nature's great debt I have paid,
My eyes fhall be ftrangers to fleep.
She inftantly quitted the grove,
And all the long night wept and figh'd
O'er the fod that fequefter'd her love,
Till the morn, when fhe ficken'd and died.

SONG 1285.

THE CAMP-MEDLEY.

THE lark was up, the morning grey,
The drum had beat a revelly,
And jolly foldiers on the ground,
In peaceful camp flept fafe and found:
Only one poor foldier, who,
Nought but love could e'er fubdue,
Wander'd to a neighbouring grove,
There to vent his plaints of love.

For women are whimfical, changeable things,
Their fweets, like the bee's, are mingled with
    ftings;
They're not to be got without toil, care and coft,
They're hard to be won and are eafily loft.
In feeking a fair-one, I found, to my fmart,
I know not the way, but I loft my own heart.

Ah! haplefs, haplefs day,
That e'er I faw fair Biddy;
My heart fhe ftole away,
My head fhe turn'd quite giddy.
The world may laugh and ftare,
'Tis truly ftrange to fee,
A lover fo fincere,
A fwain admir'd like me.

She's graceful, tall and flender,
She's brighter than the fun;
Her looks are foft and tender,
But oh! her heart's of ftone:
Nor tears, nor fighs can move her;
My bleeding heart fhe fees,
She knows too well I love her,
In vain I ftrive to pleafe.

Too vainly once I thought
To gain the lovely charmer,
And ev'ry method fought,
In hopes to win and warm her;
But all my hopes are over!
What charms then can I try?
But, like a haplefs lover,
I'll fet me down and die.

As on the ground he lay,
Minerva came that way,
In armour bright and gay,
And thus to him did fay :

Rife, foldier, rife,
The drum has beat to arms,
Hark to her loud alarms!
  Hang her beauty,
  Mind your duty,
Think not of her charms.

Rife, foldier, rife;
I'll take you by the hand,
And I'll lead you through the land ;
I'll give you the command
Of a well chofen band.
  Don't be ftupid,
  Drive away Cupid,
Follow Minerva's wife advice.

Soldier, go home, go home,
Nor mind your miftrefs's fcorn ;
Slight, flight her again ;
For flighted vows fhould flight return.

The foldier thus rous'd from his amorous floth,
Hafted away to his duty;
Swore to Minerva a terrible oath,
He'd never more think of her beauty.
Batchelor bluff, batchelor bluff;
Heigh for a heart that is rugged and tough.

He that is fingle can never wear horns ;
  He that is fingle is happy ;
He that is married lays upon thorns,
  And always is ragged and fhabby.
Batchelor bluff, &c.

He that is fingle, he fears not the rout,
  Nothing to him can be fweeter ;
He has no wife that can wimper and pout,
  Or cry, Can you leave me, dear creature.
Batchelor bluff, batchelor bluff;
Heigh for a heart that is rugged and tough.

Ye belles and flirts, fo fmart and fair,
  Say, are not foldiers form'd for love ?
For you fhall find them all fincere,
  Would you but kind and conftant prove :
But if you flight their paffion ftill,
  And tyrannife o'er hearts fo true,

Depend upon't they'll all rebel,
  And will not care one fig for you.

Ah! hold your foolifh tongue
A little laughing Cupid faid,
  Have you not heard it fung,
That conftancy will win a maid ?
  And what on earth would ever prove
  Superior to the joys of love !

Let wifdom preach in fchools,
For what has fhe with love to do;
  We go not by fuch rules :
Unbounded pleafures we purfue;
  On rofy wine our fancies fly;
  We ev'ry wordly care defy.

Let Mars in council boaft,
Of refolution, ftrength, and art ;
  Love comes without a hoft,
And fteals away the foldier's heart :
  Love breaks the bow, the fword and fpear,
  And turns the angry face of war.

E'en mighty Jove above
Hath been by Cupid's pow'r o'ercome ;
  There's none can conquer love,
Tho' arm'd with fword and fpear, or gun.
  Then ground your arms, ye fons of war;
  None can refift the Britifh fair.

SONG 1286.

Written by the EDITOR.

MY Nancy quits the rural plain,
  And kindly feeks her faithful fwain ;
Who, 'midft the din of war's alarms,
His much-lov'd country calls to arms.

Of old, when heroes fally'd forth,
To refcue innocence and worth,
The fair-one's image in the heart,
Could vigour to their nerves impart :

Then what fuperior laurels, now,
Muft grace the happy foldier's brow ;
Bleft with her prefence in the field,
To whom alone his heart can yield !

F I N I S.

INDEX.

a

INDEX.

INDEX.

INDEX.

b

INDEX.

b 2

INDEX.

INDEX.

I N D E X.

INDEX.

www.ingramcontent.com/pod-product-compliance
Lightning Source LLC
Chambersburg PA
CBHW030902270326
41929CB00008B/536